The Regulation of Hedge Funds

"*The Regulation of Hedge Funds: A Global Perspective* represents a timely and well-argued contribution to the scientific literature on this subject. It provides a comprehensive review of recent development in hedge fund regulation and legislation, with an appropriate study of comparative law of hedge funds in several jurisdictions. Written by Ana Maria Fagetan, this book is a very valuable tool for understanding the guidelines of regulation in this area, including protection of investor interests, risk prevention, and market freedom."

—Domenico Siclari, *Full Professor of Banking and Financial Regulation, Sapienza University of Rome, Italy*

Ana Maria Fagetan

The Regulation of Hedge Funds

A Global Perspective

palgrave
macmillan

Ana Maria Fagetan
Sapienza University of Rome
Rome, Italy

ISBN 978-3-030-63705-7 ISBN 978-3-030-63706-4 (eBook)
https://doi.org/10.1007/978-3-030-63706-4

This Palgrave Macmillan imprint is published by the registered company Springer Nature Switzerland AG
The registered company address is: Gewerbestrasse 11, 6330 Cham, Switzerland

I dedicate this book to my family.
I love you dearly.

Foreword

In recent years we have witnessed seismic changes in international capital markets both with regard to the entities that dominate the financial system and the volume and nature of the transactions. Fund management has grown exponentially and hedge funds in particular have become mainstream players. Their growth and systemic potential have featured prominently in the media, as well as in regulatory and policy circles.

The question of whether hedge funds should be further regulated or not has become hotly contested in the aftermath of the global financial crisis (GFC). Those in favor of tighter public regulation claim that hedge funds are a potential source of financial instability while those that suggest that self-regulation or light touch regulation suffice point to the fact that the hedge fund industry was not subject to the bailouts that characterized bank rescues—and associated moral hazard incentives—during the GFC. If the costs of failure are internalized and the entity (the hedge fund) is wound down when 'the money runs out' rather than expecting or demanding official protection, then—the latter ague—there is no moral hazard and consequently no need for further regulation.

In her book *The Regulation of Hedge Funds. A Global Perspective* Ana Maria Fagetan provides a comprehensive review of recent development in hedge fund regulation and legislation post GFC, including the Dodd Frank Act in the US and key directives in the EU such as the Alternative Investment Funds Managers Directive (AIFMD), the Markets in Financial Instruments Directive (MiFID II), the new EU Prospectus Regulation

(2019) and UCITS IV and V Directives. The book covers historical developments, regulatory changes and trends, the dangers of over-regulation and the demand for greater transparency.

The book assesses the current state of the regulation of hedge funds in several onshore jurisdictions: UK, Italy, France, Ireland, Luxembourg, Malta, Switzerland, and offshore jurisdictions: Cayman Islands, British Virgin Islands, Mauritius and Delaware, considering how the law should balance investor protection, integrity in the conduct of the business and prevention and the prevention and containment of systemic risk.

The author argues that there are several gaps in the existing literature on hedge funds. Why countries which were in the past in favor of lighter regulations emerged as supporters of a tighter regulation after the international crisis? And, why, a decade after the crisis, populist policies in the US and UK (post Brexit) create regulatory divergence instead of convergence? She answers all these challenging questions in this timely book.

This volume provides a much needed, comprehensive and economically-sophisticated overview of hedge fund regulation The book represents a significant contribution to the literature in the field and will appeal to both financial law scholars and students on the one hand and regulators and practitioners on the other hand. Many of the findings are not narrowly limited to the field of hedge fund regulation but are more broadly applicable to the evolution of financial regulation generally.

September 2020

Professor Rosa Maria Lastra
Sir John Lubbock Chair in Banking Law
CCLS, Queen Mary University of London
London, UK

Preface

Providing a comprehensive review of the recent development of hedge funds regulation, *The Regulation of Hedge Funds: A Global Perspective* reveals the dynamic legislative challenges to which the financial sector across the globe has been subject to, providing up-to-date insights into the ever-changing legislation of hedge funds. The book guides the reader through the complex interplay of the many state laws and regulations—the Dodd Frank, the AIFMD, the UCITS IV and V Directives, the MiFID II, along with national regulations of each country analyzed. Additionally, the regulatory analysis of the selected jurisdictions, located both onshore and offshore, include the US, the UK, several EU jurisdictions and also particular offshore jurisdictions, offers an understanding of the historical developments, current regulatory changes and further possible perspectives and shifts expected to happen, most of these measures being stemmed from the crisis regulatory overreaction.

By assessing the current state of the regulation of hedge funds and considering the regulatory position of hedge funds in different states of the globe, the author intends to provide an answer to the question of whether hedge funds should be regulated (tight regulation) or not (light touch). The author underlines the role of prominent player such as the EU and the US in the aftermath of the global financial crisis.

This book comprehensively analyses all legal investor protection-based regulations, approaching the possible shift in the hedge funds regulation paradigms, from an interdisciplinary point of view. The core of the book is represented by the potential changes of investors' rights stemming from the financial crisis, addressing their limits also.

While severe criticism attacked hedge funds during and after the international financial crisis, due to the huge instability period which implied huge exceptional efforts on behalf of both governments and international public authorities' regulators, increasing attention was paid to risk mitigation, transparency and investors' protection globally as well as to the entire financial system.

One major aspect of the debate has been whether hedge funds should be allowed to keep their status of lightly regulated entities, and whether increased regulation is required in order to mitigate the risks induced by hedge funds. These failures resulted in losses to investors, and simultaneously negatively affected the market confidence. Under these circumstances, the investor protection concept and the struggle to restore market confidence became essential in the hedge fund debate, prompting for the proliferation of unprecedented regulatory measures.

This book depicts an overview of the financial regulatory systems before the 2007–2009 crisis, a view of the complex regulatory changes stemmed after the international crisis, and a perspective on recent regulatory frameworks in various jurisdictions, namely, the US, the UK and the EU and single jurisdictions. The author argues that there are several gaps in the existing literature on hedge funds: first, why countries which were in the past in favor of lighter regulations emerged as supporters of a tighter regulation after the international crisis? Second, the lack of systematic researches of regulatory changes post-crisis, analyzed in a comparative and contrastive manner with major focus on regulatory shifts in order to provide a global perspective. Third, a decade after the crisis, recent views on regulations are challenging against the financial system: Trump's populist approach and UK's Brexit, threatening with disintegration of the international and EU system of regulation.

To address these main gaps, the author carried a systematic contrastive and comparative approach, which is demonstrated in the seven chapters of the book, by analyzing the various onshore and offshore jurisdictions. The regulation and legal structure are critically examined, checked and evaluated. This research pursues also to contribute to a better understanding of the hedge funds development during volatile times, focusing on investor protection and to provide a global framework for the most frequent available alternative investment tools.

Also, the book has a twofold aim: to find out similarities and differences, choosing between different regulatory models, and to evaluate the supreme regulatory version of hedge funds in order to provide the best answer to a global financial area. The ultimate goal is an international hedge funds regulation focused on providing investor protection and mitigating the risk. The book analyses the US and the EU hedge funds regulatory frameworks and also focuses on several local onshore jurisdictions such as UK, Italy, France, Ireland, Luxembourg, Malta, Switzerland, but also on offshore jurisdictions: Cayman Islands, British Virgin Islands, Mauritius and Delaware. The main aim is to measure the consequences of local rules on hedge fund investor protection-based regulation and their effect on the spreading of hedge funds in this area.

Pursuant to the financial crisis, the investors' interests emergence on the agenda of legal debates besides stronger supervisory regulations is unsurprising, questioning the sufficiency of traditional means and instruments in avoiding such problems in the future. The book points out the similarities and particularities of the analyzed financial regulatory frameworks emphasizing investor protection, before and after the financial crisis of 2007–2009, by different methodological and contrastive approaches, analytical and comparative studies.

The significance of investors' protection on the global financial stage is highlighted in this research, together with the role of the lessons learnt from several countries' past and present regulatory experiences. The construction of a comparative approach in such a complex field of interest requires the thorough study and examination of hedge fund regulatory systems in the US, the UK, the EU and single jurisdictions (Italy, France, Ireland, Luxembourg, Malta and Switzerland), but also in offshore jurisdictions: Cayman Islands, British Virgin Islands, Mauritius and Delaware. In Europe, new laws or directives are on the agenda to protect investors and customers, such as the Alternative Investment Funds Managers Directive (AIFMD), the Markets in Financial Instruments Directive (MiFID), the new EU Prospectus Regulation (2019). However, the overregulation of markets by defending the investors' rights could result in an uneconomical underproduction of new financial products. The perfect balance between these two poles seems to be difficult to find by legislators.

With the increase in complexity and innovation of financial products, the creative and proactive nature of financial regulation and insurance of investors' rights protection needs to be the highest. In this context, the key pieces of legislation adopted in the aftermath of the financial crisis (the Dodd-Frank Act in the US and the AIFM Directive in the EU) are compared and analyzed in a critical manner.

In choosing this topic, one presumed that hedge funds legal characteristics could be defined by studying their regulatory forms, features and strategies in the American and European systems, aiming to understand how they may lead to similar regulatory frameworks (and in the end to one single global regulation), enabling risk mitigation, greater transparency and investors' protection in the US and the European countries, both onshore and offshore jurisdictions.

The book aims to empirically determine the guidelines and techniques used by hedge fund regulators worldwide in the context of the rapidly changing regulatory field, particularly addressing investor protection. Various types of hedge fund regulatory codes applicable in the analyzed countries are identified by the author of the book, who also addresses the regulatory factors that could motivate or inhibit the development of the hedge fund industry.

It is undeniable that the research is of great interest nowadays. The hedge funds supervision and the evaluation of their regulatory bodies surface and surpass the national regulators and reveal themselves at the international level. The same reform process occurs not only within the EU through the *Alternative Investment Fund Managers Directive* (AIFM Directive), with major focus on Brexit, but also in the US, through the *Dodd-Frank Act Wall Street Reform and Consumer Protection Act* (Dodd-Frank Act). The offshore jurisdictions have also been impacted by the regulatory changes during the past decade. This makes the author of this book consider and promote internationally the subject of regulation and supervision of hedge funds, with major focus on investors' protection. The reform of hedge funds regulation which aimed to mitigate the risk and increase the level of investors' interests protection is not over yet. However, inherently, the different regulatory approach of the selected countries analyzed in this book implies a clear grouping of the sets of hedge funds regulation.

Of major interest are the UK's post-crisis actions and the shifting regulatory environment. From a supporter of financial deregulations, in the pre-crisis period, the UK or the City of London, a huge financial center of hedge funds, has opted for Brexit, which prompts us to analyze how powerful interests shape negotiations and national strategies. UK's decision of withdrawal from the construction of the European Union will be thoroughly analyzed, UK's position with respect to finance, generally, and hedge funds, particularly being carefully scrutinized.

The law is stated as of 1 January 2020, and all forthcoming changes are mentioned, where important. Website citations are applicable to 1 September 2020.

Rome, Italy

Ana Maria Fagetan

Acknowledgments

My special appreciation and my sincere, heartily gratitude go to my esteemed Professor Rosa Maria Lastra, who supported me so enthusiastically from the very beginning, first, as my Ph.D. Supervisor, providing me an opportunity to complete my Ph.D. thesis, and later, when I first decided to start this book project, and convert my Ph.D. thesis into a book. I have benefited a lot from her guidance, critical comments and suggestions. Professor Rosa Maria Lastra has been a constant inspiration to me. Her determined support, firm encouragement, reflective guidance, prodigious insights into analysis and dedication have contributed enormously to the completion of this project. Her help has been invaluable and enormously appreciated. For all these, I feel very much indebted to my Professor. She has been and will remain my best role model for a scholar, mentor and professor.

I would especially like to express my gratitude and appreciation to Professor Domenico Siclari for encouraging me to publish my Ph.D. thesis and for tirelessly supporting my endeavour to do so.

My acknowledgement would be incomplete without thanking the biggest source of my strength, my family. Writing this book would have been so much more difficult without you by my side. Your dreams for me have resulted in this achievement! Thank you for rekindling dreams.

Contents

List of Figures

List of Tables

CHAPTER 1

The Rationales of Hedge Fund Regulation

1.1 Introduction to Hedge Funds

In the last decennium, there have been many changes in the asset management industry, the last year representing a critical point for the hedge fund industry. Thus, important hedge funds shut down,[1] meanwhile other managers decided in favor of mergers.[2] There were also managers who acquired other firms.[3] These changes were dictated by different reasons, as we shall see below. Indexation and also fee constrain have forced mutual funds to advance brand new models of investment strategies which used to be dictated in the past by hedge funds. A main characteristic of the last decade is that numerous corporate investors are currently choosing an inactive investing manner.[4] Another feature, observed mainly in the United States, refers to the fact that hedge funds' investment discretion

[1] See New York-based Hoplite Capital Management and also London-based Arrowgrass Capital Partners.

[2] See in this vein the case of Nordea Asset Management, part of Helsinki-based financial services group Nordea, forced to close one fund for reducing operational costs and afterwards, to merge the capital into another fund.

[3] See the case of Sabre Fund Management bought by Trium Capital (a London-based alternative asset manager).

[4] Lewis, C. M. (2016). *Liquid alternative mutual funds: An asset class that expands opportunities for diversification* (Working Paper). Vanderbilt University Owen Graduate School of Management.

A. M. Fagetan, *The Regulation of Hedge Funds*,
https://doi.org/10.1007/978-3-030-63706-4_1

was strongly reduced by the requirements that were imposed lately, such as new registration and other reporting requests, all these measures having as main aim the increase of transparency. In addition, Brexit and everything referring to it that is still unknown to investors, also impact the industry. Also, adding value is becoming more difficult for hedge fund managers and investors, since the market is defined through both strong equity and bond markets. These changes are constantly challenging hedge funds industry, raising doubts and unanswerable inquiries for investors concerning the future of hedge funds.

According to Barclay Hedge, and their Global Hedge Fund Database as of March 26, 2020, currently, the situation can be found in Table 1.1.

Figure 1.1 illustrates the global hedge funds managers percentage according to their domicile, as of March 26, 2020.

All tendencies noticed above are reflected in the growth of the hedge funds' AUM, as seen in Fig. 1.2. Thus, after the crisis, the growth of AUM for hedge funds was constant, but it has however reached 8.4% yearly in comparison to a rate of 20.3%, registered between 2000 and 2010. Therefore, even if hedge funds are on a growing tendency, this last 10 years were characterized by difficulties. Additionally, their liquidations grew very much in comparison to the years before the financial crisis.

If it were also to examine launches of hedge funds as compared to liquidations, "between 2012 and 2018, new hedge fund launches outpaced liquidations. But, as the industry has grown, the number of fund launches has trailed liquidations. Just 529 hedge funds and CTAs launched in

Table 1.1 The global hedge funds databases as of March 2020

Number of reporting funds	7091
Number of reporting management companies	1982
Number of funds added in previous month	116
Managers domiciled in United States	57.62%
Managers domiciled in Europe	24.32%
Managers domiciled in Caribbean	15.74%
Managers domiciled in Rest of World	2.32%
% of Funds with February Returns	94.43%
% of Funds with January Returns	99.01%

Source BarclayHedge (2020a)

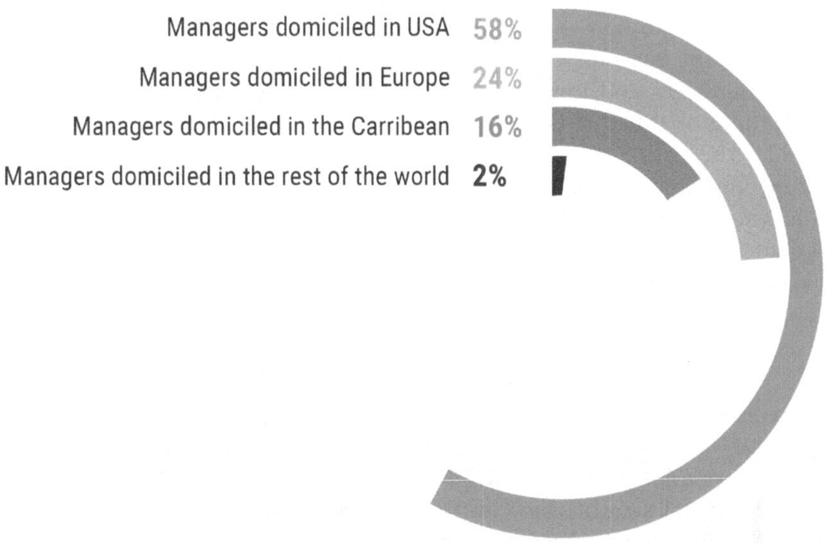

Fig. 1.1 Global hedge funds managers as of March 26, 2020 according to their domicile (*Source* BarclayHedge 2020a)

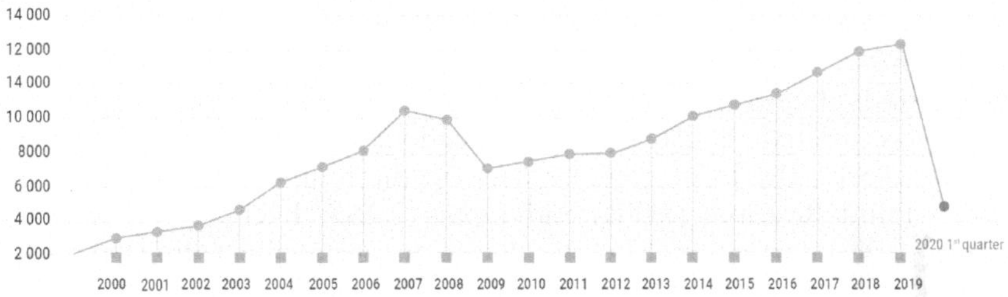

Fig. 1.2 Assets under management in the global hedge fund industry (*Source* BarclayHedge 2020b)

2019, fewer than half the number (1169) that launched in 2018."[5] On one hand, the reasons for these are that, some of liquidations occurred due to high fees and low performance[6] in the last period. On the other hand, the global hedge fund landscape seems saturated, particularly if we consider the major trends which defined the industry last year: "consolidation and investor concerns over market volatility growing focus on ethical investment and the higher costs of starting a fund amid increasing regulation – all while maintaining performance."[7]

1.2 The Worldwide Total Size of the Hedge Funds Industry

The world's total size of the industry remains yet uncertain. Even though regulators have been paying increased attention and have been constantly adjusting regulation concerning hedge funds since LTCM's failure in 1998, the total size of this industry is yet questionable. As Barth et al. (2020) assess in their research paper "The Hedge Fund Industry Is Bigger (and Has Performed Better) Than You Think," "the potential data gaps in hedge fund activities are not confined to questions of size; the extent to which hedge fund performance and investor flows have been comprehensively measured is similarly uncertain."[8]

Of course, there are several reliable estimates regarding the size of hedge funds, but their ambiguity resides in the fact that, until recently, there were limited regulatory data collections on hedge fund activities. In this respect, the most accurate data on the industry are provided by Hedge Fund Research (HFR) and Lipper TASS. Even these databases collect their information from funds on an essentially voluntary basis,

[5] Preqin. (2020). *Global hedge fund report*. https://www.preqin.com/insights/global-reports/2020-preqin-global-hedge-fund-report. Accessed 20 June 2020.

[6] McCahery, J. A., & de Roode, Al. (2019). *The lost decade for hedge funds: Three threats* (TILEC Discussion Paper No. DP2019-027. Working Paper No. 486/2019). European Corporate Governance Institute—Law. SSRN: https://ssrn.com/abstract=3501551. Accessed 20 June 2020.

[7] Preqin. (2020). *Global hedge fund report*. https://www.preqin.com/insights/global-reports/2020-preqin-global-hedge-fund-report. Accessed 20 June 2020.

[8] Barth, D., Joenvaara, J., Kauppila, M., & Wermers, R. R. (2020). *The hedge fund industry is bigger (and has performed better) than you think* (Working Paper 20-01). Office of Financial Research. https://ssrn.com/abstract=3544181. Accessed 20 June 2020.

the biggest hedge funds usually choosing not to list in these databases.[9] This idea is also supported by Cary who underlines that, "access to transparency likewise depends on the bargaining power of investors as hedge fund advisers are not obligated to provide any such information to investors."[10] Contemporary regulation both in Europe and the United States try to fill this gap, still, data are not complete because of a lack of jurisdictional overlap. We mention in this respect the differences in these data. According to Eurekahedge the world total size of the industry is around 2.33 trillion US dollars.[11] Meanwhile, HFR estimates around 3.21 trillion US dollars. Also, eVestment estimates 3.31 trillion US dollars, while Barclay Hedge asses the total AUM industry at USD 3.54 trillion. Also, Preqin estimates the industry at USD 3.55 trillion.[12] As seen above, most of these estimates are between USD 3.0 and 3.55 trillion.[13] The biggest estimates come from the SEC, around USD 3.89 trillion.[14]

Indeed, scholars generally rely on hedge fund indices in the evaluation of their performance, which in itself raises various limitations, because, as already observed above, "these indices rely on hedge funds that are self-reporting because these entities are not required to disclose returns pursuant to any regulatory mandate."[15]

[9] Edelman, D., Fung, W., & Hsieh, D. A. (2013). Exploring uncharted territories of the hedge fund Industry: Empirical characteristics of mega hedge fund firms. *Journal of Financial Economics, 109*(3), 734–758.

[10] Shelby, C. M. (2019). How did we get here? Dissecting the hedge fund conundrum through an institutional theory lens. *Bus Law, 74*(3), 735–787.

[11] Eureka. (2019). *The Eureka hedge report April 2019*. https://static1.squarespace.com/static/5a02fa72bff200aa6a54edd9/t/5cc1449515fcc0de796a5b6f/1556169910440/Eureka+Hedge+Report_Apr-2019.pdf. Accessed 12 June 2020.

[12] These estimates are for 2017. Eurekahedge offers estimated for the third quarter, meanwhile the other estimates are for the fourth quarter.

[13] https://www.evestment.com/news/2020-begins-with-allocations-into-hedge-funds/, on 12.06.2020.

[14] See SEC. (2017). SEC's private fund statistics. US Securities and Exchange Commission. https://www.sec.gov/divisions/investment/private-funds-statistics/private-funds-statistics-2017-q4.pdf. Accessed 12 June 2020.

[15] Shelby, C. M. (2019). How did we get here? Dissecting the hedge fund conundrum through an institutional theory lens. *Bus Law, 74*(3), 735–787.

1.3 Rationales of Financial Regulation Applicable to Hedge Funds

The vast literature[16] on the issue suggests that there are three objectives that provide the rationale for financial regulation in general and for hedge fund regulation in particular. These objectives are: (a) protection of investors, (b) promotion of market integrity, but also (c) preservation of financial stability.[17]

As remarked by various observers, such as Sander Van Berkel, Peter Cartwight, Niamh Moloney, Phoebus Athanassiou, the above-mentioned aims are connected and they overlap, in certain regards. For instance, the provision and insurance of fair, efficient, and transparent markets need some requirements, which are also used for investor protection and mitigation of systemic risk. Similarly, some of the systemic risk mitigation measures afford investor protection.[18]

Consequently, capital flows to hedge funds in various countries are influenced by the strength and the enforcement of investor protection laws in these countries. All the above-mentioned principles are being addressed in the current chapter, in relation to the apparent validity of their application to hedge funds, not only within European borders, but also outside Europe. Further on, the chapter makes a clear organization of the different sets of regulation applicable to hedge funds aiming to protect investors, market integrity, and financial system stability.

[16] Athanassiou, Ph. (2009). *Hedge fund regulation in the EU: Current trends and future prospects*. The Netherlands: Wolters Kluwer; Aragon, G. O., Nanda, V. K., & Zhao, H. (2019). *Investor protection and capital fragility: Evidence from hedge funds around the world*. https://ssrn.com/abstract=3207064 or http://dx.doi.org/10.2139/ssrn.3207064. Accessed 1 July 2020.

[17] Van Berkel, S. (2008). Should hedge funds be regulated? *Journal of Banking Regulation, 9*, 196–223. https://doi.org/10.1057/jbr.2008.10; Cartwright, P. (2004). *Banks, consumers and regulation* (pp. 30–42). London: Hart Publishing; Moloney, N. (2006). *EC securities regulation*. New York: Oxford University Press; Farrell, D. (2018). Increasing investor protection through improving hedge fund valuation. *St. John's Law Review, 92*(1), 149–172.

[18] IOSCO. (2003). Objectives and Principles of Securities Regulation: 5. These are by no means the only regulatory rationales: the case for regulating financial markets also rests on a number of additional grounds including particularly, the need to ensure correct competitiveness for the financial intermediation industry.

1.3.1 *Investor Protection as Rationale of Hedge Fund Regulation*

Investor protection concerns the strand of regulatory attention directed toward making sure that investors' interests are conducted against market failure or unfavorable behavior within institutions possessing investors' funds. Non-compliance to "investor rights" may have so far-reaching results that the investor protection-based law has consistently featured among the main components of most capital market regulatory schemes, with national arrangements differing from one another only in terms of pointing out the specific investments that best suit them, based on the information that product providers are mandated to disclose by law.[19] This evidence is also supported by Aragon et al. (2019), who conclude that, "in countries with weak investor protection, poor fund performance exposes investors to a greater risk of fraud and legal jeopardy, thus triggering a larger outflow of capital."[20]

There are some factors that turned the protection of investors into one of the most visible objectives pursued by financial market supervisors and lawmakers worldwide.[21] Among these, one needs to mention: the

[19] Edwards differentiates between top-down and bottom-up investor protection regimes, of which the former is based on the exhaustive authorisation of the available investment products, while the latter is disclosure based, relying on rules requiring product vendors to explain the features of their products, their risks and returns, allowing investors the freedom to determine whether these are suitable for them (Edwards, F. R. (2006). Hedge fund and investor protection regulation. *Federal Reserve Bank of Atlanta Economic Review, 91*(4), 35–48).

[20] Aragon, G. O., Nanda, V. K., & Zhao, H. (2019). *Investor protection and capital fragility: Evidence from hedge funds around the world.* https://ssrn.com/abstract=3207064 or http://dx.doi.org/10.2139/ssrn.3207064. Accessed 1 July 2020.

[21] The importance of investor protection as a ground for financial regulation is reflected both in the statutory objectives of several of the EU Member States' financial market supervisory authorities, including the FSA (FSMA 2000, sections 2(2)(c) and 5), and in the score of investor protection-oriented Community legislative measures adopted in recent years. See Garcia, G., & Prast, H. (2003). *Depositor and investor protection in the EU and the Netherlands: A brief history.* Netherlands Central Bank Research Series Supervision (discontinued) 54. Netherlands Central Bank, Directorate Supervision.

noneconomic,[22] paternal[23] basis of many of the current financial market regulatory frameworks, the public desire for outer (governmental) regulation, together with the supervision of private self-regulation (mainly in crucial times of crisis), the prejudicial economic results emerging from the "loss of investor confidence in the aftermath of market failures,"[24] but also from the high amount of empirical proof or researches stating that there is a causal connection between tighter investor protection regulation and financial market increase.[25] This is even more relevant in the context of "institutional investment vehicles," where, as Franklin Edwards emphasized, *investor protection* represents the top-priority goal of public policy underlying regulation.[26]

Many aspects need to be considered regarding the meaning of hedge fund-specific legal transparency requirements for the investor protection-related data. This is because there is a lack of a realistic comprehension by (several) investors (mainly less-experienced ones) of hedge fund investment strategies and imminent conflict of interests that emerge between managers of the fund and individuals investing capital in it. This is to be performed even in the EU Member States where hedge fund-specific legal transparency requirements are applied.

[22] Academics often distinguish between the economic and social rationales for external regulation. The conceptual difficulty of differentiating between the two may serve little practical purpose: measures justified on social grounds (e.g. consumer protection) may also improve the functioning of markets and vice versa (Ramsay, I. (1995). Consumer credit law, distributive justice and the welfare state. *Oxford Journal of Legal Studies, 15*(2), 177–197 (1995). https://doi.org/10.1093/ojls/15.2.177).

[23] Cartwright, P. (2004). Op. Cit., pp. 19–22. For the classical statement of paternalism as a legal concept see Dworkin, G. (1971). Paternalism. In R. Wasserstrom (Ed.), *Morality and the law* (pp. 107–126). Belmont: Wadsworth Pub. Co.

[24] Davies, H. (1999). Financial regulation: Why bother? Mimeo, society of Business Economists lecture, London.

[25] Financial markets appear to perform better where adequate investor protection conditions prevail (La Porta, R., et al. (1997). Legal determinants of external finance. *Journal of Finance, 52*(3), 1131–1150 (1997). https://doi.org/10.1111/j.1540-6261.1997.tb02727.x). Empirical evidence also links consumer protection guarantees with greater external financing opportunities (La Porta, R., et al. (1999). Corporate ownership around the world. *Journal of Finance, 54*(2), 471–517. https://doi.org/10.1111/0022-1082.00115).

[26] Edwards, F. R. (1999). Hedge funds and the collapse of long-term capital management. *The Journal of Economic Prospectives, 13*(2), 189–210.

One must consider the case of *single-manager* hedge funds regulation based on investor protection rights claiming that this premise is highly unrealistic and that the existence of relevant barriers might go a long path to approaching whatever legitimate investors risks a realistic regulator might have wanted to keep against in this area.[27] Following the example of the US hedge fund situation, despite the huge dimension and the absolute relevance of its onshore industry (which surpasses by far the European industry), the compulsory transparency actions aiming to protect the investor were not considered necessary. This impressive "exempted status" that the American hedge funds take advantage relies on the general apprehension that the so-called "accredited" (also known under the name of qualified) investors, who owned most of the hedge funds industry established somewhere on the Atlantic shore, tend to be highly sophisticated and therefore they afford to make professional investment options and bear their costs. This makes the protection through regulations pointless. Meanwhile, retail investors are protected by the very fact that they are denied the access to hedge funds.[28]

However, in some cases, qualified investors may need protective guaranty as well, where there is an objective *leverage* deficiency in setting up their investing conditions and in assessing their risk outline.[29] The promoters of transparency regulations inspired by investor protection still have to prove that real investor transparency safeguards can be implemented. They have to identify the costs and benefits and their practical purpose, taking into consideration the complex framework of hedge fund strategies and the flexibility of their investments capable of making sound

[27] Spangler, Timothy et al. (2010). Op. Cit., p. 23.

[28] Paredes, T. A. (2006). On the decision to regulate hedge funds: The SEC's regulatory philosophy, style and mission. *University of Illinois Law Review, 5*, 975–1036. It is nevertheless interesting to note that the SEC's rationale for adopting Rule 203 (b)(3)-2, requiring the registration, by 1 February 2006, as investment advisers (within the meaning of the Investment Advisors Act of 1940) of most hedge fund managers was inter alia motivated by the need to protect investors in hedge funds and to enhance the Commission's ability to protect our nation's securities markets in the face of the industry's retailisation and of the growing incidence of fraud amongst hedge fund managers (SEC. 17 CFR Parts 275 and 279. Release No. IA-2333 (File No. S7-30-04). https://www.sec.gov/rules/final/ia-2333.htm. Accessed 12 June 2020).

[29] SEC. (2003). Implications of the Growth of Hedge Funds, Staff Report, 47. For a more systematic discussion see McVea, H. (2007). Hedge funds and the new regulatory agenda. *Legal Studies, 27*(4), 709–739. https://doi.org/10.1111/j.1748-121x.2007.00069.x.

antique even the most comprehensive, mandatory investor transparency data in a *de facto* short period.[30]

In addition, good incentives are offered to hedge fund investors to gather the necessary information for their self-protection. If they assess the information to be inadequate, they have all the rights and power to withdraw their assets and redeem their investments (with the exception, maybe, of an extremely long "lock-up" time).[31]

Public concerns have been expressed as additional grounds for investor protection-based regulation, regarding the major increase of capital allocations of ***institutional*** investors in alternative investment products. All the above represent legitimate concerns attributed ***inter alia*** to the indirect retail investor exposure produced by the organizational investor allotments. However, the fact that hedge fund regulation is justified or not by these concerns is a different matter.[32]

Despite the numerical increase of organizational investors who assign parts of their own liquid assets to hedge funds (they can do this either directly or indirectly, by means of the FoHF[33]), increasing pension funds into an international hedge fund industry major financial suppliers, institutional investor allocations to hedge funds continued to be limited and did not change lately.

Without damaging the quantitative dimension of recent institutional investor interest in hedge fund investments, at first glance, it seems that however useful the inclusion in the regulatory arsenal of basic conflict of interest prevention safeguards might be, a feasible solution for the investor protection connected concerns brought about by institutional investor allotments to hedge funds stands in their own hands. There

[30] The MWGED, composed of the Basel Committee, the IOSCO, the International Association of Insurance Supervisors and the Committee on the Global Financial System, presented recommendations on enhancing disclosure practices by financial institutions and hedge funds in April 2001 (MWGED. (2001). Final Report of the Multidisciplinary Working Group on Enhanced Disclosure, Report). The moment when the Joint Forum tried to follow up in 2003 on the implementation status of its 2001 recommendations it was unable to publish its findings as it could not secure cooperation from a sufficient number of hedge funds (Basel Committee on Banking Supervision (2004). The Joint Forum, Final Disclosure in the Banking, Insurance and Securities Sectors: Issues and Analysis. https://www.bis.org/publ/joint08.htm. Accessed 20 June 2020).

[31] Spangler, T., & Scholer, K. (2010). Op. Cit., p. 27.

[32] Spangler, T., & Scholer, K. (2010). Op. Cit., p. 27.

[33] Funds of Hedge Funds.

is a very relevant conflict of interests between pension fund managers, who are ready to take risks in order to increase their funds' returns (and their own compensation, too) and their beneficiaries, who have an interest in funds, adopting more conservative investment policies. This is an effective institutional oversight and governance mechanism to rectify the noticed conflict of interest arising between the managers of a fund and its beneficiaries.[34]

This contrast is more an issue for pension fund regulation (or, more properly, for the enforcement of existing pension fund-related corporate governance rules) than it is for hedge fund regulation. As Franklin Edwards has competently observed "... hedge funds are not the source of this conflict, only its latest manifestation."[35] If the problem is more relevant to the relationship between pension fund managers (as agents) and beneficiaries (as principals), then the appropriate answer is in terms of tighter institutional investor governance, so that fund beneficiaries may control fund managers more efficiently.

Lately, the focus has been on increasing investor protection in direct relation to improving hedge fund valuation,[36] particularly because an accurate valuation appears as critical on several grounds. Thus, on the one hand, measuring and reporting the performance of hedge funds to investors is done according to the changes over time of the fair value of their assets.[37] Nowadays, investors carefully track a fund's performance in order to make accurate decisions of whether keeping or not their capital with the fund, meanwhile when investing in a new fund, they also analyze

[34] Spangler, T., & Scholer, K. (2010). *A practitioner's guide to alternative investment funds* (p. 30). City & Financial Publishing.

[35] Edwards, F. (2006). Op. Cit., p. 47.

[36] Hoffmann, B., & Paetzmann, K. (2018). Investor protection, valuation methods and the German alternative funds industry. *Journal of Risk Finance, 19*(2), 174–189. https://doi.org/10.1108/jrf-06-2017-0101.

[37] Maxey, D. (2014, February 4). If a security isn't trading, what is it really worth? *The Wall Street Journal*. https://www.wsj.com/articles/sec-looking-at-how-alternative-funds-value-investments-1391096281?tesla=y. Accessed 12 June 2020.

its past performance[38] before making a decision of investing or not with the fund.[39]

On the other hand, "hedge fund managers are compensated based on the net asset valuation and the performance of the fund."[40] Still, many conflicts of interest may rise from this form of compensation making it possible for managers to stimulate marking up the fund's valuation with the main purpose of increasing their compensation.[41] However, standardization and supervision of valuation for hedge funds are insufficient, which makes it problematic for investors to follow and set side by side fund valuations.

More recently, the second iteration of the EU's Markets in Financial Instruments Directive (MiFID II) came into being on January 3, 2018, having as initial objective to strengthen investor protection and improve the functioning of financial markets by making them more efficient, resilient, and transparent.[42] This transparency into buying and selling activities across all the major asset classes in the capital markets industry stands as a major factor, although MiFID II has not been universally welcomed. From time to time, the European Securities and Markets Authority (ESMA) updates its Questions and Answers on the implementation of investor protection topics under the Market in Financial Instruments Directive and Regulation (MiFID II/MiFIR). The purpose of the MiFID II/MiFIR investor protection Q&As is to promote common supervisory approaches and practices in the application of MiFID II

[38] It is true that past performance of funds are not trustable data of future results, but in spite of this, investors carefully scrutinize fund's past performance especially when investing their capital. Soe, A. M., & Poirier, R. (2018). *Does past performance matter? The persistence scorecard*. https://www.spglobal.com/en/research-insights/articles/does-past-performance-matter-the-persistence-scorecard. Accessed 12 June 2020.

[39] AIMA. (2013). AIMA's Guide to Sound Practices for Hedge Fund Valuation 45, at 17. "From the [i]nvestor's perspective, fair valuation is the foundation on which analysis of the portfolio's performance and volatility of returns is based… [A]n [i]nvestor would normally expect that the amount of cash paid to take an equity interest in the portfolio and the amount of cash received on withdrawal of an equity interest is based on a formal and fair valuation of the portfolio's assets and liabilities."

[40] Sklar, R. (2009). Hedges or thickets: Protecting investors from hedge fund managers' conflicts of interest. *Fordham Law Review, 77*(6), 3251–3323.

[41] Idem at 3269.

[42] Gortsos, C. (2018). *Stricto sensu investor protection under the MiFID II: A systematic overview of Articles 24–30*. Newcastle upon Tyne: Cambridge Scholars Publishing.

and MiFIR. This stands as a proof that strengthening the protection of investors is of major interest for regulators.[43]

As Lannoo Karel states "generally speaking, the new conduct rules deal with soft rules on the behavior of market participants and hard rules prohibiting distortive practices."[44] This opinion is supported also by Bordellini, who states when referring to US regulatory framework that "although Dodd-Frank includes among its legislative purposes the protection of consumers from abusive financial services practices, its new provisions do not seem to be able to achieve this result."[45]

1.3.2 Market Integrity and Hedge Fund Fraud as Rationales for Hedge Fund Regulation

The protection of market integrity represents the second aspect of regulatory interest in the field of financial investments.[46] This occurs as one major determinant concerning each investor's capability to transact the business he/she manages in a transparent, fair background, and in the absence of discrimination, manipulative market conduct, secret agreements, and different abusive conducts.[47] In this vein, financial market misconduct of hedge fund managers is seen "as being very costly to financial markets and, thus, is an active area of scholarly study."[48] At

[43] Gillet, R., Ligot, St., & Firouzi, H. (2017). The challenges and implications of the Markets in Financial Instruments Directive (MiFID) and of its revision (MiFID II, MiFIR) on the efficiency of financial markets. In R. Douady, C. Goulet, & P. C. Pradier (Eds.), *Financial regulation in the EU* (pp. 151–198). London: Palgrave Macmillan.

[44] Lannoo, K. (2017). *MiFID II and the new market conduct rules for financial intermediaries: Will complexity bring transparency?* ECMI Policy Brief. European Capital Markets Institute. https://www.ceps.eu/wp-content/uploads/2017/05/ECMI%20PB%20No%2024%20KL_MarketConductRules.pdf. Accessed 12 July 2020.

[45] Bodellini, M. (2017). From systemic risk to financial scandals: The shortcomings of US hedge fund regulation. *Brooklyn Journal of Corporate, Financial & Commercial Law, 11*, 417. https://brooklynworks.brooklaw.edu/bjcfcl/vol11/iss2/6. Accessed 15 June 2020.

[46] Shelby, C. M. (2016). Are hedge funds still private? Exploring publicness in the face of incoherency. *SMU Law Review, 69*(2), 405–452.

[47] Athanassiou, Ph. (2009). *Hedge fund regulation in the EU: Current trends and future prospects*. The Netherlands: Wolters Kluwer.

[48] Dimmock, S. G., & Gerken, W. (2016). Regulatory oversight and return misreporting by hedge funds. *Review of Finance, 20*(2), 795–821. https://doi.org/10.1093/rof/rfv025.

the same time, another aspect which raised important questions among academicians[49] is whether "hedge fund managers fraudulently manipulate their performance results."[50] Considering the structure and requests of reporting for hedge funds, they are perceived by the financial market as rather opaque investment instruments, thus decreasing the efficiency in their pricing and reported performance.[51] According to Patton et al., "as informational asymmetries between investors and the managers of their investments increase,"[52] there is a deterioration in terms of trust between these two parties. Due to this aspect, important debates emerged concerning "whether hedge fund managers intentionally smooth their performance results to deceive investors, whether this smoothing behavior is more a result of the opaque and illiquid nature of the underlying assets contained within these funds or whether there are other explanations for this performance smoothing."[53]

One cannot underestimate the ramifications of market integrity infringements. Factors like the misuse of insider information, "the misevaluation of complex instruments" or the predilection manifested by brokers toward specific funds may reduce the investors' confidence but may also lead to the deterring of the business, since either "*bona fide* investors" are deprived of their money or their costs are increased. This can have a knock-on effect on market activity.[54] Also, loosening regulation can lead to "unintended consequences related to compromising market integrity and exposing investors to undue risk."[55] According to Professor Shelby, "hedge funds can still pose a systemic threat to the

[49] Aragon, G. O., & Nanda, V. (2017). Strategic delays and clustering in hedge fund reported returns. *Journal of Financial and Quantitative Analysis, 52*(1), 1–35.

[50] Smith, Z. Al., & Mumtaz, M. Z. (2017). Hedge fund managers and deceit: Is the accusation of performance manipulation valid? *Chinese Management Studies, 11*(3), 387–414 (2017). https://doi.org/10.1108/cms-02-2017-0035.

[51] Aragon, G. O., & Nanda, V. (2017). Strategic delays and clustering in hedge fund reported returns. *Journal of Financial and Quantitative Analysis 52*,(1): 1–35.

[52] Patton, A., Ramadorai, T., & Stratfield, M. (2013). Change you can believe in? Hedge fund data revisions. *Journal of Finance, 70*(3), 963–999.

[53] Jorion, P., & Schwartz, C. (2014). Are hedge fund managers systematically misreporting? Or not? *Journal of Financial Economics, 111*, 311–27.

[54] Rydge, J., & Comerton-Forde, C. (2004, September 7). *The Importance of market integrity. An analysis of ASX self-regulation.*

[55] Shelby, C. M. (2019). How did we get here? Dissecting the hedge fund conundrum through an institutional theory lens. *Bus Law, 74*(3), 735–787.

economy" and therefore, "enhancing transparency to hedge fund counterparties and investors can decrease systemic risk by empowering such market participants to better protect themselves against risk."[56]

As the economic relevance of these results might be significant and wide-ranging, financial market regulators have issued and enforced scores that are inspired from market integrity norms, which focus on the interdiction of insider exchanging together with market manipulation, on management of business problems, as well as on the governance together with fiduciary assignments of financial intermediaries. Resources and initiatives of regulated markets also contribute to maintain market integrity.[57]

The need to make sure that hedge funds cannot control or manipulate markets is, undoubtedly, pertinent. The suggestion that market integrity breaches are widespread to the hedge fund industry is nevertheless, misleading. Some of the real issues across markets are insider information, wrongful appraisals regarding either profit or loss (or both), and the incomplete exchange records. These tend to be mainly concentrated in the hedge fund industry and consequently, need to be removed from other, tighter regulated industries.[58] Recently, due to all the abovementioned problems encountered in the hedge funds industry, this industry has become overregulated, which makes even more stringent the necessity to truly determinate and comprehend hedge funds' performance and dynamic before certifying that managers tend to dishonestly manipulate their performance results.[59]

Hedge funds have undoubtedly highlighted some shortcomings in the existing market integrity protective framework and their operation has added to the urgency of revising monitoring mechanisms. However, literature states that the occurrence of "insider trading and market manipulation" within hedge fund managers tends to be extravagantly prominent lately if we consider recent US cases which have resulted in convictions

[56] Shelby, C. M. (2017). Closing the hedge fund loophole: The SEC as the primary regulator of systemic risk. *B.C.L. Review, 58*(2), 639–701.

[57] Edwards, F. (2006). Op. Cit., p. 47.

[58] Edwards, F. (2006). Op. Cit., p. 47.

[59] Smith, Z. Al., & Mumtaz, M. Z. (2017). Hedge fund managers and deceit: Is the accusation of performance manipulation valid? *Chinese Management Studies, 11*(3), 387–414. https://doi.org/10.1108/cms-02-2017-0035, on 15.06.2020.

and have shown a clear involvement in market manipulation and insider dealing of hedge funds.[60]

Also, it seems less probable that hedge funds could include the market integrity threat that some appear to believe that they do, if only because, despite the higher incidence, among hedge funds of more concentrated portfolios, a large part of them are not that powerful so that to manipulate prices.

The large hedge funds managers' tendency for manipulative behavior toward the markets cannot be assumed to be stronger than that of other financial market professionals to do so. This is both because the generous financial rewards received by the hedge fund administrators capable of generating abusive behavior represent no monopoly of this industry, but also because hedge fund managers cannot simply and spontaneously be expected to appreciate their prestige to a lesser extent than their counterparts from other financial organizations.[61]

Also, it is worth remembering that laws like those governing insider trading, notifiable holdings, and share registers are already implemented to *all* market participants, especially to hedge funds and their managers. This means that hedge fund-specific market integrity issues can be solved using common tools such as those applied to fraud or collusion in the banking or securities field, despite the relative difficulty of providing, in the case of hedge funds, evidence to substantiate unlawful conduct, due to the insufficient transparency or regulation within the sector and the complexity of its trading strategies.[62]

Regarding specifically hedge funds, dealings in tools accepted to enlist in regulated markets in the EU, these would fall under the MAD,[63] regardless of the inexistence of homogenous hedge fund regulation framework in other respects, they would be subjected squarely to the Community law security guarantee together with their managers and

[60] SEC v. Rajaratnam. (2012). SEC v. Rajaratnam 622 F.3d 159, 188 (2d Cir. 2010). https://www.courtlistener.com/opinion/176129/sec-v-rajaratnam/. Accessed 12 June 2020.

[61] Smith, Z. Al., & Mumtaz, M. Z. (2017). Hedge fund managers and deceit: Is the accusation of performance manipulation valid? *Chinese Management Studies, 11*(3), 387–414. https://doi.org/10.1108/cms-02-2017-0035, on 15.06.2020.

[62] Spangler, T., & Scholer, K. (2010). *A practitioner's guide to alternative investment funds* (2nd ed., p. 32). London: Sweet & Maxwell.

[63] Market Abuse Directive.

would be conditioned by very much alike conformity responsibilities just like the other industry participants, *inter alia* regarding market manipulation.[64]

The solution of market integrity problems raised by hedge fund market activities should be searched in: (a) the effective implementation of the existing rules rather than in the introduction of new ones, devised with hedge funds and their operations in mind and (b) the investors' accomplishment of the regular due diligence checklist suggested by sound investing procedures and constant precaution.[65]

Due to the financial crisis, systemic risk and its importance for stability and economy have been reviewed.[66] Nevertheless, neither systemic risk, nor the intentions to mitigate are new. Academic reviews[67] confirm that hedge funds can transmit risk to the financial system, which prompted specific measures, particularly after the financial crisis, in order to mitigate part of these risks. Thus, when referring to hedge funds, systemic risk, and financial stability, it appears that during the last decade, "hedge funds themselves have adjusted their business models, and international regulations, such as the Financial Stability Board's derivative reforms, have limited the risks that hedge funds pose to the financial system."[68] In this respect, many researches pointed out that "hedge funds could create and transmit systemic risk given their respective freedoms to trade in derivatives and carry unlimited leverage."[69] However, scholars focused mainly on the manner in which regulations can "be updated to regulate the growing threat of systemic risk, and many such solutions have sought to navigate how the fractured nature of our regulatory system

[64] Directive (EC) 2003/6, [2003] OJ L 96/16.

[65] FSA. (2005). *Hedge funds: A discussion of risk and regulatory engagement*. Financial Services Authority (Discussion Paper 05/4, 54); and McVea, H. (2007). Hedge funds and the new regulatory agenda. *Legal Studies, 27*(4): 709–739. https://doi.org/10.1111/j.1748-121x.2007.00069.x.

[66] Hilary, J. A. (2014). Putting the 'Financial Stability' in Financial Stability Oversight Council. *SSRN Electronic Journal*. https://doi.org/10.2139/ssrn.2485949. Accessed 12 June 2020.

[67] Kenny, F., & Mallaburn, D. (2017). Hedge funds and their prime brokers: developments since the financial crisis. *Bank of England Quarterly Bulletin Q4*, 1–12.

[68] Idem.

[69] Shelby, C. M. (2017). Closing the hedge fund loophole: The SEC as the primary regulator of systemic risk. *B.C.L. Review, 58*(2), 639–701.

could effectively regulate the blurred distinctions between hedge funds and banks."[70]

This is the main reason why quite a lot of the reform recommendations underline this need for macroprudential orientation of classical micro-prudential regimes. Otherwise said, such new regulatory regimes would not only focus on the solvency and other elements (in banking CAMEL) of commercial banks and other individual financial institutions (micro-prudential), but would also take into consideration the impact of financial institutions' activities on the financial system and real economy (macroprudential).[71]

In addition, one should take into consideration that at least some of the abuses associated with "hedge funds" imply leaks of internal information attributable to investment banks, making the receiving hedge fund managers "accomplices rather than the chief offenders."[72] After the financial crisis, all financial newspapers pointed fingers toward hedge funds, although the crisis must not be attributed to the hedge funds sector. Thus, the role and the effect of hedge funds on the crises raised opposing academic views.[73] They may have contributed to spread the chaos on the financial market, but they are not the ones to blame. In the aftermath of the financial crisis, all international organizations called for more regulation toward the shadow banking sector. Only if hedge funds continue to rely on investment banks for data related to market conditions and for the purpose of placing their trades, the "front running"[74] threat to market integrity often associated to these funds is still unapproachable, except through the wider use of electronic trading which becomes accessible only in the context of assets, when trade depends on exchanges.[75]

[70] Shelby, C. M. (2019). How did we get here? Dissecting the hedge fund conundrum through an institutional theory lens. *Bus Law, 74*(3), 735–787.

[71] McVea, H. (2007). Op. Cit., pp. 725–727.

[72] Mallaby, S. (2007). Op. Cit., p. 95.

[73] Stoforos, Ch., Degiannakis, St., & Palaskas, Th. (2017). Hedge fund returns under crisis scenarios: A holistic approach. *Research in International Business and Finance, 42,* 1196–207. https://doi.org/10.1016/j.ribaf.2017.07.056.

[74] Front running—i.e. the practice of trading ahead of a large buy or sell order placed by an institution or a mutual fund—is something that hedge fund managers can only do if they receive inside information form executing brokers who are probably more to blame than the hedge funds themselves for front-running.

[75] Eichengreen, B. (1999). The regulator's dilemma: Hedge funds in the international financial architecture. *International Finance, 2*(3), 411–440. Hildebrand commented that,

1.3.3 *Financial Stability as Rationale for Hedge Fund Regulation*

More than ten years after the financial crisis, the long shadow it has cast has started to fade. Most post-crisis prudential policies have already been decided, financial stability being one major issue in this respect. Thus, the protection of the financial system stability,[76] by means of ongoing systemic risk mitigation represents the third major motivation concerning financial market regulation and its primary objective, as some commentators, such as Phoebus Athanassiou, would say.[77]

Generally, active industry participants like hedge funds offer advantages for securities industries through liquidity promotion, but also through performance. In addition, they can be relevant for financial new products and for the reshuffle of fiscal risk. Nevertheless, there are several funds, which just like various highly leveraged organizations can throw into confusion or even worse, rupture every financial markets operation. Hedge funds were indeed considered causative of excessive but also, at certain times, turbulent industry processes emerging within vulnerable financial systems.[78] Many academic researchers considered that hedge funds did not have a major significance for the propagation of the financial market crises during the last several years.[79] Thus, Dixon et al. (2012)[80] analyze the measure in which HFs contributed to the increase of systemic risk and also to the 2009 financial crisis, concluding that although HFs can contribute to systemic risk, they "are not the primary cause of the financial crisis."[81]

in the interests of ensuring anonymity and avoiding front-running, the largest hedge funds should be made to deal with several prime brokers and that higher Chinese Walls should be erected between the prime brokers' proprietary trading and execution desks (Hildebrand, P. M. (2007). Hedge funds and prime broker dealers: Steps towards a best practice proposal. *Banque de France Financial Stability Review, 10,* 67–76).

[76] Athanassiou, Ph. (2009). Op. Cit., p. 64.

[77] Idem.

[78] Brown, J., et al. (1998). *Hedge funds and the Asian currency crisis of 1997* (NBER Working Paper No. 6427). https://doi.org/10.3386/w6427.

[79] Ibid.

[80] Dixon, L., Clancy, N., & Kumar, K. B. (2012). *Hedge funds and systemic risk.* Rand Corporation.

[81] Kalak, I., Azevedo, A., & Hudson, R. (2016). Reviewing the hedge funds literature II: Hedge funds' returns and risk management characteristics. *International Review of Financial Analysis, 48,* 55–66. https://doi.org/10.1016/j.irfa.2016.09.006.

"Systemic risk" is an ambiguous concept of particular major importance to the financial stability rationale. This term has been clearly defined as the occurrence ability of one crucial *systemic event* leading to several connected failures within financial entities, capable to adversely affect most operations of financial markets *as systems* (and not at the level of each of their participants). This capacity may also lead to the deterioration of the real economy[82] by, *inter alia*, the abruption of payments, the collapse of financial markets, the insufficiency of credit supply (market liquidity) and, ultimately, the occurrence of conditions favorable to deflation and recession.[83]

A report to the G 20 by the IMF,[84] BIS,[85] and FSB[86] describes the *systemic risk* concept in terms of "the disruption to the flow of financial services as (a) generated by a distortion of all parts of the financial system; and (b) capable of causing serious negative consequences for the real economy."[87]

The following definition of "systemic events" was provided: situations in which "…shocks to one part of the financial system lead to shocks elsewhere, impinging in turn upon the stability of the real economy."[88] Emphasizing the role of a loss for the real economy as a key feature of the economic crisis concept, the CRMPG[89] identified a financial event, which differed from a "systemic event" according to whether or not its consequences entail significant damages which hit not only financial systems but also real economies.[90] They defined the term as a drop occurring within

[82] De Bandt, O., Hartmann, P. (2002). Systemic risk: A survey. In C. Goodhart & G. Illing (Eds.), *Financial crisis, contagion and the lender of last resort: A book of readings* (pp. 11–28). London: Oxford University Press, p. 11.

[83] Danielsson, Jon et al. Op. Cit., pp. 538–539.

[84] International Monetary Fund.

[85] Bank for International Settlements.

[86] Financial Stability Board.

[87] IMF, BIS, & FSB (2009). Guidance to Assess the Systemic Importance of Financial Institutions, Markets and Instruments: Initial Considerations, at 5–6.

[88] Bordo, M. D. et al. (1998). Real versus pseudo-international systemic risk: Some lessons from history. *Review of Pacific Basin Financial Markets and Policies, 1*(1), 31–58. https://doi.org/10.1142/s0219091598000053.

[89] Counterparty Risk Management Policy Group.

[90] CRMPG II. (2005). Toward greater financial stability: A private sector perspective. Report 5. http://www.crmpolicygroup.org/. Accessed 15 June 2020.

productive investments, subsequent to the decrease in credit provisions, and the loss of balance as far as the financial, but also economic activities are concerned.[91]

Some aspects were considered very important in terms of financial stability: recurring financial crises during the last two decades, in association with the progressive liberalization ("deregulation") and increasing integration and interdependence of global capital markets. These have progressively shifted the focus of the contemporary regulatory policy debate from micro-prudential (investor-related) to macroprudential (systemic stability-related) issues.

One of the most important lessons to be learnt from the economic depression consists of the fact that previous financial regulation took exaggerated measures to preserve the integrity of private corporations, while it reduced the interdependence between financial organizations, not focusing at all on what this interdependence really symbolized in terms of systematic security. Essential causes creating systematic insecurity imply: "counterparty risk, the risk of default on the part of counterparties to OTC transactions, and fire-sale risk."[92] Indeed, many post-crisis scholarly researches have confirmed that systemic risk can be enhanced by hedge funds. As a consequence, international authorities, among which we mention the Financial Stability Board ("FSB") and the International Organization of Securities Commissions ("IOSCO") support the opinion that hedge funds "could in fact enhance systemic risk irrespective of the existing regulations over counterparties and OTC derivatives."[93] In this respect, the FSB and IOSCO stated in a consultation paper that: "[I]t is still possible for an investment fund to become highly leveraged through derivatives that are not centrally-cleared, particularly if margining practices for the non-centrally cleared derivatives are inadequate. Hence

[91] National Research Council. (2007). *New Directions for understanding systemic risk: A report on a conference cosponsored by the Federal Reserve Bank of New York and the National Academy of Sciences*. Washington, DC: The National Academies Press. https://doi.org/10.17226/11914.

[92] Goddard, J., et al. (2009). The financial crisis in Europe: Evolution, policy responses and lessons for the future. *Journal of Financial Regulation and Compliance, 17*(4), 362–380. https://doi.org/10.1108/13581980911004352.

[93] Shelby, C. M. (2017). Closing the hedge fund loophole: The SEC as the primary regulator of systemic risk. *B.C.L. Review, 58*(2), 639–701.

leverage constitutes a central component in the analysis of the counterparty channel, particularly for those funds that are not subject to any restrictions and may build up significant leverage positions (e.g. private funds)."[94]

As a consequence of the need for financial stability, both European and US regulatory bodies carefully scrutinized the shadow banking system during the last decade, and especially unregulated hedge funds in direct connection to international systemic risk. According to Mhalla et al. (2020), this "preoccupation stems from the high probability that these funds suffer extreme losses, which in turn would cause funds' closures, fire-sale of assets, and eventually, financial distress of systemically important institutions."[95] The current turmoils regarding the repo market[96] clearly exhibit the role that hedge funds play with regard to financial stability, as well as the change of trading activities involving systemic risks from commercial banks to hedge funds. According to Mhalla et al. (2020), "combined with their intense lobbying efforts to escape regulations, this highlights the need to define improved regulatory policies."[97]

It was Brunnermeier et al. (2009) who have asserted the measurement of systemic risks with a variable named $CoVaR$. This is composed of "*the value at risk*" (VaR) of financial entities depending on other entities which are at risk. A growth of $CoVaR$ relative to VaR reveals

[94] Financial Stability Board. (2015). Consultative Document (2nd): Assessment Methodologies for Identifying Non-Bank Non-Insurer Global Systemically Important Financial Institutions 33. https://www.fsb.org/2015/03/assessment-methodologies-for-identifying-non-bank-non-insurer-global-systemically-important-financial-institutions/. Accessed 15 June 2020.

[95] Mhalla, L., Hambuckers, J., & Lambert, M. (2020). *Extremal connectedness and systemic risk of hedge funds*. https://ssrn.com/abstract=3519295 or http://dx.doi.org/10.2139/ssrn.3519295. Accessed 12 June 2020.

[96] Financial Times. (2019, January 19). Hedge fund leverage risk comes under scrutiny. *Financial Times*. https://www.ft.com/content/156023df-0c22-3945-aad0-6140113a9ee6. Accessed 15 June 2020.

[97] Mhalla, L., Hambuckers, J., & Lambert, M. (2020). Extremal connectedness and systemic risk of hedge funds. https://ssrn.com/abstract=3519295 or http://dx.doi.org/10.2139/ssrn.3519295. Accessed 12 June 2020.

the growth in systemic risks.[98] Another group[99] proposes that credit institutions receive the authority to oversee systemic security. This delegation completes the already enforced responsibilities regarding inflation constancy and (for instance, if one refers to "the US Federal Reserve") unemployment mitigation. Several issues must be considered in terms of supervising: the analysis of data and information collection regarding the asset positions, but also risk vulnerability in a standardized form enabling the contrast between entities; the public issue of information, subjected to periodic intervals which provide a balance between disclosure and transparency goals, but also rightful concerns regarding financial innovative techniques, and proprietary business models protection; and last but not least, the elaboration of a yearly report on systemic security and risk.[100]

Hedge fund operations and entities also need to have financial stability, as this is the main reason for their coming under the spotlight in much the same way as the other financial market participants because of the fact that their operations might have undermining effects. The other way around, comparing a hedge fund with an investment credit institution, the first one is probably by far the most changing of comparable leverage because it may fight the whole financial market by means of its strong advantages.

When addressing the systemic stability risk usually generated by hedge funds, the main scenario considered by policy makers is failure. Instead of the downfall of an individual large fund, the collapse of several funds might be more credible and pertinent; regardless of their form or features, breaking down during the same period, disseminating confusion and alarm throughout the economy, and involving systemic risk. The former situation described is called "contagion." The issues directly related to the latter consist of "liquidity risk" (the request of cutting loose investments after some important deficit), "risk to counterparties," and "herding" (possibly unsuccessful various funds investing in similar areas). Concerns regarding the fact that market might fail from contagion are mainly hypothetical. Lately, a plethora of academic studies on hedge funds address

[98] Brunnermeier, M., & Cheridito, P. (2019). Measuring and allocating systemic risk. *Risks, 7*(2), 46. https://doi.org/10.3390/risks7020046, p. 31.

[99] Squam Lake Working Group on Financial Regulation.

[100] Hedge Funds. (1999). *Leverage, and the lessons of long-term capital management.* Op. Cit.

systemic risk directly,[101] but neither of them concludes the gravity of the threat, nor even provides a definitive measure or assessment. As Bodellini underlines, "hedge funds have demonstrated that they can pose and spread systemic risk across the financial markets, and that their managers can use them to commit fraud and misappropriation of fund assets."[102] According to him, the regulation in force nowadays seems inconsistent and largely inappropriate to prevent and face systemic risks of hedge funds.

The previously mentioned so-called "direct" channel which can result in systemic contagion has also an "indirect" channel. This channel represents another way for hedge funds to affect financial stability, characterized by: "…a forced hedge fund liquidation [that] exacerbates market volatility and reduces liquidity in key markets (especially where the hedge fund under threat was the prime provider of liquidity)." Systemic correlations between asset classes increase in times of stress and market movements amplified by the potential for herding.[103]

The transmission mechanisms of systemic risk are one of the issues debated in an article by Professor Rosa Lastra[104] describing how "the channels of contagion or transmission mechanisms can be classified into at least four categories […]: a) the inter-bank, inter-institution, inter-instrument channel; b) the payment systems channel; c) the information channel; and d) the psychological channel."[105] These transmission channels contribute to disseminate the systemic risk across the financial markets globally. As Professor Lastra explains, "what makes a crisis of a systemic nature is not so much the trigger event (*causa proxima*), but these transmission mechanisms, domestically and internationally. If the

[101] Bodellini, M. (2017). From systemic risk to financial scandals: The shortcomings of US hedge fund regulation. *Brooklyn Journal of Corporate, Financial & Commercial Law, 11,* 417. https://brooklynworks.brooklaw.edu/bjcfcl/vol11/iss2/6. Accessed 15 June 2020.

[102] Idem.

[103] King, M. R., & Maier, P. (2007). *Hedge funds and financial stability: The state of the debate* (Discussion Paper 9). Bank of Canada. https://www.bankofcanada.ca/2007/09/discussion-paper-2007-9/. Accessed 12 July 2020.

[104] See Lastra, R. M. (2011a). Systemic risk, SIFIs and financial stability. *Capital Markets Law Journal, 6*(2), 197–213.

[105] Lastra, R. M. (2011a). Op. Cit., pp. 197–213.

linkages are strong, the potential for systemic instability increases. If the connections are weak, there is less of a threat of systemic risk."[106]

The systemic implications of the industry's operation and its potential to generate, precipitate or propagate systemically relevant shocks include three main reasons which have recently stepped forward. These are: (a) the public prominence hedge fund failure experiences starting with 1998 and the possibility that they reoccur within the next future, (b) the ongoing increase of the hedge funds' segments of the asset management industry, together with the insufficiency of accessible data for the public reported in their balance sheets, but also the quite recent decrease of the industry profits in conjunction with (c) the function and impact of hedge funds within the credit risk transfer markets.[107] This does not consider these guaranteed concerns and the relevance of hedge fund late developments for the determination of the applicability of the systemic stability rationale of financial regulation to hedge funds.

The financial crisis of 2007–2009 has led to an increase in regulation regarding hedge funds. All international organizations pointed the fingers toward the shadow-banking sector as being the one to blame for the recent financial crisis. For the reasons illustrated above, hedge funds were not to blame, as they spread systemic risk, but they did not create it. Thus, two major arguments support this affirmation. On the one hand, they were not involved in the forming of the toxic securities at the center of the crisis since they had nothing to do with nonconforming mortgages, as their repackage into securities, the bundle of these securities along with other securities as collateral for yet other securities, have provided a rating to the structured credit securities or have distributed

[106] Lastra, R. M. (2011a). Op. Cit., pp. 197–213.

[107] These are by no means the only ones. A paper highlights the following reasons for concerns over the external effects of hedge funds: the risk that hedge funds might be a source of market vulnerability because of their use of high-risk strategies or the deterioration of the quality of investment managers following an increase in transactions and a reduction in profit opportunities; the risk that hedge funds might trigger steep price fluctuations, especially in low liquidity markets, and that prime brokers' counterparty-risk-management standards for hedge funds are lowered as the prime brokerage business becomes more competitive; and the concern that the emergence of risks will go undetected because of the constraints imposed by quantitative data and secondary related information of hedge funds and the limitations of available analytical methods (Bank of Japan (2006) Recent Developments in Hedge Funds, 48).

the above-mentioned securities.[108] On the other hand, there were many others that bought the high yield bearing subprime-backed securities and among these one can find: pension and mutual funds, insurance corporations, as well as European and Asian banks, all having been similarly convinced into buying them.[109] It is the view of the author of this book thinks that an increase of regulation towards the hedge fund sector will not be the right answer for the shadow-banking problem. Hedge funds should be more regulated, but according to certain criteria, more transparency and disclosure should be asked to hedge fund managers bearing in mind that the risk of overregulation is high. Private investors will find alternative ways to invest their money. An example of this statement belongs to the renowned George Soros, who has decided to gradually diminish his hedge fund on claims that in the aftermath of "the Dodd-Frank Act" there is too much regulation affecting the hedge fund sector in the United States. What Soros did was to give back money to his investors and establish a family office. According to the new "provisions of the Dodd-Frank Act" in the United States, a family office will not incur the risk of being supervised by the Federal Reserve as the large hedge funds currently may incur this risk in the event of being considered a systemically important financial institution.[110]

Issues involving systemic stability produced a major regulatory impact to date[111] and are likely to provide an ongoing focus of regulatory attention with the increase of financial risks within the banking sector. However, regulatory authorities must carefully consider that stricter regulation implies more constraints for the hedge funds industry and consequently limit the number of services provided. Regulators should consider adjusting the tolerance parameter, in order to reach "the right level of stringency for an optimal balance between financial stability and

[108] Kirchgaessner, S., & Sender, H. (2008, November 13). Hedge fund chiefs blame the system for financial crisis. *Financial Times*. www.ft.com/cms/s/0/0f8c0216-b193-11dd-b97a-0000779fd18c.html#axzz1hB5fGiqm. Accessed 12 July 2020.

[109] Shadab, H. (2008, November 13). Hedge funds and the financial market. In *Testimony before the House Committee on Oversight and Government Reform*. Washington, DC. http://mercatus.org/publication/hedge-funds-and-financial-market. Accessed 15 June 2020.

[110] See Chapter 6 on Regulation of hedge funds in US.

[111] Market transparency, deposit insurance, capital adequacy and bank failure resolution regulatory measures, to name a few, are premised (at least to an extent) on financial stability considerations as a justification for financial market regulation.

enough flexibility for the financial sector to operate efficiently."[112] This has to be achieved in an iterative process in which the regulator fine-tunes the tolerance parameter and monitors the response from the financial sector and the effects on the rest of the economy.

1.4 Regulatory Response at International Level

In 1999, in the United States, immediately after the 1998 LTCM collapse, "the President's Working Group on Financial Markets" (which has become the Financial Stability Oversight Council) released an initial study.[113] The Working Group issued subsequent premises, but also guidance on private pools of capital starting with 2007.[114] "The Basel Committee" had released its first study on credit institution and "*Highly Leveraged Institutions*" (HLIs) in 1999 with a support paper on sound practices and a follow-up paper in January 2000.[115] IOSCO issued an initial paper in November 1999, comparing work of the Basel Committee with a joint Basel/IOSCO report in 2001.[116] IOSCO issued subsequent surveys in 2006 and 2007 on hedge funds.[117] In 2005, the

[112] Brunnermeier, M., & Cheridito, P. (2019). Measuring and allocating systemic risk. *Risks, 7*(2), 46. https://doi.org/10.3390/risks7020046.

[113] PWG. (1999). Hedge funds, leverage and the lessons of long term capital management. In *Report of the President's Working Group on Financial Markets*. https://www.treasury.gov/press-center/press-releases/Pages/report3097.aspx. Accessed 20 June 2020.

[114] PWG. (2007). Principles and guidelines regarding private pools of capital. President's Working Group on Financial Markets. https://www.treasury.gov/press-center/press-releases/Pages/hp272.aspx. Accessed 20 June 2020.

[115] Several articles and reports need to be consulted: Basel Committee on Banking Supervision (1999a). Banks' Interaction with Highly Leveraged Institutions; and Basel Committee on Banking Supervision (1999b). Sound Practices for Banks' Interactions with Highly Leveraged Institutions. See also Basel Committee on Banking Supervision (2000). Banks' Interaction with Highly Leveraged Institutions: Implementation of the Basel Committee's Sound Practices Paper.

[116] Basel Committee and IOSCO (2001). Review of Issues Relating to Highly Leveraged Institutions.

[117] Several articles and reports need to be consulted: IOSCO, The Regulatory Environment for Hedge Funds: A Survey and Comparison, 2006; and IOSCO (2008). Report on Funds of Hedge Funds—Final Report. International Organization of Securities Commissions. https://www.iosco.org/library/pubdocs/pdf/IOSCOPD276.pdf. Accessed 15 August 2020.

"Banking Supervision Committee" (BSC)[118] issued a separate paper on the vulnerability of EU credit institutions "to hedge funds."[119]

Similarly, the *"Financial Stability Board"* (FSB) issued an important document on HLIs in 2000, which was updated seven years later. The 2000 report was mainly concerned with systemic risk and leverage following the collapse of LTCM in 1998.[120] The FSB recommended mainly a market discipline rather than a direct regulation based approach. Specific recommendations were made on risk management, oversight, disclosure, and surveillance.[121]

While the 2007 report accepted that substantial improvements had been made in prudential supervision and risk management capacity, a number of changes had arisen within the hedge fund system a short time ago, while further specific factors increased the threat of systemic exposure. Summing up, after the collapse of Long-Term Capital Management L.P. it became obvious that hedge funds can lead to the appearance of risks and therefore shatter the financial stability "due to their close relationship with large and complex financial institutions (LCFIs), especially commercial and investment banks."[122] These aspects are still forcing regulators to date, to increase the control of hedge fund activities.[123] Another instrument which may offer positive response to controlling risks posed by hedge funds is their indirect regulation by "constraining their counterparties is often considered to be the most effective mechanism."[124]

[118] Of the European System of Central Banks (ESCB).

[119] European Central Bank. (2005). Large EU Banks' Exposures to Hedge Funds.

[120] Financial Stability Forum. (2000). Report of the Working Group on Highly Leveraged Institutions.

[121] Eight specific recommendations were made concerning; (a) stronger counter party risk management; (b) stronger risk management by hedge funds; (c) enhanced regulatory oversight of credit providers; (d) greater risk sensitivity in credit institution capital adequacy regulations; (e) sustaining industry progress (f) building a firmer infrastructure; (i) enhanced national supervision of financial market activities; and (j) good practice recommendations for foreign exchange trading.

[122] Bowe, M., Kolokolova, O., & Yu, L. (2019). *The Volcker rule and the hedge fund liquidity circle*. http://dx.doi.org/10.2139/ssrn.3486305. Accessed 15 June 2020.

[123] Kaal, W. A., & Krause, T. A. (2016). Hedge funds and systematic risk. *Handbook on hedge funds*. http://dx.doi.org/10.2139/ssrn.2748096.

[124] Nabilou, H., & Pacces, A. M. (2015). The hedge fund regulation dilemma: Direct vs. indirect regulation. *William and Mary Business Law Review, 6*(1), 183–236.

After the 2008 depression, the discoveries related to Madoff Ponzi scheme and the discoveries regarding plenty of declared frauds brought to trial by SEC,[125] it is not difficult at all to comprehend the active, increasing the attention of regulators, legislators, and investors. While the industry press and academic literature have well-covered some specific features of the Madoff saga, it is of no use to observe that those alleged operational risks and their evaluation have been and continue to be a major item within the hedge funds sector. At the same time, after more than a decade, "Ponzi schemes and the courts efforts to address them and to recover funds for defrauded investors continue."[126]

Regulation of hedge funds apart from straighter reinforcement for existing laws will progress in the directions presented in Fig. 1.3.

In this respect, primary legislators and regulators need to continue to directly address hedge fund regulations. "The Dodd-Frank Act" for the United States and the AIFMD II[127] for Europe continue to adopt more uptight regulations on hedge fund industry.

Other national and industry initiatives have also been continued. The FCA replaced the FSA, in charge of the maintenance and supervision of the UK financial and banking industry.[128] These processes and measures are implemented through the fact that the FCA makes sure that the pertinent markets function in a suitable manner, offering an appropriate degree

[125] Lidstone, H. K. (2019, January 9). *Bernie Madoff after ten years; recent Ponzi scheme cases, and the Uniform Fraudulent Transactions Act*. https://ssrn.com/abstract=3313045 or http://dx.doi.org/10.2139/ssrn.3313045. Accessed 15 June 2020.

[126] Idem.

[127] Following the March 2018 European Commission proposal to amend the Alternative Investment Fund Managers Directive ("AIFMD") to provide for a uniform regime for "pre-marketing" of alternative investment funds ("AIFs") across the European Union ("EU") an agreement has now been reached on the text to be implemented. A two-year national implementation period began on 2 August 2019 for the Directive to be fully transposed from 2 August 2021.

[128] The Financial Services Act 2012 (2012). c. 21 ('FSA12'), ss 6(1A) to (1T) (Amendments of Financial Services and Markets Act 2000) pt 1A, ss 1A—1T; Scheds 1ZA to Financial Services and Markets Act 2000, c. 8 (FSMA2000).

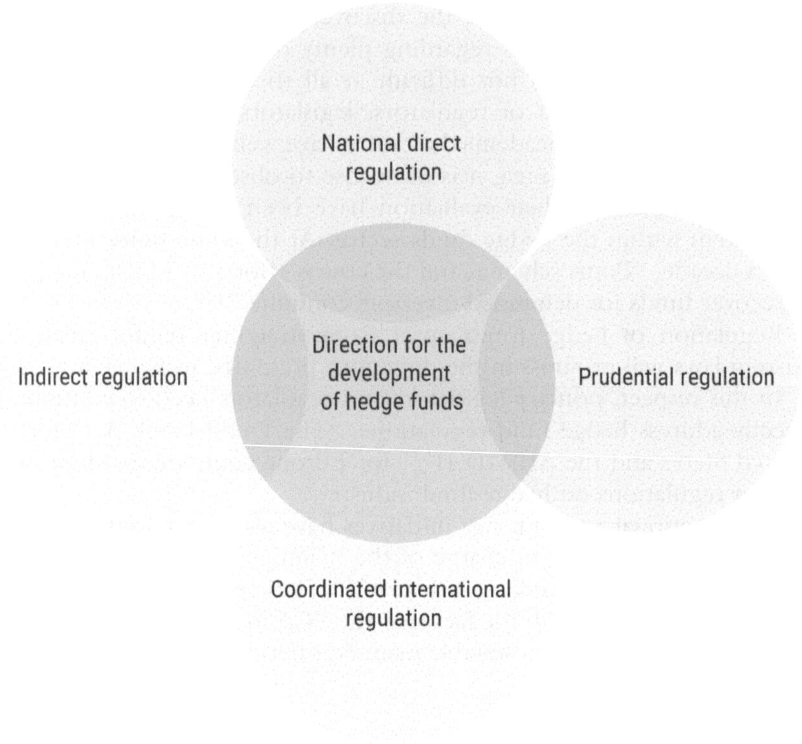

Fig. 1.3 Directions for the development of regulation of hedge funds (*Source* Kaal 2019)

of consumer safety,[129] maintaining and enhancing the stability[130] of the financial system in the United Kingdom, at the same time stimulating

[129] Ibid., ss 1 B(3)(a), and 1C.

[130] Stability is a matter for the Bank of England: Bank of England Act 1998, c. 11 (BEA98), ss 2A, 2B, 2C, 2D, and pt 1A; the Prudential Regulation Authority that has succeeded a role to stability- The Financial Services Act 2012, c. 21 ('FSA12'), ss 6(1A) to (1T) (Amendments of Financial Services and Markets Act 2000), ss 2B, 2O, and 2J. Stability—the Banking Act 2009, c. 1 ('BA09'), ss 1, 4; The Banking (Special Provisions) Act 2008 (2008) c. 2 has largely been replaced by the Banking Act 2009, ss 1, and 11-13 (Stabilisation Options); For Integrity—The Financial Services Act 2012, ss 1(3)(b), and 1 D.

competition[131] for the consumers' advantages.[132] Another attribution of the FCA consists in supervising the manner in which undertakings by authorized financial institutions occur, monitoring that the regulations are respected and correctly enforced, concerning possible lawbreaker firms.[133]

Both new authorities orchestrate their efforts. Thus, there are certain contexts, when the PRA can, in the case when it is appropriate, to require the FCA to stop exercising its authority in issues regarding bankruptcy or regulations concerning a PRA-approved entity.[134] Also, this can occur if the PRA considers that, exercising its' authority may endanger UK's security concerning the financial system, or may conduct to the collapse of a PRA-approved institution, so that the entire British banking and financial system can be damaged.[135] Actually, both the FCA and the PRA cooperate with the Bank of England, in order to ease the bank's mission concerning the preservation of financial stability. This subject will be further addressed in Chapter 4.

The IMF[136] argued in its April 2020 GFSR with direct reference to asset managers that "regulators should ensure that risk management frameworks are being applied in a robust and effective manner. Regulators should support the availability of the widest possible set of liquidity management tools (such as gates/deferred redemptions, swing pricing) and encourage fund managers to make full use of the available tools where it would be in the interests of unitholders to do so."[137] According to this report, authorities must carefully monitor fund managers and help them solve their difficulties concerning "obtaining timely and reliable valuations."[138] At the same time, IMF advices them to "monitor developments and seek to provide clarity to fund managers on their expectations,

[131] The Financial Services Act 2012, s 1(3)(c).

[132] Kovas, A. (2014). *Understanding the financial conduct authority—A guide for senior managers*. Leicestershire: Troubador Publishing.

[133] FSMA2000, pt 6, s 73.

[134] The Financial Services Act 2012, c. 21, pt 4.

[135] Ibid., s 74; see, FSMA2000, sched 1ZB.

[136] International Monetary Fund. (2020). *Global financial stability report: Markets in the time of COVID-19*, Chapter 1, p. 26.

[137] Idem.

[138] Idem.

including on the circumstances in which use of liquidity management tools, including a (temporary) suspension of redemptions, may become appropriate."[139]

As far as financial markets and their stability, the IMF report focuses on the use of appropriate definitions, good communication, efficient and well-calibrated measures. It also refers to the authorities' obligation to carefully consider the adoption of temporary restrictions,[140] and their possible negative impact on liquidity and price discovery, the final aim of authorities being to make sure that they are justified in the measures they take by the increase of market confidence and of financial stability. This IMF also advices that these restrictions must be taken for short periods of time and "implemented within a predictable and reliable framework."[141]

The interconnectedness issue among financial system players is to be addressed mainly through broader macroprudential coverage, and reinforcement of the capital and liquidity requirements for the global banking industry. As the financial crisis was caused not by the lack of capital, but rather by a liquidity crisis induced by concerns about asset quality and transparency, the "*Basel Committee on Banking Supervision*"(BCBS) developed enhanced risk-weighted capital adequacy standards (the "Basel III" framework). To strengthen the resilience of banks to loan losses, hybrid "Tier 1" capital is to be phased out for more conventional forms of permanent equity capital (that is common shares and retained earnings). More capital will be needed for contingent calls on capital arising from derivative instruments. Additionally, the capital adequacy framework will incorporate a non-risk weighted (or "simple") leverage ratio intended to identify leverage buildup from any gaming of the capital adequacy rules, and minimum liquidity standards (both short and long-term coverage ratios). Considerable attention was paid to pro-cyclicality in bank lending and provisioning practices. In December 2017, BCBS published one last report concerning Basel III regulations: Basel III: Finalizing post-crisis reforms,[142] aiming at reducing excessive variability of risk-weighted assets

[139] Idem.

[140] Such as the use of short selling.

[141] International Monetary Fund. (2020). Global financial stability report: Markets in the time of COVID-19, Chapter 1, p. 26.

[142] Basel Committee on Banking Supervision (2017). Bank for International Settlements. Basel III: Finalising post-crisis reforms. https://www.bis.org/bcbs/publ/d424.pdf. Accessed 15 June 2020.

through the introduction of "transitional arrangements to implement the new standards to ensure an orderly and timely implementation by jurisdictions and adjustment by banks."[143]

At the inaugural 2008 summit of the "Group of Twenty," leaders called for the development of best practices to enhance transparency, both at market and counterparty levels, for hedge funds and other systemically significant financial institutions. The G-20's subsequent declaration on the 2nd of April 2009 also favored increased regulatory oversight for hedge funds, and for other private capital pools to improve investor protection but also systemic risks management.[144] In this respect, IOSCO's Technical Committee was established in November 2008 and released its final report outlining six principles for regulation of hedge funds in June 2009.[145] In response to G20's declaration of 2009, IOSCO started publishing, every two years, a report on hedge funds. This year, IOSCO published its Report on the Fifth IOSCO Hedge Funds Survey,[146] gathering information as on September 30, 2018. This survey provides insight into the hedge funds industry at an international level, "making it an integral part of IOSCO's policy work in the investment management sector,"[147] focusing on "the markets in which hedge funds operate, their trading activities, leverage, funding and counterparty information,"[148] in this manner, IOSCO supporting the G20 initiative for risk mitigating connected with hedge funds.

Among other international initiatives aiming at understanding and monitoring risks in the hedge fund sector, we also mention Financial Stability Board (FSB) Policy Recommendations to Address Structural Vulnerabilities from Asset Management Activities. These recommendations published in January 2017 were addressing structural vulnerabilities having to do with asset management activities. One of the central points

[143] Idem, p. 2.

[144] Excerpt from Declaration Summit on Financial Markets and the World Economy, Action Plan to Implement Principles of Reform, G-20, 15 November 2008.

[145] For further details see IOSCO Final Report 2009.

[146] IOSCO. (2020). Report on the fifth IOSCO hedge funds survey. Final Report. International Organization of Securities Commissions. https://www.iosco.org/library/pubdocs/pdf/IOSCOPD653.pdf. Accessed 17 June 2020.

[147] Idem.

[148] Bank of England. (2017). Hedge funds and their prime brokers: Developments since the financial crisis. *Quarterly Bulletin Q4*, p. 7.

of the report was leverage, seen as the most important vulnerability in the hedge funds industry. Two major risks were underlined by these recommendations, which require policy response:

a. "the lack of consistent and available data on leverage; and
b. wide variation in limits imposed on financial and synthetic leverage across jurisdictions."[149]

In this vein, the FSB proposed to regulatory bodies (conducted by IOSCO) that before the end of 2018, they should "identify and/or develop consistent measures of leverage in funds, to facilitate more meaningful monitoring of leverage."[150]

It remains to be seen whether future solution will take the form of mere regulatory reforms, such as adaptations to and reinforcement of the current framework while respecting the existing principles, or regulatory revolution, eventually necessary changes to the current regulations. In any case, whatever the legal form and details of the new supervisory approach, all actors involved will have to make one compromise or another, and they have to manifest a willingness to find rapid solutions to the obvious political difficulties that any attempt to move in the direction of more integrated supervision and more shared powers at the Community level can be expected to entail.

1.5 Concluding Remarks

While the current regulatory environment appears more settled compared to the recent past, regulators across the world continue to set high expectations intended to maintain a strong, resilient financial sector through hedge fund firms having robust financial and operational resilience, supported by strong risk management and compliance capabilities. In our view, this may provide an opportunity for leading financial firms to pivot from having to build frameworks to reflect a barrage of new regulations to optimising through taking advantage of new technologies and operating models.

[149] Idem, p. 7.
[150] Idem, p. 7.

This chapter groups and illustrates different sets of regulations applicable to hedge funds aiming the protection of investors, the market integrity, and the financial system stability.

The relevance of economic activities regulation can only be highlighted if the process takes into account the risks of market failure, which can be limited by regulation without excessively interfering with the associated legitimate advantages. The decision-making process implies whether (and the manner in which) certain given economic activities are supposed to be regulated. During this process, one must also assess not only its risks and advantages, how they correspond to one or more of the financial regulation rationales, but also whether there is any empirical evidence and a wider, *lato sensu* "philosophical" disagreement regarding the regulation.

Disagreement evidently exists; the question is where does it emerge from? According to analyses performed throughout this chapter, this emerges mainly from the highly ambiguous role of hedge funds in the financial crisis. Following the crash of LTCM in 1998, many dealer-banks requested overall collateralization of hedge fund undertakings. In agreement with this, hedge funds used to be less levered as compared to credit institutions. Afterward, the collapse of significant hedge funds, among which one can mention Amaranth in 2006, and the major redemptions by investors during but also after the crisis, which did not lead to systemic problems. Furthermore, hedge funds have fewer assets and less leverage as compared to credit institutions. This could diminish the probability that hedge funds might be a causal agent of any future crisis, such as the current pandemic one. In the absence of the systemic risk threat and of an exact delineation of social externalities brought about by hedge funds, the aim of direct hedge fund regulation is not so clear. However, in the light of the above-mentioned events, requests for a tighter regulation start to make sense, as the supervisors started to face four major issues: investors' protection, transparency, market integrity, and risk mitigation.

Regarding the financial crisis, the author does not attribute it to the hedge funds. However, the blame belongs to hedge funds in terms of their involvement and responsibility during the crisis, having turned into a whim for the problems that affect many issues regarding financial markets. International regulators examined hedge funds closely and to a great extent, and consequently implemented, alongside other measures, registration requests, limitations on leverage, and increasing disclosure and transparency for protecting investors.

So far, there has been harsh criticism regarding the new regulation in the Dodd-Frank Act due to the fact that it is reactive, but also narrow-minded. Similar criticisms emerged also about the AIFMD Directive. As already seen, scholars have suggested a wide range of possible solutions to address the concerns in the debate on hedge funds and hedge fund regulation. Some favor regulatory arbitrage as a measure against systemic failure. Other scholars state that the pre-Dodd-Frank Act approach dealing with allowing advisers to voluntarily register would be the most effective in this respect, proposing an approach based on trust that would let funds having previously earned general trust from the public to develop on the grounds of that trust, with less or no interference of regulation.

The author argues that this debate on the most suitable type of hedge fund regulation appears to be very controversial. The shift of the criteria dealing with hedge fund investments, the appointment of one self-regulatory authority, the application of higher disclosure criteria to counterparties, and the increase of leverage limitation as well as of the transparency disclosure are some of the recommendations discussed in this chapter. The author continues her argumentation as regarding the benefit of fees from hedge funds, regulation of hedge fund creditors, and the moderation of the mutual funds regulation for the increase of the competitiveness between hedge funds.

Thus, the author states that hedge funds regulators worldwide face an increasing dichotomy. The major concern of the regulators is the investors' protection in conjunction with making sure that the industry is operating properly. With this in mind, regulators try not to tightly regulate the industry while tailoring measures and recommendations for avoiding systemic risks.

One very frequently mentioned argument of individuals against each type of external intervention in the industry processes is that not all types of regulation are compatible with the hedge fund industry's basic role and characteristics. This is the main reason to presume that regulation would be bound to affect negatively their development and performance, not in terms of the imminent growth in compliance costs entailed by its introduction.

Other often cited argument opposing to regulation of the industry consists of the fact that normative compulsion might dissuade hedge funds or their managers from locating in the EU, forcing them to leave Europe in order to find locations that are more "favorable." In the event that this might happen, the argument further develops as follows: regulatory arbitrage would be reinforced and the sector's effective supervision diminished. Finally, the argument continues as regulating the industry would not serve a meaningful function, as the purpose of each normative initiative would prove unsuccessful in covering offshore hedge fund jurisdictions, regardless of the "extraterritorial" nature of its consequence.

On the other side, a professor experienced in financial law notes that: "We should also beware of the excesses of regulation and the dangers of overregulating a given sector or type of institutions, creating incentives for businesses to move outside the regulatory framework. Any regulatory perimeter brings its own shadows and loopholes."[151]

Considering the arguments stated above in this chapter, hedge fund regulation appears not only as a necessity, but also as a wise issue. From the author's point of view, moderation, and good sense should prevail, and therefore, nothing would come to indicate that this kind of implementation could prove unfeasible. There is one major aspect that should not be overseen: it is likely that moderation or sound judgment would not prevail within these funds structure in two cases. The first one is if this emerging chance to eventually implement harmonized norms applicable to onshore hedge funds had been offered as a consequence of an important European or global financial crisis a priori their operation. The second is if its norms had not been the result of observation but rather, the outcome of extreme hurry, together with urgency in the aftermath of the disorderly unwinding of the positions of one or more hedge funds. Moreover, the regulatory process could become a scapegoat to the caprices of political tensions, together with the vagaries of public perceptions regarding the image of ideal hedge fund regulatory overview.[152]

Current efforts that aim to regulate hedge funds through their registration with regulators together with requesting disclosure of pertinent data might aid minimizing moral hazard, social externalities, and systemic risk that the hedge fund industry is generating, making all the efforts

[151] Lastra, R. M. (2011b, March 23). *The quest for international financial regulation*. Inaugural Lecture presented at Charterhouse Square.

[152] ...restructuring in response to a regulatory failure is probably the weakest ground for reform' (Carmichael, Jeffrey, Australia's Approach to Regulatory Reform in Carmichel, J., et al. (2004). *Aligning financial supervisory structures with countries' needs* (p. 95). Washington: WBI Learning Resources.

to improve investor protection. So far, hedge funds' involvement in the ongoing financial crisis is still not clear. In this respect, dissymmetric hedge fund regulation emerging from the Dodd-Frank Act together with the AIFM Directive becomes in the author's perspective disadvantageous and even undermining, this requiring a global regulation of hedge funds with major attention on investor protection.

From a global point of view, the AIFM Directive might develop incentives for regulatory arbitrage, might lead to retaliatory action by states from outside the EU and might lead to the achievement of an appropriate level of investor protection. In the long term, this might prove counterproductive for the competitiveness of the EU alternative investment community in conjunction with financial markets in Europe, while keeping an adequate standard of protection of investors' interests. In this regard, the author considers that investors would benefit in terms of protection from the AIFM Directive mainly because of the disclosure and operational requirements that it stipulates. Thus, this disclosure would not only provide investors with up-to-date material data about their funds, but, at the same time, would also offer features of the potential conflicts of interests and risk factors the investors could be subjected to.

In the Dodd-Frank Act, the SEC received the authorization from the Congress to adopt norms in order to interpret the exemptions for hedge funds. The SEC needs to use its discretion to provide the vital-needed guiding. In the author's opinion, many of the regulatory dilemmas in the AIFM Directive, but also in the Dodd-Frank Act might have been prevented or even entirely avoided if the Basel Committee had introduced a fee for credit institutions' lending exposure to hedge funds. Basel III capital requests that credit institutions implement a fee for banks' assets according to their systemic risk contribution. The Basel III measure for hedge fund lending exposure could have been associated with a focus on the exposure of credit institutions to complex financial products. This might prove of great benefit in addressing the connection between market failure in terms of financial instruments, and in augmenting the significance of hedge funds within the market for financial instruments.

Due to these reasons, the author acknowledges the cross-border nature of the hedge funds sector and therefore the need to create a harmonized international hedge funds regulation regime. This is exactly what the MiFID II is planning to do. In October 2019 the European Securities and Markets Authority (ESMA) updated its Questions and Answers (Q&As) regarding transparency issues under MiFID II. These Q&As aim to promote common supervisory approaches and practices in the application of MiFID II, and provide responses to questions posed by the general public and market participants relating to hedge funds transparency, investor protection, and market structures issues. Not only will these be updated on an ongoing basis, but authorities in some of the biggest European countries—United Kingdom, Germany, France, and Italy—are assessing the impact and success of MiFID II. Brussels is believed to be considering changes to standards. What is constant is the requirement to be compliant with MiFID II.

As a concluding remark, the governments, central banks, but also every regulating authority need to choose between the effectiveness of a regulation, on the one hand and the price implied in complying with it, on the other hand. As far as the hedge funds sector is concerned, an investment area careful to watchdogs after decades of being unregulated, regulators will have to convince fund managers that a continuous free in/out data flow, together with open communication are of major importance, and that active intervention will occur if market stability and investor protection are at risk.

Therefore, the greatest challenge that regulators will have to face is finding an ideal suitable manner to increase compliance in conjunction with *investors' protection* without forcing hedge fund managers to move to unregulated jurisdictions.

In the author's opinion, the trend towards the new architecture of financial regulation has three similar ways with important different characteristics referring to the US, the UK, particularly in the Brexit context, and the EU financial regulatory frameworks.

References

AIMA. (2013). AIMA's guide to sound practices for hedge fund valuation 45. Alternative Investment Management Association. https://www.aima.org/sound-practices/guides-to-sound-practices.html. Accessed 1 July 2020.

Aragon, G. O., & Nanda, V. (2017). Strategic delays and clustering in hedge fund reported returns. *Journal of Financial and Quantitative Analysis, 52*(1), 1–35.

Aragon, G. O., Nanda, V. K., Zhao, H. (2019). *Investor protection and capital fragility: Evidence from hedge funds around the world*. https://ssrn.com/abstract=3207064 or http://dx.doi.org/10.2139/ssrn.3207064. Accessed 1 July 2020.

Athanassiou, Ph. (2009). *Hedge fund regulation in the EU: Current trends and future prospects*. The Netherlands: Wolters Kluwer.
Bank of England. (2017). Hedge funds and their prime brokers: Developments since the financial crisis. *Quarterly Bulletin Q4*. https://www.bankofengland.co.uk/quarterly-bulletin/2017/q4/hedge-funds-and-their-prime-brokers-developments-since-the-financial-crisis. Accessed 12 June 2020.
Bank of Japan. (2006). *Recent developments in hedge funds*. https://www.boj.or.jp/en/research/brp/ron_2006/ron0606a.htm/. Accessed 12 June 2020.
BarclayHedge. (2020a). *Global hedge fund database*. https://www.barclayhedge.com/databases/global-database. Accessed 12 June 2020.
BarclayHedge. (2020b). *Hedge fund industry: Assets under management—Historical growth of assets*. https://www.barclayhedge.com/solutions/assets-under-management/hedge-fund-assets-under-management/hedge-fund-industry. Accessed 12 June 2020.
Barth, D., Joenvaara, J., Kauppila, M., & Wermers, R. R. (2020). *The hedge fund industry is bigger (and has performed better) than you think* (Working Paper 20-01). Office of Financial Research. https://ssrn.com/abstract=3544181. Accessed 20 June 2020.
Basel Committee on Banking Supervision. (1999a). *Banks' interaction with highly leveraged institutions*. https://www.bis.org/publ/bcbs45.htm. Accessed 20 June 2020.
Basel Committee on Banking Supervision. (1999b). *Sound practices for banks' interactions with highly leveraged institutions*. https://www.bis.org/publ/bcbs46.htm. Accessed 20 June 2020.
Basel Committee on Banking Supervision. (2000). *Banks' interaction with highly leveraged institutions: Implementation of the Basel committee's sound practices paper*. https://www.bis.org/publ/bcbs68.htm. Accessed 20 June 2020.
Basel Committee on Banking Supervision. (2004). *The joint forum, final disclosure in the banking, insurance and securities sectors: Issues and analysis*. https://www.bis.org/publ/joint08.htm. Accessed 20 June 2020.
Basel Committee on Banking Supervision. (2017). *Bank for international settlements*. Basel III: Finalising post-crisis reforms. https://www.bis.org/bcbs/publ/d424.pdf. Accessed 15 June 2020.
Basel Committee & IOSCO. (2001). Review of issues relating to highly leveraged institutions. Basel Committee on Banking Supervision and the International Organization of Securities Commissions (IOSCO). https://www.bis.org/publ/bcbs79.htm. Accessed 20 June 2020.
Bodellini, M. (2017). From systemic risk to financial scandals: The shortcomings of US hedge fund regulation. *Brooklyn Journal of Corporate, Financial & Commercial Law, 11*, 417. https://brooklynworks.brooklaw.edu/bjcfcl/vol11/iss2/6. Accessed 15 June 2020.

Bordo, M. D., et al. (1998). Real versus pseudo-international systemic risk: Some lessons from history. *Review of Pacific Basin Financial Markets and Policies, 1*(1), 31–58. https://doi.org/10.1142/s0219091598000053.

Bowe, M., Kolokolova, O., & Yu, L. (2019). *The Volcker rule and the hedge fund liquidity circle*. http://dx.doi.org/10.2139/ssrn.3486305. Accessed 15 June 2020.

Brown, J., et al. (1998). *Hedge funds and the Asian currency crisis of 1997* (NBER Working Paper No. 6427). https://doi.org/10.3386/w6427.

Brunnermeier, M., & Cheridito, P. (2019). Measuring and allocating systemic risk. *Risks, 7*(2), 46. https://doi.org/10.3390/risks7020046.

Brunnermeier, M., et al. (2009). *The fundamental principles of financial regulation*. International Centre for Monetary and Banking Studies. https://www.google.com/url?sa=t&rct=j&q=&esrc=s&source=web&cd=&ved=2ahUKEwi_kb64_vHqAhUvA2MBHbo4DjwQFjABegQIAxAB&url=https%3A%2F%2Fcepr.org%2Fsites%2Fdefault%2Ffiles%2Fgeneva_reports%2FGenevaP197.pdf&usg=AOvVaw0LdeNJGiwnJbLU0DIGDY6V. Accessed 15 June 2020.

Carmichel, J., et al. (2004). *Aligning financial supervisory structures with countries' needs*. Washington: WBI Learning Resources.

Cartwright, P. (2004). *Banks, consumers and regulation*. London: Hart Publishing.

CRMPG II. (2005). Toward greater financial stability: A private sector perspective. Report 5. http://www.crmpolicygroup.org/. Accessed 15 June 2020.

Davies, H. (1999). Financial regulation: Why bother? Mimeo, society of business economists lecture. London. https://www.google.com/url?sa=t&rct=j&q=&esrc=s&source=web&cd=&ved=2ahUKEwixxPnnpo7rAhVH_SoKHezuCBcQFjAAegQIBBAB&url=https%3A%2F%2Fwww.fep.up.pt%2Fdisciplinas%2Fpgaf924%2FPGAF%2FTexto_2_David_Llewellyn.pdf&usg=AOvVaw1wZ9UcGtdUeXKcxxd4pszC. Accessed 15 June 2020.

De Bandt, O., & Hartmann, P. (2002). Systemic Risk: A Survey. In C. Goodhart & G. Illing (Eds.), *Financial crisis, contagion and the lender of last resort: A book of readings* (pp. 11–28). London: Oxford University Press.

Dimmock, S. G., & Gerken, W. (2016). Regulatory oversight and return misreporting by hedge funds. *Review of Finance, 20*(2), 795–821. https://doi.org/10.1093/rof/rfv025.

Dixon, L., Clancy, N., & Kumar, K. B. (2012). *Hedge funds and systemic risk*. Rand Corporation. https://www.rand.org/pubs/monographs/MG1236.html. Accessed 12 July 2020.

Directive (EC) 2003/6, [2003] OJ L 96/16.

Dworkin, G. (1971). Paternalism. In R. Wasserstrom (Ed.), *Morality and the law*. Belmont: Wadsworth Pub. Co.

Edelman, D., Fung, W., & Hsieh, D. A. (2013). Exploring uncharted territories of the hedge fund industry: Empirical characteristics of mega hedge fund firms. *Journal of Financial Economics, 109*(3), 734–758.

Edwards, F. R. (1999). Hedge funds and the collapse of long-term capital management. *The Journal of Economic Prospectives, 13*(2), 189–210.

Edwards, F. R. (2006). Hedge fund and investor protection regulation. *Federal Reserve Bank of Atlanta Economic Review, 91*(4), 35–48.

Eichengreen, B. (1999). The regulator's dilemma: Hedge funds in the international financial architecture. *International Finance, 2*(3), 411–440.

Eureka. (2019). *The Eureka hedge report April 2019*. https://static1.squarespace.com/static/5a02fa72bff200aa6a54edd9/t/5cc1449515fcc0de796a5b6f/1556169910440/Eureka+Hedge+Report_Apr-2019.pdf. Accessed 12 June 2020.

European Central Bank. (2005). *Large EU banks' exposures to hedge funds*. https://www.ecb.europa.eu/press/pr/date/2005/html/pr051125_1.en.html. Accessed 12 June 2020.

Farrell, D. (2018). Increasing investor protection through improving hedge fund valuation. *St. John's Law Review, 92*(1), 149–172.

Financial Stability Board. (2015). *Consultative document (2nd): Assessment methodologies for identifying non-bank non-insurer global systemically important financial institutions*, 33. https://www.fsb.org/2015/03/assessment-methodologies-for-identifying-non-bank-non-insurer-global-systemically-important-financial-institutions/. Accessed 15 June 2020.

Financial Stability Forum. (2000). *Report of the working group on highly leveraged institutions*. https://www.fsb.org/2000/04/r_0004a/. Accessed 15 June 2020.

Financial Times. (2019, January 19). Hedge fund leverage risk comes under scrutiny. *Financial Times*. https://www.ft.com/content/156023df-0c22-3945-aad0-6140113a9ee6. Accessed 15 June 2020.

FSA. (2005). *Hedge funds: A discussion of risk and regulatory engagement*. Financial Services Authority (Discussion Paper 05/4, 54). https://www.google.com/url?sa=t&rct=j&q=&esrc=s&source=web&cd=&ved=2ahUKEwj5kZPfyr_rAhUpD2MBHesWCMEQFjAAegQIARAB&url=https%3A%2F%2Fuk.practicallaw.thomsonreuters.com%2F8-200-9311&usg=AOvVaw3Io1B8JB1NtxMi4RqHwbU4. Accessed 15 June 2020.

Garcia, G., & Prast, H. (2003). *Depositor and investor protection in the EU and the Netherlands: A brief history*. Netherlands Central Bank Research Series Supervision (discontinued) 54. Netherlands Central Bank, Directorate Supervision. https://www.google.com/url?sa=t&rct=j&q=&esrc=s&source=web&cd=&cad=rja&uact=8&ved=2ahUKEwiQk4v8yr_rAhW1DmMBHfppBDwQFjAAegQIAxAB&url=https%3A%2F%2Fideas.repec.org%2Fp%2Fdnb%2Fressup%2F54.html&usg=AOvVaw0-qhvc4XsokA1LfDO2RMH0. Accessed 15 June 2020.

Gillet, R., Ligot, St., & Firouzi, H. (2017). The challenges and implications of the Markets in Financial Instruments Directive (MiFID) and of its revision (MiFID II, MiFIR) on the efficiency of financial markets. In R. Douady, C. Goulet, & P. C. Pradier (Eds.), *Financial Regulation in the EU* (pp. 151–198). London: Palgrave Macmillan.

Goddard, J., et al. (2009). The financial crisis in Europe: Evolution, policy responses and lessons for the future. *Journal of Financial Regulation and Compliance, 17*(4), 362–380. https://doi.org/10.1108/13581980911004352.

Gortsos, C. (2018). *Stricto sensu investor protection under the MiFID II: A systematic overview of Articles 24–30*. Newcastle upon Tyne: Cambridge Scholars Publishing.

Hilary, J. A. (2014). Putting the 'financial stability' in financial stability oversight council. *SSRN Electronic Journal*. https://doi.org/10.2139/ssrn.2485949. Accessed 12 June 2020.

Hildebrand, P. M. (2007). Hedge funds and prime broker dealers: Steps towards a best practice proposal. *Banque de France Financial Stability Review, 10*, 67–76.

Hoffmann, B., & Paetzmann, K. (2018). Investor protection, valuation methods and the German alternative funds industry. *Journal of Risk Finance, 19*(2), 174–189. https://doi.org/10.1108/jrf-06-2017-0101.

IMF, BIS, & FSB. (2009). *Guidance to assess the systemic importance of financial institutions, markets and instruments: Initial considerations*. Report to the G-20 Finance Ministers and Central Bank Governors. Financial Stability Board, International Monetary Fund, Bank for International Settlements. https://www.google.com/url?sa=t&rct=j&q=&esrc=s&source=web&cd=&ved=2ahUKEwiWtN-z9o_rAhXRyaQKHQiXBdEQFjAAegQIBRAB&url=https%3A%2F%2Fwww.imf.org%2Fexternal%2Fnp%2Fg20%2Fpdf%2F100109.pdf&usg=AOvVaw0xlMldT2IFHtMJUfln-VaS. Accessed 15 June 2020.

International Monetary Fund. (2020). Global financial stability report: Markets in the time of COVID-19, Chapter 1. https://www.imf.org/~/media/Files/Publications/GFSR/2020/April/English/text.ashx?la=en. Accessed 15 June 2020.

IOSCO. (2003). *Objectives and principles of securities regulation*. International Organization of Securities Commissions. https://www.google.com/url?sa=t&rct=j&q=&esrc=s&source=web&cd=&cad=rja&uact=8&ved=2ahUKEwjxw8Oj-Y_rAhWF_qQKHYkXDLEQFjAFegQIBBAB&url=https%3A%2F%2Fwww.legco.gov.hk%2Fyr04-05%2Fenglish%2Fpanels%2Ffa%2Fpapers%2Ffa0217cb1-880-9e.pdf&usg=AOvVaw3eFJc6fhdvH9dHGqByEHeN. Accessed 17 June 2020.

IOSCO. (2008). *Report on funds of hedge funds—Final report*. International Organization of Securities Commissions. https://www.iosco.org/library/pubdocs/pdf/IOSCOPD276.pdf. Accessed 15 August 2020.

IOSCO. (2020). *Report on the fifth IOSCO hedge funds survey: Final report*. International Organization of Securities Commissions. https://www.iosco.org/library/pubdocs/pdf/IOSCOPD653.pdf. Accessed 17 June 2020.

Jorion, P., & Schwartz, C. (2014). Are hedge fund managers systematically misreporting? Or not? *Journal of Financial Economics, 111,* 311–327.

Kaal, W. A., & Krause, T. A. (2016). Hedge funds and systematic risk. *Handbook on Hedge Funds*. https://doi.org/10.2139/ssrn.2748096.

Kaal, W. A. (2019). *Indirect regulation of hedge funds*. Oxford Handbook of Hedge Funds. https://ssrn.com/abstract=3405660. Accessed 15 June 2020.

Kalak, I., Azevedo, A., & Hudson, R. (2016). Reviewing the hedge funds literature II: Hedge funds' returns and risk management characteristics. *International Review of Financial Analysis, 48*, 55–66. https://doi.org/10.1016/j.irfa.2016.09.006.

Kenny, F., & Mallaburn, D. (2017). Hedge funds and their prime brokers: Developments since the financial crisis. *Bank of England Quarterly Bulletin, Q4*, 1–12.

King, M. R., & Maier, P. (2007). *Hedge funds and financial stability: The state of the debate* (Discussion Paper 9). Bank of Canada. https://www.bankofcanada.ca/2007/09/discussion-paper-2007-9/. Accessed 12 July 2020.

Kirchgaessner, S., & Sender, H. (2008, November 13). Hedge fund chiefs blame the system for financial crisis. *Financial Times*. www.ft.com/cms/s/0/0f8c0216-b193-11dd-b97a-0000779fd18c.html#axzz1hB5fGiqm. Accessed 12 July 2020.

Kovas, A. (2014). *Understanding the financial conduct authority—A guide for senior managers*. Leicestershire: Troubador Publishing.

La Porta, R., et al. (1997). Legal determinants of external finance. *Journal of Finance, 52*(3), 1131–1150. https://doi.org/10.1111/j.1540-6261.1997.tb02727.x.

La Porta, R., et al. (1999). Corporate ownership around the world. *Journal of Finance, 54*(2), 471–517. https://doi.org/10.1111/0022-1082.00115.

Lannoo, K. (2017). *MiFID II and the new market conduct rules for financial intermediaries: Will complexity bring transparency?* ECMI Policy Brief. European Capital Markets Institute. https://www.ceps.eu/wp-content/uploads/2017/05/ECMI%20PB%20No%2024%20KL_MarketConductRules.pdf. Accessed 12 July 2020.

Lastra, R. M. (2011a). Systemic risk, SIFIs and financial stability. *Capital Markets Law Journal, 6*(2), 197–213.

Lastra, R. M. (2011b, March 23). *The quest for international financial regulation*. Inaugural Lecture presented at Charterhouse Square.

Lewis, C. M. (2016). *Liquid alternative mutual funds: An asset class that expands opportunities for diversification* (Working Paper). https://www.google.com/url?sa=t&rct=j&q=&esrc=s&source=web&cd=&ved=2ahUKEwj3loL065LrAhXUN8AKHcQ4DF8QFjAAegQIBRAB&url=https%3A%2F%2Fwww.sec.gov%2Fcomments%2Fs7-24-15%2Fs72415-96.pdf&usg=AOvVaw13ZlRZSPR882Oag7Oy7Uit. Accessed 12 July 2020.

Lidstone, H. K. (2019, January 9). *Bernie Madoff after ten years; recent Ponzi scheme cases, and the Uniform Fraudulent Transactions Act*. https://ssrn.com/abstract=3313045 or http://dx.doi.org/10.2139/ssrn.3313045. Accessed 15 June 2020.

Maxey, D. (2014, February 4). If a security isn't trading, what is it really worth? *The Wall Street Journal*. https://www.wsj.com/articles/sec-looking-at-how-alternative-funds-value-investments-1391096281?tesla=y. Accessed 12 June 2020.

McCahery, J. A., & de Roode, Al. (2019). *The lost decade for hedge funds: Three threats* (TILEC Discussion Paper No. DP2019-027. Working Paper No. 486/2019). European Corporate Governance Institute – Law. SSRN: https://ssrn.com/abstract=3501551. Accessed 20 June 2020.

McVea, H. (2007). Hedge funds and the new regulatory agenda. *Legal Studies, 27*(4), 709–739 (2007). https://doi.org/10.1111/j.1748-121x.2007.00069.x.

Mhalla, L., Hambuckers, J., & Lambert, M. (2020). *Extremal connectedness and systemic risk of hedge funds*. https://ssrn.com/abstract=3519295 or http://dx.doi.org/10.2139/ssrn.3519295. Accessed 12 June 2020.

Moloney, N. (2006). *EC securities regulation*. New York: Oxford University Press.

Nabilou, H., & Pacces, A. M. (2015). The hedge fund regulation dilemma: Direct vs. indirect regulation. *William and Mary Business Law Review, 6*(1), 183–236.

National Research Council. (2007). *New directions for understanding systemic risk: A report on a conference cosponsored by the Federal Reserve Bank of New York and the National Academy of Sciences*. Washington, DC: The National Academies Press. https://doi.org/10.17226/11914.

Paredes, T. A. (2006). On the decision to regulate hedge funds: The SEC's regulatory philosophy, style and mission. *University of Illinois Law Review, 5*, 975–1036.

Patton, A., Ramadorai, T., & Stratfield, M. (2013). Change you can believe in? Hedge fund data revisions. *Journal of Finance, 70*(3), 963–999.

Preqin. (2020). *Global hedge fund report*. https://www.preqin.com/insights/global-reports/2020-preqin-global-hedge-fund-report. Accessed 20 June 2020.

PWG. (1999). Hedge funds, leverage and the lessons of long term capital management. In *Report of the President's Working Group on Financial Markets*. https://www.treasury.gov/press-center/press-releases/Pages/report3097.aspx. Accessed 20 June 2020.

PWG. (2007). Principles and guidelines regarding private pools of capital. President's Working Group on Financial Markets. https://www.treasury.gov/press-center/press-releases/Pages/hp272.aspx. Accessed 20 June 2020.

Ramsay, I. (1995). Consumer credit law, distributive justice and the welfare state. *Oxford Journal of Legal Studies, 15*(2), 177–197. https://doi.org/10.1093/ojls/15.2.177.

Rydge, J., & Comerton-Forde, C. (2004). *The importance of market integrity: An analysis of ASX self-regulation.* https://www.google.com/url?sa=t&rct=j&q=&esrc=s&source=web&cd=&ved=2ahUKEwiss5XZ8ZLrAhXjo4sKHUNKByEQFjABegQIBxAB&url=http%3A%2F%2Fciteseerx.ist.psu.edu%2Fviewdoc%2Fdownload%3Fdoi%3D10.1.1.175.4322%26rep%3Drep1%26type%3Dpdf&usg=AOvVaw2dARyVneZQ4rdqayt85NK3. Accessed 20 June 2020.

SEC. (2003). *Implications of the growth of hedge funds.* Staff Report 47. US Securities and Exchange Commission. https://www.google.com/url?sa=t&rct=j&q=&esrc=s&source=web&cd=&ved=2ahUKEwiVndKB8pLrAhVxoVwKHZwrC2IQFjABegQIBBAB&url=https%3A%2F%2Fwww.sec.gov%2Ffiles%2Fimplications-growth-hedge-funds-09292003.pdf&usg=AOvVaw0xWmtBMdBKzQCWGMFTydKP. Accessed 20 June 2020.

SEC v. Rajaratnam. (2012). SEC v. Rajaratnam 622 F.3d 159, 188 (2d Cir. 2010). https://www.courtlistener.com/opinion/176129/sec-v-rajaratnam/. Accessed 12 June 2020.

SEC. (2017). SEC's private fund statistics. US Securities and Exchange Commission. https://www.sec.gov/divisions/investment/private-funds-statistics/private-funds-statistics-2017-q4.pdf. Accessed 12 June 2020.

SEC. 17 CFR Parts 275 and 279. Release No. IA-2333 (File No. S7-30-04). https://www.sec.gov/rules/final/ia-2333.htm. Accessed 12 June 2020.

Shadab, H. (2008, November 13). Hedge funds and the financial market. In *Testimony before the House Committee on Oversight and Government Reform.* Washington, DC. http://mercatus.org/publication/hedge-funds-and-financial-market. Accessed 15 June 2020.

Shelby, C. M. (2016). Are hedge funds still private? Exploring publicness in the face of incoherency. *SMU Law Review, 69*(2), 405–452.

Shelby, C. M. (2017). Closing the hedge fund loophole: The SEC as the primary regulator of systemic risk. *B.C.L. Review, 58*(2), 639–701.

Shelby, C. M. (2019). How did we get here? Dissecting the hedge fund conundrum through an institutional theory lens. *Bus Law, 74*(3), 735–787.

Sklar, R. (2009). Hedges or thickets: Protecting investors from hedge fund managers' conflicts of interest. *Fordham Law Review, 77*(6), 3251–3323.

Smith, Z. Al., & Mumtaz, M. Z. (2017). Hedge fund managers and deceit: Is the accusation of performance manipulation valid? *Chinese Management Studies, 11*(3), 387–414. https://doi.org/10.1108/cms-02-2017-0035.

Soe, A. M., & Poirier, R. (2018). *Does past performance matter? The persistence scorecard*. https://www.spglobal.com/en/research-insights/articles/does-past-performance-matter-the-persistence-scorecard. Accessed 12 June 2020.

Spangler, T., & Scholer, K. (2010). *A practitioner's guide to alternative investment funds* (2nd ed.). London: Sweet & Maxwell.

Stoforos, Ch., Degiannakis, St., & Palaskas, Th. (2017). Hedge fund returns under crisis scenarios: A holistic approach. *Research in International Business and Finance, 42,* 1196–1207. https://doi.org/10.1016/j.ribaf.2017.07.056.

Van Berkel, S. (2008). Should hedge funds be regulated? *Journal of Banking Regulation, 9,* 196–223. https://doi.org/10.1057/jbr.2008.https://doi.org/10.s.

CHAPTER 2

Regulation of Hedge Funds in the EU

2.1 Introduction

As the primary source of harmonized rules relevant to hedge funds, the current European regulatory framework comprises: the "*Undertakings for Collective Investment in Transferable Securities*" (UCITS) Directives and the "*Markets in Financial Instruments Directive*" (MiFID) together with the "*Alternative Investment Fund Managers*" (AIFM Directive). The following sections examine how the contemporary UCITS Directives from the first until their last version UCITS V, and the MiFID (I and II) and AIFM Directives together with a number of other Community legal acts, could affect first of all, investor protection, then, the marketing and distribution of hedge fund shares and units and the activities of their managers and last, the shaping of the European hedge fund industry's regulatory future as a result of their evolution and implementation. Hence, the major aim of this chapter is to study the latest evolutions in terms of regulatory integration of the EU economic market analyzing mainly the protection of investors' rights.

This chapter is organized as follows: first, it explains the dynamics of the financial security structure within the EU in connection to the European regulatory framework, more precisely, an overview of the UCITS Directives, focusing on investor protection. This section also explains the European law evolution from the single market concept, the Single European Act, to the Lamfalussy framework and De Larosière Report.

A. M. Fagetan, *The Regulation of Hedge Funds*,
https://doi.org/10.1007/978-3-030-63706-4_2

The next section deals with valuable information learned from the financial crisis, it addresses the main recent regulatory reforming trends and assesses investor's interests protection, but also the UCITS Directives. The third part presents the UCITS IV Directive and the UCITS V Directive, as well as key changes compared to UCITS IV. The fourth section presents a critical overview of "the AIFM Directive." The fifth and the sixth parts focus generally on the MiFID Directive components in relation with funds regulation. The analysis of the AIFM Directive approved in the turmoil of the financial crisis is valuable in order to comprehend the new rules regarding hedge funds in the European market. The impact of this Directive on the hedge fund sector and particularly on investor protection is the main reason for the author's decision to provide an overview of the critical evaluation of the Directive. This review includes also several critical analyzes, which exceed the mere presentation of the legislative integration operation. After examining other sources of Community legal rules regarding the protection of investing parties within the regulation of hedge funds, the chapter ends with some concluding remarks.

The chapter points out that the major objective of the reform is in line with that of the book theme, namely the creation of uniform market conditions across the EU (although the book addresses the making of uniform market conditions at the international level), by increasing investor protection, investor confidence, and the safeguard of the UCITS market integrity worldwide.

2.2 The European Regulatory Framework: An Overview of the UCITS Directives

Over time, Directive 85/611/EEC was updated four times, Directive 2014/91/EU of July 23, 2014 ("UCITS V"[1]) being the last one.

The history of UCITS Directives dates back to 1985, when UCITS I was issued with the aim of creating a single European regulatory framework for mutual funds.[2] In 2001, this Directive was incorporated under

[1] The UCITS acronym stands for Undertaking for Collective Investment in Transferable Securities.

[2] The so-called European passport for funds, which would allow the distribution of investment funds in order to be sold within the European Economic Area (EEA) on a cross-border basis, having as main request to be authorized in a European Union Member State.

Fig. 2.1 The history of the UCITS Directive—From UCITS I to UCITS V (*Source* Author's analysis)

the form of Directives 2001/107/EC and 2001/108/ES, also known as UCITS II and UCITS III. The original Directive was further amended, by UCITS IV Directive of January 13, 2009, in a new text.[3]

In 2012 the European Commission issued a consultation paper concerning UCITS which had as main purpose receiving market feedback on several issues, among which, of major relevance was UCITS investment policy having to do with eight key aspects: "eligible assets for UCITS; efficient portfolio management techniques; over-the-counter (OTC) derivatives; extraordinary liquidity management rules; depositary passports; money market funds (MMFs); long-term investments; and UCITS IV updates."[4]

There was a tendency at that time for referring to this as UCITS VI directive,[5] being thought that this consultation paper would later turn into further amendments to UCITS framework, "seen as part of the EC's wider strategy to regain investors' confidence and deepen the integration of financial markets."[6] However, up to date, no information regarding this potential UCITS VI Directive was issued by the EU Commissions (Fig. 2.1).

[3] Directive 2009/65/EC.

[4] Muller, C., & Braunstein, C. (2014). UCITS VI: In practice. *Journal of Securities Operations & Custody, 6*(3), 220–227.

[5] Joenvaara, J., & Kosowski, R. (2015). *The effect of regulatory constraints on fund performance: New evidence from UCITS hedge funds*. https://ssrn.com/abstract=2598012 or http://dx.doi.org/10.2139/ssrn.2598012. Accessed 20 June 2020.

[6] Muller, C., & Braunstein, C. (2014). Op. Cit., p. 220.

As already seen, the UCITS have been the subject of many changes over time,[7] just as most areas of European financial market regulation, several updates being made, of different types with the aim of completing and/or detailing some aspects, updates which will be further discussed.

The regulatory integration includes several phases. The first lasts until 2001, and this is the *single market* phase,[8] followed by the harmonization process and afterwards by the shift to a collective admission procedure. Still, during the same year, the *Lamfalussy process* occurred, which represented a significant "institutional innovation within the EU."[9]

Secondly, until the adoption of the Lamfalussy procedure, the EU policy focused on the adoption of directives stipulating regulatory rules, but the supervision necessity appeared with the Lamfalussy procedure. The Lamfalussy committees setup a regulatory framework and engaged in the supervisory practices process that would ensure the consistent enforcement of EU regulations in all EU member states.[10]

This subsection is structured chronologically and follows the phases presented above. For the general overview of each regulatory phase, relevant regulatory policy contexts were summarized and the most important directives approved during the given period were noted. Exclusive consideration was given to the Lamfalussy procedure and the De Larosière Report.

The author starts her analysis with the *single market* concept, initiated in 1985, when the EC's White Paper introduced the single market

[7] For further details see Annunziata, F. (2019, March 3). Investment services and investment funds. In M. Ventoruzzo & F. Fabbrini (Eds.), *Research handbook on European Economic Law*. Edward Elgar; Bocconi Legal Studies Research Paper No. 3345943. https://ssrn.com/abstract=3345943 or http://dx.doi.org/10.2139/ssrn.3345943, on 12.05.2020.

[8] Council Directive 85/611/EEC of 20 December 1985 on the coordination of laws, regulations and administrative provisions relating to undertakings for collective investment in transferable securities (UCITS). https://eur-lex.europa.eu/legal-content/EN/TXT/?uri=celex%3A31985L0611, on 02.05.2020.

[9] Kudrna, Z. (2009). *The EU financial market policy: Evolution, innovation and research outlook* (Working Paper No. 04:1-35) Institute for European Integration Research. https://www.academia.edu/975557/The_EU_Financial_Market_Policy_Evolution_Innovation_and_Research_Outlook. Accessed 15 June 2020.

[10] Idem.

approach to financial services.[11] This document included political availability to undertake economic reformation, in the sense of market liberalization and additional market integration in the EU.[12] Later on, the framework for EMU[13] and the single currency framework were developed by the Maastricht Treaty of 1992. This also involved the establishment of the ECB and the "*European System of Central Banks*" (ESCB).[14]

In the summer of 2000, the Lamfalussy Committee issued several assessments regarding the regulatory adoption for securities as "mechanisms for regulating securities markets and practices to ensure: timely adjustments, faster convergence and better cooperation."[15]

The Lamfalussy Committee distinguished between the legislation framework and its enforcing rules and the reallocated responsibility for each of them, by a four-level governance mechanism. They include old and new bodies, which would eventually determine the implementation of better communication between the EU and the national bodies dealing with financial regulations. This process was introduced in 2001 in the securities field. Four years later, it expanded to banking and insurance.[16] Due to "the Lamfalussy" report, a new European regulatory framework regarding the single financial market was setup in 2003. The current organizational framework would represent the basis of this regulatory system and this would not involve any abilities transfer or any Treaty alteration.

The High-Level Group[17] appointed by the EC, issued a report on the 25th of February 2009,[18] recommending 31 measures necessary

[11] European Commission. (1985). Completing the Internal Market, White Paper to the European Council of 28/29 June 1985 in Milan, COM (85) 310 final.

[12] Recine, F., & Teixeira, P. G. (2009). The new financial stability architecture in the EU. Frankfurt Institute for Law and Finance. *Working Paper Series, 110*(12), 1–36, p. 3.

[13] European Market Union.

[14] Recine, F., Teixeira, P. G., Op. Cit., p. 5.

[15] Recine, F., et al., Op. Cit., p. 9. For further details see Gortsos, C. (2019). *The evolution of European (EU) Banking Law under the influence of (public) International Banking Law: A comprehensive overview research study*. Prague: Faculty of Law, Charles University. http://dx.doi.org/10.2139/ssrn.3334493.

[16] Idem.

[17] Garicano, L., & Lastra, R. M. (2010). Towards a new architecture for financial stability: Seven principles. *Journal of International Economic Law, 13*(3), 597–621. https://doi.org/10.1093/jiel/jgq041.

[18] Report of the High-Level Group on Financial Supervision in the EU. (2009). Brussels. http://ec.europa.eu/, on 17.06.2020.

to establish the "*European Financial Supervisory Architecture.*" Accordingly, the EC[19] (2009) proposed the reform of "the European financial supervisory" framework, with the implementation of two pillars: Pillar I—"*European Systemic Risk Council*" (ESRC) and Pillar II—the "*European System of Financial Supervisors*" (ESFS).

Even nowadays, EU member states have decentralized prudential monitoring, based on the home country supervision key element, combined with prior regulatory harmonization-related mutual recognition.[20]

The 4th Framework Directives of the Lamfalussy Process represented one step forward in pledging for an effective and active operation of the EU's securities sector. Several directives and regulations have been enacted since and further shifts have been proposed by now.

"The UCITS" represents a group of "European Directives" whose purpose is to let "Collective Investment Schemes" function within the EU without restriction due to one "authorization" provided by a member state. Indeed, several member states have introduced secondary regulatory requirements limiting the independent process of hedge funds so that to ensure the protection of local asset managers.[21]

This subsection of the chapter provides an overview of the UCITS Directives framework as the author will first explain its origins and evolution until the UCITS IV version of the directive. UCITS II refers to the UCITS reform from the '90s that was never adopted. Several scholars considered "that the management company directive was UCITS II with the product directive as UCITS III."[22] A separate subsection is dedicated to the latest version of the directive, the UCITS V Directive, promoting significant changes to the UCITS framework. UCITS V stands as the latest recital of the initial Directive, imposing new remuneration rules, sanctions regime and depositary role on the fund industry.

[19] European Commission. (2009). *European financial supervision*. Impact Assessment. http://ec.europa.eu/. Accessed 17 May 2011.

[20] Thiemann, M., & Tröger, T. (2019). *It's the tail-risk, stupid! Precluding regulatory arbitrage in shadow banking with a normatively charged approach to supervision capitalizing on multipolar regulatory dialogues* (SAFE Working Paper, No. 260). Frankfurt a. M.: Goethe University Frankfurt, SAFE—Sustainable Architecture for Finance in Europe.

[21] Moloney, N. (2006). Op. Cit., p. 883.

[22] Kovas, A. (2006). UCITS—Past, present and future in a world of increasing product diversity. *Working Paper Series, 44*(2), 1–33, p. 11.

The original UCITS I Directive aimed to integrate the European sector for investment funds, with advantages for investors, and expansive entrepreneurial advantages for asset managers. One main priority was to enable the distribution of a previously authorized fund within an EU country in another country. A "product passport" was implemented.[23] The regulation of investment services would be dominated by the regulatory passport in the securities regulation field, using the UCITS I Directive as a model.[24]

Three main ideas influence the financial governance of the EU: "harmonization of rules, mutual recognition and national supervision."[25] Home country control and the single passport are the key pillars accompanying harmonization and mutual recognition.

From an organizational point of view, some academicians pointed out that supervisory authorities' collaboration represented a normal repercussion after the establishment of similar norms at the EU level. This is mainly due to the existence of a necessity to implement EC[26] norms uniformly, and secondary, to the growing number of transnational exchanges motivations for cross-border mutual actions to prevent undertaking from breaking away of prudential surveillance.[27]

Theory proved different from practice because of the particular marketing standards from every EU state, leading to impediments for UCITS cross-border marketing.[28] Moreover, the restrictive manner of defining investments enabled UCITS to reduce their overall marketing possibilities. New proposals were released in the 1990s to correct the 1985 Directive in harmonization of European regulations. Although they lead toward the making of a draft UCITS II Directive, these debates were

[23] Moloney, N. (2006). The EC and the hedge fund challenge: A test case for EC securities policy after the financial services action plan. *Journal of Corporate Law Studies, 6*(1), 1–38. https://doi.org/10.1080/14735970.2006.11419945.

[24] Ferran, E. (2004). *Building an EU securities market*. Cambridge University Press. https://papers.ssrn.com/sol3/papers.cfm?abstract_id=604047. Accessed 15 June 2020.

[25] Wymeersch, E. (2005). The future of financial regulation and supervision in Europe. *Common Market Law Review, 42*(4), 987–1010.

[26] European Commission.

[27] Moloney, N. (2002). *EC securities regulation*. Oxford: Oxford University Press.

[28] Alshaleel, M. K. (2016). Undertakings for the collective investment in transferable securities directive V: Increased protection for investors. *European Company Law, 13*, 14–22.

not continued because they were excessively ambitious at that moment when the Council of Ministers could not reach a common viewpoint.[29]

The UCITS III Directive aims to promote the free movement of collective investment schemes and to make it easier for a CIS[30] located in an EU country to trade its units in other EU countries. Article 47(2) EC (former Article 57(2) EC), setting the basis of the Directive is part of the Treaty's free movement structure and it is designated to facilitate the freedom of establishment.

The Directive stipulates that UCITS can be established in two forms: investment companies or unit trusts,[31] depending on whether they are in a corporate form. Three entirely individual entities compose a unit trust under the Directive: the capital rose from unit-holders; the management company administering the trust's assets and marketing the trust; and the depositary with custody of the trust's assets.

Greater inter-relations of securities markets are fostered by the Directive, by granting a UCITS regulatory passport to act in a cross-border manner in the EU (in host member states), without further regulations except the local marketing rules, if authorized by the member state of its location (home of the EU Member) according to the Directive. Article 4(1) provides that a UCITS is unable to perform any activities without previous authorization from the EU country where it is located. Once the authorization is granted, it is available for all member states.

2.3 Regulation of Hedge Funds and the UCITS Regime

The main goal established by "the UCITS Directive" resides in providing a universal regulatory context capable of enabling harmonized and open-ended CIS, hence facilitating the "free" pursuance of business within the EU and the marketing of their shares or units. This can be performed based on a single authorization issued by the competent "home" member

[29] Hertig, G. (2003). Four predictions about the future of EU securities regulation. *Journal of Corporate Law Studies, 3*, 1–25. http://dx.doi.org/10.2139/ssrn.3334493.

[30] Collective Investment Scheme.

[31] Unit trusts as regulated by the Directive are not limited to trust structures. The Directive includes contractual arrangements such as common funds or fonds commun de placement under the umbrella of unit trusts. The defining feature of a unit trust in this context is that the common fund or the trust is managed by a management company.

states authorities. This effect of the UCITS "product passport" was undermined through the diverging interpretation and implementation by its addressees with regard to several of its provisions on the one hand, and through the lack of a unified marketing regime, on the other hand, with severe restrictions pertaining the type of assets that UCITS could invest in the diverse member state and tax regimes for retail funds. As a result, the ensemble of such provisions has led to the obstruction of the establishment of an effective Single Market for designated asset management products.

In the early 1990s, the proposals issued by the EC to help overcome these shortcomings[32] did not reach their scope until January 2002, when the European Council finally approved two modernizing directives: "the Product Directive"[33] and "the Management Directive"[34] (jointly, "UCITS III").

A major effect of the Product Directive has been the extended scale of eligible UCITS investments, and, consequently, of those UCITS funds marketed on a cross-border basis.

The introduction of the Management Directive, on the other hand, has brought about a single "European passport" providing the UCITS management companies the possibility to expand activities in EU countries, other than those of their establishment, subject to conditions similar to those applicable to investment services firms under the Investment Service Directive.[35] At present day, the provisions of the ISD provisions are captured by CRD IV, which also applies to hedge funds.[36]

Notwithstanding the increase in the list of UCITS investments, the combination of individual strategic mechanisms pursued by alternative investment vehicles under the UCITS roof, the theoretical similarities

[32] Commission Proposal for an European Parliament and Council Directive Amending Directive 85/611/EEC, COM (93) 37 final [1993] OJ C59/14, as amended by COM (94) 329 final [1994] OJ C242/4.

[33] Directive (EC) 2001/108 [2002] OJ L41/35.

[34] Directive (EC) 2001/107 [2002] OJ L41/20.

[35] Council Directive (EEC) 93/22 [1993] OJ L141/27. The ISD, covering some of the same area as the MiFID was repealed on November 1, 2007, the date of the MiFID's entry into force.

[36] Annunziata, F. (2019). Investment services and investment funds. In F. Fabbrini & M. Ventoruzzo (Eds.), *Research handbook on European economic law* (p. 477). Cheltenham: Edward Elgar.

between UCITS and non-harmonized funds, and the gradual convergence of their respective investment strategies,[37] hedge funds continue to be excluded from the harmonized funds' framework.

The present version of the UCITS III discipline does not allow genuine short positions,[38] preventing the establishment of onshore, UCITS—compliant hedge fund-type vehicles. Consequently, the UCITS framework might influence the European hedge funds in light of its evolution impetus and subsequent indirect "institutionalization" of investments in onshore hedge funds. The main implication of the UCITS funds investment discretion widening is indirect, with the lately regulatory modifications having brought within the reach of UCITS fund managers derivatives trading and, indirectly, leverage, enabling them to offer retail investors partial benefits of sophisticated portfolio diversification (through funds of hedge funds investing) and higher returns promises (through recourse to derivatives).[39]

Recent surveys regarding definition of UCITS "eligible assets," further to Article 2 of the product Directive, outlined an insertion opportunity of additional hedge fund-related features in the revised UCITS framework.[40] Moreover, they highlighted ways to distribute *indirectly* non-harmonized

[37] The trend towards enhanced convergence of mutual and hedge funds has been particularly pronounced in Europe since the adoption of the UCITS III (Alternative Investment Expert Group. (2006). *Managing, servicing and marketing hedge funds in Europe, report*).

[38] Article 19(1)(g) from the revised UCITS Directive allows for the creation of synthetic short equity positions, permitting funds to run short derivative positions on equities provide, however, that these are cash-settled. To establish such positions, a UCITS manager could either buy a put option on a particular security and hold cash on cover (instead of holding the specific underlying security) or, alternatively, make use of an equity swap. By simultaneously increasing the fund's leverage on the long side, a UCITS fund manager could, de facto, replicate a long/short strategy (incurring, nevertheless, the relevant transaction costs).

[39] The changing composition of eligible UCITS investments is linked to the increasing penetration of hedge fund investment and risk management techniques in the traditional asset management industry and to the impact of changing investment trends and investor demands on the regulatory treatment of UCITS funds. A report for the European Commission has found that the effect of hedge funds on the classical asset management market extends beyond the mere demand-side substitution effect and has encouraged traditional asset managers to adapt their business models in accordance with the hedge fund paradigm (Oxera Consulting. (2006). *Current trends in asset management*. Report, October, 46).

[40] As a commentator has observed, the possibility of a pan-European distribution of hedge funds has indirectly surfaced with the implementation of UCITS III and, more

products, like hedge funds, on an EU-wide basis, as eligible UCITS assets. One must also specify that the definition of eligible assets was considered one of the most problematic part of UCITS III,[41] as this is the main reason for the adoption of an implementing directive by the Commission, to address this weak point of the revised harmonized funds' framework.[42]

Although the original scope did not relate to hedge funds, the "*Committee of European Securities Regulators*" CESR) (now substituted by the "*European Banking Authority*" (EBA) operating as of the 1st of January 2011)—already involved in the Directive implementation process of the EC—examined the issue of the inclusion of credit derivatives in the amended UCITS framework[43] and, more significantly for the purpose of the present research, of hedge fund indices (HFIs).[44] Despite the fact that the Product Directive acknowledged "index tracking" as a legitimate investment management option for UCITS funds,[45] in its last recommendation on the understanding of concepts regarding "eligible assets for UCITS" investments, CESR reserved its viewpoint on the issue of

specifically, during the consultation phase organized by the Committee of European Security Regulators regarding the eligible assets of the UCITS III funds (L'Habitant, F. S. (2006). Hedge fund indices for retail investors: UCITS eligible or not eligible? *Derivatives Uses, Trading and Regulation, 12,* 275–289).

[41] A Green paper identified as essential defining UCITS eligible assets as one of the Commission's priorities, European Commission, Green Paper on the Enhancement of the EU framework for Investment Funds, Brussels, 2005, COM (2005) 314 final, 4.

[42] Commission Directive (EC) 2007/16 [2007] OJ L79/11.

[43] The Product Directive provided little guidance on the eligibility of specific derivative instruments. The importance attributed by the Commission to avoiding potential inconsistencies between member states on the use of derivatives as UCITS eligible assets and to the correct implementation of the Product Directive is clear from a Commission Recommendation (EC) 2004/383 regarding the use of financial derivative instruments for UCITS [2004] OJ L144/33, followed by a July 2005 CESR report on its implementation (Ref: CESR/05-302b).

[44] The Commission implementing directive qualified, in recital 11, the issue of a clarification of the state of play with regard to derivatives on financial indices as particularly pressing (Commission Directive (EC) 2007/16, n.237).

[45] UCITS Directive, Articles 19(1)(g) and Article 21(3). These provide that harmonised funds may invest in several instruments, including derivative instruments on financial indices if these indices full fill some minimum criteria.

their eligibility as UCITS-compliant "financial indices."[46] Such instance was subsequently approached in a CESR "issues paper,"[47] whose publication has led to a consultation addressing the criteria under which HFIs might be subjected to UCITS III definition regarding "financial indices." However, in its feedback statement, CESR did confirm HFIs as eligible assets in case they fulfil the common criteria specified by Article 9 of the Directive 2007/16/EC,[48] with several secondary requirements concerning index methodology and information disclosure. The implications of the increase of the HFIs from UCITS funds must be understood by the remainder of the analysis, first for the investing policy of harmonized funds and second, for the larger acceptability of the onshore hedge fund industry.

2.4 The UCITS IV Directive

UCITS IV stands as a major step forward to the achievement of a single market for financial products. This might change the asset management industry in a manner similar to that of MiFID changing the broker-dealers and investment credit institutions.[49] Since 1985 when they appeared, until their later modifications six years later, UCITS funds have turned into an international brand, as they became well known for their adjustability and reliability.

[46] CESR. (2006b, January). *Advice to the European Commission on the clarification of definitions concerning eligible assets for investments in UCITS*. CESR/06-005, para. 158 et seq. To include HFIs in the list of UCITS eligible assets means that any non-approved offshore hedge fund could be distributed indirectly to retail investors via a UCITS vehicle, as long as such a fund belonged to a HFI, inevitably challenging the utility of the UCITS label.

[47] CESR. (2006a, October). *Can hedge fund indices be classified as financial indices for the purposes of UCITS?* Ref: CESR/06-530. The issues paper sought the views of market participants on questions concerning the ability of hedge fund indices to fall within the definition of financial indices contained in UCITS III.

[48] CESR. (2007, February). *Clarification on the definitions concerning eligible assets for investment by UCITS: Can hedge fund indices be classified as financial indices for the purposes of UCITS?* Ref: CESR/07-045.

[49] Dejmek, P. (2009). The EU internal market for financial services—A look at the first regulatory responses to the financial crisis and a view to the future. *The Columbia Journal of European Law, 15*(3), 455.

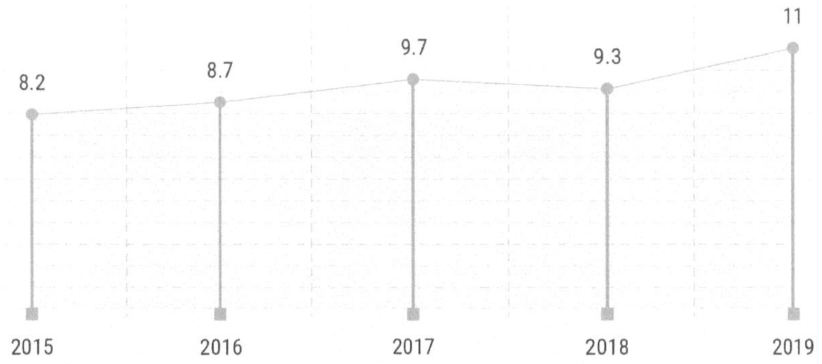

Fig. 2.2 Evolution of total net assets of UCITS domiciled in the European Union between 2015 and 2019 (*Source* EFAMA 2020)

According to a recent EFAMA report, the total net assets of UCITS domiciled in the European Union reached EUR 11 trillion in 2019 (Fig. 2.2).[50]

Also, as far as net sales of UCITS are concerned, if in 2018 they reached EUR 121 billion, in 2019 they grew strongly up to EUR 394 billion (Fig. 2.3).[51]

As already seen above, the UCITS offer "many important advantages to European investors, including professional management services, access to global markets, the benefit of regulation and supervisory oversight, and access to a wide array of investment options via passporting."[52]

The top ten domiciles in 2019 in terms of net assets were as presented in Fig. 2.4.

The top ten domiciles in 2019 in terms of net sales are presented in Fig. 2.5.

The new measures included in the UCITS IV Directive enabled the free operation of asset managers within Europe based on a single authorization received from an EU member state. Accordingly, the aim of the

[50] EFAMA. (2020). Trends in the European Investment Fund Industry in the fourth quarter of 2019 & results for the full year of 2019. In B. Delbecque, T. Tilley & H. Yang (Eds.), The European fund and asset management association. *Quarterly Statistical Release, 80,* 1–22.

[51] Idem.

[52] Duvall, J., & Swan, G. (2019). Ongoing charges of UCITS in the European Union. *ICI Research Perspective, 25*(7). www.ici.org/pdf/per25-07.pdf. Accessed 7 May 2020.

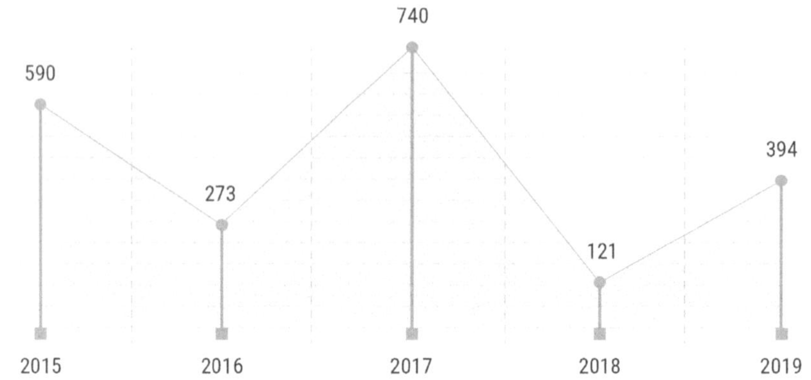

Fig. 2.3 Evolution of total net sales of UCITS domiciled in the European Union between 2015 and 2019 (*Source* EFAMA 2020)

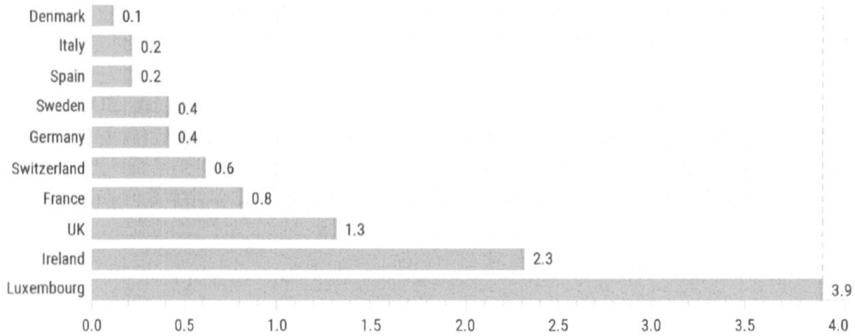

Fig. 2.4 Top ten domiciles in 2019 in terms of net assets (*Source* EFAMA 2020)

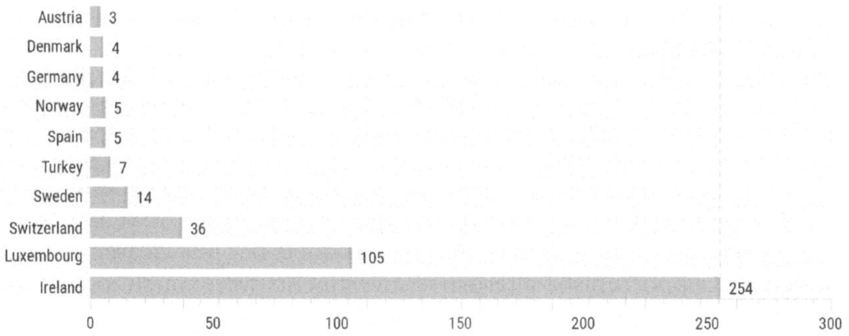

Fig. 2.5 Top ten domiciles in 2019 in terms of net sales (*Source* EFAMA 2020)

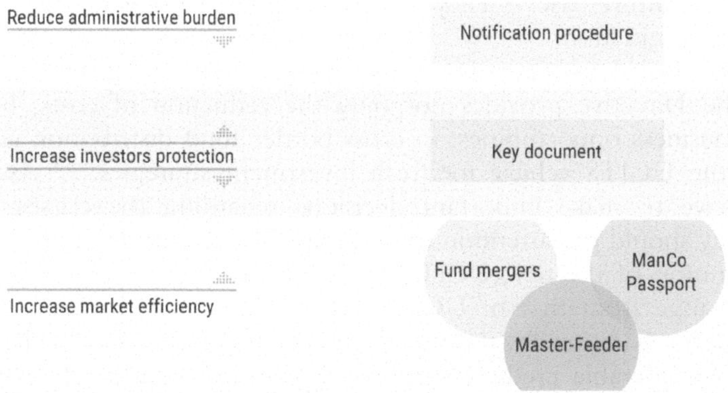

Fig. 2.6 Objectives and topics of UCITS IV (*Source* Author's analysis)

UCITS IV is the increase of the efficiency/investor protection as well as of the flexibility of the European fund industry, reducing administrative burden at lower total costs.[53] Figure 2.6 presents the three objectives and five topics of UCITS IV.

[53] Dejmek, P. (2009). The EU internal market for financial services—A look at the first regulatory responses to the financial crisis and a view to the future. *The Columbia Journal of European Law, 15*(3), 455.

By its five essential measures, the Directive will favor fund mergers and master-feeder structures on the one hand and it will enable centralized fund management throughout Europe, on the other hand. At the same time, this will also shorten the time available for asset managers to inform regulators of new products.

Since 2005, market conditions have significantly changed. Due to the serious ongoing crisis, the worth of equities and other asset structures greatly decreased. Complicated financial products became clearer, risk was avoided and opportunistic alternative investments were much looked for. Currently, pressure is placed on asset managers who earn less as subscriptions slow down, assets perform inappropriately, while expenses increase. An expenses cut simulation alone is not enough. Asset managers are forced to reposition themselves strategically, but they must also restructure their expenditure base.[54] They have to consider the best practices of using the new legislation.

UCITS IV provides support to asset managers in reshaping their fund strategy. The Directive provides not only the reduction of costs, but also "new business opportunities: in cross-border fund distribution and leveraging the UCITS vehicle for fresh investment strategies."[55] Asset managers have to make important decisions regarding the classes of investors they should pay attention to, either within or outside the EU.[56]

The definition of the new UCITS Directive's depositary importance does not change from that of UCITS III, as this still remains in the fund's domicile. Additionally, their role has been emphasized in the light of current considerable credit institution failure and fraudulent activities. Hence, the EC's AIFM Directive tends to impose that a depositary employment for every particular fund is necessary, not only for UCITS. Those debates can lead to an increase in the degree of the depositaries'

[54] Mertzanis, H. (2011, April 7). *The UCITS IV directive, the need for rationalization, and master-feeder structures.* Paper presented at the Workshop on master-feeder funds and key investor information, Capital Markets Board of Turkey, Ankara.

[55] BNP Paribas Securities Services. (2010). Op. Cit., p. 55.

[56] Ibid.

liabilities, which might further result in higher costs. The "AIFM Directive's depositary returns create at present intense debate in the alternatives industry."[57]

As stated above, the forth version of the UCITS Directive represents a courageous move to a single market for financial products from Europe. Every measure gathered in the provisions of the Directive under debate has been meant for the reinforcement of the competitiveness of the hedge funds industry in Europe. The buy-side is going to change, in a similar manner as the "MiFID" made for the sell-side. The transnational distribution of funds and activities represents the Directive's key concept. This should enable the transnational distribution of funds,[58] and it should also ensure higher protection to the investor.

2.4.1 The Management Company Passport

Another important measure to increase efficiency enforced by the UCITS IV Directive refers to the asset management entity pan-European passport. This passport enables a management company to provide the UCITS funds a wide variety of collective portfolio services, while these funds are registered in a different EU country, without necessarily being entirely set up in another EU country. There are two ways to do this. The first is on a full/remote basis. The second is through setting up a secondary office where the UCITS are domiciled. Regardless of the chosen option, the management company will be forced to move not only the managerial, but also the accounting departments to the UCITS domicile location.

The controlling responsibilities need to be split between the home regulator of the management firm and that of the fund, as below:

- The regulator in the UCITS fund home location will control all facets related to the authorization and operation of the fund;

[57] Ernst&Young. (2012). Viewpoint: AIFM Directive: Get ready for European depositary reform. *European Asset Management Viewpoint Series*. Ernst & Young Global Limited. www.ey.com/nn/en/home/pr_aifmd—depositary-reform-and-the-impact-on-jersey. Accessed 17 May 2019.

[58] Cumming, D., Imad'Eddine, G., & Schwienbacher, A. (2012). Harmonized regulatory standards, international distribution of investment funds and the recent financial crisis. *The European Journal of Finance, 18*(3–4), 261–292.

- The compliance of the management entity to all rules of its EU home country is compulsory;
- The compliance of the management company regarding all facets from the administrative and accounting tasks to the regulations of the fund's domicile, comprising those related to the net asset valuation is compulsory.[59]

2.4.2 *"Master-Feeder Fund Structures"—Pooling*

"Master-feeder structures" are meant to bring an increase to the performance of the sector, by reducing the product's selling cost made possible by the large size of the business. The performance is also increased by pooling of master, as well as feeder fund assets. A secondary advantage resides in fostering cross-border funds trade. The feeder fund is forced to invest minimum 85% of its assets in entities of a single master UCITS fund, while the rest of the 15% must be placed in other current assets or derivative instruments, excepting the case when the derivatives tend to be employed for hedging. In addition, it is compulsory that master funds are UCITS funds, as these do not have permission to be another feeder funds. Similarly, master funds do not have permission to invest in/hold units in feeder funds. Besides, "the investors in the master fund can be feeder funds and/or direct unit holders of the master fund."[60]

2.4.3 *Key Investor Information*

The simplified prospectus needs to be replaced for the improvement of investor protection through better cost disclosures. The new proposal stipulates that the asset management company has not only to disclose a paper of two pages containing "*Key Investor Information*" (KII) expressed in a nontechnical manner, in the specific language employed by the distribution state, but this needs to be intelligible so that the investors are enabled to draw comparisons. Therefore, this KII needs to be "clear, understandable and not misleading."[61]

[59] BNP Paribas Securities Services. (2010). Op. Cit., p. 58.

[60] Ibidem.

[61] Ibidem.

2.4.4 UCITS Supervision

Wishing to eliminate administrative barriers and interruptions, and to make sure that all instruments are applicable, this new Directive brings around complex proposals to increase collaboration between national and overseas authorities. For instance, they are adopting proposals such as instant examinations, but also checks and a process for transferring data between regulators. Therefore, regulators are able to exercise surveillance, but also examine powers, in cooperation with other officials, through delegation or via the regulatory system. The author's firm opinion is that, if nothing was done on harmonizing the regulation of hedge funds, the investors' confidence in the safety of assets invested through a collective investment vehicle would remain shattered.

The UCITS supervision aims to address lessons learned from the financial crisis, relating mainly to the Madoff incident which highlighted several issues dealing with the inconsistency of regulation existing between "member states" in enforcing the provisions of the UCITS Directive.

2.4.5 Conclusions

The UCITS IV Directive is meant to lead to the performance development of the asset management industry for the increase of EU competitiveness. Undoubtedly, the Directive will lead to the changing of the present situation of asset management firms, as these are structured in vertical set-ups to a structure where the set ups are rather pan-European, centralized, but also horizontal. Currently, asset managers distributed in six EU states are forced to have six different management firms, administer six different funds, and employ six various depositaries. According to UCITS IV, this situation changes as for the same distribution coverage, a single management entity, two funds, two feeder funds, or four depositaries may be owned by the same asset manager.[62]

Advantages for asset managers will differ from one state to another in terms of asset manager entrepreneurial standard and dimension. Alternatives will flourish coming from different markets influenced by the local community and tax system. Asset managers need to know how to consider their investors' needs and their own organizations' features when approaching each country. Each country will continue to have specific

[62] Ibidem.

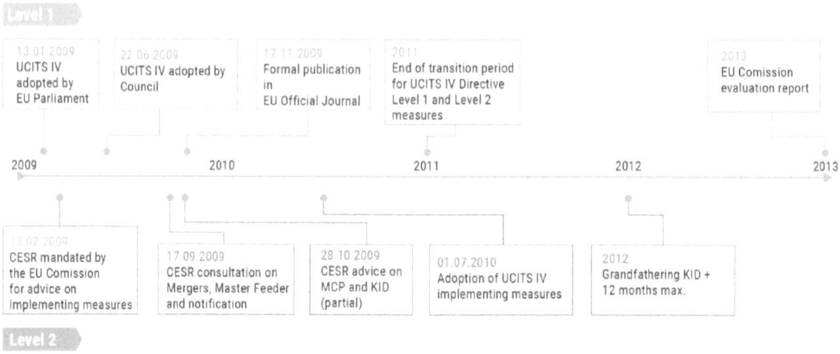

Fig. 2.7 The UCITS IV legislative framework (*Source* Author's analysis)

accounting rules, tax treatment, and regulatory reporting and that is exactly why the regional monitoring of asset-servicing providers is going to be highly pursued.[63]

Asset managers need to take advantages from the UCITS IV Directive and, therefore, they need to approach it from a strategic point of view. First, if they deal not only with UCITS, but also with non-UCITS, they need to focus on resemblances, as well as on dissimilarities brought forth by the AIFM Directive and the UCITS Directives, in order to enable regulatory arbitrage. Besides, local knowledge should not be underrated. Most of the time, a global view but also a local expertise is needed in order to choose the adoption of the best strategy, no matter if the asset manager is developing across—or rationalizing in—Europe.

Further on, the Legislative framework of UCITS IV will be presented as a timeline (Fig. 2.7).

The EC published consultation document dating from July 26, 2012, "Product Rules, Liquidity Management, Depositary, Money Market Funds, Long-term Investments,"[64] recognizes that there were several measures introduced under UCITS IV that do not operate as expected. In this respect, through this consultation paper, the EC emphasizes

[63] BNP Parisbas Securities Services. (2010). Op. Cit., p. 58.

[64] European Commission. (2012a). *Consultation on the undertakings for collective investment in transferable securities (UCITS)—Product rules, liquidity management, depositary, money market funds, long-term investments*. https://ec.europa.eu/finance/consultations/2012/ucits/index_en.htm. Accessed 3 April 2020.

some specific areas where further enhancement may be appropriate, inter alia: (a) recommending more detailed organizational norms for self-managed organizations; (b) some modifications to the dynamics of operating master-feeder structures; (c) certain changes to the mechanics of operating fund mergers; and (d) several improvement revisions of the transnational notification procedures.

2.5 The UCITS V Directive

Towards the middle of the year 2012, more precisely in July, a recommendation for reviewing the UCITS regime was published by the EC concerning depositary functions, payment principles, but also penalties concerning the UCITS (UCITS V).

Overall, the recommended proposals in addition to the already existing UCITS regime are directed toward the lessons learned from the financial crises, especially connected to the Madoff's fraud, which revealed several problems concerning lack of consistency between the member states regarding the application of the UCITS Directive provisions. The main goal related to the reform consists of creating uniform market facilities within the EU, thus generating the increase of the investors' protection, which leads to the increase of the investors' reliability, but also to the UCITS sector's integrity protection at international level.

The UCITS V Directive has the purpose to adapt the UCITS to the depositary and the AIFM Directive provisions regarding the remuneration and to contain a harmonized clearance framework. The harmonized UCITS policy overlooked the fundamentals of remuneration and sanctions compatible with other financial services fields.

Thus, there are several main objectives of the UCITS V Directive, respectively: (a) clear understanding of the "UCITS depositary's functions" and "liability in circumstances where assets are lost in custody, (b) rules governing remuneration policies that the UCITS will be obliged to introduce, and (c) the harmonization of the minimum administrative sanctions regime across the Member States."[65]

The UCITS V legislative timeline is presented in Fig. 2.8.

[65] http://ec.europa.eu/internal_market/investment/docs/ucits/20120703-proposal_en.pdf. Accessed 20 April 2020.

Fig. 2.8 The UCITS V legislative timeline (*Source* Author's analysis)

During the summer of 2012, on the 26th of July, the EC issued a consultation paper under the name of "Product Rules, Liquidity Management, Depositary, Money Market Funds, Long-term Investments."[66] This paper would improve, by means of adjustment, every further amendment to the UCITS regime forming at the same time the basis of "UCITS VI" to build on and revise the introduced UCITS IV, as well as the UCITS V.

The abovementioned consultation represents the beginning of a process for UCITS regime shifts whose process of becoming effective would last at least two years (or even more). However, one should take into account that there is a certain disillusion in the industry regarding the forthcoming changes to the UCITS regulation recommended by the EC before the completion of the UCITS V Directive. Nevertheless, a positive part of this initiative consists of the fact that the EC formulated this initial stage of UCITS VI as a consultation, asking questions on ways of enhancing the present model. There were no further steps made after this consultation paper.

Among the key changes compared to UCITS IV are:

- The introduction of stricter criteria for entities allowed to act as a depositary (now restricted to credit institutions, national central banks and other legal entities authorized under the laws of EU member states to carry out depositary activities and subject to harmonized additional conditions under UCITS V).

[66] Dalhuisen, J. H. (2019). *Dalhuisen on transnational comparative, commercial, financial and trade law* (7th ed.). Oxford: Hart Publishing.

- The obligation for the depositary and the asset manager/UCITS fund to enter into an agreement whose content is specified in the level 2 text.
- For depositaries, the strict liability regime for assets held in custody and the introduction of new duties: cash monitoring, record-keeping for assets not held in custody and oversight duties for UCITS funds that have a legal personality.[67]

The focus of the UCITS V Directive is mainly on finding solutions for the increase of investor protection for UCITS funds, as a consequence of the fact that these are sold to the general public.[68] Directive 2014/91/EU[69] ("UCITS V Directive") was adopted on July 23, 2014, amending the UCITS Directive with respect to depositary rules, remuneration, and sanctions.

In this respect, this Directive (UCITS V) is globally aligned with the AIFMD on regulations having to do with asset manager remuneration and the duties and liabilities of depositaries. The key differences from the earlier UCITS Directives consist in the fact that this Directive imposes a stricter depositary regime, at the same time introducing a harmonized sanctions regime. Also, as far as key changes compared to AIFMD are concerned, the following provisions need to be underlined:

- First, the independence requirement between the UCITS asset manager and the depositary;
- Second, the insolvency protection regime when the custody function has been delegated by the depositary although recent amendments of AIFMD delegated acts on safekeeping duties of depositaries,

[67] https://securities.bnpparibas.com/insights/ucits-v-regulation-memo.html. Accessed 12 April 2020.

[68] Idem.

[69] The Directive 2014/91/EU of the European Parliament and of the Council of 23 July 2014 amending Directive 2009/65/EC on the coordination of laws, regulations and administrative provisions relating to undertakings for collective investment in transferable securities (UCITS) as regards depositary functions, remuneration policies and sanctions Text with EEA relevance, Official Journal of the European Union, L 257/186. https://eur-lex.europa.eu/legal-content/EN/TXT/?uri=CELEX%3A32014L0091. Accessed 5 June 2020.

which will enter into application in April 2021 will remove this gap between AIFMD and UCITS V.

2.5.1 Depositaries

2.5.1.1 Eligibility Criteria

The present UCITS overview does not offer much clarity regarding those entities which are allowed to behave like UCITS depositaries and therefore give a certain degree of discretion to the member states in this regard. This has led to divergent approaches across the EU. The UCITS V Directive draft provides that only two types of companies are going to be capable of acting as UCITS depositaries, such as:

- (i) EU certified banks;
- (ii) investment entities authorized by MiFID, which provide safekeeping and administration services. The draft contains a two-year grandfathering period during which the UCITS will be allowed to use a non-compliant depositary. However, these provisions are not final and the funds industry intends to propose additional eligible depositaries categories to be included as per the AIFM Directive and the Irish Central Bank's rules for UCITS and non-UCITS.

2.5.2 Delegation of Custody

Nowadays, UCITS invest by far in more states using also more elaborated instruments as compared to 1985. This increases the obligation of appointing sub-custodians in various jurisdictions. The EC notes that the current UCITS framework lacks clarity in relation to the conditions that apply to the delegation of custody to sub-custodians. In this context, new due diligence and current controlling requirements are introduced. Consequently, the draft of the Directive stipulates the concepts upon which the assurance obligations of the depositary may be entrusted to a tutor. Moreover, the UCITS depositaries can hand over their safekeeping obligations to third parties under certain conditions and requirements compliant with those applicable to the AIFM Directive.[70] Similarly, one

[70] http://Euro-lex.europa.eu/LexUriServ/LexUriServ.do?uri=COM:2012:0350:FIN:EN:HTML. Accessed 3 April 2020.

needs to mention that, in case of the securities held by a delegate in a state of insolvency of safekeeping, it will not be available for distribution to their creditors. According to the UCITS V Directive, the EC holds the power to further define the first, but also continuous due diligence obligations of the depositary. The abovementioned duties include also the aspects related to the selection and appointment of a sub-custodian.[71]

2.5.3 *Liability*

The existing loss commitment standard of a monetary tool under custodianship resides in its emergence in cases of failure justification impossibility in performing duties or performances related to unsuitable obligations. These norms have been interpreted differently in various member states, which has led to diverging levels of investor protection. The UCITS V Directive implements a rigorous liability criterion forcing depositaries to give back financial tools lost in custody, regardless of the fact they were lost due to fault or neglect, except those losses caused by an outsider event beyond the depositary's rational supervising. Depositaries will remain liable for the loss of assets in cases where safekeeping duties have been entrusted to third parties. Accordingly, the UCITS V Directive, in contrast to the AIFM Directive, makes the depositary responsible for the return of the financial tool, despite the loss occurred to the sub-custodian, without the possibility to discharge the liability by contract.

2.5.4 *Prospectus Disclosure*

The inclusion of a characterization of any safekeeping functions that the depositary entrusted in favor of a third party within the UCITS prospectus was proposed. Such disclosure will be required to identify the representative but also additional "conflicts of interest" which might occur due to the delegation. While this provision corresponds to the disclosure requirement included in the AIFM Directive in terms of the required disclosure level, it goes further in requiring that this information

[71] European Commission. (2012b). Proposal for a Directive of the European Parliament and of the Council Amending Directive 2009/65/EC on the Coordination of Laws, Regulations and Administrative Provisions Relating to Undertakings for Collective Investment in Transferable Securities (UCITS) as Regards Depositary Functions, Remuneration Policies and Sanctions, Strasbourg, 3.7.2012 COM (2012) 350 final.

be provided in the prospectus of a UCITS, not that it simply be provided to investors, as stated in the AIFM Directive. This provision will pose both practical and operational challenges and, as such, will be the subject of intense lobbying by industry bodies, such as the IFIA.[72]

2.5.5 Remuneration of UCITS Managers

The EC proposes the introduction of a requirement for UCITS management companies to adopt "remuneration policies consistent with sound risk management,"[73] which discourages disproportionate exposure to risk. Increased risk exposes investors to greater possible losses, which could be presumed due to the risk profile disclosed to the investors. These policies and practices will apply not only to senior management, but also to those persons who affect the risk profile of the Management Company or UCITS through their services. These provisions of the draft Directive correspond to the relevant provisions of the AIFM Directive. The EC has not confirmed if the requirement to implement the remuneration policies described in the draft Directive will be applicable when a self-managed UCITS or UCITS management entity receives no asset-based tax.

2.5.6 Administrative Sanctions

After investigating the national norms regarding penalties for infringements of the UCITS Directive, the EC has concluded that there is a significant divergence between jurisdictions, both regarding the criteria applied to issuing sanctions and the level of sanctions applied to specific breaches. The UCITS V Directive requires that member states of the EU invest their regulatory bodies with power, as well as with the diversified inspecting powers but also administrative penalties set out in the draft Directive covering a range of breaches of regulatory provisions. The Directive proposes harmonization of the sanctioning regimes by requiring the national regulators to introduce catalogues of sanctions and other punitive measures, and lists of sanctioning criteria.

[72] Irish Funds Industry Association.

[73] http://ec.europa.eu/.

2.5.7 *Implementation*

Directive 2014/91/EU[74] ("UCITS V Directive"), adopted on July 23, 2014, has amended the UCITS Directive with respect to depositary rules, remuneration, and sanctions. UCITS new depositary requirements mirror, to a large extent, the provisions on depositaries that were introduced in the Alternative Investment Fund Managers Directive 2011/61/EU ("AIFMD").[75] The UCITS V Directive entered into force on September 17, 2014.

2.5.8 *PRIIPs—Packaged Retail Investment and Insurance Products*

Another major regulation is the PRIIPs—Packaged Retail Investment and Insurance Products (Table 2.1).

The Packaged Retail Investment and Insurance Products (PRIIPs) Regulation[76] has a main goal providing a pre-contractual standardized disclosure text for all retail financial products, in order to increase product

Table 2.1 The PRIIPs—Packaged retail investment and insurance products

IMPACT	*Asset Managers, Insurers, Issuers, Consumers*
31 DEC 2017	The PRIIPS Regulation took effect
2019	Review of the application of the PRIIPs to be completed by the European Commission.
DEC 2019	Original expiry for UCITS exemption from PRIIPs application
DEC 2021	New expected expiry date for UCITS exemption (pending formal amendments to existing texts)

[74] The Directive 2014/91/EU of the European Parliament and of the Council of 23 July 2014 amending Directive 2009/65/EC on the coordination of laws, regulations, and administrative provisions relating to undertakings for collective investment in transferable securities (UCITS) as regards depositary functions, remuneration policies, and sanctions Text with EEA relevance (OJ L 257, 28.8.2014, pp. 186–213).

[75] Directive 2011/61/EU of the European Parliament and of the Council of 8 June 2011 on Alternative Investment Fund Managers and amending Directives 2003/41/EC and 2009/65/EC and Regulations (EC) No 1060/2009 and (EU) No 1095/2010 (OJ L 174, 1.7.2011, pp. 1–73).

[76] Regulation (EU) No 1286/2014 of the European Parliament and of the Council of November 26, 2014 on key information documents for packaged retail and insurance-based investment products (PRIIPs) OJ L 352, 9.12.2014, pp. 1–23.

comparability and transparency. The Regulation controls various products such as: corporate bonds, structured notes, retail investment funds (other than UCITS), and insurance products with an investment component. Pension products are not included due to their different nature of the underlying investment process. Industry and consumer organizations required the necessity of reviewing the PRIIPs Key Information Document (KID) since its adoption, due to methodological issues with the presentation of performance and cost figures and uncertainty concerning the aim of the Regulation.

PRIIPs offer a transitional period where prospective retail investors in UCITS will continue to receive a UCITS KIID until the end of 2019. The PRIIPs Regulation envisaged that the application of the PRIIPs KID standards to UCITS funds would be subject to a review, potentially leading to the replacement of the UCITS KIID with the PRIIPS KID, or to retaining both documents.[77]

Comparable and meaningful information for all savings products will foster consumer appetite for investing across Europe, contributing to the creation of a deep Capital Markets Union. However, information must be fair, clear, and not misleading. A full review of the PRIIPs regime must therefore be undertaken before extending it further.

EU supervisors have underlined the need to maintain the original sequencing of the review to ensure that PRIIPs KID disclosure standards are suitable for UCITS disclosures, and that consumers will benefit from replacing the UCITS KIID with the PRIIPs KID. More recently, the European Supervisory Authorities (ESAs) expressed concerns about consumers receiving duplicative information from both a UCITS KID and a PRIIPs KID when investing in UCITS fund as of January 1, 2020.[78] Consumers would require further explanations. To expedite a single document, the ESAs announced they would make targeted revisions to the PRIIPs KID, in order to meet the 2020 deadline. However, they currently only consider performance scenarios and changes that can

[77] Kokoris, A., Archontakis, F., & Grose, C. (2020). Market risk assessment: Evidence from packaged retail and insurance-based investment products. *Journal of Risk Finance, 21*(2), 111–126. https://doi.org/10.1108/jrf-05-2019-0078.

[78] Münchhalfen, P., & Gaschler, R. (2020). *Attention distribution of current key investor documents—Standardization as a long-term goal of the PRIIPS regulation*. https://ssrn.com/abstract=3607872 or http://dx.doi.org/10.2139/ssrn.3607872. Accessed 2 June 2020.

be addressed through further guidance. They have not mentioned the very contentious issue of transaction cost disclosures, which imply new adjustments.

Various legislative initiatives are currently underway, including a European Parliament proposal to extend the UCITS exemption for two years, allowing for a full review of PRIIPs and possible corrections to methodological issues.

Summing up, the key features of PRIIPs are:

- A standardized Key Information Document for all retail financial products (except pension products).
- The PRIIPs KID provides standardized information, including a synthetic risk indicator, future performance scenarios, and aggregate charges and costs incurred over a given holding period.

2.6 The Alternative Investment Fund Managers Directive

The AIFM Directive was enacted on July 21, 2012 (level I). The AIFM Directive timeline can be seen in Fig. 2.9, and this will be discussed further on.

The AIFMD is extremely important because it regulates, at Union level, the management and marketing activities of alternative investment funds to professional investors. Before the adoption of the AIFMD, these activities and the firms performing them were unregulated or they were

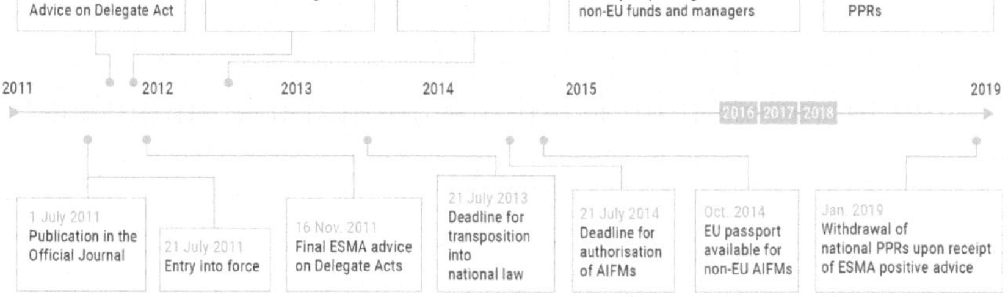

Fig. 2.9 The AIFM Directive timeline (*Source* Author's analysis)

regulated only at national level. This means that it introduced a new regulation regarding a part of the financial sector that earlier was either unregulated or regulated (lightly or fully) only at national level.

This AIFM Directive implements harmonized requirements for financial intermediaries involved in the management of AIFs[79] in the EU. The Directive defines an AIF as any collective investment scheme that requires no authorization in compliance with the UCITS Directive.[80] This extended definition was meant to include institutional vehicles which previously did not fit the perimeter of the EU financial regulation, among which one can mention "hedge funds/absolute return' funds, private equity funds/collective investment schemes, real estate funds/fixed property funds"[81] and others. AIFs management and administration experience certain limited exceptions, especially for the EU-domiciled AIFMs[82] authorized as per the Directive.[83]

The purpose of the AIFM Directive is to regulate all major risk sources in the alternative investment value chain by guaranteeing that AIFMs are authorized and undergo periodical and continuous governing and that robust regulatory standards govern the key service providers, including depositaries and administrators. The Directive seeks to attain also the improvement of the transparency of AIFMs and their managed funds in front of supervisors, investors, and other key stakeholders. In addition, the Directive needs to guarantee that all governed bodies comply with the appropriate governance standards and benefit of robust systems for the risk, liquidity, and conflicts of interest management. The Directive also intends to enable AIFMs to market funds to professional investors

[79] Alternative Investment Funds.

[80] 2009/65/EC, Article 3 (a).

[81] Directive on Alternative Investment Fund Managers (AIFM Directive): Frequently Asked Questions, Memo/10/572 (November, 2010) (FAQ). The breadth of this definition is curtailed somewhat by a number of exceptions. Specifically, the Directive does not apply to collective investment schemes regulated under the UCITS Directive, EU credit institutions, pension funds, life assurance or reinsurance companies or sovereign wealth funds; Article 2, s. 2(c)–(g). The Directive also does not apply to an AIFM EU-located but that does not offer management services to an AIF located or marketed within the EU; Article 2, s. 2(b). That is not to say, however, that these institutions fell outside the perimeter of regulation in their home member states.

[82] Alternative Investment Fund Managers.

[83] Article 18 and 36.

throughout the EU, subjected to compliance with imperative regulatory standards.

The authorization received from the responsible authorities in its EU home member state is compulsory to every AIFM intending to manage or market an AIF, according to the provisions of the Directive.[84] The Directive contains a *de minimus* exemption for managers who directly or indirectly manage AIF portfolios holding minimum EUR100 million integral assets.[85] This threshold is raised to EUR500 million for managers who: (a) only manage AIFs without employing any leverage, and (b) do not assure investors the right to redemption for minimum five years from the day of a fund's inception.[86] One of the preconditions of authorization is that an AIFM should provide all officials in charge, detailed information observing, inter alia, ownerships' details, features of the AIFs the company intends to trade, all adjustments for the delegation of management functions and the appraisal, as well as safekeeping of portfolio assets.[87] More broadly, the AIFM has to assure the competent authorities that it is able to observe all the basic requests of this Directive.[88] After receiving the authorization, the AIFM is enabled to provide management activities to AIFs settled in any member states,[89] but also to market the securities

[84] Article 4, s. 1. An AIFM might become authorised in providing management services in respect of all or only some forms of AIF; Article 4, s. 2.

[85] Article 2, s. 2(a). There is a potential ambiguity in the English language version of the Directive respecting whether the thresholds apply at the fund or manager levels. The Commission estimates that the EUR100 million threshold will capture 30% of all hedge fund managers of EU-domiciled hedge funds; Proposal for a Directive on Alternative Investment Funds, 2009/0064 (April 30, 2009) (AIFM Proposal).

[86] Article 2, s. 2 (a).

[87] Article 5.

[88] Article 6, s. 1.

[89] Straight or through the setting up of a branch, subject to (1) the scope of its original authorization, (2) the communication of its intention to do so to the competent officials in its home EU State, and (3) meeting the relevant procedural requirements; Article 34, s. 1–3.

of the AIFs managed to professional investors[90] within the EU.[91] In the short term, this passport will only be accessible to EU-domiciled AIFs and AIFMs. However, it is carefully considered at present that the passport extends to the non-EU-domiciled managers and funds in 2013.[92] On May 29, 2014, the European Securities and Markets Authority (ESMA) published a new multilateral memorandum of understanding (MMoU) between EEA national competent authorities, national competent authorities, and the ESMA. This has been signed by 31 authorities in the securities and markets area (Fig. 2.10).[93]

Once an AIFM receives authorization under the Directive, it must provide full compliance with substantive requirements observing, inter alia, (a) conduct of business, governance, and risk management, (b) third-party appraisal and safekeeping, but also (c) open, periodical, and event-driven disclosure to investors, competent official bodies, but also to some third parties stakeholders.[94] The Directive also empowers the EC and, if absolutely necessary, the official representatives from EU member states, so that they can act for the restriction of the use of leverage by AIFs.

[90] As defined in Annex II of the MIFID; Article 2, s. 1. The Directive permits EU States to allow the marketing of securities of AIFs to retail investors in their territory and, for that purpose, to impose requirements on AIFMs and/or AIF more strict than those imposed by the Directive; Article 34, s. 1.

[91] Again, subject to communicating its intention to do so to the delegated regulators in its jurisdictional EU country (who must then pass the information on to entitled professionals in the applicable jurisdictional EU States), and meeting the relevant procedural requirements; Article 33, s. 1–2.

[92] Provided that, inter alia: (1) the Commission has determined that the legislation regarding prudential regulation and ongoing supervision in the relevant third party country is equivalent to the Directive and effectively enforced, (2) the third party jurisdiction has granted EU-domiciled AIFMs reciprocal market access, and (3) the supervisor of the AIFM has signed a cooperation agreement with the competent authorities of the relevant member state; Article 39, s. 1 and 3. The EU has characterized this phase-in period as necessary to ensure appropriate controls and cooperation agreements are put in place to enable regulators to effectively supervise non-EU domiciled AIFMs; See FAQ supra at 35.

[93] Spendzharova, A. (2017). Becoming a powerful regulator: The European Securities and Markets Authority (ESMA) in European financial sector governance. *TARN Working Paper Series, 8*, 1–19. http://dx.doi.org/10.2139/ssrn.2965429.

[94] Awrey, D. (2011). Regulating financial innovation: A more principles-based alternative? *Brooklyn Journal of Corporate. Financial and Commercial Law, 5*(2), 273–315.

Before AIFMD

No authorization required	Authorization	Required to authorize business with national supervisory
Neither remuneration policy required nor conflicts of interest need to be identified	Remuneration and conflict of interest	Remuneration policy required and potential conflicts of interest need to be identified
No defaults	Risk and liquidity managemet Leverage rules	Required according to the AIFMD
No defaults	Valuation	Units and assets as well as changes on level of the investments or fund need to be valuated at least once a year
No defaults	Delegation	Specific notification requirements in case functions are delegated by the AIFM to third party provider
No defaults	Depository	External depository for controlling cash flows and ownership is required
Neither supervisory of the AIFM nor the AIF. Solely review of fund prospectus by the supervisory	Transparency	Several transparency requirements regarding annual reports, monthly reporting requirements, etc
Marketing of AIFs by non-EU AIFMs not possible	Passport regulation	Marketing of AIFs by non-EU possible

Fig. 2.10 Regulation of alternative investment funds before and post implementation of the AIFMD (*Source* Author's analysis)

The Directive causes controversy at various levels. The uniform regime that the Directive intends to enforce on a wide range of distinct AIFs is one of the controversial issues. This implies purely national funds without any evident systemic security relevance. Many of these are regulated at national level by now. However, credit institutions or insurance companies are excluded.[95]

Another major source of concern is the similarity of the draft directive and other previous European directives. Thus, an example could be "the Prospectus," "the Transparency," and "the Market Abuse Directives." As an alternative, the other way round, MiFID already regulates

[95] ECB. (2009). Opinion of 16 October 2009 on a Proposal for a Directive on Alternative Investment Fund Managers and amending Directives 2004/39/EC and 2009/.../EC. paragraph 7.

"open-ended and listed, closed-ended investment funds." In addition, the assertion of the necessity to require a double license on management firms operating simultaneously UCITS and non-UCITS funds,[96] the directive brings forth arguable issues in the regulation of such sectors where clearness is an essential element.

The intent of the AIMF Directive to regulate both authorization and advertising across the EU, as well as the funds located outside the EU is disturbing and, to some point, even offensive, from a double perspective. The requirements, according to which the competent member state official bodies issue this authorization, and the activation of the foreign funds' exchanging capability three years after the enactment of the directive, reduce the chances for non-EU AIFM to achieve such authorization.[97] If this approach has the slight chance of being defended prima facie due to its possible consideration in compliance with the objective of the "*G-20 Pittsburgh Summit*," which is to offer "transparency" around overseas areas, the limitations imposed to third state funds and administrators represent a major issue. The first restriction is upon the investors' choice. To this, one might add the fact that they tend to contradict the "*G-20 London Summit's*" demand that both regulators and supervising persons must reduce their aim for regulatory arbitrage while promoting international trade and investment and rejecting protectionism. The legitimacy of the internal market regulation objective of the "passport-driven opening of the European fund market to offshore funds and their managers"[98] is questioned.

One major problem revealed by the AIFM Directive resides in its chaotic and confused regulatory framework. The emphasized concept is hardly understood: either "*financial stability*" (individuals tend to consider this as target point) or *investor protection*. In this case, investor protection seems to be to some point improper under the AIFs circumstances due to the fact that the aim of the proposal tends to be limited to the funds marketing and AIFM's services offering only to professional investors. Also, financial stability seems to provide a more compelling basis for regulation in this area. The parallel pursuit of these two mutually

[96] Athanassiou, P. (2010). The draft AIFM Directive and the future of European alternative investment fund regulation. *CESifo DICE Report, 8*(1), 8–13.

[97] Athanassiou, P. (2010). Op. Cit., p. 10.

[98] Ibid.

exclusive regulatory rationales is capable of reducing the chances of the directive to fulfil any of these rationales.

On the one hand, if "the Directive" would mainly focus on financial stability, this would be more than enough for the limitation of the scope of the Directive to transnational, very high leveraged funds with significant AUMs, so that systemically relevant funds are accessed.[99] On the other hand, if its fundamental focus was the protection of investors, then it would definitely need the revision of some investor disclosure rules, which are not tailored to professional investors, but rather to the needs of retail.[100]

The Directive includes the following requirements on transparency: yearly reporting (Article 22), disclosure to investors (Articles 23 and 43), and reporting to competent authorities (Article 24).

On July 12, the Official Journal of the European Union published the new EU cross-border fund distribution directive and regulation:

- Directive (EU) 2019/1160 of 20 June 2019, amending the UCITS and Alternative Investment Fund Manager directives ("UCITSD" and "AIFMD") (the "Directive").[101]
- Regulation (EU) 2019/1156 of 20 June 2019,[102] on facilitating cross-border distribution of collective investment undertakings and amending European social entrepreneurship funds ("EuSEF"), European venture capital funds ("EuVECA") and packaged retail and insurance-based investment products ("PRIIPs") regulations (the "Regulation").

[99] Ibid.

[100] Ibid.

[101] Directive (EU) 2019/1160 of the European Parliament and of the Council of 20 June 2019 amending Directives 2009/65/EC and 2011/61/EU with regard to cross-border distribution of collective investment undertakings (Text with EEA relevance.) PE/53/2019/REV/1, OJ L 188, 12.7.2019, pp. 106–115.

[102] Regulation (EU) 2019/1156 of the European Parliament and of the Council of 20 June 2019 on facilitating cross-border distribution of collective investment undertakings and amending Regulations (EU) No 345/2013, (EU) No 346/2013 and (EU) No 1286/2014 (Text with EEA relevance.), PE/54/2019/REV/1, OJ L 188, 12.7.2019, pp. 55–66.

EU member states have to include the Directive into national law by August 2, 2021. It will apply as from that date to cross-border distribution of UCITS, AIFs, EuSEF, and EuVECA.

The aims of MiFID II and PRIIPs are "to increase transparency through greater disclosure of cost and charges."[103] Especially the key information document (KID), as part of the PRIIPs regulation, was highly criticized because it obliged asset managers to offer informative estimates of future performance, based on five-year historic performance.

PRIIPs replaces the Undertakings for the Collective Investment of Transferable Securities (UCITS) regime at the end of 2019, targeting a greater number of investment products and demands more details to be documented than the previous regime.[104]

The main changes to the UCITSD and AIFMD are the following:

1. Removal of requirement to appoint a local entity fulfilling the paying—and/or information agent function for UCITS and AIFs distributed to retail investors.

UCITS and AIFMs marketing AIFs to retail investors "have to ensure that payments, subscription and redemption requests, procedures detailing such payment or request processes, fund documents, etc. are available to investors in the marketing countries, but they are no longer required to fulfil these tasks by appointing a local physical presence."[105]

2. Implementation of uniform rules for the de-notification process, in case UCITS or AIFs shall no longer be marketed in a member state.

Host regulators must allow "UCITS and AIFs to be de-notified, even with remaining local investors, provided certain conditions are met. Such conditions include informing investors about the marketing termination in a specific way, fulfilling ongoing disclosure obligations toward remaining investors also following the de-notification and the terminating contracts with local distributors on the de-notification effective date.

[103] Olly, J. (2018). Unintended impact of Priips, MIFID to be reviewed for asset managers. *International Financial Law Review*. https://www.iflr.com/article/b1lp1wcsjk8tqt/unintended-impact-of-priips-mifid-to-be-reviewed-for-asset-managers. Accessed 15 June 2020.

[104] Ibid.

[105] Fihri, S. (2019). *New EU regulation and directive amending the UCITS and AIFM directives as well as the EuSEF, EuVECA and PRIIPs regulations, KPMG*. https://kpmgfundnews.eu/european-union/2019/07/new-eu-regulation-and-directive-amending-the-ucits-and-aifm-directives-as-well-as-the-eusef-euveca-and-priips-regulations/. Accessed 3 June 2020.

The de-notification request for UCITS and AIFs has to be submitted to the relevant home state regulator, which will forward it to the impacted host state regulators."[106]

3. Implementation of uniform definition and conditions for AIF "premarketing" to professional investors.

The presentation of "an investment idea without providing final documents and information about an AIF to potential professional investors to assess their potential interest in an AIF (or its sub-fund), without giving such investors the possibility to take an investment decision and subscribe to shares of the relevant AIF would be considered as 'pre-marketing' and could be conducted before the relevant AIFMD notification has been submitted to the home state regulator. AIFM must send an informal communication to their home state regulator, informing the home state regulator about the premarketing activities."[107]

The main new requirements introduced by the new Regulation, which was effective as of August 1, 2019, are as follows:

1. Extension of the deadline for UCITS and AIFs under the same exemption to provide PRIIPs-KIDs up to December 31, 2021. The previous data was December 31, 2019.
2. Requirement for host regulators to send invoices or any other individual payment instruction relating to regulatory fees to the impacted UCITS' or AIFM's contact details indicated in the notification letter, thereby abolishing local requirement to calculate and pay regulatory fees without prior notification by host regulators.
3. Implementation of a 10-business-day review period and deadline for marketing material reviews conducted by host regulators.
4. Request for host regulators to publish summaries on local requirements[108] in English on their websites.
5. Making and keeping of ESMA databases detailing local requirements.

Starting with February 2, 2022, ESMA is going to publish databases to provide overviews on local regulatory fees, local requirements, and a

[106] Idem.

[107] Idem.

[108] Laws, regulations, administrative provisions, regulatory fees.

central UCITS and AIF register, listing all cross-border distributed funds and their European marketing countries.

Such databases will be based on regular reporting that regulators have to file to ESMA.

In addition, the new Regulation[109] introduces the following new rules, which will be applied only after August 2, 2021:

1. Introduction of common rules on marketing communications. As of August 2, 2021, "UCITS and AIFs marketing material has to describe potential risks and rewards arising from the investment in an equally prominent manner; be fair, clear and not misleading; and contain references to available fund documentation and investor rights as well as information on the possibility to terminate marketing in a member state.
2. Amending the EuSEF and EuVECA regulations to include the description and requirements for 'pre-marketing' (the same requirements apply as introduced in the AIFMD)."[110]

Currently, the Directive is applied to all individuals who manage hedge funds, existing however an exemption for those managers who manage smaller funds whose portfolios do not surpass "100million or 500million euros when unleveraged and having limited redemption rights. To be authorized under the Directive, managers have to provide a significant amount of information concerning their investment strategies, risk, and leverage positions. Moreover, managers fall under supervision regarding authorization of management, capital, conduct of business, delegation, marketing, and leveraging requirements."[111] Still, European

[109] Regulation (EU) 2019/1156 Of The European Parliament And Of The Council of 20 June 2019 on facilitating cross-border distribution of collective investment undertakings and amending Regulations (EU) No 345/2013, (EU) No 346/2013 and (EU) No 1286/2014, Official Journal of the European Union L 188/55.

[110] Fihri, S. (2019). *New EU regulation and directive amending the UCITS and AIFM directives as well as the EuSEF, EuVECA and PRIIPs regulations, KPMG.* https://kpmgfundnews.eu/european-union/2019/07/new-eu-regulation-and-directive-amending-the-ucits-and-aifm-directives-as-well-as-the-eusef-euveca-and-priips-regulations/, on 03.06.2020.

[111] Stowell, D. P. (2018). Risk, regulation, and organizational structure. In D. P. Stowell (Ed.), *Investment banks, hedge funds, and private equity* (3rd ed., pp. 309–322). Cambridge: Academic Press.

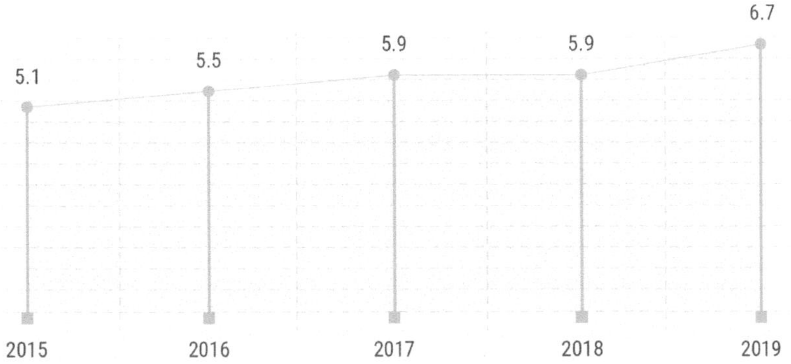

Fig. 2.11 Evolution of total net assets of AIFs domiciled in the European Union between 2015 and 2019 (*Source* EFAMA 2020)

Union hedge fund managers have the advantage of the EU Passport, offering them the possibility of managing and marketing authorized funds in each member state.

According to a recent EFAMA report, total net assets of AIFs domiciled in the European Union reached EUR 6.7 trillion in 2019 (Fig. 2.11).[112]

This growth of the EU AIF industry is a consequence of the launch of new AIFs in 2019 and it is not due to valuation effects. It should also be mentioned that, hedge funds are almost exclusively owned by professional investors. Also, as far as net sales of AIFs are concerned, if in 2018 they reached EUR 137 billion, in 2019 they grew strongly up to EUR 152 billion (Fig. 2.12).[113]

The top ten domiciles in 2019 in terms of net assets of AIFs are presented in Fig. 2.13.

The top ten domiciles in 2019 in terms of net sales (AIFs) are presented in Fig. 2.14.

As seen in Fig. 2.14, the AIF market is highly concentrated in Germany due to the role played by German special funds ("Spezialfonds").

[112] EFAMA. (2020). Trends in the European Investment Fund Industry in the fourth quarter of 2019 & results for the full year of 2019. In B. Delbecque, T. Tilley & H. Yang (Eds.), The European fund and asset management association. *Quarterly Statistical Release, 80,* 1–22.

[113] Idem.

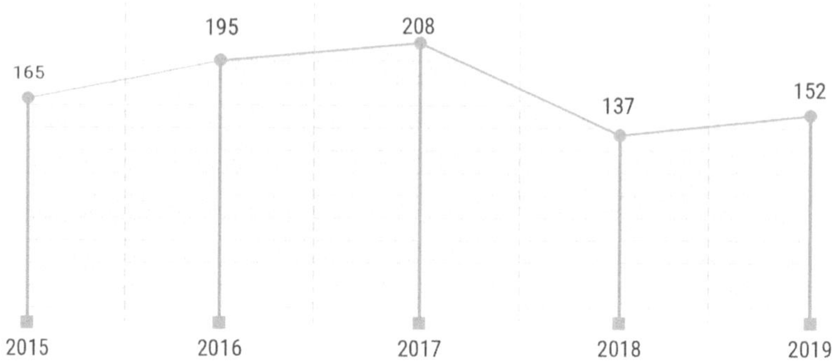

Fig. 2.12 Evolution of total net sales of AIFs domiciled in the European Union between 2015 and 2019 (*Source* EFAMA 2020)

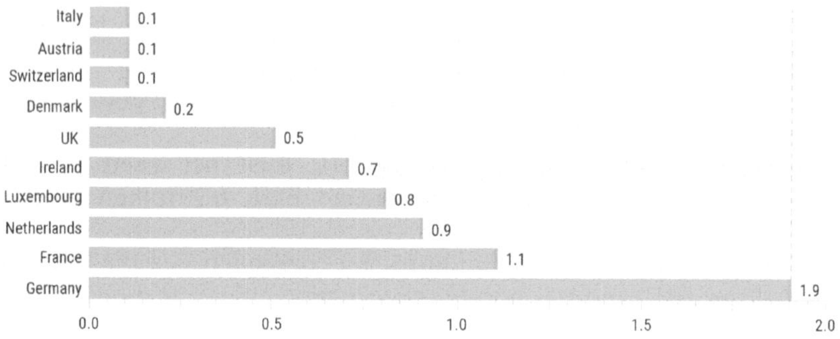

Fig. 2.13 Top ten domiciles in 2019 in terms of net assets (AIFs) (*Source* EFAMA 2020)

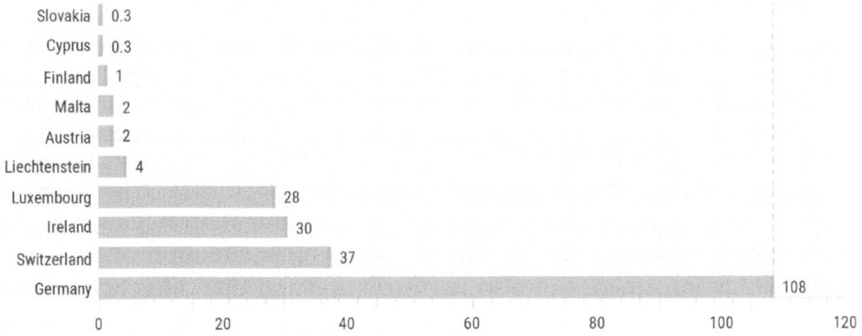

Fig. 2.14 Top ten domiciles in 2019 in terms of net sales (AIFs) (*Source* EFAMA 2020)

2.6.1 Conduct of Business, Governance, and Risk Management Requirements

The Directive imposes uniform care and loyalty duties upon authorized AIFMs. Specifically, it mandates AIFMs to: "(i) act honestly, with due skill, care and diligence and fairly in conducting its activities, (ii) act in the best interest of the AIFs it manages, the investors in those AIFs and the integrity of the market, and (iii) ensure that all AIF investors are treated fairly."[114]

An AIFM must also take all acceptable actions in order to identify "conflicts of interest"[115] but also, thereafter keep and operate efficient institutional and administrative adjustments to stop these conflicts from negatively affecting the interests of an AIF or its investors.[116] When an AIFM identifies material conflict of interest within its operations—or

[114]This includes a prohibition against any undisclosed preferential treatment of investors; Article 9, s. 1 (a)–(c).

[115]This includes conflicts (a) between an AIFM (including its managers, employees, and those able to exercise direct or indirect control) and AIF investors, and (b) between different AIF investors; Article 10, s. 1.

[116]Article 10, s. 1. This is in fact a purposive interpretation of what, it must be said, is a tortured piece of legislative drafting that contemplates the maintenance of effective adjustments with a view to taking all reasonable steps designed to prevent conflicts of interest. It remains to be seen how authorities will interpret the interplay between the requirement of effectiveness, the subsequent reasonable qualifier, and the notion that the arrangements need only be designed for preventing conflicts of interest.

when it determines that its conflict arrangements do not have enough power to ensure the adversely impact of AIF investors interests in a reasonable and confident manner—it must disclose this fact to AIF investors.[117]

The Directive stipulates that an AIFM should adopt risk management systems designed to measure and supervise overall risks induced to the AIFs it manages by virtue of their investment strategies.[118] This requirement contemplates, inter alia, (a) the implementation of an appropriate, highly informed, but also regularly updated due diligence process for investments, (b) accurately identification, measurement, and monitoring of risks by means of appropriate stress testing procedures, (c) the compatibility between the risk profile of each AIF and its size, structure, investment strategies, and objectives,[119] and (d) the implementation of risk management procedures to an AIF engaged in short selling.[120] The Directive also requires an AIFM to implement systems designed to manage liquidity risk and to conduct regular "stress tests of these systems under both normal and exceptional market conditions."[121] It further asks for the separation of portfolio and risk management functions—along with their respective review process—within the operational environment of an AIFM.[122] These risk management requirements are augmented by

[117] Article 10, s. 1–2. This is once again, a purposive interpretation of an ambiguously drafted provision. Specifically, the Directive contemplates disclosure where an AIFM's conflict arrangements are not sufficient to ensure, with reasonable confidence, that the risks of damage to investors' interests will be prevented. However, if one acknowledges that preventing the risk of damage is not the same thing as preventing the damage itself, this language is potentially inconsistent with the adverse effects standards articulated in the same Article.

[118] Article 11, s. 2.

[119] Article 11, s. 3 (a)–(c).

[120] Article 11, s. 4. The Directive further provides that EU States shall guarantee that an AIFM has in place procedures which provide its access to securities/financial instruments on the date it is required to deliver them pursuant to any short selling arrangement.

[121] Article 12, s. 1. As a corollary, an AIFM must ensure that the redemption policy of each AIF it manages is appropriate given the liquidity profile of its portfolio assets; Article 12, s. 2.

[122] Article 11, s. 1.

a requirement that an AIFM should adopt payment policies that tend to be compatible with and to encourage sound risk management.[123]

Lastly, the AIFM Directive institutes simple incipient and evolving capital requirements. All AIFMs are required to keep their own funds of minimum EUR 125,000.[124] Additionally, when the AIFs' aggregate portfolio worth exceeds EUR 250 million, an AIFM must set aside an extra amount of 0.02% of the total surpassing the quarter-million EUR threshold of the portfolio value.[125] Accordingly, for an AIF with a EUR 1 billion worth portfolio value, an AIFM would be required to put aside capital totaling EUR 275,000. The capital requirements mentioned above according to any very important duties comply with Article 21 of the Capital Requirements Directive governing the money ability of investment companies, but also of banks.[126]

2.6.2 Third-Party Valuation and Safekeeping Requirements

The Directive requires that "an AIFM appoints an independent third party to value both the portfolio assets of the AIFs it manages and their issued securities."[127] This valuation exercise must be undertaken at least once a year and every time the securities of an AIF are traded or redeemed.[128] An AIFM must also appoint a depositary for the purposes of, *inter alia*, "(i) receiving subscription proceeds from AIF investors and depositing them into a segregated account, and (ii) safekeeping AIF portfolio assets."[129] The depositary shall be a credit institution whose

[123] The remuneration requirement does not appear in the most recent draft of the directive made available by the Commission. However, it is described in the more recent FAQ, and more broadly, is consistent with the EU's emerging position on remuneration within financial institutions; http://ec.EUROpa.eu/.

[124] Article 14.

[125] Seretakis, A. L. (2012). The new EU Directive on the regulation of private equity. *Columbia Journal of European Law Online, 18*(3), Forthcoming. https://ssrn.com/abstract=2035997. Accessed 4 June 2020.

[126] 2006/49/EC.

[127] Article 16, s. 1. Third party valuators domiciled in jurisdictions outside the EU must be subject to regulatory standards equivalent to those applicable within the EU; Article 37, s. 1(b).

[128] Article 16, s. 1.

[129] Article 17, s. 1(a)–(c).

registered office must be in the EU.[130] The depositary is obliged to act freely and only in support and on behalf of "AIF investors." He will be responsible to the AIF investors for any damages inflicted upon them due to its failure to perform its obligations according to the Directive.[131]

2.6.3 Disclosure Requirements

The Directive sets up a series of initial, periodic, and event-driven disclosure requirements designed to increase the transparency of AIF activities to investors, competent authorities, and certain other stakeholder constituencies. "MiFID requires investment firms to provide,"[132] *inter alia*, a description of the relevant AIF's (a) investment strategy and objectives,[133] (b) valuation and redemption policies, (c) custody, valuation, administration, and risk management activities, but also (d) investment taxes, charges, and costs.[134] Thereafter, an AIFM will be required to provide the investors with a yearly audited report comprising the AIF's balance sheet, income statement, activity report, and auditor's report.[135] The AIFM should also submit these annual reports to the empowered officials from its home EU country.[136]

The Directive contemplates additional periodic disclosure to both investors and competent officials with respect to: (a) the special arrangements percentage of AIF portfolio assets emerging from their illiquid type, (b) every new liquidity management settlements, and (c) the current risk profile of each AIF and the AIFM's risk management systems.[137] An AIFM will be required to provide aggregated data for empowered officials according to a certain pattern, observing not only main markets and tools

[130] Article 17, s. 3. An AIFM cannot, however, act as a depositary; Article 17, s. 2.

[131] Article 17, s. 2 and 5.

[132] http://www.esma.europa.eu/system/files/07_050b.pdf.

[133] Including descriptions of (1) the permitted assets and techniques and their attendant risks, (2) any investment restrictions, and (3) the circumstances under which the AIF may use leverage and the types and sources of permitted leverage; Article 20, s. 1.

[134] COM/2009/0207, Article 20, s. 1.

[135] Article 19, s. 1–3.

[136] Article 21, s. 3 (a).

[137] Article 20, s. 2 and Article 21, s. 2.

of AIFs' trade, but also their fundamental vulnerabilities, and significant risk concentration.[138]

In addition, an AIFM must report to the competent officials the main forms of assets where its AIFs are invested but also, when important, the employment of short selling.[139] The Directive contemplates that the EC is going to adopt implementing measures which ensure the adaptation of the nature and frequency of these periodic disclosures—or at least those targeted at investors—to every AIF species.[140]

Finally, the Directive imposes event-driven and subsequent periodic disclosure obligations on an AIFM related to the acquisition of "a controlling interest in a company domiciled in the EU which employs more than 250 persons, has an annual turnover exceeding EUR50 million,"[141] but also a balance sheet surpassing EUR 43 million. An AIFM will be thought to have acquired a "controlling interest" if either it or any of the AIFs it manages holds either separately or totally "30% of the voting rights"[142] of the target corporation. In case an AIFM acquires a controlling interest, this shall offer certain prescribed data[143] to the corporation, its shareholders, and employees (or their representatives). In addition, the yearly report of an AIFM is going to contain data regarding every entity where it holds a controlling interest. More specifically, the report must include information observing, inter alia: "(i) its operational and financial affairs, (ii) any financial risks associated with its capital structure, (iii) employee turnover, termination and recruitment, and (iv) any significant divestment of assets."[144]

[138] Article 21, s. 1.

[139] Article 21, s. 2(d)–(e).

[140] Article 20, s. 3.

[141] Articles 26–29. This provision applies to both listed and non-listed companies, and includes the conclusion of an agreement, which would enable an acquisition.

[142] Article 26, s. 1 (a)–(b).

[143] The nature of the information required will depend on whether the company is listed or non-listed; see Articles 27–28.

[144] Article 29.

2.6.4 Leverage Requirements

The Directive empowers the EC to establish leverage requirements for AIFs where these are considered imperative for guaranteeing security and "integrity of the financial system."[145] It further empowers national officials to prevent the use of leverage for individual AIFMs and AIFs in exceptional circumstances.[146] The Directive mandates that an AIFM is evaluated once every four months if any of the AIFs it manages uses "high levels of leverage on a systematic basis."[147] An AIF is considered to have passed this test if its merged leverage from overall elements exceeds its amount of "equity capital in two out of the past four quarters."[148] When an AIF transcends this threshold, its manager must make prescribed disclosures to both AIF investors[149] and the properly qualified officials in its EU residence countries.[150]

2.6.5 Closing Remarks

To conclude, the AIFM Directive is an important piece of legislation and needs to be carefully analyzed because of its relevance and especially because of its effects. After the financial crisis, it became clear that rushing

[145] According to the Directive, leverage represents any method by which an AIFM increases the exposure of an AIF to a particular investment, whether through borrowing of cash or securities, leverage embedded in derivative positions or any other means; Article 3(1). The Directive contemplates that the Commission will adopt implementing measures setting limits on the leverage an AIFM can employ taking into account, inter alia, the type of AIF, its investment strategy and sources of leverage; Article 25, s. 3.

[146] Provided that they are temporary in nature and comply with the Commission's leverage limits; Article 25, s. 4.

[147] Article 22.

[148] Article 22, s. 4.

[149] An AIFM managing an AIF with high levels of leverage on a systematic basis must disclose to investors (1) the maximum level of leverage which the AIFM may employ as well as the right of reuse of collateral or any guarantee granted under the leveraging arrangement; and (2) on a quarterly basis, the total amount of leverage employed in the preceding quarter; Article 23.

[150] An AIFM must regularly provide to competent authorities information respecting the level of leverage and a breakdown between leverage arising from borrowed cash or securities and that embedded in financial derivatives; Article 24, s. 1. This information must include the identity of the five largest sources of borrowed cash or securities for each AIF and the amounts of leverage received; Article 24, s. 2.

regulation not only does not help or serve any public interest, but it might even be more dangerous or damaging than no action at all. Therefore, the author considers that further negotiations and debates could be needed when transposing it into national law, in order to achieve the correct equilibrium between the two main parties involved: the international or global nature of this market, on the one hand and the local nature of the investors, on the other hand. The AIFM Directive, will definitely: (a) diminish systemic risks and the leverage use; (b) improve investor protection while increasing the transparency, too; (c) enhance the integrity and the efficiency of the sector; (d) promote the sector for the supervision of corporations.

In spite of the fact that hedge funds regulation was quite basic both in the United States and in the United Kingdom, regulators from Europe continuously pursued tighter regulation after the global financial crisis. In this respect, the EU imposed new regulatory framework for hedge fund managers, and the AIFMD is part of it. The hedge fund industry strongly criticized the Directive due to its "inadequate approach to regulation, not responding to the specific needs of the industry and for curtailing its market operations."[151]

2.7 Similarities and Differences Between UCITS and AIFMD

In terms of disclosure and transparency both Directives try to ensure "that investors are adequately informed on the risks and nature of their investment, and that they receive regular updates on the fund's situation."[152] The nature of the fund is directly involved in this case, either the UCITS or the AIFs, each falling under a different regulatory regime. At the same time, there are also similarities in terms of governance and controls in these regulations, although they do not find a common basis in both

[151] Stowell, D. P. (2018). *Investment banks, hedge funds, and private equity* (3rd ed., pp. 309–322). Chapter 14: Risk, regulation, and organizational structure. Academic Press. http://dx.doi.org/10.1016/B978-0-12-804723-1.00014-1. Accessed 5 May 2020.

[152] Annunziata, F. (2019, March 3). Investment services and investment funds. In F. Fabbrini & M. Ventoruzzo (Eds.), *Research handbook on European economic law*. Edward Elgar; Bocconi Legal Studies Research Paper No. 3345943. https://ssrn.com/abstract=3345943 or http://dx.doi.org/10.2139/ssrn.3345943. Accessed 12 May 2020.

Directives even though, inevitably, with approaches that are not identical, but rather have some common points. Once the UCITS V and the AIFMD came into force, gradually, "collective investment management saw the gradual inclusion of rules concerning the composition and role of the board of directors of the manager, and the implementation of the three internal control functions typical of other financial sectors as well: internal audit, compliance and risk management."[153]

Thus, if in the first versions of the UCITS, risk management was practically absent; in the last one it became a central element both in defining collective investment undertaking and in terms of internal controls. Consequently, Supervisors are the ones responsible for government processes that force them to have a well-defined structure of the investment process.

The two directives complete each other in terms of risk prevention, since the UCITS is centered on products' aspect, meanwhile the AIFMD focuses on the regulation of the asset manager. Indeed, risks of the Directives are various and quite different. On the one hand, because UCITS funds being open-ended funds are "addressed and targeted to retail investors,"[154] which makes risk even more important especially if we consider its liquidity profile. On the other hand, the AIFMD regulates distinct risk types, namely, those implying just professional investors.

Another important subject to be discussed is that of asset protection which did not previously apply to investment financial services being rather subject to special standards. No matter how they are structured from a legal point of view, CIUs represent pooled assets, controlled by the asset manager, still, being subject to various patterns of disjunction or segregation from the assets of the manager itself. These directions concerning the separation and segregation are most of the times enforced by national regulatory bodies, being, however, "first of all, grounded in general law on contract, trust, or corporations (the three basic forms that a CIU may actually have in the EU context, although other forms are also present). Especially for CIUs incorporated by way of a trust deed, or having a statutory form, the segregation issued is solved by the general rules applicable in these cases: the assets in trust are, in fact, structurally

[153] Idem.

[154] Idem.

segregated from those of the trustee; if the CIU has the form of a corporation, general corporate law shall apply. A further model would provide a more distinct form of segregation: this happens particularly when the statutory CIU is managed externally by an external asset manager (a solution typical of many legal systems and broadly used in Luxembourg and Ireland, where a considerable part of the EU industry of investment funds is located)."[155]

Some problems emerge concerning purely contractual funds, where both AIFMD and UCITS Directive are not specific, simply because they leave this matter in the hand of the national regulatory authorities. Indeed, both directives are silent on this issue because their approach is simply functional. This leads, however, to inconsistencies in regulations that prove sometimes, unclear.

In spite of this, regulations on separation of assets are aided by a complex set of EU rules on custody. In this vein, both UCITS and AIFMD are very much alike: the assets of a CIU are completely separated from the assets of the asset manager, and at the same time, they are also materially handed over to a third-party custodian, performing two main functions: supervising and controlling. This is the solution found so that the asset manager does not control the assets of the CIU, which diminishes the risks of self-allocation or "loss of control over those assets."[156] According to Annunziata, the custodians existed even from the first form of the UCITS Directive. Meanwhile, the market of alternative funds was highly unregulated globally speaking until the end of 1999–2000, when it "had evolved alongside schemes mostly non-coincident with those of the UCITS industry. The AIFMD therefore had to deal with a different standard from the industry, but at the same time, had to enforce the role of the custodian."[157] This was particularly stringent after the Madoff scandal, especially. At present day, due to the enactment of UCITS V, the standards of the two Directives are very much alike.

[155] Idem.

[156] Idem.

[157] Idem.

2.8 The MiFID Directive: An Overview of the Framework

The "*Markets in Financial Instruments Directive*" (MiFID)[158] was enforced in 2004, being the earliest in the financial services area, or the so-called "Lamfalussy-formatted," which cleared the way for several thoroughly implemented Directives or Regulations and became effective in the EU on November 1, 2017.[159] The MiFID Directive, "a key element of the FSAP, belongs to a group of four-part regulatory reforms. The other three regulations are: the Prospectus Directive, the Market Abuse Directive, and the Transparency Directive."[160]

MiFID relates to securities that are still under implementation nowadays in the credit institutions and insurance area in particular. The MiFID represents the most exhaustive exemplification of the "Lamfalussy approach" up to now, with the aim of making regulation more effective.[161] MiFID I "was aimed at fostering competition between trading avenues, promoting market integration, enhancing transparency and strengthening market integrity."[162]

The European supervisory architecture has changed in the aftermath of 2007–2009 financial crisis. In terms of financial supervising, a simultaneous accomplishment of single financial market and financial stability is very difficult, maintaining at the same time a higher supervision level

[158] Directive 2004/39/EC of the European Parliament and of the Council of April 21, 2004 on Markets in Financial Instruments amending Council Directives 85/611/EC and 96/6/EEC and Directive 2000/12/EC of the European Parliament and of the Council and repealing Council Directive 93/22/EEC, OJ L145, p. 1.

[159] European Commission (EC), 2004.

[160] Aghanya, D., Agarwal, V., & Poshakwale, S. (2020). Market in Financial Instruments Directive (MiFID), stock price informativeness and liquidity. *Journal of Banking & Finance, 113*(C), 105730. https://doi.org/10.1016/j.jbankfin.2019.105730.

[161] Cumming, D., & Johan, S. (2019). Capital-market effects of securities regulation: Prior conditions, implementation, and enforcement revisited. *Finance Research Letters, 31*(C). https://doi.org/10.1016/j.frl.2018.12.013.

[162] Thakor, A. V. (2018). *The economic consequences of regulatory protection and extraterritorial reach* (Center for Capital Markets Paper Spring 2018). www.centerforcapitalmarkets.com/wpcontent/.../2018/.../CCMC_EconCon_v8. Accessed 12 May 2020.

at the national position.[163] Schoenmaker called these inconsistent goals "trilemma," as far as the financial monitoring is concerned: the security of the financial system, the harmonized financial sector, and the national financial monitoring.[164]

Within the EU, prudential supervising is decentralized in each member state, due to the home country control principle combined with prior regulatory harmonization-based mutual recognition.[165] As a consequence of regulatory harmonization, the EU banking policy presents a rather unified picture. This is one of the reasons why Tommaso Padoa-Schioppa considered that the current approach was based on national supervision European regulation. The *Lamfalussy framework* set up many committees, while the new supervisory structure was established by the De Larosière Report.

The following framework sets the grounds for the new European Supervisory Authorities: five regulations approved by the European Parliament and the European Council on September 22, 2010, each of them establishing the following new bodies[166]: the "*European Systemic Risk Board*" (ESRB), assigning tasks to the ECB in relation to the ESRB, establishing EBA and the "*European Insurance and Occupational Pensions Authority*" (EIOPA), but also, finally setting up the "*European Securities and Markets Authority*" (ESMA).

The new objectives of the ESFS are: the adequate implementation of the rules to the financial sector, the maintenance of financial stability, and confidence in the financial system, but also the financial services consumers' protection. This shall account for the European Parliament and the European Council (ECOFIN).[167]

[163] Thygesen, N. (2003). The political economy of financial harmonisation in Europe: Comments. In J. J. M. Kremers, D. Schoenmaker, & P. J. Wierts (Eds.), *Financial supervision in Europe* (pp. 142–150). Cheltenham, UK: Edward Elgar.

[164] Schoenmaker, D. (2009). A new financial stability framework for Europe. *The Financial Regulator, 13*(3), 748–774. https://doi.org/10.1017/cbo9781139151184.036.

[165] Garicano, L., & Lastra, R. M. (2010). Towards a new architecture for financial stability: Seven principles. *Journal of International Economic Law, 13*(3), 597–621. https://doi.org/10.1093/jiel/jgq041.

[166] Regulation (EC) N. 1093/2010 by the European Parliament and the Council on November 24, 2010.

[167] www.ftseglobalmarkets.com/.

The ESRB will perform *inter alia* the following tasks: (a) define, access, and collect the relevant data supporting "the systemic risk" assessment at European level, (b) identify and assess the risks to financial security within the EU, relating to developments within "the financial system" focusing on its interaction with "the real economy," (c) prioritize the risks and insurance of risks warning to be considered by public authorities (central banks, supervisors, Ministers of Finance), or made available to the public, (d) issue recommendations (including in the legislative field) or advice on identified risks to stability, (e) "supervising of follow-ups to warnings as well as suggestions" ("comply or explain"), (f) connection with international bodies ("IMF, FSB") and third-country counterparties.

The EBA was founded on January 1, 2011. It was entrusted overall tasks and duties of the CEBS.[168] EBA's role is to guard and preserve the financial system stability, the markets and financial products transparency and the depositor and investor protection, acting as a hub and spoke network of the EU and national bodies.[169]

Also, among its core abilities, the author mentions: prevention of regulatory arbitrage, promise of a level playing sector, reinforcement of global surveillance coordination, promotion of surveillance convergence, and provision of advice to the EU authorities in the credit institutions, remuneration, and e-money legal fields,[170] but also on matters concerning corporation governance, control and "financial reporting." The amendment of the EBA Regulation was done by Regulation (EU) No 1022/2013 of October 22, 2013[171] regulating the offering of particular supervisory tasks to the ECB within the Single Supervisory Mechanism.

[168] Committee of European Banking Supervisors.

[169] http://www.eba.europa.eu/. Accessed 3 April 2020.

[170] Ibid.

[171] Regulation (EU) No 1022/2013 of the European Parliament and of the Council of 22 October 2013 amending Regulation (EU) No 1093/2010 establishing a European Supervisory Authority (European Banking Authority) as regards the conferral of specific tasks on the European Central Bank pursuant to Council Regulation (EU) No 1024/2013, OJ L 287.

The coordination of three entities: EBA, the ESMA and the EIOPA occur within the "Joint Committee," established pursuant to Articles 54–57 of the Regulations establishing these three Authorities.[172] These three Regulations governing the ESAs are currently under amendment, mainly in view of the need to further enhance and (in certain cases) clarify their powers, improve their governance, and enhance their funding base.[173]

2.8.1 Regulation of Hedge Funds and the MiFID

MiFID's impact seems actual due to its passport far wider objective.[174] The wide range of changes to the *status quo ante* caused by the MiFID, due to the abolition of the "concentration rule"[175] together with its ambitious desire to bring within its fold the widest available spectrum of organizations[176] have led to uncertainty in relation to its accurate remit in conjunction with its interrelation with other community legal documents (especially, UCITS III). From a broad perspective, while it is quite difficult to acknowledge MiFID's degree of influence on the European framework in terms of the financial services provision, little uncertainty is associated with the significant changes the entire asset management industry will have to undergo. For a correct assessment of MiFID's possible impact upon the unregulated vehicles together with products, which are not harmonized, having to do with hedge funds, the

[172] Gortsos, C. (2019). *The evolution of European (EU) Banking Law under the influence of (public) International Banking Law: A comprehensive overview research study*. Prague: Faculty of Law, Charles University. http://dx.doi.org/10.2139/ssrn.3334493.

[173] COM (2017) 536 final (20.9.2017).

[174] The MiFID passport covers the provision of investment advice as a core activity, the operation of multilateral trading facilities, or MTFs, trading platforms similar to electronic communication networks—(ECNs) in the United States—and the provision of investment services on commodity and credit derivatives.

[175] See Penn, B. (2007). MiFID and market infrastructure: Convergence of exchange and broker regulation. *Buttherworths Journal of International Banking and Financial Law, 22*(3), 155–158.

[176] Entities that are not subject to the MiFID involve: insurance undertakings (e.g., re-insurers), employee schemes (when dealing in the administration of employee-participation schemes), persons administering their own assets and undertakings which not providing investment services and/or performing investment activities; there is also an exemption for incidental business in the course of the pursuit of a professional activity regulated by legal or regulatory provisions or a code of ethics (MiFID, Article 2).

examination of several question marks raised by its stipulations becomes imperative.

A major source of doubt concerning the MiFID implies its potential significance for the transnational promotion and distribution of *products that are not harmonized*.[177]

Contrary to the UCITS Directive dealing only with harmonized funds, the MiFID's requests are also concerned with investments in "units in collective investment undertakings," regardless of the harmonized or non-harmonized nature of the entity involved.[178] Also, opposite to the ISD, which cover mainly conditional on the stipulation of "investment services," MiFID deals with investment advice and portfolio management and investment processes.[179]

On the one hand, the introduction of MiFID made the European asset management industry think that this was an excellent possibility for its non-harmonized products to take the benefits of novel, EU broad distribution potentiality, free of the duty to comply with the requirements of the national regulations, related either to their products or to their managers. On the other hand, both the CESR and several market associations and stakeholders[180] have presented the so-called "diversion" of the MiFID as an opposite image within an indirect path in terms of non-harmonized product marketing. It was believed that the impact of this "liberal" perspective regarding its aim would be harmful for the *effet utile* of the UCITS scheme and that it would damage the interests of the European harmonized hedge funds industry. It is really difficult to see how the guarantees, together with protections built into the UCITS regime would be dismissed within the framework of frequently *light regulated* hedge funds in the absence of reasons for the existence of the harmonized funds regime which is currently under examination. Despite the fact that there is hardly any indication of MiFID providing intentional grounds for the transnational promotion of non-harmonized products, regardless of the host member state where it has been registered or other various

[177] MiFID, Article 2(1)(h), read in conjunction with Recital 15 thereof, are indicative of the indiscriminate bundling together by the MiFID of harmonized and non-harmonized funds.

[178] MiFID, Annex I, Section C.

[179] Ibid., Annex I, Section A.

[180] Assogestioni apud De Phoebus Athanassiou. (2009). *Hedge fund regulation in the European Union: Current trends and future prospects*. Netherlands: Wolters Kluwer.

national distribution requirements,[181] an explanation of its interaction with UCITS III is a major objective. This objective was given particular interest by a 2006 European Parliament Resolution emphasizing that "the interaction between UCITS III and MiFID and its Level 2 implementing measures leave undesirable scope for interpretation and require clarification and consolidation."[182]

A second important issue to consider refers to the assessment of the regulatory treatment of particular functions related to hedge funds. The text of the provision does not clarify at all, for instance, if subscriptions, together with redemptions of hedge fund shares or units should be dealing with the "best execution" obligation of Article 21 of the MiFID Directive. When the process concerning the subscription and redemption of hedge fund shares or units differs qualitatively from that concerning the buying but also selling of financial tools, subjected to the best execution obligation, the subscription, and redemption of the shares or units of the hedge fund could prove problematic regarding its coverage by the aim of the MiFID's definition of "execution of orders."[183] This signifies that this limitation could not apply in the context of a hedge fund.[184] Similarly, ambiguity encompasses the degree to which the subscription and the redemption of hedge fund shares/units might qualify as "reception and/or transmission of orders,"[185] whether hedge fund managers

[181] Janin, S. (2007). MiFID impact on investment managers. *Journal of Financial Regulation and Compliance, 15*(1), 90–98.

[182] European Parliament. (2006). Resolution on Asset Management (2006/2037/INI), 27 April 2006, A recent White Paper is, however, silent on the issue (European Commission, White Paper on Enhancing the Single Market Framework for Investment Funds, Brussels, 15 November 2006, COM [2006] 689 final).

[183] MiFID, Article 4(1) and (5).

[184] Janin, S. (2007). Op. Cit., 97. The element that distinguishes the subscription from the redemption of hedge fund shares or units from the buying and selling of other financial instruments is the different degree of discretion performed by the financial intermediary in each of these two contexts.

[185] Only in the event of a positive answer to that question then the subscription and redemption of hedge fund shares or units would be covered by the best execution obligation. Subscribing and redeeming funds' units may be difficult to bring within the definition of the reception and transmission of orders since, according to Articles 45 (2), (4), (5), and (6) of the MiFID, that service is always connected to the subsequent service of execution of orders which may not be applicable to the process of subscribing and redeeming funds' units.

can be considered "investment firms"[186] or what the MiFID's definition of "investment activity" supposes.[187] Considering the fact that "the definition of an investment activity is far from clear"[188] and that it is not easy to establish the difference between the follow-up of an "investment activity" and the provision of an "investment service,"[189] there are ambiguities about the location of hedge fund activities on the "service"—"activity" sequence. The conclusive assessment of the MiFID's rules on transparency, outsourcing, and investor classification is difficult, despite the fact that the better view is that fund managers make investment advice and portfolio management functions falling within the scope of the MiFID.[190]

For the moment, one cannot say much about the impact of the MiFID on hedge funds, at least not until some of these questions would have been answered. Also, little can be said of the extent to which its occurrence will eliminate the need to adopt EU-wide hedge fund-specific rules or, on the contrary, require their even more urgent implementation in order to cope with the "hedge fund exception" to harmonized EU financial regulatory framework.

2.8.2 *The Regulation of Hedge Funds and Other Sources of Community Legal Rules*

The UCITS Directives and MiFID are not the only European Directives with direct/indirect effects regarding the evolution of asset management business in the EU. The other community legal acts significant

[186] While there is no indication that the MiFID was intended to regulate hedge funds by treating them as investment firms, its Article 4(1)(1) definition thereof is very broad, leaving much to the interpretative discretion of the individual member states Authorities.

[187] These include conduct of business obligations (MiFID, Article 19), obligations relating to conflicts of interest (ibid., Article 18), best execution (ibid., Article 21) and client order handing (ibid, Article 22).

[188] Penn, B. (2007). Op. Cit., p. 21.

[189] Considering the MiFID's definition of client in Article 4(1) thereof, those of the MiFID requirements that apply to clients would not seem to come into play where an entity merely undertakes an investment activity.

[190] Moloney, N. (2006). Op. Cit., p. 8.

to the market activities of hedge funds include the "*E-Commerce Directive*,"[191] the "*Prospectus Directive*,"[192] and the "*Savings Tax Directive*."[193] Considering the specific aspects of the cross-border provision of alternative asset management services addressed by these directives and the fact that they facilitate the hedge fund products marketing in the member states that do not specifically regulate their public marketing, these acts need to be briefly described.[194]

The rules employed for electronic cross-border consumer transactions have been adopted by means of the E-Commerce Directive. This adoption was explained by the EC's intention to establish a set of basic rules to promote E-commerce activity and EU-wide information society services. Based on mutual acknowledgment and the home country norms, the E-Commerce Directive could prima facie seem at first sight to let the transnational marketing of domestic hedge fund shares/units on the internet based on the tenderer's home country authorization.

The application of the "E-Commerce Directive" to financial services has led to many concerns regarding both the account of their highly regulated nature and the risk that could be brought up by market players to surround host European member state product regulations together with marketing norms (implying rules relevant for non-harmonized products).[195] Nevertheless, this "country of origin principle application" of "the E-Commerce Directive" is restricted by derogations concerning, in particular, obligations stipulated in a contract of a client, advertising the UCITS investments,[196] the act of issuing E-money through the "waived" electronic money institutions[197] and other rules in the insurance field.

From the point of view of the impact on hedge funds, it should be noted that the EU E-Commerce Directive, once it has been completely adopted by the member states, can highly impact on-line cross-border

[191] Directive EC 2000/31, [2000] OJ L178/1.

[192] Directive EC 2003/71, [2003] OJ L345/64.

[193] Directive EC 2003/48/EC, [2003] OJ L 96/16.

[194] See Phillis, G., & Dawson, J. (2003). The regulation and distribution of hedge funds in Europe—Changes and challenges. *Balance Sheet, 11*(4), 36–43.

[195] Taylor, K. (2002). The impact of the E-Commerce Directive in the area of financial services. *Journal of Financial Services Marketing, 6*, 391–396. https://doi.org/10.1057/palgrave.fsm.4770067.

[196] UCITS Directive, Article 44(2).

[197] Directive EC 2000/46, [2000] OJ L275/39, Article 8.

hedge funds marketing. However, the E-Commerce Directive imposes a "country of origin" approach to regulation, in the sense that, for instance, UK managers marketing funds in other EU member states are to be subject to the applicable UK marketing rules instead of having to comply with the regulations of the other countries. Nevertheless, this is only going to apply to promotion via the Internet; other regulations, among which laws on tax and information protection or against unsolicited email, still need to be observed.

The Prospectus, Market Abuse Directive and *Savings Tax Directives* represent other sources of community legal rules relevant to the business activities of onshore alternative investment vehicles.[198] As far as the MAD is concerned, it seems obvious that the insider handling with market manipulation interdictions enclosed therein could treat the dealings of onshore hedge funds in tools allowed to enlist in regulated markets functioning in the EU, "particularly with respect to potential market manipulation."[199] This reform mirrors several recent cases and discussions both in the United States and in Europe that will be analyzed in the last chapter. In the United States, for example, the conviction and sentencing of the hedge fund manager Raj Rajaratnam to eleven years in prison due to insider dealing, as well as the payment of USD 25 million by Moore Capital Management to settle charges of market manipulation were carefully considered. These cases concern the MAD.[200] Under MAD, regulators try to protect investors against market abuse and to expand supervisory and enforcement possibilities.

In the end, regarding the Savings Tax Directive and considering that its scope is to make sure that where an "interest payment" is made to a particular "beneficial owner"[201] located in an EU country by a "paying

[198] Bremus, F., & Kliatskova, T. (2018). *Legal harmonization, institutional quality, and countries' external positions: A sectoral analysis* (DIW Discussion Papers, No. 1768). https://doi.org/10.2139/ssrn.3287798.

[199] Persson, M. (2009). *The EU's AIFM Directive: Likely impact and best way forward* (p. 51). London: Open Europe.

[200] Market Abuse Directive.

[201] Savings Tax Directive, Article 2. The notion of beneficial owner captures individuals only.

agent"[202] domiciled in a jurisdiction falling within the scope of the Directive, the paying agent is going to provide data on the interest payment toward the tax authorities from the jurisdiction in the tax residence place of the beneficial holder. The most desirable perspective is that this should not affect the payments *received* by hedge funds (the latter cannot qualify as "beneficial owners" since they are not individuals). It could continue to be important to payments *made* by funds investing in fixed interest instruments, where the involved funds are deemed to fall within the Directive's *rationae personae* scope. Meanwhile, the largest part of hedge funds could not be apprehended through the Savings Tax Directive, due to their classification as non-UCITS or UCITS equivalent funds in most jurisdictions. It is still unclear how the competent authorities are going to investigate its provisions and how changes in the national categorization of hedge funds could impact their treatment from the point of view of their (possible) interest payment duties.[203]

2.8.3 MiFID II

Recently, ESMA issued a Consultation Paper, in which admits that investors, or most of them, could question their financial decisions as these possibly conduct to sub-optimal results.[204] This document "is addressed to authorities and firms subject to MiFID II, and the guidelines seek to implement enhanced provisions to ensure investor protection,

[202] Ibid., Article 4. Paying agent means any economic operator paying interest to or securing the payment of interest for the immediate benefit of the beneficial owner, whether the operator is the debtor of the debt claim which produces the interest, or the operator charged by the debtor or the beneficial owner with paying interest or securing the payment of interest.

[203] Question marks also occur in connection with the onshore hedge fund implications of the Third Anti-Money Laundering Directive (which, although imposing a detailed set of customer due diligence, reporting and record-keeping requirements, inter alia on collective investment undertakings marketing [their] shares or units', does not specify whether its reference to CIS captures harmonised funds only) and of the recast Capital Adequacy Directive (which, while applicable to prime brokers, is bound to also affect hedge funds themselves where its national implementation expressly covers alternative investment vehicles).

[204] ESMA. (2017). *Consultation paper, 13 July 2017, 35-43-748*, p. 9.

such as updating the investor suitability assessment questionnaires to take into account clients' behavioral biases."[205]

According to some scholars, "it may seem that transparency has simply become a sole legislative measure assuring values such as consumer protection, market stability or – most of all – high-quality governance."[206] It is obvious that transparency contributes to the quality of governance through various aspects, but at the same time some standards need to be met in order that their implementation can lead to the desired outcomes, particularly concerning hedge funds. In spite of the fact that transparency stands as a central element in the EU regulatory environment, the existence of increased transparency obligation for hedge funds is not. In this vein, "some doubts may arise as to the question whether the principle of transparency actually adds much to existing rules and principles."[207]

According to the European Commission after reviewing MiFID I, there were major needs to upgrade its rules,[208] which conducted to a new Directive proposal: MiFID II.[209] Stafford underlined that "the complexity and scale of the MiFID II proposal contributed to the delay in its implementation."[210] Consequently, when MiFID II (2014) came into

[205] Krokida, S. I., Makrychoriti, P., & Spyrou, S. (2020). Monetary policy and herd behavior: International evidence. *Journal of Economic Behavior and Organization, 170,* 386–417.

[206] Ostrowska, M. (2018). Transparency regime within the financial institutions: Does it really work. In S. Grima & P. Marano (Eds.), *Governance and regulations' contemporary issues. Contemporary studies in economic and financial analysis* (Vol. 99, pp. 293–313). Emerald Publishing Limited.

[207] Idem.

[208] European Commission. (2010, December 8). *Public consultation: Review of the markets in financial instruments directive (MiFID).* EC Public Consultation Document. European Commission. www.ec.ruropa.eu/finance/consultations/2010/mifid/index_en.htm. Accessed 5 May 2020.

[209] ESMA. (2014, May). *Consultation paper on MIFID II/MIFIR, European Securities and Markets Authority (ESMA)* (EC Consultation Paper). www.esma.europa.eu/press-news/consultations/consultation-paper-mifid-iimifir. Accessed 12 June 2020.

[210] Stafford, P. (2017, June 7). No more MiFID II delays-European markets regulator. *Financial Times.* www.ft.com/content/663b3629-764-34de-892d-5062d515643. Accessed 4 June 2020.

force on January 3, 2018, only half of the 28 EU member states "fully transposed the directive into national laws."[211]

MiFID II is in line with the original objectives of MiFID I, focusing mainly on investor protection, transparency, and clarifications concerning the regulation of investment products.[212] Amending and restating MiFID I, this new Directive was accompanied by another regulation, the Markets in Financial Instruments Regulation,[213] which dealt with regulating the mandatory trading of derivatives in organized venues, but also with requirements of "services from third-country firms without branches, new powers for European regulators and the enhanced requirements for trade transparency."[214]

Still, MiFID II is far stricter than MiFID I. Three particular aims of MiFID II differentiate it from MiFID I. Thus, (a) MiFID II sets up more rigorous regulatory requirements, which would supervise the technological evolutions and market infrastructure in the financial industry; (b) MiFID II intends to enhance investor protection as a result of the major collapses occurred during the credit crisis; (c) the target of MiFID II is to increase transparency as much as possible, and at the same time decrease the fragmentation of information. Due to these three targets, the strategic, commercial, and technological implications of the MiFID II are wider than those of the MiFID I.

Effective from January 3, 2018, the new requirements aimed at creating a regulated, transparent, and accountable financial atmosphere within the EU. The European MiFID I and MiFID II directives "differentiate between complex and non-complex products, and include two criteria for determining when a product is complex: (i) the product is illiquid because it is not listed on any organized financial market, and (ii)

[211] Stafford, P., & Smith, P. (2018, January 1). Europe begins countdown to MiFID I: Sweeping changes to EU rules on financial instruments come into force on January 3. *Financial Times*. www.ft.com/content/b8a9a634-e116-11e7-a8a4-0a1e63a52f9c. Accessed 5 June 2020.

[212] Prorokowski, L. (2015). MiFID II compliance-Are we ready? *Journal of Financial Regulation and Compliance, 23*(2), 196–206.

[213] Regulation (EU) No 600/2014 OF THE EUROPEAN PARLIAMENT AND OF THE COUNCIL of 15 May 2014 on markets in financial instruments and amending Regulation (EU) No 648/2012, Official Journal of the European Union L 173/84.

[214] Yeoh, P. (2019). MiFID II key concerns. *Journal of Financial Regulation and Compliance, 27*(1), 110–123.

the product contains some kind of financial derivative embedded in its design, as a future, option, or swap."[215]

The legislation provides a legislative framework to ensure that financial products are traded on regulated venues, increase transparency of trading, limit speculation on commodities, and protect investors through very strict organizational and conduct of business requirements. Its main scope is to strengthen market integrity, reduce risk, and foster stability in the financial markets.

Article 5 of Regulation (EU) No 600/2014 of the European Parliament and the Council stipulates that its main aim is "to strengthen confidence in the transparency of markets across the Union, to reduce regulatory complexity and investment firms' compliance costs, especially for financial institutions operating on a cross-border basis, and to contribute to the elimination of distortions of competition."[216] Consequently, increasing confidence and investor protection as well as high transparency are the key objectives of this regulation. According to Busch and Ferrarini (2017), the Directive mainly offered the rules framework governing market participants,[217] also providing different exemptions.[218] In comparison to MiFID I, this new Directive does not focus solely on security market efficiency and increasing competition, but also pays increased attention to market integrity.[219] Accordingly, the Directive enlarged the general perspective of MiFID I, capturing also other trading

[215] Méndez-Suárez, M., Monfort, A., & Gallardo, F. (2020). Sustainable banking: New forms of investing under the umbrella of the 2030 agenda. *Sustainability, 12*(5), 2096. https://doi.org/10.3390/su12052096.

[216] Article 5 of Regulation (EU) No 600/2014 OF THE EUROPEAN PARLIAMENT AND OF THE COUNCIL of 15 May 2014 on markets in financial instruments and amending Regulation (EU) No 648/2012, Official Journal of the European Union L 173/84.

[217] Busch, D., & Ferrarini, G. (2017). Who's afraid of MiFID II: An introduction. In D. Busch & G. Ferrarini (Eds.), *Regulation of the EU financial markets: MiFID II and MiFIR* (pp. 3–24). Oxford: Oxford University Press.

[218] Lieverse, K. (2017). Investments firms and investment services. In D. Bush & G. Ferrarini (Eds.), *Regulation of the EU financial markets: MiFID II and MiFIR*. Oxford: Oxford University Press.

[219] Lannoo, K. (2017). *MiFID II and the new market conduct rules for financial intermediaries: Will complexity bring transparency?* Belgium: European Capital Markets Institute (ECMI) Policy Brief. https://www.ceps.eu/ceps-publications/new-market-conduct-rules-financial-intermediaries-will-complexity-bring-transparency/. Accessed 15 June 2020.

activities and systems of the derivatives industry, offering pre- and post-trade stipulations concerning transparency, a rigorous equivalence regime for third country firms as well as new regulatory powers for national bodies in imposing sanctions or restrictions regarding sales.[220]

Some particular innovative concepts introduced were those of the OTF, representing a new trading venue and also the "Data Reporting Services Providers" (DRSPs), an entity collecting data and providing information on the market and transactions within the industry, for a better monitoring of the financial system. Also, another preoccupation of regulators was commodity derivatives due to their high volatility problems. This makes this Directive extremely important in terms possible repercussions on "market conduct risk."[221]

Major critics on MiFID II came from banks and brokerages, who stated that this Directive tends to overregulate, particularly on the transparency aspect.[222] According to them, the profitability of the market could be seriously damaged, due to forcing the disclosure of prices. Also, this could negatively impact trading and diminish market liquidity. At the same time, the new rules regarding the limitation of the amount of trade stocks in dark pools might force investors in favor of anonymity to find new loopholes. Regulators answered these critics and mentioned the financial traumas experienced in the last decennium, which urged for stricter trading rules.

Other concerns regarding MiFID II implied costs and charges reporting, firm and product governance, transaction reporting, and others. So far, there are no specific regulations dealing with the manner in which firms could discharge their disclosure obligations for MiFID II.

At the same if, while increasing transparency might enhance financial stability, it is also possible that MiFID II diminishes liquidity and even damage financial stability, representing therefore other issue for

[220] Directive 2004/39/EU, sections. 5-162.

[221] Nilson, B., Schff, R., & Williams, D. (2018). *Perspectives on conduct risk in wealth management*. www.mkinsey.com/.../risk/.../perspectives-on-conduct-risk-inwealth-management. Accessed 17 June 2020.

[222] Schumacher, D. (2018, January 3). Quicktake: MiFID II. *Bloomber*. www.bloomberg.com/quicktake/mifid-making-markets-fair. Accessed 4 June 2020.

concern.[223] The debate is still open: some argue that MiFID II could reduce the risk of fragmentation to a certain extent, while others claim that, although without intention, it can enhance risk.

2.9 Concluding Remarks

The current chapter presented a comprehensive overview of the European legislative framework regarding, inter alia, hedge funds: UCITS Directives (IV, V, and VI), AIFM Directive and MiFID (Level I and II), and other major sources of community Legal Rules. The UCITS Directives, the AIFMD, and the MiFID introduce a harmonized investment protection and product regulation framework, focusing on improved investor disclosure and transparency in order to enhance financial stability of the market.

In the author's opinion, the AIFM Directive has a great potential to overturn the alternative investment market within and beyond the borders of the EU, proposing a way to redesign the UCITS investor protection architecture.

The most attractive option in the author's opinion, seen also as a *quid pro quo* in favor of the adhesion to the new coordinated standards, is that EU AIFMs would be provided the favorable circumstances to market their AIFs in the EU by means of a passport. New distribution channels will develop while providing their access to markets that found it invariably difficult and even impossible (at times) to enter.

However, the author considers that both managers and investors welcome the option of allowing them to perform both tasks. The Directives are considered to become in time a brand for *investor protection* in relation to high-standards, in a similar manner the UCITS funds proved successfully not only inside, but also outside the EU. There is no doubt that the UCITS Directives are a successful instrument for facilitating cross-border investments in AUM schemes while offering at the same time a high level of investor protection. However, when the industry and regulators refer to the success of UCITS in reaching a high standard of investors' interests protection, they are mainly referring to a product that tightly regulates the asset management company on the one hand and

[223] Thakor, A. V. (2018). *The economic consequences of regulatory protection and extraterritorial reach* (Center for Capital Markets Paper Spring 2018). www.centerforcapitalmarkets.com/wp-content/../2018/.../CCMC_EconCon_v8. Accessed 4 June 2020.

the depositary on the other hand, in order to mitigate possible conflicts of interest, operational risk, as well as other risks connected to entrusting a person's savings to a money manager. This does not exclude the fact that the AIFM Directive might pose several major challenges regarding the compliance costs that will affect especially the small managers.

Meanwhile, Article 3 of the Directive establishes minimum AUM threshold norms regulating leverage calculation and the lack of certainty regarding the possibility for member states to impose very exact limits for the small manager exemption—both situations lead to the opinion that these thresholds could not prove very efficient in practical applications. *Ad consequentiam*, negative impacts are expected under certain circumstances: costs related to the appointment of a depositary according to the new liability rules stipulated in Article 21, the lack of certainty over delegation, the lack of compatibility with MiFID, and the remuneration controls together with the third country cooperation settlements issues. Overall, there are major concerns regarding an efficient and balanced implementation. In this respect, the successful implementation of the AIFM Directive requires the maintenance of a level playing area between EU and non-EU organizations.

The author identified several important disadvantages so far: the AIFMs located in EU are already required to obtain authorization according to the MiFID. Therefore, they are already subjected to registration, regulatory capital, compliance, and reporting requests. At the same time, the AIFM Directive will apply similar standards and requests, even if this directive establishes by far more oppressive reporting requests. In this respect, the author would like to underline that the EU regulatory authorities from Brussels, including the EC, have explicitly inserted within the AIFM Directive many of the principles stipulated within the MiFID and overall UCITS Directives (IV, V, and even VI), most of the times using exactly the same words. Positive and negative comments were provided as the abovementioned approach proved the EU's willingness to harmonize the norms in the financial services field, but at the same time proved, to a certain extent, its low comprehension level regarding the AIFs operation, requiring the AIFMs to comply with the norms set up for the UCITS funds managers (fund tools particularly meant for retail investors), unlike the most part of AIFs.

Further on, the author proposes a brief comparison of the three major directives analyzed herein: UCITS Directive, MiFID Directive, and AIFM Directive, all focused on ensuring investor protection.

The convergences of these three directives represent major issues in addressing them. Therefore, overlaps regarding MiFID and the UCITS Directive imply the regulatory framework regarding the sales of UCITS, because the UCITS sale is included in the aim of MiFID's conduct of business norms. So far, MiFID II considers that the UCITS are either "complex" or "non-complex." From this point of view, there are significant distinctions between MiFID II and the UCITS Directive. Therefore, according to MiFID, only the non-complex particular financial instruments may be sold to clients based on an execution ground in the absence of the tool suitability control for the client. The abovementioned issue contradicts the UCITS Directive, as UCITS tend to be particularly considered appropriate for retail investment, tightly regulated by the UCITS Directive. Conclusively, the conflict emerging between these two directives becomes very clear in this context. The author considers that these issues should be carefully considered and that the distinction between UCITS/non-UCITS should be made.

Nonetheless, while an AIFM is outside the aim of MiFID, one anticipates that similarly to UCITS, many of the investor management activities of alternative investment funds will occur in investment companies, subjected to the regulation of the MiFID. Consequently, managers will manage funds covered not only by MiFID, but also by the AIFM Directive, and this implies the fact that they will be compelled to comply with both directives. This raises the significant question whether tracing refined differentiations between these two directives makes any sense.

On the other hand, as far as MiFID is concerned, it is necessary that several approaches are implemented when developing MiFID II: the prevention of the duplication between the two directives; in case the duplication cannot be avoided; the clarification of stipulation guides so that these are easily comprehended in terms of which directive should be followed or is going to prevail, or at least a clear sign of the more rigorous requests observance; the notification of direct remarks to both UCITS and AIFM Directives where appropriate, as the major aim is to prevent the occurrence of overlaps between the two directives.

This chapter focuses, on the one hand on investment services and activities, and, on the other hand, on collective investment management, which stands as an important part of the EU regulatory architecture articulating financial markets legislation. In spite of their different origins, particularly during the last decade, the framework for investment services regulation in the EU has turned more and more articulated, and investment fund rules have been extended to all CIUs falling under the definition of the 2011 AIFM Directive. At the same time, various issues, typical of investment services approach (mainly those emerging from MiFID I and more recently MiFID II) were incorporated into the UCITS and AIFMD Directives, and the MiFID approach being currently influencing several other areas of EU Financial Services regulation. Lately, a trans-sectorial standard for investor protection and transparency enhancement is starting to emerge, and may stand as the foundation for future developments and integration of EU legislation.

As one could see, the UCITS Directives, the AIFM Directive, and the MiFID all have negative and positive impacts. As a final concluding remark, the real advantages of these directives will be observed in the forthcoming future, as a follow-up of dust settlement and of the passport availability to a broader extent—if such be the case.

The author considers that disclosure and operating provisions must be at the core of investor protection architecture, as they will ensure a gold standard applied worldwide.

References

Aghanya, D., Agarwal, V., & Poshakwale, S. (2020). Market in Financial Instruments Directive (MiFID), stock price informativeness and liquidity. *Journal of Banking & Finance, 113*(C), 105730. https://doi.org/10.1016/j.jbankfin.2019.105730.

Alshaleel, M. K. (2016). Undertakings for the collective investment in transferable securities directive V: Increased protection for investors. *European Company Law, 13,* 14–22.

Annunziata, F. (2019). Investment services and investment funds. In F. Fabbrini & M. Ventoruzzo (Eds.), *Research handbook on European economic law* (p. 477). Cheltenham: Edward Elgar.

Assogestioni apud De Phoebus Athanassiou. (2009). *Hedge fund regulation in the European Union: Current trends and future prospects.* Netherlands: Wolters Kluwer.

Athanassiou, P. (2010). The draft AIFM Directive and the future of European alternative investment fund regulation. *CESifo DICE Report, 8*(1), 8–13.

Awrey, D. (2011). Regulating financial innovation: A more principles-based alternative? *Brooklyn Journal of Corporate. Financial and Commercial Law, 5*(2), 273–315.

Bremus, F., & Kliatskova, T. (2018). *Legal harmonization, institutional quality, and countries' external positions: A sectoral analysis* (DIW Discussion Papers, No. 1768). https://doi.org/10.2139/ssrn.3287798.

Busch, D., & Ferrarini, G. (2017). Who's afraid of MiFID II: An introduction. In D. Busch & G. Ferrarini (Eds.), *Regulation of the EU Financial Markets: MiFID II and MiFIR* (pp. 3–24). Oxford: Oxford University Press.

CESR. (2006a, October). *Can hedge fund indices be classified as financial indices for the purposes of UCITS?* The Committee of European Security Regulators. CESR/06–530. https://www.esma.europa.eu/press-news/consultations/cesrs-issues-paper-can-hedge-fund-indices-be-classified-financial-indices. Accessed 15 June 2020.

CESR. (2006b, January). *Advice to the European Commission on the clarification of definitions concerning eligible assets for investments in UCITS*. The Committee of European Security Regulators. CESR/06–005, para. 158 et seq. https://www.esma.europa.eu/document/cesr%E2%80%99s-advice-european-commission-clarification-definitions-concerning-eligible-assets. Accessed 15 June 2020.

CESR. (2007, February). *Clarification on the definitions concerning eligible assets for investment by UCITS: Can hedge fund indices be classified as financial indices for the purposes of UCITS?* The Committee of European Security Regulators. CESR/07-045. https://www.esma.europa.eu/press-news/consultations/clarification-definitions-concerning-eligible-assets-investment-ucits-canv. Accessed 15 June 2020.

COM (2017) 536 final (20.9.2017).

COM/2009/0207, Article 20, s. 1.

Commission Directive (EC) 2007/16 [2007] OJ L79/11.

Commission Proposal for an European Parliament and Council Directive Amending Directive 85/611/EEC, COM (93) 37 final [1993] OJ C59/14, as amended by COM (94) 329 final [1994] OJ C242/4.

Council Directive (EEC) 93/22, [1993] OJ L141/27.

Council Directive 85/611/EEC of 20 December 1985 on the coordination of laws, regulations and administrative provisions relating to undertakings for collective investment in transferable securities (UCITS). https://eur-lex.europa.eu/legal-content/EN/TXT/?uri=celex%3A31985L0611. Accessed 2 May 2020.

Cumming, D., Imad'Eddine, G., & Schwienbacher, A. (2012). Harmonized regulatory standards, international distribution of investment funds and the recent financial crisis. *The European Journal of Finance, 18*(3–4), 261–292.

Cumming, D., & Johan, S. (2019). Capital-market effects of securities regulation: Prior conditions, implementation, and enforcement revisited. *Finance Research Letters, 31*(C). https://doi.org/10.1016/j.frl.2018.12.013.

Dalhuisen, J. H. (2019). *Dalhuisen on transnational comparative, commercial, financial and trade law* (7th ed.). Oxford: Hart Publishing.
Dejmek, P. (2009). The EU internal market for financial services—A look at the first regulatory responses to the financial crisis and a view to the future. *The Columbia Journal of European Law, 15*(3), 455.
Directive (EC) 2001/107 [2002] OJ L41/20.
Directive (EC) 2001/108 [2002] OJ L41/35.
Directive (EU) 2019/1160 of the European Parliament and of the Council of 20 June 2019 amending Directives 2009/65/EC and 2011/61/EU with regard to cross-border distribution of collective investment undertakings (Text with EEA relevance.) PE/53/2019/REV/1, OJ L 188, 12.7.2019, pp. 106–115.
Directive 2004/39/EC of the European Parliament and of the Council of April 21, 2004 on Markets in Financial Instruments amending Council Directives 85/611/EC and 96/6/EEC and Directive 2000/12/EC of the European Parliament and of the Council and repealing Council Directive 93/22/EEC, OJ L145, p. 1.
Directive 2009/65/EC on the coordination of laws, regulations and administrative provisions relating to undertakings for collective investment in transferable securities (UCITS) as regards depositary functions, remuneration policies and sanctions Text with EEA relevance, Official Journal of the European Union, L 257/186. https://eur-lex.europa.eu/legal-content/EN/TXT/?uri=CELEX%3A32014L0091. Accessed 5 June 2020.
Directive 2009/65/EC on the coordination of laws, regulations and administrative provisions relating to undertakings for collective investment in transferable securities (UCITS) as regards depositary functions, remuneration policies and sanctions Text with EEA relevance (OJ L 257, 28.8.2014, pp. 186–213).
Directive 2011/61/EU of the European Parliament and of the Council of 8 June 2011 on Alternative Investment Fund Managers and amending Directives 2003/41/EC and 2009/65/EC and Regulations (EC) No 1060/2009 and (EU) No 1095/2010 (OJ L 174, 1.7.2011, pp. 1–73).
Directive on Alternative Investment Fund Managers (AIFM Directive): Frequently Asked Questions, Memo/10/572 (November, 2010) (FAQ).
Duvall, J., & Swan, G. (2019). Ongoing charges of UCITS in the European Union. *ICI Research Perspective, 25*(7). www.ici.org/pdf/per25-07.pdf. Accessed 7 May 2020.
ECB. (2009). Opinion of 16 October 2009 on a Proposal for a Directive on Alternative Investment Fund Managers and amending Directives 2004/39/EC and 2009/.../EC. paragraph 7.
EFAMA. (2020). Trends in the European Investment Fund Industry in the fourth quarter of 2019 & results for the full year of 2019. In B. Delbecque, T. Tilley & H. Yang (Eds.), The European fund and asset management association. *Quarterly Statistical Release, 80*, 1–22.

Ernst&Young. (2012). Viewpoint: AIFM Directive: Get ready for European depositary reform. *European Asset Management Viewpoint Series* (p. 1).

ESMA. (2014, May). *Consultation paper on MIFID II/MIFIR, European Securities and Markets Authority (ESMA)* (EC Consultation Paper). www.esma.europa.eu/press-news/consultations/consultation-paper-mifid-iimifir. Accessed 12 June 2020.

ESMA. (2017). *Consultation paper, 13 July 2017, 35-43-748*, p. 9.

European Commission. (1985). Completing the Internal Market. White Paper to the European Council of 28/29 June 1985 in Milan. COM (85) 310 final.

European Commission. (2005). Green Paper on the Enhancement of the EU framework for Investment Funds, Brussels, 2005, COM (2005) 314 final, 4.

European Commission. (2009). *European financial supervision*. Impact Assessment. http://ec.europa.eu/. Accessed 17 May 2011.

European Commission. (2010, December 8). *Public consultation: Review of the markets in financial instruments directive (MiFID)*. EC Public Consultation Document. www.ec.ruropa.eu/finance/consultations/2010/mifid/index_en.htm. Accessed 5 May 2020.

European Commission. (2012a). *Consultation on the undertakings for collective investment in transferable securities (UCITS)—Product rules, liquidity management, depositary, money market funds, long-term investments*. https://ec.europa.eu/finance/consultations/2012/ucits/index_en.htm. Accessed 3 April 2020.

European Commission. (2012b). Proposal for a Directive of the European Parliament and of the Council Amending Directive 2009/65/EC on the Coordination of Laws, Regulations and Administrative Provisions Relating to Undertakings for Collective Investment in Transferable Securities (UCITS) as Regards Depositary Functions, Remuneration Policies and Sanctions, Strasbourg, 3.7.2012 COM (2012) 350 final.

European Parliament. (2006). Resolution on Asset Management (2006/2037/INI), 27 April 2006, A recent White Paper is, however, silent on the issue (European Commission, White Paper on Enhancing the Single Market Framework for Investment Funds, Brussels, 15 November 2006, COM [2006] 689 final).

Ferran, E. (2004). *Building an EU securities market*. Cambridge University Press. https://papers.ssrn.com/sol3/papers.cfm?abstract_id=604047. Accessed 15 June 2020.

Fihri, S. (2019). *New EU regulation and directive amending the UCITS and AIFM directives as well as the EuSEF, EuVECA and PRIIPs regulations, KPMG*. https://kpmgfundnews.eu/european-union/2019/07/new-eu-regulation-and-directive-amending-the-ucits-and-aifm-directives-as-well-as-the-eusef-euveca-and-priips-regulations/. Accessed 3 June 2020.

Garicano, L., & Lastra, R. M. (2010). Towards a new architecture for financial stability: Seven principles. *Journal of International Economic Law, 13*(3), 597–621. https://doi.org/10.1093/jiel/jgq041.

Gortsos, C. (2019). *The evolution of European (EU) Banking Law under the influence of (public) International Banking Law: A comprehensive overview research study*. Prague: Faculty of Law, Charles University. https://doi.org/10.2139/ssrn.3334493.

Hertig, G. (2003). Four predictions about the future of EU securities regulation. *Journal of Corporate Law Studies, 3,* 1–25. http://dx.doi.org/10.2139/ssrn.3334493.

Janin, S. (2007). MiFID impact on investment managers. *Journal of Financial Regulation and Compliance, 15*(1), 90–98.

Joenvaara, J., & Kosowski, R. (2015). *The effect of regulatory constraints on fund performance: New evidence from UCITS hedge funds*. https://ssrn.com/abstract=2598012 or http://dx.doi.org/10.2139/ssrn.2598012. Accessed 20 June 2020.

Kokoris, A., Archontakis, F., & Grose, C. (2020). Market risk assessment: Evidence from packaged retail and insurance-based investment products. *Journal of Risk Finance, 21(*2), 111–126. https://doi.org/10.1108/jrf-05-2019-0078.

Kovas, A. (2006). UCITS—Past, present and future in a world of increasing product diversity. *Working Paper Series, 44*(2), 1–33.

Krokida, S. I., Makrychoriti, P., & Spyrou, S. (2020). Monetary policy and herd behavior: International evidence. *Journal of Economic Behavior & Organization, 170,* 386–417.

Kudrna, Z. (2009). *The EU financial market policy: Evolution, innovation and research outlook* (Working Paper No. 04:1-35). Institute for European Integration Research. https://www.academia.edu/975557/The_EU_Financial_Market_Policy_Evolution_Innovation_and_Research_Outlook. Accessed 15 June 2020.

L'Habitant, F. S. (2006). Hedge fund indices for retail investors: UCITS eligible or not eligible? *Derivatives Uses, Trading and Regulation, 12,* 275–289.

Lannoo, K. (2017). *MiFID II and the new market conduct rules for financial intermediaries: Will complexity bring transparency?* Belgium: European Capital Markets Institute (ECMI) Policy Brief. https://www.ceps.eu/ceps-publications/new-market-conduct-rules-financial-intermediaries-will-complexity-bring-transparency/. Accessed 15 June 2020.

Lieverse, K. (2017). Investments firms and investment services. In D. Bush & G. Ferrarini (Eds.), *Regulation of the EU financial markets: MiFID II and MiFIR*. Oxford: Oxford University Press.

Méndez-Suárez, M., Monfort, A., & Gallardo, F. (2020). Sustainable banking: New forms of investing under the umbrella of the 2030 agenda. *Sustainability, 12*(5), 2096. https://doi.org/10.3390/su12052096.

Mertzanis, H. (2011, April 7). *The UCITS IV directive, the need for rationalization, and master-feeder structures*. Paper presented at the Workshop on master-feeder funds and key investor information, Capital Markets Board of Turkey, Ankara.

Moloney, N. (2002). *EC securities regulation*. Oxford: Oxford University Press.

Moloney, N. (2006). The EC and the hedge fund challenge: A test case for EC securities policy after the financial services action plan. *Journal of Corporate Law Studies, 6*(1), 1–38. https://doi.org/10.1080/14735970.2006.11419945.

Muller, C., & Braunstein, C. (2014). UCITS VI: In practice. *Journal of Securities Operations & Custody, 6*(3), 220–227.

Münchhalfen, P., & Gaschler, R. (2020). *Attention distribution of current key investor documents—Standardization as a long-term goal of the PRIIPS regulation*. https://ssrn.com/abstract=3607872 or http://dx.doi.org/10.2139/ssrn.3607872. Accessed 2 June 2020.

Nilson, B., Schff, R., & Williams, D. (2018). *Perspectives on conduct risk in wealth management*. www.mkinsey.com/.../risk/.../perspectives-on-conduct-risk-inwealth-management. Accessed 17 June 2020.

Olly, J. (2018). Unintended impact of Priips, MIFID to be reviewed for asset managers. *International Financial Law Review*. https://www.iflr.com/article/b1lp1wcsjk8tqt/unintended-impact-of-priips-mifid-to-be-reviewed-for-asset-managers. Accessed 15 June 2020.

Ostrowska, M. (2018). Transparency regime within the financial institutions: Does it really work. In S. Grima & P. Marano (Eds.), *Governance and regulations' contemporary issues: Contemporary studies in economic and financial analysis Vol. 99* (pp. 293–313). Emerald Publishing Limited.

Oxera Consulting. (2006). *Current trends in asset management*. Report prepared for European Commission DG Internal Market and Services. https://www.google.com/url?sa=t&rct=j&q=&esrc=s&source=web&cd=&ved=2ahUKEwjPv_i59qbrAhV-REEAHcehC28QFjAAegQIAhAB&url=https%3A%2F%2Fwww.oxera.com%2Fwp-content%2Fuploads%2F2018%2F03%2FCurrent-trends-in-asset-management.pdf&usg=AOvVaw0XxwFc2XYLZ5LF6OA6RsGe. Accessed 15 June 2020.

Penn, B. (2007). MiFID and market infrastructure: Convergence of exchange and broker regulation. *Buttherworths Journal of International Banking and Financial Law, 22*(3), 155–158.

Persson, M. (2009). *The EU's AIFM Directive: Likely impact and best way forward*. London: Open Europe.

Phillis, G., & Dawson, J. (2003). The regulation and distribution of hedge funds in Europe—Changes and challenges. *Balance Sheet, 11*(4), 36–43.

Prorokowski, L. (2015). MiFID II compliance-Are we ready? *Journal of Financial Regulation and Compliance, 23*(2), 196–206.

Recine, F., & Teixeira, P. G. (2009). The new financial stability architecture in the EU. Frankfurt Institute for Law and Finance. *Working Paper Series, 110*(12), 1–36.

Regulation (EC) N. 1093/2010 by the European Parliament and the Council on 24 November 2010.

Regulation (EU) No 600/2014 OF THE EUROPEAN PARLIAMENT AND OF THE COUNCIL of 15 May 2014 on markets in financial instruments and amending Regulation (EU) No 648/2012, Official Journal of the European Union L 173/84.

Regulation (EU) 2019/1156 of the European Parliament and of the Council of 20 June 2019 on facilitating cross-border distribution of collective investment undertakings and amending Regulations (EU) No 345/2013, (EU) No 346/2013 and (EU) No 1286/2014 (Text with EEA relevance.), PE/54/2019/REV/1, OJ L 188, 12.7.2019, pp. 55–66.

Regulation (EU) No 1022/2013 of the European Parliament and of the Council of 22 October 2013 amending Regulation (EU) No 1093/2010 establishing a European Supervisory Authority (European Banking Authority) as regards the conferral of specific tasks on the European Central Bank pursuant to Council Regulation (EU) No 1024/2013, OJ L 287.

Schoenmaker, D. (2009). A new financial stability framework for Europe. *The Financial Regulator, 13*(3), 748–774. https://doi.org/10.1017/cbo9781139151184.036.

Schumacher, D. (2018, January 3). Quicktake: MiFID II. *Bloomber*. www.bloomberg.com/quicktake/mifid-making-markets-fair. Accessed 4 June 2020.

Seretakis, A. L. (2012). The new EU Directive on the regulation of private equity. *Columbia Journal of European Law Online, 18*(3), Forthcoming. https://ssrn.com/abstract=2035997. Accessed 4 June 2020.

Spendzharova, A. (2017). Becoming a powerful regulator: The European Securities and Markets Authority (ESMA) in European financial sector governance. *TARN Working Paper Series, 8*, 1–19. http://dx.doi.org/10.2139/ssrn.2965429.

Stafford, P. (2017, June 7). No more MiFID II delays-European markets regulator. *Financial Times*. www.ft.com/content/663b3629-764-34de-892d-5062d515643. Accessed 4 June 2020.

Stafford. P., & Smith, P. (2018, January 1). Europe begins countdown to MiFID I: Sweeping changes to EU rules on financial instruments come into force on January 3. *Financial Times*. www.ft.com/content/b8a9a634-e116-11e7-a8a4-0a1e63a52f9c. Accessed 5 June 2020.

Stowell, D. P. (2018). Risk, regulation, and organizational structure. In D. P. Stowell (Ed.), *Investment banks, hedge funds, and private equity* (3rd ed., pp. 309–322). Cambridge: Academic Press.

Taylor, K. (2002). The impact of the E-Commerce Directive in the area of financial services. *Journal of Financial Services Marketing, 6*, 391–396. https://doi.org/10.1057/palgrave.fsm.4770067.

Thakor, A. V. (2018). *The economic consequences of regulatory protection and extraterritorial reach* (Center for Capital Markets Paper Spring 2018). www.centerforcapitalmarkets.com/wp-content/../2018/.../CCMC_EconCon_v8. Accessed 4 June 2020.

Thygesen, N. (2003). The political economy of financial harmonisation in Europe: Comments. In J. J. M. Kremers, D. Schoenmaker, & P. J. Wierts (Eds.), *Financial supervision in Europe* (pp. 142–150). Cheltenham, UK: Edward Elgar.

Wymeersch, E. (2005). The future of financial regulation and supervision in Europe. *Common Market Law Review, 42*(4), 987–1010.

Yeoh, P. (2019). MiFID II key concerns. *Journal of Financial Regulation and Compliance, 27*(1), 110–123.

CHAPTER 3

Regulation of Hedge Funds in Selected Single European Jurisdictions: Italy, France, Ireland, Luxembourg, Malta, and Switzerland—The Impact of the AIFM Directive

3.1 Introduction

Investor protection was a priority throughout 2018, through the implementation of MiFID II and the Packaged Retail and Insurance-based Investment Products (PRIIPs) Regulation, which have prompted operational changes by financial service providers targeting improved transparency, retrocession bans, and more robust suitability assessments. In parallel, the European Commission continues work on reducing barriers to competition in the provision of cross-border financial services in a number of areas.

Elsewhere, market structure is in a period of reform and will adapt as MiFID II continues to bed in. The refinement of the MiFID framework under the new EU legislature is expected, and for financial stability more broadly to remain under discussion at both a regional and global level. Preparations for a post-Brexit financial system in Europe have influenced the regulatory agendas in the United Kingdom, and to a certain extent in the EU27. Since negotiations are still ongoing, it is important to see whether, when the United Kingdom leaves the EU, it will decide

A. M. Fagetan, *The Regulation of Hedge Funds*,
https://doi.org/10.1007/978-3-030-63706-4_3

to remain in EEA[1] country or not. As a consequence of the United Kingdom's withdrawal from the EU, different EU member states, including those analyzed in the current chapter are competing to attract hedge funds in their financial centers. Brexit prompts hard choices for both the United Kingdom and the EU member states. Policy makers have sought to gain some control of their borders by reviewing the supervisory infrastructure in Europe through the ESA Review, and ensuring alignment of cross-border practices. In this respect, on December 27, 2019, the revised version of ESMA's founding Regulation was published in the EU Official Journal.[2]

This chapter provides a comparative overview of how different and diverse the hedge fund regulation throughout Europe is. Even if the author does not go into details when describing the laws identified in the different selected single European jurisdictions: Italy, France, Ireland, Luxembourg, Malta, and Switzerland. The intention is to give the reader an idea of how diverse and dissimilar the different legislators' approaches can be, instead of presenting a detailed description. Also, such a description would not correspond to the scope of this chapter that aims to focus on investor protection principles, not on the detailed international rules.

3.2 Hedge Funds Regulation in Italy

3.2.1 Overview of Hedge Funds Regulatory Regime

Italy is among the first European jurisdictions to explicitly adopt, in 1999, specific regulations for hedge funds as well as FoHF.[3] According to statistics, in the first quarter of 2019, the total AUM reached a new record, summing up more than EUR 2 billion—approximately 120% of Italy's GDP.[4] This major growth reflects an equally major growth of wealth

[1] European Economic Area.

[2] The new Regulations founding the European Supervisory Authorities (ESAs) and in particular ESMA, are applicable as of January 1, 2020.

[3] Calderoni, C. (2006). *Hedge funds in Italy: An industry update*. Alternative Investment Management Association. https://www.aima.org/article/hedge-funds-in-italy--an-update.html. Accessed 14 July 2020.

[4] Rumi, G., Ubaldini, R., Dimonte, M., Ferrari, C., & Vece, G. (2019). Italy. In *The asset management review* (8th ed.). https://thelawreviews.co.uk/edition/the-asset-management-review-edition-8/1197347/italy. Accessed 12 August 2020.

of investors', clients, and also investment industry.[5] Over the medium terms, it looks like Italy will maintain this increasing tendency—increase of AUM.[6]

Hedge funds represent not a legally defined term under the Italian law, known rather as "speculative funds" ("*fondi speculativi*"),[7] a designation making no difference between single-manager funds or FoHF.[8]

The key norm is Treasury Decree no. 228, as amended (the "Treasury Decree"),[9] further developed, mainly through the 1999 and 2005 Bank of Italy Regulations[10] with the latter indicating the adoption of a somewhat more liberal approach to alternative investment fund regulation. There were several regulations acknowledging hedge funds, or for a better accuracy, their Italian synonym: *fondi speculativi/speculative funds* in compliance with the Italian regulatory system. These regulations were the Decree n° 58/98 and the already mentioned Ministerial Decree n° 228.[11] Therefore, it was only in 2008, with the enactment of the Law Decree n° 185, that the international concept of hedge fund started to be acknowledged in Italy, too.[12] These will be further approached in this chapter. The minimum initial investment or threshold for speculative funds was set at EUR 500,000 while the Italian law also stipulated a

[5] Idem.

[6] Alvaro, S., & Annunziata, F. (2019). *Shareholdings of alternative investment funds in listed companies and in banks: A legal perspective.*

[7] Treasury Decree, Article 16. "Decreto del Ministero del Tesoro n° 228" del 1999.

[8] In February 2006, almost 97% of the Italian onshore hedge fund market consisted of Fund of Hedge Funds: The effective lack of an Italian single-manager hedge fund market is due to exogenous and endogenous factors.

[9] Decreto del Ministro del Tesoro, del Bilancio e della Programmazione Economica del 24 maggio 1999, no 228, G.U. no 164 del 15 luglio 1999, inter alia adopted on the basis of Article 37 of the Decreto Legislativo del 24 febbraio 1998, n° 58 Testo Unico della Finanza.

[10] Banca d'Italia. (1999a). Provvedimento del Governatore della Banca d'Italia del 20 settembre 1999 (Regolamento recante disposizioni per le società di gestione del risparmio), and to the Banca d'Italia. (2005). Provvedimento della Banca d'Italia del 14 aprile 2005 (Regolamento sulla gestione colletiva del risparmio). The latter flashes out several of the provisions of Decreto Legislativo 1 agosto 2003, n° 274, transposing UCTIS III.

[11] Of 24 May 1999.

[12] Opromolla, G. (2009). Facing the financial crisis: Bank of Italy's implementing regulation on hedge funds. *Journal of Investment Compliance, 10*(2), 41–44. https://doi.org/10.1108/15285810910971274.

maximum of 200 investors per fund.[13] Moreover, speculative funds could only be distributed on a private placement basis, with authorization of CONSOB[14]—the regulator for Italian securities.[15] Hence, while Italian law did not statutorily restrict hedge funds to designated categories of professional investors—the Treasury Decree did not explicitly require that the 200 investors should be "qualified investors"—its effect was to limit the marketing of speculative funds exclusively to those public or private investors having increased net value.

In terms of investment policy, speculative funds can invest freely, without any restrictions, adopting the investment strategy of their choice, without being subjected to the prudential supervision rules of the "*Bank of Italy*" (BoI), which apply to common collective investment schemes.[16] Similarly, there are no restrictions regarding the portfolio diversification applicable to Italian speculative funds.

However, Italy is the only EU jurisdiction examined herein, where the offer of hedge fund products is reserved to specialized asset management companies, appointed as "*Società di gestione del risparmio speculative*" ("speculative SGRs"), endowed with legal personality and established under the law of contract.[17]

The fee rate levied for speculative funds reaches 12.5% in terms of the accumulated managerial outcomes toward the end of the year. According to the Italian main norms, the return acquired through any investment fund is levied before deductions by withholding fees at source or swap fees. Similarly, both the capital subjected to the deduction fee at source

[13] Treasury Decree, Articles 16.3 and 16.2. A July 2008 report advocated a decrease by half of the investment threshold and the elimination of the maximum amount of investors allowed within one fund. This threshold was the result of the amendment brought by Ministry of Treasury Decree N° 47 of 2003 (Gruppo di Lavoro sui Fondi Comuni Italiani. [2008]. *Fondi Comuni Italiani: Situazione attuale e Possibili Linee di Intervento.* Rapporto [pp. 41–42]).

[14] Commissione Nazionale per le Società e la Borsa.

[15] Treasury Decree, Article 16.4.

[16] Treasury Decree, Article 16.1.

[17] Although speculative SGRs only differ from ordinary ones in terms of their objective, with Italian law prescribing no special requirements for speculative SGRs to secure a BoI management license. Banca d'Italia. (1999b). Regolamento della Banca d'Italia 20 settembre 1999, pubblicato nella Gazzetta Ufficiale n° 230 del 30 settembre 1999, sostituito dal provvedimento della Banca d'Italia 14 aprile 2005, pubblicato nel supplemento ordinario alla Gazzetta Ufficiale n° 109 del 12 maggio 2005.

and the fee-exempted capital in Italy tend to be removed from the managerial outcome, falling under the 12.5% fee.

Italian law submits the distribution of foreign non-UCTIS funds in Italy to the same BoI prior authorization requirement. The grant of an authorization is explicitly made conditional.[18]

Further on, "speculative funds are regulated by article 16 of the Ministry Decree n° 228 of 24 May 1999, as amended by the Ministry Decree n° 256 of 14 October 2005 and the Ministry Decree n° 47 of 31 January 2003 (Decree n° 228) that implement article 37, paragraph 1 of the Consolidated Finance Act."[19] Similarly, there are also secondary norms regulating speculative funds, namely:

- "the BoI regulations of 14 April 2005, as amended by the BoI Order of 16 December 2008 that provides the implementing rules of the EU Directive 2007/16/EC on eligible assets."[20] These regulations contain typical norms with regard to SGRs and the manner they are managed;
- the "BoI Order of 21 June 2007, amending April 2005 BoI Regulations,"[21] with regard to scopes concerning SGRs but also the regulation of funds;
- "the BoI and the CONSOB joint regulations of 29 October 2007 providing the MiFID Directive 2004/39/EC implementing rules;
- the Decree n° 185 and the implementing December 2008 BoI Regulations."[22]

To ensure a very effective operation of Italian hedge funds on the financial industries' liquidity crises but also, simultaneously, to guarantee similar interests and support for all invested individuals, the BoI issued

[18] Testo Unico della Finanza, Article 42(5).

[19] Lener, R. (2010). *Italian national report to the IACL*. Paper presented at the International Academy of Comparative Law Congress, Washington, July 27, 2010.

[20] Ibid.

[21] Ibid.

[22] Ibid.

Regulation 785/08[23] on December 16, 2008, adopting "Section 14, paragraphs 6, 7, 8 and 9, of Law Decree n° 185 of November 29, 2008."

In agreement with Law Decree n° 185,[24] taking on Italy's finances and coming up against this financial tumult,[25] several recommendations were made by Italian regulatory texts, up to the end of 2009:

i. First, in case the SGRs receive overall redemption requirements higher than 15% of the NAV,[26] at some particular date or extent of time, then the SGRs will be able to perform partial redemptions. According to this, all units that were not repaid—surpassing all thresholds that were previously mentioned, also named entries/gates—are going to be seen like reimbursement requirements that the investors newly submit during the first day following that above-mentioned partial redemptions[27];
ii. Second, if it is absolutely compulsory for SGRs to satisfy every redemption request, sell "the fund's illiquid assets, and if this may adversely affect the interests of the investors, the SGR can solve a withdrawal thereof and transfer the illiquid assets in a new closed-end fund, whose units are assigned to each participant to the original fund proportionally to the amount of units owned in the latter."[28] These newly created funds, also named side-pockets, are not allowed to release new units, while the old ones are going to face reimbursement when the assets liquidation will occur.

Provisions find that an SGR is able to face problems in the reimbursement of customers meaning that these are going to need to divest every illiquid asset.[29]

[23] The BoI Regulation 785/08 was published on December 22, 2008 in the Italian Official Gazette and entered into force on the same date.

[24] Law N° 2 of 28 January 2009 (Decree 185) (so-called "Anti-Crisis Decree").

[25] Opromolla, G. (2009). Op. Cit., pp. 41–42.

[26] Net asset value

[27] Law Decree 185. (2008). Law Decree no 185 of 28 November 2008. Ordinary Supplement no. 263/L, Official Gazette no. 280 of 29.11.2008.

[28] Ibid.

[29] Opromolla, G. (2009). Op. Cit., p. 14.

The highest amount of participants in hedge funds is set at 200. In fact, the previously mentioned limit had led to the making of similar duplicates of hedge funds. Such innovation has been suggested in a recent study advanced by the Group responsible with the hedge funds reform in Italy, as this was also established before the BoI.

According to the previous statements, Regulation n° 785 of December 2008, adopted by BoI focuses generally on features regarding side-pockets, definition of *illiquid assets*, estimation of the manner in which new norms affect the industry, especially at the time the unitary worth is below half a million EUR and last but not least, regarding the approval act of "procedures for the amendments to the fund's regulation."[30]

"*Characteristics regarding side-pockets.*" Article 14[31] of the above-mentioned Decree, considers that side-pockets represent closed-end funds. According to this, they focus on the disinvestment of their assets which are difficult to sell in compliance with a given disinvestment program previously confirmed by the managers of the SGR. Similarly, they are forbidden to make a single transfer or to merge. However, they might ask for loans but not more than 10% of its net worth, while the allowed period is half a year, the most.

The creation of a fund implies several conditions for SGR, which must first clarify the main motivation regarding the illiquid assets transfers. Secondly, this must acknowledge all norms imposed by side-pockets. Thirdly, the individualization of those illiquid assets that need to be moved to the side-pockets is necessary. In the fourth place, the solving of the hedge fund separation and the transference concerning illiquid assets to side-pockets shall be ensured. In the fifth place, one needs to establish fundamental appraisal standards regarding illiquid assets, and then to receive the approval of a controlling strategy regarding the illiquid assets transfer. Lastly, the approval of the study regarding the establishment of side-pockets will be forwarded toward the investors.[32]

Defining "*illiquid assets.*" Several standards need to be promoted to assess the fund in terms of its financial tools liquidity:

[30] Idem.

[31] Regulation n° 785 of December 2008, Paragraph 6, let. (b).

[32] Opromolla, G. (2009). Op. Cit., p. 43.

(i) Undertakings for UCITS or other similar financial tools:

- long-term act of suspending regarding calculations of the shares' worth;
- sectional or overall act of suspending redemptions;
- fund termination;
- making side-pockets/similar tools;
- the act of amending regular buybacks of the shares;
- worth rates instability due to assets difficult to sell, to whom this industry is not pointing out trustworthy costs.

(ii) Secondary financial tools. The following data are considered:

- size, regularity, and trading firm;
- a consistent price;
- buying tendency as well as selling costs during a given interval;
- distribution of costs by means of trustworthy materials.[33]

These recent rules affect the market for two reasons, especially when the unitary price exceeds EUR 500,000:

(i) The hedge fund can be separated. At that time, the investor, who is by no means guilty of the unitary price decrease, cannot be forced to replace the minimal amount mentioned;
(ii) Adding a *gate*, when the redemption is verified, with regard to the subsequent expiration periods until the last redemption, the only exception accepted is when the investor subscribes for the amount requested to reinstate minimal thresholds.[34]

The processes confirming all rectifications *of the fund's regulation* to the hedge fund's norms regarding the introduction of the so-called *gate*, regarding the setup of side-pockets, but also/or regarding the cancelation of the norm lowering the upper limit of the amount of hedge funds investors tend to be similar to those for normal amendments to the fund's norms.[35]

[33] Idem.

[34] Idem.

[35] Ibid., p. 43.

Due to the financial crisis, as well as to the systemic generated risks bursting out generally due to low mastery instruments for alternative investments,[36] there was a general agreement about EU, which expected to introduce an innovating system of rules. Therefore, the published Directive 2011/61/EC of the European Parliament and of the Council of June 8, 2011 on Alternative Investment Fund Managers, as well as the amending Directives 2003/41/EC and 2009/65/EC and Regulations (EC) n° 1060/2009 and (EU) n° 1095/2010[37] focus on regulating managers of alternative investment funds. These imply the overall collective investment institutions that are not included in the UCITS directive, or in other words, that cannot be defined as harmonized investment funds.[38]

The principles governing asset management are contained in the Italian Financial Act,[39] and were implemented—after the adoption of the AIFMD and the UCITS V[40] rules—by Ministerial Decree No. 30/2015, which set out the general criteria applicable to Italian UCIs; the Bank of

[36] Catelani, E., & Sequi, G. (2010, October 15–16). *Alternative investment funds: The case of hedge funds, private equity funds and real estate funds in the Italian context*. Paper presented at the 10th Global Conference on Business and Economics, Rome, Italy, 10th Global Conference on Business and Economics.

[37] AIFM Directive. (2011). Alternative Investment Fund Managers Directive 2011/61/EU. Official Journal of the European Union L 174/1 of July 1, 2011.

[38] The AIFM Directive is analyzed in detail in Chapter 2.

[39] Legislative Decree 58. (1998). Legislative Decree 58/1998 last amended by Italian Decree Law no. 23 of 8.4.2020, in force from April 9, 2020, "Liquidity Decree" published in the Official Gazette General Series no. 94 of 08-04-2020 which provides additional urgent tax measures in response to COVID-19.

[40] The key principles and general rules of the UCITS V (EU Directive 2014/91) were enacted in Italy in June 2016 (Legislative Decree No. 71/2016) when the Italian Financial Act was amended. The main changes concerned cooperation between ESMA and the competent national authorities, activities that can be carried out by a custodian, remuneration policies and sanctions for infringing the relevant legal provisions. After the implementation at primary legislation level through the amendment of the Italian Financial Act by Legislative Decree no. 71/2016, on April 27, 2017 CONSOB approved the amendments to "CONSOB Regulation on issuers" (11971/1999) and to the "Joint CONSOB-Bank of Italy Regulation dated October 29, 2007" on the organization and procedures of intermediaries providing investment services or collective investment management services, as required in order to adapt also the Italian secondary legislation to the European Directive no. 2014/91 relating to the undertakings for collective investment in transferable securities ("UCITS V").

Italy's regulation of January 19, 2015[41] on the collective asset management rules and the relevant explanatory notes; and regulations issued by Consob.[42]

The main supervisors on asset management in Italy are:

- the Bank of Italy, which ensures the sound and prudent management of banks and intermediaries[43];
- the National Commission for Companies and the Stock Exchange (Consob) which supervises, among other things, the provision of investment services, and ensures transparency and correctness of conduct toward investors;
- the Institution for the Supervision of Insurance (IVASS)[44]; and
- the Pension Funds Supervisory Commission (COVIP).[45]

The marketing of AIF units or shares in Italy fully reflect the regime set out in the AIFMD[46]:

- EU AIFs to professional investors: the EU AIFM must (1) get prior authorization in an EU jurisdiction where the AIFMD is implemented already and (2) notify Consob and
- EU AIFs to retail investors: the EU AIFM is required to, additionally to getting the authorization in an EU jurisdiction where the AIFMD is implemented already, ask for Consob's authorization.

[41] Regulation on the organization and procedures of intermediaries who provide investment services or collective investment management services (Adopted by the Bank of Italy and CONSOB by provision of October 29, 2007 as subsequently amended by joint deeds of the Bank of Italy/CONSOB of May 9, 2012, of July 25, 2012, of January 19, 2015 and of April 27, 2017), published in the Official Journal of the Republic no. 106 of May 9, 2017 and in the CONSOB fortnightly Bulletin no. 4 of April 2, 2017; For the transitional rules, see art. 4 of the joint Bank of Italy/CONSOB deed of April 27, 2017.

[42] Papa, A., Alfano, N., Iaselli, G., & Benigni, C. (2016). *Investment funds in Italy: Regulatory overview*. https://uk.practicallaw.thomsonreuters.com/7-501-3065?transitionType=Default&contextData=(sc.Default)#co_anchor_a459255. Accessed 12 August 2020.

[43] Including Italian asset management companies and joint-stock companies.

[44] The insurance regulator and supervisory authority since January 1, 2013.

[45] The supervisory authority for the private pension funds sector.

[46] Including the marketing of non-EU AIFs or AIFs by non-EU AIFMs.

The marketing of foreign collective investment schemes under the UCITS framework, the home country regulator is obliged to notify Consob before marketing.

The implementation of MiFID II, which came into force in January 2018 also impacted Italy's asset management companies. During the period of application of the legislative decree n. 129 of 2017, implementing EU Directive 2014/65/EU ("MiFID II") and EU Regulation 2014/600/EU ("MiFIR") in the Italian legal system, national Supervisory Authorities spotted certain issues in the transposing legislation and reported them to the Ministry of Finance ("MEF").

Following a public consultation launched by MEF, the Italian Council of Ministers approved the legislative decree n.165/2019 ("Corrective Decree"),[47] which introduces additional and corrective measures (mainly dealing with organizational and sanctioning framework) to the Italian Financial Act ("TUF") as previously amended to implement MiFID II. The key amendments are:

1. Repealing of KID filing obligation.
2. Supervisory powers.
3. Off-site offer of financial instruments.
4. Crowdfunding.

3.2.2 *The Italian Regulatory Regime: Scope and Objectives*

An important aspect of the regulatory landscape on hedge funds in Italy is "supervision," divided by purpose between CONSOB and the Bank of Italy. The former carries out checks relating to relations with investors (rules of conduct, disclosure, etc.), while the second authorizes the asset management companies and supervises as regards the prudential and systemic risk profiles, inherent to collective management of savings. In both cases, it involves information, inspection and regulatory supervision, assisted, among other things, by criminal sanctions.[48]

[47] The amendments introduced by the Corrective Decree, published in the Italian Official Journal n. 6 of January 9, 2020, entered into force on January 24, 2020.

[48] Art. 2632 of the Italian Civil Code and art. 170-bis of the Consolidated Law on Finance (TUF).

Also, the Italian regulator introduced also several limits that have impacted the distribution of and investment in hedge funds. The main aim was, of course, investor protection from higher risks. In this vein, we mention a fund's regulation which must expressly set out the maximum level of leverage and flag the risks of the investment. At the same time, the initial minimum subscription amount for nonprofessional investors is EUR 500,000, and hedge fund units cannot be exclusively distributed to retail investors through the individual portfolio management service.[49] Due to these structural constraints, hedge funds have developed more slowly in the Italian market compared to other countries and are still mainly targeted to institutional investors.

Also, the MiFID II has the following major objectives: "making the system more transparent and improving service quality."[50]

3.2.3 The Advantages and Disadvantages of the Italian Regulatory Regime

The new regulatory framework implemented by Italy after the 2007–2008 crisis increased transparency toward investors and regulatory authorities through the implementation of the reporting and went on to delineate in a precise way issues hitherto neglected, such as the use of leverage. This legislation at EU level, however, has not hindered the great freedom of management that characterized alternative investment funds, not comparable to that provided to mutual funds (due to the greater level of regulation and supervision that they are required to bear). Furthermore, the introduction of the "European passport," provided for by the AIFM Directive, has had many positive effects in the Italian context where the hedge fund market is still underdeveloped, but has led to greater competition in contexts where this category of funds is more present and well-established.

[49] Decree 30. (2015). The Ministry of Finance Decree no. 30 of March 5, 2015, setting out the general criteria the undertakings in collective investments must comply with, published in the Official Gazette no. 65 of March 19, 2015.

[50] Deloitte. (2017). *Asset management in Italy: A snapshot in an evolutive context*. https://www2.deloitte.com/content/dam/Deloitte/lu/Documents/int-markets/lu-asset-management-italy-snapshot-evolutive-context-whitepaper.pdf. Accessed 12 August 2020.

A major driver of a fund's net performance resides in "the cost that investors must bear to have the fund in their portfolio."[51] According to current research, Italian funds "are generally more expensive than European funds."[52] In the context in which investors are particularly interested of the amount and the nature of fees, high costs are a negative aspect.

Also, there is a tendency to consider that MiFID II polarized the market to the two extremes: pure passive players and pure active fund managers.

3.2.4 Could a More Regulated Hedge Funds Industry at European Level Lead to an Increase of This Sector?

During the last decade, particularly after the financial crisis, regulators were very attentive, particularly regarding hedge funds which were always on the top of regulators' agenda. After implementing the provisions of AIFMD, the most debated regulation was the Market in Financial Instruments Directive (MiFID II), which covers many areas of the industry and brings major shifts to the table. The Directive has the following major objectives: "making the system more transparent and improving service quality. To meet the first goal, along with other provisions, regulators have imposed costs and retrocessions disclosure requirements and banned inducements in case of independent advisory. To achieve the second objective, they introduced standards on product governance and imposed minimum qualifications to agents operating as financial advisors."[53] In spite of the fact that most operators strive to be sufficiently ready to implement all the changes implied, there will definitely be unexpected consequences ahead for some players, particularly for the smallest, who could consider compliance, to a certain extent burdensome.

The general opinion among investors is that, a more regulated industry at European level could turn into an obstacle to future development of the Italian hedge funds market. Additionally, the more regulated the hedge funds industry will be, the less appealing hedge funds managers will find to settle their funds in Italy.

[51] Idem.

[52] Idem.

[53] Deloitte. (2017). *Asset management in Italy: A snapshot in an evolutive context*. https://www2.deloitte.com/content/dam/Deloitte/lu/Documents/int-markets/lu-asset-management-italy-snapshot-evolutive-context-whitepaper.pdf. Accessed 12 August 2020.

3.2.5 *The AIFM Directive Impact on the Italian Regulatory Regime*

The AIFM Directive aims to prevent any negative consequences for all financial market participants, as well as the underlying market security through specific rules regarding *inter alia*, own funds, gearing ratio, conduct of business rules, rules regarding manager's remuneration, information and/or disclosure rules, financial accounts provisions.

The transposition of AIFM Directive into the Italian law was characterized by a long regulatory procedure. The Legislative Decree n. 44 of March 4, 2014 initiated the procedure and made profound changes to the Consolidated Law on Finance (TUF), regarding the regulatory framework for the discipline of collective asset management. In this long process many changes have been made to the TUF, including: the introduction of new types of products and subjects (previously not regulated by this regulatory source), the redefinition of the collective asset management service (as required by Article 1, paragraph 1, k[54] of the TUF) and the review of the regulations relating to the depositary (admissible subjects, tasks, and responsibilities). This process of implementation was completed with a series of provisions by CONSOB, by the Bank of Italy and the Ministry of Economy and Finance. Specifically, these Authorities intervened, each in their own areas of competence, in the following documents:

[54] Undertaking for Collective Investment (UCI): body set up to provide the service of the collective management of assets, the capital of which is obtained from multiple investors by the issue and offer of units or shares, managed upstream in the investors' interests and independently by the same and also invested in financial instruments, credit, including credit backed, in favor of subjects other than consumers, by the UCITS capital, equity, or other fixed or non-fixed assets, on the basis of a predetermined investment policy. Letter first replaced by Art. 1 of Legislative Decree no. 44 of 4.3.2014 and then amended by Art. 22, section 5 of Italian Decree Law no. 91 of 24.6.2014, converted with amendments by Italian Law no. 116 of 11.8.2014, which after the word "credits" has introduced the words "included those issued from the capital of the UCITS" and by paragraph 1 of art. 17 Legislative Decree no. 18 of 14.2.2016, converted with amendments by Italian Law no. 49 of 8.4.2016, which, after the words: "included in those issued" has included the words "in favour of subjects other than consumers." Law no. 296 of 27.12.2006, as amended by Decree Law no. 133 of 12.9.2014, converted with amendments by Law no. 164 of 11.11.2014, has ruled (with Art. 1, Section 119-ter) that "The SIIQ are not collective investment bodies pursuant to Legislative Decree 58 (1998)". Legislative Decree 58/1998 last amended by Italian Decree Law no. 23 of 8.4.2020, in force from 9 April 2020, "Liquidity Decree". Official Gazette General Series no. 94 of 08-04-2020.

- Regulation on collective asset management ("Bank of Italy Regulation"), as regards the regulation of the various types of UCITS, cross-border operations and the depositary, in addition to the provisions relating to the authorization procedure.
- Joint Bank of Italy—CONSOB Regulation ("Joint Regulation"), regarding the organization and controls of intermediaries presenting investment and collective management services;
- Intermediaries Regulation, with regard to the rules of conduct that must be observed in the marketing of UCIs;
- Issuers' Regulation, regarding the rules relating to the public offer of shares or units of UCIs.

Finally, these changes were followed by the definitive version of the new Decree of the Ministry of Economy and Finance no. 30 of March 5, 2015, in implementation of Article 39 of the TUF, concerning the determination of the general criteria, which Italian UCIs must comply. This Decree, which will be analyzed later, has played a fundamental role in the new legislation relating to hedge funds, in fact, with its entry into force there has been a radical change in the world of collective savings management. The regulation implements Article 39 of the Legislative Decree n. 58 of February 24, 1998, concerning the determination of the general criteria to which the Italian collective investment schemes (UCITS) had to comply. The great importance of the legislation derives from the fact that this decree of April 3, 2015 (date of entry into force), repeals the decree of the Ministry of the Treasury, Budget and Economic Planning n. 228 of May 24, 1999, (regulation relating to the general standardization criteria of mutual investment funds). Above all, it redefines the "structure of the categories of Italian UCIs" by reclassifying the different types of Italian UCIs into five macro-categories:

1. UCITS;
2. closed-ended or open-ended AIFs;
3. real estate AIFs;
4. reserved AIFs;
5. guaranteed UCIs.

The new category in which hedge funds were reclassified, by virtue of the changes made by the implementation of the AIFMD, was the generic class of "Italian alternative investment funds (AIFs)." If, as a rule, investment in the fund was allowed only to professional investors, the TUF classified the hedge funds in a more specific type known as "alternative Italian AIFs."[55]

After the AIFMD was implemented in the Italian law, Italian hedge funds were classified as a subcategory of reserved AIFs (closed-ended or open-ended). Reserved AIFs may carry out a wide spectrum of investment strategies, not limited to the typical policies of hedge funds.

The Italian regulator introduced also several limits that have impacted the distribution of and investment in hedge funds. The main aim was, of course, investor protection from higher risks. In this vein, we mention a fund's regulation which must expressly set out the maximum level of leverage and flag the risks of the investment. At the same time, the initial minimum subscription amount for nonprofessional investors is EUR 500,000, and hedge fund units cannot be exclusively distributed to retail investors through the individual portfolio management service.[56] Due to these structural constraints, hedge funds have developed more slowly in the Italian market compared to other countries and are still mainly targeted to institutional investors.

Through the transposition of the AIFMD in the Italian regulations, Italy shifted from a national regulatory system to a community one. The work carried out by the European legislator had as its ultimate goal the harmonization of the regulatory system at EU level, trying to provide a unitary direction that would regulate the entire sector of alternative investment funds. In addition, it has implemented the protection of savers and investors, introducing rules capable of renewing confidence in the entire financial system after the serious crises of 2007–2008. The receipt of Decree 30/2015, in fact, with the consequent abolition of the previous national discipline that regulated speculative funds (Decree 228/1999), increased transparency toward investors and regulatory authorities through the implementation of the reporting and went

[55] Art. 1, para. 1, m-ter "Italian alternative UCI" (Italian AIF): investment funds, SICAVs and SICAFs falling within the scope of application of Directive 2011/61/EU. Letter first included by art. 1 of Legislative Decree no. 47 of 16.4.2012 and subsequently thus replaced by art. 1 of Legislative Decree no. 44 of 4.3.2014.

[56] Decree 30. (2015). The Ministry of Finance Decree no. 30 of March 5, 2015, setting out the general criteria the undertakings in collective investments must comply with, published in the Official Gazette no. 65 of March 19, 2015.

on to delineate in a precise way issues either neglected, such as the use of leverage. This legislation at EU level, however, has not hindered the great freedom of management that characterized alternative investment funds, not comparable to that provided to mutual funds (due to the greater level of regulation and supervision that they are required to bear). Furthermore, the introduction of the "European passport," provided for by the AIFM Directive, has had many positive effects in the Italian context where the hedge fund market is still underdeveloped, but has led to greater competition in contexts where this category of funds is more present and well-established.

Summing up, as already stated, according to statistics, in the first quarter of 2019, the total AUM reached a new record, summing up more than EUR 2 billion—approximately 120% of Italy's GDP.[57] This major growth reflects an equally major growth of wealth of investors, clients and also investment industry.[58] Over the medium term, it looks like Italy will maintain this increasing tendency—increase of AUM.[59] This proves a positive effect of the AIFMD implementation in Italy. The implementation of this Directive (AIFMD) has played a key role in increasing investment opportunities for investment funds[60] meanwhile shifting the sector into a more trustworthy one for less sophisticated investors.

All in all, the Italian hedge fund industry is still low, and some scholars consider that this occurs due to the fact that, "traditionally, Italian investors tend to be risk-averse, and although this helped them protect their assets during the financial crisis, it has also hindered Italy's ability to compete in innovative market segments (such as that of hedge funds)."[61]

[57] Rumi, G., Ubaldini, R., Dimonte, M., Ferrari, C., & Vece, G. (2019). Italy. In *The asset management review* (8th ed.). https://thelawreviews.co.uk/edition/the-asset-management-review-edition-8/1197347/italy. Accessed 12 August 2020.

[58] Idem.

[59] Alvaro, S., & Annunziata, F. (2019). *Shareholdings of alternative investment funds in listed companies and in banks: A legal perspective*. Roma: Consob.

[60] For instance, by allowing alternative investment funds (AIFs) to acquire loans from non-customer originators against their own capital.

[61] Rumi, G., Ubaldini, R., Dimonte, M., Ferrari, C., & Vece, G. (2019). Italy. In *The asset management review* (8th ed.). https://thelawreviews.co.uk/edition/the-asset-management-review-edition-8/1197347/italy. Accessed 12 August 2020.

3.2.6 *The Impact of Brexit on the Alternative Investment Funds in Italy*

The potential effects of Brexit forced the adoption of new regulations on March 23, 2019.[62] This new legislation approves comprehensive provisions aimed at regulating the possible impacts on multiple stakeholders in the event that the United Kingdom (UK) exits from the European Union (EU) without an accord with the EU (UK withdrawal).

The new Law provides that, following the UK withdrawal, UK banks that are authorized to conduct operations in Italy in the same terms that Italian banks are authorized to carry out activities in the United Kingdom may continue carrying out such activities after notifying the Bank of Italy.[63]

UK banks and UK investment firms that, on the UK withdrawal date, provide investment services and activities in Italy, may continue to perform the same activities only with respect to qualified counterparties and professional clients as provided in the applicable legislation.[64]

Banking, financial, and other related entities operating in Italy remain bound by contractual extrajudicial dispute resolution mechanisms after the date of the UK withdrawal. Alternatively, these entities may adhere to other mechanisms established by the EU Commission-approved Fin-Net network.[65]

UK banking institutions operating in Italy through branches will continue to be members of the guarantee systems established for Italian depositors regulated by current banking legislation.[66]

UK payment institutions, fund managers, and investment banks operating in Italy under the current freedom of service regime at the time of the UK withdrawal must cease their activities on that date.[67] To

[62] Decree-Law No. 22 of March 25, 2019, Urgent Measures to Ensure Safety, Financial Stability and the Integrity of Markets as well as the Protection of the Health and Freedom of Residence of Italian Citizens and United Kingdom Citizens in case of Brexit (Decree Law No. 22), published in the Official gazette on March 25, 2019.

[63] Decree Law No. 22 of March 25, 2019, art. 3(1)–(2).

[64] Id. art. 3(3).

[65] Id. art. 7(2).

[66] Id. art. 8(1).

[67] Id. art. 4(1).

avoid prejudice to their existing clients, these institutions are authorized to carry out operations necessary to close their activities within the shortest possible time and within a maximum of six months from the UK withdrawal date, after complying with applicable contractual notices.[68]

As an exception, UK banks and investment firms remain authorized to manage existing derivative over-the-counter contracts even if such activities involve the modification of existing contracts or the execution of new contracts.[69]

UK payment institutions, fund managers, and investment banks that are registered in Italy and that on the date of the UK withdrawal conduct businesses in the United Kingdom may continue to operate during the transitional period in accordance with UK legislation.[70]

3.3 France: Overview of Hedge Funds Regulatory Framework

3.3.1 The Hedge Funds Regulatory Framework Evolution in France

In France, the most important authorities of rules which regulate hedge funds are:

- French Monetary and Financial Code.[71]
- General Regulation[72] of the Financial Markets Authority (AMF), as amended and supplemented by AMF instructions ad recommendations.

The adoption in France of Directive 2011/61/EU on alternative investment fund managers (AIFM Directive) has changed the framework of the European hedge funds industry. As a consequence, there has been a limitation of the range of available vehicles for hedge funds. Currently there are only several vehicles that may be used for hedge funds:

[68] Id.

[69] Id. art. 4(4).

[70] Id. art. 5(1).

[71] Code Monétaire et Financier (CMF).

[72] AMF. (2016). Order of 14 December 2016, Official Journal of 17 December 2016. https://reglement-general.amf-france.org/eli/fr/aai/amf/rg/20161218/en.pdf. Accessed 12 August 2012.

- Alternative funds of funds, which can be used by nonprofessional investors.
- General purpose funds[73] and specialized professional funds,[74] which are only for professional investors falling under the scope of Annex II of Directive 2014/65/EU on markets in financial instruments (MiFID II) (Professional Investors).

The AMF "replicates the European principles in its General Regulation and its policy,"[75] at the same time adapting them to the French asset management perspective. A key place is held by risk management with regard to hedge funds. In this respect, the AMF issued Position-Recommendation 2014-06[76] specifying the requirements dealing with identification and management of the risks to which the funds are potentially exposed.[77] At the same time, Instruction 2012–01[78] (Organization of the UCITS and real estate Collective Investment Undertakings—OPCI—management activity and discretionary portfolio management investment service regarding risk management), applicable from January 31, 2018 to January 23, 2019, required that all AMCs should have a permanent risk management function,[79] provided with the necessary resources to accomplish its mission (Article 2).

[73] Fonds professionnels à vocation general.

[74] Fonds professionnels spécialisés.

[75] Darpeix, P. M., Le Moign, C., Même, N., & Novakovic, M. (2020). *Overview and inventory of French funds' liquidity management tools* (Working Paper #775). Banque de France. http://dx.doi.org/10.2139/ssrn.3659260.

[76] AMF. (2018b). *Position—Recommendation DOC-2014-06, Applicable from January 31, 2018 to January 23, 2019*. Autorité des Marchés Financiers (AMF). https://doctrine.amf-france.org/en_US/Reglementation/Doctrine/Doctrine-list/Doctrine?docVersion=4.0&docId=workspace%3A%2F%2FSpacesStore%2F8be6d64a-e78e-4487-90ad-8ac0d832d636#fragment-1. Accessed 12 August 2020.

[77] Regular risk mapping exercise.

[78] AMF. (2018a). *Risk management organization for collective investment undertaking management activities and discretionary portfolio management investment services*. Autorité des Marchés Financiers (AMF). DOC-2012-01. https://doctrine.amf-france.org/en_US/Reglementation/Doctrine/Doctrine-list/Doctrine?category=III+-+Providers&docId=workspace%3A%2F%2FSpacesStore%2Fa6710d0b-3944-43eb-979c-677ef69d8fef. Accessed 12 August 2020.

[79] In accordance with Article 39 of Delegated Regulation (EU) No. 231/2013 (AIFs) and Article 321-77 of the AMF GR (UCITS).

Inspired by the Luxembourg special limited partnership, a French new corporate vehicle of limited partnership was introduced by Law 2015-990 dated August 6, 2015 for economic growth, activity, and equal opportunities. This law came into force on August 8, 2015. The main scope was to particularly address the needs of the AIF industry, being restricted to Professional Investors and for specialized professional funds,[80] not for general purpose professional funds.[81]

According to this new regulation, these UCIs are very flexible, especially regarding their investment policies. In this vein, general purpose professional funds are allowed to invest 100% of their assets in other UCIs, the main condition being that they invest maximum 20% of their assets in particular types of instruments issued by particular categories of UCIs, comprising (between others):

- Foreign UCIs.
- Undertakings for collective investments in transferable securities (UCITS).
- AIFs available to retail to clients.[82]
- Venture capital AIFs.

At the same time, professional funds too are more flexible concerning the amount of shares or units to which they can invest. Such an example is that they can invest no more than 50% of their assets in a French UCI, a foreign UCITS, an AIF established under the laws of another EU member state or a foreign UCI; and can invest no more than 35% in liquid instruments of the same issuer.

[80] CMF, Article L. 214-154, French Monetary and Financial Code (CMF).

[81] CMF, Article L. 214-24-25 and L. 214-24-29.

[82] Even if figures for 2019 have been issued so far, the value of AUMs in France for 2018 decreased by EUR 170 billion compared to 2017. See in this vein—AMF. (2018c). Annual Report. Autorité des Marchés Financiers. https://www.amf-france.org/Publications/Rapports-annuels/Rapports-annuels-de-l-AMF/annee-2015-2019?xtcr=1&isSearch=true&docId=workspace%3A%2F%2FSpacesStore%2F64a1c9f1-dcdd-47b3-a099-d885dfd560ed&lastSearchPage=https%3A%2F%2Fwww.amf-france.org%2FmagnoliaPublic%2Famf%2FResultat-de-recherche%3FTEXT%3DChiffres%2Bcl%25C3%25A9s%2B2019%2Bde%2Bla%2Bgestion%2Bd%2527actifs%26LANGUAGE%3Dfr%26isSearch%3Dtrue%26simpleSearch%3Dtrue%26valid_recherche%3DValider&xtmc=Chiffres-cles-2019-de-la-gestion-d-actifs&docVersion=1.0. Accessed 31 July 2020.

3.3.2 The French Regulatory Framework: Scope and Objectives

The advantages of hedge funds are widely recognized.[83] In France, the 1990–2000 period led to significant reforms for the financial industry, concerning deregulating matters, but also liberalizing financial processes.[84] The tendency to become highly diversified financial markets widely accessible for various investment vehicles, starting from a classical bank-fundamental standard, occurred together with different regulatory limitations regarding hedge funds. Besides, this issue resulted in major political debates in France concerning major risks associated to asset industries. Thus, France currently demanded for a tighter legal regime[85] for hedge funds, with the purpose of mitigating the prudential risks associated to *extremely* leveraged institutions.

It is supposed that there are three basic subjects to be regulated in terms of hedge funds. Thus, the primary objective of the strategic plan established by France is the investor protection. The second objective is to reinforce their risk policy,[86] and the third objective is to encourage Paris as a capital, but also France as a financial crossroad develop a fine relation involving the investor security and a dynamic financial market, particularly due to Brexit, as this new opportunity emerged.[87]

French hedge funds together with their portfolio management companies (PMCs) must follow several risk control measures, which consist on the one hand in the ratios applicable to the funds and on the other hand, on the type of financial instruments that they are allowed to purchase.

[83] Mustier, J. P., & Dubois, A. (2007). Risks and return of banking activities related to hedge funds. Banque de France. *Financial Stability Review–Special Issue on Hedge Funds* (pp. 85–94).

[84] O'Sullivan, M. (2007). Acting out institutional change: Understanding the recent transformation of the French financial system. *Socio-Economic Review*, 5(3), 389–436.

[85] France stated that it has 'long wanted stricter scrutiny of funds and more harmonisation of asset management rules across Europe', 'London's Asset Managers Fret over Prospect of EU Raids', *Financial Times*, January 12, 2018.

[86] AMF. (2018a). *Risk management organization for collective investment undertaking management activities and discretionary portfolio management investment services*. Autorité des Marchés Financiers (AMF). DOC-2012-01. https://doctrine.amf-france.org/en_US/Reglementation/Doctrine/Doctrine-list/Doctrine?category=III+-+Providers&docId=workspace%3A%2F%2FSpacesStore%2Fa6710d0b-3944-43eb-979c-677ef69d8fef. Accessed 12 August 2020.

[87] Howarth, D., & Quaglia, L. (2018). Brexit and the battle for financial services. *Journal of European Public Policy, 25*, 1118–1136.

All PMCs which manage these funds need to be licensed by the AMF within a particular program of activity having to do with the use of specific financial instruments.[88] In terms of valuation and pricing, the rules are very strict, namely that hedge fund's PMC or an external valuer is obliged to publish the net asset value (NAV) and communicate it to every individual who is interested, if required. At the same time, the AMF must evaluate periodically the PMC's license, and correctly assess if the PMC is able to adequately evaluate the AUMs.

In terms of controls, there are internal controls, according to which the PMC must make sure that it follows ethical rules,[89] which can be done through the appointment of a compliance and internal control officer, who is held responsible for complying and monitoring.[90]

In terms of the UCI's depositary, this one needs to view the PMC's decisions and make sure that the hedge fund obeys the law, both internal and external regulations, at the same time reporting to the AMF.[91]

Other forms of control over hedge funds are the auditor and also mandatory periodic reporting, the last one done to investors. Auditor can involve the AMF, and reporting also.

With regard to insider dealing and market abuse, the breach of these laws could lead to criminal prosecution and/or administrative proceedings in front of the AMF.

Hedge funds and their PMCs must obey the standard money laundering regulations just like every UCI. In this vein, the PMC must:

- Get and check the identity of each investor before accepting him/her to the hedge fund.
- Assess each uncommon or major transaction which seems as having no economic justification.
- Report doubtful amounts and transactions.
- Keep written records of the supervising activities.

[88] For instance, complex derivatives and credit derivatives.

[89] Article 318-1, AMF General Regulation.

[90] Article 318-5, AMF General Regulation; Article 61, Commission Delegated Regulation (EU) No. 231/2013 dated 19 December 2012.

[91] Articles L. 214-24-3 and 214-24-12, CMF; Article 323-23, AMF General Regulation.

In France, the money laundering regulations were strengthened after Directive 2015/849/EU[92] was adopted, on the prevention of the use of the financial system for the purposes of money laundering or terrorist financing. Still, these requirements need to fit the PMC's marketing, especially where the PMC does not have a direct relationship with the last investors.

3.3.3 *The Advantages and Disadvantages of French Regulatory Framework*

France has always been a regulated country with a fervent legislative agenda, focusing very much on strengthening regulations.[93] Indeed, establishing a hedge fund in France is difficult because France limited very much the establishment of hedge funds on its territory, the manager's biggest advantage being that investors are attracted by "super protective" regulatory regimes. Still, hedge fund managers acknowledge the fact that France is an atypical country to set up a hedge fund, but it can be a good idea as competition is not an issue, since hedge funds managers usually avoid France.

At the same time, another negative aspect is, according to Grec and Marquais (2020), France "failed to take legislative measures and provide judicial guidance, and essentially let professional bodies develop professional and ethical standards to guide counsels in their interactions with funders."[94]

On the one hand, AMF makes its presence felt through control rather than proactive attendance in encouraging new fund management business. In this respect, instead of being encouraging, the Financial Markets Authority behaves somewhat impartial while having to do with advancement and ambitious development of hedge fund managers but also it does not look like forthcoming with regard to supporting new arrivals. Thus, it will be extremely difficult for France to compete with major European

[92] Fourth EU Anti-Money Laundering Directive.

[93] Grec, A., & Marquais, O. (2020). Investment management and corporate structuring considerations for third-party litigation funders in Luxembourg. *ASA Bulletin, 38*(2), 296–413.

[94] Marquais, O., & Grec, A. (2020). Do's and don'ts of regulating third-party litigation funding: Singapore vs. France. *Asian International Arbitration Journal, 16*(1), 49–68.

alternative hubs. Therefore, the comparisons between France and other UK or Luxembourg located funds are useless.

Nevertheless, the AMF's reputation for being strict can be beneficial. Many investors, among which "the high net worth individuals" and private investor's targets rely on the French regulatory system and the sense of security that it provides. France also has a good reputation in terms of the quality of its service providers. It is true that France may not be able to compete with England and Luxembourg in terms of numbers, but it could develop a distinct competitive edge.

At the same time, currently, the French AIF industry is also positively impacted by favorable shifts concerning national regulatory aspects. New French laws and regulations enable the creation of new types of investment funds offering incentives to develop the French AIFs industry (such as the new PACTE law in 2019).[95]

This positive trend is also supplemented by the regulatory EU framework, since recent EU regulations are also in favor of the creation of new types of investment funds. In this vein, one can mention the recently adopted EU Regulation No. 2019/1238 on the creation of a pan-European Personal Pension Product (PEPP), the ELTIF Regulation, EuVECa and EuSEF Regulations, and others.

3.3.4 *Could a More Regulated Hedge Fund Industry at European Level Lead to an Increase of This Sector?*

The French regulations of hedge funds reduced their development. Nevertheless, if the last improvements were to be taken into account there would be indeed a major shift on behalf of the officials from France. In compliance with these improvements, significant progresses and numerical increases are expected in the future for the French hedge funds market. Accordingly, this particular market has the necessary resources, but also the professionalism to help customers create new funds. Nevertheless, a more regulated industry at European level could lead to a small increase of the sector in Europe, or even to stagnation.

However, currently, the regulators' opinion is that, due the highly interdependencies and interactions between the various sectors of the

[95] Law 486. (2019). The PACTE act for the business growth and transformation action plan. Official Journal, May 23, 2019 (Law No. 2019-486 of May 22, 2019).

financial world, active discussions developed by the various national regulators "has proved to be a crucial asset. The process of harmonizing the rules and applying them across the different European jurisdictions, along with coordinating efforts effectively, must continue in order to deal effectively with the frequent cases where there is a difference between the asset management company's country of registration, the fund's country of domicile and the fund's country of marketing."[96]

3.3.5 The Impact of the AIFM Directive on the French Regulatory Framework

France is somehow in the middle of a battle against the United Kingdom due to its over-zealous government controlled by beliefs and national concerns. Some British observers tended to appreciate that the AIFM Directive represents a straight assault on the United Kingdom, orchestrated by French officials.[97] Since around "80% of the hedge fund industry is located in London or more generally in UK," while for France there remain few funds to settle in, it becomes clear why the French did not have too much to lose,[98] at least before BREXIT. At the same time, a French–German alliance (for the single market in financial services they joined forces[99]) in terms of regulation reform in global finance appeared to be crucial for the AIFM negotiations. If at first, the common concern in hedge fund regulation started in "2007, in Heiligendamm, the city where the G8 summit took place,"[100] at the time the French request for a stricter regulatory approach had little impact. Later on, when the financial crisis became visible, French politicians understood this was their chance

[96] AMF. (2020). *2020 Markets and risk outlook: Risks and trend mapping*. Autorité des Marchés Financiers. https://www.amf-france.org/sites/default/files/2020-07/cartographie-2020-consolidee_en_2.pdf. Accessed 12 August 2020.

[97] Tait, N. (2011, March 11). UK nominee grilled on EU markets role. *Financial Times*. https://www.ft.com/content/3df42a5e-50b8-11e0-9227-00144feab49a. Accessed 17 August 2020.

[98] Woll, C. (2011). Beyond ideological battles: A strategic analysis of hedge fund regulation in Europe. *Les Cahiers Européens de Sciences Po, 2*, 2–20.

[99] Rittelmeyer, Y. S. (2017). *Will Brexit revive the Franco-German engine?* https://www.europe-solidarity.eu/documents/ES_brexitfranco-germanengine.pdf. Accessed 16 August 2020.

[100] Stiglitz, J. E., & Griffith-Jones, St. (2007). Growth with responsibility in a globalized world—Findings of the Shadow G-8. *Dialogue on Globalization*, 31.

to proclaim their main goals. Nevertheless, in the end, France failed in casting offshore funds out of the European market. It has however acquired a regulatory frame of reference with regard to hedge funds looking very much alike to that which at first supported the structure of the retail mutual funds industry.[101] Still, as the French government insisted, the main issue is not the origin of funds, if legislative requests imposed on "hedge fund managers" are being respected. Accordingly, any comprehensive regulatory framework is appealing, as they hold the minimum number of their industry's financial interests at stake.

The AIFM Directive should not significantly affect French managers because the French regulators already control investment managers. Since French regulatory framework is strict, an even stricter one will not affect managers that much. However, the French authorities are deeply aware of the improvement in the UCITS area, as this is the main cause that makes many French asset managers prefer to move their operations to Luxembourg. With the growing employment of the UCITS tools by alternatives managers, the development of Luxembourg as a major fund center appears quite probable. Against this, France is keen to retain its very large and well-developed funds sector. Several French asset managers are not only major players at home, but the owners of leading asset managers based elsewhere around the world. The interaction between the AFM and these global giants gives the regulator a uniquely well-informed image on developments across the investment management sector.

A recent report from January 2019 states that at the end of 2017 there are 5168 AIFs, representing EUR 688 billion in net assets and EUR 915 billion in exposure.[102] The AMF study was conducted on the basis of AIFM reporting through to the end of 2017 and other data at the disposal of the regulator, and according to it, the following trends can be observed:

- hedge funds represent a small proportion of the AIFs subject to reporting in France (0.6% of total net assets). Most of the AIFs have similar characteristics to those of more traditional, lower-risk funds:

[101] Woll, C. (2011). Op. Cit., p. 9.

[102] AMF. (2019). *First results from AIFM reporting*. Autorité des Marchés Financiers (AMF). https://www.amf-france.org/en_US/Actualites/Communiques-de-presse/AMF/annee-2019?docId=workspace%3A%2F%2FSpacesStore%2Ff6c171e6-9bae-4c1f-b355-b9a4bf7cba64. Accessed 12 August 2020.

59% of total net assets are made up of equity, bond or diversified funds;

- the portfolios are sufficiently liquid to cope with investor redemption frequencies in normal market conditions. With the exception of real estate and private equity funds, whose assets are held on a long-term basis, the AIFs can liquidate the majority of their assets within one day or less;
- leverage levels are in line with the investment strategies employed, on the whole;
- exposures are consistent with the strategies of the AIFs: for real estate funds, 71% of their exposure is to physical assets, for private equity funds 85% to securities, for funds of funds 58% to collective investment undertakings, and 'other' strategy funds 60% to Securities.[103]

In France, the Directive impacted the management companies "domiciled in France and that manage one or more AIFs, regardless of whether these AIFs are French, EU, or third-country AIFs."[104] Table 3.1 presents the regulatory reporting requirements that these companies must respect. At the same time, the reporting frequency depends on the value of net AUMs.

In terms of regulatory changes impacting France, at the EU level the EU directive 2019/1160 of June 20, 2019 amending the AIFMD can be mentioned. This new directive implies a new definition of premarketing, its key aim being of harmonizing the rules on marketing of AIFs. On August 2, 2019, started a two-year national implementation period for this Directive which must be fully transposed starting with August 2, 2021.

If we consider strictly France, the PACTE law mentions new provisions with major positive impact on investment funds, especially on:

(i) the eligibility of professional AIFs for units account of life-insurance contract and

[103] AMF. (2019). *First results from AIFM reporting*. Autorité des Marchés Financiers (AMF). https://www.amf-france.org/en_US/Actualites/Communiques-de-presse/AMF/annee-2019?docId=workspace%3A%2F%2FSpacesStore%2Ff6c171e6-9bae-4c1f-b355-b9a4bf7cba64. Accessed 12 August 2020.

[104] Idem.

Table 3.1 The regulatory reporting requirements for management companies domiciled in France

Type of reporting	*Net asset value <= thresholds (EUR 100 M and EUR 500 M)*	*Net asset value > thresholds but <= EUR 1bn*	*Net asset value > EUR 1bn*
AIFM basic reporting[a]	Yearly	Biannual	Once every three months
AIF "lighter" reporting[b]	Yearly (for each AIF managed)	Biannual (for each AIF managed)	Once every three months (for each AIF managed)
AIF "full" reporting[c]	Yearly only if opt-in	Biannual (for each AIF managed)	Once every three months (for each AIF managed)
Leverage[d]	Yearly only if opt-in and leverage > 3	Biannual if leverage > 3	Once every three months if lêverage > 3
Workforce of French AMCs that transmitted at least one report at end-2017	280	68	96

Source Darpeix et al. (2020)
[a]Articles 3(3)(d) and 24(1) of Directive 2011/61/EU
[b]Articles 3(3)(d) and 24(1) of Directive 2011/61/EU
[c]Article 24(2) of Directive 2011/61/EU
[d]Article 24(4) of Directive 2011/61/EU

(ii) the possibility for some professional AIFs de jure (FPS, SLP, OFS, and FPCI) to invest straight in crypto-assets.

As far as the AMF is concerned:

- There were brought amendments to the General Regulations of the AMF for including new provisions on OFS—in this respect, a new AMF instruction is going to supplement these new provisions; and
- So far, AMF is bringing updates to its documents (instructions, positions, and recommendations) so that it can adapt to the implementation of MiFID[105] into French law.

[105]Which occurred as of January 2018.

As a final comment, France will protect national benefits and current industry organizations. Also, the French government is deeply concerned with the industry claims and takes all possible actions to ensure the protection of important components of economy against the supervision recommendations.

3.3.6 Brexit Impact of the French Hedge Funds

In early February 2019, Ordinance no. 2019-750 introduced into legislation rules according to which France does "not offer a broad continuity regime for UK firms. Instead, regulatory authorities devised a small number of targeted concessions especially relevant to the French economy (insurance, derivatives, UK inter-bank settlements, etc.)."[106] Indeed, France was the single EU state "willing to accept the consequences of a no-deal Brexit and maintain a hard-line negotiation stance (excepting, of course, the array of EU-level protections already agreed)."[107] Due to the fact that a last-minute extension was agreed by negotiators to push back the Brexit deadline to October 2019, these plans did not turn into reality.

If we take into consideration the level of the French portfolio management industry, over the past five years, according to AMF, the number of new portfolio management firms appears as remaining stable, in spite of the convergence of portfolio management companies (under the form of either mergers or aggregation). There are done either due to their margins diminishment or due to the powerful competition from the industry. An important trend has, so far, been noticed by the AMF toward the end of 2018: a major growth in the number of authorization requests—more precisely, around 60 authorization requests or even more were filed in 2018. According to the AMF, this growth in authorization requests is due to the political and economic changes around the world, more precisely due to Brexit. In this vein, "Paris benefitted in 2018 and 2019 from

[106] Allen & Overy. (2019). *Brexit law: New French Brexit-related ordinance*. https://www.allenovery.com. Accessed 14 August 2020.

[107] Kalaitzake, M. (2020). Brexit for finance? Structural interdependence as a source of financial political power within UK-EU withdrawal negotiations. *Review of International Political Economy*. https://doi.org/10.1080/09692290.2020.1734856.

Brexit, which has so far led to partial or total relocation of activities of some British investment firms and British investment managers."[108]

In the light of Brexit there are major power battles currently taking place over hedge funds. In this respect, France, maintaining its strict regulatory perspectives, has publicly pleaded in favor of tighter regulation within the AIFMD, imposing its own gold plating regarding the third country regime and maintaining that there is need for reinforcing of the existing equivalence framework.[109] In spite of this, it also fights for ensuring "a larger slice of the EU fund management pie in Paris."[110] Indeed, there is currently a "battle emerging amongst the Member States with respect to promoting their financial hubs and competing to attract business from the UK."[111]

Referring strictly to hedge funds, due to the fact that France also competes with other countries that already have a firm foot in the door with management companies domiciled in Luxembourg, Dublin, or Frankfurt, this could well add further nuance to its position.[112] In direct competition with Germany, whose domestic politics dominate EU, France was back drowned by Germany, who publicly opposed wider French moves toward greater levels of European integration.[113] In spite of working together in the past decade, lately, "presupposing

[108] Tatar, L. R. (2019). *Law and practice*. https://practiceguides.chambers.com/practice-guides/alternative-funds-2019/france/2-funds. Accessed 4 August 2020.

[109] In particular France states that it has 'long wanted stricter scrutiny of funds and more harmonisation of asset management rules across Europe', 'London's Asset Managers Fret over Prospect of EU Raids', *Financial Times*, 12 January 2018.

[110] Howarth, D., & Quaglia, L. (2018). Brexit and the battle for financial services. *Journal of European Public Policy, 25,* 1118–1136; See also Latham, M. (2018). *French regulator cranks up Brexit pressure on UK asset managers*. https://www.funds-europe.com/news/french-regulator-cranks-up-brexit-pressure-on-uk-asset-manager. Accessed 5 August 2020.

[111] Howell, E. (2020). Post Brexit UK fund regulation: Equivalence, divergence or convergence? *European Business Organization Law Review*. https://doi.org/10.1007/s40804-020-00177-w.

[112] Dohle, M. (2017). *Battle for Brexit business: Frankfurt's aim to attract firms leaving the UK*. http://www.investmenteurope.net/regions/germany/battle-brexit-business-frankfurts-aim-attract-firms-leaving-uk/. Accessed 2 August 2020.

[113] Münchau, W. (2018, April 13). Germany is frustrating Emmanuel Macron's grand ambitions. *Financial Times*. https://www.ft.com/content/4db75b80-3f1e-11e8-b7e0-52972418fec4. Accessed 13 August 2020.

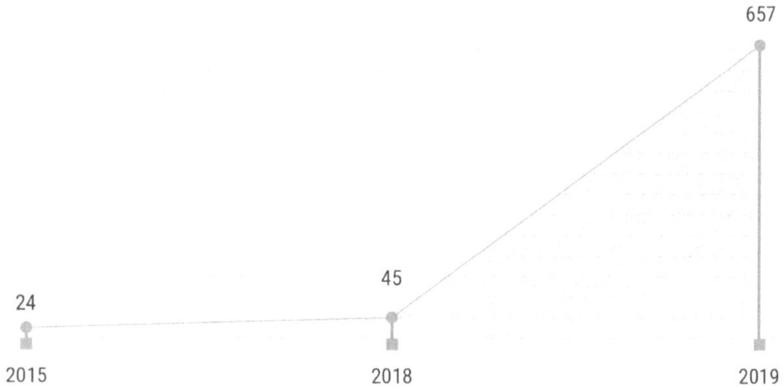

Fig. 3.1 Evolution of asset management companies in France between 2017 and 2019 (*Source* Authors' research)

a commonality of interests between France and Germany can be erroneous."[114] Domestic elections, as well as Brexit, will definitely impact many competing preferences of these two mentioned countries, influencing and affecting the regulatory response of each country. Therefore, given shifting hedge funds landscape, France is expected to adjust its policies.

However, according to the AFG, "the number of asset management companies jumped to 657 at the end of 2019, as a significant number of companies secured licenses during the year (45 compared with 24 in 2018)"[115] (Fig. 3.1).

The responsibility for this huge increase falls on the shoulders of "the large number of asset management companies created in France in preparation for Brexit."[116]

Currently, French asset management companies are ranked first in continental Europe in the management of investments.[117] Assessments

[114] Howell, E., (2020). Post Brexit UK fund regulation: Equivalence, divergence or convergence? *European Business Organization Law Review*. https://doi.org/10.1007/s40804-020-00177-w.

[115] AFG. (2020). Annual overview of the French asset management market. *French Asset Management Association* (p. 2).

[116] Idem.

[117] Investment funds and discretionary mandates.

show that French asset managers hold around 27% share of the European market (the United Kingdom not being included). At the same time, when referring to the domicile of the fund, France is ranked second in Europe (the United Kingdom being included) concerning AIFs (16.8% market share) and fourth regarding UCITS (7.5%).

In France, assets invested through foreign funds managed by almost 140 asset management companies increased in 2019 reaching currently EUR 580 billion. This represents a quadruple growth since the 2008 crisis.[118]

As a consequence, what the AMF estimated, that 2010 would imply a historic record of new French portfolio management companies, exceeded in 2019, was actually true. France currently has the second highest number of AIFs in Europe (including the United Kingdom).

3.4 Ireland: Overview of Hedge Funds Regulatory System

3.4.1 The Irish Hedge Funds Regulatory System Evolution

In terms of regulations, The Central Bank Reform Act 2010[119] was enacted on October 1, 2010. This document merged roles held by "the Central Bank and the IFSRA,"[120] setting the foundation for the Central Bank of Ireland. Accordingly, "IFSRA" was dissolved. Therefore, currently, the Central Bank is the regulatory body responsible for the initial authorization and ongoing supervision of all Irish QIAIFs and AIFMs. Also, AIFs established in Ireland are authorized under the following pieces of national regulation:

- the Unit Trusts Act 1990[121] which regulates Unit trusts.

[118] Tatar, L. R. (2019). *Law and practice, chambers and partners*. https://practiceguides.chambers.com/practice-guides/alternative-funds-2019/france/2-funds. Accessed 4 August 2020.

[119] http://www.irishstatutebook.ie/pdf/2010/en.act.2010.0023.PDF. Accessed 12 August 2020.

[120] Irish Financial Services Regulatory Authority, in "Opinion of the European Central Bank of 7 April 2010 on the restructuring of the Central Bank and Financial Services Authority of Ireland" (CON/2010/30).

[121] S.I. No. 37 of 1990.

- the Investment Limited Partnerships Act 1994[122] which regulates investment limited partnerships.
- the Investment Funds, Companies, and Miscellaneous Provisions Act 2005[123] regulating Common Contractual Funds.
- the Irish Collective Asset-management Vehicles Act 2015[124] regulating ICAVs, introduced in the post-AIFMD era, "when new legal forms for funds and thereby improved their 'fund toolbox.'"[125]
- the Companies Act 2014,[126] regulating Investment Companies.
- The Investment Limited Partnership (Amendment) Bill 2019 ("ILP Bill").[127]

AIFs are authorized in the following categories, both authorized by the Central Bank:

- A Retail Investor AIF ("RIAIF")—which may be marketed to retail investors.
- A Qualifying Investor AIF ("QIAIF")—which may be marketed to Qualifying Investors.

In Ireland, UCITS and AIFs can be established as follows (Figs. 3.2 and 3.3).

[122] S.I. No. 12 of 2005.

[123] S.I. No. 371 of 2015.

[124] S.I. No. 258 of 2015.

[125] Hooghiemstra, S. N. (2019). Towards modernization of the Luxembourg legal form 'Toolbox' for funds. *JurisNews Investment, 8*(3–4), 135–144. http://dx.doi.org/10.2139/ssrn.3509731.

[126] S.I. Number 38 of 2014.

[127] In June 2019, the Irish Government subsequently approved the publication of the Investment Limited Partnership (Amendment) Bill 2019 ("ILP Bill"). The Irish Minister for Finance & Public Expenditure and Reform, Paschal Donohoe TD indicated that "This is a further step towards ensuring that Ireland remains one of the leading funds domiciles in Europe. The revised Investment Limited Partnership structure will stand alongside the Irish Collective Asset-management Vehicle as a symbol of Ireland's responsiveness to business needs and a sound regulatory environment."

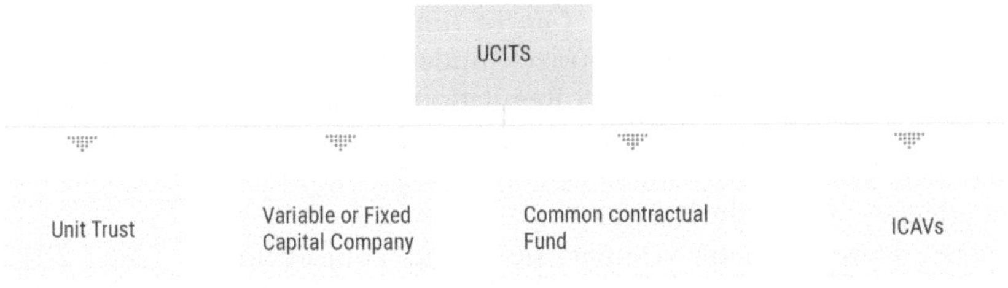

Fig. 3.2 Legal structures of UCITS in Ireland (*Source* Author's analysis)

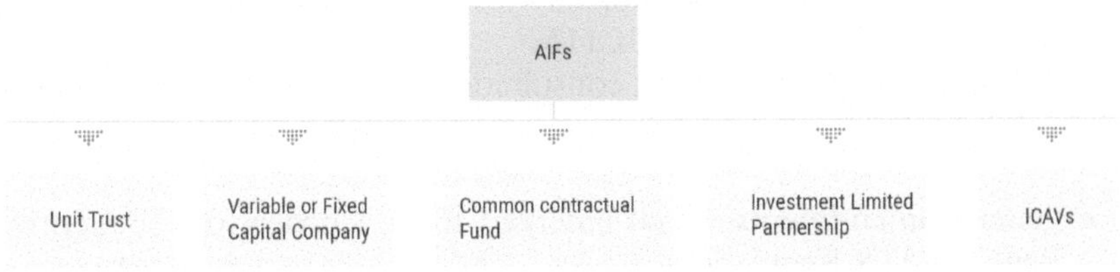

Fig. 3.3 Legal structures of AIFs in Ireland (*Source* Author's analysis)

Ireland is an alternative asset management jurisdiction, with major global alternative investment administrators who have significant operations in Ireland. The legislation concerning the establishment of non-UCTIS collective investment schemes was introduced in this jurisdiction one year after the transposition of the UCTIS I Directive into the Irish law.[128] The legal alternatives were extended in the middle of 1990s with the enactment of a law regulation Irish non-UCTIS investment limited partnerships[129] and, more recently, through the adoption

[128] Non-UCTIS vehicles were first regulated under the "Unit Trusts Act 1990" (S.I. No. 37 of 1990) as non-UCTIS unit trusts and under "Part XIII of the Companies Act 1990" (S.I. n° 336 of 1990) as non-UCTIS open-ended variable capital investment companies.

[129] Investment Limited Partnership (ILP) Act 1994 ("S.I. n° 24 of 1994"). A parallel development was that of the amendment, by "Section 80 of the Investment Intermediaries Act 1995" (S.I. n° 11 of 1995), extending its provisions to closed ended investment companies.

of a law regulating "*Common Contractual Funds*" (CCFs).[130] UCITS established in Ireland are authorized under the European Communities Regulations 2011 ("the UCITS Regulations"). The UCITS Regulations, which transpose Council Directive 2009/65/EC, Commission Directive 2010/43/EC, and Commission Directive 2010/44/EC into Irish law, are effective from July 1, 2011.

The Central Bank (Supervision and Enforcement) Act 2013 (Section 48(1)) (Undertakings for Collective Investment in Transferable Securities) (Amendment) Regulations 2019[131] (the "Central Bank UCITS Regulations") consolidate into one location all of the requirements which the Central Bank imposes on UCITS, UCITS management companies and depositories of UCITS.

This follows the Central Bank consultation CP119,[132] focusing mainly on:

- general amendments which emerged from a review of the Central Bank UCITS Regulations.
- amendments to UCITS Share Class Provisions in order to reflect the ESMA Opinion.
- amendments dealing with performance fees of UCITS.
- amendments having to do with the implementation of the EU Money Market Fund Regulation.

More recently, on July 13, 2020, the Central Bank issued the 29th edition of the Central Bank UCITS Q&A, including new Q&A IDs 1095, 1096, and 1097 in relation to liquidity stress testing in UCITS.[133]

[130] "Investment Funds, Companies and Miscellaneous Provisions Act 2005" (S.I. n° 12 of 2005).

[131] Central Bank. (2019). S.I. No. 230 of 2019, Central Bank (Supervision and Enforcement) Act 2013 (Section 48(1)) (Undertakings for Collective Investment in Transferable Securities) Regulations 2019.

[132] Central Bank of Ireland. (2018b). *CP119—Consultation on amendments (and consolidation) to the Central Bank UCITS Regulations*. https://www.centralbank.ie/publication/consultation-papers/consultation-paper detail/cp119---consultation-on-amendments-(and-consolidation)-to-the-central-bank-ucits-regulations. Accessed 13 August 2020.

[133] Central Bank of Ireland. (2020b). *UCITS questions and answers* (29th ed.). https://www.centralbank.ie/docs/default-source/regulation/industry-market-sectors/funds/ucits/guidance/ucits-qa-29-edition.pdf?sfvrsn=2. Accessed 13 August 2020.

The Q&As clarify the Central Bank's expectations in relation to liquidity stress testing (LST) in UCITS, focusing mainly on the application of the ESMA "Guidelines on liquidity stress testing in UCITS and AIFs."

Currently, Ireland's hedge funds market is a very mature one, in spite of product or regulatory changes. Last year it has seen a remarkable growth not only from the point of view of new market entrants but also from the point of view of continued growth. In this respect, the growing interest in Ireland regarding private debt and private equity fund managers can be mentioned, particularly due to the highly anticipated amended Irish Investment Limited Partnership (ILP) Bill 2019.[134] The Bill's intention is the update of the existing framework for regulated limited partnerships, set out in the ILP Act 1994, for a better reflection of changes in the global private equity market, both in terms of the modernization of the Irish ILP structure and in terms of applicable EU legislation. The Bill intends also to contribute to achieving the Irish Government's aim to convert Ireland into a global location for private equity funds. A major change that the Bill brings to the 1994 Act implies the proposal to allow an Investment Limited Partnership to be structured as an umbrella fund with segregated liability between sub-funds. At the same time the Bill clarifies limited partners' obligations with regard to capital contributions and facilitates the replacement of a General Partner.

AIFs are regulated by the Central Bank pursuant to the AIFMD Regulations, which are supplemented by the Central Bank's AIF Rulebook.[135]

The most important documents under which AIFs are regulated are:

- European Union (Alternative Investment Fund Managers) Regulations 2013.[136]
- European Union (Alternative Investment Fund Managers) (Amendment) Regulations 2014.[137]

[134] Which was published by the Irish Government on June 20, 2019.

[135] Central Bank of Ireland. (2018a). *AIF rulebook*. https://www.centralbank.ie/docs/default-source/regulation/industry-market-sectors/funds/aifs/guidance/aif-rulebook-march-2018.pdf?sfvrsn=6. Accessed 8 August 2020.

[136] S.I. No. 257 of 2013.

[137] S.I. No. 379 of 2014.

- Irish Collective Asset-management Vehicles Act 2015.[138]
- European Union (Alternative Investment Fund Managers) (Amendment) Regulations 2019.[139]
- European Union (Key Information Document for Packaged Retail and Insurance-Based Investment Products [PRIIPS]) Regulations 2017.[140]

Recently, on July 13, 2020, the Central Bank issued the 34th edition of the Central Bank AIFMD Q&A,[141] including new Q&A IDs 1131 and 1132 in relation to liquidity stress testing in AIFs.

3.4.2 *The Irish Regulatory System: Scope and Objectives*

The hedge funds regulatory background in Ireland is essential in terms of the next dynamics of the funds market. Pragmatic regulation of hedge funds is vital if substitute investment products are to grow in the flexible environment in which they must work to achieve their objectives. In this context, there are several major objectives: first, to make sure that suitable, but also efficient regulation will be enacted for financial entities but also for the entire industry; second, to minimize all risks that might lead to failure. This could be achieved by ensuring the observance of prudential conformation and other requests.[142] The third will be to make sure that all actions will be taken for the well-being and best protection of clients involved in financial services. The certain way to do this is by taking care of clients but also of investors through business norms conduct and other protective procedures.[143]

[138] S.I. No. 2 of 2015.

[139] S.I. No. 428 of 2019.

[140] S.I. No. 629 of 2017.

[141] Central Bank of Ireland. (2020a). *AIFMD questions and answers* (34th ed.). https://www.centralbank.ie/docs/default-source/regulation/industry-market-sectors/funds/aifs/guidance/qa/aifmd-qa-34-edition.pdf?sfvrsn=2. Accessed 13 August 2020.

[142] Central Bank of Ireland. (2010). *Enforcement strategy 2011–2012* (p. 8). http://www.centralbank.ie/regulation/processes/enforcement/documents/enforcement%20strategy%202011-2012.pdf. Accessed 4 March 2012.

[143] Ibid.

3.4.3 The Advantages and Disadvantages of the Irish Regulatory System

Ireland's reputation of international leader in hedge funds and management center for international alternative investment funds (AIFs) signifies that any legislation related to the management of funds will be analyzed to determine whether it will convey negative costs for what has been a flourishing industry in Ireland. Its attractive tax regime, under which UCITS and other alternative funds remain entirely tax free, also offers it a key advantage over its competitors.

Irish hedge funds structure alternatives, the present regulatory framework and also the strong management model represent an advantage for investors, to whom Irish regulation of hedge funds offer the necessary transparency[144] and comfort levels. Ireland's regulations offer structures that fit well the different investor profiles, various fund strategies, and aims.

The major issue in maintaining the confidence of hedge funds investors has to be Ireland's ability to control the current wave of international regulatory reform. Currently, Ireland is experiencing what could be called a continuous regulatory change. In this vein, "the Irish Collective Asset Management Vehicle (ICAV) was introduced in 2015 to complement a wide range of Irish-regulated funds and more than 500 have been registered since its launch. There has also been a recent push to enhance the attractiveness of the Irish investment limited partnership (ILP), which will improve the environment for private equity investing."[145]

Ireland's success as an onshore domicile for investment funds is well-known, and the development of Ireland's funds industry continues to be an area of strategic importance for the Irish economy.

Statistics show that Irish-domiciled investment funds had over EUR 3.04 trillion in net assets in 2019 (up 26% from EUR 2.4 trillion at the end of 2018).[146] This means the industry has now quadrupled in size over the last decade.

[144] IFIA. (2010). *Why? Ireland excellence in alternative investments*. Irish Funds Industry Association Dublin, p. 5.

[145] Lardner, P. (2019). *A portal of Europe: Ireland 2019 special report*. https://irishfunds-secure.s3.amazonaws.com/1550237958-HFM-Ireland-2019.pdf. Accessed 5 October 2020.

[146] Irish Funds. (2020). *Irish domiciled funds*. https://www.irishfunds.ie/facts-figures/irish-domiciled-funds. Accessed 15 August 2020.

While the majority of assets under management are held in UCITS funds, Irish-domiciled AIFs had in excess of EUR 748 billion in net assets in May 2020[147] (Fig. 3.4).

The majority of the investments in these regulated investment funds comes from non-Irish institutional investors (Fig. 3.5).

In Ireland, AIFs reached almost EUR 1tn, being around 2000[148] in number according to a current report issued by the Central Bank of Ireland. Most of equity, bond, and mixed funds are established under UCITS, while hedge funds, property funds, and "other" funds are typically AIFs.

As on December 2018, Ireland had a total of 13,941 funds, of which 7920 were Irish-domiciled Funds and 6624 were non-domiciled and it distributes its funds to over ninety countries. It has a large range of fund

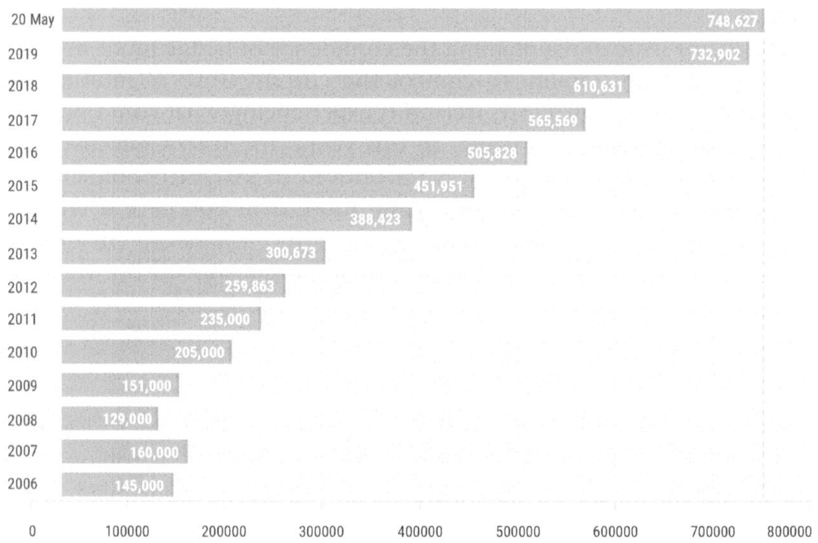

Fig. 3.4 Irish-domiciled AIFs funds total net assets (EUR million) (*Source* Irish Funds 2020)

[147] Ibid.

[148] Cima, S., Killeen, N., & Madouros, V. (2019). Mapping market-based finance in Ireland. *Financial Stability Notes, 17,* 1–26.

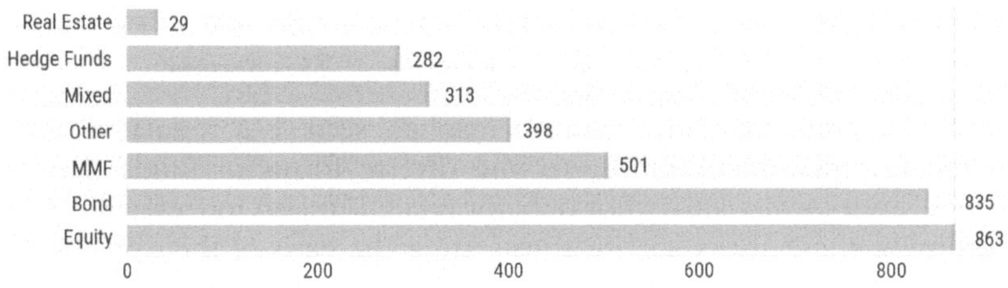

Fig. 3.5 Total assets of funds domiciled in Ireland, by fund type (Q2 2019) (*Source* Cima and Madouros 2019)

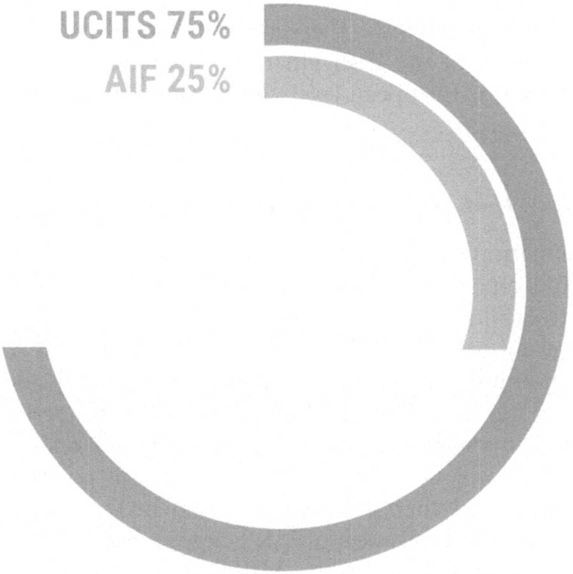

Fig. 3.6 Breakdown in assets between UCITS and AIFs in Ireland (*Source* Irish Funds 2020)

types, an efficient tax structure and puts priority on investor protection. The Central Bank is responsible for the approval and supervision of the Investment funds. Today 75% of Irish-domiciled funds are UCITS and 25% are AIFs (Fig. 3.6).

3.4.4 Could a More Regulated Hedge Funds Industry at European Level Lead to an Increase of This Sector?

Ireland is apprehended in a positive manner, seen as a regulated environment for investment funds, serving diverse forms of funds. It also provides cautious regulatory not only for retail, but also for refined funds. Accordingly, these are crucial reasons setting the basis of their prosperity in Ireland. Moreover, the Irish Financial Regulator tends to be acknowledged as adaptable, accessible, but also as receiving ideas favorable for fixed time limits for exempting the funds. A wide range of persons wishing to invest seek exposure to alternative asset classes. Still, they lack the desire to invest in lightly regulated jurisdictions (for instance British Virgin Islands, Cayman). Apparently, they currently value their status of being under authorization of the Irish Financial Regulator. Therefore, a more regulated industry at European level could lead to a growth of the hedge funds sector in Europe.

3.4.5 The AIFM Directive Impact on the Irish Regulatory System

The implementation of AIFMD has had a significant impact on the Irish regulatory landscape for alternative investment funds. A key scope of the AIFMD is "to facilitate the harmonization of financial services across EU Member States by giving an AIF managed by an authorized AIFM an 'EU passport,' enabling its units or shares to be marketed and sold in all other EU Member States."[149] This AIFMD passport is restricted to marketing to professional investors only. Taken into account Brexit and that the United Kingdom will become a third country, this passport will be an important aspect, together with general Irish hedge funds regulations, which will impact the relocation of UK hedge funds in Ireland.[150]

However, to a certain extent, the AIFMD framework is "in many ways reflective of pre-existing requirements in Ireland relating to supervisory

[149] Matheson. (2019). *Ireland as a fund domicile*. https://www.matheson.com/images/uploads/publications/Ireland_as_a_Fund_Domicile.pdf. Accessed 14 August 2020.

[150] Bisciari, P. (2019). *A survey of the long-term impact of Brexit on the UK and the EU27 economies* (Working Paper, No. 366). Brussels: National Bank of Belgium. https://www.nbb.be/en/articles/survey-long-term-impact-brexit-uk-and-eu27-economies. Accessed 12 July 2020.

oversight, an independent depositary, corporate governance, valuations and investor disclosure."[151]

Current researches state that "EU initiatives have tightened the regulatory apparatus in recent years. Most hedge fund activity is now regulated by the authorities in Ireland or elsewhere, and the Alternative Investment Funds Managers Directive (AIFMD) 2011, among other EU schemes."[152] Both local and European regulations have extended the aim of financial regulation putting some light onto the shadow banking industry. However, according to Griffin and Brenan, "the international scale of finance and the complexity of regulatory jurisdictions demand much more active monitoring and international coordination than national oversight agencies can normally muster."[153] In this vein, experts consider that "there is still considerable scope for international regulatory and tax arbitrage, and the Irish financial services sector has become a significant player in exactly this field."[154]

3.4.6 MiFID II Implementation in Ireland

MiFID II/MiFIR applies from January 3, 2018. This new regulation aims at strengthening investor protection and improving the functioning of financial markets. As for Ireland, regulation has increased significantly since the financial crisis. In line with the FCA's final MiFID II regulation, most Irish hedge funds have observed the January 2018 deadline. In this respect, the separation of execution and research services was implemented in Ireland. At the same time, MiFID II imposes other

[151] Irish Funds. (2015). *A guide to establishing alternative investment funds in Ireland, Dublin*. https://irishfunds-secure.s3.amazonaws.com/1525962428-Irish-AIFs_web.pdf. Accessed 15 August 2020.

[152] Hardiman, N., & Metinsoy, S. (2019). Power, ideas, and national preferences: Ireland and the FTT. *Journal of European Public Policy, 26*(11), 1600–1619. https://doi.org/10.1080/13501763.2018.1539117.

[153] Griffin, D., & Brennan, J. (2016, June 25). Russian bank collapse shines light into shadowy corners of Irish finance. *Irish Independent*. https://www.independent.ie/business/irish/russian-bank-collapse-shines-light-into-shadowy-corners-of-irish-finance-34482531.html. Accessed 11 August 2020.

[154] Brennan, J. (2017, September 4). Russia's growing banking crisis to hit IFSC vehicles, experts warn. *Irish Times*. https://www.irishtimes.com/business/financial-services/russia-s-growing-banking-crisis-to-hit-ifsc-vehicles-experts-warn-1.3208132. Accessed 15 July 2020.

major new rules on MiFID-regulated firms, having to do mainly with (1) product governance rules (according to which firms must define their investor target market), (2) enhanced marketing communication requirements (focusing mainly on the manner in which information regarding past performance can be presented and mandatory disclosure of costs and charges).

3.4.7 Brexit Impact on Irish Hedge Funds

Brexit continues to be the most significant development affecting the financial services sector in Ireland and across the EU.

Ireland has proven to be a popular destination for UK firms looking to relocate or establish fund management companies in advance of Brexit. In addition, the Irish government has continued to commit its strategic support to the financial services sector. On April 26, 2019, the Irish government unveiled its new "Ireland for Finance" strategy (IFS 2025)[155] for the further development of the financial services sector in Ireland to 2025 (building on its previous IFS 2020 strategy). The vision of the strategy is to continue the development of Ireland as a top-tier location of choice for specialist international financial services. According to this new strategy, 2019 has been very successful for Ireland: "with over EUR 4 trillion in fund assets under administration, Ireland is the 3rd largest global investment funds domicile, the largest European domicile for ETFs, and a leading location worldwide for hedge fund administration."[156]

Therefore, while Brexit has been challenging for the financial services sector, Ireland has been and continues to be well-placed to offer solutions for UK-based financial services firms and, with the strategic support of the Irish government the Irish financial sector is well-positioned to continue its rapid development over the coming years.[157]

[155] Government of Ireland. (2019). *Ireland for finance—The strategy for the development of Ireland's international financial services sector to 2025*. https://www.ifsireland.com/BlankSite/media/IFSMedia/Documents/Ireland-for-Finance.pdf. Accessed 13 August 2020.

[156] Idem, p. 1.

[157] Bisciari, P. (2019). *A survey of the long-term impact of Brexit on the UK and the EU27 economies* (Working Paper, No. 366). National Bank of Belgium, Brussels. https://www.nbb.be/en/articles/survey-long-term-impact-brexit-uk-and-eu27-economies. Accessed 12 July 2020.

Ireland is one of the leading EEA jurisdictions for cross-border fund distribution and is home to funds collectively valued at over EUR 2 trillion. Ireland is also a leading location for fund management companies ("FMCs"), particularly Alternative Investment Fund Managers ("AIFMs") and UCITS Management Companies ("UCITS ManCos"), which are drawn by the numerous advantages Ireland has to offer as a domicile for cross-border management companies.

Ireland is a natural home for UK investment managers that wish to continue to avail of UCITS and AIFMD passports post-Brexit and to retain the right to distribute into EEA markets. Recent changes to Central Bank of Ireland regulations around fund governance mean that it is now easier to set up a dual authorized Irish AIFM/ UCITS ManCo, also known under the name of a "Super ManCo."[158] This is expected to become attractive not only for FMCs, but also for some MiFID authorized investment managers. In a similar manner, a UK AIFM cannot benefit anymore after Brexit from the AIFMD passport and could consider establishing an AIFM in an EEA jurisdiction (this could be the case of Ireland) for making sure that the AIFs it manages keep on benefiting from AIFMD passporting rights.

There are several advantages offered by Ireland, which are going to be mentioned further on. Thus, "an Irish UCITS ManCo or AIFM may delegate the day-to-day portfolio management function to an investment manager located outside of Ireland (either within or outside the EU) as long as the investment manager is subject to a comparative level of prudential supervision as that which would exist under the EU MiFID regime. Provided the UCITS ManCo or AIFM does not become a 'letter box entity' as a result of this delegation, the Irish FMC model permits the day-to-day investment decisions to be taken outside of Ireland, while at the same time, enabling the funds themselves (whether UCITS or AIFs) to be passported for sale throughout the EU pursuant to the respective UCITS and AIFMD regimes. UK-based investment managers authorized

[158] Mulcahy, A., & De Feu, F. (2020). Changes in the Irish asset management landscape. *AIMA Journal*. https://www.aima.org/journal/aima-journal---edition-121/article/changes-in-the-irish-asset-management-landscape.html. Accessed 12 August 2020.

under MiFID frequently carry out portfolio management on behalf of FMCs located in Ireland and elsewhere in the EEA."[159]

At the moment of this writing, MiFID does not regulate the manner in which a third country entity can provide MiFID services into the EEA. Consequently, this is left to the relevant member state. It is true that this is going to be modified under MiFID II, but there will be some time before the MiFID II will apply entirely. Therefore, "both the UCITS ManCo and AIFM regimes permit those entities to apply to be licensed to undertake certain additional MiFID type services such as individual portfolio management, investment advice, and receipt and transmission of orders. In order to continue to access EU markets, a UK investment manager may consider adding those additional MiFID services to an EU entity that has a UCITS ManCo/AIFM authorization."[160]

Taking into consideration retaining its current access to the EEA market, UK investment managers could consider the establishment of a Super ManCo in Ireland. As previously mentioned, both the UCITS and AIFM Directives allow dual authorization so that a UCITS ManCo can also be authorized to hold an AIFM license and vice versa. Therefore, this issue is of high importance for investment managers, who can therefore get access to the passporting regimes for UCITS and AIF products without being obliged to establish two separately regulated and capitalized entities. Furthermore, "as the CBI has recently streamlined the authorization, on-going supervision, managerial functions and governance of AIFMs and UCITS ManCos, establishing an Irish Super ManCo is now an attractive option. Overall, depending on the regulated services which a firm intends to carry on, an Irish Super ManCo may offer a regulated solution within a single regulated entity which would allow a UK investment manager to manage and sell AIFs and UCITS funds throughout the EEA on a passported basis while at the same time being authorized to provide individual portfolio management, investment advice and receipt and transmission services to clients throughout the EEA on a passported basis."[161] Therefore, Ireland offers a solution for avoiding the separate establishment of a MiFID firm, a UCITS ManCo

[159] White, M., Darragh, M., Spratt, T., Beattie, H., & Ferguson, I. (2020). *Brexit: Establishing a fund management company in Ireland*. https://www.mccannfitzgerald.com/uploads/7769-Brexit_Establishing_a_Fund_Management_Company_0.pdf. Accessed 12 August 2020.

[160] Idem.

[161] Idem.

or AIFM. Summing up, Ireland stands as a first choice for UK managers, who are trying to retain access to the EEA due to Brexit. Ireland stands out as distinguished distribution hub for both UCITS and AIFs, having a deep and well-established professional services environment, at the same time sharing a language with the United Kingdom, together with a common law legal system.

Another important aspect was underlined by S&P Global Ratings' second edition of "Brexit Sensitivity Index 2019: Who Has The Most To Lose?" where Ireland scored 2.9, implying major reverberations in the Irish economy due to Brexit, particularly if this exit would occur without a formal agreement including period of transition (Fig. 3.7).

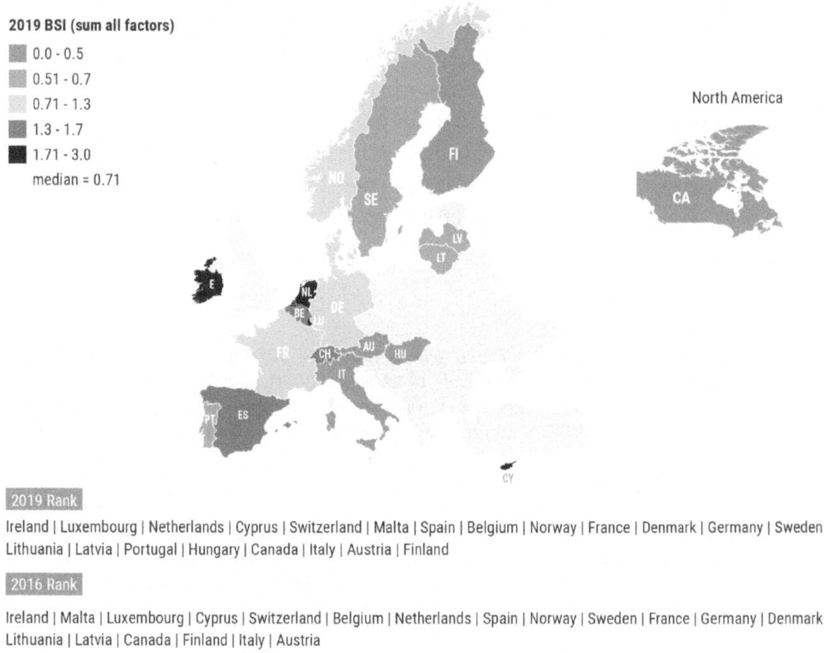

Fig. 3.7 2019 Brexit sensitivity index (*Source* S&P Global Ratings 2019)

The Report analyzed several factors which imply Irelands' exposure to the United Kingdom. Putting aside aspects,[162] which although important, are not in focus for the current paper, we consider of major importance "Ireland's financial sector's exposure to the UK," ranking "the fourth highest of all 21 economies surveyed, reflecting the size of Irish banking subsidiaries operating in the UK."[163] Nevertheless, if we compare this position with that held by Ireland in 2016, financial sector claims are lower since the Irish banking system keeps on diminishing its UK footprint.

Summing up, the report concludes that the relationships between Ireland and the United Kingdom would be highly impacted, in a negative (economic point of view) way, in the case of a hard Brexit. Still, authors consider also that "Ireland is well placed to attract some of the FDI displaced from a post-Brexit UK, should UK-based financial subsidiaries and branches lose their coveted EU passporting rights, which currently enable them to sell financial services in the EU market."[164]

As a concluding remark, as Brexit plans matured into implemented in late 2019 and early 2020, for many investment firms in the United Kingdom and some global investment firms, Ireland is currently emerging as a favored EU hub due to its relative advantages it has over a number of

[162] S&P Global Ratings.(2019). *Brexit sensitivity index 2019: Who has the most to lose?* www.spglobal.com/ratingsdirect. Accessed 14 August 2020. In this report it is stated that there are several major aspects which put Ireland on top of UK preferences after Brexit, such as: "Ireland's 499-kilometer border with the UK encourages vigorous trade in merchandise and services, as well as substantial migratory flows between the two countries. At 8.5% of GDP, Ireland exports more goods and services to the UK than any other sovereign on the index. Deep supply chains extend between Ireland and Northern Ireland, not least in agro and food processing. Indeed, Northern Ireland is the UK region with the closest trade links with Ireland, making up around 15% of total trade.

Another by-product of Ireland's location is the large bidirectional immigration between it and the UK. The sum of Irish residents in the UK and vice versa totals 16.7% of Ireland's population, according to data from the ONS and the UN's Department of Economic and Social Affairs. That figure is twice that of the next largest bidirectional migratory figure, namely 8.35% for Malta, and far exceeds two-way migratory flows from southern European countries such as Spain (1% of Spain's population), the seventh most vulnerable nation on our BSI."

[163] S&P Global Ratings. (2019). *Brexit sensitivity index 2019: Who has the most to lose?* www.spglobal.com/ratingsdirect. Accessed 14 August 2020.

[164] Idem.

other EU countries across a number of metrics including tax, legal system, labor laws but also regulation.[165]

3.5 Luxembourg: Overview of Hedge Funds Regulatory Framework

3.5.1 *The Evolution of Hedge Funds Regulatory Framework in Luxembourg*

The Grand Duchy of Luxembourg has built up a strong name as a consequence of the fact that it provides various types of investors with a highly attractive fund product structuring solutions. According to EFAMA, Luxembourg stands as one of the countries which is home to the highest number of asset management companies.[166] As a consequence of the variety of investment vehicles, Luxembourg allows implementation of a large scale of alternative investment strategies.

Looking back, Luxembourg has always found investment solutions, having an innovative and consistent regulatory approach. According to Cojocaru and Vostricov (2018), "apart from maintaining a stable and well-working financial market infrastructure and providing high quality legal services, from the regulatory perspective, Luxembourg's legislator has always been very responsive to the needs of investors providing flexible and attractive investment vehicles, often allowing things that were not permitted in other jurisdictions,"[167] for instance, setting up various compartments and sub-funds but also various share classes.[168]

In the mid-1980s by anticipating again a new opportunity, Luxembourg was a pioneer being the first country that implemented the UCITS

[165] Murphy, K., Bothwell, E., O'Shea, D., et al. (2019). Ireland. In *The asset management review* (8th ed.). https://thelawreviews.co.uk/edition/the-asset-management-review-edition-8/1197346/ireland. Accessed 12 August 2020.

[166] EFAMA. (2017). *Asset management in Europe* (9th ed.). European Fund and Asset Management Association. https://www.efama.org/Publications/Statistics/Asset%20Management%20Report/EFAMA%20Asset%20. Accessed 12 July 2020.

[167] Cojocaru, V., & Vostricov, D. (2018, May 18–19). *Implementation of AIFs' regulation in the Republic of Moldova, based on Luxembourg experience*. Paper presented at the International Conference on European Financial Regulation Eufire, Iasi, Romania.

[168] Professional Wealth Management Ltd. (2017). *Inside the toolbox for investment products: Spotlight on Luxembourg—Chapter 3*. https://www.youtube.com/watch?v=uqUXMf_xY4I. Accessed 13 August 2020.

Directive into national law. Thus, in 1983 the first complex "investment fund legislation in Luxembourg" was implemented. Ever since, investment funds developed thoroughly, under the name of "*Undertakings for Collective Investment*" (UCI). As a consequence of this Directive, Luxembourg initiated to market funds across the EU (European Union) and later across the globe.[169] This is one major reason for Luxembourg's currently second ranking in the world's Investment fund center after the United States, and the global leader in terms of offering cross-border funds.[170]

In addition to the foregoing, Luxembourg has also considerable experience in administering non-Luxembourg domiciled hedge funds but also FoHF. The main aspects that attract the international promoters of Luxembourg investment funds are the favorable legal environment, the know-how of well-established service providers, and the pragmatism and reactivity of the supervisory authority.

The establishment of onshore non-UCTIS funds in Luxembourg was made possible with the enactment of the 1988 UCTIS law,[171] complemented soon thereafter by a law on non-publicly traded institutional investor funds (the "1991 Law").[172]

Currently, as shown in Fig. 3.4, 61% of all UCITS registered in at least 3 countries are Luxembourg funds.

Luxembourg's non-UCTIS legal framework was silence on a number of key issues handled on item-by-item by the CSSF[173] (for example, prime brokerage and short sales) and the discretionary nature of the approval of domestic non-UCTIS collective investment schemes launching. These prompted the *Commission de Surveillance du Secteur Financier* (CSSF), Luxembourg's financial sector supervisor, to adopt

[169] ALFI. (2014a). *Luxembourg: A financial center at the service of the European economy*. Association of the Luxembourg Fund Industry. https://www.alfi.lu/getattachment/f75643a4-c132-4471-9168-2cb2c9697ab7/alfi-alfi-abbl-brochure-final-web.pdf. Accessed 14 August 2020.

[170] Idem.

[171] Loi du 30 mars 1988 relative aux organismes de placement collectif.

[172] Loi du 19 juillet concernant les organismes de placement collectif dont les titres ne sont pas destines au placement dans le public (the "1991 Law", Mémorial A, 1991-49, du 2 aout 1991, 996). The 1991 Law was to be read in conjunction with the 1988 CIS Law.

[173] Commission de Surveillance du Secteur Financier.

a Circular in December 2002, laying down rules that apply to funds pursuing alternative investment strategies (the "2002 Circular").[174]

Luxembourg's regulatory regime was complemented with the adoption, at the beginning of 2007, of a regulation regarding the specialized investment funds,[175] which repealed "the Law of July 19, 1991." Other significant developments included the abrogation of the restrictions imposed by a 1991 Circular[176] on the listing of offshore funds' units on the "*Luxembourg Stock Exchange*" (LuSE) and the issuance of a Ministerial Order amending its internal regulations on the listing of foreign funds,[177] as well as the adoption of a subsequent CSSF Circular laying down the contents of the prospectus of foreign funds intending to become listed on the LuSE.[178]

This being said, the Luxembourg regulator has created an innovative and flexible framework for qualified investors. The introduction of the new Law on "*Specialized Investment Funds*" (SIF) in Luxembourg means that there are now the following possibilities for launching an undertaking for collective investment structure.

In Luxembourg, there is no particular type of vehicle dedicated to hedge funds. Luxembourg hedge funds can be classified according to their being regulated and by consequence, subject to the supervision of the financial regulator, the Commission de Surveillance du Secteur Financier (CSSF), or according to their non-regulated nature, being managed by a regulated alternative investment fund manager (AIFM) itself subject to CSSF supervision. In Luxembourg, the hedge fund sector has grown

[174] Circulaire CSSF 02/80.

[175] SIF Law. (2007). Loi du 13 février 2007 relative aux fonds d'investissements specialisés (Mémorial A 2007-13 du 13 février 2007). This SIF Law supersedes the 1991 Law and amends the 2002 CIS Law, introducing an alternative to established Luxembourg law vehicles (notably, hedge funds) and broadening the pool of investors eligible to invest in non-publicly traded UCTIS.

[176] Circulaire CSSF 04/132 concernant l'abrogation de la circulaire CAB 91/3 du 17 juillet 1991 concernant l'admission à la cote officielle de la Bourse de Luxembourg d'organismes de placement collective ("OPC") étrangers.

[177] Arreté ministerial du 11 Juin 2004 portant approbation de modifications du règlement d'ordre intériEuro de la Bourse de Luxembourg (Mémorial A, 2004-104 du 5 juillet 2004, 1640).

[178] Circulaire CSSF 04/151 concernant les dates devant figurer dans le prospectus d'admission à la cote officielle.

rapidly over the last years. Luxembourg "regulated hedge funds are essentially tax-exempt vehicles, with the exception of registration duty and the annual subscription tax."[179]

Accordingly, the most common investment fund structures for hedge funds are:

- Strongly regulated investment vehicles, such as:
  - undertakings for collective investment in transferable securities (UCITS). Sophisticated and complex UCITS are subject to Part I of the Law of December 17, 2010 relating to undertakings for collective investment (UCI Law)[180];
  - undertakings for collective investment (UCIs) pursuing alternative investment strategies (Part II UCIs). These are subject to Part II of the UCI Law, these being currently used although to a lesser extent.
- More lightly regulated investment vehicles, such as:
  - specialized investment funds (SIFs), subject to the Law of February 13, 2007, relating to specialized investment funds (SIF Law).[181] SIFs provide high flexibility concerning asset eligibility and diversification;
  - reserved alternative investment funds (RAIFs), subject to the Law of July 23, 2016, on RAIFs (RAIF Law).[182] RAIFs do not need authorization from the CSSF at the same time not being supervised but need to be managed by an authorized external AIFM. Also, after five days of formation, a RAIF needs to be acknowledged by a notarial deed and by consequence registered with the Luxembourg Trade and Companies Register (RCS).

[179] ALFI. (2018). *Luxembourg investment vehicles: An overview of the legal and regulatory requirements*. https://www.alfi.lu/getattachment/9d6077df-e6db-438a-b77a-ba3fd7a39f1d/alfi-alfi-luxembourg-investment-vehicles-final.pdf. Accessed 14 August 2020.

[180] Law of 17 December 2010 relating to undertakings for collective investment as amended (2010). Mém. A 2010, No. 239.

[181] Law of 13 February 2007 relating to specialised investment funds. (2007). Mém. A 2007, No. 13.

[182] Law of 23 July 2016 on Reserved Alternative Investment Funds. (2016). Mém. A 2016, No. 140.

By now, after four years of existence of RAIFs, nearly 1,000 were established in Luxembourg.[183]

- The Law of July 16, 2019[184] aims to designate the competent authority, i.e., the CSSF, and provides supervisory and administrative sanctions powers granted to such authorities for the specific needs of the EU Regulations. In respect to the power of investigation, the Law of July 16, 2019 distinguishes between:
  - EuVECA, EuSEF, MMF in respect of which the CSSF is vested with the supervisory and investigation powers necessary to perform its functions;
  - ELTIFs where the CSSF is vested with the supervisory and investigation powers provided by Article 50 of the Law of July 12, 2013 on alternative investment fund managers (the "AIFM Law").

Lately, the vast majority of hedge funds in Luxembourg have been set up as SIFs. However, currently they were highly challenged due to the flexibility offered by the RAIF.

It is worth noting that Part II UCIs, SIFs, and RAIFs fall within the scope of Directive 2011/61/EU on alternative investment fund managers (AIFM Directive). The AIFM Directive was transposed in Luxembourg by the Law of July 12, 2013 on alternative investment fund managers (AIFM Law).

As a result, a Luxembourg hedge fund qualifying as alternative investment fund (AIF) (that is, a collective investment undertaking [but not a UCITS] which seeks to raise capital from a number of investors with a view to investing it in accordance with a defined investment policy for the benefit of such investors) must be managed by an AIFM and must comply with organizational and procedural requirements.

[183] Luxembourg Trade and Company Register, access on 14 August 2020. https://www.lbr.lu/mjrcs/jsp/webapp/static/mjrcs/en/mjrcs/pdf/listeFIAR.pdf. Accessed 14 August 2020.

[184] Loi du 16 juillet 2019 portant mise en œuvre des règlements EuVECA, EuSEF, MMF, ELTIF et Titrisation STS. Publication: 18/07/2019, Prise d'effet: 22/07/2019, Mémorial: A514. http://www.legilux.lu/eli/etat/leg/loi/2019/07/16/a514/jo. Accessed 24 May 2020.

Table 3.2 Aggregated national balance sheet of euro area investment funds in billions of euros (June 2019)

Country	*Assets (EUR billions)*
Belgium	170.5
Germany	2341.0
Estonia	1.1
Ireland	2584.7
Greece	6.4
Spain	303.6
France	143.6
Italy	389.1
Cyprus	5.2
Latvia	0.4
Lithuania	1.2
Luxembourg	**4566.2**
Malta	19.7
Netherlands	905.5
Austria	183.4
Portugal	29.0
Slovenia	2.7
Slovakia	7.0
Finland	132.6
Euro Area Total	**13,102.9**

Source European Central Bank (2019)

Currently, "the Luxembourg hedge fund sector has grown rapidly making Luxembourg a recognized premier hedge fund domicile."[185]

Table 3.2 shows the aggregated national balance sheet of Investment funds in the Euro Area in mid-2019 (billions of euros). Luxembourg surpassed EUR 4500 billion in net assets being, by consequence, the largest investment center in Europe. The second rank is occupied by Ireland (EUR 2584.7 billion), third by Germany (EUR 2341.0 billion), and fourth by France (EUR 1453.6 billion).

As the second-largest fund servicing jurisdiction in the world after the United States, Luxembourg is a favored destination for investment fund managers (IFMs) and investors alike, thanks to its stable political and social environment, versatile fund products, leadership in investor protection, and experienced and responsive regulator and service

[185] ALFI. (2020). *Luxembourg: Your hedge fund domicile*. Association of the Luxembourg Fund Industry. https://www.alfi.lu/Alfi/media/Statements/2020/HedgeFund-Flyer-2020-20201302-8.pdf. Accessed 13 August 2020.

providers. AuM in Luxembourg-regulated collective investment undertakings reached EUR 4.3 trillion at the end of May 2019.[186] Meanwhile AuM increase during the last period, Luxembourg also consolidated the total number of entities, being currently "3,871 entities that are subject to regulatory supervision, of which 2,513 are umbrella funds consisting of 13,553 sub-funds. In addition, 1,358 entities have adopted a standalone structure, bringing the total number of active fund units to 14,911 as of April 2019."[187] In addition to 14 internally authorized managers, 207 UCITS management companies, 263 authorized alternative investment fund managers (AIFMs), and 165 other IFMs are authorized as of July 2019.[188] There are 570 other IFMs that are registered as below threshold AIFMs.

Over the past few years, government efforts have been mainly directed at increasing transparency, protecting market stability and preventing the build-up of systemic risk in the financial system. Those large-scale reforms have been, to a large extent, driven by European initiatives.

UCITS and Part II UCIs that may be marketed to retail investors in Luxembourg are subject to the UCITS V Directive depositary regime.[189] Their depositary must be a credit institution with its registered office in Luxembourg or a Luxembourg branch of a credit institution with its registered office in another EEA country.

Part II UCIs whose offering documents prohibit marketing to retail investors in Luxembourg are subject to the AIFMD depositary regime.[190] SIFs, SICARs, RAIFs, and other AIFs managed by authorized AIFMs, and internally managed AIFs that are subject to the AIFM Law, are also subject to the AIFMD regime. They must appoint a Luxembourg credit institution or Luxembourg branch of an EEA credit institution, a Luxembourg investment firm, a Luxembourg branch of an EEA investment firm, or—under certain conditions detailed below—a Luxembourg professional depositary of assets other than financial instruments.

[186] Association of the Luxembourg Fund Industry. (2020). *Net assets under management in Luxembourg funds*. https://www.alfi.lu/en-GB/Pages/Industry-statistics/Luxembourg. Accessed 13 August 2020.

[187] Idem.

[188] Idem.

[189] AIFMD, Article 19.

[190] AIFMD, Articles 31 and 33.

Introduced by the AIFM Law, professional depositaries of assets other than financial instruments may only be used by AIFs that have no redemption rights for a period of five years from the date of the initial investments and either do not invest in financial instruments that must be held in custody in accordance with the AIFM Law (typically real estate funds), or invest in issuers or non-listed companies in order to potentially acquire control over such companies under the AIFM Law (typically private equity and venture capital funds).

Finally, the CSSF has issued guidance on reverse solicitation and marketing in respect of AIFs in Luxembourg.[191]

Luxembourg's fund center has a strong international orientation: over 97% of funds under management in Luxembourg (around EUR 4.2 trillion) are from overseas. In addition, more than 90% of the large- and medium-sized asset management firms in Luxembourg are owned by overseas investors.[192]

Luxembourg funds are distributed to investors in more than 70 countries, making the cross-border dimension of Luxembourg's fund center unequaled.[193] Nearly two-thirds of the funds authorized for cross-border distribution are domiciled in Luxembourg.[194]

UCITS provide the majority of funds under management in Luxembourg, contributing to more than 82% of total funds in 2018. The share of assets under management of regulated AIFs managed by authorized IFMs is more modest in terms of managed assets (EUR 704.1 billion). IFMs established in other EEA countries and managing Luxembourg

[191] CSSF. (2019). Frequently Asked Questions (version 15, 27 September 2019) concerning the Luxembourg Law of 12 July 2013 on alternative investment fund managers as well as the Commission Delegated Regulation (EU) No. 231/2013 of 19 December 2012 supplementing Directive 2011/61/EU of the European Parliament and of the Council with regard to exemptions, general operating conditions, depositaries, leverage transparency and supervision. http://www.cssf.lu/fileadmin/files/AIFM/FAQ_AIFMD.pdf. Accessed 12 August 2020.

[192] CSSF. (2018a). *Annual report 2018*. Commission de Surveillance du Secteur Financier. Luxembourg: Imprimerie Centrale.

[193] PricewaterhouseCoopers. (2019). *Global fund distribution*. https://www.pwc.lu/en/fund-distribution/docs/pwc-publ-gfd-march-2019.pdf. Accessed 14 August 2020.

[194] Idem.

UCITS or AIFs under UCI Law or AIFM Law hold EUR 591.1 billion of assets combined.[195]

Although a limited number of UCITS employing hedge fund strategies may be marketed to retail investors on the same basis as other UCITS funds, hedge fund strategies are usually pursued under Part II of the UCI Law, the SIF Law, or the RAIF Law.

CSSF Circular 02/80 sets forth specific rules applicable to Luxembourg UCIs pursuing alternative investment strategies. The Circular determines the investment restrictions generally applicable to these types of Luxembourg UCIs.

SIFs and RAIFs are not subject to any investment eligibility requirements, and are therefore best suited to accommodate all sorts of alternative strategies. They are both, however, required to diversify their investments to 30% of their assets (except for certain fund of funds or feeder funds) as further set out in CSSF Circular 07/309.

CSSF Circular 08/372 specifies the rules on the appointment of prime brokers, the relationship between the depositary and the appointed prime brokers, and the liability of the depositary in that respect.

3.5.2 The Luxembourg Regulatory System: Scope and Objectives

Over the past few years, the Luxembourg government efforts have been mainly directed at increasing transparency, protecting market stability, and preventing the build-up of systemic risk in the financial system. Those large-scale reforms have been, to a large extent, driven by European initiatives.

The "Commission de Surveillance du Secteur Financier" (CSSF) is the Luxembourg regulatory authority which supervises all Luxembourg registered funds. It is a public law body established with legal status by the Luxembourg state. Generally speaking, the CSSF promotes transparency and fairness in the financial products and services, protects the final consumers, and fights against money laundering and the financing terrorism.

[195] CSSF. (2018b). *Commission de Surveillance du Secteur Financier*. Development of Net Assets and Number of UCIs. Commission de Surveillance du Secteur Financier. https://www.cssf.lu/en/supervision/ivm/ucits/statistics/annual-statistics/development-of-net-assets-and-number-of-ucis-over-the-last-years/. Accessed 13 August 2020.

3.5.3 The Advantages and Disadvantages of Luxembourg's Regulatory Framework

In view of the alleged Madoff fraud,[196] the Stanford International Bank fraud[197] and the financial crisis, the increasingly regulated funds will be considered by investors the best choice for hedge fund investment. Accordingly, several institutional investors decided to move to onshore vehicles and address the larger, more regulated industries, such as Luxembourg. In this particular situation, it seems that regulation is an advantage, mainly due to this ongoing trend in hedge funds to settle down to better, investor friendly regulated jurisdictions like Luxembourg. Still, even if the measurement of the force of trans-jurisdictional regulations is pursued, most of the time there are concerns regarding the failure to find out overall significant inputs of regulation.

The mixture of Luxembourg's pragmatic regulatory expansions, strengthening of efforts between classical and alternative asset classes and new marketing favorable circumstances in areas such as the United Kingdom are all to the country's advantage.

More recently driven by the adoption of the AIFM Directive in 2013, ManCos in Luxembourg have successfully shifted from traditional to alternative strategy assets and even more recently from regulated to unregulated assets. The successes of RAIFs and SCS/SCSps in Luxembourg confirm this trend. Thus, the new regulations positively impacted Luxemburg Assets under Management (AuMs), which reached EUR 4718 billion, representing a year-on-year increase of 16%, according to PwC 2020 Report.[198] Figure 3.8 shows the evolution of UCITS Management companies and licensed AIFMs in Luxembourg. As of December 2018, Luxembourg had 257 licensed AIFMs, representing an increase of 15 over a year, 196 UCITS ManCos and 136 Super ManCos. Super ManCos are Management companies that have both UCITS and AIFM licenses.

[196] Bollen, N. P., et al. (2007). Op. Cit., p. 1.

[197] US v. Stanford, Criminal Action no H-09-342-1 (S.D. Tex. 2009). http://www.justice.gov/criminal/vns/docs/2009/jun/06-18-09Stanford.pdf. Accessed 5 March 2012.

[198] PricewaterhouseCoopers. (2020). *ManCos observatory barometer*. https://www.pwc.lu/en/asset-management/docs/pwc-observatory-management-companies-barometer.pdf. Accessed 14 August 2020.

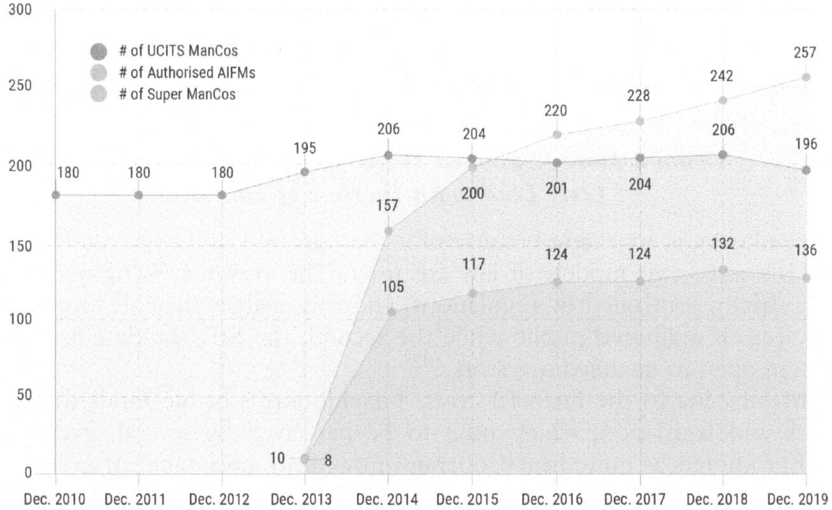

Fig. 3.8 Evolution of UCITS management companies and licensed AIFMs in Luxembourg (*Source* PricewaterhouseCoopers 2020)

Thus, the year began with positive trends for ManCos, who have assimilated a dense regulatory agenda over the past 18 months with, among others, the implementation of the CSSF Circular 18/698.[199] 2020 promised to be a challenging year for ManCos with great opportunities to seize with the development of the alternatives sector. However, it began with an entirely different unpredictable challenge, the COVID-19 pandemic, which presents significant challenges to people and organizations around the globe.

An important challenge for ManCos will be managing their profitability, which, together with a decrease of their AuM following the crisis[200] will be on the top of the ManCos main challenges. Also, according to PwC, "valuation exercises for closing end of March 2020

[199] CSSF Circular 18/698 Authorisation and organization of investment fund managers incorporated under Luxembourg law; Specific provisions on the fight against money laundering and terrorist financing applicable to investment fund managers and entities carrying out the activity of registrar agent.

[200] AuM in Luxembourg decreased by 12% from December 2019 to March 2020, representing 569bn EUR.

and end of June 2020 for Alternative Investments will be crucial in this period of instability and promise to be a very delicate exercise for players exposed to illiquid assets."[201]

3.5.4 *Could a More Regulated Hedge Fund Industry at European Level Lead to an Increase of This Sector?*

Luxembourg is appealing because of its background on hedge funds and FoHFs since two models of law are used. The very first is tighter but also strictly controlled by regulations, and this enables their distribution towards an unlimited public while the second, the SIF, stands a flexible system open to qualified investors.[202]

Mainly due to the financial crisis, Luxembourg's hedge funds framework and legislation, which used to be perceived by several investors and promoters as quite heavy, operates now to its advantage. At present, both the Luxembourg Government and the CSSF have a good record in implementing EU directives, by regulation and clear understanding, expressing optimism in supporting industry guidance and new best practices. Accordingly, a more regulated industry at European level could lead to an increase of the sector in Europe, particularly in Luxembourg, and this can be seen at the level of RAIF Law. Indeed, "Luxembourg modernized and refined its legal system to offer a unique variety of tools for investors to set up their (regulated or unregulated) structures, with or without a distinct legal personality, allowing managers to set up the vehicle which best fits their needs."[203] Also, from the point of view of litigations and arbitrations, there are many voices who "welcome the addition of this latest tool in Luxembourg's investment fund toolbox as it is perfectly suited to the needs of third-party funders which may be required

[201] PwC: PricewaterhouseCoopers. (2020). *ManCos observatory barometer* [Brochure]. https://www.pwc.lu/en/asset-management/docs/pwc-observatory-management-companies-barometer.pdf. Accessed 14 August 2020.

[202] http://www.hedgefundsreview.com/hedge-funds-review/feature/1554476/flight-quality-defines-luxembourg-regime. Accessed 6 May 2012.

[203] Grec, A., & Marquais, O. (2020). Investment management and corporate structuring considerations for third-party litigation funders in Luxembourg. *ASA Bulletin, 38*(2), 296–413.

to react quickly to market trends and dedicate substantial resources to specific types of disputes."[204]

3.5.5 *The Impact of the AIFM Directive on the Hedge Funds Regulatory Framework in Luxembourg*

Luxembourg has transposed the AIFMD Law into its national law on July 12, 2013 with the major aim of strengthening its position as a global investment fund center.[205]

The AIFM Law contains several principle-biased rules as the one laid down in the UCITS Directive. As an example, an AIFM must "act honestly, with due skill, care and diligence and in the best interest of the AIF or its investors and in the integrity of the market."[206]

The AIFMs must "manage three internal control functions such as a permanent compliance function, a risk management function and an internal audit function."[207]

The AIFM Law applies to Lux/EU AIFMs managing one or more EU AIFs/non-EU AIFs; Non-EU AIFMs managing one or more EU AIFs; Non-EU AIFMs marketing AIFs in the EU (ALFI 2014c). The only scenario which does not fall within the scope of the AIFM regime is the situation of a non-EU AIFM managing and/or marketing a non-EU AIF outside the EU.[208]

Authorized AIFMs will be allowed to perform core functions such as portfolio management, risk management, administration, marketing, and activities related to the assets of the AIF.[209]

The most important advantage of having an authorized AIFM is the passport it benefits from, a passport which allows it to marketing its EU-based AIFs to professional investors in the EU on a cross-border basis. An authorized Luxembourg AIFM "may also hold a UCITS ManCo

[204] Idem.

[205] ALFI. (2014b). *The alternative Investment Fund Managers Directive: Luxembourg implementation*. Association of the Luxembourg Fund Industry. https://www.alfi.lu/getattachment/00ea7075-a4ab-4208-8d9e-321ac7c09c9e/alfi-aifmd-luxembourg-implementation-2013-final-web.pdf. Accessed 12 May 2019.

[206] Idem, p. 10.

[207] Idem.

[208] Idem.

[209] Idem.

(Management Company) license, and therefore market and manage on a cross-border basis both EU AIFs and UCITS funds."[210]

Summing up, the implementation of the AIFMD into Luxembourg legislation was seen as a step forward in stabilizing the key role held by Luxemburg in the global investments industry, therefore it was not an end to the traditional private placement regime. The most important aspect of all is that currently, the two regimes coexist, the distribution passport under the AIFM Law and the private placement regime of EU AIF on the Luxembourg territory. Therefore, "Luxembourg modernized its limited partnership regime, at the same time as transposing the AIFMD into its national law."[211]

The Luxembourg regulator of the financial sector ("CSSF") gave some guidance as to when an offering of securities could be considered as not being made to the public (and hence be within the traditional private placement regime):

- whether the offer is made to (i) EU professional investors[212];
- whether the securities have a high nominal amount[213];
- whether the offer is made to a small circle of persons[214];
- the form of the offer, e.g., targeting existing customers, high sales amount, no advertisement;
- the use of a "wrapper" that is initially offered on a private placement basis, but ultimately offered to the public does not benefit from the private placement regime.

However, within Luxembourg territory, the CSSF must be informed in advance of the marketing of any AIF by non-EU alternative investment

[210] ALFI. (2018). *Luxembourg investment vehicles: An overview of the legal and regulatory requirements*. Association of the Luxembourg Fund Industry. https://www.alfi.lu/getattachment/9d6077df-e6db-438a-b77a-ba3fd7a39f1d/alfi-alfi-luxembourg-investment-vehicles-final.pdf. Accessed 14 August 2020.

[211] Repiquet, M. D. (2018a). Regulatory competition in European partnership law: A case of alternative investment funds. *Amsterdam Law Forum, 10*(1). http://130.37.92.72/article/view/427.

[212] As defined under Annex II of Directive 2014 / 65 / EU (mifid).

[213] Equivalent or higher of EUR 125,000.

[214] The CSSF evaluates cases on an individual basis, since no maximum number of investors is stipulated so far.

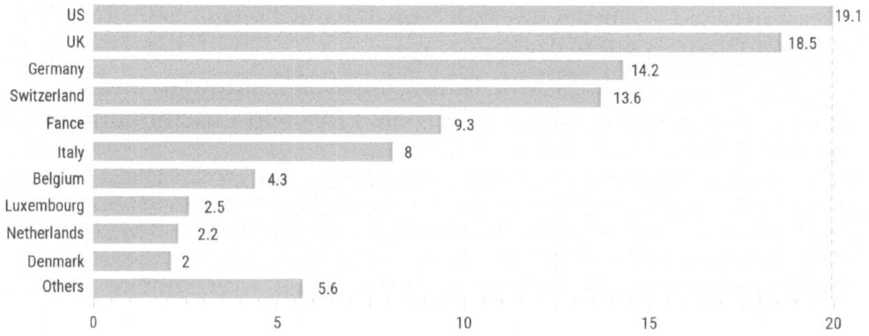

Fig. 3.9 Market share of fund initiator's home countries in terms of AuM (*Source* CSSF 2019)

fund managers ("AIFM"). The CSSF has set out the steps to be followed for such notification procedure for marketing either EU or non-EU AIFs managed by a non-EU AIFM. While there is no statutory time-limit for the administrative procedure with the CSSF, the marketing of the AIFs can start from the date of the notification. The non-EU AIFM is subject to certain reporting obligations to the CSSF, publication of an annual report, and compliance with the Consumer Code.

The introduction of the EU Alternative Investment Management Directive in 2013 boosted the development of hedge funds in Luxembourg. Figure 3.9 shows market share (in %) of fund initiators' home countries in terms of AuM.

Asset managers from all over the globe perceive Luxembourg as a gateway to the European Union market and the global investment fund industry. Currently, as seen in Fig. 3.9, fund initiators from the United States and the United Kingdom hold the biggest market shares in terms of AuMs.

3.5.6 *Brexit Impact on Luxembourg Hedge Funds*

The "Brexit sensitivity index" that the rating agency Standard & Poor's calculated in 2019, revealed that, "the three most exposed European countries at Brexit are, Ireland, Luxembourg and the Netherlands and the least exposed countries are Italy, Austria and Finland."[215] Regarding the Grand Duchy, S&P believes that its second position is linked to "Luxembourg's important links with British financial institutions and its high exports (many of which have been rerouted through Luxembourg for tax purposes)."[216]

The rating agency also believes that Luxembourg, as a financial intermediary for many international companies, could have significant repercussions in financial services and commerce.

S&P specifies, however, that its index could overestimate Luxembourg's vulnerability to Brexit. Indeed, the rating agency excluded from its calculation of FDI the common funds of claims (or SPE, special purpose entities). However, these represent more than 95% of Luxembourg's FDI in the United Kingdom.

The tight connection between the two is clear. Even from the moment when Brexit was not yet clear to occur, the Luxembourg Government stated that relations with the United Kingdom were of major importance and will remain as such.

The United Kingdom stands as a key partner of Luxembourg since they are both supporters of the economic liberalism, their relationship being also important in the field of transnational European cooperation.

Assuming that the United Kingdom will become the third country after its withdrawal from the EU, the Luxembourg Parliament has passed on April 8, 2019 two laws that aim to mitigate disruptions caused by Brexit: hard versus soft Brexit.

The first Brexit law (hard Brexit) would only apply if the United Kingdom leaves the EU without an agreement. It introduces a form of EU passport for UK financial service providers currently operating in Luxembourg during a transitional period of 21 months in line with EU contingency plans.[217] The bill 7401 "covers services in the financial sector, payment services, the fund industry, hedge funds and the insurance sector. The legislation also concerns the two financial supervisory

[215] Fort, L. (2019). *Le Luxembourg, deuxième pays le plus exposé au Brexit*. Paperjam Business Zu Letzebuerg. https://paperjam.lu/article/le-luxembourg-2e-pays-le-plus. Accessed 12 August 2020.

[216] Idem.

[217] Bill no. 7401—Luxembourg, Parliament. Bill no. 7401 on measures to be taken in relation to the financial sector in case of the withdrawal of the United Kingdom of Great Britain and Northern Ireland from the European Union.

bodies in Luxembourg: the Financial Sector Supervisory Commission (CSSF) and the Insurance Commissariat (CAA). They might take temporary emergency measures to ensure the proper functioning of the financial markets, and have the power to issue, on a case-by-case basis, a European passport to UK service providers."[218]

The second Brexit law (soft Brexit) applies whether the United Kingdom leaves the EU with or without an agreement with the EU. The law sets out a 12-month grace period for IFMs of Luxembourg UCITS, Part II UCIs and SIFs to address breaches of investment rules resulting from the United Kingdom's withdrawal, such as divesting from positions in UK UCITS which could no longer be deemed compliant due to Brexit. It also authorizes UK UCITS to continue to be marketed to retail investors in Luxembourg during the grace period. Where the UK UCITS is managed from outside the United Kingdom by an EEA IFM also authorized as an AIFM, then the UK UCITS will be considered an AIF for these purposes and permitted to be marketed to retail investors in Luxembourg under local AIF rules after the grace period.[219]

The one-year delay enables Luxembourg funds to modify their portfolio composition as well as their investment strategies and prospectuses.[220] The law also allows UK Management Companies, authorized as AIFMs, to continue selling their UK UCITS in Luxembourg for maximum one year, until getting a Management Company in the EU. The law will enter into force starting from the date of the United Kingdom's departure from the EU.[221]

Brexit has led investment managers to decide to open their next fund in Luxembourg or Ireland. Luxembourg has a solid reputation as Investment fund domicile and has business-friendly tax systems. UK asset managers may appoint a third-party AIFM in Luxembourg that would

[218] Vysotskaya, V., Vukovich, L., Bissinger, J., Sommarribas, A., & Nienaber, B. (2019). *To be or not to be: How the Luxembourgish government is preparing for Brexit*. https://orbilu.uni.lu/bitstream/10993/39325/1/working%20paper%20brexit-lu.pdf. Accessed 15 August 2020.

[219] Backer, P., & Bauer, E. (2019). Luxembourg. In P. Dickson (Ed.), *The asset management review* (8th ed., pp. 212–229). London: Law Business Research Ltd.

[220] Veeckmans, C. (2019). *New Luxembourg law protects fund sector from Brexit*. https://blog.kpmg.lu/new-luxembourg-law-protects-fund-sector-from-brexit/. Accessed 14 August 2020.

[221] Idem.

manage their EU-based AIFs to continue to have access to the EU passporting regime.

One major advantage for Luxembourg is the SCSp form.[222]

On the other side, Luxemburg's Investment funds benefit from increased flexibility due to new laws introduced by the Government.[223]

UK funds managers have clear advantages in reallocating their business to Luxembourg as it is the largest Investment fund center in Europe and has adequate international human resources and infrastructures. Moreover, most of the UK fund managers already have subsidiaries located in Luxembourg.

The reallocation of UK fund managers to Luxembourg would increase the attractiveness for multinational companies in Luxembourg. This could also mean for Luxembourg an increase in its population and therefore in the real estate prices, possibly also requiring certain adaptations of the infrastructures.

According to ALFI, a number of 23 asset management companies based in the United Kingdom announced that they will move or strengthen their presence in Luxembourg. And several examples are: "JPMorgan, Blackstone, MJ Hudson, Columbia Threadneedle, M&G Investment Ltd."[224]

Since the Brexit referendum, major new inflows reached Dublin and Luxembourg. Thus, "Dublin has received EUR 48 billions of net inflows from the UK since June 2016, with Luxembourg receiving only EUR 23 billion."[225]

Reports acknowledge currently "that Dublin comes up as the clear winner in terms of attracting business from the UK, with 100 firms

[222] Idem.

[223] Idem.

[224] Di Pillo, N. (2019). Pour la première fois depuis plusieurs années, l'industrie luxembourgeoise des fonds d'investissement a enregistré en 2018 une baisse de 2,28% de ses actifs sous gestion. *Luxemburger Wort*. https://www.wort.lu/fr/economie/fonds-premiere-baisse-depuis-2011-5c51b659da2cc1784e33cbce. Accessed 12 August 2020.

[225] Taylor, C. (2019, April 10). Dublin big winner as UK investors place 'wall of money' in offshore funds. *The Irish Times*. https://www.irishtimes.com/business/financial-services/dublin-big-winner-as-uk-investors-place-wall-of-money-in-offshore-funds-1.3855596. Accessed 12 August 2020.

choosing the Irish capital as a post-Brexit location. 60 have chosen Luxembourg, 41 Paris, 40 Frankfurt and 32 Amsterdam."[226]

More recently, the uncertainties surrounding Brexit caused a number of British and international operators with a significant presence in the United Kingdom to relocate all or part of their operations to Luxembourg or to establish Luxembourg investment funds. Of those firms that have publicly communicated their plans, more than 60 firms—half of which are in the asset management industry—have chosen to relocate to Luxembourg.

Companies from all over the world use Luxembourg as their gateway to Europe and the rest of the world. The two countries with the largest market share of assets under management in Luxembourg are the United States and United Kingdom.

As a concluding remark, after the adoption of the AIFM Directive, Luxembourg proposed a new legal structure to be used by investment funds in order to attract international investors and fund managers, a model which comes very close in terms of flexibility and tax-transparency. In spite of the fact that the management rights of investors are more limited than under the UK model, a Luxembourg special limited partnership provides "an efficient structure as regards the time-to market and the absence of regulatory oversight," which "enables fund managers to quickly set up an investment fund and engage in sophisticated, almost unlimited investment strategies."[227] This stands as very important in the post-Brexit era when fund managers and investors are expected to engage in forum-shopping within the EU. Since after leaving the EU the United Kingdom will be considered a third country, UK fund managers are expected "to look for an EU jurisdiction to move their operations to if they wish to market their funds to the EU investors. It goes without saying that Luxembourg offers an interesting choice in terms of a limited

[226] Wright, W., Benson, C., & Hamre, E. F. (2019). Report: Brexit & the City—The impact so far. *New Financial*. https://newfinancial.org/the-impact-of-brexit-on-the-city/. Accessed 12 August 2020.

[227] Repiquet, M. D. (2018). Regulatory competition in European partnership law: A case of alternative investment funds. *The Amsterdam Law Forum, 10*(1). For further data, see Repiquet, M. D. (2018b). Report from Luxembourg: New alternative investment funds regulation in Luxembourg—Basis for an attractive domicile in the post-brexit era? *European Company Law, 15*(1), 25–29.

partnership structure, the importance of which will only increase after the UK exits the EU."[228]

3.6 Malta: Overview of Hedge Funds Regulatory System

3.6.1 *The Funds Regulatory System Evolution in Malta*

In Malta, ISA[229] enacted in 1994[230] sets up a particularly regime regulating the approval of CIS, but also fund administrators, paving this road for the establishment of "retail funds and local fund managers." Six years later, MFSA[231] issued particular standards for the so-called "*Professional Investors Funds*" (PIF) with the purpose of putting Malta in the role of "European hedge fund location."

Currently, the regulatory body responsible for investment services in Malta is the Malta Financial Services Authority (the "MFSA"). According to MFSA, "the Investment Services Act (the "Act") establishes the framework for two types of licenses: Investment Services Licenses and Collective Investment Schemes Licenses. It also transposes the legislation issued by the EU in terms of investment services, including the Markets in Financial Instruments Directive ("MiFID"),[232] the UCITS Directive and the AIFMD."[233] To this end, the MFSA licenses regulate and supervise investment services providers and collective investment schemes. It has also issued (and continues to issue as circumstances require) various sets of dedicated Investment Services Rules which lay down the requirements and conditions relative both to initial licensing and to license holders' ongoing operations.

Summing up, the law and regulations which regulate hedge funds are:

[228] Idem.

[229] The Investment Services Act.

[230] As amended in 2011.

[231] Malta Financial Services Authority.

[232] Directive 2004.39/EC of the European Parliament and of the Council of 21 April 2004 on Markets in Financial Instruments.

[233] Malta Financial Services Authority. (2019a). *A guide to establishing an alternative investment fund manager in Malta*. https://www.mfsa.mt/wp-content/uploads/2019/01/A_Guide_on_Establishing_an_Alternative_Investment_Fund_Manager_in_Malta.pdf. Accessed 16 August 2020.

- The Investment Services Act[234] (as amended) and all subsidiary legislation which are also applied to retail funds.
- The Companies Act of 1995 as amended[235] and all subsidiary legislation which are also applied to retail funds.
- Part A and B of the Rules for Professional Investor Funds (in case of professional investor funds).
- Part A and B of the Rules for Alternative Investor Funds (in case of alternative investment funds).
- The Listing Rules (Admissibility requirements for Collective Investment Schemes)[236] issued by MFSA which are applicable to collective investment schemes listed on the Malta Stock Exchange.

3.6.2 The Maltese Regulatory System: Scope and Objectives

Malta's law on hedge funds is complex and flexible. Most of the island states consider it a model for onshore directive of hedge funds and think international and European measures in regulation of industry would probably bring other countries closer to the Maltese model. Its major advantage is its bilingual legislation. All laws in Malta are issued both in

[234] As amended by Acts: XXIV, XXV of 1995; Legal Notices 191 of 1998 and 46 of 1999; Acts XVII of 2002, IV of 2003, XIII of 2004, XII of 2006; Legal Notice 318 of 2006; Act XX of2007; Legal Notice 425 of 2007; Acts XVII of 2009, XIX of 2010, Xof 2011; Legal Notice 251 of 2013; Act XX of 2013; Legal Notice147 of 2014; Acts XXII of 2014, XXI of 2015, XIX of 2016 and XXXIof 2017, XLIV of 2018 and V of 2020.

[235] By Acts XXIV of 1995, IX, XXX of 1997, XVII of 1998, XXII of 2000, XVII of 2002, IV, IX of 2003, II, XIII of 2004; Legal Notices 390, 391 of2005, 181, 186 of 2006; Acts V, XII of 2006, XV of 2007; 425 of 2007; Acts IX of 2008, III of 2009 and XIX of 2010; Legal Notice 561 of 2010; Acts X and XVI of 2011; Legal Notices 171, 337, 338 of 2012; Acts III, XX of 2013, XXII of 2014; Legal Notice 478 of2014; Acts XXXI, XXXIII of 2015, XIX, XXXVI, LIV of 2016, Act XIXXXI of 2017 and XXXVI of 2018 and XXVI of 2019 and V and XXXI of 2020.

[236] Malta Financial Services Authority. (2019b). *Admissibility requirements for collective investment schemes*. https://www.mfsa.mt/wp-content/uploads/2019/01/Listing-Rules-CHAPTER-8-25.05.pdf. Accessed 12 August 2020.

English and in Maltese,[237] the official languages in the Maltese state.[238] This legislation provides clarity and simplicity of understanding, sometimes absent in some other onshore jurisdictions. An advantage resides in the fact that Malta melded the legal traditions of the continent with the Anglo-Saxon model.[239]

During the last decade and a half, the Maltese regulatory body was thoroughly modernized. This complex regulatory outcome was meant to attract investments from abroad and firms across Malta.

The country has a single financial services regulator, the MFSA. From November 1, 2018, the MFSA also began regulating virtual financial assets.[240] Until 2018, the MFSA additionally housed the Registry of Companies and the Listing Authority. The structure of the MFSA changed in 2019, when, the Maltese Parliament approved amendments to the MFSA Act and to the Financial Markets Act which, according to the MFSA's 2018 Annual Report, "will strengthen and streamline the MFSA's decision-making processes, and boost the supervision of compliance to prevent money laundering and the financing of terrorism."[241] In implementing these changes, the MFSA established: (i) an Executive Committee; (ii) an Enforcement Decisions Committee; (iii) an Enforcement Directorate; (iv) a Financial Crime Compliance Team; (v) an Anti-Money Laundering and Combating the Financing of Terrorism

[237] Malta Financial Services Authority. (2013). *A guide to investment services*. https://www.google.com/url?sa=t&rct=j&q=&esrc=s&source=web&cd=&ved=2ahUKEwin---1tK_rAhVUlFwKHdCVBvkQFjAAegQIBBAB&url=http%3A%2F%2Fwww.mfsa.com.mt%2FGetFile.php%3Ftype%3Dsite%26file%3DPublications%2FBrochures%2FSecurities%2FInvestment%252520Services%252520Brochure04_02_2013.pdf&usg=AOvVaw0etQlo0NgR17vhhOLa8-5y. Accessed 19 March 2020.

[238] Cremona, A. (2010). Malta: Foundations-the new vehicle of choice? *Trusts & Trustees, 16*(6), 479–489.

[239] Galgoczi, B., Lafoucriere, C., & Magnusson, L. (Eds.) (2004). *The enlargement of social Europe—The role of social partners in the European employment strategy*. Brussels: ETUI (pp. 77–95).

[240] Malta Financial Services Authority. (2018b, November). Virtual Financial Assets Act (Chapter 590 of the Laws of Malta) "MFSA Virtual Financial Assets". http://www.justiceservices.gov.mt/DownloadDocument.aspx?app=lom&itemid=12872&l=1. Accessed 13 August 2020.

[241] Malta Financial Services Authority. (2018a). *Annual report 2018*. Management%20Report%202017.pdf. Accessed 16 August 2020.

Committee (AML/CFT); (vi) a Risk Committee; and (vii) a Financial Services Stakeholder Panel.[242]

In contrast to many of its counterparts, it can quickly modify the existing rules and change the old ones in order to make sure that regulation complies with industry innovations. The principal proposer and driver of new financial services legislative initiatives, MFSA succeeds in winning new business within the tough competition by ensuring of both a robust and yet highly flexible regulatory framework.

Generally, the legislation makes available a wide-ranging, flexible regulatory structure for the establishment, licensing, and marketing of all kinds of CIS and institutional funds and investment service providers. The laws also provide a guideline for several selected financial processes of non-credit institutions and for the establishment, but also multinational identification. Maltese company law[243] is side by side with all applicable EU corporation laws. The island state is well-known for the prompt adoption and harmonization of EU directives. This means the state is fully compatible with all EU legislation and that it provides companies established in Malta many of the benefits these laws provide to companies thriving to develop in other EU member states.

In addition to the adoption of EU directives, Malta's laws also comply with OECD provisions on the control and stop of money laundering[244] and insider dealing.

The government considers that foreign investors are completely reassured by the consolidation of the various provisions in Maltese law on professional secrecy, without obstructing the supervision of fiscal and regulatory compliance or the investigation of serious crimes such as money laundering and insider dealing.

Malta encourages an environment that stimulates the development of investment in a professional and sound manner. The protection of

[242] Idem.

[243] Which is essentially based on the UK's company law.

[244] Prevention of Money Laundering Act. (1994). Act XIX of 1994 as amended by: Act II of 1998; Legal Notice 71 of 1999; Acts XXXI of 2001, III of 2002, and III and XIII of 2004; Legal Notice 176 of 2005; Acts VI of 2005 and XXVIII of 2006; Legal Notice 425 of 2007; Act XXXI of 2007; Legal Notice 105 of 2008; Act VII of 2010; Legal Notice 426 of 2012; and Acts XXXVIII of 2014, III, VIII of 2015, XXVIII of 2017, XLII of 2018, VII and XXXI of 2019 and I and VIII of 2020. http://justiceservices.gov.mt/DownloadDocument.aspx?app=lom&itemid=8842&l=1. Accessed 13 August 2020.

investors' interests is extremely important. This shows that MFSA has been given full powers to act. At the same time, the MFSA understands the importance of enabling the financial services, and especially the fund sector to autonomously innovate but also develop new products.

Whenever pleased with a candidate or firm candidate, the MFSA offers a certificate, each of its principal and secondary connected parts are "fit and proper." Generally, there are three criteria that need to be fulfilled: integrity, competence, and solvency.

In spite of the minute legislation, the culture existing in Malta tends to make things happen rather than stop them. Combined with the accessibility and proactive development at the MFSA, this makes Malta an alternative jurisdiction by many funds, and especially start-ups.

3.6.3 The Advantages and Disadvantages of the Maltese Regulatory System

The small Mediterranean financial center of Malta "prides itself on innovation. The latest trend to be embraced is technology-themed investment, with the launch of virtual currency funds, which regulators at the Malta Financial Services Authority (MFSA) hope will attract new business."[245]

Hedge funds managers consider that the regulation in Malta is very flexible and also knowledgeable. Its rivals do not look as good as Malta. Although Malta is a long way behind Luxembourg and Ireland, the jurisdiction is moving in the right direction and the country's advantages of low cost and highly skilled workforce, together with an accessible and flexible regulator will attract more funds.

Even if the cost advantage is transitory and will eventually disappear as Malta's economic growth equals that of its EU counterparts, it does provide the jurisdiction a short-term advantage that Malta is eager to exploit. The domicile-related costs in Malta are lower by a half to a third than in the other states of Europe. However, cost is not the only important issue for hedge fund managers and promoters of the island. The MFSA has made a name for flexibility together with meticulous attention to detail. Although the regulation was considered too strict by many—especially as compared to Luxembourg and even Ireland—in a world

[245] Bender, Y. (2019). Malta fears fallout from disorderly Brexit. *Professional Wealth Management*. https://search-proquest-com.am.e-nformation.ro/docview/2210967341?accountid=136549. Accessed 12 July 2020.

distressed by negligent regulation, it is quickly gaining advocates. As an onshore EU authority with advantageous tax rates could make Malta win even more businesses during the next period. Even though the total number of funds domiciled in the jurisdiction is still small as compared to the more established centers, the industry started to grow.

Malta is creating a niche for itself. This state builds its reputation as the jurisdiction chosen by smaller, start-up funds that consider the high costs and crowded service sectors of Dublin and Luxembourg to be unfriendly. Under the circumstances of a cost-dependent world, funds intend to show investors that their goal is to keep management fees low. Indeed, in a recent report, it is stated that "its services sector regarding financial services [...] has seen stable growth however financial services have been in focus for the nation considering recent tax avoidance discussions in Europe, due to the countries low tax policies."[246] In Malta, size is not important.

3.6.4 Could a More Regulated Hedge Funds Industry at European Level Lead to an Increase of This Sector?

MFSA is considered stricter as compared to Ireland and Luxembourg, although it has a reputation for approachable and flexible authority. Malta's position is very good to capitalize on its reputation, as well as its clear legislation. The real challenge for Malta will be to ensure that it has the necessary skills to provide quality services for the industry. Malta's legislation is pragmatic and well-organized and at the same time it provides strong and efficient regulation.

The Maltese regulatory authorities have stated that they are committed to guarantee market participation in compliance with regulations but, at the same time, they have confirmed a pro-business attitude and the adaptability that can only survive in a small-sized jurisdiction. As part of the EU, Malta is almost certainly closer to Ireland or Luxembourg in terms of strength and depth of its rules than Bermuda or the Caribbean jurisdictions. Of course, regulation within the EU is more coherent and stronger than that in more classical "offshore" countries. On the other hand, as mentioned above, Malta enjoys the advantage of being a small

[246] Syeda, A., Syeda, A. F., & Latha, K. (2020). Impact of loan portfolio diversification on Central Bank performance and risk mitigation. *International Journal of Management, 11*(5), 644–661.

jurisdiction, which has the pragmatic complete authority in implementing legislation and regulation. The Maltese regulator continuously encourages more custodians to establish in their jurisdiction.

3.6.5 The AIFM Directive Impact on the Maltese Regulatory System

According to Zerafa and Scicluna, "Malta was the first EU Member State to complete the transposition of the AIFMD into national law and started accepting applications from start-up AIFMs as of the date the AIFMD entered into force."[247]

Lately, Malta has a reputation of home-based EU land, which has the ability to draw together investment from funds in Europe. The AIFMD regulation appeared like a major opportunity for Malta to take place as one of Europe's prime financial centers. According to Lawrence Gonzi, in 2012, Malta "ranked among the top five emerging financial centers in the world in the City of London's Global Financial Index."[248]

Malta provides a perfect entry opportunity for hedge funds managers who desire to establish an onshore fund, because the Maltese law is strict and in line with EU requirements. Additionally, the MFSA has proved itself practical and business-friendly, providing an active support to find a key within the context of the laws and legislations.

As the Finance Minister, Tonio Fenech, said, "Malta has witnessed a rapid growth in the number of domiciled funds in the past year,"[249] a tendency which will probably continue in the years to come. Malta's pragmatic approach to regulating its funds industry, its growing economy, its deep pool of talent (both local and overseas), its small but well-connected ecosystem of high-quality service providers, all of whom understand the cost pressures and demands of hedge fund managers, and its range of fund structuring options to meet the different distribution and marketing

[247] Zerafa, A., Scicluna, M. C., & Piazza, S. (2015). L'impatto dell'articolo 19 della Direttiva AIFM sul framework della valutazione degli asset. *MondoAlternative*. https://ganadoadvocates.com/wp-content/uploads/2015/04/MondoAlternative-Malta-Dossier.pdf. Accessed 12 August 2020.

[248] Opening Speech by the Hon Lawrence Gonzi, Prime Minister, During the Finance Malta 3rd Annual Conference—Floriana—Friday 30th April 2010. https://opm.gov.mt/finance_malta?l=2. Accessed 9 March 2012.

[249] Fenech, T. (2012, March 7). Malta's minister of finance, economy and investment. *Times of Malta*. https://timesofmalta.com/articles/view/malta-witnesses-rapid-growth-in-domiciled-funds.410105. Accessed 12 March 2020.

needs of managers, are all key ingredients. And as UK fund managers look for a Plan B in response to Brexit, all the signs would appear to be that Malta is primed and ready to welcome UK managers with open arms.[250]

In a research[251] which investigates the impact of the Alternative Investment Fund Managers Directive (AIFMD) on the financial services industry after its transposition into Maltese national law,[252] it is stated that the aim of the Directive was that of increasing investor protection and confidence, at the same time being seen as a change that would bring about major shifts not only for local industry investors but for the entire fund industry. According to this study, "so far, the AIFMD has certainly benefitted investors through improved transparency yet it has also significantly increased costs for market players as a result. The growth and reputation of the financial sector appears to have been affected negatively over the short-term. But [...] there is still time and the possibility for it to yield further benefits; a view that is strongly endorsed by local entities, who believe that certain benefits have already been gained through features such as the ability to 'passport' alternative investment funds (AIFs) throughout the European Union (EU)."[253] This study also found that major impacts occurred in relation to depository requirements, risk management, valuation, transparency, and marketing.

However, one thing should be remembered: the Maltese hedge funds industry is still significantly small as compared to medium-sized hedge funds markets in Europe and not only. At the same time, Malta's industry attracts especially small hedge funds.

3.6.6 *Brexit Impact on the Maltese Hedge Funds*

According to a recent article, "Malta's low costs, innovative mindset and robust regulatory environment bode well for its future as a financial center, but the island worries about the potential impact of Brexit

[250] Williams, J. (2018). *Malta in a post-Brexit world*. https://www.privateequitywire.co.uk/2018/06/26/265711/malta-post-brexit-world. Accessed 12 September 2019.

[251] Sammut Alessi, D. (2016). *The impacts of the Alternative Investment Fund Managers Directive (AIFMD) on the Maltese financial sector*. https://www.um.edu.mt/library/oar//handle/123456789/13718. Accessed 17 August 2020.

[252] On June 27, 2013.

[253] Sammut Alessi, D. (2016). Op. Cit.

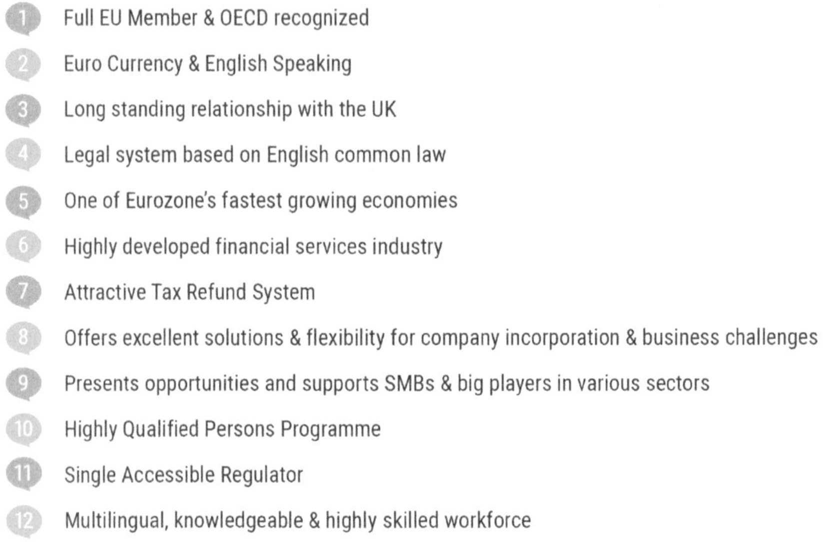

Fig. 3.10 12 reasons to choose Malta (*Source* Werber & Partner 2020)

shock waves."[254] In a similar line, recent studies found "12 reasons to choose Malta," which can be found in Fig. 3.10.

Therefore, Malta can stand as a viable solution for investors post-Brexit, particularly if we consider "Malta's straightforward and transparent process, constructive attitude and ever-growing financial services industry offers the leanest, pro-business jurisdiction in Europe." In addition, the Maltese legal system is very much based on English common law, which makes this jurisdiction even more appealing for UK hedge fund services managers. Also, this prompts Malta to provide the best of each system and by consequence to offer asset managers "with the opportunity to smoothly continue their activities within the EU."[255] Therefore, it can be said the Single Accessible Regulator is very attractive, being

[254] Malta fears fallout from disorderly Brexit. (2019). *Professional Wealth Management 16*. https://search-proquest-com.am.e-nformation.ro/docview/2210967341?accountid=136549. Accessed 12 July 2020.

[255] Werber & Partner. (2020). *Malta—A viable Brexit solution for businesses*. https://www.drwerner.com/en/malta-a-viable-brexit-solution-for-businesses/. Accessed 12 July 2020.

modeled on the then UK FSA: "Credits for Malta's success as a financial services hub merely go the Malta Financial Services Authority ('MFSA'). The adoption of an open-door policy not only provides asset managers with the opportunity to directly and informally communicate with the Regulator, but the latter offers instant advice and is flexible to incentivize those who wish to do business in Malta. Additionally, to decrease bureaucracy, the MFSA is presently improving the manner it regulates and serves individuals and businesses."[256]

Malta is currently a niche destination. Still, if we consider Malta's residency scheme, namely the new Golden Visa Programme,[257] this might turn into a key aspect for investors when choosing their next state of relocation. Other way round, Malta has often been named "Europe's gateway"[258] due to offering "third-country nationals with visa-free access to the European Schengen Area."[259]

In the MFSA's report "Supervision Priorities 2020," as far as Brexit is concerned, both EU and the MFSA keep on preparing for both soft and hard Brexit scenario, the major focus of the latter being on managing the immediate risks and key aspects. According to this report, the impact of a no-deal Brexit on licensed entities on investment services has been assessed by the MFSA in 2019 and in this respect different circulars on this subject have been issued. According to this report, "the MFSA will continue to monitor the level of preparedness, taking into account the public communications issued by the European Commission and the ESAs. In a no-deal Brexit scenario, the MFSA will focus on ensuring that the immediate risks and issues are managed. In the scenario where a withdrawal agreement is in place, the MFSA will have more time to implement any relevant actions in relation to Brexit, taking into account the discussions on the future relationship being held between the political

[256] Idem.

[257] Additionally to the citizenship-by-investment program.

[258] Goudner, N., & Scicluna, L. (2018). Malta: UK's gateway to Europe. *International Tax Review*, 29, 53. https://heinonline.org/HOL/LandingPage?handle=hein.journals/intaxr29&div=59&id=&page. Accessed 15 August 2020.

[259] Werber & Partner. (2020). *Malta—A viable Brexit solution for businesses*. https://www.drwerner.com/en/malta-a-viable-brexit-solution-for-businesses/. Accessed 12 July 2020.

negotiators."[260] According to the MFSA, the most important priorities for 2020 are going to be: on the one hand relocations and local setups, and on the other hand, the United Kingdom firms passporting in Malta but also Malta firms passporting in the United Kingdom.

For the first priority, the duties of the MFSA are going to be "monitoring and applying a substance-based approach to any applications for entities relocating from the UK to the Malta, withdrawal from the EU. The Authority will also ensure that the business models and structures that involve UK entities can continue to adhere to supervisory expectations. This will be done through meetings and engagement with applicants and licensed entities."[261]

As far as the second objective is concerned, the MFSA is going to keep on monitoring important entities which "operate on a cross-border basis and their applications for the domestic or UK TPR, as well as the exposure of local market participants and clients to the UK. This will include the implementation of Malta TPR for securities, engagement with UK authorities on the UK TPR and engagement with affected entities on their contingency plans."[262]

3.7 Switzerland: Overview of Hedge Funds Regulatory System

3.7.1 *The Funds Regulatory System Evolution in Switzerland*

With its long tradition of banking and finance, Switzerland is one of the leaders at the international level in the asset management industry. Swiss asset management constitutes one of the main pillars of the Swiss financial center.

The asset management industry in Switzerland is heterogeneous and applies different business models. Large banking institutions active in wealth management (private banking) coexist with a number of smaller niche players.

[260] Malta Financial Services Authority. (2019c). *Supervision priorities 2020*. https://www.mfsa.mt/wp-content/uploads/2019/12/20191204_Supervision_Priorities-2020.pdf. Accessed 17 August 2020.

[261] Idem.

[262] Idem.

There is no specific legal regime that applies to hedge funds and private equity in Switzerland. Assets invested in hedge fund products represent approximately 5% of the assets invested in Switzerland at present time. This is partially due to the fact that fewer restrictions are applied to hedge funds than any other investment vehicles in terms of the investment types they can make.[263]

The main Swiss legal and regulatory overview in terms of hedge funds is represented by the "*Collective Investment Schemes Act*" of June 23, 2006 ("CISA") enacted on January 1, 2007 and adopted by the Swiss Federal Council and the "*Swiss Financial Market Supervisory Authority*" ("FINMA").[264] FINMA issued several circulars relevant decisions, respectively, on August 29, 2007 updated guides on public offering and private placement enacted on October 1, 2007, regarding the private employment of non-Swiss collective investment schemes.

Up to now, Switzerland has been a less significant domicile for single hedge funds. Still, Switzerland does represent an important market for the placement of funds of offshore hedge fund products and an attractive jurisdiction for the management and distribution of foreign hedge funds. The Cayman Islands stands as the central incorporation place for the biggest part of Swiss-managed hedge funds.

The regulatory framework of hedge funds in Switzerland both for foreign hedge funds as well as Swiss funds are the following:

- Swiss Collective Investment Schemes Act (CISA).[265]
- Swiss Collective Investment Schemes Ordinance (CISO).[266]

[263] Senn, M. (2010). *The regulation of hedge funds, private equity and sovereign wealth funds, hedge funds, private equity and sovereign funds*. https://www.researchgate.net/publication/228126099_The_Regulation_of_Hedge_Funds_Private_Equity_and_Sovereign_Wealth_Funds. Accessed 16 August 2020.

[264] The FINMA replaced the Swiss Federal Banking Commission (SFBC) as the regulator responsible for the oversight of the financial markets as of January 2009.

[265] CISA. (2006). Federal Act of 23 June 2006 on Collective Investment Schemes. Collective Investment Schemes Act (CISA), which came into force on 1 January 2007, replacing the Federal Act on Investment Funds (Investment Fund Act, IFA) of 18 March 1994. https://www.admin.ch/opc/en/classified-compilation/20052154/index.html. Accessed 12 August 2020.

[266] Ordinance of 22 November 2006 on Collective Investment Schemes Collective Investment Schemes Ordinance, CISO.

- Swiss Collective Investment Schemes Ordinance of the Swiss Financial Market Supervisory Authority (FINMA) (CISO-FINMA).[267]
- Swiss Ordinance of FINMA on Bankruptcy of Collective Investment Schemes (CISBO-FINMA).

The revised versions of the CISA, the CISO, and CISBO-FINMA entered into force on March 1, 2013. In addition, "the revised provisions in the law governing qualified investors and the Key Investor Information Document (KIID) replacing the simplified prospectus (Art. 10, 76 and 77 CISA) are also part of this recent revision and entered into force subsequently after a set delay on June 1, 2013. The same applies to the provisions on the duty to keep documentary records when distributing collective investment schemes set out in both the law and the ordinance (Art. 24 para. 3 CISA and Art. 34a CISO), which entered into force on January 1, 2014 and have been added to the Code of Conduct."[268]

In addition, FINMA issued several circulars which are also part of the current regulations:

- FINMA Circ. 2013/9 Distribution of Collective Investment Schemes.
- FINMA Circ. 2013/8 Market conduct rules.
- FINMA Circ. 2013/3 Auditing.
- FINMA Circ. 2009/1 Guidelines on asset management.
- FINMA Circ. 2008/10 Self-regulation as a minimum standard.

For Swiss hedge funds the regulatory bodies are the: Swiss Financial Market Supervisory Authority (FINMA) and Swiss Funds and Asset Management Association (SFAMA).

FINMA is the competent regulatory body and supervisory authority for hedge funds domiciled in Switzerland, being responsible for the:

[267] Ordinance of 27 August 2014 of the Swiss Financial Market Supervisory Authority on Collective Investment Schemes (FINMA Collective Investment Schemes Ordinance, CISO-FINMA).

[268] SFAMA. (2020). *Collective investment schemes legislation*. Swiss Fund and Asset Management Association. https://www.sfama.ch/en/regulation/collective-investment-schemes-legislation. Accessed 15 August 2020.

- authorization and supervision of fund management companies, asset managers of Swiss collective investment schemes and foreign collective investment schemes, distributors and representatives of foreign collective investment schemes[269];
- the approval of fund products.[270]

SFAMA is the representative industry association of collective investment schemes and their managers in Switzerland. The industry standards of SFAMA are of great significance. Indeed, the importance of SFAMA was admitted by FINMA, which recognized plenty of industry standards as minimum standards for all market participants.

In the past years, the Swiss financial market regulation changed very much. Existing rules already have been complemented or replaced by new laws, and we refer to the following:

- Financial Market Infrastructure Act (FMIA).
- FinSA.
- FinIA.

The FMIA entered into force on January 1, 2016, while the Swiss Federal Council's dispatch including revised draft bills for the FinSA and FinIA was published in late 2015. The Swiss Parliament adopted both bills in the final votes on June 15, 2018, which are expected to enter into force on January 1, 2020.

The latest regulatory change in Switzerland occurred on January 1, 2020, when, two financial laws: the Financial Services Act (FINSA) and the Financial Institutions Act (FINIA) were enacted. Their enactment was done by taking into account the global trends to regulate and supervise financial services and their providers.[271] This "new Swiss regulation introduces prudential supervision for asset managers and trustees who have only been subject to Anti-Money Laundering (AML) regulation

[269] Section 4 FMSA.

[270] If approval is required for distributing the respective fund product in or from Switzerland.

[271] Such as Markets in Financial Instruments Directive (MiFID) II, Prospectus Directive, Packaged Retail and Insurance-based Investment Products (PRIIPs).

in Switzerland until now. Foreign trustees will also be affected by the FINSA/FINIA if they engage in activities in Switzerland."[272]

The FinSA[273] stands as "a new modernised prospectus regime"[274] for the capital markets in Switzerland. Summing up some customizations for debt and equity instruments, but also for collective investment schemes, derivatives, and structured products, this new Swiss prospectus regulation intends to be applied to all financial instruments, in a uniform manner.

3.7.2 Swiss Regulatory Regime: Scope and Objectives

Current challenges to the asset management industry in Switzerland include a wave of new regulatory activity and regulatory developments occurring at the EU level. The Swiss legal and regulatory framework is being adjusted on an ongoing basis to ensure its euro-compatibility to keep it in line with international standards and to enhance the protection granted to investors.

The regulatory framework for the regulated hedge funds focuses mainly on investor protection. This is achieved primarily through transparency and control of the professional qualifications of fund managers and representatives.

The protection of investment advisory and asset managers' clients has been at the top of the Swiss regulator's agenda for several years now, and will be one of the most important legislative projects in the financial services sector for the years to come.

In November 2015, the Federal Council published the draft of the Financial Services Act (FinSA) and the Financial Institution Act (FinIA). The FinSA deals with the relationship between the financial intermediary and investors, essentially provides for rules of conduct aiming at protecting investors upon the provision, upon a professional basis, of financial services or financial instruments in Switzerland. Those rules

[272] Blumenfeld, M. (2020). FINSA/FINIA-new regulation for foreign trustees in Switzerland. *Trusts & Trustees, 26*(5), 400–403. https://doi.org/10.1093/tandt/ttaa025.

[273] The new regime came into effect on January 1, 2020, some provisions of the new regime applying with immediate effect; others only after certain transition periods.

[274] Bosch, R., Leisinger, B., & Janett-Seiler, P. (2020). Exchange offers under Switzerland's new prospectus regime: A guide. *International Financial Law Review*. https://www.iflr.com/article/b1mb1yfxdfz5m8/exchange-offers-under-switzerlands-new-prospectus-regime-a-guide. Accessed 15 July 2020.

are primarily based on the EU's MiFID regulations. By contrast, the FinIA includes provisions concerning the relationship between the financial intermediary and the regulatory authority, and imposes general licensing and organizational requirements, irrespective of the authorization regime. The Parliament adopted both bills in the final votes on June 15, 2018. During its meeting on November 6, 2019, the Federal Council brought the FinSA and the FinIA—together with the implementing ordinances—into force with effect from January 1, 2020.[275]

Scholars consider that the main aim of the two regulations is to increase "customer protection in the financial market"[276] but also investor protection.[277] Besides increasing investor protection, the FinSA aims at ensuring that "Swiss financial market law complies with applicable international standards and that a level playing field for the supervised financial service providers is created through uniform competitive conditions. Owing to the close intertwining of the Swiss financial market with European financial markets, the rules of the FinSA are based on EU regulations such as the Markets in Financial Instruments Directive II, the Prospectus Directive and the PRIIPs regulation, which simplifies matters for financial service providers serving clients both in Switzerland as well as in the EU."[278] It should also be noted that, although the FinSA tries to intervene intertwine European directives into the Swiss law, it also aims at maintaining special characteristics of the Swiss financial market and as a consequence the simple adoption of the European regulatory is not done as a whole. Under the current law, financial service providers are treated differently with regard to the intensity of the regulation and their

[275] FINMA. (2020). *FinSA/FinIA: Follow-up regulation by FINMA*. Swiss Financial Market Supervisory Authority (FINMA). https://www.finma.ch/en/news/2020/02/20200207-mm-finiv/. Accessed 16 August 2020.

[276] Bosch, R., Leisinger, B., & Janett-Seiler, P. (2020). Exchange offers under Switzerland's new prospectus regime: A guide. *International Financial Law Review*. https://www.iflr.com/article/b1mb1yfxdfz5m8/exchange-offers-under-switzerlands-new-prospectus-regime-a-guide. Accessed 15 July 2020.

[277] Goekmen, A. S. (2019). Where is the safe haven? *The International Family Offices Journal*, 13. Globe Law and Business. www.globelawandbusiness.com. Accessed 13 August 2020, p. 53.

[278] Liebi. M., & Haldemann, M. (2020). The new rules for providing financial services in Switzerland: Fundamental changes to the cross-border provision of financial services for non-Swiss financial service providers and producers of financial instruments for the Swiss market. *Business Law International, 21*(1), 23–40.

supervision. This inconsistent design of the regulatory requirements for financial service providers leads to unequal conditions of competition for the provision of financial services.

Apart from investor protection, transparency was also taken into account, as a means of insuring investor protection. However, under FinSA, disadvantages exist "in the areas of code of conduct and product regulations. For example, it is common that clients are not well-informed about financial service providers and their services or products and are not being asked about their knowledge and experience. Furthermore, prospectuses used in public market transactions are often very detailed and hard for clients to understand. The FinSA addresses this issue by increasing information requirements and financial service providers have to, *inter alia*, give clients appropriate explanations and advice and to supply a KID to retail clients with regard to financial instruments."[279] This increased client protection raised many controversies, but this new regulation supports clients in a manner which is "more tailored to their needs when engaging in businesses on the financial markets and thereby enhanced level client protection is afforded in comparison to the *status quo*."[280]

3.7.3 *The Advantages and Disadvantages of the Swiss Regulatory Regime*

Switzerland stands for neutrality and "a strong financial services sector,"[281] also being "one of the oldest tax havens in the world.[282] Lighter regulation and less costly compliance in present Switzerland appeared to be an alternative to more strictly regulated EU member states from the perspective of asset management. But with the new regulations enacted, namely FinSA and FinIA and also with the fact that "recognition of Swiss stock market equivalence was discontinued by the European

[279] Idem.

[280] Dispatch on the Financial Services Act (FinSA) and Financial Institutions Act (FinIA) of 4 November 2015, Federal Gazette 2015, p. 8912 et seq, p. 8919.

[281] Syeda, A., Syeda, A. F., & Latha, K. (2020). Impact of loan portfolio diversification on Central Bank performance and risk mitigation. *International Journal of Management, 11*(5), 644–661.

[282] Idem.

Union on June 30, 2019,"[283] new administrative burdens were put on investors.

If we speak of disadvantages, the FINIA "increases the regulatory and compliance burden for foreign trustees in Switzerland. However, the accomplishable standards allow even very small trustees to meet the regulatory expectations of the FINIA in time."[284]

On the opposite side, there are also positive aspects of the new legislative measures adopted residing in the fact that they offer more clarity, which is of great help, particularly "in a cross-border context, where expectations by the different competent regulators are sometimes difficult to align. A stringent operational setup (for example in respect to intra-group services) is key to minimize the administrative burden."[285]

"Except for the AIFM Directive, Switzerland is a very stable country."[286] It is a country with very stable and static regulatory and tax system.

3.7.4 A More Regulated Hedge Funds Industry at European Level Could Lead to an Increase of This Sector?

Switzerland is very important with respect to investor base, enabling hedge funds to be close to their main client segments, which is a vital advantage, especially in times of crisis when demand for accessibility of managers increases. Switzerland hosts a wide range of hedge funds (FoHF), and it also provides managers broad exposure to institutional clients, in terms of sizeable pension funds, family offices and very large diversity of independent asset managers. Apart from this proximity to customers, Switzerland overruns many of its European counterparts in terms of political stability and quality of life, which are frequently considered by managers as a central reason for relocating.

The expected hedge funds migration from London to Switzerland and the exodus of entire organizations has not started yet, but managers are expected to keep opening offices in Switzerland.

[283] Idem.

[284] Blumenfeld, M. (2020). FINSA/FINIA-new regulation for foreign trustees in Switzerland. *Trusts & Trustees, 26*(5), 400–403. https://doi.org/10.1093/tandt/ttaa025.

[285] Idem.

[286] Ibid.

While profitable functions such as trading will be moved to Switzerland, many hedge funds have started, and are likely to continue, to keep at least parts of their staff in their original locations. Interest in Swiss-domiciled fund structures could increase because Switzerland is not directly under the jurisdiction of the AIFM Directive. The Swiss Collective Investment Schemes Act also provides relevant favorable circumstances with its moderately flexible investment boundaries for alternative funds.

In Switzerland, as in many other jurisdictions, hedge funds were carefully scrutinized after the financial crisis of 2007–2008. Thus, FINMA carefully analyzed clients in Switzerland being impacted by the subsidiaries of Lehman Brothers Holdings Inc. and found that clients were exposed to high risk.[287]

Investigations proved "the existence of a big deficiency in the law: the former Swiss Federal Act on Collective Investment Schemes, in force at the time, provided that a simplified prospectus was to be made available at the issuance of a structured product in the secondary market phase."[288]

Based on these findings, FINMA reached the conclusion that, at that time, investor protection provisions were not efficient.[289] Thus, after issuing several recommendations, CISA was revised, including Section 5 that is currently found in the law and which entered into force on March 31, 2013.[290]

In spite of the regulatory changes from 2013, the framework of financial regulations in Switzerland, including hedge funds regulations were still seen as inconsistent and incomplete, especially those dealing with behavioral rules and the regulation of financial products.[291] The

[287] FINMA. (2010). *Madoff deal and distribution of Lehman products: Impact on investment advisory and wealth management activities*. Report of 2 March 2010. Swiss Financial Market Supervisory Authority (FINMA), pp. 4–21.

[288] Lecocq, D., & Cesareo-Hostettler, L. (2019). The structured products law review—Switzerland. *The Law Reviews*. https://thelawreviews.co.uk/edition/the-structured-products-law-review/1212191/switzerland. Accessed 16 August 2020.

[289] FINMA report of 2 March 2010, p. 3/21.

[290] RO 2013 585, p. 603.

[291] Federal Council. (2015, November 4). Message on the Financial Services Act (FIDLEG) and the Financial Institutions Act (FINIG) (pp. 8–112).

prospectus information was seen as divergent and incomplete, too detailed and not clear enough for clients.[292]

In respect of the above, the aim of the legislator when adopting FinSA was to provide a clear and comprehensible framework for investors through imposing disclosure requirements on financial service providers.[293] Scholars consider that "the new prospectus regime introduced by FinSA and FinSO will positively impact the Swiss capital markets in the long-run."[294]

3.7.5 The Impact of the AIFM Directive on the Swiss Regulatory Regime

The AIFM Directive does not apply because Switzerland is not a member of the EU.[295]

The AIFM Directive had a direct impact on the Swiss alternative market: Switzerland has become more appealing to the EU managers, mainly to those managers in the United Kingdom that seem to be most adversely affected by the new rules, besides the impending tax reform adopted in the country. Since the implementation of the AIFM Directive, local consultants and lawyers have been overwhelmed with inquiries from UK asset managers questioning about setting up in Switzerland. The Swiss law has become more attractive as a result of its light regulation background. Cantons such as Zug or the city of Pfaeffikon in the canton of Zurich will become more attractive to hedge fund managers from the United Kingdom. Nevertheless, recommended changes to be incorporated within the laws of investment market in Switzerland raised

[292] Idem.

[293] Abegglen, S., & Bianchi, L. (2016). *Regulation of the point of sale—An update on the rules of conduct of financial services providers under the proposed FIDLEG*. CapLaw-2016-3. Swiss Capital Markets Law. https://www.caplaw.ch/2016/regulation-of-the-point-of-sale-an-update-on-the-rules-of-conduct-of-financial-services-providers-under-the-proposed-fidleg/. Accessed 15 August 2020.

[294] Weber, Ph., & Del Vecchio, Ch. (2020). *Licensing of the reviewing bodies pursuant to the financial services act—An initial view*. CapLaw-2020-21. https://www.caplaw.ch/2020/licensing-of-the-reviewing-bodies-pursuant-to-the-financial-services-act-an-initial-view/#more-2328. Accessed 16 August 2020.

[295] Risoldi, M. (2018). *Distributing foreign investment funds in Switzerland*. https://www.aima.org/article/distributing-foreign-investment-funds-in-switzerland.html. Accessed 13 July 2020.

several concerns because European regulation is already very strict and it seems that this country intends to implement even stricter regulations.

Nearly nine years ago, the European legislature responded to the financial market crisis of 2007/2008 with the AIFM Directive, and European Alternative Investment Funds Manager (AIFM) proposed comprehensive and uniform regulation and supervision. The new Swiss regulation enforced on January 1, 2020 should unfold this single legal framework for all AIFM validity, i.e., it will also extend to AIFM, which has its headquarters in a third country (such as Switzerland). The future extension of the passport regime to asset managers from third countries poses numerous challenges for Swiss cross-border asset managers. There is, however, a certain amount of tension, especially Swiss AIFM doubling up and possibly colliding surveillance arrangements.

1. EU passport for Swiss asset manager

The AIFMD is, due to its wide scope of application, which regulates the regulation of relations with third countries and the competence of the member states, of great importance also for the Swiss fund industry. The scope of application of the AIFMD on AIFM based outside the EU (so-called non-EU AIFM[296]), insofar as there is a relevant reference to the EU area. This also affects the asset managers in Switzerland of the third state regulation of the AIFMD. As a non-EU AIFM, they are directly subordinated to the AIFMD. The current rules for market access of AIFM (for example Swiss asset managers) domiciled in third countries provide for the expulsion of the so-called (EU and non-EU) AIF national Private Placement Regimes shares managed by them. However, it is up to the discretion of the member states to allow such private placements at all.[297] In view of Switzerland, ESMA has already made several positive

[296] A "non-EU AIFM" is an AIFM that is not an EU AIFM (Art. 4 Para. 1 from AIFMD). The term "EU AIFM" denotes an AIFM with a registered office in one Member State (Art. 4 Para. 1 point 1 AIFMD).

[297] See Art. 42 Para. 1 AIFMD. If a member state permits such private placements, the AIFMD sets certain minimum requirements with regard to the third country and the AIFM domiciled there (cf. Art. 42 Paragraphs 1 and 2 AIFMD). The practice of private placement regimes in the individual member states was, however, extremely restrictive even before the AIFM Directive was passed; With the introduction of the AIFMD, various countries have narrowed their previous private placement regimes even more or in fact canceled them (Haldner, F. [2016]. Wie wird Schweizer Private Equity Management

recommendations.[298] It is now up to the European Commission to issue a corresponding delegate act and to extend the application of the administrative passport to AIFM from Switzerland (and possibly other states), for which the AIFMD actually had a three-month deadline after the entry of the positive recommendation by the ESMA.[299] In view of the United Kingdom's exit from the EU, the Commission's decision will continue to be delayed. Against the background of Brexit, the whole concept of third country relations should be examined in the light of more integration in supervision within the EU-27. This ensures that all financial sector risks are properly managed.[300]

For Swiss asset managers, the extension of the passport regime would be of great benefit if: after approval as a non-EU AIFM in accordance with Article 37 of the AIFMD could, in their reference member state or cross-border with EU passport, either manage EU-AIF and/or shares the AIF managed by them according to the requirements of Article 39 or 40 of the AIFMD after they have passed the notification procedure[301] in the EU.

Swiss AIFMs would be subject to the AIFMD directly if they were to use the EU passport. While the recognition of equivalence provided for in other legal acts implies that the financial market players concerned are generally only subject to their domestic legal system, the future passport regime according to the AIFMD means for Swiss asset managers that they—based on the authorization and supervision by FINMA as well as the approval of the competent authorities of their reference member

exportfähig? In D Gericke [Ed.], *Private equity* [pp. 7–18]. Zurich: Schulthess Verlag, p. 12).

[298] See ESMA's advice to the European Parliament, the Council and the Commission on the application of the AIFMD passport to non-EU AIFMs and AIFs, July 30, 2015, ESMA / 2015/1236 (ESMA Advice 2015), no. 114; ESMA's advice to the European Parliament, the Council and the Commission on the application of the AIFMD passport to non-EU AIFMs and AIFs, 9/12/2016, ESMA / 2016/1140 (ESMA Advice 2016), no. 129.

[299] Art. 67 para. 3 AIFMD.

[300] COM. (2017, September 20). 542 final Communication from the Commission to the European Parliament, the Council, the European Central Bank, the European Economic and Social Committee and the Committee of the Regions Reinforcing integrated supervision to strengthen Capital Markets Union and financial integration in a changing environment, Brussels.

[301] Art. 39 Paragraphs 2 and 4 as well as Art. 40 Paragraphs 3 and 5, AIFMD.

state—basically have to observe both the requirements of the Swiss collective investment scheme and those of the AIFM Directive. This results in a certain tension, as Swiss AIFMs could possibly be subject to double or even conflicting requirements with regard to authorization, supervision, and enforcement. The double burden of possibly diverging regulations will also (compared to the equivalence approach) cause additional work that will ultimately be passed on to the customer. The less the regulations in the EU and Switzerland congruent with one another, the higher the burden.[302]

The expansion of the passport regime to include Swiss asset managers would still result in an enormous improvement in the status of the currently applicable national private placement regimes. This is because such private placements may also involve the simultaneous application of different legal systems. In addition, the effect of the sales opportunity obtained in the context of private placement is limited locally only to the territory of the respective member state. So if a Swiss asset manager wants to work *de lege lata* in several EU countries, he/she has to keep an eye on several different legal systems.

Since Switzerland in particular should benefit from the expansion of the passport regime—as a result of the already mentioned positive recommendation by ESMA—, against the background of the associated direct subordination of Swiss asset managers to the AIFMD. It is already asked to what extent—despite the partial revision of the CISA of 2013—there will be a need for adjustment and additional compliance costs. In the following, some compliance-relevant requirements of the AIFMD for the operating activities of an AIFM are presented as examples and compared with the requirements of the Swiss Collective Investment Schemes Act (KAG).

2. Standard Compliance function

With the revision of the Swiss Collective Investments Regulation (KKV) in 2013, the requirements for the operational organization of the

[302] Jutzi, T., & Wess, K. (2018). *Compliance-Anforderungen für Schweizer Asset Manager alternativer Investmentfonds Parallele Anwendung europäischer und nationaler Regulierungen*. SZW / RSDA 5/2018 (pp. 496–516).

licensee[303] were regulated in detail in Article 12 point a.[304] The licensee must in principle have an appropriate risk management system, an internal control system and a compliance office, which cover all business activities. The main focus of the provision is the separation of the operational from control functions. The principle of proportionality should, however, be taken into account—comparable to the AIFM Directive.[305] For example, asset managers with a small organizational structure can apply to FINMA for an exception to the independence requirements. However, the establishment of the compliance office cannot be dispensed within Switzerland either.

It should be noted that Swiss asset managers as financial institutions according to Article 2 Para. 1 point c in conjunction with Article 24 of FinIA will be subject to FinIA. In its Article 9 Paragraph 1, the FinIA lays down the general requirement that all financial institutions must be organized in such a way that they can fulfill their statutory obligations. In addition, all financial institutions (within the meaning of FinIA) must have an effective internal control system in accordance with Article 9 Para. 2 FinIA, which ultimately reflects the provisions of the CISA. The Federal Council will regulate the details of the organization of the financial institutions in accordance with Article 9 Para. 3 of FinIA. The FinSA also provides for general organizational measures in Article 21.

3. Risk management

Article 12a of the CISO, which was revised in line with international standards in 2013, provides that the operational organization of each licensee must have an appropriate risk management system, which is intended to cover all business activities. The core elements of the regulation in Article 12a CISO[306] include (i) the separation of the risk management system from operational functions and in particular those of portfolio management as well as (ii) the principle of proportionality.

[303] Art. 14 para. 1 point c Swiss Collective Investments Regulation.

[304] Explanatory report on the revision of the Ordinance on Collective Investment Schemes (KKV) dated February 13, 2013 (Detailed report CISO), 8.

[305] Final report KKV/CISO, 8.

[306] The Swiss Financial Market Supervisory Authority FINMA has opened the consultation on the FINMA Collective Investment Schemes Ordinance, art. 9&43.

The minimum requirements of Article 12a of the CISO are specified in the completely revised CISO-FINMA, which entered into force on January 1, 2015 whose requirements must be met by January 1, 2017, whereby the international principles (AIFMD and CESR-Guideline 09-963 for UCITS) have been adopted with regard to the desired market access. Since the design of the risk management functions was inconsistent in the past, the definition of the principles of risk management in the ordinance corresponded to a need in practice.[307] As a result of the alignment with international standards, the requirements of Article 67 from CISO-FINMA must meet risk management comparable to that of the AIFMD. The latter, however, devotes significantly more attention to the prevention of conflicts of interest and the independence of the risk management function: The AIFMD required taking special precautions with regard to the independent exercise of risk management measures. In addition, Article 42 of the AIFMD defines how the functional and hierarchical separation of the risk management function is to be carried out. The regulation in Switzerland, on the other hand, is limited to the general requirement of functional and hierarchical separation of control and operational functions[308] and the requirement for the independence of risk control.[309] While FINMA can grant deviations from these requirements in justified cases,[310] the AIFMD in contrast to its provisions on the compliance function, does not provide any exemption options with regard to the independence requirements of the risk management function.[311] In view of the fact that the Swiss asset management industry has not yet established any standards for the implementation of the regulatory requirements in the area of established risk management, SFAMA issued a risk management recommendation on September 7, 2018. The aim of the technical recommendation is to specify the regulatory requirements of the CISO and the CISO-FINMA with regard to the risk management function and to provide the fund and asset management industry with a standard that is compatible with other domestic and foreign rules. These

[307] CISO-FINMA (Fn. 202), 43.

[308] CISO, Art. 12a.

[309] CISO-FINMA (Fn. 202), Art. 70.

[310] CISO, Art. 12a.

[311] For exemption from the independence requirement at the compliance function cf. Art. 61 para. 3 subpar. 2 in conjunction with Paragraph 3 subpar. 1 point c. of AIFMD.

are recommendations for the governance, organization, and positioning of the risk management function, for the delegation of risk and asset management as well as for the identification, assessment, control, and monitoring of risks, whereby a holistic approach is pursued with regard to the last aspect. Both investment and corporate risks must be taken into account. More recently, the risk management function is regulated in the FinIA (and in the ordinance on the FinIA). According to Article 9 Para. 2 of FinIA, a finance institution must measure, manage, and monitor its risks (including legal and reputational risks) and ensure effective controls. The ordinance on the FinIA elaborates on this provision.

A central regulatory area of the AIFMD is the definition of comprehensive information and disclosure obligations,[312] which, in view of their scope and frequency, have posed major challenges for the fund industry. This concerns periodic reporting by means of an annual report,[313] before and post-contractual investor information[314] and, finally, information requirements vis-à-vis supervisory authorities.[315]

AIFMs from third countries and therefore also Swiss asset managers must already comply with these transparency requirements if they sell the AIFs they manage in individual EU member states under private placement regimes.[316] For reasons of space, a detailed presentation of the transparency obligations is waived. Only a few special features need to be pointed out. Although the AIFMD only regulates distribution to qualified investors, it provides for a prospectus of minimum information that must be presented to investors in any case before subscribing for shares.[317] In contrast to the disclosure requirements of UCITS IV[318] and

[312] Dornseifer, F., Klebeck, U., Jesch, T. A., & Tollmann, C. (Eds.). (2013). Commentary on AIFM Directive, Directive 2011/61/EU on Managers alternative investment funds with references to investment management, Munich.

[313] AIFMD, art. 22.

[314] AIFMD, art. 23.

[315] AIFMD, art. 24.

[316] AIFMD, Art. 42, para. 1, point a.

[317] AIFMD, Art. 23.

[318] European Commission. (2009). Directive 2009/65/EC of the European Parliament and of the Council of 13 July 2009 on the coordination of laws, regulations and administrative provisions relating to undertakings for collective investment in transferable securities (UCITS), Art. 68 para. 1 point a, Art. 69 para. 1 and 2.

the Prospectus,[319] however, there is no standardized disclosure procedure and format for AIFMs across the EU. The individual disclosure modalities are agreed in the respective contractual conditions or articles of association of the AIF.[320]

In Switzerland, however, the pre-contractual investor information is provided in the prospectus,[321] which, as a rule, does not have to be actively offered.[322] In terms of content, the prospectus under Swiss law largely corresponds to the information that must be presented to investors prior to subscription under Article 23 (1) of the AIFM Directive, even if the AIFMD attaches greater importance to information on leverage. In contrast to the AIFM Directive, there are no regular subsequent information obligations in Switzerland: the information claims of investors are limited to information in the semi-annual and annual reports as well as individual rights of inspection and information specific to collective investment schemes.[323] The obligation is introduced by the Financial Services Act (FIDLEG) entered into force on January 1, 2020, stipulating to

[319] Regulation (EU) 2017/1129 of the European Parliament and of the Council on the prospectus to be published when securities are offered to the public or admitted to trading on a regulated market, and repealing Directive 2003/71/EC ('the Prospectus Regulation') was published in the Official Journal of the European Union on June 30, 2017. The Regulation entered into force 20 days after its publication and shall apply from July 21, 2019 except for Article 1(3) and Article 3(2) which shall apply from July 21, 2018 and points (a), (b) and (c) of the first subparagraph of Article 1(5) and the second subparagraph of Article 1(5) which apply from July 20, 2017.

[320] Art. 23 para. 1 AIFMD; see Zetzsche, D. A., & Eckner, D. (2015). Investor information and reporting. In D. A. Zetzsche (Ed.), *The alternative Investment Fund Managers Directive* (2nd ed., pp. 391–429). The Netherlands: Kluwer Law International. However, if AIFMs sell AIF units to retail investors, they are subject to Regulation (EU) No. 1286/2014, OJ. L 352/1 of December 9, 2014 (PRIIPs) and must therefore create and publish a basic information sheet (cf. Art. 5 and 14 PRIIPs; on this, Zetzsche, D. A., & Eckner, D. (2015). Chapter 15, p. 422.

[321] For Switzerland, for the fund management companies and the SICAV: Art. 75 of CISA; for the SICAF: Art. 116 in conjunction with Art. 75 and 77 of CISA; for the Limited Partnerships: Art. 102 CISA. These principles can be found in Art. 48 of FinSA.

[322] The only exception is for other funds for alternative investments, the prospectus of which must be offered to interested persons free of charge (cf. Art. 71 Para. 4 of CISA; see De Zordi, E., & Haeberli, D. [2015]. In R. Bösch, F. Rayroux, Ch. Winzeler, & E. Stupp [Eds.], *Basler Kommentar Kollektivanlagengesetz* (2nd ed., p. 32). Basel 2015, Art. 71).

[323] See Art. 84 Para. 1 and 2 from CISA, Art. 106 from CISA, Art. 697 for shareholders of SICAF.

prepare a supplement to the prospectus if new facts arise or are established between the approval of the prospectus and the final closing of a public offer and these facts could significantly influence the valuation.[324]

3.7.6 *The Brexit Impact on Swiss Hedge Funds*

The "Brexit sensitivity index" that the rating agency Standard & Poor's calculated in 2019, revealed that, "Switzerland's exposure to the UK is primarily via sizable FDI holdings and large financial sector subsidiaries and branches in the UK. These entities book trading positions and engage in wholesale funding operations with UK counterparties."[325] In the 2019 Report, Switzerland ranks 5th place, and compared with 2016, "the Swiss financial sector's claims (on an ultimate basis) on UK counterparties have declined by 14%, although the downsizing of Swiss financial operations in the UK predates the Brexit referendum."[326]

However, since Switzerland is not in the EU, it does not benefit from the EU passport, as this is available only for EU member countries. Without this passport, investment funds are not likely to move to Switzerland as a consequence to Brexit, in spite of the somewhat lighter hedge funds regulation in this country.

3.8 Conclusions Drawn from the Comparison of National Hedge Fund Regulatory Regimes in Single Selected European Jurisdictions

This chapter has examined the laws and regulations governing the marketing of hedge funds in Italy, France, Ireland, Luxembourg, Malta, and Switzerland. Given the lack of harmonization of such laws and regulations, the author raised a series of questions to order and to compare, at least to a certain extent, the position in these different jurisdictions mentioned above.

[324] Art. 56 para. 1 FinSA.

[325] S&P Global Ratings. (2019). *Brexit sensitivity index 2019: Who has the most to lose?* www.spglobal.com/ratingsdirect. Accessed 14 August 2020.

[326] Idem.

This chapter provides a comparative summary of the legal forms applicable to hedge funds in six jurisdictions. It focuses on and explores five EU member states' hedge fund regulations plus Switzerland.

The author has chosen Ireland, France, Luxembourg, Malta, and Italy because they are relevant from the point of view of the diversity of regulatory frameworks that coexist in the EU. In addition, the chosen European countries represent the countries with highly developed financial sectors inside the EU. Although Switzerland is not an EU member, it is also included in the analysis, mainly because, in the international financial world, Switzerland is an important player and accordingly, especially as a consequence of its foreign policy, many, if not all global financial organizations, are to some extent present in Switzerland.

If before 2008, countries benefitted from high degree of discretion regarding the shaping of their local regulatory framework dealing with hedge funds, currently due to the fact that it was certified that financial institutions can create systemic risk and, consequently, destabilize markets far beyond national boundaries, regulators, clients, and investors are far more prudent. Wishing to avoid situations as the one in 2008, risk mitigation, investor protection, and transparency have climbed up on the international political agenda of each country of those analyzed, and this resulted in the implementation of new, regulatory standards. As seen in this chapter, in the analyzed EU countries, the agenda was dominated by introducing new regulations such as the EU Alternative Investment Fund Managers Directive (AIFMD), the EU European Market Infrastructure Regulation (EMIR), and the revised EU Markets in Financial Instruments Directive (MiFID II). At the same time, Brexit was the subject of fervent discussions for the last four years, at least, and will continue to be one of the most disputed issues for some years from now on.

As already mentioned by the author, in terms of legal regime, *regulating hedge funds* experienced two phases: before the financial crisis, when the largest part of the jurisdictions had not implemented particular regulations regarding hedge funds, and after the crisis, when the implementation of the AIFMD, UCITS IV and V, and MiFID II has started. Currently, regulation turned into a key strategic factor as it enhanced increased transparency, which lead to the enforceability of compliance and thus protected both clients and investors. In light of this, regulation needs to be comprehended as a major responsibility in risk prevention and investor protection.

The investment funds in the Euro Area in Q2-2020 (billions of euros) reached a total of 13,765.8 (billions of euros). The first rank is occupied by Luxembourg, which surpassed EUR 4500 billion in net assets, consequently being the largest investment center in Europe. Second in ranking comes Ireland (EUR 2905.5 billion), on the fourth France (EUR 1439.5 billion), on the 6th Italy, and on the 12th rank is Malta. Since Switzerland is not an EU member, it is not included in this list (Table 3.3).

In terms of hedge funds, if we consider investment fund shares issued broken down by investment policy, strictly focusing on hedge funds (Table 3.4).

The regulatory bodies in the analyzed countries are presented in Table 3.5.

Currently, none of the countries subjected to study has a clear definition of the term hedge funds, and this conclusion could be applied to all the countries in the world (Table 3.6).

Table 3.3 Aggregated national balance sheet of euro area investment funds in billions of euros (Q2-2020)

Country	*Investment funds*	*Rank*
Malta	18.7	12
Italy	396.6	6
France	1439.5	4
Ireland	2905.5	2
Luxembourg	4714.7	1
Euro Area Total	13,765.8	

Source European Central Bank (2020)

Table 3.4 Investment fund shares issued broken down by investment policy, strictly focusing on hedge funds in billions of euros (June 2020)

Country	*Funds by investment policy Hedge funds*	*Rank*
Ireland	192.3	1
Luxembourg	173.4	2
Italy	6.7	4
France	1.3	6
Malta	0.1	11
Euro Area Total	394.1	

Source European Central Bank (2020)

Table 3.5 The main bodies of rules regulating hedge funds

Country	*Regulatory bodies*
France	1. French Monetary and Financial Code (Code Monétaire et Financier) (CMF)
	2. Financial Markets Authority (AMF)
Ireland	1. The Central Bank
Italy	1. The Bank of Italy
	2. The National Commission for Companies and the Stock Exchange (Consob) which supervises, among other things, the provision of investment services, and ensures transparency and correctness of conduct toward investors
	3. The Institution for the Supervision of Insurance (IVASS)
	4. The Pension Funds Supervisory Commission (COVIP)
Luxembourg	1. The Commission de Surveillance du Secteur Financier (CSSF)
Switzerland	1. Swiss Financial Market Supervisory Authority (FINMA)
	2. Swiss Funds and Asset Management Association (SFAMA)
Malta	1. The Financial Services Authority (the "MFSA")

Table 3.6 Definition of the hedge fund concept

France	*No*
Ireland	No
Italy	No
Luxembourg	No
Switzerland	No
Malta	No

For instance, hedge funds in France are called "multi-market category of funds," while in Italy, they are known as "*fondi speculativi*" (or speculative funds). It seems that all nations agree on the broad concept that hedge funds represent "other fund additional to the ones defined," which can actually mean anything.

The EU can define hedge funds and make a regulation proposal to enable and facilitate hedge funds trading outside borders, similar to UCITS funds. Currently, "a hedge fund" undeniably represents "an investment vehicle." The lack of interdictions is the main reason for not being defined according to its features, but rather according to what it

Table 3.7 Categories of hedge funds which may be set up

Country	*Single hedge fund (SHF)*	*Fund of hedge funds (FoHF)*
France	Yes	Yes
Ireland	Yes	Yes
Italy	Yes	Yes
Luxembourg	Yes	Yes
Switzerland	Yes	Yes
Malta	Yes	Yes

Table 3.8 Hedge funds allowed to advertise

Country	*Single hedge fund (SHF)*
France	Yes, if the fund is registered
Ireland	Yes, if the fund is registered
Italy	No
Luxembourg	Yes, if the fund is registered
Switzerland	Yes, if the fund is registered
Malta	Yes, if the fund is registered

is not. Still, "the EC's Expert Group on hedge funds"[327] proposed to "the EC" to start regulating mainly because this will positively affect the trading of FoHF across frontiers. However, this Group considers that "the EC" should not start the negotiations again regarding essential proposals of the UCITS directive and consequently change it one more time, but instead it should start to authorize "UCITS to invest in derivatives on fund indicators"[328] (Table 3.7).

Every country enables the setting up of funds, by means of its regulation. They do it because there are many returns and knowledge coming from the hedge funds, and if they would not, the market and the investment professionals would abandon the countries moving to a more auspicious location. For this purpose, countries do not wish a tightened hedge funds rule (excerpt for France, maybe, from the analyzed countries), mainly due to their high relevance for liquidity and portfolio diversity (Table 3.8).

[327] http://www.Euroactiv.com/financial-services/eu-expert-group-calls-tightened-financial-supervision/article-179770. Accessed 12 March 2012.

[328] Ibid.

Accordingly, various states anticipate the risks connected to hedge funds in various ways. The only country that does not allow advertising at all is Italy, while countries like France, Ireland, Luxembourg, Malta, and Switzerland do not consider that advertising represents a problem if the funds are properly registered. One can notice in the above table that various states use different standards. Quite often, domestic funds are limited by a certain concentration and therefore have to obey rules concerning risk spreading.

The rules for marketing hedge funds in the local analyzed jurisdictions are presented in Table 3.9.

However, in order to mitigate risk, limitations can frequently be found in the funds' way of investing their financial assets. All the analyzed states regulate the hedge fund administrator in order to mitigate the risks. The hedge fund manager is regulated in the following countries: France, Ireland, Italy, Luxembourg, Switzerland, and Malta.

All the analyzed states preferred to regulate the funds directly for risk mitigation. The hedge fund itself is regulated in the following countries: France, Ireland, Italy, Luxembourg, Switzerland, and Malta.

Since Luxembourg and Ireland accommodate a significant part of the EU-based investment funds, it is important to provide an efficient framework on their regulatory regime, particularly taking into account Brexit, if they want to attract more hedge funds from the United Kingdom. One should not forget that regulation from Luxembourg and Ireland was introduced with the aim of allowing them to set up and thus re-domicile within their own jurisdictions.

Luxembourg stands as the fastest growing alternative investment funds domicile globally speaking, and the second-largest investment fund center after the United States. This expansion is the consequence of a robust legal and regulatory framework, of the country's economic and fiscal stability, but also due to the fact that Malta recently introduced the special limited partnership structure and the reserved alternative investment fund.

The Irish hedge funds, known as qualifying investor alternative investment funds (QIAIFs) are regulated under the AIFM Directive, as all funds analyzed in this chapter. What needs to be pointed out is that the Central Bank of Ireland (Central Bank) was the first European regulator to implement new rules under the AIFM Directive. This led to Ireland's keeping the leading EU domicile for hedge funds. Ireland was also the first EU member state to introduce a specific regulatory framework for

Table 3.9 Rules for the marketing of local hedge funds

Jurisdiction	*Can local hedge funds be marketed in your jurisdiction?*	*Who can legally market these funds?*	*Who can these funds legally be marketed to?*
France	Yes	Authorized PMCs (internal or external to the fund) Authorized financial investment advisers Authorized investment service providers	Funds of hedge funds can be marketed to any investor including retail investors Professional funds with general purpose can be marketed to investors fulfilling the criteria of Article 423-2 of the AMF General Regulation Specialized professional funds can be marketed to investors fulfilling the criteria of Article 423-27 of the AMF General Regulation

(continued)

Table 3.9 (continued)

Jurisdiction	*Can local hedge funds be marketed in your jurisdiction?*	*Who can legally market these funds?*	*Who can these funds legally be marketed to?*
Ireland	Yes	Whether fund is domiciled in Ireland or abroad, an entity that provides any of the following activities must be regulated under MiFID: Investment advice Receiving, transmitting, or executing orders Funds must also be registered for sale in Ireland	QIAIFs are generally subject to a minimum subscription of EUR 100,000 and can only be marketed to qualifying investors. Qualifying investors are: Investors who are professional clients within the meaning of MiFID Investors who receive an appraisal from an EU credit institution, a MiFID firm, or a UCITS management company stating that the investor has the appropriate expertise, experience, and knowledge to adequately understand the investment in the QIAIF Investors who self-certify that they have the appropriate expertise, experience, and knowledge to adequately understand the investment in the QIAIF

Jurisdiction	*Can local hedge funds be marketed in your jurisdiction?*	*Who can legally market these funds?*	*Who can these funds legally be marketed to?*
Luxembourg	Yes	A hedge fund can be marketed by the fund itself; by its management company or its AIFM (if any)	A hedge fund can be marketed to retail institutional, or professional investors depending on the chosen investment vehicle Hedge funds are generally considered as alternative funds and are therefore only marketable to well-informed investors However, it is possible to structure hedge funds as UCITS or Part II UCIs to reach retail investors too
Switzerland	Yes	Any person/entity with a distribution license from FINMA (or other FINMA license which includes the right to distribute collective investment schemes, such as a banking license or an asset managers' license for collective investment schemes) can market Swiss collective investment schemes in Switzerland	Non-Qualified Investors (retail investors) provided the Swiss collective investment scheme is approved by FINMA Qualified Investors
Italy	Yes	Marketing in Italy of Italian AIFs carried out by an Italian AIFM or by EU AIFM	Professional investors Under certain conditions (and if contemplated by the rules of management), to other categories of nonprofessional investors (such as retail investors)

(continued)

Table 3.9 (continued)

Jurisdiction	*Can local hedge funds be marketed in your jurisdiction?*	*Who can legally market these funds?*	*Who can these funds legally be marketed to?*
Malta	Yes	Professional investor funds (PIFs) and Alternative investment funds (AIFs)	Professional investor funds (PIFs) and Alternative investment funds (AIFs)

loan origination funds benefitting from the pan-European passport under the AIFM Directive. Also, the Irish hedge funds are regulated by the Central Bank of Ireland (CBI) which ensures a transparent process with clear timelines for fund and promoter authorizations, all these transposing into very fast approval timelines as compared to other EU jurisdictions. Also, the fact the Brexit conducted to an increasing number of AIFMs setting up in Ireland is of major importance.

Additionally, the Irish tax regime keeps on playing an important role in the successful growth of the funds industry, being entirely compliant with OECD regulations and EU legislation. At the same time, Irish-domiciled funds are exempt from Irish tax on income and gains derived from their investment not being subject to any Irish tax on their net asset value.

Malta represents one of the EU's top domiciles for asset management and investment funds. Well-established as the jurisdiction of choice for hedge funds and alternative funds within the EU, Malta allows managers to run a wide spectrum of funds, from the national Professional Investor Fund (PIF) regime that is not subject to the EU directives, Alternative Investment Funds (AIF) under the AIFMD, as well as the EU hallmark and internationally recognized UCITS schemes. During the past years, since the Brexit referendum, Malta has witnessed record inflows of license applications to the MFSA on behalf of UK-based funds in search for a post-Brexit strategy.

Many states are very restrictive with hedge funds on their territory, and this is particularly France's case from those analyzed by us. In addition, some countries have enacted detailed regulation, while others have not, and try to preserve their individuality, such as Switzerland, Luxembourg, and to a certain extent, Ireland.

Among the studied countries, the most affected during the last years was Switzerland due to it not being a member of the EU. Thus, even if Switzerland has, for many decades, pursued a successful strategy of implementing efficient regulatory regime governing hedge funds, lately, this approach was not in line with international developments, creating gaps in investor protection. The passporting or third country admission aspect prompted Switzerland (to a certain extent as a consequence of Brexit, also) to adopt new regulation equivalent to that from their home countries. Therefore, major changes took place lately, the legislative framework of Switzerland following a course of harmonization with EU standards.

French hedge funds are historically regulated and follow the general international standards of the EU. Even before the enactment of the

AIFM Directive, French hedge funds and their portfolio management companies (PMCs) had to follow a developed set of rules. Indeed, France has always had a fervent legislative agenda, focusing very much on strengthening regulations. Indeed, establishing a hedge fund in France is difficult because France limited very much the establishment of hedge funds on its territory, the manager's biggest advantage being that investors are attracted by "super protective" regulatory regimes.

During the last decade, Italy has strived very much to adopt all regulations that the EU implemented in the hedge funds industry, but there are still uncertainties concerning the readiness of the Italian hedge funds market to address all the changes implied. Thus, all in all, these new regulations are perceived, to a certain extent burdensome or even an obstacle to future development of the Italian hedge funds market. Additionally, the more regulated the hedge funds industry will be, the less appealing hedge funds managers will find to settle their funds in Italy.

The financial industry has become so complicated and innovative that it takes particular amount of intelligence and professionalism to understand it. Innovative services are often discovered and exchanged due to their high request by investors and individuals who try to manage risks. Therefore, is the inability of the officials to regulate rapidly enough or stop financial services from being traded a good enough reason to allow the parliaments and policy makers located in the EU stop the aforementioned individuals from handling their risks? Or is the inability of the former to understand the latter and therefore, their fear of them, a good enough reason?

References

Abegglen, S., & Bianchi, L. (2016). *Regulation of the point of sale—An update on the rules of conduct of financial services providers under the proposed FIDLEG*. CapLaw-2016-3. Swiss Capital Markets Law. https://www.caplaw.ch/2016/regulation-of-the-point-of-sale-an-update-on-the-rules-of-conduct-of-financial-services-providers-under-the-proposed-fidleg/. Accessed 15 August 2020.

AFG. (2020). *Annual overview of the French asset management market*. French Asset Management Association. https://www.google.com/url?sa=t&rct=j&q=&esrc=s&source=web&cd=&ved=2ahUKEwjK2fHUkK_rAhUTesAKHSWfBvcQFjAAegQIAxAB&url=https%3A%2F%2Fwww.afg.asso.fr%2Fen%2Fdocument_afg%2Fannual-overview-of-the-french-asset-management-market%2F&usg=AOvVaw1sWbW4wtwDJllcf29iZXYz. Accessed 15 August 2020.

AIFM Directive. (2011). Alternative Investment Fund Managers Directive 2011/61/EU. Official Journal of the European Union L 174/1 of 1 July 2011.

ALFI. (2014a). *Luxembourg: A financial center at the service of the European economy*. Association of the Luxembourg Fund Industry. https://www.alfi.lu/getattachment/f75643a4-c132-4471-9168-2cb2c9697ab7/alfi-alfi-abbl-brochure-final-web.pdf. Accessed 14 August 2020.

ALFI. (2014b). *The alternative Investment Fund Managers Directive: Luxembourg implementation*. Association of the Luxembourg Fund Industry. https://www.alfi.lu/getattachment/00ea7075-a4ab-4208-8d9e-321ac7c09c9e/alfi-aifmd-luxembourg-implementation-2013-final-web.pdf. Accessed 12 May 2019.

ALFI. (2018). *Luxembourg investment vehicles: An overview of the legal and regulatory requirements*. Association of the Luxembourg Fund Industry. https://www.alfi.lu/getattachment/9d6077df-e6db-438a-b77a-ba3fd7a39f1d/alfi-alfi-luxembourg-investment-vehicles-final.pdf. Accessed 14 August 2020.

ALFI. (2020). *Luxembourg: Your hedge fund domicile*. Association of the Luxembourg Fund Industry. https://www.alfi.lu/Alfi/media/Statements/2020/HedgeFund-Flyer-2020-20201302-8.pdf. Accessed 13 August 2020.

Allen & Overy. (2019). *Brexit law: New French Brexit-related ordinance*. https://www.allenovery.com. Accessed 14 August 2020.

Alvaro, S., & Annunziata, F. (2019). *Shareholdings of alternative investment funds in listed companies and in banks: A legal perspective*. https://www.google.com/url?sa=t&rct=j&q=&esrc=s&source=web&cd=&ved=2ahUKEwjQy_vwk6_rAhXtAxAIHe03ASYQFjAAegQIAxAB&url=http%3A%2F%2Fwww.consob.it%2Fdocuments%2F46180%2F46181%2Flp17.pdf%2F2ca235bc-17a1-4bda-9efb-569d9ff361b8&usg=AOvVaw00HegV75UIZ8xdkLD3Bkcp. Accessed 12 April 2020.

AMF. (2016). Order of 14 December 2016, Official Journal of 17 December 2016. https://reglement-general.amf-france.org/eli/fr/aai/amf/rg/20161218/en.pdf. Accessed 12 August 2012.

AMF. (2018a). *Risk management organization for collective investment undertaking management activities and discretionary portfolio management investment services*. Autorité des Marchés Financiers (AMF). DOC-2012-01.https://doctrine.amf-france.org/en_US/Reglementation/Doctrine/Doctrine-list/Doctrine?category=III+-+Providers&docId=workspace%3A%2F%2FSpacesStore%2Fa6710d0b-3944-43eb-979c-677ef69d8fef. Accessed 12 August 2020.

AMF. (2018b). *Position—Recommendation DOC-2014-06, applicable from January 31, 2018 to January 23, 2019*. Autorité des Marchés Financiers (AMF). https://doctrine.amf-france.org/en_US/Reglementation/Doctrine/

Doctrine-list/Doctrine?docVersion=4.0&docId=workspace%3A%2F%2FSpacesStore%2F8be6d64a-e78e-4487-90ad-8ac0d832d636#fragment-1. Accessed 12 August 2020.

AMF. (2018c). *Annual report*. Autorité des Marchés Financiers. https://www.amf-france.org/Publications/Rapports-annuels/Rapports-annuels-de-l-AMF/annee-2015-2019?xtcr=1&isSearch=true&docId=workspace%3A%2F%2FSpacesStore%2F64a1c9f1-dcdd-47b3-a099-d885dfd560ed&lastSearchPage=https%3A%2F%2Fwww.amf-france.org%2FmagnoliaPublic%2Famf%2FResultat-de-recherche%3FTEXT%3DChiffres%2Bcl%25C3%25A9s%2B2019%2Bde%2Bla%2Bgestion%2Bd%2527actifs%26LANGUAGE%3Dfr%26isSearch%3Dtrue%26simpleSearch%3Dtrue%26valid_recherche%3DValider&xtmc=Chiffres-cles-2019-de-la-gestion-d-actifs&docVersion=1.0. Accessed 31 July 2020.

AMF. (2019). *First results from AIFM reporting*. Autorité des Marchés Financiers (AMF). https://www.amf-france.org/en_US/Actualites/Communiques-de-presse/AMF/annee-2019?docId=workspace%3A%2F%2FSpacesStore%2Ff6c171e6-9bae-4c1f-b355-b9a4bf7cba64. Accessed 12 August 2020.

AMF. (2020). *2020 Markets and risk outlook: Risks and trend mapping*. Autorité des Marchés Financiers. https://www.amf-france.org/sites/default/files/2020-07/cartographie-2020-consolidee_en_2.pdf. Accessed 12 August 2020.

Arreté ministerial du 11 Juin 2004 portant approbation de modifications du règlement d'ordre intériEuro de la Bourse de Luxembourg (Mémorial A, 2004-104 du 5 juillet 2004, 1640). http://legilux.public.lu/eli/etat/leg/amin/2004/06/11/n1/jo. Accessed 12 April 2020.

Backer, P., & Bauer, E. (2019). Luxembourg. In P. Dickson (Ed.), *The asset management review* (8th ed., pp. 212–229). London: Law Business Research Ltd.

Banca d'Italia. (1999a). Provvedimento del Governatore della Banca d'Italia del 20 settembre 1999 (Regolamento recante disposizioni per le società di gestione del risparmio). http://52.57.218.2/modules/documenti_it/regolamentazione_bancaria_finanziaria/compendio_tuif/Provvedimento_20.09.1999.pdf. Accessed 12 July 2020.

Banca d'Italia. (1999b). Regolamento della Banca d'Italia 20 settembre 1999, pubblicato nella Gazzetta Ufficiale no 230 del 30 settembre 1999, sostituito dal provvedimento della Banca d'Italia 14 aprile 2005, pubblicato nel supplemento ordinario alla Gazzetta Ufficiale no 109 del 12 maggio 2005.

Banca d'Italia. (2005). Provvedimento della Banca d'Italia del 14 aprile 2005 (Regolamento sulla gestione colletiva del risparmio). http://www.dt.mef.gov.it/modules/documenti_it/regolamentazione_bancaria_finanziaria/compendio_tuif/Provvedimento_14042005.pdf. Accessed 12 July 2020.

Banca d'Italia. (2008). Rapporto del Gruppo di lavoro sui fondi comuni italiani. *Fondi comuni italiani: Situazione attuale e possibili linee di intervento, Luglio*. https://www.bancaditalia.it/vigilanza/pubblicazioni/altri_doc/rapp_risparmio_gestito.pdf. Accessed 12 April 2017.

Bender, Y. (2019). Malta fears fallout from disorderly Brexit. *Professional Wealth Management*. https://search-proquest-com.am.e-nformation.ro/docview/2210967341?accountid=136549. Accessed 12 July 2020.

Bisciari, P. (2019). *A survey of the long-term impact of Brexit on the UK and the EU27 economies* (Working Paper, No. 366). Brussels: National Bank of Belgium. https://www.nbb.be/en/articles/survey-long-term-impact-brexit-uk-and-eu27-economies. Accessed 12 July 2020.

Blumenfeld, M. (2020). FINSA/FINIA-new regulation for foreign trustees in Switzerland. *Trusts & Trustees, 26*(5), 400–403. https://doi.org/10.1093/tandt/ttaa025.

Bosch, R., Leisinger, B., & Janett-Seiler, P. (2020). Exchange offers under Switzerland's new prospectus regime: A guide. *International Financial Law Review*. https://www.iflr.com/article/b1mb1yfxdfz5m8/exchange-offers-under-switzerlands-new-prospectus-regime-a-guide. Accessed 15 July 2020.

Brennan, J. (2017, September 4). Russia's growing banking crisis to hit IFSC vehicles, experts warn. *Irish Times*. https://www.irishtimes.com/business/financial-services/russia-s-growing-banking-crisis-to-hit-ifsc-vehicles-experts-warn-1.3208132. Accessed 15 July 2020.

Calderoni, C. (2006). *Hedge funds in Italy: An industry update*. Alternative Investment Management Association. https://www.aima.org/article/hedge-funds-in-italy–an-update.html. Accessed 14 July 2020.

Catelani, E., & Sequi, G. (2010, October 15–16). *Alternative investment funds: The case of hedge funds, private equity funds and real estate funds in the Italian context*. Paper presented at the 10th Global Conference on Business and Economics, Rome, Italy, 10th Global Conference on Business and Economics.

Central Bank. (2019). S.I. No. 230 of 2019, Central Bank (Supervision and Enforcement) Act 2013 (Section 48(1)) (Undertakings for Collective Investment in Transferable Securities) Regulations 2019 published in the Official Gazette of 31th May, 2019. http://www.irishstatutebook.ie/eli/2019/si/230/made/en/print. Accessed 12 August 2020.

Central Bank of Ireland. (2018a). *AIF rulebook*. https://www.centralbank.ie/docs/default-source/regulation/industry-market-sectors/funds/aifs/guidance/aif-rulebook-march-2018.pdf?sfvrsn=6. Accessed 8 August 2020.

Central Bank of Ireland. (2018b). *CP119—Consultation on amendments (and consolidation) to the Central Bank UCITS Regulations*. https://www.centralbank.ie/publication/consultation-papers/consultation-paper-detail/cp119—consultation-on-amendments-(and-consolidation)-to-the-central-bank-ucits-regulations. Accessed 13 August 2020.

Central Bank of Ireland. (2020a). *AIFMD questions and answers* (34 ed.). https://www.centralbank.ie/docs/default-source/regulation/industry-market-sectors/funds/aifs/guidance/qa/aifmd-qa-34-edition.pdf?sfvrsn=2. Accessed 13 August 2020.

Central Bank of Ireland. (2020b). *UCITS questions and answers* (29 ed.). https://www.centralbank.ie/docs/default-source/regulation/industry-market-sectors/funds/ucits/guidance/ucits-qa-29-edition.pdf?sfvrsn=2. Accessed 13 August 2020.

Cima, S., Killeen, N., & Madouros, V. (2019). Mapping market-based finance in Ireland. *Financial Stability Notes, 17,* 1–26.

CISA. (2006). Federal Act of 23 June 2006 on Collective Investment Schemes. Collective Investment Schemes Act (CISA), which came into force on 1 January 2007, replacing the Federal Act on Investment Funds (Investment Fund Act, IFA) of 18 March 1994. https://www.admin.ch/opc/en/classified-compilation/20052154/index.html. Accessed 12 August 2020.

Cojocaru, V., & Vostricov, D. (2018, May 18–19). *Implementation of AIFs' regulation in the Republic of Moldova, based on Luxembourg experience.* Paper presented at the International Conference on European Financial Regulation Eufire, Iasi, Romania.

COM. (2017, September 20). 542 final Communication from the Commission to the European Parliament, the Council, the European Central Bank, the European Economic and Social Committee and the Committee of the Regions Reinforcing integrated supervision to strengthen Capital Markets Union and financial integration in a changing environment, Brussels.

Cremona, A. (2010). Malta: Foundations-the new vehicle of choice? *Trusts and Trustees, 16*(6), 479–489.

CSSF. (2018a). *Annual report 2018.* Commission de Surveillance du Secteur Financier. Luxembourg: Imprimerie Centrale.

CSSF. (2018b). *Commission de Surveillance du Secteur Financier.* Development of Net Assets and Number of UCIs. Commission de Surveillance du Secteur Financier. https://www.cssf.lu/en/supervision/ivm/ucits/statistics/annual-statistics/development-of-net-assets-and-number-of-ucis-over-the-last-years/. Accessed 13 August 2020.

CSSF. (2019). *Frequently asked questions.* Commission de Surveillance du Secteur Financier. http://www.cssf.lu/fileadmin/files/AIFM/FAQ_AIFMD.pdf. Accessed 12 August 2020.

Darpeix, P.M., Le Moign, C., Même, N., & Novakovic, M. (2020). *Overview and inventory of French funds' liquidity management tools* (Working Paper #775). Banque de France. http://dx.doi.org/10.2139/ssrn.3659260.

Decree 30. (2015). The Ministry of Finance Decree no. 30 of 5 March 2015. Published in the Official Gazette no. 65 of 19 March 2015.

Decree-Law No. 22 of March 25, 2019, Urgent Measures to Ensure Safety, Financial Stability and the Integrity of Markets as well as the Protection of the Health and Freedom of Residence of Italian Citizens and United Kingdom Citizens in case of Brexit (Decree Law No. 22), published in the Official gazette on Mar. 25, 2019.

Decreto del Ministro del Tesoro, del Bilancio e della Programmazione Economica del 24 maggio 1999, no 228, G.U. no 164 del 15 luglio 1999.

Deloitte. (2017). *Asset management in Italy: A snapshot in an evolutive context*. https://www2.deloitte.com/content/dam/Deloitte/lu/Documents/int-markets/lu-asset-management-italy-snapshot-evolutive-context-whitepaper.pdf. Accessed 12 August 2020.

De Zordi, E., & Haeberli, D. (2015). In R. Bösch, F. Rayroux, Ch. Winzeler, & E. Stupp (Eds.), *Basler Kommentar Kollektivanlagengesetz* (2nd ed., p. 32). Basel 2015, Art. 71.

Di Pillo, N. (2019). Pour la première fois depuis plusieurs années, l'industrie luxembourgeoise des fonds d'investissement a enregistré en 2018 une baisse de 2,28% de ses actifs sous gestion. *Luxemburger Wort*. https://www.wort.lu/fr/economie/fonds-premiere-baisse-depuis-2011-5c51b659da2cc1784e33cbce. Accessed 12 August 2020.

Dohle, M. (2017). *Battle for Brexit business: Frankfurt's aim to attract firms leaving the UK*. http://www.investmenteurope.net/regions/germany/battle-brexit-business-frankfurts-aim-attract-firms-leaving-uk/. Accessed 2 August 2020.

Dornseifer, F., Klebeck, U., Jesch, T. A., & Tollmann, C. (Eds.). (2013). *Kommentar zur AIFM-Richtlinie, Richtlinie 2011/61/EU über Verwalter alternativer Investmentfonds mit Bezügen zum KAGB-E* (pp. 5, 1470). München, Art. 6.

EFAMA. (2017). *Asset management in Europe* (9th ed.). European Fund and Asset Management Association. https://www.efama.org/Publications/Statistics/Asset%20Management%20Report/EFAMA%20Asset%20. Accessed 12 July 2020.

ESMA. (2015, July 30). Advice ESMA's advice to the European Parliament, the Council and the Commission on the application of the AIFMD passport to non-EU AIFMs and AIFs. ESMA/2015/1236 (ESMA Advice 2015). https://www.esma.europa.eu/sites/default/files/library/2015/11/2015-1236_advice_to_ep-council-com_on_aifmd_passport.pdf. Accessed 12 July 2020.

ESMA. (2016, September 12). Advice ESMA's advice to the European Parliament, the Council and the Commission on the application of the AIFMD passport to non-EU AIFMs and AIFs. ESMA/2016/1140. https://www.esma.europa.eu/search/site/FINAL%20ADVICE%20ON%20AIFMD%20PASSPORT. Accessed 12 July 2020.

European Central Bank. (2019). *Aggregated national balance sheets of euro area investment funds*. http://sdw.ecb.europa.eu/reports.do?node=1000003517. Accessed 12 August 2020.

European Commission. (2009). Directive 2009/65/EC of the European Parliament and of the Council of 13 July 2009 on the coordination of laws, regulations and administrative provisions relating to undertakings for collective investment in transferable securities (UCITS).

Federal Council. (2015, November 4). Message on the Financial Services Act (FIDLEG) and the Financial Institutions Act (FINIG) (pp. 8–112).

Fenech, T. (2012, March 7). Malta's minister of finance, economy and investment. *Times of Malta*. https://timesofmalta.com/articles/view/malta-witnesses-rapid-growth-in-domiciled-funds.410105. Accessed 12 March 2020.

FINMA. (2010). Madoff deal and distribution of Lehman products: Impact on investment advisory and wealth management activities. Report of 2 March 2010. Swiss Financial Market Supervisory Authority (FINMA) (pp. 4–21).

FINMA. (2020). *FinSA/FinIA: Follow-up regulation by FINMA*. Swiss Financial Market Supervisory Authority (FINMA). https://www.finma.ch/en/news/2020/02/20200207-mm-finiv/. Accessed 16 August 2020.

Fort, L. (2019). *Le Luxembourg, deuxième pays le plus exposé au Brexit*. Paperjam Business Zu Letzebuerg. https://paperjam.lu/article/le-luxembourg-2e-pays-le-plus. Accessed 12 August 2020.

Galgoczi, B., Lafoucriere, C., & Magnusson, L. (Eds.). (2004). *The enlargement of social Europe—The role of social partners in the European employment strategy*. Brussels: ETUI (pp. 77–95).

Goekmen, A. S. (2019). Where is the safe haven? *The International Family Offices Journal*, 13. Globe Law and Business. www.globelawandbusiness.com. Accessed 13 August 2020.

Goudner, N., & Scicluna, L. (2018). Malta: UK's Gateway to Europe. *International Tax Review*, 29, 53. https://heinonline.org/HOL/LandingPage?handle=hein.journals/intaxr29&div=59&id=&page. Accessed 15 August 2020.

Government of Ireland. (2019). *Ireland for finance—The strategy for the development of Ireland's international financial services sector to 2025*. https://www.ifsireland.com/BlankSite/media/IFSMedia/Documents/Ireland-for-Finance.pdf. Accessed 13 August 2020.

Grec, A., & Marquais, O. (2020). Investment management and corporate structuring considerations for third-party litigation funders in Luxembourg. *ASA Bulletin, 38*(2), 296–413.

Griffin, D., & Brennan, J. (2016, June 25). Russian bank collapse shines light into shadowy corners of Irish finance. *Irish Independent*. https://www.independent.ie/business/irish/russian-bank-collapse-shines-light-into-shadowy-corners-of-irish-finance-34482531.html. Accessed 11 August 2020.

Gruppo di Lavoro sui Fondi Comuni Italiani. (2008). *Fondi Comuni Italiani: Situazione attuale e Possibili Linee di Intervento*. Rapporto (pp. 41–42).

Haldner, F. (2016). Wie wird Schweizer Private Equity Management exportfähig? In D. Gericke (Ed.), *Private equity* (pp. 7–18). Zurich: Schulthess Verlag.

Hardiman, N., & Metinsoy, S. (2019). Power, ideas, and national preferences: Ireland and the FTT. *Journal of European Public Policy, 26*(11), 1600–1619. https://doi.org/10.1080/13501763.2018.1539117.

Hooghiemstra, S. N. (2019). Towards modernization of the Luxembourg legal form 'Toolbox' for funds. *JurisNews Investment, 8*(3–4), 135–144. http://dx.doi.org/10.2139/ssrn.3509731.

Howarth, D., & Quaglia, L. (2018). Brexit and the battle for financial services. *Journal of European Public Policy, 25*, 1118–1136.

Howell, E. (2020). Post-Brexit UK fund regulation: Equivalence, divergence or convergence? *European Business Organization Law Review*. https://doi.org/10.1007/s40804-020-00177-w.

IFIA. (2010). *Why? Ireland excellence in alternative investments*. Irish Funds Industry Association Dublin. https://www.google.com/url?sa=t&rct=j&q=&esrc=s&source=web&cd=&ved=2ahUKEwjm2YaYrq_rAhVOPcAKHXuvDvUQFjAAegQIARAB&url=https%3A%2F%2Firishfunds-secure.s3.amazonaws.com%2F1551880566-5648-Irish-Funds-Why-Ireland-Brochure_EU_WEB.pdf&usg=AOvVaw2BbBWDrOt0E6Xq-PB-Posd. Accessed 11 August 2020.

Investment Funds, Companies and Miscellaneous Provisions Act. (2005). S.I. no. 12 of 2005. http://www.irishstatutebook.ie/eli/2005/act/12/enacted/en/html. Accessed 11 August 2020.

Irish Funds. (2015). *A guide to establishing alternative investment funds in Ireland, Dublin*. https://irishfunds-secure.s3.amazonaws.com/1525962428-Irish-AIFs_web.pdf. Accessed 15 August 2020.

Irish Funds. (2020). *Irish domiciled funds*. https://www.irishfunds.ie/facts-figures/irish-domiciled-funds. Accessed 15 August 2020.

Jutzi, T., & Wess, K. (2018). Compliance-Anforderungen für Schweizer Asset Manager alternativer Investmentfonds Parallele Anwendung europäischer und nationaler Regulierungen. SZW / RSDA 5/2018 (pp. 496–516).

Kalaitzake, M. (2020). Brexit for finance? Structural interdependence as a source of financial political power within UK-EU withdrawal negotiations. *Review of International Political Economy*. https://doi.org/10.1080/09692290.2020.1734856.

Lardner, P. (2019). *A portal of Europe*. Ireland 2019 Special Report. https://irishfunds-secure.s3.amazonaws.com/1550237958-HFM-Ireland-2019.pdf. Accessed 5 October 2020.

Latham, M. (2018). *French regulator cranks up Brexit pressure on UK asset managers*. https://www.funds-europe.com/news/french-regulator-cranks-up-brexit-pressure-on-uk-asset-manager. Accessed 5 August 2020.

Law 486. (2019, May 23). The PACTE Act for the Business Growth and Transformation Action Plan. Official Journal (Law No. 2019-486 of May 22, 2019).

Law Decree 185. (2008). Law Decree no 185 of 28 November 2008. Ordinary Supplement no. 263/L, Official Gazette no. 280 of 29.11.2008.

Lecocq, D., & Cesareo-Hostettler, L. (2019). The structured products law review—Switzerland. *The Law Reviews*. https://thelawreviews.co.uk/edition/the-structured-products-law-review/1212191/switzerland. Accessed 16 August 2020.

Legislative Decree 58. (1998). Legislative Decree 58/1998 last amended by Italian Decree Law no. 23 of 8.4.2020, in force from 9 April 2020, "Liquidity Decree". Official Gazette General Series no. 94 of 08-04-2020.

Lener, R. (2010, July 27). *Italian national report to the IACL*. Paper presented at the International Academy of Comparative Law Congress, Washington.

Liebi. M., & Haldemann, M. (2020). The new rules for providing financial services in Switzerland: Fundamental changes to the cross-border provision of financial services for non-Swiss financial service providers and producers of financial instruments for the Swiss market. *Business Law International, 21*(1), 23–40.

Loi du 16 juillet 2019 portant mise en œuvre des règlements EuVECA, EuSEF, MMF, ELTIF et Titrisation STS. Publication: 18/07/2019, Prise d'effet: 22/07/2019, Mémorial: A514. http://www.legilux.lu/eli/etat/leg/loi/2019/07/16/a514/jo. Accessed 24 May 2020.

Malta Financial Services Authority. (2013). *A guide to investment services*. https://www.google.com/url?sa=t&rct=j&q=&esrc=s&source=web&cd=&ved=2ahUKEwin---1tK_rAhVUlFwKHdCVBvkQFjAAegQIBBAB&url=http%3A%2F%2Fwww.mfsa.com.mt%2FGetFile.php%3Ftype%3Dsite%26file%3DPublications%2FBrochures%2FSecurities%2FInvestment%252520Services%252520Brochure04_02_2013.pdf&usg=AOvVaw0etQlo0NgR17vhhOLa8-5y. Accessed 19 March 2020.

Malta Financial Services Authority. (2018a). *Annual report 2018*. https://www.mfsa.mt/news-item/the-virtual-financial-assets-act-comes-into-force/. Accessed 16 August 2020.

Malta Financial Services Authority. (2018b, November). Virtual Financial Assets Act (Chapter 590 of the Laws of Malta) "MFSA Virtual Financial Assets". http://www.justiceservices.gov.mt/DownloadDocument.aspx?app=lom&itemid=12872&l=1. Accessed 13 August 2020.

Malta Financial Services Authority. (2019a). *A guide to establishing an alternative investment fund manager in Malta*. https://www.mfsa.mt/wp-content/uploads/2019/01/A_Guide_on_Establishing_an_Alternative_Investment_Fund_Manager_in_Malta.pdf. Accessed 16 August 2020.

Malta Financial Services Authority. (2019b). *Admissibility requirements for collective investment schemes*. https://www.mfsa.mt/wp-content/uploads/2019/01/Listing-Rules-CHAPTER-8-25.05.pdf. Accessed 12 August 2020.

Malta Financial Services Authority. (2019c). *Supervision priorities 2020*. https://www.mfsa.mt/wp-content/uploads/2019/12/20191204_Supervision_Priorities-2020.pdf. Accessed 17 August 2020.

Marquais, O., & Grec, A. (2020). Do's and don'ts of regulating third-party litigation funding: Singapore vs France. *Asian International Arbitration Journal, 16*(1), 49–68.

Matheson. (2019). *Ireland as a fund domicile*. https://www.matheson.com/images/uploads/publications/Ireland_as_a_Fund_Domicile.pdf. Accessed 14 August 2020.

Mulcahy, A., & De Feu, F. (2020). Changes in the Irish asset management landscape. *AIMA Journal*. https://www.aima.org/journal/aima-journal—edition-121/article/changes-in-the-irish-asset-management-landscape.html. Accessed 12 August 2020.

Münchau, W. (2018, April 13). Germany is frustrating Emmanuel Macron's grand ambitions. *Financial Times*. https://www.ft.com/content/4db75b80-3f1e-11e8-b7e0-52972418fec4. Accessed 13 August 2020.

Murphy, K., Bothwell, E., O'Shea, D., et al. (2019). Ireland. In *The asset management review* (8th ed.). https://thelawreviews.co.uk/edition/the-asset-management-review-edition-8/1197346/ireland. Accessed 12 August 2020.

Mustier, J. P., & Dubois, A. (2007). Risks and return of banking activities related to hedge funds. Banque de France. *Financial Stability Review—Special Issue on Hedge Funds* (pp. 85–94).

Opromolla, G. (2009). Facing the financial crisis: Bank of Italy's implementing regulation on hedge funds. *Journal of Investment Compliance, 10*(2), 41–44. https://doi.org/10.1108/15285810910971274.

O'Sullivan, M. (2007). Acting out institutional change: Understanding the recent transformation of the French financial system. *Socio-Economic Review, 5*(3), 389–436.

Papa, A., Alfano, N., Iaselli, G., & Benigni, C. (2016). *Investment funds in Italy: Regulatory overview*. https://uk.practicallaw.thomsonreuters.com/7-501-3065?transitionType=Default&contextData=(sc.Default)#co_anchor_a459255. Accessed 12 August 2020.

Prevention of Money Laundering Act. (1994). Act XIX of 1994 as amended by: Act II of 1998; Legal Notice 71 of 1999; Acts XXXI of 2001, III of 2002, and III and XIII of 2004; Legal Notice 176 of 2005; Acts VI of 2005 and XXVIII of 2006; Legal Notice 425 of 2007; Act XXXI of 2007; Legal Notice 105 of 2008; Act VII of 2010; Legal Notice 426 of 2012; and Acts XXXVIII of 2014, III, VIII of 2015, XXVIII of 2017, XLII of 2018, VII and XXXI of

2019 and I and VIII of 2020. http://justiceservices.gov.mt/DownloadDocument.aspx?app=lom&itemid=8842&l=1. Accessed 13 August 2020.

Professional Wealth Management Ltd. (2017). *Inside the toolbox for investment products: Spotlight on Luxembourg—Chapter 3*. https://www.youtube.com/watch?v=uqUXMf_xY4I. Accessed 13 August 2020.

PricewaterhouseCoopers. (2019). *Global fund distribution*. https://www.pwc.lu/en/fund-distribution/docs/pwc-publ-gfd-march-2019.pdf. Accessed 14 August 2020.

PricewaterhouseCoopers. (2020). *ManCos observatory barometer*. https://www.pwc.lu/en/asset-management/docs/pwc-observatory-management-companies-barometer.pdf. Accessed 14 August 2020.

Repiquet, M. D. (2018a). Regulatory competition in European partnership law: A case of alternative investment funds. *Amsterdam Law Forum, 10*(1). http://130.37.92.72/article/view/427.

Repiquet, M. D. (2018b). Report from Luxembourg: New alternative investment funds regulation in Luxembourg—Basis for an attractive domicile in the post-Brexit Era? *European Company Law, 15*(1), 25–29.

Risoldi, M. (2018). *Distributing foreign investment funds in Switzerland*. https://www.aima.org/article/distributing-foreign-investment-funds-in-switzerland.html. Accessed 13 July 2020.

Rittelmeyer, Y. S. (2017). *Will Brexit revive the Franco-German engine?* https://www.europe-solidarity.eu/documents/ES_brexitfranco-germanengine.pdf. Accessed 16 August 2020.

Rumi, G., Ubaldini, R., Dimonte, M., Ferrari, C., & Vece, G. (2019). Italy. In *The asset management review* (8th ed.). https://thelawreviews.co.uk/edition/the-asset-management-review-edition-8/1197347/italy. Accessed 12 August 2020.

S&P Global Ratings. (2019). *Brexit sensitivity index 2019: Who has the most to lose?* www.spglobal.com/ratingsdirect. Accessed 14 August 2020.

Sammut Alessi, D. (2016). *The impacts of the Alternative Investment Fund Managers Directive (AIFMD) on the Maltese financial sector*. https://www.um.edu.mt/library/oar//handle/123456789/13718. Accessed 17 August 2020.

Senn, M. (2010). *The regulation of hedge funds, private equity and sovereign wealth funds, hedge funds, private equity and sovereign funds*. https://www.researchgate.net/publication/228126099_The_Regulation_of_Hedge_Funds_Private_Equity_and_Sovereign_Wealth_Funds. Accessed 16 August 2020.

SFAMA. (2020). *Collective investment schemes legislation*. Swiss Fund and Asset Management Association. https://www.sfama.ch/en/regulation/collective-investment-schemes-legislation. Accessed 15 August 2020.

SIF Law. (2007). Loi du 13 février 2007 relative aux fonds d'investissement specializes. Mémorial A 2007-13 du 13 février 2007. http://legilux.public.lu/eli/etat/leg/loi/2007/02/13/n1/jo. Accessed 15 August 2020.

Stiglitz, J. E., & Griffith-Jones, St. (2007). Growth with responsibility in a globalized world—Findings of the Shadow G-8. *Dialogue on Globalization*, 31. https://www.google.com/url?sa=t&rct=j&q=&esrc=s&source=web&cd=&ved=2ahUKEwiVsfORv6_rAhUDhlwKHcrHCPkQFjAAegQIChAB&url=http%3A%2F%2Flibrary.fes.de%2Fpdf-files%2Fiez%2Fglobal%2F04472.pdf&usg=AOvVaw1wkSRphsN8mf_ux9p65Qnu. Accessed 15 August 2020.

Syeda, A., Syeda, A. F., & Latha, K. (2020). Impact of loan portfolio diversification on Central Bank performance and risk mitigation. *International Journal of Management, 11*(5), 644–661.

Tait, N. (2011, March 11). UK nominee grilled on EU markets role. *Financial Times*. https://www.ft.com/content/3df42a5e-50b8-11e0-9227-00144feab49a. Accessed 17 August 2020.

Tatar, L. R. (2019). *Law and practice*. https://practiceguides.chambers.com/practice-guides/alternative-funds-2019/france/2-funds. Accessed 4 August 2020.

Taylor, C. (2019, April 10). Dublin big winner as UK investors place 'wall of money' in offshore funds. *The Irish Times*. https://www.irishtimes.com/business/financial-services/dublin-big-winner-as-uk-investors-place-wall-of-money-in-offshore-funds-1.3855596. Accessed 12 August 2020.

US v. Stanford, Criminal Action no H-09-342-1 (S.D. Tex. 2009). http://www.justice.gov/criminal/vns/docs/2009/jun/06-18-09Stanford.pdf. Accessed 5 March 2012.

Veeckmans, C. (2019). *New Luxembourg law protects fund sector from Brexit*. https://blog.kpmg.lu/new-luxembourg-law-protects-fund-sector-from-brexit/. Accessed 14 August 2020.

Vysotskaya, V., Vukovich, L., Bissinger, J., Sommarribas, A., & Nienaber, B. (2019). *To be or not to be: How the Luxembourgish government is preparing for Brexit*. https://orbilu.uni.lu/bitstream/10993/39325/1/working%20paper%20brexit-lu.pdf. Accessed 15 August 2020.

Weber, Ph., & Del Vecchio, Ch. (2020). *Licensing of the reviewing bodies pursuant to the financial services act—An initial view*. Caplaw-2020-21. https://www.caplaw.ch/2020/licensing-of-the-reviewing-bodies-pursuant-to-the-financial-services-act-an-initial-view/#more-2328. Accessed 16 August 2020.

Werber & Partner. (2020). *Malta—A viable Brexit solution for businesses*. https://www.drwerner.com/en/malta-a-viable-brexit-solution-for-businesses/. Accessed 12 July 2020.

White, M., Darragh, M., Spratt, T., Beattie, H., & Ferguson, I. (2020). *Brexit: Establishing a fund management company in Ireland*. https://www.mccannfitzgerald.com/uploads/7769-Brexit_Establishing_a_Fund_Management_Company_0.pdf. Accessed 12 August 2020.

Williams, J. (2018). *Malta in a post-Brexit world*. https://www.privateequitywire.co.uk/2018/06/26/265711/malta-post-brexit-world. Accessed 12 September 2019.

Woll, C. (2011). Beyond ideological battles: A strategic analysis of hedge fund regulation in Europe. *Les Cahiers Européens de Sciences Po, 2*, 2–20.

Wright, W., Benson, C., & Hamre, E. F. (2019). Report: Brexit & the City—The impact so far. *New Financial*. https://newfinancial.org/the-impact-of-brexit-on-the-city/. Accessed 12 August 2020.

Zerafa, A., Scicluna, M.C., & Piazza, S. (2015). *L'impatto dell'articolo 19 della Direttiva AIFM sul framework della valutazione degli asset*. MondoAlternative. https://ganadoadvocates.com/wp-content/uploads/2015/04/MondoAlternative-Malta-Dossier.pdf. Accessed 12 August 2020.

Zetzsche, D. A., & Eckner, D. (2015). Investor information and reporting. In D. A. Zetzsche (Ed.), *The alternative Investment Fund Managers Directive* (2nd ed., pp. 391–429). The Netherlands: Kluwer Law International.

CHAPTER 4

The Regulation of Hedge Funds in the United Kingdom and the Impact of Brexit

4.1 The New Supervisory Model Introduced with the Financial Reform of 2012: The Creation of the Financial Conduct Authority and the Prudential Regulatory Authority

The British financial system almost collided after the 2007–2009 global financial crisis, which made it urgent for the United Kingdom to deeply reform its regulation of financial services. The weaknesses revealed by the crisis in the regulatory architecture, established the agenda for new regulatory hedge funds reform. As Lopez and Saeidinezhad state, "2012 was a turning point for the UK regulatory architecture. The Financial Services Act completed the regulatory structural reform by abolishing the UK Financial Service Authority and creating three new financial regulators: the Financial Conduct Authority (FCA), the Prudential Regulation Authority (PRA), and the Financial Policy Committee (FPC)."[1]

[1] Lopez, C., & Saeidinezhad, E. (2016). *UK financial reforms: Bank of England 2.0*. https://doi.org/10.2139/ssrn.2911914. Accessed 15 June 2020.

A. M. Fagetan, *The Regulation of Hedge Funds*,
https://doi.org/10.1007/978-3-030-63706-4_4

4.1.1 Regulatory Reform 2010 Onwards

In 2010, the moment when the coalition government came into power, in a speech of the new Chancellor of the Exchequer, held at Mansion House, the Chancellor noted that the UK regulatory regime was going to be completely renewed.[2] However, as Georgosouli (2013) puts it, "the initial enthusiasm that came with the Government's plans to set up focus-specific regulatory agencies in place of the FSA has been followed with skepticism regarding the actual ability of the PRA and the FCA to work together in a non-adversarial and coherent manner."[3] This opinion was supported also by Ferran who claimed that this breaking up conducted to many controversies and disputes concerning the current reform.[4]

As stated by the new Chancellor of the Exchequer, in 2010, two years later, in 2012, the FSA was abolished, this becoming effective one year later, in 2013, and as a consequence, the FSA's power was split into two regulatory bodies: "the Prudential Regulation Authority (PRA, a subsidiary of the Bank of England) responsible for the prudential regulation and supervision of financial entities, and the independent Financial Conduct Authority (FCA) devoted to protecting consumers and promoting competition in the financial sector but with a subordinated role to the general competition authority,"[5] Therefore, the regulatory architecture was modified, from the FSA regulator, to the so-called "twin peaks" construction previously mentioned.[6] This change occurred quickly and it was completed on April 1, 2013.

[2] Osborne, G. (2010). *Speech at The Lord Mayor's Dinner for Bankers & Merchants of the City of London by The Chancellor of the Exchequer, The Rt Hon George Osborne MP, at Mansion House*. https://www.gov.uk/government/speeches/speech-by-the-chancellor-of-the-exchequer-rt-hon-george-osborne-mp-at-mansion-house. Accessed 12 May 2020.

[3] Georgosouli, A. (2013). The FCA-PRA coordination scheme and the challenge of policy coherence. *Capital Markets Law Journal, 8*(1), 62–76. http://dx.doi.org.am.e-nformation.ro/10.1093/cmlj/kms044.

[4] Ferran, E. (2011a). The breaking-up of the financial services authority. *Oxford Journal of Legal Studies, 31*(3), 455–480. https://doi.org/10.1093/ojls/gqr006.

[5] Vives, X. (2016). Competition policy, regulatory architecture, and public intervention in the crisis. In X. Vives (Ed.), *Competition and stability in banking: The role of regulation and competition policy* (pp. 183–221). Princeton: Princeton University Press. https://doi.org/10.2307/j.ctt1q1xs80.12.

[6] HM Treasury. (2011). *A new approach to financial regulation: Building a stronger system*. https://www.gov.uk/government/consultations/a-new-approach-to-financial-regulation-building-a-stronger-system. Accessed 15 June 2020.

These two new authorities were assigned roles and responsibilities broadly defined both in several consultation papers but also in the draft legislation of the Financial Services Bill, which has received Royal Assent toward the end of 2012.

As Putnis acknowledges, the Banking Reform Act 2013 offered actually the scheme for the implementation of ICB's[7] recommendations. ICB was a committee formed by the Government in 2010, with the aim of developing recommendations for the reformation of the British banking sector.[8] These "recommendations that were put forward into the Banking Reform Act 2013 included a plan to make sure that, in the future, catastrophic losses in the investment banking of large banking groups would not harm the viability of its high street banking operations."[9] However, the solution found consisted in the "ring fence" of retail bank services from investment banking services.[10] Still, this could involve additional costs, as we shall see.

Through these changes, the main aim of the Financial Policy Committee is supporting the Bank of England's lawful goal to "protect and enhance the stability of the financial system of the United Kingdom."[11] The newly formed FCA, stands as an independent authority, having the scope of protecting and increasing the confidence in the UK's financial industry. Also, the PRA's key mission consists in the promotion of the safety and integrity of regulated financial authorities. What needs to be highlighted is that in the making of the PRA, 1100 staff members were transferred to the Bank of England,[12] since the PRA represents a

[7] The Independent Commission on Banking.

[8] Putnis, J. (2014). *The banking regulation review* (5th ed.). London: Law Business Research.

[9] Parise, T. V., & Shenai, V. (2018). The value effect of financial reform on UK banks and insurance companies. *International Journal of Financial Studies, 6*(81), 1–28. https://doi.org/10.3390/ijfs6030081.

[10] Mashiandaro, D., & Suardi, M. (2014). Public interest and lobbies in reforming banking regulation: Three tales of ring fencing. *International Review of Economics, 61*, 305–328; Casu, B., Girardone, C., & Molyneux, P. (2015). *Introduction to banking* (2nd ed.). Harlow: Pearson Education Limited.

[11] HM Treasury. (2010). *A new approach to financial regulation: Judgement, focus and stability*. hm-treasury.gov.uk. Accessed 15 June 2020.

[12] FSB. (2012a). *Increasing the intensity and effectiveness of SIFI supervision: Progress report to the G20 Ministers and Governors*. Financial Stability Board.

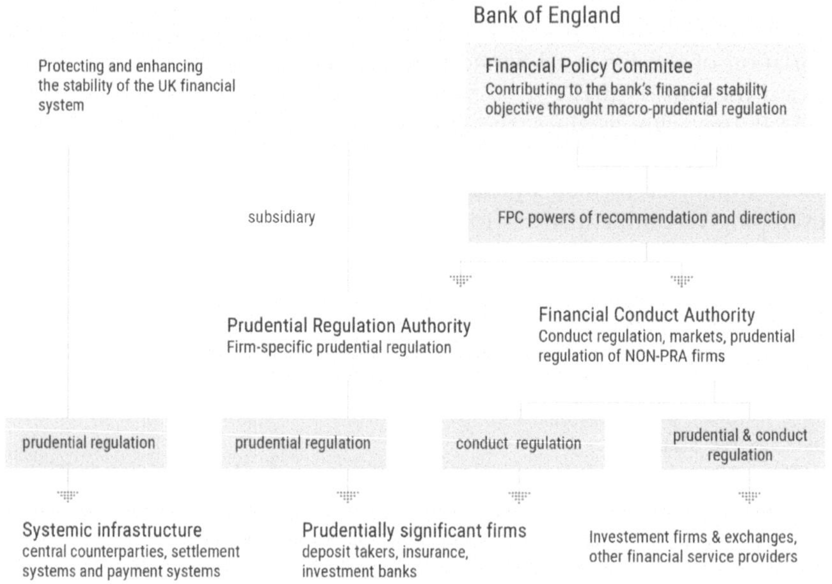

Fig. 4.1 The new UK regulatory architecture (*Source* HM Treasury 2011)

subsidiary of the Bank of England. Figure 4.1 comprises the changes in the regulatory construction as well as the relationship developed between the different authorities.

Therefore, starting on April 1, 2013, two new regulators emerged, each having a various group of goals. In order to smooth this change, the FSA underwent an internal reorganization and consequently, two units: the Conduct Business Unit and the Prudential Business Unit replaced the Risk and Supervision Business Units. Also, another step was the making of "two separate but coordinated supervisors for banks, insurers and major investment firms covering prudential and conduct."[13] The entire

https://www.google.com/url?sa=t&rct=j&q=&esrc=s&source=web&cd=&cad=rja&uact=8&ved=2ahUKEwi1tab9n6frAhVElYsKHa1CAJMQFjAAegQIAxAB&url=http%3A%2F%2Fwww.fsb.org%2Fwp-content%2Fuploads%2Fr_121031ab.pdf&usg=AOvVaw0bOz6kMiPXFGFGnv-UsiwH. Accessed 1 June 2020.

[13] Idem, p. 14.

renewal process finished on the April 1, 2013, when all fieldwork interviews ended, the new legal constructions were functioning, and the PRA was supervising banks.

Consequently, the new coalition government did not only extensively reorganize the regulatory landscape of the UK legislative framework, but at the same time, this immense change claimed a break with the soft regulatory style. From the very beginning of this reform, it has been emphasized by the HM Treasury the necessity for a more complex supervisory framework, taking into account the previous crisis, as well the international request for all financial organizations in favor of the compliance. Even the FSA admitted this need, and just before the former CEO, Hector Sants was demised, he highlighted the need for such a conduct, as the focus on more invasive and "outcome focused" supervision was of high importance.[14] Starting from these pillars, the new document setting out the manner in which this new Prudential Regulatory Authority would be conducted was issued: "the PRA's approach to supervisory assessment will be based on forward looking judgments, with supervisory interventions clearly directed at reducing the major risks to the stability of the system."[15] In accordance to this, the PRA was designed to proceed with the risk-related modus operandi to legislative resource assignment, at the same time, performing the assessment of the risk in relation to more forthcoming risks, together with the risk to its lawful objective of financial stability.

According to Vives, "the regulatory agencies have well-defined missions: the PRA (depending also of the Bank of England) is responsible for micro-prudential regulation, and the FCA of conduct regulation with a competition remit. This structure integrates micro- and macroprudential supervision under one roof, the central bank (which is good for information exchange) at the potential cost of conflicts between supervision and

[14] FCA. (2010). *CP10/17 Strengthening capital standards 3.* Financial Services Authority. https://www.google.com/url?sa=t&rct=j&q=&esrc=s&source=web&cd=&ved=2ahUKEwj5hL6Tn6frAhXhlIsKHRLIAiEQFjAAegQIAxAB&url=https%3A%2F%2Fwww.fca.org.uk%2Fpublication%2Fconsultation%2Fcp10_17.pdf&usg=AOvVaw0oTH7zt3NiqpWYmdVDdO4M. Accessed 15 May 2020.

[15] Bank of England & FSA. (2012). *The PRA's approach to banking supervision.* London: Bank of England & Financial Services Authority. https://www.bankofengland.co.uk/-/media/boe/files/prudential-regulation/approach/banking-approach-2012.pdf?la=en&hash=6C1E1C6BFE2BF79263AC7A7D89278D9EBE0A73EF. Accessed 5 May 2020.

monetary policy. FCA's competition remit will need coordination with the PRA (and the CMA)."[16]

The PRA's supervisory modus operandi text established not only the PRA's duties, but also its expectations of their regulated entities. Accordingly, the PRA was entitled to request "firms to submit sufficient data, of appropriate quality, to inform their [supervisors'] judgments about key risks."[17] Additionally, in the case when the PRA recommends remedial actions for the reduction of identified risks, the expectations are that the firms "implement these recommendations in the spirit as well as to the letter."[18] In the end, the document concludes that "firms should not approach their relationship with the PRA as a negotiation,"[19] warning to a certain extent firms, that the PRA intentions were connected to a more powerful and challenging approach.

According to Ferran, this growth in judgment-led supervision, allowing an important discretion from the supervisory point of view, did not meet the regulatory imposed or at least requested by the EU, which were much more prescriptive.[20] In contrast to the Basel 2 implementation, a process in which national authorities had space to operate; the Capital Requirements Regulation IV was enforced straightaway in the United Kingdom, the PRA being therefore obliged to change its principles. In this vein, one consultation paper and several supervisory statements[21] were released by the PRA, which clarified the manner in which CRD IV would be put into practice for credit risk, counterparty

[16] Vives, X. (2016). Competition policy, regulatory architecture, and public intervention in the crisis. In *Competition and stability in banking: The role of regulation and competition policy* (pp. 183–221). Princeton and Oxford: Princeton University Press. https://doi.org/10.2307/j.ctt1q1xs80.12.

[17] Bank of England, & Financial Services Authority. (2012). *The PRA's approach to banking supervision* (p. 31). London: Bank of England, FSA.

[18] Idem, p. 30.

[19] Idem, p. 35.

[20] Ferran, E. (2012). Understanding the new institutional architecture of EU financial market supervision. In E. Wymeersch, K. J. Hopt, & G. Ferrarini (Eds.), *Financial regulation and supervision: A post-crisis analysis*. Oxford: Oxford University Pres.

[21] Supervisory statements articulate the PRA's expectations for firms to help firms determine whether they are meeting those expectations. They do not have the status of legal regulatory requirements.

risk, systemic risk, and others.[22] It was in December 2013 that this was finalized. In 2014[23] and 2015[24] other statements and upgraded information by the PRA were implemented, concerning the EU authorized acts regarding liquidity and the leverage ratio. Figure 4.1 presents most of the final regulations and in-depth standards which were implemented by both EU and the UK.

These two new regulatory agencies have well-established missions: "the PRA (depending also of the Bank of England) is responsible for micro-prudential regulation, and the FCA of conduct regulation with a competition remit. This structure integrates micro- and macro-prudential supervision under one roof, the central bank (which is good for information exchange) at the potential cost of conflicts between supervision and monetary policy. FCA's competition remit will need coordination with the PRA (and the CMA). The development of a banking union in the eurozone will present a challenge for the UK architecture."[25]

4.1.2 *Financial Conduct Authority*

Created in 2013 by Parliament the FCA is the "regulator of the conduct of financial services in the UK."[26] The FCA has three functional goals which are in line with the Parliament's strategic goal for FCA, namely, ensuring the good functioning of the relevant markets, as exposed in Fig. 4.2.

[22] Prudential Regulation Authority. (2013a). *Strengthening capital standards: Implementing CRD IV* (Vol. CP5/13). London: Bank of England. Prudential Regulation Authority. (2013b). *Supervisory statement 11/13 internal ratings-based approaches*. London: Bank of England. Prudential Regulation Authority. (2013c). *Supervisory statement 12/13 counterparty credit risk*. London: Bank of England. Prudential Regulation Authority. (2013d). *Supervisory statement 13/13 market risk*. London: Bank of England.

[23] Prudential Regulation Authority. (2014). *CRD IV: Liquidity* (Vol. CP27/14). London: Bank of England.

[24] Prudential Regulation Authority. (2015). *Implementing a UK leverage ratio framework* (Vol. CP24/15). London: Bank of England.

[25] Vives, X. (2016). Competition policy, regulatory architecture, and public intervention in the crisis. In X. Vives (Ed.), *Competition and stability in banking: The role of regulation and competition policy* (pp. 183–221). Princeton: Princeton University Press. https://doi.org/10.2307/j.ctt1q1xs80.12.

[26] FCA. (2017). *Our mission 2017: How we regulate financial services*. Financial Conduct Authority. https://www.fca.org.uk/publication/corporate/our-mission-2017.pdf. Accessed 12 May 2020.

Fig. 4.2 FCA's functional goals (*Source* FCA 2017)

Therefore, there are three main goals of the FCA:

- Costumers' protection—ensuring suitable protection for consumers.
- Integrity, protecting and enhancing the integrity of the financial markets in the United Kingdom.
- Promoting competition—that is promoting efficient competition in the best interest of consumers.

As far as the aim of the FCA regulation is concerned, this resides in serving consumers' interest by helping them improve the manner in which financial systems operate and the manner in which entities run their businesses, this offering advantages not only to individuals, businesses, and the economy, but also to the whole public.

The Financial Conduct Authority holds responsibility for the regulation of firms' conduct, as well as for the effective supervision of non-Prudential Regulation Authority (PRA) financial entities, among which the investment entities which are lower, exchanges, together with secondary suppliers of financial services.

All in all, the FCA replaced the FSA, in charge of the maintenance and supervision of the UK financial and banking industry.[27] These processes and measures are implemented through the fact that the FCA makes sure that the pertinent markets function in a suitable manner, offering an appropriate degree of consumer safety,[28] maintaining and enhancing the stability[29] of the financial system in the United Kingdom, at the same time stimulating competition[30] for the consumers' advantages.[31]

Another attribution of the FCA consists in supervising the manner in which undertakings by authorized financial institutions occur, monitoring that the regulations are observed and correctly enforced, concerning possible lawbreaker firms.[32]

Both these new authorities orchestrate their efforts. Thus, there are certain contexts, when the PRA can, in the case when it is appropriate, require the FCA to stop exercising its authority in issues regarding bankruptcy or regulations concerning a PRA-approved entity.[33] Also, this can occur if the PRA considers that, exercising its authority may endanger UK's security concerning the financial system, or may conduct to the collapse of a PRA-approved institution, so that the entire British banking

[27] The Financial Services Act 2012 (2012). c. 21 (=FSA12'), ss 6(1A) to (1T) (Amendments of Financial Services and Markets Act 2000) pt 1A, ss 1A–1T; Scheds 1ZA to Financial Services and Markets Act 2000, c. 8 (FSMA2000). (http://www.legislation.gov.uk/ukpga/2000/8/schedule/1ZA. Accessed 12 June 2020).

[28] Ibid., ss 1B(3)(a), and 1C.

[29] Stability is a matter for the Bank of England: Bank of England Act 1998 (http://www.legislation.gov.uk/ukpga/1998/11/contents. Accessed 12 June 2020), c. 11 (BEA98), ss 2A, 2B, 2C, 2D, and pt 1A; the Prudential Regulation Authority that has succeeded a role to stability—The Financial Services Act 2012, c. 21 (FSA12'), ss 6(1A) to (1T) (Amendments of Financial Services and Markets Act 2000), ss 2B, 2O, and 2J. Stability—the Banking Act 2009, c. 1 (BA09'), ss 1, 4; The Banking (Special Provisions) Act 2008 (http://www.legislation.gov.uk/ukpga/2008/2/contents, on 12.06.2020), (2008) c. 2 has largely been replaced by the Banking Act 2009 (http://www.legislation.gov.uk/ukpga/2009/1/contents. Accessed 12 June 2020), ss 1, and 11-13 (Stabilization Options); For Integrity—The Financial Services Act 2012, ss 1(3)(b), and 1D.

[30] The Financial Services Act 2012, s 1(3)(c). http://www.legislation.gov.uk/ukpga/2012/21/contents/enacted. Accessed 12 June 2020.

[31] Kovas, A. (2014). *Understanding the financial conduct authority—A guide for senior managers*. Leicestershire: Troubador Publishing.

[32] FSMA2000, pt 6, s 73.

[33] The Financial Services Act 2012, c. 21, pt 4.

and financial system can be damaged.[34] Actually, both the FCA and the PRA cooperate with the Bank of England, in order to ease the bank's mission concerning the preservation of financial stability.

4.1.3 Prudential Regulation Authority

The Prudential Regulation Authority (PRA) represents a secondary authority to the Bank of England (BoE),[35] being responsible for regulating deposit takers, investment entities but also insurance firms.[36] At the same time, the PRA deals with the increase of safety as well as the stability of accredited financial institutions. This is done by lowering the adverse results connected with their shortcomings, affecting the stability of the banking and financial system of the United Kingdom.[37]

The most important goal of the PRA is "to promote the safety and soundness of regulated firms and, in so doing, to minimize any adverse effects of firm failure on the UK financial system. The PRA would not be required to ensure that no authorized firm fails, which would remain the responsibility of firm management, board, and shareholders."[38] Therefore, PRA needs to supervise entities' resilience, interventions, and resolution, with the main scope of diminishing the possibility of failure.[39] For providing a stronger oversight of the system, the PRA would cooperate with the Financial Policy Committee (FPC).[40] The PRA's approach to supervisory evaluation is founded on "forward-looking [judgments]," in accordance with "supervisory interventions," with the main purpose of

[34] Ibid., s 74; see, FSMA2000, sched 1ZB.

[35] FSMA2000, ss 2A–2P; also, Sched 1ZB. For more information about the role and functions of Prudential Regulation Authority, see www.bankofengland.co.uk/pra/Pages/about/default.aspx.

[36] FSMA2000 (n5), ss 2B–2D.

[37] Ibid., s 2H.

[38] Walker, G. A. (2012). UK regulatory revision—A new blueprint for reform. *The International Lawyer, 46*(3), 787–828.

[39] Bank of England & FSA. (2011). *The Bank of England, Prudential Regulation Authority: Our approach to banking supervision*. Bank of England & Financial Services Authority. http://www.bankofengland.co.uk/publications/Docu-ments/other/financialstability/uk_reg_framework/pra_approach.pdf. Accessed 5 May 2020.

[40] Idem, 7.

diminishing the important risks that would endanger the stability of the system.[41]

Concerning the PRA's authorizations, these applications for authorization[42] would be dealt after an evaluation of resolvability which would be "embedded into the [authorization] process."[43] The granting of the authorization would be made on a "'whole firm' basis,"[44] after the FCA consents regarding the grant of adequate permission.[45]

Also, the PRA's aim resides in nurturing and protecting PRA-approved financial entities. For fulfilling this responsibility, the PRA must make sure that PRA-approved entities' work is done by having in view the insurance of the soundness of the British financial blueprint.

At the same time, safeguarding PRA-approved entities from the collapse of an entity is another goal of the PRA, particularly since any collapse would affect in a negative manner the state of the British financial market. For accomplishing these goals, both the PRA and the FCA, follow regulatory standards that are alike, in order to eliminate negative competition repercussions in the financial and banking systems.

Vives (2016) presents these attributions broadly: "with respect to mergers and acquisitions, any acquiring bank needs to be properly authorized by the PRA after consulting with the FCA. The PRA assesses the financial soundness and prudent management of the acquirer before approving a takeover. The FCA evaluates the capability of the acquiring firm and the financial soundness of the acquisition, among other matters. It also may request the CMA to consider if the acquisition restricts or distorts competition."[46]

[41] Id. X 37.

[42] Id. X HO.

[43] Id. X 113.

[44] Id. X 112.

[45] Id. X 114.

[46] Vives, X. (2016). Competition policy, regulatory architecture, and public intervention in the crisis. In X. Vives (Ed.), *Competition and stability in banking: The role of regulation and competition policy* (pp. 183–221). Princeton: Princeton University Press. https://doi.org/10.2307/j.ctt1q1xs80.12.

The PRA, along with the CMA,[47] FCA, and the PSR,[48] are all empowered to ensure the regulation of the British financial services industry. Still, as already observed, there is a huge debate on whether the foregoing authorities are going to be capable of meeting their regulatory requests, among others, facilitating efficient competition in this industry.

4.2 The Regulation of Hedge Funds in the United Kingdom

Generally, hedge funds are domiciled in offshore jurisdictions (mainly because offshore hedge funds enable entities to avoid domestic regulatory, at the same time having a favorable tax treatment), as the UK-based hedge funds are relatively few. Nevertheless, after New York, London remains the second-largest international center for hedge fund managers.[49] Practically, there was a tendency for the regulation of hedge funds in the United Kingdom to target managers themselves, instead of targeting the hedge fund entities, in order to reach also the funds located outside UK's jurisdictional reach. Fund managers in the United Kingdom, similar to other investment managers, must be developing activities which represent a regulated activity under the FSMA and also under the Regulated Activities Order.[50] Therefore, in order to be able to carry out such activities, hedge funds must hold the necessary FCA authorizations.

The current regulations allow some funds that invest in underlying hedge funds (funds of funds) to be domiciled in the United Kingdom and also to be listed on the London Stock Exchange under the form of investment trusts. As Dickson stipulates, "investment trusts are not CISs for the purposes of the FSMA and do not require FCA authorization themselves. Nonetheless, the investment manager of an investment trust will still need

[47] Competition and Markets Authority.

[48] Payment Systems Regulator.

[49] McVea, H. (2018). Targeting hedge funds and "repo runs." In I. H.-Y. Chiu & I. G. MacNeil (Eds.), *Research handbook on shadow banking* (p. 189). London: Edward Elgar (Research Handbooks in Financial Law). London: Edward Elgar. https://www.eelgar.com/shop/research-handbook-on-shadow-banking, on 12.04.2020.

[50] For instance, these managers are likely to manage investments as stipulated in Article 37 of the Regulated Activities Order, to advise on investments in conformity to Article 53 of the Regulated Activities Order and also to manage an AIF in accordance to Article 51ZC of the Regulated Activities Order.

to be authorized. The advantage of a UK-listed fund of funds is that it can provide an indirect route to investment in multiple underlying hedge funds while still requiring adherence to the continuing obligations and reporting requirements contained in the UK Listing Authority's Listing Rules."[51]

Before the FCA, there was the FSA, which generally considered that hedge fund managers, as a result of their management of offshore funds, do not impact much the UK financial markets, consequently, representing low risk to UK investors.[52] Currently, risks connected with hedge funds are constantly assessed on an ongoing basis, in addition, the FCA having remarkably grew its critical observation and examination of the hedge fund industry, also with the help of the enforcement of regulations against hedge fund managers and their staff.

Apart from the FCA, the UK hedge funds are also subject to regulations that the EU introduced, such as the AIFMD. Lately, the number of UCITS-compliant hedge funds[53] concerning the number of the managers that are not forced to comply with the AIFMD increased. However, in spite of this advantage, they will have to request authorization from FCA in order to be able to carry out regulated activities similar to those presented before.[54] In addition, "non-UCITS hedge funds are likely to fall within the definition of AIFs; the managers of such funds, as AIFMs, are subject to the requirements of that regime."[55]

It was in the year 2008, when the Standards Board for Alternative Investments (SBAI)[56] was settled to act under the form of an industry institution, being appointed to represent hedge funds and also to increase standards in this sector. The Hedge Funds Standards are therefore published by the SBAI, being meant to stimulate the development of higher transparency and efficient governance in the hedge fund industry

[51] Dickson, P. (2019). *Asset management review* (8th ed., p. 403). London: Law Business Research.

[52] FSA, Hedge funds and the FSA at Paragraph 4.24, August 2002.

[53] The CityUK, Hedge Funds, May 2013.

[54] Ibid.

[55] Dickson, P. (2019). *Asset management review* (8th ed., p. 404). London: Law Business Research.

[56] The Hedge Fund Standards Board, at that time.

with the major goal of preempting the desideratum for stronger regulation and legislative implication.[57] Currently, all hedge funds adopting the Hedge Fund Standards must "adhere to a 'comply or explain' regime, ensuring that certain information is disclosed to investors about how the standards have been complied with, or why certain requirements have otherwise not been met or are not appropriate in the context of a particular fund."[58] At the end of 2018, more than 130 hedge fund managers with combined AuM estimated at more than US$1 trillion had pledged to the Hedge Fund Standards.[59]

4.2.1 Market Overview

Further on, the structure of the hedge funds market in the United Kingdom and the main trends lately will be analyzed. The hedge funds industry from UK stands as the largest in Europe, due to its important margin. The industry size is measured by "assets being managed through hedge fund strategies from the UK, rather than by the place of establishment of hedge funds, which is still largely offshore."[60]

In terms of regulations that impact hedge funds and their managers, the most important still come from the European Union. Thus, since Directive 2011/61/EU[61] on alternative investment fund managers is currently strongly implemented, the "AIFMD II" is now carefully scrutinized by industry participants, particularly since it anticipates changes regarding the European passport, but also private placement provisions of the AIFMD.

The European regulation applying generally to hedge fund managers from United Kingdom is mentioned in Table 4.1.

[57] SBAI. (2015, November 5). *The hedge fund standards (11/2015).*

[58] Dickson, P. (2019). *Asset management review* (8th ed., p. 404). London: Law Business Research.

[59] SBAI. (2018). *Annual report 2018.* Standards Board for Alternative Investments. https://www.sbai.org/about-us/reports/. Accessed 12 May 2020.

[60] Pitt, C., & Cavers, M. (2018). *Hedge funds in the UK (England and Wales): Regulatory overview.* https://uk.practicallaw.thomsonreuters.com/w-009-9984?transitionType=Default&contextData=(sc.Default)&firstPage=true&bhcp=1#co_anchor_a337973. Accessed 20 May 2020.

[61] AIFM Directive.

Table 4.1 European regulation applying to date to hedge fund managers in the United Kingdom

Directive 2014/65/EU on markets in financial instruments	*MiFID II*
Regulation (EU) 236/2012 on short selling and certain aspects of credit default swaps	Short Selling Regulation
Regulation (EU) 2015/3565 on securities financing transactions reporting	SFT Regulation
Regulation (EU) 648/2012 on OTC derivatives, central counterparties, and trade repositories, including the Regulation's margining, risk mitigation, and clearing requirements relating to over-the-counter (OTC) and exchange-traded derivatives, and accompanying regulatory technical standards	European Market Infrastructure Regulation

Source Author's analyses

Before 2011, member states from the European Union were free to decide whether to regulate or not alternative investment funds.[62] Consequently, these funds had unregulated or "lightly" regulated activities.[63] Because of this light regulation, but also as a consequence of the crisis, the necessity to reshape the regulatory framework appeared. In 2011, the European Parliament and the Council adopted the so-called Alternative Investment Fund Managers Directive (hereinafter AIFMD)[64] having the main goal of providing harmonization of the regulation of alternative investment funds within member states.[65]

This new Directive increases transparency as well as security in the manner in which these funds are managed and operated, which enlarges stability of the entire financial system.[66] Therefore, this regulation

[62] MacGregor, B., Schulz, R., & Green, R. K. (2018). *Routledge companion to real estate investment*. London: Routledge. https://doi.org/10.1201/9781315775579.

[63] Zetzsche, D. A. (2015). *The alternative investment fund managers directive* (2nd ed.). The Netherlands: Kluwer Law International.

[64] Directive 2011/61/EU of the European Parliament and the Council of 8 June 2011.

[65] Zetzsche, D. A. (2017). *The anatomy of European investment fund law*. http://dx.doi.org/10.2139/ssrn.2951681. Accessed 12 April 2020.

[66] European Commission statement at the occasion of the European Parliament vote on the directive on hedge funds and private equity, MEMO/10/573, 11 November, 2010.

emerged especially because "hedge funds have demonstrated the capability to create two main different kinds of issues. On one hand, they can pose and spread systemic risk across the financial markets, and on the other hand, their managers can use them to commit fraud and misappropriation of the fund's assets, which, in turn, can cause serious damages to the investors."[67]

The AIFMD regulates, therefore the so-called "shadow banking system," including, among others, the hedge funds.[68] Therefore, the AIFMD "increases the disclosure requirements and implements certain capital requirements. In addition, since the financial crisis, a number of other changes have been introduced to mitigate potential risks in the hedge fund industry."[69]

The UK regulator of hedge funds managed so far, to a certain extent, to find a fund-friendly[70] manner for the transposition of the AIFMD, in order that the United Kingdom can continue being an attractive market for hedge funds,[71] particularly when taking into consideration Brexit.

Also, it should be mentioned that Brexit involved negotiation and possible measures impacting hedge funds, at a particular level, as well as the future of the UK's next participation in the single market for financial

[67] Bodellini, M. (2017). From systemic risk to financial scandals: The shortcomings of US hedge fund regulation. *Brooklyn Journal of Corporate, Financial and Commercial Law, 11*(2), 417–467.

[68] Zetzsche, D. A. (2015). *The alternative investment fund managers directive* (2nd ed., p. 3). The Netherlands: Kluwer Law International.

[69] Kenny, F., & Mallaburn, D. (2017). *Hedge funds and their prime brokers: Developments since the financial crisis* (Bank of England Quarterly Bulletin 2017, Q4). SSRN: https://ssrn.com/abstract=3095892. Accessed 15 June 2020.

[70] Quaglia, L. (2015). The politics of "third country equivalence" in postcrisis financial services regulation in the European Union. *West European Politics, 38*(1), 167–184. https://doi.org/10.1080/01402382.2014.920984. It has been observed a high concern regarding the adoption of the AIFMD and its' implementation in the United Kingdom, mainly because after its adoption, many hedge funds could have left the United Kingdom and move to less regulated jurisdictions, the so-called offshore jurisdictions. The same opinion is shared also by Bourne, C., & Edwards, L. (2012). Producing trust, knowledge, and expertise in financial markets: The global hedge fund industry "re-presents" itself. *Culture and Organisation, 18*(2), 107–122. https://doi.org/10.1080/14759551.2011.636614.

[71] Buller, J., & Lindstrom, N. (2012). Hedging its bets: The UK and The politics of European financial services regulation. *New Political Economy, 18*(3), 391–409. https://doi.org/10.1080/13563467.2012.700924. They highlight that the industry of alternative investment funds from the United Kingdom was against the adoption of the AIFMD.

services, at a more general level, are not yet known due to the uncertainty reigning in the market of financial services. Particularly, if fund managers regulated in the United Kingdom are going to be capable to manage and market funds in the EU post-Brexit is not clear so far. However, when this regulation was being negotiated, "the debate over the proposed AIFMD third country provisions, including the passport system for non-EU fund managers, was especially fractious. A more liberal approach to the EU's third country access rules was supported particularly by the UK, as well as the international hedge fund industry." This position emerged from UK's openness to the international hedge fund industry. Currently, it is possible for the United Kingdom to become a third country.

4.2.2 Regulatory Framework and Bodies

As far as regulatory framework of hedge funds in the United Kingdom is concerned, from the very beginning it should be made clear that not many hedge funds are established in the United Kingdom. Consequently, the basic regulations are, on the one hand, those impacting hedge funds operating in the United kingdom and, on the other hand, those impacting hedge funds' marketing in the United Kingdom.

Hedge fund entities which are domiciled in the United Kingdom need to be authorized by the Financial Conduct Authority (FCA) in accordance with the AIFM Directive, except for the availability of an exemption. The fund that are managed by an alternative investment fund manager (AIFM) are alternative investment funds (AIFs) under the regulation of the AIFM Directive, being impacted by its provisions in a direct manner, and in this vein the necessity to report the requirements and also the requirement for funds to designate a trustee can be mentioned. Generally, hedge fund managers are at the same time "investment entities," regulated by the MiFID, being also subject to the provisions subsequent to the implementation of MiFID II in the United Kingdom. Marketing and investment strategies are impacted by these regulations.

As far as regulatory bodies are concerned, the FCA represents the most important regulatory body, responsible for hedge funds' regulation; no matter if they operate in the United Kingdom or they are domiciled or marketed in the United Kingdom. Table 4.2 presents the rules for the marketing of local hedge funds.

Table 4.2 Rules for the marketing of local hedge funds

Jurisdiction	*Marketing of local hedge funds in this jurisdiction*	*These funds can be marketed by*	*These funds can be marketed to*	*These funds cannot be marketed to*
United Kingdom, England, and Wales	Yes	If it involves a regulated activity, can be performed only by persons authorized by the FCA If it involves marketing an AIF, needs notification or consent from the FCA[a]	Institutions, professional investors, and high net worth companies; High net worth or sophisticated investors if some conditions are accomplished	Retail investors
United Kingdom–Scotland	Yes	Authorized persons can market alternative funds, in accordance with COBS 4.12, which provides exemptions to the restrictions on marketing collective investment schemes in section 238 of the FSMA Non-authorized persons can market alternative funds of this type, provided the recipient falls within one or more of the exemptions contained in the Financial Services and Markets Act 2000 (Financial Promotion) Order 2005 (FPO)	Some categories of qualified investors, such as: • Certified high net worth investors • Certified sophisticated investors • Investment professionals High net worth companies and unincorporated associations There are cases, when a certification process must be complied with	

[a]Depending on whether the fund is in the UK or not
Source Pitt and Cavers (2018)

For the reform of hedge funds regulation, there have been made some proposals for the amendment of the AIFM Directive, on the March 12, 2018. Thus, a proposed directive and a proposed regulation amending, among other things, the AIFM Directive was proposed by the European Commission with the main aim to simplify cross-border marketing of funds.[72] These amendments are going to be adopted in May 2019 and it is only in May 2021, that they will be implemented. Thus, since no "marketing" definition exists in the AIFM Directive, and consequently a harmonized approach regarding this issue does not exist in the EU, local regulators were constrained to implement various approaches concerning legal "pre-marketing" activities.[73] This issue is going to be solved by the proposed amendments to the AIFM Directive. Consequently, the proposals include:

- A definition of "pre-marketing", broadly as providing information to professional investors before the AIF is established.
- For pre-marketing by an EU AIFM to be allowed by EU member states provided the marketing does not relate to or refer to an established AIF.[74]

Other amendments include the Senior Managers and Certification Regime (SM&CR).[75] Accordingly, the FCA is planning to expand this SM&CR to most of the FCA-regulated firms, comprising also asset managers. Therefore, hedge fund managers regulated by the FCA would fall under this new amendment. In terms of the levels of impact, at a general approach, there are three:

[72] Debevoise & Plimpton. (2018). *European Commission proposes harmonised premarketing rules for funds*. https://www.debevoise.com/insights/publications/2018/03/european-commission-proposes-harmonised. Accessed 12 May 2020.

[73] Schnittker Möllman Partners. (2018). *EU Commission proposal: Narrowing the 'pre-marketing' concept*. https://www.smp.law/EN/Briefing/Fund_Briefing_EU_Commission_proposal_copy.php. Accessed 23 May 2020.

[74] Pitt, C., & Cavers, M. (2018). *Hedge funds in the UK (England and Wales): Regulatory overview*. https://uk.practicallaw.thomsonreuters.com/w-009-9984?transitionType=Default&contextData=(sc.Default)&firstPage=true&bhcp=1#co_anchor_a337973. Accessed 20 May 2020.

[75] FCA. (2019). *The senior managers and certification regime: Guide for FCA solo-regulated firms*. Financial Conduct Authority. https://www.fca.org.uk/publication/policy/guide-for-fca-solo-regulated-firms.pdf. Accessed 20 May 2020.

- Senior management must remain subject to pre-vetting and be held accountable for a firm's conduct.
- A firm must be satisfied that key staff is fit and proper. This covers individuals who make decisions that could adversely impact either it, such as functional heads and risk managers, or its customers, such as dealers and advisers. They must promise to act competently and with integrity, and to treat customers fairly.
- All other staff (with limited exceptions) must also make the same promises.[76]

In December 2018 the Approved Persons regime for dual-regulated insurers (those regulated by both the PRA and FCA) was replaced by SM&CR. Also, from the 9th of December 2019, SM&CR must be complied with by all regulated financial entities.

4.2.3 Hedge Funds and Compliance with General International Standards

In terms of risks, the hedge funds UK regulatory regime transposes the AIFMD provisions, focusing mainly on two key aspects: increasing financial stability and ensuring investor protection particularly after the 2008 crisis. Indeed, the financial crisis urged for a new regulatory framework of the financial industry together with its players. There was an imperative need for the regulation of the shadow banking system,[77] hedge funds[78] being also considered. Indeed, most were encouraging the new

[76] Pitt, C., & Cavers, M. (2018). *Hedge funds in the UK (England and Wales): Regulatory overview*. https://uk.practicallaw.thomsonreuters.com/w-009-9984?transitionType=Default&contextData=(sc.Default)&firstPage=true&bhcp=1#co_anchor_a337973. Accessed 20 May 2020.

[77] Seen as "credit intermediation involving entities and activities (fully or partially) outside the regular banking system." FSB. (2011, April 12). *Shadow banking: Scoping the issues*.

[78] Awrey, D. (2011). The limits of EU hedge fund regulation. *Law and Financial Markets Review*, *5*(2), 119–128; Zetzsche, D. A. (2012). Introduction: Overview, regulatory history and technique, transition. In D. A. Zetzsche (Ed.), *The alternative investment fund managers directive: European regulation of investment funds* (pp. 1–20). The Netherlands: Wolters Kluwer Law and Business; Ferran, E. (2011b). *The regulation of hedge funds and private equity: A case study in the development of the EU's regulatory response to the financial crisis* (University of Cambridge Faculty of Law Research Paper No. 10/2011, ECGI—Law Working Paper No. 176/2011). http://dx.doi.org/10.2139/ssrn.1762119.

regulations due to the fact it was proved that the risks brought out by the financial crisis could move very quickly from one financial market to another, spreading in the international market, with the help of the managers of alternative funds. In 2010, in his speech, the President of the European Commission concluded that "the adoption of the directive means that hedge funds and private equity will no longer operate in a regulatory void outside the scope of supervisors. The new regime brings transparency and security to the way these funds are managed and operate, which adds to the overall stability of our financial system."[79]

Therefore, risk management became an import issue, being considered an important aspect in the achievement of its goals and in accordance, a requirement for all AIFMs was made, for the necessity to assure a functional and hierarchical distinction concerning risk and portfolio management. Additionally, AIFMs can delegate only one of these above-mentioned management types, not both at the same time.

Also, risk management is applied not only at the level of the AIFM but also at that of the AIFs it manages. Thus, the AIFM needs to assess its operational risk vulnerabilities and harmonize this with capital and/or professional responsibility requests. Liquidity risk is the most important type of risk for hedge funds, risk that AIFMs need to manage for making sure that all AIFs are able to conform to its liquidity provisions.

In terms of the risks of the AIFs they manage, AIFMs need to establish the risk tolerance for each, in order to establish suitable instruments for their strict, careful, and continuous monitoring. In this vein, reporting is used for monitoring and comparing current risk to the preestablished tolerance.

Accessed 15 May 2020; Horan, S. (2012). White collar crime, money laundering, and taxation: The AIFMD and hedge funds—An international and Irish perspective. In D. A. Zetzsche (Ed.), *The alternative investment fund managers directive: European regulation of investment funds* (pp. 109–138). International Banking and Finance Law Series. The Netherlands: Wolters Kluwer Law and Business, p. 113, according to which, "hedge funds managers seek to protect their trading activity methods and as consequence they disclose limited information to the public" and, at the same time, "hedge funds founders tend to refuse to discuss their trading strategies because they do not want competitors to imitate their moves."

[79] European Commission Statement at the Occasion of the European Parliament Vote on the Directive on Hedge Funds and Private Equity, 11 November 2010 (Reference: Memo/10/573).

In a more comprehensive analysis, the following rules are stipulated into the FCA Investment Fund (FUND) Sourcebook[80] harmonizing the laws with the AIFM Directive:

- Conflict management;
- Record-keeping and reporting;
- The requirement for an AIF to appoint a depositary;
- Investor disclosure;
- The delegation and risk management requirements noted above.

In terms of valuation and pricing, the rules according to which AIFM Directive stipulations concerning valuation were adopted in the United Kingdom, are also to be found in the FUND Sourcebook. According to this, an AIFM is in charge with the following aspects:

- Valuation of AIF assets;
- Calculation of the net asset value;
- Publication of that net asset value;
- This valuation must be performed impartially and with all due skill, care, and diligence.

Assets valuations for open-ended funds need to be completed minim once per year, at a frequency suitable not only to the assets held by the AIF but also to its liquidity action lines. The valuation function can be performed by the AIFM itself or it can be delegated to an external evaluator. In the first case, when the AIFM performs the valuation, the ones which respond for that valuation need to be operationally independent with regard to the portfolio management function, and at the same time, there should be taken into account the mitigation of the conflicts of interest.[81]

In the second case, when valuation is performed by an external valuer, this one needs to be independent of the AIF and the AIFM. There are other provisions enforced in the case it is proposed that the depositary of an AIF is also nominated external valuer. Additionally, an external valuer

[80] FCA. (2020d). *Investment funds sourcebook 3.9*. Financial Conduct Authority. https://www.handbook.fca.org.uk/handbook/FUND.pdf. Accessed 12 June 2020.

[81] Such as under the AIFM's remuneration policy.

is governed by professional registration or legislation. Just as stipulated for all delegations, the AIFM needs to be capable to explain or justify the delegation in an objective manner. Also, another provision has to do with the external valuer who cannot "delegate it to a third party."[82]

Hedge fund managers authorized by the British are regulated by Senior Management Arrangements, Systems and Controls (SYSC) Sourcebook of the FCA Rules.[83] Changes in SYSC regulations are constant, depending upon MiFID II implementation, and also on the FCA's extension requests. Thus, the Senior Managers and Certification Regime (SM&CR) was extended[84] to entities solo-regulated by the FCA.

According to Izaguirre (2020), the British SMCR "seeks to improve conduct by encouraging individuals to take responsibility for their actions. The regime aims to ensure that firms and staff clearly understand and can demonstrate 'who does what.' Its provisions have applied to banking firms since 2016, insurers since 2018, and FCA-regulated firms (e.g., credit unions, consumer credit firms) since December 2019 in a tiered approach: core, enhanced, and of limited scope."[85] This is made up of 3 parts:

1. According to the Senior Managers Regime, particular senior management functions must exist, and in this vein there can be mentioned: executive directors and compliance oversight officers, all being subject to FCA's approval, before performing those functions. There are two main obligations on behalf of managers: to meet fit-and-proper standards and to reach an agreement concerning a statement of responsibility on accountability.[86] In case an entity does not comply the FCA law, the responsible will be the senior manager, also likely to be subject to punitive provisions, pecuniary penalty, or

[82] Zetzsche, D. A. (2015). *The alternative investment fund managers directive* (2nd ed., p. 3). The Netherlands: Kluwer Law International.

[83] https://www.handbook.fca.org.uk/handbook/SYSC/. Accessed 12 June 2020.

[84] With effect from 9 December 2019.

[85] Izaguirre, J. C. (2020). *Making consumer protection regulation more customer-centric* (p. 16) (Working Paper). Washington, DC: CGAP. https://www.cgap.org/research/publication/making-consumer-protection-regulation-more-customer-centric. Accessed 13 June 2020.

[86] FCA. (2018). *FCA mission: Our approach to supervision*. Financial Conduct Authority. https://www.fca.org.uk/publication/corporate/our-approach-supervision.pdf. Accessed 12 May 2020.

public reprimand for not being able to avoid or eliminate a breach and failing to accomplish responsibilities.[87]

2. The Certification Regime is applied to all employees, even to business unit managers or retail advisers, since any of them can harm the firm or its customers.[88] The approval from the FCA approval is not imposed. However, every year senior management must certify that employees are suited to performing their roles.[89]
3. Conduct Rules guarantee that entities are responsible for treating customers correctly, that their employees are trained on regulations, and that FCA receives information once rules are violated.[90] The employees must obey five Individual Conduct Rules:

    i. act with integrity;
    ii. act with due care, skill, and diligence;
    iii. be open and cooperative with FCA, the Prudential Regulation Authority, and other regulators;
    iv. pay due regards to the interests of customers and treat them fairly; and
    v. observe proper standards of market conduct. Additional Senior Manager Conduct Rules also apply.[91]

[87] FCA. (2019). *The senior managers and certification regime: Guide for FCA solo-regulated firms*. Financial Conduct Authority. https://www.fca.org.uk/publication/policy/guide-for-fca-solo-regulated-firms.pdf. Accessed 20 May 2020; FCA. (2020c, April). *Decision procedure and penalties manual*. Manual, Release 49. Financial Conduct Authority. https://www.handbook.fca.org.uk/handbook/DEPP.pdf. Accessed 12 May 2020. A decision by a senior manager that causes a UK banking firm to fail may amount to a criminal offense. See UK Financial Services (Banking Reform) Act 2013, http://www.legislation.gov.uk/ukpga/2013/33/section/36/enacted.

[88] FCA. (2020b). *SYSC 27 Senior managers and certification regime: Certification regime*. Financial Conduct Authority.

[89] FCA. (2018). *FCA mission: Our approach to supervision*. Financial Conduct Authority. https://www.fca.org.uk/publication/corporate/our-approach-supervision.pdf. Accessed 12 May 2020.

[90] The Code also applies to firms that indirectly deal with retail customers (e.g., through distribution networks) and to regulated and unregulated financial services activities (e.g., ancillary activities).

[91] FCA. (2020a, March). *Code of Conduct (COCON) handbook*. Handbook, Release 48. Financial Conduct Authority. https://www.handbook.fca.org.uk.handbook/COCON.pdf. Accessed 12 May 2020.

In spite of the fact that there were many controversies in the beginning, there are UK banks which reported positive benefits, like increased awareness by senior managers on the manner in which entities function. In addition, there has been a decrease of cases concerning irresponsible risk-taking.

MiFID II was enforced in January 2018. The Directive implements systems and controls important for the entire securities market. Provisions concerning the following aspects are very important for hedge fund managers:

- High frequency and algorithmic trading.
- Best execution.
- The use of dealing commission to pay for broker research.
- Disclosure of fees and costs to clients.
- Transaction reporting to the FCA.
- Trade reporting to the market.
- Product governance, assessment of target market and appropriate distribution channels.
- Insider dealing and market abuse.

In terms of insider dealing and market abuse, just as all users of British systems, hedge funds managers must obey the UK's regulations concerning insider dealing and market abuse. The regulations on this subject are:

- Regulation (EU) 596/2014 on market abuse,[92] a European Union regulation imposing civil penalties.
- The insider dealing provisions stipulated in the Criminal Justice Act 1993, a British regulation imposing criminal penalties.

In terms of transparency, hedge fund managers have several issues that they need to be transparent about: "investor disclosures, trade reporting and regulatory reporting."[93] The first one, investor disclosures is subject to regulations under the AIFM Directive, according to which, investors

[92] Market Abuse Regulation.

[93] Pitt, C., & Cavers, M. (2018). *Hedge funds in the UK (England and Wales): Regulatory overview*. https://uk.practicallaw.thomsonreuters.com/w-009-9984?transitionType=Default&contextData=(sc.Default)&firstPage=true&bhcp=1#co_anchor_a337973. Accessed 20 May 2020.

must report not just pre-investment, but also continuous investments. This is available for every AIF that is managed or marketed on the British market.

Product governance and reporting requests imposing that fabricators, as well as product distributors must identify a suitable target industry for new financial products introduced by MiFID II. In addition to the former regulations, these enforce extra requirements, some complex products being designated to be offered to retail investors. Taken into account the specialized definition of "retail"[94] in that respect, encompassing high net worth individuals and several kinds of pension schemes, there must be precaution on behalf of managers in determining the target market for units in hedge funds.

Additionally, PRIIPs Regulation[95] imposes that retail investors are provided with a Key Information Document (KID) prior to investing in a product subject to this Regulation. There have been many criticisms on the fact that the content of the KID is heavily set, and on the necessary methodologies used in the calculation of costs and performance within the industry.[96] Instead of producing a KID, plenty of hedge fund managers would rather make sure their fund is not sold to retail investors.

In terms of trade reporting, according to the European Market Infrastructure Regulation, hedge funds need to report a trade repository that is either registered or recognized, all details of each derivative contract,[97] be it signed, changed, or finished.

As they are regulated according to the SFT Regulation, hedge funds have to "report details of securities financing transactions to a trade repository (including repurchase, securities and commodities lending and

[94] A 'retail client' is defined as (a) a retail client as defined in Article 4(1)11 MiFID II, or (b) a customer within the meaning of IDD, where that customer would not qualify as a professional client as defined in MiFID II (Article 6(4) PRIIPs Regulation).

[95] Regulation (EU) No. 1286/2014 of the European Parliament and of the Council of November 26, 2014 on key information documents for packaged retail and insurance-based investment products (PRIIPs) [2014] OJ L 352/1.

[96] Colaert, V. A. (2016). MiFID II in relation to other investor protection regulation: Picking up the crumbs of a piecemeal approach. In D. Busch & G. Ferrarini (Eds.), *Regulation of the EU Financial Markets: MiFID II and MiFIR* (pp. 864–894). Oxford: Oxford University Press.

[97] OTC or exchange-traded.

borrowing, buy/sell-back and margin lending transactions)."[98] Additional disclosure requirements are also obligatory for AIFMs concerning their use of securities financing transactions.

In terms of money laundering, for hedge funds, the main responsibility in order to obey anti-money laundering laws belongs to the administrator of the fund, in charge with the management of redemptions and subscriptions for units. Generally, these administrators tend to be located offshore in an equivalent jurisdiction as the involved fund is thus subject to regulation in that jurisdiction. Still, hedge fund managers that operate in the United Kingdom will probably fall under the Money Laundering Regulations 2017.

Also, short selling for hedge funds falls under the Short Selling Regulation, hedge funds must report and reveal net short positions in European Union shares and European Union sovereign debt sold on European Union trading venues (above some thresholds).[99] Also, the Short Selling Regulation limit exposed short sales of European Union shares, EU sovereign debt, and sovereign credit default swaps.

4.3 The European Union Withdrawal Agreement Act of 2020 and the Transition Period Laws Impacting the Regulation of Hedge Fund

As soon as the formalization of Brexit took place, both the UK and the EU started their preparation for the negotiation phase, a key role in this 2 years negotiation process concerning "the common market's access for UK financial entities and products."[100] From these products, hedge funds will for sure attract the attention of both parties, especially since there is a long tradition for London to be on the first ranks next to New

[98] Pitt, C., & Cavers, M. (2018). *Hedge funds in the UK (England and Wales): Regulatory overview*. https://uk.practicallaw.thomsonreuters.com/w-009-9984?transitionType=Default&contextData=(sc.Default)&firstPage=true&bhcp=1#co_anchor_a337973. Accessed 20 May 2020.

[99] Koehl, A. (2016). *Brexit and short-selling disclosures*. http://dx.doi.org/10.2139/ssrn.2808498. Accessed 20 June 2020.

[100] Olivares-Caminal, R., & Bodellini, M. (2017a). The impact of Brexit on the UK alternative investment fund industry. *Law and Economics Yearly Review*, *6*(1), 79–103.

York.[101] However, according to McVea,[102] in Europe, London stands as the biggest hedge funds center.

If the United Kingdom remains in the EEA, the impact will be lower since both British managers and funds will continue to be seen as similar to EU entities; meanwhile, if the United Kingdom leaves the EEA, they will be considered third country entities, which will make it more difficult to access the EU market. However, a first step was made, since there was also possible the possibility of a hard—no-deal Brexit. So far, politics developed in the United Kingdom, but also in the Western part of the world since Donald Trump's election, are quite difficult to predict, which makes it impossible to cover all possibilities of how financial services in general, and hedge funds in particular, will be impacted by Brexit.

[101] Globally, hedge funds' AUM reached in 2014, $2.7 trillion, surpassing the precrisis peak which was in 2007 at $2.4trillion. In spite of the fact that London remains the second-largest global center for hedge funds managers, after New York, holding about 17% share of the global hedge fund industry, UK's capital emerges as the largest center for hedge funds in Europe, holding more than 2/3s of European single manager hedge fund AUM. In this vein, see TheCityUK. (2015, November). *UK fund management: An attractive proposition for international funds* (pp. 24–25). (https://www.thecityuk.com/research/uk-fund-management-an-attractive-proposition-for-international-funds/. Accessed 12 April 2020). See also, Sowels, N. (2017). Brexit and UK-based financial services. *Revue Française de Civilisation Britannique* [Online] (XXII-2), 1. http://rfcb.revues.org/1331. Accessed 12 April 2020. The author acknowledges that "London is one of the world's top two leading financial services centers, jockeying year-in, year-out with New York for top place. Its position stems largely from the very high level of international, offshore financial activities operating in the City, and more generally in Britain's capital markets." Also, in another paper: Sennholz-Weinhardt, B. (2014). Regulatory competition as a social fact: Constructing and contesting the threat of hedge fund managers relocation from Britain. *Review of International Political Economy, 21*(6), 1240–1274. https://doi.org/10.1080/09692290.2013.844722, it is highlighted most hedge funds assets in Europe are being managed from the United Kingdom. McVea, H. (2018). Targeting hedge funds and "repo runs". In I. H.-Y. Chiu & I. G. MacNeil (Eds.), *Research handbook on shadow banking. Research handbooks in financial law* (p. 189). London: Edward Elgar. Additionally, ESMA, in Opinion to the European Parliament, Council and Commission and responses to the call for evidence on the functioning of the AIFMD EU passport and on the National Private Placement Regimes, on the 30th of July 2015, stipulated that from a total of 7868 EU AIFs which were notified for marketing in other EU member states in accordance with Article 32 AIFMD, the biggest number of outbound notifications come from the United Kingdom, i.e., 5027, 2013 (July) to 2015 (March).

[102] McVea, H. (2018). Targeting hedge funds and "repo runs." In I. H.-Y. Chiu & I. G. MacNeil (Eds.), *Research handbook on shadow banking* (p. 189). London: Edward Elgar.

The Brexit steps were very complex. In March 2018 a draft withdrawal agreement was published by the government, providing a transition period of almost two years (the end date being December 31, 2020). Up to the end of this transition period, the United Kingdom remains subject to EU law, at the same time benefiting of similar rights as those they have now (for instance, passporting). However, this draft withdrawal agreement was rejected three times by the House of Commons, in the end, on 24 January, being finally signed the Brexit withdrawal agreement known under the name of Agreement on the withdrawal of the United Kingdom of Great Britain and Northern Ireland from the European Union and the European Atomic Energy Community,[103] which established the terms and conditions of the withdrawal from the EU and Euratom.

There are still many uncertainties concerning this withdrawal, and the first impacts on hedge funds can already be seen. Thus, in March 2019, although asset managers have already implemented their contingency plans, the IA was highly disappointed by all the failures of the House of Commons in passing the withdrawal agreement together with the other uncertainties concerning Brexit.[104] According to the IA, British savers have withdrawn nearly £15 billion from UK equity funds since the date of the referendum.[105] At the same time, in 2017, the IA pointed out the paramount of avoiding a no-deal exit. At the same time, "statements made by ESMA in July 2017 raised doubts about the continuing viability post-Brexit of the 'delegation model' employed by many international fund management groups, in which a fund manager authorized in one country delegates fund management or advisory duties to an affiliate in another jurisdiction (which may be outside the EU)."[106] In a recent keynote address, the Chair of ESMA, highlighted that the delegation model is under no way undermined or doubted by ESMA. This model stands as a basic, important characteristic of the investment funds market at the same time contributing to its success through the ability to organizing

[103] https://assets.publishing.service.gov.uk/government/uploads/system/uploads/attachment_data/file/862063/TS3202_1.PDF. Accessed 12 May 2020.

[104] IA, Investment Association responds to the meaningful vote, 12 March 2019.

[105] Idem.

[106] Dickson, P. (2019). *Asset management review* (8th ed.). London: Law Business Research. See also European Securities and Markets Authority, Opinion to support supervisory convergence in the area of investment management in the context of the United Kingdom withdrawing from the European Union, 13 July 2017.

centers of excellence in various jurisdictions. At the same time, ESMA clarified that "it does not envisage changing the legal requirements, but is rather seeking to aid their practical application and help authorities when supervising delegation arrangements so that national regulators would be able to interpret the requirements consistently."[107] On the side of this, in February 2019, a memorandum of understanding (MOU) was signed by ESMA with the FCA, making sure that the delegation model will be employed further on by asset managers in the scenario in which the United Kingdom would have left the EU without an agreement. However, this is no longer the case.

In the hereby context it can be assumed that British banks will be found in difficulty as far as accessing the European markets is involved, after the Brexit transition period ends. So far, there is few, if any, literature concerning hedge funds regulations after the Brexit, particularly because there are many uncertainties in the industry. Still, as Olivares-Caminal and Bodellini (2017b) put it, "Brexit is likely to have a significant impact on the UK investment fund industry and for the same reason the UK negotiators should not underestimate the importance of the free access on the common market and of the delegation of functions to UK managers for the success of London as an international center for investment fund activities."[108]

As already stated in the beginning of the chapter, there could be three alternative scenarios concerning the access to the common market of UK financial entities.[109] One scenario, the positive one, has to do with the

[107] ESMA. (2018). *Keynote address, CMU, Brexit, and ESA review—What's next?* European Securities and Markets Authorities.

[108] Olivares-Caminal, R., & Bodellini, M. (2017b). The UK regulation on alternative investment fund managers: A difficult compromise between two different legislative approaches. *Journal of Banking Regulation, 19*(1), 73–85. https://doi.org/10.1057/s41261-017-0052-1.

[109] Moloney, N. (2016). Financial services, the EU, and Brexit: An uncertain future for the city? *German Law Journal, 17,* 75–82, stating that the only reason for the United Kingdom to leave the EEA status is "the possibility of lower levels of financial regulation." According to him, the relationship between the UK and the EU has not been determined yet. According to him, "On exit from the EU, the UK's ability to influence and impose its preferences on these international standards will be severely diminished." Also, regulatory changes and their impact on the international financial community are analyzed by Alexander, K., Barnard, C., Ferran, E., Lang, A., & Moloney, N. (2018). *Brexit and financial services law and policy.* Oxford: Hart Publishing, according to which: "Treaties, legislation, and regulation, at UK, EU, and international levels, and the many

UK's decision to keep its status of a country belonging to the European Economic Area (EEA).[110] According to Armour (2017), if during or after the transition period the United Kingdom would sign up to the EEA Agreement, "UK-authorized financial services firms would keep their EU passports."[111] In this case, "UK-registered companies founded by entrepreneurs in other EU member states ... would continue to have their existence recognized by other EU jurisdictions."[112] If this will be the situation, hedge funds will not be impacted too much since both British AIFMs and AIFs will be able use the EU AIFMD passport because this is offered to both EU and EEA entities. However, according to Amour (2017) this scenario is impossible because "EEA membership entails acceptance of the 'four freedoms' including continued free movement of persons which has been ruled out by the UK Government. Nevertheless, given the level of UK–EU activity described above, there are clear benefits to both sides in coming to some sort of bilateral agreement regarding financial services."[113]

At the same time, if we consider the fact that, after its withdrawal from the EU on January 31, 2020, the United Kingdom terminated being a Contracting Party to the EEA Agreement, this scenario becomes indeed impossible, not to mention the fact that, on January 28, 2020, the EEA EFTA States and the United Kingdom signed a Separation Agreement.[114] Also, the UK government has so far stated quite firmly that it has no intention to apply for membership of EFTA. Therefore, only in case the United Kingdom would seek to rejoin EFTA, this scenario would become possible again.

dynamics and interests which drive them, will frame and shape the ultimate settlement between the UK and the EU. Law will also shape how the EU financial system develops post-Brexit and how the international financial system responds."

[110] In spite of the fact that all the EU member states are members of the European Economic Area (EEA) as well, the last one implies a separate agreement from the rest of the EU Treaties.

[111] Armour, J. (2017). Brexit and financial services. *Oxford Review of Economic Policy, 33*(1), S54–S69. https://doi.org/10.1093/oxrep/grx014.

[112] Idem.

[113] Idem.

[114] In this respect, a separation agreement was signed between the EEA EFTA States and the UK on the 28 January 2020. https://www.efta.int/sites/default/files/documents/eea/eea/legal-texts/2020_01_28_UK-EEA-EFTA_separation_agreement.pdf.pdf. Accessed 5 May 2020.

In this case, we reach the second scenario, which is the most probable now.[115] Thus, after signing the Withdrawal Agreement, the United Kingdom ceased being a Contracting Party to the EEA Agreement. This comes as a consequence of the two-pillar structure in accordance with Article 126 of the EEA Agreement, where it is stipulated that the EEA Agreement can be applied only to the EU member states and, in addition, the three EEA EFTA States. Nevertheless, the United Kingdom will continue to be treated as an EEA State during the transition period.

In the Withdrawal Agreement[116] between the EU and the UK, Article 126 stipulates a transition period until December 31, 2020. Article 129 provides that, during this period, the United Kingdom would be subject to the UE regulations, being therefore bound by the obligations stemming from all global agreements signed by the EU, along with the EEA Agreement. At the same time, the EEA EFTA States accepted treating the United Kingdom as an EU member state during transition. Consequently, all rights and obligations stipulated in the EEA Agreement[117] shall apply prior to December 31, 2020.

As soon as this transition period ends, the United Kingdom will be considered as a third country according to the EEA Agreement. Consequently, both AIFMs and AIFs will need a decision of the European Commission concerning the possibility of extending the AIFMD passport to non-EU AIFMs and AIFs. In this case, unless there will be changes in the domestic regulation, there is possible for the United Kingdom to get a positive assessment from ESMA particularly because UK's regulation is based on the AIFMD, therefore can be seen as similar. At the same time, this might easier convince the European Commission to offer to the United Kingdom the third country passport according to the AIFMD.

[115] Apart from the reasons which will be presented in the chapter further on in favor of this scenario, ESMA's opinion was even from 2017, quite similar; ESMA, General principles to support supervisory convergence in the context of the United Kingdom withdrawing from the European Union, Opinion published on 31 May 2017, www.esma.europa.eu, p. 2. According to ESMA, "the opinion assumes that the UK will become a third country after its withdrawal from the EU. This is without prejudice to any specific arrangements that may be reached between the UK and the EU".

[116] House of Lords. (2020). *European Union (Withdrawal Agreement) Bill, Ordered to be printed 13 January 2020 and published 14 January 2020*. London: Authority of the House of Lords. https://publications.parliament.uk/pa/ld5801/ldselect/ldconst/5/5.pdf. Accessed 12 May 2020.

[117] Between the UK and the EEA EFTA States.

A third scenario might involve the negotiation for a particular agreement between the United Kingdom and the European Union so that the British financial entities can access the common market.[118] So far, this did not happen. Thus, if we consider that, until the transition period ends, the parties find themselves in the impossibility of reaching a specific agreement which should permit UK financial players to access the EU market freely, taking into consideration that the United Kingdom is not going to preserve its status of an EEA Country,[119] then the AIFMD passport is going to cease its availability.[120] Armour (2017) is also in favor of the last two scenarios. In his opinion, "the loss of this ability to 'passport' services throughout the EU is at the center of the financial sector's concerns over Brexit,"[121] particularly because this would mean that UK entities "will no longer be able to rely on the freedom of establishment, or on EU passporting rights under financial services legislation."[122] Accordingly, immediately after Brexit, UK-based AIFMs and AIFs are going to lose both passporting according to current regulation and their status as EU entities. In consequence, it becomes obvious that a first issue on the UK alternative investment fund industry agenda should be persuading the European Commission to be seen in time a similar system. In doing so, the United Kingdom must rely on the total harmonization of its regulation with the EU legislation.

Therefore, so far, the United Kingdom is trapped between "equivalence" or direct regulation. This means that harmonizing its regulation,

[118] Ringe, W. G. (2017). The irrelevance of Brexit for the European financial market. *European Business Organization Law Review*. http://dx.doi.org/10.2139/ssrn.2902715. The author argues that this can is a possible result of negotiations, so that each party can get advantages through the free access of financial entities to the common market. There EU and the UK might opt for an agreement of this type.

[119] In this respect, a separation agreement was signed between the EEA EFTA States and the United Kingdom on the January 28, 2020. https://www.efta.int/sites/default/files/documents/eea/eea/legal-texts/2020_01_28_UK-EEA-EFTA_separation_agreement.pdf.pdf. Accessed 5 May 2020.

[120] Moloney, N. (2016). Financial services, the EU, and Brexit: An uncertain future for the city? *German Law Journal, 17,* 75–82, arguing that this is one of the few certainties about the post-Brexit scenario.

[121] Armour, J. (2017). Brexit and financial services. *Oxford Review of Economic Policy, 33,* S58. www.law.ox.ac.uk/business-law-blog. Accessed 12 May 2020.

[122] Idem.

would bring UK (in the position of third country) real advantages for financial firms.

The European Union's financial regulatory regime for third country access in many sectors relies on a framework of "equivalence," whereby institutions based in approved non-EU countries with similar standards may have varying degrees of access to EU markets or investors, depending on the extent to which their laws and regulations achieve equivalent outcomes to those of EU law.[123] The EU's equivalence regimes have been given increased prominence as a result of Brexit, since they are the means by which the EU's formerly largest financial center, in London, would access EU investors and vice versa.

Summing up, entities domiciled in equivalent third countries benefit from exemptions contained in national authorizations, in this case, the regulatory impact being that they are not obliged to open a subsidiary in the EU to manage their operations in the Single market.[124] The main problem resides in the fact that "the European Commission maintains a list of current 3CE determinations, which details 39 different equivalence regimes under 14 different pieces of EU financial services legislation,"[125] which can be a problem for the United Kingdom.

An important document was published by the Commission immediately after the Brexit referendum, concerning the equivalence decisions in financial services policy. In this paper, although Brexit is not mentioned, the new legislative guidelines appear as dealing with the UK financial market when the withdrawal would finish.[126] Accordingly, offering this equivalence "label" to a third country stands as a political choice based on a technical assessment that the European Supervisory Authority has to perform.[127] In this case, the difficult relations between the EU and

[123] Lehmann, M., & Zetzsche, D. A. (2018). *How does it feel to be a third country? The consequences of Brexit for financial market law* (CIGI & BIICL, Brexit: The International Legal Implications, Paper No. 14). https://ssrn.com/abstract=3155355. Accessed 15 June 2020.

[124] Armour, J. (2017). Brexit and financial services. *Oxford Review of Economic Policy, 33,* S58 www.law.ox.ac.uk/business-law-blog. Accessed 12 May 2020.

[125] Idem.

[126] European Commission. (2017, February 27). *Commission Staff Working Document—EU equivalence decisions in financial services policy: An assessment*. Brussels. www.ec.europa.eu.

[127] Idem.

the UK could determine the Commission's position,[128] this equivalence proving to be very difficult to get.[129] Brexit prompts hard choices for both UK and the EU.

4.4 Concluding Remarks

The UK's hedge funds industry is a major part of UK financial services. Also, as a consequence of the UK's withdrawal from the EU, it turned into a politically outstanding area, with different EU member states competing to attract hedge funds in their financial centers. Brexit prompts hard choices for both UK and the EU. In the middle of all these changes, a major question concerning hedge funds emerges: will/should the United Kingdom keep on coexisting under the EU regulations or it can consider applying a certain divergence from them.

From this analysis, it becomes obvious that Brexit is going to introduce additional, complex layers of regulations but also costs for the UK hedge funds market. At the same time, there is little, if any guarantee concerning the future Single market access rights. In a more positive note, markets and financial regulation are constantly changing and co-evolving. Consequently, Brexit can have also a positive aspect for the United Kingdom, and new benefits can be found in terms of hedge funds regulation.

The UK's future choices regarding the hedge funds regulations are important in the context of UK's maintaining the key, top position on international financial markets, as a global financial center. As already seen, "over the short to medium term, the UK should ensure it is likely to be deemed equivalent under EU law."[130] In this case, the current access to the European Single market can continue as much as possible, and consequently, the UK's hedge funds industry can market and manage funds at least to some point within the Common market.

[128] Moloney, N. (2016). Financial services, the EU, and Brexit: An uncertain future for the city? *German Law Journal, 17,* 78.

[129] Ringe, W.-G. (2017). The irrelevance of Brexit for the European financial market (January 2, 2018). *European Business Organization Law Review*, Forthcoming; Oxford Legal Studies Research Paper No. 10/2017. SSRN: https://ssrn.com/abstract=2902715 or http://dx.doi.org/10.2139/ssrn.2902715. Accessed 12 May 2020.

[130] Howell, E. (2020). Post-Brexit UK fund regulation: Equivalence, divergence or convergence? *European Business Organization Law Review*. https://doi.org/10.1007/s40804-020-00177-w.

Nevertheless, there can be sections within UK hedge funds regulation, in which some limited divergence can emerge. This can occur "provided that the UK remains in line with international standards, and (ideally) continues to be recognizably similar to remain equivalent. This certainly holds true in the event that equivalence is interpreted as more of a holistic assessment that could extend to embrace an element of regulatory competition."[131]

In the long term, Brexit should, on behalf of both EU and the UK, stimulate broader negotiations concerning longer-term challenges that the hedge funds market is going to face in the post-Brexit era. From this perspective, the Brexit should also imply innovative and proportionate solutions for the reinforcement and strengthening of this important industry.

References

Agreement on Arrangements MS No. 1/2020. (2020). *Presented to Parliament by the Secretary of State for Foreign and Commonwealth Affairs by Command of Her Majesty January 2020*. https://assets.publishing.service.gov.uk/government/uploads/system/uploads/attachment_data/file/861908/MS_1.2020_Agreement_on_arrangements_between_Iceland__Liechtenstein__Norway_and_UK_following_withdrawal_of_UK_from_EU__EEA_agreement_and_other_agreements_applicable_UK_and_EEA_EFTA_States.pdf. Accessed 23 August 2020.

Armour, J. (2017). Brexit and financial services. *Oxford Review of Economic Policy, 33*(1), S54–S69. https://doi.org/10.1093/oxrep/grx014.

Awrey, D. (2011). The limits of EU hedge fund regulation. *Law and Financial Markets Review, 5*(2), 119–128.

Bank of England & FSA. (2011). *The Bank of England, Prudential Regulation Authority: Our approach to banking supervision*. Bank of England & Financial Services Authority. http://www.bankofengland.co.uk/publications/Docu-ments/other/financialstability/uk_reg_framework/pra_approach.pdf. Accessed 5 May 2020.

Bank of England & FSA. (2012). *The PRA's approach to banking supervision*. London: Bank of England & Financial Services Authority. https://www.bankofengland.co.uk/-/media/boe/files/prudential-regulation/approach/banking-approach-2012.pdf?la=en&hash=6C1E1C6BFE2BF79263AC7A7D89278D9EBE0A73EF. Accessed 5 May 2020.

[131] Idem.

Bodellini, M. (2017). From systemic risk to financial scandals: The shortcomings of US hedge fund regulation. *Brooklyn Journal of Corporate, Financial and Commercial Law, 11*(2), 417–467.

Bourne, C., & Edwards, L. (2012). Producing trust, knowledge and expertise in financial markets: The global hedge fund industry 're-presents' itself. *Culture and Organisation, 18*(2), 107–122. https://doi.org/10.1080/14759551.2011.636614.

Buller, J., & Lindstrom, N. (2012). Hedging its bets: The UK and the politics of European financial services regulation. *New Political Economy, 18*(3), 391–409. https://doi.org/10.1080/13563467.2012.700924.

Casu, B., Girardone, C., & Molyneux, P. (2015). *Introduction to banking* (2nd ed.). Harlow: Pearson Education.

Cleary, G. (2018). *EU Commission proposals to harmonise the cross-border distribution of funds and define 'pre-marketing'*. https://www.clearygottlieb.com/-/media/files/alert-memos-2018/eu-proposals-to-harmonize-cross-border-fund-distribution-and-regulate-pre-marketing.pdf. Accessed 23 July 2020.

Colaert, V. A. (2016). MiFID II in relation to other investor protection regulation: Picking up the crumbs of a piecemeal approach. In D. Busch & G. Ferrarini (Eds.), *Regulation of the EU financial markets: MiFID II and MiFIR* (pp. 864–894). Oxford: Oxford University Press.

Debevoise & Plimpton. (2018). *European Commission proposes harmonised pre-marketing rules for funds*. https://www.debevoise.com/insights/publications/2018/03/european-commission-proposes-harmonised. Accessed 12 May 2020.

Dickson, P. (2019). *Asset management review* (8th ed.). London: Law Business Research.

ESMA. (2018). *Keynote address, CMU, Brexit and ESA review—What's next?* European Securities and Markets Authorities. https://www.google.com/url?sa=t&rct=j&q=&esrc=s&source=web&cd=&cad=rja&uact=8&ved=2ahUKEwiHiYfxm6frAhXilosKHbFJALMQFjABegQIBhAB&url=https%3A%2F%2Fwww.esma.europa.eu%2Fdocument%2Fcmu-brexit-and-esa-review-%25E2%2580%2593-what%25E2%2580%2599s-next-steven-maijoor-bvi-keynote&usg=AOvVaw0GlKMpyxpC4Zg-3Y8B1wEE. Accessed 12 May 2020.

FCA. (2010). *CP10/17 Strengthening capital standards 3*. Financial Services Authority. https://www.google.com/url?sa=t&rct=j&q=&esrc=s&source=web&cd=&ved=2ahUKEwj5hL6Tn6frAhXhlIsKHRLIAiEQFjAAegQIAxAB&url=https%3A%2F%2Fwww.fca.org.uk%2Fpublication%2Fconsultation%2Fcp10_17.pdf&usg=AOvVaw0oTH7zt3NiqpWYmdVDdO4M. Accessed 15 May 2020.

FCA. (2017). *Our mission 2017: How we regulate financial services*. Financial Conduct Authority. https://www.fca.org.uk/publication/corporate/our-mission-2017.pdf. Accessed 12 May 2020.

FCA. (2018). *FCA mission: Our approach to supervision*. Financial Conduct Authority. https://www.fca.org.uk/publication/corporate/our-approach-supervision.pdf. Accessed 12 May 2020.

FCA. (2019). *The senior managers and certification regime: Guide for FCA solo-regulated firms*. Financial Conduct Authority. https://www.fca.org.uk/publication/policy/guide-for-fca-solo-regulated-firms.pdf. Accessed 20 May 2020.

FCA. (2020a, March). *Code of Conduct (COCON) handbook*. Handbook, Release 48. Financial Conduct Authority. https://www.handbook.fca.org.uk.handbook/COCON.pdf. Accessed 12 May 2020.

FCA. (2020b). *SYSC 27 Senior managers and certification regime: Certification regime*. Financial Conduct Authority. https://www.google.com/url?sa=t&rct=j&q=&esrc=s&source=web&cd=&cad=rja&uact=8&ved=2ahUKEwijnvaEnafrAhXxsosKHQ4lDOwQFjAAegQIAhAB&url=https%3A%2F%2Fwww.handbook.fca.org.uk%2Fhandbook%2FSYSC%2F27.pdf&usg=AOvVaw214_GYCaxrLAEzCfe8LGtT. Accessed 12 May 2020.

FCA. (2020c, April). *Decision procedure and penalties manual*. Manual, Release 49. Financial Conduct Authority. https://www.handbook.fca.org.uk/handbook/DEPP.pdf. Accessed 12 May 2020.

FCA. (2020d). *Investment funds sourcebook 3.9*. Financial Conduct Authority. https://www.handbook.fca.org.uk/handbook/FUND.pdf. Accessed 12 June 2020.

Ferran, E. (2011a). The breaking-up of the financial services authority. *Oxford Journal of Legal Studies, 31*(3), 455–480. https://doi.org/10.1093/ojls/gqr006.

Ferran, E. (2011b). *The regulation of hedge funds and private equity: A case study in the development of the EU's regulatory response to the financial crisis* (University of Cambridge Faculty of Law Research Paper No. 10/2011, ECGI—Law Working Paper No. 176/2011). http://dx.doi.org/10.2139/ssrn.1762119. Accessed 15 May 2020.

Ferran, E. (2012). Understanding the new institutional architecture of EU financial market supervision. In E. Wymeersch, K. J. Hopt, & G. Ferrarini (Eds.), *Financial regulation and supervision: A post-crisis analysis*. Oxford: Oxford University Press.

FSB. (2011). *Shadow banking: Scoping the issues*. Financial Stability Board. https://www.google.com/url?sa=t&rct=j&q=&esrc=s&source=web&cd=&cad=rja&uact=8&ved=2ahUKEwjs647Hn6frAhVwtIsKHQXdBOIQFjAAegQIBBAB&url=https%3A%2F%2Fwww.fsb.org%2Fwp-content%2Fuploads%2Fr_110412a.pdf&usg=AOvVaw0NydyBv3uxCDCreofBeC2E. Accessed 1 June 2020.

FSB. (2012a). *Increasing the intensity and effectiveness of SIFI supervision: Progress report to the G20 Ministers and Governors*. Financial Stability Board. https://www.google.com/url?sa=t&rct=j&q=&esrc=s&source=web&cd=&cad=rja&uact=8&ved=2ahUKEwi1tab9n6frAhVElYsKHa1CAJMQFjAAegQIAxAB&url=http%3A%2F%2Fwww.fsb.org%2Fwp-content%2Fuploads%2Fr_121031ab.pdf&usg=AOvVaw0bOz6kMiPXFGFGnv-UsiwH. Accessed 1 June 2020.

Georgosouli, A. (2013). The FCA-PRA coordination scheme and the challenge of policy coherence. *Capital Markets Law Journal, 8*(1), 62–76. http://dx.doi.org.am.e-nformation.ro/10.1093/cmlj/kms044.

HM Treasury. (2010). *A new approach to financial regulation: Judgement, focus and stability*. hm-treasury.gov.uk. Accessed 15 June 2020.

HM Treasury. (2011). *A new approach to financial regulation: Building a stronger system*. https://www.gov.uk/government/consultations/a-new-approach-to-financial-regulation-building-a-stronger-system. Accessed 15 June 2020.

Horan, S. (2012). White collar crime, money laundering and taxation: The AIFMD and hedge funds—An international and Irish perspective. In D. A. Zetzsche (Ed.), *The alternative investment fund managers directive: European regulation of investment funds* (pp. 109–138). International Banking and Finance Law Series. The Netherlands: Wolters Kluwer Law and Business.

House of Lords. (2020). *European Union (Withdrawal Agreement) Bill, Ordered to be printed 13 January 2020 and published 14 January 2020*. London: Authority of the House of Lords. https://publications.parliament.uk/pa/ld5801/ldselect/ldconst/5/5.pdf. Accessed 12 May 2020.

Howell, E. (2020). Post-Brexit UK fund regulation: Equivalence, divergence or convergence? *European Business Organization Law Review*. https://doi.org/10.1007/s40804-020-00177-w.

Izaguirre, J. C. (2020). *Making consumer protection regulation more customer-centric* (Working Paper). Washington, DC: CGAP. https://www.cgap.org/research/publication/making-consumer-protection-regulation-more-customer-centric. Accessed 13 June 2020.

Kenny, F., & Mallaburn, D. (2017). *Hedge funds and their prime brokers: Developments since the financial crisis*. Bank of England Quarterly Bulletin 2017, Q4. SSRN: https://ssrn.com/abstract=3095892. Accessed 15 June 2020.

Koehl, A. (2016). *Brexit and short-selling disclosures*. http://dx.doi.org/10.2139/ssrn.2808498. Accessed 20 June 2020.

Kovas, A. (2014). *Understanding the financial conduct authority—A guide for senior managers*. Leicestershire: Troubador Publishing.

Lehmann, M., & Zetzsche, D. A. (2018). *How does it feel to be a third country? The consequences of Brexit for financial market law* (CIGI & BIICL, Brexit: The International Legal Implications, Paper No. 14). https://ssrn.com/abstract=3155355. Accessed 15 June 2020.

Lopez, C., & Saeidinezhad, E. (2016). *UK financial reforms: Bank of England 2.0*. https://doi.org/10.2139/ssrn.2911914. Accessed 15 June 2020.

MacGregor, B., Schulz, R., & Green, R. K. (2018). *Routledge companion to real estate investment*. London: Routledge. https://doi.org/10.1201/9781315775579.

Mashiandaro, D., & Suardi, M. (2014). Public interest and lobbies in reforming banking regulation: Three tales of ring fencing. *International Review of Economics, 61*, 305–328.

McVea, H. (2018). Targeting hedge funds and 'repo runs'. In I. H.-Y. Chiu & I. G. MacNeil (Eds.), *Research handbook on shadow banking* (p. 189). London: Edward Elgar.

Moloney, N. (2016). Financial services, the EU, and Brexit: An uncertain future for the city? *German Law Journal, 17*, 75–82.

Olivares-Caminal, R., & Bodellini, M. (2017a). The impact of Brexit on the UK alternative investment fund industry. *Law and Economics Yearly Review, 6*(1), 79–103.

Olivares-Caminal, R., & Bodellini, M. (2017b). The UK regulation on alternative investment fund managers: A difficult compromise between two different legislative approaches. *Journal of Banking Regulation, 19*(1), 73–85. https://doi.org/10.1057/s41261-017-0052-1.

Osborne, G. (2010). *Speech at The Lord Mayor's Dinner for Bankers & Merchants of the City of London by The Chancellor of the Exchequer, The Rt Hon George Osborne MP, at Mansion House*. https://www.gov.uk/government/speeches/speech-by-the-chancellor-of-the-exchequer-rt-hon-george-osborne-mp-at-mansion-house. Accessed 12 May 2020.

Pitt, C., & Cavers, M. (2018). *Hedge funds in the UK (England and Wales): Regulatory overview*. https://uk.practicallaw.thomsonreuters.com/w-009-9984?transitionType=Default&contextData=(sc.Default)&firstPage=true&bhcp=1#co_anchor_a337973. Accessed 20 May 2020.

Prudential Regulation Authority. (2013a). *Strengthening capital standards: Implementing CRD IV* (Vol. CP5/13). London: Bank of England. https://www.google.com/url?sa=t&rct=j&q=&esrc=s&source=web&cd=&ved=2ahUKEwjEirbzyqfrAhUWilwKHbjWBHUQFjABegQIAxAB&url=https%3A%2F%2Fwww.bankofengland.co.uk%2F-%2Fmedia%2Fboe%2Ffiles%2Fprudential-regulation%2Fconsultation-paper%2F2013%2Fcp513.pdf&usg=AOvVaw1dAoa1tDRqLmNYXMWe2rCV. Accessed 20 May 2020.

Prudential Regulation Authority. (2013b). *Supervisory statement 11/13 internal ratings based approaches*. London: Bank of England. https://www.google.com/url?sa=t&rct=j&q=&esrc=s&source=web&cd=&ved=2ahUKEwiKv-D6y6frAhVBlFwKHZ-6AHAQFjABegQIAxAB&url=https%3A%2F%2Fwww.bankofengland.co.uk%2F-%2Fmedia%2Fboe%2Ffiles%2Fprudential-regulation%2Fsupervisory-statement%2F2013%2Fss1113.pdf%3Fla%3Den%26hash%3DB

7AD49D3B53B2DCAEA20D7C39AE43EF60B11A174&usg=AOvVaw3e4 4AONyo_RY1OXw5Phaqj. Accessed 20 May 2020.

Prudential Regulation Authority. (2013c). *Supervisory statement 12/13 counterparty credit risk*. London: Bank of England. https://www.google.com/url?sa=t&rct=j&q=&esrc=s&source=web&cd=&ved=2ahUKEwjaitmczKfrAhWLOcAKHSenCXMQFjAAegQIBRAB&url=https%3A%2F%2Fwww.bankofengland.co.uk%2F-%2Fmedia%2Fboe%2Ffiles%2Fprudential-regulation%2Fsupervisory-statement%2F2013%2Fss1213.pdf&usg=AOvVaw3zooCy2vB_w9_vzsijVdFx. Accessed 20 May 2020.

Prudential Regulation Authority. (2013d). *Supervisory statement 13/13 market risk*. London: Bank of England. https://www.google.com/url?sa=t&rct=j&q=&esrc=s&source=web&cd=&ved=2ahUKEwjhh-jzzKfrAhXxlFwKHURsC3IQFjABegQIBRAB&url=https%3A%2F%2Fwww.bankofengland.co.uk%2F-%2Fmedia%2Fboe%2Ffiles%2Fprudential-regulation%2Fsupervisory-statement%2F2013%2Fss1313.pdf%3Fla%3Den%26hash%3DDED4889473DAE9A668D0279E1B8037B1B8ED59EC&usg=AOvVaw0lK5iaibmDWT8Cf5YwMn_E. Accessed 20 May 2020.

Prudential Regulation Authority. (2014). *CRD IV: Liquidity* (Vol. CP27/14). London: Bank of England. https://www.google.com/url?sa=t&rct=j&q=&esrc=s&source=web&cd=&ved=2ahUKEwiTh8KgzafrAhXRa8AKHf8-CXQQFjAAegQIBhAB&url=https%3A%2F%2Fwww.bankofengland.co.uk%2F-%2Fmedia%2Fboe%2Ffiles%2Fprudential-regulation%2Fconsultation-paper%2F2014%2Fcp2714&usg=AOvVaw2jKjiSoUyJPJiGkwX2H1d8. Accessed 20 May 2020.

Prudential Regulation Authority. (2015). *Implementing a UK leverage ratio framework* (Vol. CP24/15). London: Bank of England. https://www.google.com/url?sa=t&rct=j&q=&esrc=s&source=web&cd=&ved=2ahUKEwjgrIW-zafrAhUJYsAKHSLNBnAQFjABegQIAhAB&url=https%3A%2F%2Fwww.bankofengland.co.uk%2F-%2Fmedia%2Fboe%2Ffiles%2Fprudential-regulation%2Fconsultation-paper%2F2015%2Fcp2415&usg=AOvVaw0QrktAdqlAoFPj9id8V2_9. Accessed 20 May 2020.

Quaglia, L. (2015). The politics of 'third country equivalence' in post-crisis financial services regulation in the European Union. *West European Politics, 38*(1), 167–184. https://doi.org/10.1080/01402382.2014.920984.

Putnis, J. (2014). *The banking regulation review* (5th ed.). London: Law Business Research.

Parise, T. V., & Shenai, V. (2018). The value effect of financial reform on UK banks and insurance companies. *International Journal of Financial Studies, 6*(81), 1–28. https://doi.org/10.3390/ijfs6030081.

Ringe, W. G. (2017). The irrelevance of Brexit for the European financial market. *European Business Organization Law Review*. https://doi.org/10.2139/ssrn.2902715.

SBAI. (2015). *The hedge fund standards (11/2015)*. Standards Board for Alternative Investments. https://www.google.com/url?sa=t&rct=j&q=&esrc=s&source=web&cd=&ved=2ahUKEwjxrLa706frAhVPecAKHQepCm4QFjAAegQIAxAB&url=http%3A%2F%2Fwww.sbai.org%2Fwp-content%2Fuploads%2F2016%2F04%2FHedge-Fund-Standards-as-at-November-2015.pdf&usg=AOvVaw3sM_3rL7Rafn6_2VIyoK7Z. Accessed 12 April 2020.

SBAI. (2018). *Annual report 2018*. Standards Board for Alternative Investments. https://www.sbai.org/about-us/reports/. Accessed 12 May 2020.

Schnittker Möllman Partners. (2018). *EU Commission proposal: Narrowing the 'pre-marketing' concept*. https://www.smp.law/EN/Briefing/Fund_Briefing_EU_Commission_proposal_copy.php. Accessed 23 May 2020.

Sennholz-Weinhardt, B. (2014). Regulatory competition as a social fact: Constructing and contesting the threat of hedge fund managers relocation from Britain. *Review of International Political Economy, 21*(6), 1240–1274. https://doi.org/10.1080/09692290.2013.844722.

Sowels, N. (2017). Brexit and UK-based financial services. *Revue Française de Civilisation Britannique* [Online] (XXII-2), 1. http://rfcb.revues.org/1331. Accessed 12 April 2020.

Vives, X. (2016). Competition policy, regulatory architecture, and public intervention in the crisis. In X. Vives (Ed.), *Competition and stability in banking: The role of regulation and competition policy* (pp. 183–221). Princeton: Princeton University Press. https://doi.org/10.2307/j.ctt1q1xs80.12.

Walker, G. A. (2012). UK regulatory revision—A new blueprint for reform. *The International Lawyer, 46*(3), 787–828.

Zetzsche, D. A. (2012). Introduction: Overview, regulatory history and technique, transition. In D. A. Zetzsche (Ed.), *The alternative investment fund managers directive: European regulation of investment funds* (pp. 1–20). The Netherlands: Wolters Kluwer Law and Business.

Zetzsche, D. A. (2015). *The alternative investment fund managers directive* (2nd ed.). The Netherlands: Kluwer Law International.

Zetzsche, D. A. (2017). *The anatomy of European investment fund law*. http://dx.doi.org/10.2139/ssrn.2951681. Accessed 12 April 2020.

CHAPTER 5

The Non Regulation of Hedge Funds in Offshores Jurisdictions: Cayman Islands, British Virgin Islands, Mauritius, and Delaware

5.1 Coining the Terms: Offshore Hedge Funds

Palan (1998) offers one of the most precise definitions of the term "offshore" depicting it "as legal enclaves distinguished from their 'on-shore' brethren, not necessarily because of their location, but because they define a territory or a realm of activities in which states choose to withhold some or all of their regulations and taxation. In that sense, offshore signals a profound fissure in the life of the state system: it denotes nothing less than the bifurcation of the juridical space of sovereignty into mutually dependent relative spaces".[1] In a similar definition, this time more recent, an "offshore hedge fund is called offshore when its manager creates a legal entity in a country other than that of the management company in order to profit from its low income tax and financial benefits.[2]

Offshore hedge funds tend to be set up by sponsors expecting to manage a significant amount of capital from non-US investors and/or

[1] Palan, R. (1998). Trying to have your cake and eating it: How and why the state system has created offshore. *International Studies Quarterly, 42*(4), 625–644.

[2] Khelifa, S. B., & Hmaied, D. M. (2014). European hedge funds industry: An overview. *The Journal of Private Equity, 18*(1), 46–59.

A. M. Fagetan, *The Regulation of Hedge Funds*,
https://doi.org/10.1007/978-3-030-63706-4_5

from US-based tax-exempt investors which want to avoid UBTI,[3] most of the time domiciled in tax-light or even no-tax jurisdictions.

At the same time, more recently, Palan et al., associate offshore and the Cayman Islands,[4] in their report Cayman being the fourth largest international banking center in the world.[5] Indeed, there are many sources which claim that more than $2.6 trillion in untaxed profits of US companies can be found in offshore jurisdictions.[6] These jurisdictions which are usually small, mild islands with little permanent workforce, became lately, as Palan et al. observed, major financial havens hosting hedge funds and not only.[7] In this respect, it is estimated that the Cayman Islands[8] host more than 60% of the world's hedge fund assets,[9] and currently reported as the third-largest holder of US government debt.[10] This is encouraged

[3] Unrelated Business Taxable Income (I.R.C. Section 511(a)(1)). The definition of the UBTI regards the gross income derived either directly, or indirectly, through a partnership with any organization; this is chargeable on the profit its unrelated trade activity or other business regularly carried on by it (I.R.C. Section 512), minus the deductions directly connected with carrying out such activity. Both the gross income and the deductions are computed with certain modifications and are subject to certain exclusions.

In general, UBTI does not imply: interest, dividends, or gains from the sale or exchange of capital assets. As a consequence, a tax-exempt investor's distributive share from a hedge fund does not class as UBTI, which does not make it subject to federal income tax.

[4] Palan, R., Murphy, R., & Chavagneux, C. (2010). *Tax havens: How globalization really works*. New York: Cornell University Press.

[5] Palan, R. (2015). The second British Empire: The British Empire and the re-emergence of global finance. In S. Halperin & R. Palan (Eds.), *Legacies of empire imperial roots of the contemporary global order* (pp. 40–68). Cambridge: Cambridge University Press.

[6] Browning, L. (2017b, June 12). *Trump's offshore tax plan may mean perk for Apple, Pfizer*. Bloomberg. http://www.bloomberg.com/news/articles/2017-06-12/trump-s-offshore-tax-plan-may-mean-extra-perk-for-apple-pfizer. Accessed 12 March 2020.

[7] Palan, R., Murphy, R., & Chavagneux, C. (2010). *Tax havens: How globalization really works*. New York: Cornell University Press.

[8] Located in the Western Caribbean.

[9] Fichtner, J. (2016). The anatomy of the Cayman Islands Offshore Financial Center: Anglo-America, Japan, and the role of hedge funds. *Review of International Political Economy, 23*, 1034 ("About 60% of global hedge fund assets are legally domiciled in Cayman").

[10] Ronalds-Hannon, E. (2016, June 21). *Hedge funds' misery exposed as Caribbean proxies dump treasuries*. Bloomberg. https://www.bloomberg.com/news/articles/2016-06-21/hedge-funds-misery-exposed-as-caribbean-proxies-dump-treasuries. Accessed 6 April 2020.

mainly by law firms which are interested in providing full-service services, starting with offshore mergers and acquisitions and ending with offshore fund formations.[11] This captivated the attention of many academics but also of lawmakers, particularly due to the fact that small islands transformed into hubs of modern hedge funds imply major efforts to diminish tax evasion or avoidance.[12] A similar opinion is supported also by De Brouwer, who states that "most hedge funds are incorporated offshore, in exotic places such as Grand Cayman and Bermuda, to minimize taxes paid."[13]

Indeed, offshore hedge funds enable entities to avoid domestic regulatory laws, especially "under recent US Supreme Court case law strengthening the presumption against applying federal statutes in cases with both domestic and foreign facts."[14]

5.2 Comparative Perspective Offshore Versus Onshore

In a research paper written in 2013, Fichtner spoke about inequalities existing between offshore and onshore hedge funds, "inequality between nearly unregulated hedge funds and the regulated rest of financial market actors; inequality between offshore financial centers that provide minimal regulation and low taxation to hedge funds, and onshore jurisdiction that

[11] Corporate. (2018). *APPLEBY*. http://www.applebyglobal.com/services/corporate.aspx. Accessed 12 March 2020; Fitzgibbon, W. (2017, November 5). Appleby, the offshore law firm with a record of compliance failures. *Irish Times*. https://www.irishtimes.com/business/appleby-the-offshore-law-firm-with-a-record-of-compliance-failures-1.3280860. Accessed 12 March 2020; see also Valencia, M. (2013, February 16). Storm survivors. *The Economist*. http://www.economist.com/news/special-report/21571549-offshore-financial-centres-have-taken-battering-recently-they-have-shown-remarkable. Accessed 6 April 2020 (assessing that offshore financial havens grew "often with help from lawyers based in Wall Street or the City of London").

[12] Clarke, C. (2016). What are tax havens and why are they bad? *Texas Law Review, 95*, 59–68.

[13] De Brouwer, G. (2001). *Hedge funds in emerging markets*. Cambridge: Cambridge University Press.

[14] Fichtner, J. (2016). The anatomy of the Cayman Islands Offshore Financial Center: Anglo-America, Japan, and the role of hedge funds. *Review of International Political Economy, 23*, 1037.

do not."[15] In his opinion, there are two countries that allow "this unequal regulation of hedge funds,"[16] namely the United States and the United Kingdom. In his opinion, these countries "refrain from any strict direct regulation of the funds' activities and also provide the important offshore legal domiciles."[17]

Indeed, in a 2014 analysis concerning offshore and onshore hedge funds it is stated that "at the end of 2012, 76.74% of European hedge funds were domiciled offshore, especially in tax havens such as the British Virgin Islands, Luxembourg, the Cayman Islands, and Guernsey."[18] According to the same report, funds that are domiciled in the United States reach almost 50%, more precisely 47.19%, dominating mainly in the Cayman Islands. This Cayman Island domination is explained by the tax benefits offered by this territory.[19] In addition, "the rest of offshore hedge funds, representing 29.55% of all European hedge funds are registered in European countries, including Ireland, which has the largest share. Onshore European funds represent 17.54% of the total, with a concentration of funds in Luxembourg."[20] On the other hand, Delaware ranks first place as a domicile location among the US (offshore) hedge funds.

As far as the choice of the jurisdiction is concerned, "hedge funds may select any jurisdiction to be domiciled in, although inevitable the jurisdiction chosen will be determined by more practical, operational factors."[21] In this vein, Cumming, Dai, and Johan outline that "the scope of investors that may invest in a hedge fund depends on the regulatory

[15] Fichtner, J. (2013). The rise of hedge funds: A story of inequality. *Momentum Quarterly, 2*(1), 3–20.

[16] Idem, at 4.

[17] Idem, at 4.

[18] These states have no or limited income tax and managers have broad freedom of action.

[19] First, there is no real exchange of tax information with foreign authorities, and there is insufficient transparency in the function of legal provisions. Second, there are no income taxes. Finally, the substantial local presence is not required.

[20] Khelifa, S. B., & Hmaied, D. M. (2014). European hedge funds industry: An overview. *The Journal of Private Equity, 18*(1), 46–59.

[21] Cumming, D., Dai, N., & Johan, S. A. (2015). Are hedge funds domiciled in delaware different? *Journal of Corporate Finance, 35*, 232–246.

landscape in which the fund is domiciled, therefore fund raising will be a factor in domicile choice."[22]

Although there are important differences between both regulations and investor taxes, there is little academic research differentiating between onshore (funds located in the US) and offshore hedge funds[23] (funds domiciled in low-tax jurisdictions among which one can mention the Cayman Islands and British Virgin Islands). However, US investors are usually confronted with choosing either onshore or offshore: "US investors are often confronted with the issue of investing in an offshore investment vehicle and hedge fund managers are often confronted with the issue of whether to set up a domestic fund, an offshore fund or both. Generally, US tax-exempt investors and foreign investors invest in a manager's parallel offshore hedge fund or offshore feeder fund which is classified as a corporation for US federal income tax purposes. Conventional wisdom is that US taxable investors invest in the manager's parallel domestic fund or domestic feeder fund which is classified as a partnership for US federal income tax purposes."[24] As it is known, for the avoidance of registering under the Investment Company Act of 1940, hedge funds managers must both (1) limit the number (maximum 100 or 499) and (2) type of fund investors. Also, they (3) are banned from public offerings of fund shares, and (4) may use just private placements to solicit US investors.[25] On the contrary, offshore managers do not pay attention to these aspects, particularly because their shares are not offered to US taxable investors. Hardly investing into or keeping custody of assets in

[22] Cumming, D., Dai, N., & Johan, S. A. (2013). *Hedge fund structure, regulation, and performance around the world*. Oxford: Oxford University Press.

[23] See in this vein Brown et al. (1999), who analyze offshore fund performance by using information from the US Offshore Funds Directory, Aragon, G. B., & Park, L. H. (2014). Onshore and offshore hedge funds: Are they twins? *Management Science, 60*(1), 74–91.

[24] Gross, PhS. (2004). Tax planning for offshore hedge funds—Potential benefits of investing in a PFIC. *Journal of Taxation of Investments, 21*(2), 187–195.

[25] See §§3(c)(l) and 3(c)(7) of the Investment Company Act of 1940. Although a fund can have an unlimited number of qualified investors under the §3(c)(7) exemption, a fund having more than 499 investors would trigger registration under the Security Exchange Act of 1934. Also, in addition to avoiding fund registration, managers of onshore funds further rely on an exemption from registering with the US Securities and Exchange Commission (SEC) under the Investment Advisers Act.

the United States does not imply major US regulation worries.[26] At the same time, they got access to financial assets outside the US by way of various distribution channels besides private placements, being comprised banks as well as investment managers.[27]

At the same time, there are major differences between onshore and offshore funds from the point of view of their legal structures, and particularly with regard to tax requirements. First of all, traditionally, for non-US investors, "hedge funds' legal domicile is where regulatory requirements are at a minimum, often in offshore tax havens".[28] Usually, offshore funds tend to be organized under a corporate structure avoiding UBTI, which makes them more tempting to tax-exempt investors by far, additionally to investors[29] who are not from the United States. On the contrary, according to McCrary (2002), generally, onshore funds are structured as "limited partnerships in order that taxable income is 'passed through' to fund investors instead of being taxed at both the investor and entity levels."[30]

In their work "Onshore and Offshore Hedge Funds: Are They Twins?" Aragon, Liang, and Park conduct a comparative research of onshore and offshore hedge funds during several years, between 1994 and 2010. Indeed, according to them there are several differences between these two types of hedge funds, the major differences being observed in investment strategies, share restrictions, capital flow, and performance. Also,

[26] Barth, M. H., & Blanco, M. (2001). US regulatory and tax considerations for offshore funds. In S. Barham, I. Hallsworth, & C. Bonnett (Eds.), *The capital guide to offshore funds 2001* (pp. 15–61). The Hague: ISI Publications.

[27] Cumming, D. J., & Dai, N. (2010). Local bias in venture capital investments. *Journal of Empirical Finance, 17*, 362–380. In this paper, they summarize the regulations of hedge funds across 29 countries. They discover that, in contrast to offshore fund managers, onshore fund managers are restricted to only one (private placement) of a possible seven distinct marketing channels: banks, fund distribution companies, wrappers, private placements, investment managers, other regulated financial service institutions, and nonregulated financial intermediaries.

[28] Tuchschmid, N. S., & Wallerstein, E. (2013). UCITS: Can they bring funds of hedge funds on-shore? *The Journal of Wealth Management, 15*(4), 90–109. https://doi.org/10.3905/jwm.2013.15.4.094.

[29] US taxable investors face tax rules that may discourage them from investing in offshore funds, Gross, PhS. (2004). Tax planning for offshore hedge funds—Potential benefits of investing in a PFIC. *Journal of Taxation of Investments, 21*(2), 187–195.

[30] McCrary, S. A. (2002). *How to create and manage a hedge fund—A professional's guide*. Hoboken: John Wiley & Sons.

according to them, offshore funds have grown much faster than onshore funds. In the authors' opinion, offshore funds, due to the fact that they "have access to additional funding channels, could hold more illiquid assets."[31]

Also, they conclude that "the portfolios of onshore funds contain more liquid assets and assets with lower market liquidity risk than do offshore funds. In particular, onshore funds are less common among 'illiquid' style categories, such as emerging markets, convertible arbitrage, fixed income arbitrage, and multi-strategy."[32] As far as regulatory constraints are concerned, with regard to marketing efforts of onshore funds when compared with offshore funds, this would lead to lower performance-flow sensitivity.

At the same time, the impact of current US hedge fund regulation can lead to a better understanding of the differences between onshore and offshore hedge funds. According to Aragon et al., taking into consideration the fact that new regulation under "the Dodd-Frank Act places a comparatively greater regulatory burden on onshore fund managers; this may increase the incentives for managers to circumvent regulation by opening offshore funds."[33]

To anyone's surprise, most offshore hedge funds are successful in tax havens such as the Cayman Islands, which house thousands of hedge funds[34] in spite of being only around 1.5 times Washington's size and having a population of around 58,000 people.[35]

[31] Aragon, G. B., & Park, L. H. (2014). Onshore and offshore hedge funds: Are they twins? *Management Science, 60*(1), 74–91.

[32] Fichtner, J. (2016). The anatomy of the Cayman Islands Offshore Financial Center: Anglo-America, Japan, and the role of hedge funds. *Review of International Political Economy, 23*(6), 1034–1063. https://doi.org/10.1080/09692290.2016.1243143.

[33] Ibid., p. 90.

[34] Johnston, D. C. (2007). *Free lunch: How the wealthiest Americans enrich themselves at government expense*. New York: Penguin Group ("Hedge funds are legally organized offshore, the favorite spot being the Cayman Islands Most hedge-fund managers have never even been to the Cayman Islands, making the headquarters arrangement a farce."); Deloitte (2015). *Establishing investment funds in the Cayman Islands: Key considerations*. https://www2.deloitte.com/content/dam/Deloitte/bm/Documents/financial-services/cayman-islands/establishing-investment-funds-in-the-cayman-islands.pdf. Accessed 3 April 2020.

[35] Cent. Intelligence Agency. (2018). *The World Factbook: Cayman Islands*. https://www.cia.gov/library/publications/the-world-factbook/geos/cj.html. Accessed 6 April 2020.

The difference between hedge funds industries and other industries which focus on productive services lies in the territorial issue. The hedge fund industry, being a financial activity does not need to identify a particular territory, as long as financial transactions tend to be legally constituted.[36] Therefore, since offshore hedge funds are built on a financial system of rules, there is no need for this industry to be territorial, this being generally true for entities like hedge funds which do not serve direct customers.[37]

This is the main reason why entities in the hedge funds sector could structure their operations to domicile "the head office in an offshore center with the onshore activities organized into affiliates of the offshore headquarters."[38] Thus, hedge funds entities "can be headquartered in offshore jurisdictions without (for the most part) physically moving their operations offshore"[39]—this being the case for hedge funds in the Cayman Islands.

Similar advantages of choosing as domicile for hedge funds offshore locations are also underlined by Cohen and Williams, who, in their Article *A Comparison by Practitioners of Delaware and Cayman Islands Limited Partnerships* state that "hedge fund managers, due to their trading strategies or investor bases, have long looked offshore for flexible, responsive regulation that also provides tax efficiency for their investors. An offshore domicile provides several advantages to the average hedge fund. A fund domiciled offshore will not pay taxes on the gains made by the portfolio (investors will still be taxed on such profits in their home jurisdiction upon

[36] Pistor, K. (2013). A legal theory of finance. *Journal of Comparative Economics, 41*(2), 315–330.

Private Funds Law. (2020). Law 1 of 2020 Supplement No. 1 published with Legislation Gazette No. 9 dated 7th February, 2020. https://www.cima.ky/upimages/commonfiles/PrivateFundsLaw2020_1581524961.PDF. Accessed 12 April 2020.

[37] Kleinbard, E. D. (2003). Competitive convergence in the financial services markets. *Taxes, 81*, 225–260.

[38] Philip, R. L., & Milesi-Ferretti, G. M. (2010). Cross-border investment in small international financial centers. *International Monetary Fund Working Paper, 10*(38), 1–32. In this vein, Professor William Magnuson explained that the remarkable mobility of capital has allowed "companies to operate on a global basis from headquarters in the Cayman Islands or the Seychelles, countries recognized as tax havens." Magnuson, W. (2016). Unilateral corporate regulation. *Chicago Journal of International Law, 17*, 521–537.

[39] Moon, W. J. (2019). Regulating offshore finance. *Vanderbilt Law Review, 72*(1), 1–54.

withdrawal or distribution). If a manager expects significant participation by non-US or US tax-exempt investors, an offshore domicile will provide tax efficiency since these investors will not be subject to US tax on the profits generated offshore."[40]

According to Cohen and Williams, the majority of offshore hedge funds tend to be formed using a "master-feeder" structure, which can be organized under the form of a partnership or an offshore corporation[41] in an offshore location, similar to the Cayman Islands, due to its foreign residence under the US tax code. They also acknowledge that "the master fund typically has two 'feeders' that invest in the master fund: the domestic feeder for US resident taxable investors; and the foreign feeder for non-US investors and US tax-exempt investors. The domestic feeder is a limited partnership, usually organized in Delaware, so all of its items of income, gain, deduction, or loss pass through to its partners."[42]

Another important difference is that at the level of the investment manager, who is generally hired by the offshore hedge fund to manage its assets in exchange for an incentive fee and a management fee. One major difference between offshore and onshore funds in this case resides in the fact that, unlike what is usually done in the onshore fund case, in offshore funds there is no need to segregate the recipients of the management and the performance fees, since no taxes need to be paid to the state, or taxes must not be avoided.

5.3 Major Offshore Locations for Hedge Funds

As already seen before, there are plenty of benefits for hedge funds in moving offshore, the most important being for sure the tax neutrality, these locations being known also under the name of "tax havens." Indeed, these locations offer strongly favorable tax terms as a stimulus to start up new business, taxes that lead, on the one hand to big profits and on the other hand to major benefits for the host country as well, no

[40] Cohen, A. R., & Williams, C. S. (2011). *Comparison by practitioners of Delaware and Cayman Islands Limited Partnerships*. Bloomberg Finance L.P. Law Reports—Fund Management and Bloomberg Law Reports—Securities Law.

[41] but treated as a partnership for US tax purposes via a check-the-box election.

[42] Cohen, A. R., & Williams, C. S. (2011). *Comparison by practitioners of Delaware and Cayman Islands Limited partnerships*. Bloomberg Finance L.P. Law Reports—Fund Management and Bloomberg Law Reports—Securities Law.

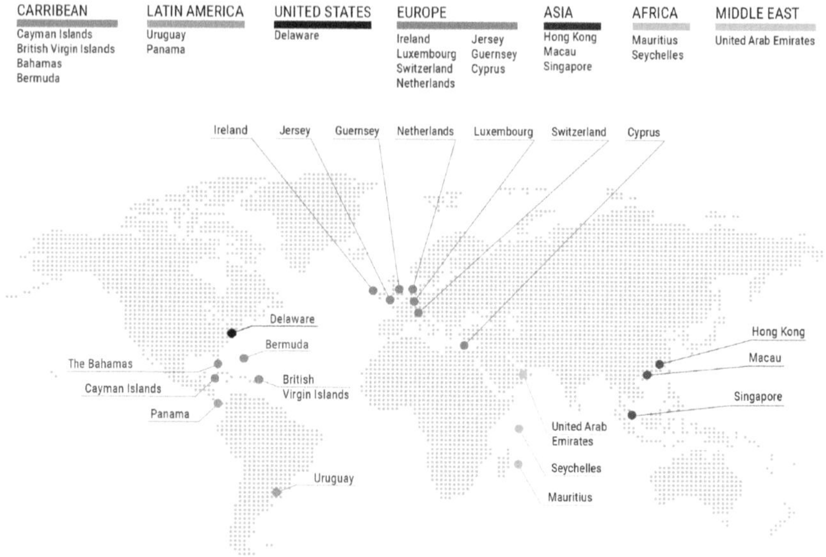

Fig. 5.1 The world's most important locations for offshore funds (*Source* Wolters Kluwer [2015])

matter if it is a small or a big country. In addition, "moving into an international market often provides companies with access to a wide variety of non-traditional investments—opportunities that may not be accessible via a domestic bank or brokerage firm."[43] Figure 5.1 presents, grouped by region, some of the world's most important locations for offshore funds.[44]

The current chapter will analyze only three of these regions: *The Caribbean*, more precisely the Cayman Islands and the British Virgin Islands, *United States*, respectively Delaware and *Africa*—Mauritius. Each of these offshore domiciles of hedge funds will be analyzed further on.

[43] Wolters Kluwer. (2015). *A guide to the top 20 offshore fund locations*. https://ct.wolterskluwer.com/sites/default/files/CT_Top_20_Offshore_Funds_0.pdf. Accessed 4 March 2020.

[44] Idem.

5.3.1 The Cayman Islands: The World's Largest Host of Hedge Funds

The Cayman Islands were accurately called "small place, big money" in the first analyses that regarded their position in the international financial system.[45] Since 1995, when this title was given to the Cayman Islands, the amount of foreign capital booked in the Cayman OFC,[46] grew bigger and bigger.[47] On the one hand, Cayman is one of the largest financial centers globally speaking, as well as a key node in contemporary global finance, standing as the legal domicile of choice for the global hedge fund industry.[48]

When analyzing the Cayman Islands, one needs to carefully consider that hedge funds represent investment funds pooling capital from either individual or institutional investors which target a positive market return by making investments in securities and other assets.[49] Further on, the research will focus on the case of the most frequently used offshore destination for hedge funds: the Cayman Islands.

For a better understanding of the manner in which the Cayman Islands, in spite of having so little stable workforce, and roughly 58,000 inhabitants,[50] turned into the world's largest host of hedge funds,[51] the key

[45] Roberts, S. (1995). Small place, big money: The Cayman Islands and the International Financial System. *Economic Geography, 71*(3), 237–256.

[46] Offshore financial center.

[47] Harrington, B. (2017). Trusts and financialization. *Socio-Economic Review, 15*, 31–63.

[48] Clarkson, D., Jaecklin, S., & Kaczmarski, K. (2014). *Domiciles of alternative investment funds*. http://docshare01.docshare.tips/files/26926/269260073.pdf. Accessed 22 April 2020.

[49] Bratton, W. W. (2007). *Hedge funds and governance targets* (Paper 862). Faculty Scholarship. http://scholarship.law.upenn.edu/faculty_scholarship/862. Accessed 12 March 2020. ("Some specialize in securities of distressed firms, while others make directional bets on the movement of currency exchange or interest rates. Still others pursue convertible arbitrage, going long in a convertible bond and shorting the underlying common stock."); Morley, J. (2013). The regulation of mutual fund debt. *Yale Journal on Regulation, 30*, 343–376.

[50] Fichtner, J. (2016). The anatomy of the Cayman Islands Offshore Financial Center: Anglo-America, Japan, and the role of hedge funds. *Review of International Political Economy, 23*(6), 1034–1063. https://doi.org/10.1080/09692290.2016.1243143.

[51] Shadab, H. B. (2013). Hedge fund governance. *Stanford Journal of Law, Business & Finance, 19*(1), 141–202. Some estimate that "around [eighty-five] percent of the world's hedge funds are domiciled in the Cayman Islands." Mourant, O. (2017). *The Cayman Islands: A guide for hedge*

legal organization of hedge funds must be understood. According to professor Shadab, there are three basic parts that make up a hedge fund: "the fund itself, the fund's management company, and the fund's equity investors."[52] However, in a classic offshore hedge fund, the entity's management is made up of professionals operating "onshore," meanwhile the hedge fund itself is set offshore.[53] The most important offshore financial centers found under the sovereignty of the United Kingdom, are the Cayman Islands, which provide political stability and the familiar Anglo-Saxon system of common law—offering low levels of regulation and taxation, and at the same time high stability. Of course, as already stated above, generally, hedge fund managers do not work in this offshore territory but rather in an onshore financial center. Thus, even if hedge funds may have offices in locations like Greenwich, Connecticut, New York City, or Mayfair, London, most of them operating worldwide are registered in the Cayman Islands.[54]

Managers who are based in the United States generally start independent business companies known under the name of "feeder funds" in offshore jurisdictions with the main aim of catering two clients: tax-exempt US companies (among which may be mentioned university endowments, but also pension funds) and foreign investors.[55] This type of funds called feeder funds play a key role as they help funds in avoiding triggering US tax liability not only for US tax-exempt companies, but

fund managers. https://www.mourant.com/file-library/media---2017/2017-guides/the-cayman-islands---a-guide-for-hedge-fund-managers.pdf. Accessed 2 April 2020.

[52] Shadab, H. B. (2013). Hedge fund governance. *Stanford Journal of Law, Business & Finance, 19*(1), 141–202.

[53] SEC v. Gruss, 859 F. Supp. 2d 653, 658 (S.D.N.Y. 2012) (describing a typical offshore fund structure, where the fund was "incorporated, administered, registered, domiciled and regulated in the Cayman Islands" whereas "the actual 'operational and investment decisions for the Offshore Fund were all made by the Offshore Fund's manager, DBZCO, primarily in DBZCO's New York office'" (quoting Complaint ¶ 20, Gruss, 859 F. Supp. 2d 653)).

[54] Cohen, A. R., & Williams, C. S. (2011). *A comparison by practitioners of Delaware and Cayman Islands Limited partnerships*. Bloomberg Finance L.P. Law Reports—Fund Management and Bloomberg Law Reports—Securities Law.

[55] Lepree, S. A. (2008). Taxation of United States tax-exempt entities' offshore hedge fund investments: Application of the Section 514 debt-financed rules to leveraged hedge funds and derivatives and the case for equalization. *Tax Law, 61*, 807–815.

also for foreign investors.[56] Further on, the regulation in the Cayman Islands helps investors to start opaque financial structures offering a certain anonymity from US lawmakers.[57]

The features or benefits presented above are the most important ones in the decision of offshore funds to maintain their appearance of foreign territorial financial operations.[58] Indeed, the offshore helps the hedge fund entity to achieve tax benefits as well, this being stated also in an often cited Article from 2007, according to which, "American fund managers legally defer domestic taxes on their personal profits by channeling them offshore through their funds."[59] In this respect, a consultant working in a hedge fund from the Cayman Islands stated that, "in order to ensure that your fund is not seen as being run within the US, it is common practice to have a majority of non-US directors on the board of the fund itself."[60] This is mostly true as the biggest part of offshore jurisdictions impose through regulations that the foreign-based funds must establish some

[56] Hammer, D. L. et al. (2005). *US regulation of hedge funds*. Chicago: ABA Book Publishing (focusing on the US tax issues for offshore hedge funds). Thus, for instance, US tax-exempt companies can face domestic tax liability on "unrelated business taxable income," generally known under the name of "UBTI." Offshore feeder funds, also known as blocker corporations, provide help in avoiding triggering this tax liability. This can be found in: Fund Associates. (2008). *Offshore hedge funds vs. onshore hedge funds*. http://fundassociates.com/pdfs/Offshore_vs_Onshore_Funds_Whitepaper.pdf. Accessed 12 April 2020. In a similar manner, meanwhile a foreign investor may trigger tax liability for the simple fact that it can be seen as being engaged in a US business, the investment in an offshore feeder fund stops this possible exposure at the offshore level. In this respect, consult: Pepper, H. (2008). *A practical guide to US tax compliance issues for hedge fund of funds*. http://www.pepperlaw.com/uploads/files/fundoffunds_schneidman_1008.pdf. Accessed 29 February 2020.

[57] Fichtner, J. (2016). The anatomy of the Cayman Islands Offshore Financial Center: Anglo-America, Japan, and the role of hedge funds. *Review of International Political Economy, 23*(6), 1034–1063. https://doi.org/10.1080/09692290.2016.1243143.

[58] Brocard, M., & Lhabitant, F. S. (2016). *A primer on the tax framework of offshore and onshore hedge fund*. Paris: EDHEC Risk Institute. https://www.edhec.edu/sites/www.edhec-portail.pprod.net/files/publications/pdf/edhec-working-paper-a-primer-on-the-tax-framework-f_1467203960443-pdfjpg. Accessed 12 March 2020.

[59] Browning, L. (2007a, July 1). Offshore tax breaks lure money managers. *New York Times*. http://www.nytimes.com/2007/07/01/business/yourmoney/01cay.html. Accessed 12 March 2020.

[60] Trang, H. K. (2015, May 9). Why hedge funds love to go offshore. *The Forbes*. https://web.archive.org/web/20150516100546/http://www.forbes.com:80/sites/trangho/2015/05/09/why-hedge-funds-love-to-go-offshore/3. Accessed 6 April 2020.

form of contact with the jurisdiction, this meaning the retaining of local directors even if they do not actually get involved into the management of the funds.[61]

If this condition would not be imposed by law, offshore funds would not differ too much in their management from onshore funds, just as Professor Houman Shadab states: "[M]anagement companies enjoy the same general plenary powers over offshore funds' investments and other operations, as they do with onshore funds."[62]

Therefore, it can be stated that offshore financial centers—known also under the name of tax havens—attract hedge funds due to their minimum levels of taxation and regulation. Such an example is that of the Cayman Islands Monetary Authority that allows in the boards of offshore hedge funds a small group of "jumbo directors," who can neither be independent nor protect investors' interests. In this vein, Fichtner is right when he states that "It seems extremely difficult to fulfill this duty for four individuals that hold more than 100 directorships each, another individual even held 567 directorships in Cayman Islands-based hedge funds."[63]

One should also keep in mind that "there is no capital required to submit only one annual statement certifying that the company operated under local law. A meeting of the board of directors must be held at least once a year in the Cayman Islands, but attorney is a widely accepted procedure. No permit is required for formation of a new society that can be completed in two to three days, regardless of its status. There is no minimum capital required and no rules requiring the ratio debt/equity. It may be single-member companies."[64]

[61] Morley, J. (2014). The separation of funds and managers: A theory of investment fund structure and regulation. *Yale Law Journal, 123*, 1228–1253 (explaining the pattern of separating funds and managers for the purpose of limiting fund investors' control rights to obtain greater profits).

[62] Shadab, H. B. (2013). Hedge fund governance. *Stanford Journal of Law, Business & Finance, 19*(1), 141–202.

[63] Fichtner, J. (2013). The rise of hedge funds: A story of inequality. *Momentum Quarterly, 2*(1), 3–20.

[64] Enea, C., & Enea, C. (2015). *Methods of taxation in the tax havens examples of taxation in the Bahamas, Bermuda, and the Cayman Islands*. Annals of the "Constantin Brâncuşi" University of Târgu Jiu. Economy Series, Special Issue ECO-TREND 2015—Performance, Competitiveness, Creativity. Targu Jiu: "Academica Brâncuşi" Publisher.

Cohen and Williams notice also a number of advantages provided by HF located in the Cayman Islands. According to them, "the flexible regulatory regime can accommodate a variety of managers. For example, first time managers with a limited track record can start as an unregistered fund relying on the Exemption and then register under the MFL as they gain marketing momentum. The Cayman Islands is home to a notable number of sophisticated professional service providers, from lawyers and accountants to fund administrators that administer the funds. Also, the Cayman Islands is a short plane ride away from the United States and situated in the same Eastern time zone as much of the US financial services industry, aiding convenience of communication. These benefits have developed into a cumulative advantage that will likely continue to make the Cayman Islands the domicile of choice for offshore hedge funds for the foreseeable future."[65]

The Cayman Islands distinguish themselves from other sunny jurisdictions such as the Bahamas, Barbados, or Belize.

Usually, the offshore funds are purposely designed and structured to avoid taxes and laws. However, as it has been noticed, this proves necessary for attracting offshore investors, and in some cases, when referring to US offshore funds, even certain tax-exempt US persons. What is however strange is that, as Lhabitant explains, in the case when "something goes awry with the fund, investors and securities regulators seem to be increasingly inclined to bring claims in US courts against the fund and its service providers (most of the time the administrator and auditors). This has the obvious advantage of being able to claim huge damage awards against defendants who have deep pockets. Defendants often argue that US courts lack subject-matter jurisdiction, because they carry out their functions entirely offshore and they have no US investors, and that forcing litigation on them in the US has the sole aim of saddling them with a heavy burden. But US courts often reject the *forum non conveniens* argument and are increasingly willing to extend their jurisdiction to securities law claims against offshore hedge fund managers and service providers."[66] In this respect, Lhabitant says that an US court can hold as sufficient for

[65] Cohen, A. R., & Williams, C. S. (2011). *A comparison by practitioners of Delaware and Cayman Islands Limited partnerships*. Bloomberg Finance L.P. Law Reports—Fund Management and Bloomberg Law Reports—Securities Law.

[66] Lhabitant F. S. (2006). *Handbook of hedge funds*. West Sussex: John Wiley & Sons Ltd., p. 28.

exercising jurisdiction "the simple fact that an offshore fund traded US securities or that some meetings took place in the US."[67]

A more complex and recent approach to offshore hedge funds focusing on the Cayman Islands is made by Brocard and Lhabitant. In their opinion, there are five important advantages[68] of the Cayman Islands. First, its robust legal system based on the English common law system. Second, a well-known position among hedge fund investors. Third, powerful privacy protection for the funds domiciled here. Fourth, a sophisticated business and legal infrastructure if it were to compare it with different offshore jurisdictions, and fifth, a zero taxation system.

As far the requirements that it has to comply, these are basic. First, the office must be registered in the Cayman Islands, second, the Board of Directors, and third, keep achieves of its Directors as well as of any security interests assumed by the company in its office from the Cayman Islands. In addition, it must hold a register of its shareholders, although this must not be kept obligatorily in the Cayman Islands.

Exempted companies from the Cayman Islands can issue various classes of shares with different redemption rights, charges, and currency denominations. There are hedge funds that issue just voting shares, meanwhile there are others issuing just a few management shares with voting rights, and a huge amount of redeemable participating shares with economic rights without voting rights or with limited voting rights. Most of the time, investors subscribe and redeem shares at their net asset value. In this respect, an offering document maps out (1) both rights and obligations of investors as shareholders in the hedge fund, but also (2) the terms of subscriptions and redemptions as well as (3) the approaches adopted for asset valuation.

5.3.1.1 Structure of Hedge Funds' Market in the Cayman Islands

The regulation concerning the Mutual Funds Law[69] identifies two types of funds: open-ended funds (generally hedge funds) and closed-ended funds (usually not hedge funds).

[67] Idem, p. 28.

[68] Brocard, M., & Lhabitant, F.S. (2016). *A primer on the tax framework of offshore and onshore hedge fund*. Paris: EDHEC Risk Institute. https://www.edhec.edu/sites/www.edhec-portail.pprod.net/files/publications/pdf/edhec-working-paper-a-primer-on-the-tax-framework-f_1467203960443-pdfjpg. Accessed 12 March 2020.

[69] MF Law.

Table 5.1 Classification of hedge funds regulated under the CIMA

Type of hedge funds	*Regulated by*
Licensed funds	• licensed under section 4(1)(a) of the MF Law
Administered funds	• licensed under section 4(1)(b) of the MF Law (Administered Funds)[a]
Registered funds	• registered under section 4(3) of the MF Law by virtue of satisfying the listing or minimum investment criteria referred to below

[a] Funds for which a CIMA-licensed mutual fund administrator provides the principal office and has delegated regulatory responsibilities

The Cayman Islands Monetary Authority[70] is the regulatory body which regulates open-ended hedge funds, which make the subject of the current chapter. The hedge funds regulated under the CIMA are of four types, as seen in Table 5.1.

On February 7, 2020, the Private Funds Law 2020 (PF Law) was enacted, as well as an amendment to the Mutual Funds Law (2020 Revision), known under the name of MFL Amendment.[71] This regulation was modified as a consequence of EU and various international recommendations with the major aim of aligning the investment fund regulatory regime from the Cayman Islands with other jurisdictions. According to the MFL Amendment, a s4(4) Fund (having 15 or fewer investors) will be required to register with CIMA by:

(i) filing a certified copy of their constitutive documents which specify that a majority of investors in number is capable of appointing or removing the operator of the fund;
(ii) filing any other information as may be required in the prescribed form; and
(iii) payment of the prescribed registration fee.[72]

[70] CIMA.

[71] By the Cayman Islands Government. The MFL Amendment came into force on February 7, 2020 and provides a six-month transitional period (to 7 August 2020) for compliance for those s4(4) Funds in existence on February 7, 2020.

[72] Private Funds Law. (2020). (Law 1 of 2020) Supplement No. 1 published with Legislation Gazette No. 9 dated 7 February, 2020. https://www.cima.ky/upimages/commonfiles/PrivateFundsLaw2020_1581524961.PDF. Accessed 12 April 2020.

At the same time, in order to register as a Registered Fund (instead of obtaining a license as a Licensed Fund or register as an Administered Fund), at least one of the following criteria must be satisfied by a fund:

- receive at least USD 100,000 as an initial investment.
- hold interests listed on an authorized stock exchange.
- be a "master fund" complying with at least one of the two conditions mentioned above.

As far as master funds are concerned, these must register with CIMA under the MF Law in the case this is an open-ended Cayman Islands vehicle trading in investments having one or more "regulated feeder funds."[73]

Usually, master funds can be registered[74] under section 4(3) of the MF Law if they meet the following requirements:

- fill a MF4 Form.
- pay the annual fee (USD 3048.78) as well as the application fee (USD 365.85).

5.3.1.2 *Regulatory Framework and Bodies*

Cayman Islands Monetary Authority (CIMA) represents the regulatory body for open-ended hedge funds, while Mutual Funds Law regulates them. Directors of corporate Regulated Funds are regulated by the Directors Registration and Licensing Law as supplemented by the Directors Registration and Licensing (Registration and Licensing) Regulations. The Securities Investment Business Law provides that the Cayman Islands Monetary Authority (CIMA) is responsible for the licensing and control of persons carrying on "securities investment business" in or from within the Cayman Islands.

[73] That is, a fund that is itself a Regulated Fund, and conducts more than 51% of its investing through the master fund.

[74] As Registered Funds.

5.3.1.3 Taxation

There will be no direct tax for a Cayman-based hedge fund based in the Cayman Islands. As we have already seen, "all available legal structures for hosting a hedge fund may register as an exempted entity, obtaining a written exemption by the Cayman Islands Governor in Cabinet of any law imposing any tax on profits, gains or appreciation, or which is in the nature of estate duty, or inheritance tax."[75] This refers to an exemption valid for either 20 years (this is the case of corporations) or 50 years (in the case of limited partnerships or trusts).

However, it is possible for Cayman-based hedge funds to be liable for taxes imposed in jurisdictions where it holds its investments. This stands as very important because the Cayman Islands have signed few Double Tax treaties.[76]

Therefore, the hedge funds can find it difficult to eliminate or minimize any foreign taxes arising on a fund's underlying investments. An example in this sense is the situation of the United States, where a foreign entity gaining profit effectively connected to the conduct of a trade or business within the United States ("ECI") is obliged to file a US tax return, at the same time being subject to US taxation for that profit at a similar progressive rate as domestic corporations.[77] Still, Section 864(b)(2)(A), provides a safe harbor "under which a foreign corporation is not treated as engaged in a trade or business within the US as a result of 'trading in stocks and securities' for its own account. This applies whether the trading is accomplished within the US directly by the taxpayer or its employees,

[75] Brocard, M., & Lhabitant, F. S. (2016). *A primer on the tax framework of offshore and onshore hedge fund*. Paris: EDHEC Risk Institute. https://www.edhec.edu/sites/www.edhec-portail.pprod.net/files/publications/pdf/edhec-working-paper-a-primer-on-the-tax-framework-f_1467203960443-pdfjpg. Accessed 12 March 2020.

[76] This is a bilateral agreement between two parties implying the abolition of double taxation on active and passive income. In this respect, the Cayman Islands have signed a comprehensive tax treaty with Japan in 2010, and limited tax treaties with the United Kingdom and New Zealand. The Cayman Islands/UK double taxation arrangement (DTA) was signed in June 2009 and it entered into force in December 2010. It started to be effective in the Cayman Islands starting with April 2011 for the corporation tax and for the income and capital gains tax and from December 2010 for other taxes. See also Trepelkov, A., Tonino, H., & Halka, D. (Eds.) (2013). *United Nations handbook on selected issues in administration of double tax treaties for developing countries*. New York: United Nations. https://doi.org/10.18356/a96cf16b-en.

[77] I.R.C. Section 882.

or through a resident broker, commission agent, custodian or other independent or dependent agent, and regardless of whether the employee or agent has discretionary authority to make decisions, or if the foreign corporation has a US office."[78] As a consequence, the hedge funds based in Cayman should usually not be subject to the regular US profit tax on none of their US investments trading incomes.[79] Still, any United States-sourced dividends that the Cayman Islands fund receives are going to be subject to the United States withholding tax at the US non-treaty rate of 30%.[80] Therefore, because the Cayman Islands and the United States have not signed a Double Tax treaty[81] so far, there is no possibility that this withholding tax to be recovered.

At the same time, hedge funds structured as Cayman entities can deliberately choose to be treated as a partnership for US federal tax aims. This implies several actions, such as getting a US taxpayer identification number for the Cayman entity and afterwards filing Form 8832.[82] Consequently, "the fund will be required to file a US federal partnership return and issue Schedules K-1 for each year in which it has had one or more US partners. In such a case, each US partner will be treated as earning a pro-rata share of the gains and losses of the 'partnership'."[83]

[78] Brocard, M., & Lhabitant, F. S. (2016). *A primer on the tax framework of offshore and onshore hedge funds*. Paris: EDHEC Risk Institute, p. 21.

[79] Exceptions include (i) gains realized from the sale or disposition of stock or non-debt securities of US real property holding corporations as defined in I.R.C. Section 897 ("USRPHCs"), including stock or securities of certain real estate investment trusts ("REITs"); and (ii) US lending activities, in particular loan negotiation and origination. See: Peaslee, J. M., & Nirenberg, D. Z. (2011). *Federal income taxation of securitization transactions and related topics* (4th ed). USA: Frank J. Fabozzi Associates Publisher.

[80] I.R.C. Section 881.

[81] The mutual legal assistance treaty between the United States and Cayman Islands specifically excludes fiscal matters.

[82] "Entity Classification Election".

[83] Brocard, M., & Lhabitant, F. S. (2016). *A primer on the tax framework of offshore and onshore hedge fund*. Paris: EDHEC Risk Institute. https://www.edhec.edu/ sites/www.edhec-portail.pprod.net/files/publications/pdf/edhec-working-paper-a-primer-on-the-tax-framework-f_1467203960443-pdfjpg. Accessed 12 March 2020.

5.3.1.4 *Advantages and Disadvantages of Cayman Islands' Legal Fund Vehicles and Structures*

There are three types of legal vehicles according to which funds can be formed (Table 5.2).

Cayman's limited partnerships resemble very much those from Delaware, as the next subchapter will highlight, and these attract many US investors due to their familiarity. In this type of partnerships, the functions of ownership and control are being divided, and this says a lot about their effectiveness at protecting assets from seizure by creditors.

As far as unit trusts are concerned, they can be perceived "as unincorporated open-ended mutual fund structures that give investors the right to purchase or redeem shares in the assets of the unit trust (called 'units')."[84] They are made up under a trust act/deed, a trustee being therefore involved, who is trustworthy for both the business and affairs of the unit trust. The trustees can widely control investments in order to accomplish the objectives of the fund, being involved in a fiduciary relationship, meaning that their actions must always be according to the best interests of the unit-holders. A 50-year tax exemption can be granted to both the exempted limited partnerships and the exempted unit trusts. Further on, the typical structure for a pure offshore hedge fund from the Cayman Islands is presented (Fig. 5.2).

The investment manager is generally hired by the hedge fund to manage its assets in exchange for an incentive fee and a management fee, being set-up either as:

(a) a Cayman exempt company or as
(b) a Cayman limited partnership.

In general, the incentive fee represents 20% of the positive performance of the fund, meanwhile the management fee is 2% of the AuM. One major difference of offshore and onshore funds in this case comes from the fact that, unlike what is usually done in the onshore fund case, in offshore funds there is no need to segregate the recipients of the management and

[84] Brocard, M., & Lhabitant, F. S. (2016). *A primer on the tax framework of offshore and onshore hedge fund*. Paris: EDHEC Risk Institute. https://www.edhec.edu/sites/www.edhec-portail.pprod.net/files/publications/pdf/edhec-working-paper-a-primer-on-the-tax-framework-f_1467203960443-pdfjpg. Accessed 12 March 2020.

Table 5.2 Regulatory overview of the legal hedge funds vehicles in the Cayman Islands

Legal hedge funds vehicles	*Regulatory overview*
Companies	Regulated open-ended funds represent about 75% of the Regulated Funds, being set up generally as exempted companies limited by shares. The biggest parts of these are standard exempted companies, only around 10% of them being segregated portfolio companies (where separate portfolios can be set up, with assets and liabilities lawfully ring-fenced). The introduction of LLCs was made in the middle of 2016, June, but up to now they have mainly been used as the vehicle for general partners of limited partnership fund vehicles, not as the fund vehicles themselves Exempted companies represent therefore the typical offshore company from the Cayman Islands. These companies and their shares "are widely understood and in addition to a body of Cayman Islands jurisprudence, the Cayman Islands courts can draw on a long tradition of relevant case law from England and the rest of the Commonwealth."[a] These companies have legal personalities separate from their shareholders, and they are able to issue shares in various classes and series. A shareholder's liability for the company's debts is limited by statute to the amount unpaid on its shares (which will generally be issued fully paid in an investment fund)
Limited partnerships	These types of hedge funds are governed by the Exempted Limited Partnership Law. Cayman Islands exempted limited partnerships are underpinned by English partnership law, although they are modified by statute in order to be made more suitable for use as investment funds. In this vein, for instance, exempted limited partnerships, since they do not have separate legal personality, can be sued and can sue on their own behalf
Unit trusts	These hedge funds are registered under the Trusts Law. They "are underpinned by English trust law, but are modified by statute to make them more suitable for use as investment funds." Such examples are STAR trusts, which are not subject to any perpetuity period, being allowed to have purposes as their objects

[a]Farley, J., & Olsen, C. (2018). *Hedge funds in the Cayman Islands: Regulatory overview*. https://uk.practicallaw.thomsonreuters.com/w-007-5747?transitionType=Default&contextData=(sc.Default)&firstPage=true&bhcp=1. Accessed 20 March 2020
[b]Special Trusts—Alternative Regime

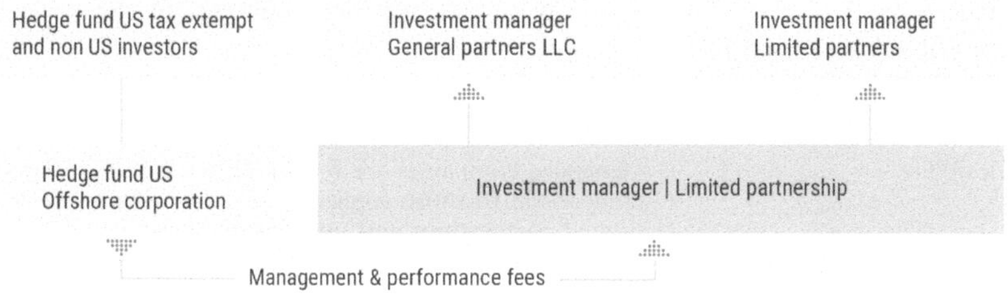

Fig. 5.2 Typical structure for a pure offshore hedge fund from the Cayman Islands (*Source* Brocard and Lhabitant [2016])

the performance fees, since no taxes need to be paid to the state, or taxes must not be avoided.

By choice, the investment manager can also be set-up as a principal, a limited partnership, or a company based outside of the Cayman Islands. As already seen earlier, no physical presence[85] in the islands is imposed. Therefore, the manager will be under no Cayman Islands laws or regulations, unless it decides registering itself in Cayman as a "foreign" company.

Therefore, the most important advantages and disadvantages of the different types of vehicles used in the Cayman Islands are (Table 5.3):

5.3.2 Delaware—Between Tax Transparency and Contractual Flexibility

Delaware is perceived as a de facto offshore financial center or as a "domestic tax haven" of the United States.[86] Just as the Cayman Islands, "Delaware performs exactly the same role as the UK tax havens by providing low levels of regulation and taxation, as well as a high degree of stability."[87] Of course, hedge fund managers usually do not work in these

[85] Office space, staff, etc.

[86] Dyreng, S., Lindsey, B., & Thornock, J. (2012). *Exploring the role Delaware plays as a tax haven* (Working Paper WP 12/12). Oxford University Centre for Business Taxation. http://www.sbs.ox.ac.uk/centres/tax/papers/Docu-ments/WP1212.pdf. Accessed 20 March 2020.

[87] Fichtner, J. (2013). The rise of hedge funds: A story of inequality. *Momentum Quarterly, 2*(1), 3–20.

Table 5.3 The most important advantages and disadvantages of the different types of vehicles used in the Cayman Islands

Principles	*Type of vehicle*
Flexibility	Generally, companies are regulated by more rigid laws in comparison to those applicable to other vehicles such as limited partnerships and unit trusts
Legal personality	Companies have separate legal personality. Unit trusts operate through their trustee, meanwhile limited partnerships operate through their general partner
Additional vehicles	Exempted limited partnerships impose that minimum one general partner establishes or registers in the Cayman Islands, while unit trusts necessitate a trustee, who will, most of the time, insert a controlled subsidiary for liability protection
Regulatory requirements	A Licensed Fund also known as a unit trust needs that a trustee is licensed under the Banks and Trust Companies Law
Overseas requirements	Usually, investors choose the vehicle depending on whether it may qualify for specific tax or regulatory treatment in an overseas jurisdiction[a]

[a]Such as example is that unit trusts are generally used for the Japanese market and limited partnerships for the Israeli market

offshore territories, but predominantly in onshore financial centers. In this section the main primary advantages of Delaware law for hedge funds will be explained. Thus, the main advantages for choosing Delaware as a HF domicile are: tax transparency corroborated with a secure and coherent legislative regime, offering contractual flexibility and at the same time enabling not only limited liability, but also active management by fund managers, investors, and service providers. Further on, these two aspects will be analyzed.

In terms of *tax transparency*, Delaware offers "an efficient platform for hedge funds to establish their pool of funds under the Delaware Limited Liability Company Acts (DLLC) and the Delaware Revised Model Uniform Limited Partnership Act (DRULPA) 1983".[88] In Delaware, the structure of hedge funds is under the form of DRULPAs. Just like in

[88]Cumming, D., Dai, N., & Johan, S. A. (2015). Are hedge funds domiciled in Delaware different? *Journal of Corporate Finance, 35*, 232–246.

the case of all limited partnerships, this allowed investors to get efficient tax flow-through, tax transparency, and limited liability, which play a key role when considering the limited supervision held by investors over the investment powers of the managers of hedge funds. Meanwhile, the structure of hedge funds themselves is under the form of DRULPAs, the general structure of hedge fund managers is as DLLCs, because of US Internal Revenue Service which allows DLLCs "to simply elect to opt-into the benefits of a flow-through tax treatment, formerly a treatment only availed to partnerships, not corporations."[89] This possibility which allowed hedge fund managers to structure themselves as DLLCs and not DRULPAs lead to extraordinary contractual flexibility. This is done generally because of the US Internal Revenue Service (IRS), which allows "to simply elect to opt into the benefits of a flow-through tax treatment, which was formerly a treatment only availed to partnerships, not corporations."[90] The IRS facilitated this only in 1997, although it was available starting with 1992[91] as Schwarts explained.

As far as the contractual flexibility is concerned, under Delaware law, DRULPA structure of hedge funds implied a general partner able to assume the entire liability of the funds since the rest of the partners had limited liability. The differences between DLLC and DRULPA are clear: "with the general partner or the hedge fund manager structured as a DLLC instead of another DRULPA the hedge fund manager is able to manage this assumption of full liability as the corporate structure, albeit enjoying the same tax flow-through privileges as a DRULPA, facilitated more protection through corporate law, instead of partnership law. The use of DLLC structure also allowed hedge fund managers to determine management and performance fee flow to management staff more efficiently, especially in view of staff turnover."[92] At the same time, there exists the possibility to delegate fund management duties without the subsequent issues connected to partnership. Still, in spite of the fact that the full liability effect of general partners, tends to be tempered with the

[89] Idem.

[90] Baker, H. K., & Filbeck, G. (2017). *Hedge funds structure, strategies, and performance*. Oxford: Oxford Scholarship Online.

[91] Schwartz, R. (2012). Delaware as a location for private funds: The why and the what. *Bloomberg World Securities Law Report, 18*, 1–8.

[92] Cumming, D., Dai, N., & Johan, S. A. (2015). Are hedge funds domiciled in Delaware different? *Journal of Corporate Finance, 35*, 242.

use of DLLCs, investors were provided by the lawmakers in Delaware with limited liability a number of measures of protection that usually are not offered to limited partners of other limited partnerships. Consequently, they are allowed several actions that do not obligatorily turn them into general partners, among which can be mentioned:

- act as a contractor on behalf of the limited partnership;
- act as a guarantor of the limited partnership;
- consult with or advise a general partner;
- sell assets of the limited partnership;
- and make determinations as far as future investments by the limited partnership, are concerned.[93]

All in all, Delaware is seen by US hedge funds as "an efficient, transparent, low-cost operational environment as there are inexpensive and simple formation processes,"[94] particularly because disclosure requirements are quite low since there is no obligation for funds and their general managers to file neither the DLLC or DRULPA Agreements, and nor the annual reports. In addition, and even more important, there is no need for managers to have a presence or office or personnel in the domicile location, which is a huge advantage for hedge funds.

Summing up, offshore financial centers analyzed so far, more precisely the Cayman Islands and also Delaware, have levels of regulation and taxation perceived as lower in comparison to onshore jurisdictions. According to Fichtner, "this provides hedge funds with an advantage over other institutional investors but also benefits very rich individuals who transfer their wealth to offshore financial centers in order to save taxes, or even to pay no taxes at all."[95]

[93] Delaware Revised Uniform Partnership Act. https://delcode.delaware.gov/title6/c015/. Accessed 3 April 2020.

[94] Cumming, D., Dai, N., & Johan, S. A. (2015). Are hedge funds domiciled in Delaware different? *Journal of Corporate Finance*, *35*, 243.

[95] Fichtner, J. (2013). The rise of hedge funds: A story of inequality. *Momentum Quarterly*, *2*(1), 3–20.

5.3.2.1 *Structure of Hedge Funds in Delaware*

Hedge funds in Delaware, the United States are registered either as the limited partnership or the limited liability corporation (LLC).

5.3.2.2 *Regulatory Framework and Bodies*

The Internal Revenue Service (IRS) is the legal entity where investors need to register when incorporating a hedge fund in Delaware. In addition, it must apply for a Federal Employer Identification Number.

A hedge fund registered in Delaware, most of the time refers to private investment companies which have several particular advantages from specific incorporation exemptions applicable under two major regulations: the Securities Act 1933 and the Investment Company Act 1940.

5.3.2.3 *Advantages and Disadvantages of Delaware's Legal Fund Vehicles and Structures*

There are two types of legal hedge funds vehicles: limited partnerships or the limited liability corporations (LLCs). One of the key reasons for investing in Delaware is that the state benefits from a court which handles cases deriving from corporate legislation in a fast manner (the Court of Chancery). Other reasons for investing here are presented in Table 5.4.

Table 5.4 The most important advantages of the different types of vehicle used in Delaware

Type of vehicle	*Advantages*
Limited partnership	Taxes such as: the income tax, the sales tax, or the property tax are not perceived in Delaware
Limited liability corporation (LLC)	The founders of an LLC benefit from a high level of privacy, because information concerning the wealth of the investors is highly secured A single investor, no matter of which nationality is allowed to create a LLC Investors benefit from very low incorporation costs, as the registration of a LLC costs approximately USD 250 No minimum share capital during its incorporation is required

5.3.3 *Hedge Funds and BVI—British Virgin Islands*

In the BVI there are three types of possible investors: (i) taxable US investors; (ii) tax-exempt US investors; and (iii) non-US investors.

In the case the investors will mainly be made up of taxable US investors, most of the times, they can rely entirely on domestic jurisdictions (and this is the case of Delaware) as a consequence of its major structuring advantages.

Still, when the investors are made up of both tax-exempt US investors and/or non-US investors, they generally consider an offshore fund within the broader structure to provide to the distinct tax concerns of such sponsors. And at this point, the British Virgin Islands (the BVI) is the choice for these investors, due to its unique set of well-regarded, innovative and cost-competitive hedge fund offers (Table 5.5).

5.3.3.1 *Taxation in BVI*

The BVI hedge funds are generally seen as the leading blue-chip jurisdiction from the cost–benefit point of view as it is a comparatively quick, painless, and cost-competitive domicile.

The most important BVI hedge funds structures are classified on the trading strategy, investment and tax considerations, and preferred tax treatment of the investment manager's performance compensation.

5.3.3.2 *Regulatory Framework and Bodies*

The BVI Financial Services Commission regulates the typical BVI hedge funds operating in BVI, most of them open-ended in nature, as a result of offering its investors the right to withdraw capital at regular periods by reference to the net asset value of the hedge fund. By contrast, a typical private equity or venture capital fund is closed-ended and this makes it avoiding the direct regulation.

5.3.3.3 *Structure of BVI Hedge Fund Products*

The incorporation of BVI hedge funds is either as business companies or as limited partnerships or unit trusts. Just as in the case of the Cayman Islands, the business company, due to its being a corporate vehicle, is generally the most common structure for BVI hedge funds.

BVI regulated hedge fund products which can be suitable for use as offshore hedge funds are: Professional Funds, Private Funds, Approved Funds, and Incubator Funds. Table 5.6 summarizes their most important characteristics.

Table 5.5 Correlations between investor base and tax considerations

Investor base and tax considerations	*General features*
Taxable US investors	Most of the time they make investments in domestic US hedge funds classified as partnerships for US tax purposes (generally Delaware limited partnerships or limited liability companies)
Tax-exempt US investors	They represent a material source of hedge fund capital. Passive investment income that these investors earn is usually exempt from US federal income tax; still, this exemption cannot be applied to "unrelated business taxable income" (UBTI). As far as hedge funds are concerned, the major potential source of UBTI lies in earnings from debt-financed investment services (for instance, trading on margin). In the case of "a tax-transparent entity such as a typical domestic hedge fund earns any UBTI, its investors shall be treated as though they earned such UBTI themselves, which may result in US tax liabilities for those otherwise tax-exempt US investors who invest in the domestic fund."[a] In opposition, offshore hedge funds (as the BVI fund) classified as corporations for US tax purposes, due to the fact that are not tax transparent vehicles, may definitely "block" this kind of attribution of UBTI. In the case the BVI hedge fund earns any UBTI, that income is not passed-through or associated with its investors. This "blocking" effect stands as the principal reason tax-exempt US investors generally prefer to invest in offshore funds
Non-US investors	Most of the time, they prefer to invest in offshore funds classified as corporations for US tax purposes in order to keep out of the US tax net (but also escape any attendant requirement to file US tax returns)
The following are exempt from the payment of income tax (Income Tax Act):	
Funds	Funds registered under the Securities and Investment Business Act 2010 It will not be liable to BVI payroll tax unless it has employees in the BVI
Resident investors	All dividends and amounts that a fund formed as a BVI company pays to investors (including redemption proceeds) Capital gains realized by investors in relation to fund interests of a fund formed as a BVI company

(continued)

Table 5.5 (continued)

Investor base and tax considerations	*General features*
Non-resident investors	"All dividends and amounts paid by a fund to non-resident investors (including redemption proceeds) Capital gains realized by non-resident investors from fund interests There are no estate, inheritance, succession or gift taxes payable in the BVI in relation to shares in funds"[b]

[a]Flaye, E. (2020). *The offshore dimension*. https://www.conyers.com/wp-content/uploads/2018/06/2018_CAY_How_to_Start_a_Hedge_Fund_in_the_US_The_Offshore_Dimension.pdf. Accessed 26 March 2020

[b]Hempel, C., & Olsen, C. (2019). *Hedge funds in the British Virgin Islands: Regulatory overview*. https://uk.practicallaw.thomsonreuters.com/w-007-6405?transitionType=Default&contextData=(sc.Default)&firstPage=true&bhcp=1. Accessed 26 March 2020

Table 5.6 Key features of the BVI hedge funds products

	Professional fund	*Private fund*	*Approved Fund*	*Incubator Fund*
Maximum AuM	Uncapped	Uncapped	USD 100 million	USD 20 million
Maximum number of sponsors	Uncapped	50 (or potentially uncapped provided the offer is made on a "private basis")	20	20
Sponsor qualification requirements	Just "professional investors"	–	–	"sophisticated private investors" only
Minimum initial investment per investor	US$100,000 (subject to exemptions for certain service providers of the fund and employees of the investment manager)	–	–	USD 20,000
Maximum term/duration	No limit	No limit	No limit	2 years[a] When this period expires, the fund needs to be converted into a Professional/Private/Approved Fund if not, be wound up
Service providers				
Mandatory Investment manager	Yes	Yes	No	No
Mandatory auditor	Yes	Yes	No	No
	No requirement for a local audit sign-off by a BVI-based auditor			
Mandatory custodian	Yes	Yes	No	No

(continued)

Table 5.6 (continued)

	Professional fund	*Private fund*	*Approved Fund*	*Incubator Fund*
	There are some conditions in which a Professional Fund or Private Fund can apply to be exempted from the requirement to appoint an investment manager, auditor, and/or custodian			
Mandatory administrator	Yes	Yes	Yes	No
Permission of foreign service providers	Yes—the United States is a "Recognized Jurisdiction" for the purposes of applicable BVI financial services regulation and as a consequence, a US investor can designate its usual US service providers as service providers to the BVI hedge fund			
Directors	At least two directors (minimum one of them must be an individual, meanwhile the other can be a corporate director). In addition, the directors do not have to be residents of the BVI			

[a]With an extension of up to 12 months available with permission from the BVI FSC

5.3.4 Mauritius Hedge Funds

5.3.4.1 Structure of Hedge Funds' Market in Mauritius

In Mauritius, there is no particular regime that applies to hedge funds, and this is particularly due to the fact that the "hedge fund" term is not used in regulatory documents. Still, several alternate investment funds generally target sophisticated investors or high net worth individuals. Consequently, they may be structured into "professional CIS" or "expert funds." These types of funds are exempt from many laws, allowing them to act quite similar to hedge funds. Usually, they are known under the name of "exempt funds."

Their authorization occurred as soon as the Securities (Collective Investment Schemes and Closed-regulation) have, as soon as the transitional period ended in September 2010, transformed into professional CIS or expert funds, in accordance to their features. Consequently, most funds established in Mauritius are either professional CIS or expert funds.

5.3.4.2 Regulatory Framework and Bodies

Just like any other fund, exempt funds function under the same regulations, the only exception being when they qualify for exemptions. As far as the regulatory framework is concerned, there are several laws applying to open-ended and closed-ended funds (Table 5.7).

In terms of regulatory bodies, there are three involved in the regulation of open-ended and closed-ended funds:

- The Financial Services Commission (FSC), which stands as the regulator for all non-bank financial services activities, regulating not only domestic, but also international funds.
- The Registrar of Companies, the regulator for all corporate issues.
- The Registrar of Limited Partnerships, which regulates limited partnerships.

Table 5.7 Regulatory framework of hedge funds from Mauritius

The Financial Services Act 2007
The Securities Act 2005
The Securities (Collective Investment Schemes and Closed-end Funds) Regulations 2008
The Financial Services (Consolidated Licensing and Fees) Rules 2008[a]
The Financial Intelligence and Anti-Money Laundering Act 2002[b]
The United Nations (Financial Prohibitions, Arms Embargo, and Travel Ban) Sanctions Act 2019
The Companies Act 2001[c]
The Trusts Act 2001[d]
The Limited Partnerships Act 2011[e]
The Protected Cell Companies Act 1999
The Guidelines for Advertising and Marketing of Financial Products 2014
The Code of Business Conduct 2015
The National Code of Corporate Governance for Mauritius 2016

Source Bhavna et al. (2019)
[a] In respect of license fees
[b] In respect of anti-money laundering provisions
[c] For funds structured as companies
[d] For funds structured as trusts
[e] For funds structured as limited partnerships

5.3.4.3 *Taxation of Hedge Funds in Mauritius*

Table 5.8 illustrates the tax treatment of hedge funds in Mauritius.

5.3.4.4 *Advantages and Disadvantages of Mauritius' Legal Fund Vehicles and Structures*

Just like in the Cayman Islands, in Mauritius there are three types of legal vehicles according to which funds can be formed: companies, limited partnerships, and trusts (Table 5.9).

As far as advantages and disadvantages are concerned, they will be presented in Table 5.10.

Table 5.8 Tax treatment of hedge funds in Mauritius

Funds	For domestic funds set-up as companies there are two taxes: (1) 15% on net business profits of corporations (capital gains are not included) and (2) 2% corporate social responsibility (CSR) levy The total amount of any contributions paid abroad can be used as tax credits against contributions that need to be paid in Mauritius. In addition, "tax credit is also allowed on foreign dividend income against any underlying tax paid if the fund holds at least 5% of the underlying investment"[a] Taxes for funds can be reduced to 0–3% and those funds which hold a GBL must not pay any CSR tax
Resident investors	A resident investor is subject to a 15% tax on its taxable income, but this excludes dividend income from Mauritius companies and capital profits. A resident investor standing as corporate body is obliged to pay a 2% CSR levy
Non-resident investors	Non-resident investors do not have to pay taxes. Withholding taxes on dividends must not be paid by non-resident investors in Mauritian funds

[a]Bhavna, R., Nafiisah, J., Senivassen, L., Robert, B. L. C., & Associates (2019). *Hedge funds in Mauritius: Regulatory overview*. https://uk.practicallaw.thomsonreuters.com/w-007-8204?transitionType=Default&contextData=(sc.Default)&firstPage=true&bhcp=1. Accessed 12 March 2020

5.3.5 Comparative View: The Nonregulation of Hedge Funds in: Cayman Islands, British Virgin Islands, Mauritius, and Delaware

According to our research, hedge funds entities "can be headquartered in offshore jurisdictions without (for the most part) physically moving their operations offshore."[96] This was the case for hedge funds in the Cayman Islands.

As already seen before, the Cayman Islands represent the largest HF offshore jurisdiction, both US and UK-based managers[97] preferring it mainly due to (1) its good reputation among institutional investors, this helping HFs with their fund raising effort, and also due to (2) its strong supporting infrastructure. Most major hedge funds tend to be domiciled in the Cayman Islands and other reasons will be discussed later on.

[96]Moon, W. J. (2019). Regulating offshore finance. *Vanderbilt Law Review, 72*(1), 1–54.

[97]Clarkson, D., Jaecklin, S., & Kaczmarski, K. (2014). *Domiciles of alternative investment funds*. http://www.alfi.lu/node/2814. Accessed 22 Apr 2020.

Table 5.9 Regulatory overview of the legal hedge funds vehicles in Mauritius

Legal hedge funds vehicles	*Regulatory overview*
Companies	The companies from Mauritius are of many types, from public to private companies, being incorporated under the Companies Act 2001. Generally, investors are issued with "shares" of the company In private companies no more than 50 shareholders are accepted, meanwhile shares cannot be offered to the public. In addition, companies can be started up as protected cell companies, being subject to the Protected Cell Companies Act 1999 and to the Companies Act. Investors "in a company or a protected cell company are issued with shares in the company they invest in or in the relevant cell. As a matter of compliance, the creation of each cell will usually require the approval of the FSC"[a]
Limited partnerships	They are governed by the Limited Partnerships Act 2011. These partnerships can be created with or without legal personality, being forced to have minimum one general partner and one or more limited partners. The responsibility of the general partner is the management of the limited partnership. Also, the general partner has unlimited liability for the debts and obligations of the partnership. At the same time, the liability of the limited partner is limited to the maximum amount of its commitment with the exception when the limited partner is not involved in the management of the partnership. Participants' interests are known under the name of "partnership interests"
Unit trusts	Unit trusts are created under the Trusts Act 2001. They can be set up as a "purpose" or "beneficiaries" trust. Generally, participants are issued with "units" in the trust

[a]Bhavna, R., Nafiisah, J., Senivassen, L., & Robert, B. L. C. & Associates. (2019). *Hedge funds in Mauritius: Regulatory overview*. https://uk.practicallaw.thomsonreuters.com/w-007-8204?transitionType=Default&contextData=(sc.Default)&firstPage=true&bhcp=1. Accessed 12 March 2020

Table 5.10 The most important advantages and disadvantages of the different types of vehicles used in the Mauritius

Type of vehicle	*Advantages*	*Disadvantages*
Companies	The limited liability criterion refers to the fact that investors benefit from liability in direct relation to investment The statutory regulations concerning filing and reporting offer transparency and accountability The governing body (board) of the company responds for their actions in front of investors, which is known as fiduciary responsibility	Their corporate procedures represent a secondary compliance cost There is no tax transparency for them: a company represents one legal person, being dealt with as one taxing unit. Additionally, investors are not taxed at their level The distribution of profit is subject to the company being financially stable
Limited partnerships	Flexibility, tax transparency, and also mitigation of fiduciary risks The ability to account for incomes and losses at investor level Limited liability as far as the debts of the partnership is concerned	The general partners are simultaneously and separately liable for the debts of the partnership[a] and individually liable to third parties[b] Normally, limited partnerships are not eligible to take benefit of tax treaties due to their tax transparency. Still, a limited partnership having a GBL can elect to be tax opaque and be liable to pay tax in Mauritius and, consequently benefit from tax treaties

(continued)

Table 5.10 (continued)

Type of vehicle	*Advantages*	*Disadvantages*
Trusts	Creating a trust is very easy since it does not require any registration or incorporation In addition, there are also the so-called "non-resident" trusts, which are not liable to tax in Mauritius, excerpt when the settler "is a non-resident of Mauritius or holds a GBL1[c] issued by the FSC, and the trust's beneficiaries are non-Mauritius residents or are holders of global business licenses"[d] Trustees are subject to fiduciary responsibilities The accomplishment of migration, restructuring, and termination is quite easy	Trusts are less transparent when compared to a company, due to the lack of formality and reporting requirements Trusts have no corporate personality

[a]Where it has legal personality

[b]In the case when the partnership has no legal personality

[c]Category 1 Global Business Licenses, governed by the Companies Act 2001 and The Financial Services Act 2007

[d]Bhavna, R., Nafiisah, J., Senivassen, L., Robert, B. L. C. & Associates. (2019). *Hedge funds in Mauritius: Regulatory overview*. https://uk.practicallaw.thomsonreuters.com/w-007-8204?transitionType=Default&contextData=(sc.Default)&firstPage=true&bhcp=1. Accessed 12 March 2020

There are many factors which explain the Cayman Islands' popularity such as: the stability of its government, the public policies oriented toward business, the advanced legal system—as well as its major various tax-free incentives with low financial regulation and oversight.

In a similar manner, Delaware's HF infrastructure is strong, being generally used by US-based HFs. Additionally, Delaware has a business-friendly legal system and its location offers a high level of confidence for institutional investors. Also, it should be stipulated that Delaware ranks first place as a domicile location among the US (offshore) hedge funds.

Both UK and US hedge funds are attracted by the British Virgin Islands, mainly because this country is historically tied to the United Kingdom and geographically close to the United States. The British Virgin Islands stands as one of the best, highly respected hedge funds' domiciles, globally speaking. In addition to its modern, efficient banking system stands the government's public policies focused mainly on developing strict money laundering and tax evasion standards, this earning for the British Virgin Islands a leading reputation in the financial world.

Mauritius is the favorite offshore center for Far East investing. The advantages offered by these jurisdictions are crystal clear. Just as Lhabitant states, they "offer well-thought-through legislation, an easy registration process, a reasonable level of confidentiality, limited reporting responsibilities, and last but not least, a benign level of taxes."[98]

Further on will be made up an analysis having in view the structure of hedge funds' market, the regulatory framework and bodies, the taxation and advantages offered by each country (Table 5.11).

[98] Lhabitant, F. S. (2006). *Handbook of hedge funds*. West Sussex: John Wiley & Sons Ltd., p. 87.

Table 5.11 Comparative view: the nonregulation of hedge funds in: Cayman Islands, British Virgin Islands, Mauritius, and Delaware

Structure of hedge funds' market			
Cayman Islands	Companies	Limited partnerships	Unit trusts
BVI	Companies limited by shares	Limited partnerships	Unit trusts
Mauritius	Companies	Limited partnerships	Unit trusts
Delaware	Companies	Limited partnerships	
Regulatory framework and bodies			
Cayman Islands	Cayman Islands Monetary Authority (CIMA) represents the regulatory body for open-ended hedge funds; meanwhile Mutual Funds Law regulates them		
BVI	The BVI Financial Services Commission regulates the typical BVI hedge funds		
Mauritius	The Financial Services Commission (FSC), which stands as the regulator for all nonbank financial services activities, regulating not only domestic, but also international funds The Registrar of Companies, the regulator for all corporate issues. The Registrar of Limited Partnerships, which regulates limited partnerships		

Structure of hedge funds' market	
Delaware	The Securities Act 1933 and the Investment Company Act 1940
Taxation	
Cayman Islands	There will be no direct tax for a Cayman-based hedge fund based in the Cayman Islands. As we have already seen, "all available legal structures for hosting a hedge fund may register as an exempted entity, obtaining a written exemption by the Cayman Islands Governor in Cabinet of any law imposing any tax on profits, gains or appreciation, or which is in the nature of estate duty, or inheritance tax"a This refers to an exemption valid for either 20 years (this is the case of corporations) or 50 years (in the case of limited partnerships or trusts)
	However, it is possible for Cayman-based hedge funds to be liable for taxes imposed in jurisdictions where it holds its investments. This stands as very important because the Cayman Islands have signed few Double Tax treaties[b]
BVI	The following are exempt from payment of income tax (Income Tax Act):
	Funds registered under the Securities and Investment Business Act 2010. It will not be liable to BVI payroll tax unless it has employees in the BVI
	The following are exempt from payment of income tax (Income Tax Act):
	All dividends and amounts that a fund formed as a BVI company pays to investors (including redemption proceeds)
	Capital gains realized by investors in relation to fund interests of a fund formed as a BVI company

(continued)

Table 5.11 (continued)

Structure of hedge funds' market		
	The following are exempt from payment of income tax (Income Tax Act): "All dividends and amounts paid by a fund to non-resident investors (including redemption proceeds) Capital gains realized by non-resident investors from fund interests There are no estate, inheritance, succession or gift taxes payable in the BVI in relation to shares in funds".[c]	
Mauritius	For domestic funds set-up as companies there are two taxes: (1) 15% on net business profits of corporations (capital gains are not included) and (2) 2% corporate social responsibility (CSR) levy A resident investor is subject to a 15% tax on its taxable income, but this excludes dividend income from Mauritius companies and capital profits. A resident investor standing as corporate body is obliged to pay a 2% CSR levy Non-resident investors do not have to pay taxes. Withholding taxes on dividends must not be paid by nonresident investors in Mauritian funds	
Delaware	Taxes such as: the income tax, the sales tax, or the property tax are not perceived in Delaware	
Advantages		
Cayman Islands		Generally, companies are regulated by more rigid laws in comparison to those applicable to other vehicles such as limited partnerships and unit trusts Companies have separate legal personality. Unit trusts operate through their trustee; meanwhile limited partnerships operate through their general partner Exempted limited partnerships impose that minimum one general partner establishes or registers in the Cayman Islands, while unit trusts necessitate a trustee, who will most of the time insert a controlled subsidiary for liability protection A Licensed Fund also known as a unit trust needs that a trustee is licensed under the Banks and Trust Companies Law Usually, investors choose the vehicle depending on whether it may qualify for specific tax or regulatory treatment in an overseas jurisdiction

Structure of hedge funds' market	
BVI	*Companies* have separate legal personality. Unit trusts operate through their trustee; meanwhile limited partnerships operate through their general partner *Limited partnerships* offer a tax transparent "pass-through" structure. It is possible to elect for the limited partnership to have (or not have) separate legal personality. Offers flexibility in relation to capital raising, allocation of distributions and carry structure Limited partners are only liable for their uncalled capital unless they take part in the management of the partnership
Mauritius	*Companies* The limited liability criterion refers to the fact that investors benefit from liability in direct relation to investment The statutory regulations concerning filing and reporting offer transparency and accountability The governing body (board) of the company responds for their actions in front of investors, which is known as fiduciary responsibility *Limited partnerships* Flexibility, tax transparency, and also mitigation of fiduciary risks The ability to account for incomes and losses at investor level Limited liability as far as the debts of the partnership is concerned *Trusts* Creating a trust is very easy since it does not require any registration or incorporation In addition, there are also the so-called "non-resident" trusts, which are not liable to tax in Mauritius, except when the settler "is a non-resident of Mauritius or holds a GBL1[d] issued by the FSC, and the trust's beneficiaries are non-Mauritius residents or are holders of global business licenses"[e] Trustees are subject to fiduciary responsibilities The accomplishment of migration, restructuring, and termination is quite easy

(continued)

Table 5.11 (continued)

Structure of hedge funds' market	
Delaware	A Licensed Fund also known as a unit trust needs that a trustee is licensed under the Banks and Trust Companies Law Usually, investors choose the vehicle depending on whether it may qualify for specific tax or regulatory treatment in an overseas jurisdiction[f]

[a]Brocard, M., & Lhabitant, F. S. (2016). A *primer on the tax framework of offshore and onshore hedge fund*. Paris: EDHEC Risk Institute. https://www.edhec.edu/ sites/www.edhec-portail.pprod.net/files/publications/pdf/edhec-working-paper-a-primer-on-the-tax-framework-f_1467203960443-pdfjpg. Accessed 12 March 2020

[b]This is a bilateral agreement between two parties implying the abolition of double taxation on active and passive income. In this respect, the Cayman Islands have signed a comprehensive tax treaty with Japan in 2010, and limited tax treaties with the United Kingdom and New Zealand. The Cayman Islands/UK double taxation arrangement (DTA) was signed in June 2009 and it entered into force in December 2010. It started to be effective in the Cayman Islands starting with April 2011 for the corporation tax and for the income and capital gains tax and from December 2010 for other taxes. See also Trepelkov, A., Tonino, H. & Halka, D. (eds.) (2013). *United Nations handbook on selected issues in administration of double tax treaties for developing countries*. UN, New York. https://doi.org/10.18356/a96cf16b-en

[c]Hempel, C., & Olsen, C. (2019). *Hedge funds in the British Virgin Islands: regulatory overview*. https://uk.practicallaw.thomsonreuters.com/w-007-6405?transitionType=Default&contextData=(sc.Default)&firstPage=true&bhcp=1. Accessed 26 March 2020

[d]Category 1 Global Business Licenses, governed by the Companies Act 2001 and The Financial Services Act 2007

[e]Bhavna, R., Nafiisah, J., Senivassen, L., Robert, B. L. C. & Associates. (2019). *Hedge funds in Mauritius: Regulatory overview*. https://uk.practicallaw.thomsonreuters.com/w-007-8204?transitionType=Default&contextData=(sc.Default)&firstPage=true&bhcp=1. Accessed 12 March 2020

[f]Such as example is that unit trusts are generally used for the Japanese market and limited partnerships for the Israeli market

References

Aragon, G. B., & Park, L. H. (2014). Onshore and offshore hedge funds: Are they twins? *Management Science, 60*(1), 74–91.

Baker, H. K., & Filbeck, G. (2017). *Hedge funds structure, strategies, and performance*. Oxford: Oxford Scholarship Online.

Barth, M. H., & Blanco, M. (2001). US regulatory and tax considerations for offshore funds. In S. Barham, I. Hallsworth, & C. Bonnett (Eds.), *The capital guide to offshore funds 2001* (pp. 15–61). The Hague: ISI Publications.

Bhavna, R., Nafiisah, J., Senivassen, L., Robert, B. L. C., & Associates. (2019). *Hedge funds in Mauritius: Regulatory overview*. https://uk.practicallaw.thomsonreuters.com/w-007-8204?transitionType=Default&contextData=(sc.Default)&firstPage=true&bhcp=1. Accessed 12 March 2020.

Bratton, W. W. (2007). *Hedge funds and governance targets* (Paper 862). Faculty Scholarship. http://scholarship.law.upenn.edu/faculty_scholarship/862. Accessed 12 March 2020.

Brocard, M., & Lhabitant, F. S. (2016). *A primer on the tax framework of offshore and onshore hedge fund*. Paris: EDHEC Risk Institute. https://www.edhec.edu/sites/www.edhec-portail.pprod.net/files/publications/pdf/edhec-working-paper-a-primer-on-the-tax-framework-f_1467203960443-pdfjpg. Accessed 12 March 2020.

Brown, St. J., Goetzmann, W. N., Ibbotson, R. G. (1999). Offshore hedge funds: Survival and performance, 1989–95. *The Journal of Business, 72*(1), 91–117.

Browning, L. (2007a, July 1). Offshore tax breaks lure money managers. *New York Times*. http://www.nytimes.com/2007/07/01/business/yourmoney/01cay.html. Accessed 12 March 2020.

Browning, L. (2017b, June 12). *Trump's offshore tax plan may mean perk for Apple, Pfizer*. Bloomberg. http://www.bloomberg.com/news/articles/2017-06-12/trump-s-offshore-tax-plan-may-mean-extra-perk-for-apple-pfizer. Accessed 12 March 2020.

Cent. Intelligence Agency. (2018). *The World Factbook: Cayman Islands*. https://www.cia.gov/library/publications/the-world-factbook/geos/cj.html. Accessed 6 April 2020.

Clarke, C. (2016). What are tax havens and why are they bad? *Texas Law Review, 95*, 59–68.

Clarkson, D., Jaecklin, S., & Kaczmarski, K. (2014). *Domiciles of alternative investment funds*. http://docshare01.docshare.tips/files/26926/269260073.pdf. Accessed 22 April 2020.

Cohen, A. R., & Williams, C. S. (2011). *A comparison by practitioners of Delaware and Cayman Islands Limited partnerships*. Bloomberg Finance L.P. Law Reports—Fund Management and Bloomberg Law Reports—Securities Law. https://www.google.com/url?sa=t&rct=j&q=&esrc=s&source=web&

cd=&cad=rja&uact=8&ved=2ahUKEwjX8aTf_6jrAhXoQhUIHR_9BUUQF jAAegQIBRAB&url=https%3A%2F%2Fwww.walkersglobal.com%2Fimages%2FPublications%2FArticles%2F2011%2F09.2011-Comparison-of-Delaware-and-Cayman-Islands-Limited-Partnerships.pdf&usg=AOvVaw1PhR_fIN3u4Kfy_j1B8vBe. Accessed 22 April 2020.

Corporate. (2018). *APPLEBY*. http://www.applebyglobal.com/services/corporate.aspx. Accessed 12 March 2020.

Cumming, D.J., & Dai, N. (2010). Local bias in venture capital investments. *Journal of Empirical Finance, 17*, 362–380.

Cumming, D., Dai, N., & Johan, S.A. (2013). *Hedge Fund structure, regulation, and performance around the world*. Oxford: Oxford University Press.

Cumming, D., Dai, N., & Johan, S. A. (2015). Are hedge funds domiciled in Delaware different? *Journal of Corporate Finance, 35*, 232–246.

De Brouwer, G. (2001). *Hedge funds in emerging markets*. Cambridge: Cambridge University Press.

Deloitte. (2015). *Establishing investment funds in the Cayman Islands: Key considerations*. https://www2.deloitte.com/content/dam/Deloitte/bm/Documents/financial-services/cayman-islands/establishing-investment-funds-in-the-cayman-islands.pdf. Accessed 3 April 2020.

Dyreng, S., Lindsey, B., & Thornock, J. (2012). *Exploring the role delaware plays as a tax haven* (Working Paper WP 12/12). Oxford University Centre for Business Taxation. http://www.sbs.ox.ac.uk/centres/tax/papers/Documents/WP1212.pdf. Accessed 20 March 2020.

Enea, C., & Enea, C. (2015). Methods of taxation in the tax havens. Examples of taxation in the Bahamas, Bermuda and the Cayman Islands. *Annals of the "Constantin Brâncuşi" University of Târgu Jiu. Economy Series, Special Issue ECO-TREND 2015—Performance, Competitiveness, Creativity*. Targu Jiu: "Academica Brâncuşi" Publisher. https://www.google.com/url?sa=t&rct=j&q=&esrc=s&source=web&cd=&ved=2ahUKEwjj6dn-g6nrAhVLMewKHYFrBxYQFjAAegQIAhAB&url=http%3A%2F%2Fwww.utgjiu.ro%2Frevista%2Fec%2Fpdf%2F2015-Special%2520ECOTREND%2F33_Enea%2C%2520Enea.pdf&usg=AOvVaw3nQSTCfMTzJjAyT7fvDQc9. Accessed 20 March 2020.

Farley, J., & Olsen, C. (2018). *Hedge funds in the Cayman Islands: Regulatory overview*. https://uk.practicallaw.thomsonreuters.com/w-007-5747?transitionType=Default&contextData=(sc.Default)&firstPage=true&bhcp=1. Accessed 20 March 2020.

Fichtner, J. (2013). The rise of hedge funds: A story of inequality. *Momentum Quarterly, 2*(1), 3–20.

Fichtner, J. (2016). The anatomy of the Cayman Islands Offshore Financial Center: Anglo-America, Japan, and the role of hedge funds. *Review of International Political Economy, 23*(6), 1034–1063. https://doi.org/10.1080/09692290.2016.1243143.

Fitzgibbon, W. (2017, November 5). Appleby, the offshore law firm with a record of compliance failures. *Irish Times*. https://www.irishtimes.com/business/appleby-the-offshore-law-firm-with-a-record-of-compliance-failures-1.3280860. Accessed 12 March 2020.

Flaye, E. (2020). *The offshore dimension*. https://www.conyers.com/wp-content/uploads/2018/06/2018_CAY_How_to_Start_a_Hedge_Fund_in_the_US_The_Offshore_Dimension.pdf. Accessed 26 March 2020.

Fund Associates. (2008). *Offshore hedge funds vs. onshore hedge funds*. http://fundassociates.com/pdfs/Offshore_vs_Onshore_Funds_Whitepaper.pdf. Accessed 12 April 2020.

Gross, PhS. (2004). Tax planning for offshore hedge funds—Potential benefits of investing in a PFIC. *Journal of Taxation of Investments, 21*(2), 187–195.

Hammer, D. L. et al. (2005). *US regulation of hedge funds*. Chicago: ABA Book Publishing.

Harrington, B. (2017). Trusts and financialization. *Socio-Economic Review, 15*, 31–63.

Hempel, C., & Olsen, C. (2019). *Hedge funds in the British Virgin Islands: Regulatory overview*. https://uk.practicallaw.thomsonreuters.com/w-007-6405?transitionType=Default&contextData=(sc.Default)&firstPage=true&bhcp=1. Accessed 26 March 2020.

Johnston, D. C. (2007). *Free lunch: How the wealthiest Americans enrich themselves at government expense*. New York: Penguin Group.

Khelifa, S. B., & Hmaied, D. M. (2014). European hedge funds industry: An overview. *The Journal of Private Equity, 18*(1), 46–59.

Kleinbard, E. D. (2003). Competitive convergence in the financial services markets. *Taxes, 81*, 225–260.

Lepree, S. A. (2008). Taxation of United States tax-exempt entities' offshore hedge fund investments: Application of the Section 514 debt-financed rules to leveraged hedge funds and derivatives and the case for equalization. *Tax Law, 61*, 807–815.

Lhabitant, F. S. (2006). *Handbook of hedge funds*. West Sussex: John Wiley & Sons Ltd.

Magnuson, W. (2016). Unilateral corporate regulation. *Chicago Journal of International Law, 17*, 521–537.

McCrary, S. A. (2002). How to create and manage a hedge fund—A professional's guide. Hoboken: John Wiley & Sons.

Moon, W. J. (2019). Regulating offshore finance. *Vanderbilt Law Review, 72*(1), 1–54.

Morley, J. (2013). The regulation of mutual fund debt. *Yale Journal on Regulation, 30*, 343–376.

Morley, J. (2014). The separation of funds and managers: A theory of investment fund structure and regulation. *Yale Law Journal, 123*, 1228–1253.

Mourant, O. (2017). *The Cayman Islands: A guide for hedge fund managers*. https://www.mourant.com/file-library/media—2017/2017-guides/the-cayman-islands—a-guide-for-hedge-fund-managers.pdf. Accessed 2 April 2020.

Palan, R. (1998). Trying to have your cake and eating it: How and why the state system has created offshore. *International Studies Quarterly, 42*(4), 625–644.

Palan, R. (2015). The second British Empire: The British Empire and the re-emergence of global finance. In S. Halperin & R. Palan (Eds.), *Legacies of empire imperial roots of the contemporary global order* (pp. 40–68). Cambridge: Cambridge University Press.

Palan, R., Murphy, R., & Chavagneux, C. (2010). *Tax havens: How globalization really works*. New York: Cornell University Press.

Peaslee, J. M., & Nirenberg, D. Z. (2011). *Federal income taxation of securitization transactions and related topics* (4th ed.). USA: Frank J. Fabozzi Associates Publisher.

Pepper, H. (2008). *A practical guide to US tax compliance issues for hedge fund of funds*. http://www.pepperlaw.com/uploads/files/fundoffunds_schneidman_1008.pdf. Accessed 29 February 2020.

Philip, R. L., & Milesi-Ferretti, G. M. (2010). Cross-border investment in small international financial centers. *International Monetary Fund Working Paper, 10*(38), 1–32.

Pistor, K. (2013). A legal theory of finance. *Journal of Comparative Economics, 41*(2), 315–330.

Private Funds Law. (2020). Law 1 of 2020 Supplement No. 1 published with Legislation Gazette No. 9 dated 7th February, 2020. https://www.cima.ky/upimages/commonfiles/PrivateFundsLaw2020_1581524961.PDF. Accessed 12 April 2020.

Roberts, S. (1995). Small place, big money: The Cayman Islands and the international financial system. *Economic Geography, 71*(3), 237–256.

Ronalds-Hannon, E. (2016, June 21). *Hedge funds' misery exposed as Caribbean proxies dump treasuries*. Bloomberg. https://www.bloomberg.com/news/articles/2016-06-21/hedge-funds-misery-exposed-as-caribbean-proxies-dump-treasuries. Accessed 6 April 2020.

Schwartz, R. (2012). Delaware as a location for private funds: The why and the what. *Bloomberg World Securities Law Report, 18*, 1–8.

SEC v. Gruss, 859 F. Supp. 2d 653, 658 (S.D.N.Y. 2012).

Shadab, H. B. (2013). Hedge fund governance. *Stanford Journal of Law, Business & Finance, 19*(1), 141–202.

Trang, H. K. (2015, May 9). Why hedge funds love to go offshore. *The Forbes*. https://web.archive.org/web/20150516100546/http://www.forbes.com:80/sites/trangho/2015/05/09/why-hedge-funds-love-to-go-offshore/3. Accessed 6 April 2020.

Trepelkov, A., Tonino, H., & Halka, D. (Eds.) (2013). *United Nations handbook on selected issues in administration of double tax treaties for developing countries*. New York: United Nations. https://doi.org/10.18356/a96cf16b-en.

Tuchschmid, N. S., & Wallerstein, E. (2013). UCITS: Can they bring funds of hedge funds on-shore? *The Journal of Wealth Management, 15*(4), 94–109. https://doi.org/10.3905/jwm.2013.15.4.094.

Valencia, M. (2013, February 16). Storm survivors. *The Economist*. http://www.economist.com/news/special-report/21571549-offshore-financial-centres-have-taken-battering-recently-they-have-shown-remarkable. Accessed 6 April 2020.

Wolters Kluwer. (2015). *A guide to the top 20 offshore fund locations*. https://ct.wolterskluwer.com/sites/default/files/CT_Top_20_Offshore_Funds_0.pdf. Accessed 4 March 2020.

CHAPTER 6

Regulation of Hedge Funds in the US

6.1 Introduction

Every regulation has its costs. What counts is whether its advantages overcome the costs.[1] Taken into consideration "the magnitude and scope of recent regulatory changes"[2] on hedge funds, this chapter examines the regulation of hedge funds before and after the implementation of the Dodd–Frank Act, focusing mainly on regulatory changes and restrictions imposed on hedge funds after the crisis.[3]

The most important "federal securities regulations" setting up the solid foundation for hedge funds' regulation on the US territory have been approved at the beginning of the Bourse collapse in 1929. The regulatory documents are:

[1] Hubbard, G. (2019). If it happened again: A road map for regulatory reform chapter. In S. O'Halloran & Th. Groll (Eds.), *After the crash: Financial crises and regulatory responses* (pp. 47–56). New York: Columbia University Press.

[2] Cumming, D., Dai, N., & Johan, S. (2019). Dodd-Franking the hedge Funds. *Journal of Banking and Finance*. https://doi.org/10.1016/j.jbankfin.2017.09.012.

[3] Hong, X. (2014). The dynamics of hedge fund share restrictions. *Journal of Banking and Finance, 49*, 82–99.

A. M. Fagetan, *The Regulation of Hedge Funds*,
https://doi.org/10.1007/978-3-030-63706-4_6

- "the Securities Act of 1933"[4];
- "the Securities Exchange Act of 1934"[5];
- "the Investment Company Act of 1940"[6];
- "the Investment Advisors Act of 1940."[7]

These acts are described in the first part of the chapter. The last part of this chapter analyses "the Dodd-Frank Act,"[8] whose enactment was the direct consequence of the financial crisis. The above-mentioned legislation stipulates under title IV[9] several recommendations which highly change the act of registering requests and investment advisers' regulation.

The vast majority of hedge funds were not compelled to fill in a registration form with the SEC, be it according to the "Investment Company Act" or in accordance with "the Investment Advisers Act," both from 1940. Also, the present chapter addresses the premises of hedge fund reforms, particularly in terms of exemption from registration for hedge funds advisers and reporting requirements, which culminated with the enactment of the "Dodd-Frank Act." The present chapter represents a survey and research regarding the hedge funds regulation in the United States, but also a general presentation of "how hedge funds together with their managers are to a large extent exempted from regulation."[10]

Since 2017, the Trump administration has been pursuing largely deregulatory agenda, including a proposed repeal of some provisions of the Dodd–Frank Act. The most significant proposals affecting investment advisers are described herein.

Hedge funds but also various private pooled investments usually try to decrease the amplitude of their regulation in the United States (and elsewhere). They have historically counted on exemptions from registering according to the most important "US Securities and Commodities

[4] 15 U.S.C. §§ 77a et seq.

[5] 15 U.S.C. §§ 78a et seq.

[6] 15 U.S.C. §§ 80a-1 et seq.

[7] 15 U.S.C. §§ 80b-1 et seq.

[8] Public Law 111-203, 124 Stat. 1376 (2010).

[9] "Regulation of Advisers to Hedge Funds and Others".

[10] Hanlon, A. P. (2002). *Proposal for reform of hedge fund regulation*. Harvard Law School.

Laws" available for PIV,[11] but also for their promoters. The present chapter adds to the research field in several ways. First of all, this study contributes to the fast-growing literature on hedge funds regulation, with a detailed research regarding the evolution of hedge funds regulations in the United States. Also, it contributes to an increased understanding of hedge funds operation during unstable periods in America. Another contribution worth mentioning is represented by the analysis of future necessity in terms of tighter regulation of the US hedge funds. This necessity is supported by the deep preoccupation for financial security and "investor protection." Also, the study considers the features of the Dodd-Frank Act focusing mainly on its accomplishments or errors. In this context, another contribution resides in the significance of the analysis for individuals interested particularly in the financial ongoing reform from the United States affecting other jurisdictions as well. The reasons for the author's belief are fully supported by the fact that the US enactment of financial regulations will definitely turn into an inevitable indicator directing the efforts toward the international development of financial regulations. Therefore, although the chapter adds to the understanding of the analysis of the US regulatory framework for hedge funds, it can also be seen as a contribution to the international regulatory development dimensions, from a comparative perspective.

The author declares that this chapter will enable academic scholars not only to discover data requested for future studies in the field, but especially, *in general*, (1) to gain comprehension with regard to general reputation of the "hedge fund" market throughout the United States, and *in particular*, (2) to gain a broad understanding of contemporary debates regarding financial regulation with focus on the protection of investors against the growing complexity of financial markets, new risks, and other changes brought about by financial innovation.

6.2 The Investment Company Act 1940

The "Investment Company Act" (hereinafter also presented as the 1940 Act) generally governs investment funds in the United States. Most alternative investment funds are defined, in the absence of an exemption, according to an "investment company" and, therefore, registered with

[11] Pooled Investment Vehicles.

the SEC.[12] Registered funds comply with several constraints incompatible with many investment strategies pursued by alternative investment funds.[13]

The 1940 Act was issued for the protection of investors who use other persons in their investments management and diversification. Every investment company[14] included in the definition without being "exempted from the act"[15] is bound to register with the SEC.[16] Only if an investment entity acts in compliance with all stipulations specified in the 1940 Act, is this entity allowed to become actively involved in some securities-related processes.[17] Also, different associations are included, but also the particular interest manifested by the managers, counsellors, as well as staff working within an investment entity.[18] Thus, for instance, investment companies are allowed to have executive principals with maximum 60 percent from individuals who are members within the entity, seen as "interested persons."[19] Also, these companies are bound to submit income and other various reports.[20]

In agreement with section 3(a) of the Investment Company Act, *investment companies* include every vehicle involved in securities investment. Alternative investment funds generally use the exemptions mentioned in sections: 3(c)(1) as well as 3(c)(7)[21] and abandon registration and its substantial associated restriction. Thus, "these private investments" firm exclusions were mentioned in two Sections.[22] According to the above-mentioned exclusions, some pooled investment vehicles are exempt from definition according to the term *investment company* and at the same

[12] Spangler, T., & Scholer, K. (2010). *A practitioner's guide to alternative investment funds* (2nd ed.). London: Sweet & Maxwell UK.

[13] Spangler, T., & Scholer, K. (2010). Op. cit., p. 115.

[14] 15 U.S.C. § 80a-3(a).

[15] Exemptions may be found at 15 U.S.C. § 80a-3(b) and (c).

[16] 15 U.S.C. §§ 80a-7 and 80a-8.

[17] 15 U.S.C. § 80a-7(a), (b), and (c).

[18] 15 U.S.C. § 80a-10.

[19] 15 U.S.C. § 80a-10(a).

[20] 15 U.S.C. § 80a-29.

[21] Goldstein, D. A., & Kelly, B. (2004). SEC proposes rules requiring offshore advisers of offshore hedge funds to register under the Advisers Act. *Journal of Investment Compliance, 5*(2), 29–33. https://doi.org/10.1108/15285810410636127.

[22] 3(c) (1) and 3(c) (7).

time, they are exempt also from substantive regulation in accordance with the Investment Company Act.

Out of the two exclusions, the oldest and most frequent seems to be Section 3(c)(1). The requests are doubled: first, interests in funds are basically placed personally to investing persons; second, the maximum acceptable number of investors is 100.

What constitutes public offerings for objectives mentioned in the 1940s Act is understood in practice to be similar subject to section 4(2) stipulated in the Securities Act.[23] As a result, funds endeavoring to count on this exemption will perform their offerings as subjected to regulation "506 of Regulation D,"[24] which is the safe harbor for section 4(2). Furthermore, private placements of fund interests in the United States complying with rule 506 from "the Securities Act" will not be incorporated with an offshore public offering of the interests. Consequently, foreign funds may have up to "100 US beneficial"[25] owners without falling under the public offering prohibition of section 7(d) as per the co-called *Touche, Remnant* & *Co* doctrine.[26]

The discussion about the counting of only up to 100 investors, for the purpose of section 3(c)(1)[27] is not entirely self-evident and is subject to various rules and clarification. In some cases, beneficial owners of distinct funds can be combined according to the integration assumption, if the two vehicles represent a distinct fund. Resemblances in investors' profiles and investment strategies are of great interest for this study. The experts of the SEC concluded that neither onshore nor offshore funds with similar investment aims cannot be merged where the vehicles concern investors with different tax positions.

Typically, only investors who are US persons are considered when a fund is organized outside of the United States. As a result, "for purposes of the 100 ownership limit,"[28] "the number of other investors in the

[23] Section 8.4 of the Securities Act of 1933.

[24] Sec. Act Release n° 6389, Fed. Sec. L. Rep. (CCH) 83,106 (1982).

[25] International Trident Trust Group. (1999). *The chancellor offshore funds manual*. London: Chancellors Publications Limited.

[26] Touche, Remnant & Co., "SEC No-Action Letter" (1984) ("Touche Remnant").

[27] Hammer, D. L., et al. (2005). *US regulation of hedge funds*. Chicago: ABA Book Publishing, p. 101.

[28] Touche, Remnant & Co., "SEC No-Action Letter".

fund would only be subject to limits imposed in the funds' jurisdiction of domicile."[29] At the same time, new regulations have been introduced regarding offshore CIS under section 7(d), as well as section 3(c)(1). According to the above-mentioned sections, all the offshore funds which are not registered have the possibility to disclose private offerings inside the US borders, while simultaneously performing public offerings outside the US borders without breaching section 7(d). There is, however, one condition which needs to be considered, namely that these offshore funds are enabled to have maximum 100 asset holders who must be American residents.[30]

The major regulatory exemption concerning hedge funds is available under the provisions of this Act. Unlike regulated investment firms, private funds do not fall under the "1940 Act" limitations regarding the participation in financial strategies among which one can enumerate: leveraging, "short selling," and making focused standings within one particular sector, company or industry. At the same time, they are exempted from worth requests generally applied to investment entities which are registered and thus forced to evaluate the entire portfolio securities daily, according to the trading price.[31]

In order to qualify for the exemption stipulated by Section 3(c)(1), the hedge fund has to fulfill two major conditions. The first one is that maximum 100 holders[32] are allowed. The second one is that public offerings[33] are not allowed.

The term "*qualified purchaser*" refers to persons with more than USD 5 million in investments/firms, but also minimum USD 25 million invested.[34] One very relevant issue is represented by the presented exceptions, according to which a fund can count on whether the fund's

[29] Rosenblum, R. H. (2003). *Investment company determination under the 1940 Act: Exemptions and exceptions* (2nd ed.). Chicago: ABA Publishing.

[30] Touche, Remnant & Co., "SEC No-Action Letter".

[31] Baums, Th., & Cahn, A. (2004). *Hedge funds—Risks and regulation. Institute for Law and Finance Series, 1.* Berlin: De Gruyter.

[32] Public Law 111-203, 124 Stat. 1376 (2010).

[33] Ritter, J. (1991). The long-run performance of initial public offerings. *Journal of Finance, 46*, 3–27.

[34] Vasavada, N. (2010). *Taxation of US Investment partnerships and hedge funds: Accounting policies.* Hoboken, NJ: Wiley Publisher.

securities are exchanged in a *private placement* according to the 1933 Act.

6.3 The Investment Advisers Act 1940

An important piece of US securities legislation, namely, "the Investment Advisers Act of 1940,"[35] is probably better known for its conciseness. Especially if it were to compare it to its companion statute, "the 1940 Act,"[36] "the Investment Advisers Act"[37] does not hinder much the entities that fall within its registration requirements. This Investment Advisers Act settles some particular prohibitions on conduct, with emphasis on broad proscription of illicit conduct by investment advisers.[38]

This Act appoints every "investment adviser" in the position of every individual paid to provide assistance to people on funds value and investments, "purchasing or selling securities,"[39] and the persons who analyze securities. Also, the Advisers Act includes fundamental requirements for some investment advisers who meet established thresholds, including: SEC registration, maintenance of business portfolios, delivery of disclosure statements for clients,[40] but also the prevention of customers deceiving because of ethical/legal confidence to act[41] in

[35] Barbash, B., & Massari, J. (2008). The Investment Advisers Act of 1940: Regulation by Accretion. *Rutgers Law Journal, 39*, 627–656.

[36] "The Investment Advisers Act" deals generally with persons providing money management advice. "Investment Advisers Act of 1940, 15 U.S.C. § 80b" (2000). This deals generally with pooled investment vehicles whose shares are available for purchase by the public. "Investment Company Act of 1940, 15 U.S.C. § 80a" (2000). Both were originally adopted as part of the same bill and reflect a complementary effort to regulate the investment management industry in the US following the turbulence of the 1930s. Sections 12, 15, and 17 of the Investment Company Act, e.g., establish comprehensive but also detailed rules of conduct for companies that come within the Act's definition of "investment company." Id. §§ 80a-12, -15, -17.

[37] E.g. "Registration Under the Advisers Act of Certain Hedge Fund Advisers, Investment Advisers Act Release n° 2333, 69 Fed. Reg. 72,054" (Advisers Act sets out minimal basic requirements for registered advisers rather than a detailed set of rules).

[38] 15 U.S.C. § 80b-6.

[39] 15 U.S.C. § 80b-2(11).

[40] "Registration under the Advisers Act of Certain Hedge Fund Advisers, 69 Fed. Reg. 72054, 72054 (Dec. 10, 2004) (to be codified at C.F.R. pt. 275)."

[41] SEC v. Capital Gains Research Bureau, Inc., 375 U.S. 180, 191 (1963).

the best interests of the client. There are however several exemptions. Thus, Section 203(b)(3) stipulates that those persons called investment counselors with maximum 15 customers "during the preceding twelve months,"[42] must not present themselves usually in front of the public as investment counselors, and they do not represent counselors for any "registered investment"[43] firm.

Nevertheless, the individuals eligible for the exemption have to follow the SEC anti-fraud provisions, but they are not required to file registration forms to identify themselves, keep business records according to SEC provisions, apply compliance plans or ethical norms or subordinate themselves to SEC supervision. Also, if it is not registered with the SEC, no investment adviser can use mails or other methods of interstate trade in relation with his/her profession of "investment adviser."[44] The latter may register by filling in particular data "with the SEC."[45]

Further on, the definition of the *investment adviser* will be presented. Section 202 (a) (11) states that this profession includes every individual involved in the marketing industry either dealing with the value of the shares, or with suitability regarding the investments in securities,[46] doing this for compensation. Therefore, the concept presented above largely includes every individual who provides advice about securities as part of a regular business, in order to get compensation.[47] In the absence of an exemption, their registration according to the Act of 1940 is required as per section 203(a).

Several exclusions from the definitions are made for persons who incidentally provide advice to their own businesses, including:

[42] Hayes, R., & Walker, R. S. (2006). Mandatory registration of hedge funds with the SEC and hedge fund activism in corporate decision. *Entrepreneurial Business Law Journal, 1*, 87–124.

[43] 15 U.S.C.A § 80b-3(b)(3) (2002).

[44] 15 U.S.C. § 80b-3(a).

[45] 15 U.S.C. § 80b-3(c).

[46] Seligman, J. (2003). The New Uniform Securities Act. *Washington University Law Quarterly, 81*, 243–299.

[47] Investment Advisers Act of 1940—Sections 203(a) and 208(d) American Bar Association, Business Law Section, January 18, 2012, "Response of the Office of Investment Adviser Regulation Division of Investment Management," http://www.sec.gov/divisions/investment/noaction/2012/aba011812.htm. Accessed 1 March 2012.

- Professional individuals, among which one can mention lawyers, as well as accountants;
- Individuals engaged in publishing printed material;
- Broker dealers;
- Credit institutions.[48]

In addition, a number of exemptions are provided for advisers with limited operations only. Of primary importance are "private investment advisers," with maximum 15 customers during the last year, who are not making them generally available like the public advisers.[49]

Registering as an investment adviser implies fiduciary duties[50] owed to clients, as well as substantial requirements that must be met. In the first case, this includes providing appropriate advice, best execution, and full disclosure of conflicts. In the second case, "a registered adviser must comply with detailed rules addressing, among other things: advertisements, custody, performance fees, record keeping and privacy."[51]

According to Paul F. Roye,[52] US SEC, managers of funds need not forget their obligation toward their customers despite their light regulation. He also warns them that not only the Commission but also other authorities and individuals pay attention to ensuring the ability of fund managers to meet all legal and ethical responsibilities.[53] This statement was triggered by suits of hedge fund fraud, which led "to regulators' investor protection concerns. Even if many enforcement litigations have implied investment registered advisers, the number of investment advisers continued to increase lately. Still, the most challenging characteristic of companies that comply to the provisions of the Investment Advisers Act does not reside in their number but rather in their variety; advisers nowadays "run the gamut from financial planners to separate accounts managers, to mutual fund advisers, to hedge or other

[48] Investment Advisers Act of 1940, Sec. 202, p. 4.

[49] Spangler, T., & Scholer, K. (2010). Op. cit., p. 111.

[50] Gibbons, G., & Stone, H. M. (2011). PE managers as registered investment advisors. *The Journal of Private Equity, 15*(1), 8–15. https://doi.org/10.3905/jpe.2011.15.1.008.

[51] Spangler, T., & Scholer, K. (2010). Op. cit., p. 112.

[52] Director of the Division of Investment Management.

[53] IA Compliance Summit and Best Practice Update (8 April 2002).

private fund managers."[54] Nowadays, litigations are filed on various grounds, from portfolio inflating, failure to achieve investment purposes, non-achievement of performing high-quality work, as well as breaching fiduciary duties.[55]

6.4 The Securities Act of 1933

One main aim of the "1933 Act" resides in protecting the investors. In this respect, it is illegal to either offer or sell securities[56] transparently if they were previously recorded under the SEC (Commission).[57] Its major occupation is represented by the first securities' distribution and less by the subsequent exchange. To reach that aim, a request of registration with the SEC needs to be submitted and data distribution of securities should be performed before being publicly exchanged. "A registration statement" turns operative 20 days after it has been submitted to the Commission, except when this is either postponed or interrupted.[58] This is composed of two parts: the first part is the prospectus, offered to each security's purchaser, and the second Part includes information and exhibits that are not compulsory, offered to purchasers and also accessible for public inquiry. Similarly, Section 7 in the 1933 Act[59] refers to

[54] Nat'l Regulatory Servs. & Inv. Advisers Ass'n. (2007). *Evolution Revolution Report 4*. http://www.investmentadviser.org/public/evolution_revolution-2007.pdf. Accessed 21 July 2020 (reporting on investment adviser industry demographics).

[55] See, SEC v. Burton G. Friedlander, Civil Action No. 01 Civ. 4658 (S.D.N.Y.), Lit. Rel. No. 17021 (June 1, 2001).

[56] The definition of the security concept can be found largely within 15 U.S.C., more precisely in Section 77b(1). According to this section, it represents each "note, stock, treasury stock, bond, debenture, evidence of indebtedness, certificate of interest or participation in any profit-sharing agreement, collateral-trust certificate, pre-organisation certificate or subscription, transferable share, investment contract, voting-trust certificate, certificate of deposit for a security, fractional undivided interest in oil, gas, or other mineral rights, any put, call straddle, option, or privilege entered into on a national securities exchange relating to foreign currency, or, in general, any instrument or instrument commonly known as a security, or any certificate of interest or participation in, temporary or interim certificate for, receipt for, guarantee of, or warrant or right to subscribe to or purchase, any of the foregoing", in Seitzinger, M.V., Overview of Major Federal Securities Laws, CRS report for Congress, p. 2.

[57] 15 U.S.C. § 77e.

[58] 15 U.S.C. § 77 h(a).

[59] 15 U.S.C. § 77g.

"Schedule A"[60] and presents data that has to be included in the registration declaration. This program demands a high amount of data, like the underwriters, business type, relevant associates, debits and possessions of the firm, and beliefs concerning legitimacy. "Section 10(a)" of the 1933 Act presents general data commonly contained by the prospectus.[61] Also, the Commission issues many rules which include new aspects regarding the possibilities of registering as per the 1933 Act.[62]

When marketing an alternative investment fund to investors from the United States, exemptions in connection with the fund's potential status as an "investment company" are necessary, simultaneously with the guarantee that every offer and trade of interests in the fund is exempt from registering according to the Securities Act. Embodied as a limited association, "a unit trust" and even a corporation, the interests of a fund will be subject to the "security" definition. In the absence of a suitable exemption, the registration with the SEC will be required for the offer and trade of such interest.[63]

The objective of the Securities Act is to provide the necessary disclosure of data to investors when offers are made to the public. Exemptions to the registration requests are reachable to some offers and trades that can take place in the secondary market or can represent private placements. Therefore, hedge funds are forbidden from general advertising and this implies securing investors through consultants, registered representatives, brokers, or investment advisors. The decreased public disclosure by hedge funds leads to decreased transparency and therefore, to a low degree of investor protection. But these new exemptions exemplify the SEC's inclination toward regulating by exemption. Still, although the SEC's purposes are laudable, the question that remains is whether this represents indeed a sound regulatory strategy.

To evade from registering their securities, a high amount of "private funds," comprising hedge funds count on exemptions stipulated "in section 4 (2)" referring to private placement. According to this section,

[60] 15 U.S.C. § 77aa.

[61] 15 U.S.C. § 77j(a).

[62] 17 C.F.R. Parts 230, 231, and 239.

[63] Spangler, T. et al. (2010). *A practitioner's guide to alternative investment funds* (2nd ed.). City & Financial Publishing, p. 115.

the exchanges that do not involve "public offerings are exempted,"[64] as per the 1933 Act. According to this, they will be exempted from registering unless the interests are traded without involving *public offering*. Usually it will not be regarded as *public offering* if the investment manager does not advertise the selling, and if the selling is available only to a limited number of experienced investors.[65]

The logic of believing this resided in the fact that it was considered that there was no need to protect the potential investors, since they could protect themselves. Still, as it can prove difficult to know what the term *public offering* actually supposes, there are many fund managers confiding in the legal safe harbor in Regulation D under the 1933 Act.[66] "Regulation D effective on April 15, 1982,"[67] provides a manner to establish that you did not make an open, "public offering" for goals stipulated at section 4(2). In this context, as an unregulated entity, the hedge fund investment manager has the freedom to undertake greater risk on more volatile positions and by doing this he can expose investors to possible substantial profit but, at the same time, to substantial losses as well.

In this respect, there are many funds trusting Rule 506[68] from Regulation D[69] to meet the particular exemption concerning the refusal of making public offerings. Accordingly, not one "public offering" occurred in the case when the institution issuing it failed to engage to an overall request of its securities. This request is available for at least "35 investors" without accreditation. This law enables selling to a limitless range "of accredited investors,"[70] like most financial organizations, which are either individuals who at that moment of purchase have a net worth surpassing

[64] Baums, Th. et al. (2004). Op. cit., p. 63.

[65] http://www.moneymanagerservices.com/tour/sales.cfm. Accessed 17 June 2020.

[66] Edwards, F. R. (2003, May 22). *The regulation of hedge funds: Financial stability and investor protection*. Paper presented at the Conference on Hedge Funds Institute for Law and Finance, Frankfurt.

[67] Securities Act Release nº 6389.

[68] 17 C.F.R. § 230.501.

[69] 15 U.S.C. § 77d(2) (1982).

[70] Meanwhile Rule 506 allows accredited investors having maximum 35 non-accredited investors, many funds find it unworthy to get involved in that particular type of investing persons.

USD 1 million, or individuals who had a profit exceeding USD 200,000 in the last 24 months.[71]

"Accredited investor" is a basic concept from Regulation D. Only if the other stipulations under Regulation D are complied with, a limitless number of accredited investors can invest in a fund without giving up the private placement exemption stipulated by Section 4(2).[72] Maximum 35 persons can invest in the fund, individuals who are not "accredited investors."[73]

Meanwhile these exemptions were a consequence of push backs against a strict and ample framework for the registration of public offerings and the governance of mutual funds, anomalies emerged in the financial markets, questionable and not in the interests of the retail investors that the SEC tries so hard to protect. The achievement of SEC exemptions was made through the use of the above-mentioned "accredited investor" approach, implemented into "Securities Act" by a Congress intolerant to the SEC's denial of being more flexible in its views of the private offering exemption.

In compliance with the Securities Act, "an accredited investor" according to stipulations under Regulation 501 stipulated by Regulation D implies the following:

(i) Somebody with a net income (the joint net income is also allowed by adding his/her wife/husband's worth) on that occasion, of investments exceeding USD 1 million (excluding the value of their main residence);
(ii) Somebody with a net worth (it is also allowed to include additional worth on behalf of his/her wife/husband) exceeding USD 200,000 during the last 24 months. At the same time, joint worth on behalf of his/her wife/husband exceeding USD 300,000 is also allowed, provided that it is gained during the last 24 months, requesting at the same time to gain similar profit during the next period[74] (current year).

[71] Baums, Th. (2004). Op. cit., p. 63.

[72] 15 U.S.C. § 77d(2) (1982).

[73] Spangler, T. et al. (2010). Op. cit., p. 115.

[74] Spangler, T. et al. (2010). Op. cit., p. 116.

Sales of interests must be limited to persons who qualify as "accredited investors," together with up to 35 additional persons who, although failing to meet that definition, qualify for "sophisticated investors." Thus, the latter represents the person with very good information and skills regarding financial and entrepreneurial issues, who is at the same time able to evaluate both advantages, but also risk processes regarding potential investments.[75] An individual might also qualify for a *sophisticated investor*, in case he/she acquired this qualification together with a purchaser representative.[76]

In addition, the issuer or his/her agent must know that the future purchaser has the financial means and sophistication to make such an investment. Even after all the potential purchasers would otherwise qualify for "accredited investors" or "sophisticated investors," the marketing of securities may still be deemed a "general solicitation" where, for example, a mass marketing is conducted. A comment needs to be added: the Madoff fraud (see Chapter 7) exposed a surprising lack of critical diligence on behalf of various sophisticated investors. And this occurred in the context of sophisticated investors having been expected to defend their own interests especially since they did have the means to do so. Thus, one cannot help to ask himself what was the reason that *so many sophisticated investors fall prey to Madoff's fraud. Why were these institutions and individuals not able to defend themselves? Why did they not ask questions? Why did they refuse to defend themselves?* As a consequence of this—and in opposition to legislative intention, the operation of the sophisticated investor exemption seems to have undermined the SEC's capability to fulfill its objective to adequately protect the public financial markets. In this vein, the author considers that a new regulatory framework focusing on increasing transparency within these industries is of great need.

What needs to be clear is that SEC proposed an increase for the accredited investor standards under the above presented Regulation only after the Goldstein decision, Regulation D, with the main purpose to *increase antifraud protection for investors.*[77] For a long time, SEC has long been

[75] Kling, L. R. et al. (1996–1997). Negotiated acquisitions of companies, subsidiaries and divisions. *Miami University Law Review, 1*(51), 5–34.

[76] Spangler, T., & Scholer, K. (2010). Op. cit., p. 118.

[77] See Prohibition of Fraud by Advisers to Certain Pooled Investment Vehicles; Accredited Investors in Certain Private Investment Vehicles, 72 Fed. Reg. 400 (proposed Jan. 4, 2007) (to be codified at 17 C.F.R. pts. 230 & 275) (proposing a new rule to allow

very clever at using its power to define terms to fill gaps or solve problems in the hedge funds laws, but as the court showed in Goldstein, such an effort needs to be reasonable. When dealing with the concept of the accredited investor maybe the SEC has been too wise and not consistent enough in defining its purposes and thinking through the results of its regulations.

6.5 The Securities Exchange Act 1934

If the 1933 Act refers mainly to offering and registration actions, the 1934 Act refers mainly to secondary trading.[78] The 1934 Act was based on the concern that hedge funds investors were provided unsatisfactory protection with regard to fraudulent schemes, misleading, but also inappropriate disclosure.[79] Hence, this Act addressed various issues, comprising also the act of disclosing the information to investors, which can be performed through permanent but also up to date filings to the Commission.[80]

Thus, this Act allows "the SEC" to require certification but also data communication at fixed intervals by authorities issuing publicly exchanged securities. Also, section 12 (g) imposes an issuer to have at least 500 owners with classes of stock,[81] but also at least 10 million dollars in holdings for registering stocked items. At the same time, the Act stipulates that every issuer with classes of securities exchanged on the NSE[82] owns also, in some given situations, overall holdings which exceed USD 1 million. Also, classes of stock[83] with minimum 500 holders need to register according to the above-mentioned Act.[84] Any authority issuing

the SEC to bring enforcement actions against investment advisers who defraud investors or prospective investors of hedge funds).

[78] 15 U.S.C. §§ 78a to 78mm (2000).

[79] S. REP. N^{O}. 73-792, at 3–4 (1934), reprinted in 5 Legislative history of the securities act of 1933 and securities exchange act of 1934, Securities Exchange Act of 1934, Item N° 17.

[80] 15 U.S.C. § 78m.

[81] Seligman, J. (2003). The New Uniform Securities Act. *Washington University Law Quarterly, 81*, 243–299.

[82] National Stock Exchange.

[83] Sterling, Th.F. (2004). *The Enron scandal*. New York: Nova Science Publishing.

[84] 15 U.S.C. § 78l.

bound to record according to "the 1934 Act" is obliged to make a repository at fixed intervals and secondary reports to the SEC.[85]

Marketing efforts in the United States may also give rise to broker-dealer registration problems. The central issues here are who of the fund manager's employees are engaged in marketing and how are they compensated. The broker is being defined according to Section 3(a)(4) as every individual involved in entrepreneurial securities trade on behalf of different investors.[86] No distinction is made between privately placed and publicly offered securities. If a fund manager's employees receive commissions from the sale of participations in a fund, they will be deemed brokers. As a result, they must be joined individuals of the 1934 Act officially recorded broker-dealer. The main reasons for tight regulation of this broker-dealer industry are "its economic importance" together with "the possibility of investor abuse." As observed along the entire Exchange Act but also in the regulation of broker-dealers, the important role of investor protection and fairness is widely spread.

Pursuant to Regulation 3(a)(4)—1 under the 1934 Act, the safe harbor can be setup, allowing counselors, managers, or employees of either the fund or the fund manager to trade involvement in a fund which does not necessarily have to register.[87]

The requirements of the safe harbor include the following:

- The individual has not been associated with a broker-dealer during the last 12 months;
- The individual must not have participated in the marketing of any fund during the last 12 months;
- The individual needs first to make considerable duties for the fund manager, others than marketing the fund;
- The individual must not be compensated for the marketing effort by officials or various remuneration due to selling securities.

[85] 15 U.S.C. §§ 78l, 78m, and 78n.

[86] Seligman, J. (2003). Op. cit., p. 4.

[87] Balotti, R. F., & Shaner, M. W. (2011). Safe harbour for officer reliance: Comparing the approaches of the Model Business Corporation Act and Delaware's General Corporation Law. *Law and Contemporary Problems, 74*(1), 161–174.

Where the safe harbor is not available, employees of the fund manager should limit their discussions with prospective investors to the investment objectives of the fund. A registered broker-dealer should be left with the responsibility to require, negotiate, and accept participations from the investors.

The major "thrust of the 1934 Act lies within Section 10b and Rule 10b-5."[88] Section 10(b),[89] one of the main anti-fraud sections, and "Rule 10b-5"[90] offer one motivation of action for damages either caused by exclusions, misstatements, or manipulations of material data within declarations different from the ones registered in reports within SEC.[91] Accordingly, these provisions have turned into powerful tools in fighting securities fraud. Still, even if the three sections of Rule 10b-5 offer wide indications of conduct violating Rule 10b, the negative issues are that no details are provided (within the text of the law) regarding the elements or conduct representing a violation of Rule 10b. In spite of Congressional desire to protect the investors, none of the two Rules mentioned above offers a cause of action for plaintiffs affected by securities fraud. Federal courts involved Congressional intention for a private cause of action according to Rule 10b, which is similar, "but is not identical to, common law actions for deceit and misrepresentation."[92]

Additionally to this aim of protecting investors, the 1934 Act also intends to authorize "adequate disclosures from companies who are being registered with the SEC under Sections 12, 13 and 15."[93]

Section 12[94] implies the registration of a comprehensive declaration regarding the firm when the latter registers for the first time under the 1934 Act. According to rule 12h-3, an issuer having more than USD 10 million in assets, which could to the contrary be submitted for filing requests in compliance with section 15(d), is exempt from offering reports

[88] 15 U.S.C. § 78j(b) and Rule 10b-5, 17 C.F.R. 204.10b-5.

[89] 15 U.S.C. § 78j(b).

[90] 17 C.F.R. § 240.10b-5.

[91] State Teachers Retirement Board v. Fluor Corp., 654 F.2d 843 (2d Cir. 1981).

[92] Pacini, C., Paterson, J., & Ghahramani, S. (2011). The uncertain liability of accountants and other professionals in securities fraud cases: The shifting sands of Central Bank. *Journal of Forensic and Investigative Accounting, 3*(3), 46–67.

[93] 15 U.S.C. §§ 78l, 78m, 78o (2007).

[94] 15 U.S.C. § 78l.

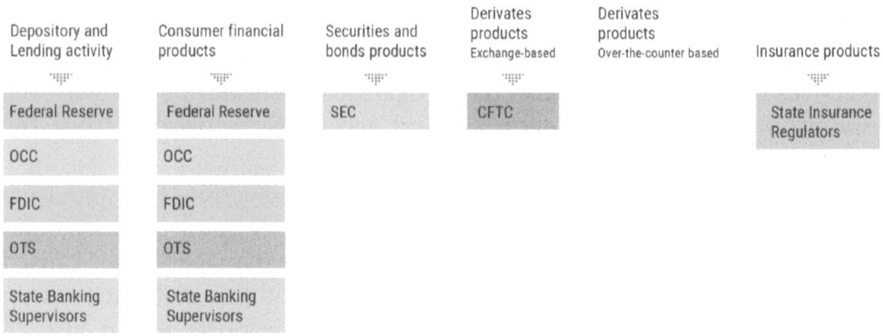

Fig. 6.1 Fragmented US regulatory structure prior to Dodd–Frank Act (*Source* Neiman and Olson [2014])

if less than 500 individuals hold its securities on record. Most of the time hedge funds try to maintain the amount of registered owners below 500 individuals to avoid falling under these registrations and reporting requirements.[95]

The regulatory system as it was prior to Dodd–Frank Act can be found in Fig. 6.1, by activity and product.

6.6 The Dodd–Frank Act of 2010

6.6.1 Introductory Lines

> It is an indisputable fact that one of the most significant contributors to our economic downturn was an unraveling of major financial institutions and the lack of adequate regulatory structures to prevent abuse and excess. A culture of irresponsibility took root from Wall Street to Washington to Main Street. And a regulatory regime basically crafted in the wake of a twentieth century economic crisis – the Great Depression – was overwhelmed by the speed, scope, and sophistication of a twenty-first century global economy.

[95] Baums & Cahn (2004). Op. cit, pp. 64–65.

> So today, the administration is proposing a sweeping overhaul of the financial regulatory system, a transformation on a scale not seen since the reforms that followed the Great Depression.[96]

In 2006, the SEC adopted a rule asking investment funds to register as investment advisers, in response to the impetuous growth of hedge funds' assets under management (AUM) and growing concern over their operations and transparency for better protecting investors. Nevertheless, during the same period, "the US Court of Columbia Circuit" abrogated this law considering that it was not compatible with the 1940s Investment Advisers Act.

Immediately after the beginning of this financial crisis, hedge funds became again a target for increased regulation. Scholars[97] believed, on the one hand, that the collapse was a result of the "lack of regulation and oversight in the United States financial markets,"[98] which led to vulnerabilities in the financial system.[99] They also considered that "the major players in the financial markets overstepped sound business practices and engaged in unhealthy practices all in anticipation of reaping huge profits through their actions."[100]

Due to the increase of negative investor feeling, hedge funds found their inclusion in the Dodd–Frank Act proposed "by the Obama administration in June 2009 in response to the post-August 2007 global financial crisis that extended throughout 2008 and 2009. In July 2010, the Dodd–Frank Act was signed into law and in March 2012, the Dodd–Frank

[96] Remarks made by Barrack Obama on twenty-first century Financial Regulatory Reform, The White House (2009). Remarks of the President on Regulatory Reform. http://www.whitehouse.gov/the_press_office/Remarks-of-the-President-on-Regulatory-Reform/. Accessed 4 June 2020.

[97] Duffie, D. (2019). Prone to fail: The pre-crisis financial system. *Journal of Economic Perspectives, 33*(1), 81–106. https://doi.org/10.1257/jep.33.1.81.

[98] Dancer, W. T., & Powell, D. (2018). Dodd-Frank repeal: Assessing the change in the day-to-day activities of financial institutions. *Journal of Accounting and Finance, 18*(7), 50–55.

[99] Aikman, D., Bridges, J., Kashyap, A., & Siegert, C. (2019). Would macroprudential regulation have prevented the last crisis? *Journal of Economic Perspectives, 33*(1), 107–130.

[100] Dancer, W. T., & Powell, D. (2018). Op. cit.

act became effective. Dodd–Frank imposes registration requirements and significantly higher disclosure of proprietary information."[101]

There were many controversies on the enactment of Dodd–Frank.[102] According to Shelby (2017) the regulation of hedge funds is not at all suitable, pleading in favor of the SEC for solving the problem. Thus, she considers as appropriate "appointing the SEC as the primary regulator of hedge funds because: (1) hedge funds can still pose a systemic threat to the economy; (2) the transparency framework inherent in the federal securities laws can supply a more effective means for mitigating systemic risk than the prudential framework currently mandated for SIFIs; and (3) appointing the SEC in this regard would reduce the fragmentation of the current regulatory structure which has been extended and complicated by the creation of FSOC."[103]

There are also scholars who consider the Dodd–Frank empowers too much the regulating authorities. In this vein, Iain Murray (2017) criticizes the CFPB stating that "it should be abolished,"[104] mentioning particularly the problem of overregulation. In spite of all these, Dodd–Frank currently stands as the most important regulatory enactment ever for the hedge fund industry. Also, even scholars who were against this law vehemently seem to appreciate the results of the legislation.[105]

[101] Cumming, D., Dai, N., & Johan, S. (2019). Dodd-Franking the hedge funds. *Journal of Banking and Finance*. https://doi.org/10.1016/j.jbankfin.2017.09.012.

[102] Urska, V. (2017). Are the SEC's administrative law judges biased? An empirical investigation. *Washington Law Review, 92*(1), 315–370.

[103] Shelby, C. M. (2017). Closing the hedge fund loophole: The SEC as the primary regulator of systemic risk. *Boston College Law Review, 58*(2), 639–701.

[104] Murray, I. (2017). *Rethinking the Consumer Financial Protection Bureau*. Competitive Enterprise Institute. https://cei.org/shrinkinggov/cfpb. Accessed 16 June 2020.

[105] Murray, I. (2015). *How Dodd–Frank Harms Main Street*. https://cei.org/content/how-dodd-frank-harms-main-street. Accessed 21 July 2020. ("The reforms enshrined in [Dodd– Frank] ... were intended to protect Main Street and consumers from financial predation by Wall Street."); United States Congress. (2016). *The Dodd-Frank Act five years later: Are we more stable? Hearing before the Committee on Financial Services*. US House of Representatives. One Hundred Fourteenth Congress. First session, July 9, 2015. (Todd Zywicki, Professor, George Mason University School of Law, stated that "An animating premise of [Dodd–Frank] was the belief that a primary source of financial instability was an inadequate consumer financial protection regime at the federal level.").

The aim of the Dodd–Frank Act was generous: to avoid another financial crisis,[106] "to promote the financial stability of the United States by improving accountability and transparency in the financial system, to end 'too big to fail', to protect the American taxpayer by ending bailouts, to protect consumers from abusive financial services practices, and for other purposes."[107] Thus, its strategy proved to be really respectable: increase transparency, investor protection, prevent credit institutions from assuming extreme risks, stop harmful financial actions but also prevent institutions apparently too large to fail through authorizing regulatory authorities to apprehend every large, collapsing financial company and gradually diminish it,[108] all with the main purpose to "facilitate greater transparency and integrity in derivatives markets."[109]

However, Dodd–Frank Act is much more complex. It has hundreds of pages[110] and it might be compared to Glass–Steagall (the famous reform following the 1929 Wall Street failure). Additionally, every page requests that regulators make further studies. Some parts of these examinations are presented on hundreds of pages. Only one tiny part, the Volcker rule, aiming at curbing risk asset exchanging by credit institutions, comprises 383 interrogations divided in no less than 1420 sub-questions.[111] All in all, the hedge fund registration and disclosure requirements stipulated in the Dodd–Frank Act increase hedge funds supervision and seem to solve

[106] Vladimer, G. V., Manvelidze, R., & Manvelidze, L. (2019, April 29–30). Big financial crisis: Analysis, assessment. In A. L. da Silva, D. Tomic, & A. Grilec (Eds.), *Book of Abstracts of the 39th International Scientific Conference on Economic and Social Development—Sustainability from an Economic and Social Perspective*. Lisbon.

[107] Dodd–Frank, 124 Stat. at 1376.

[108] Wilmarth, A. E. (2011). The Dodd-Frank Act: A flawed and inadequate response to the too big to fail problem. *Oregon Law Review, 87*, 951–1058.

[109] Giancarlo, J. C., & Tuckman, B. (2018). *US commodity futures trading Comm'n, Swaps regulation version 2.0: An assessment of the current implementation of reform and proposals for next steps*. https://www.cftc.gov/sites/default/files/2018-04/oce-chairman-swapreg. Accessed 16 June 2020.

[110] Ricks, M. (2019). *Guarantor of last resort: Is there a better alternative?* Vanderbilt Law School Faculty Publications. https://scholarship.law.vanderbilt.edu/faculty-publications/1109. Accessed 12 June 2020.

[111] Fein, M. L. (2010). *Dodd-Frank Act Wall Street Reform and Consumer Protection Act*. www.ssrn.com/abstract=1357452. Accessed 26 July 2020.

the "tension between the industry and the regulators."[112] In spite of this, Easley, O'Hara, and Yang, consider that hedge funds have a low portfolio disclosure level in the United States, in spite of the SEC and its supervision.[113] Thus, just American funds having "more than USD 1 billion in net worth are required to present quarterly reports describing their operations and portfolio positions."[114] Nevertheless, in a recent paper, it is stipulated that disclosures appear as driving behavioral changes in securities markets,[115] as we shall see further on.

From a critical point of view, adverse consequences for clients have emerged. As it often occurs, measures meant to defend investors led to harming them. Due to Dodd–Frank's breadth, these consequences vary from probable threats to privacy, as involved in the Title I section, to low investor choice as opposed to high consumer costs, as involved in the Title X and XIV sections. Taking a careful look at Title XIV section, an obvious example of a troubling trend in regulatory policy can be noticed—the opinion that government knows better than investors what is best for them. In this direction, government authorities have taken on "the paternalistic role of safely steering citizens toward "better" or "safer" products and services."[116] Consequently, investors are increasingly confronted with a one-size-fits-all market that implies higher costs and provides fewer choices.

Consequently, America urges a more intelligent approach for regulation. Thus, total major laws need to be analyzed from the "cost–benefit" point of view by an autonomous caretaker. More imperative, laws must be simplified. Regulators must propose clear laws, and they must be allowed to enforce them.

[112] Kaal, W. A. (2013). Hedge fund manager registration under the Dodd-Frank Act. *San Diego Law Review, 50*(2), 243–322.

[113] Easley, D., O'hara, M. O., & Yang, L. (2014). Opaque trading, disclosure, and asset prices: Implications for hedge fund regulation. *Review of Financial Studies, 27*(4), 1190–1237. https://doi.org/10.1093/rfs/hht079.

[114] Januzzi, F. V., Bressan, A. A., & Moreira, F. (2019). Opacity, risk, performance and inflows in hedge funds. *Revista de Administração Contemporânea, 24*(1), 77–99. https://doi.org/10.1590/1982-7849rac2020180233.

[115] Honigsberg, C. (2019). Hedge fund regulation and fund governance: Evidence on the effects of mandatory disclosure rules. *Journal of Accounting Research, 57*, 845–884.

[116] Peirce, H., & Broughel, J. (Eds.) (2012). *Dodd-Frank: What it does and why it's flawed*. Arlington: The Mercatus Center, p. 15.

Dodd–Frank's wide and equivocal data-collection purposes were interpreted by the SEC and the CFTC in the new Form PF. Because of its length, complexity, and generally unclear data requirements, Form PF represents a major burden on the advisers it is applied to. Along with other regulatory costs, the costs of these new laws are going to be passed on to investors.

The general conclusion was that, nowadays, compassion towards hedge funds is not common. On the contrary, officials understand the urgency for more regulatory enforcements. Thus, the officials' assigned job implies a lot of bureaucracy, although this represents only an example of all the requirements involving taxes but also office work used by Dodd–Frank Act to cover one ample part from the American economics.[117] Many organizations came into sight for enjoying the support of "the taxpayer" as they were said to be "too big to fail."

Policy makers and authorities in charge of "Dodd–Frank Act" appeared somewhat optimistic regarding achievements and future challenges, when addressing to the community. Still, one banker deeply involved in this matter is in agreement with lots of people while predicting a decade of turmoil, with permanent debates in court and governmental bodies, in the end exhibiting one set of rules damaged due to exemptions or shades which can, due to its complicated form, aggravate systemic risks instead of mitigating them.[118]

In the summer of 2011, on the 22 July, the American "Court of appeals for the District of Columbia" accepted one dispute between two commerce entities about a law from "Dodd–Frank Act" regarding shareholding voting promoted "by the SEC." The Tribunal considered that particular law unsupported by studies regarding the prices paid or the advantages involved. On December the 2nd, another similar case was filed at some "Washington DC District Court" versus the "*Commodities Futures Trading Commission*" (CFTC), dispute between two securities-market commercial corporations, regarding "restrictions on derivative

[117] Omarova, S. T. (2011b). The Dodd-Frank Act: A new deal for a new age? *North Carolina Banking Institute, 15*, 83–98.

[118] Jacoby, M. B. (2011). Dodd-Frank, regulatory innovation, and the safety of consumer financial products. *North Carolina Banking Institute, 15*. https://scholarship.law.unc.edu/ncbi/vol15/iss1/7. Accessed 26 July 2020.

holdings."[119] In case the tribunal pleads also in favor, litigants predict an avalanche of new lawsuits (see Chapter 7).

6.6.2 *The New Era*

July 21, 2010 was the day when the American President ratified "the Dodd–Frank Act."[120] By signing this Act, the US President initiated a new era in financial regulatory reform. In this respect, the above-mentioned regulation provides an ample regulatory reform, with the main goal of "the promotion of financial security in America"[121] through the establishment of careful observing regarding risk-exposure, through an overview of the entire system. While the Act focused primarily on banking institutions regulations and related matters, it has also significantly changed the landscape affecting investment advisers and many aspects of the investment management industry, including, among others, the regulation of domestic and foreign investment advisers assisting various types of private investment vehicles and investors.

The Dodd–Frank Act focused on:

(i) Establishing an independent and competent consumer protection authority.
(ii) Creating a more effective oversight of the financial markets by reforming the rules on the FED and the financial institutions and eliminating the system-level risks.
(iii) Ending the governmental bail-out of "too big to fail"[122] institutions, so taxpayers would not pay the cheque instead of the great firms anymore.

The enactment of the Dodd–Frank Act implied progress in solving the problem of overlapping jurisdictions (Fig. 6.2).

[119] "Too big not to fail- Flaws in the confused, bloated law passed in the aftermath of America's financial crisis become ever more apparent", *The Economist*, 18, 2012, p. 18.

[120] Public Law 111-203, 124 Stat. 1376 (2010).

[121] S. Conf. Rep. N°. 111-176, at 2-3 (2010) (Senate Committee Report).

[122] Kelleher, D. M., Hall, S. W., & Medina, F. (2016). The Dodd-Frank Act is working and will protect the American people if it is not killed before fully implemented. *North Carolina Banking Institute*, *20*(1), 127–144.

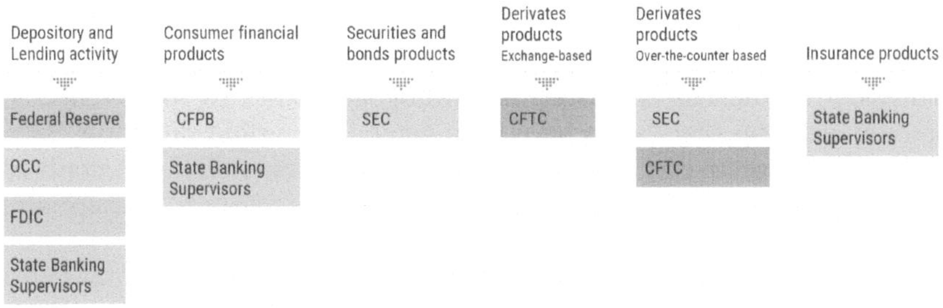

Fig. 6.2 Somewhat improved US regulatory structure after Dodd–Frank Act (*Source* Neiman and Olson [2014])

The latter provision of the Dodd–Frank Act, which is also recorded in the Preamble,[123] is one of the most debated parts of the Act.[124]

A major Dodd–Frank Act aim resides in limiting the risk of "the shadow credit institution system." Although having as main aim to implement market discipline to shadow banking, "there were too many unknown variables to create confidence in the procedures adopted, however excellent their execution."[125] In this respect, Ordoñez (2018) stated that, if the regulation is light, banks risk very much, meanwhile if the regulation is strongly enforced there is no more shadow banking, and consequently, no efficient investments either. For this reason, he argues that regulations must "allow banks to decide whether or not they want to be regulated. Banks that choose to avoid regulation would be taxed and the proceedings used to subsidize banks that choose to be regulated and operate under restrictive capital requirements."[126] According to him "there is a trade-off that regulators face between preventing efficient investments and discouraging excessive risk-taking,"[127] and he considers

[123] To [...] end "too big to fail", to protect the American taxpayer by ending bailouts [...] - The Preamble of the Dodd-Frank Act.

[124] Sandbu, M. (2015). *Europe's orphan: The future of the Euro and the politics of debt*. Princeton: Princeton University Press.

[125] Lothian, T. (2017). *Law and the wealth of nations: Finance, prosperity, and democracy*. New York: Columbia University Press.

[126] Ordoñez, G. (2018). Sustainable shadow banking. *American Economic Journal: Macroeconomics, 10*(1), 33–56. https://doi.org/10.1257/mac.20150346.

[127] Idem, p. 36.

that banks know better than regulators the dangers that need to be avoided. The shadow banking system had a key role in the 2007–2008 crisis. Up to the current date, the author subscribes to most scholars' opinion claiming that "steps have been taken in the right direction."[128]

Another objective is to limit the damages inflicted after the crash of important financial entities in order to minimize costs to society and taxpayers (negative externalities).

According to the first Title of the Act, the "*Financial Stability Oversight Council*" (FSOC) is made up of different managers which are members of the financial regulatory authorities, but there are also secondary persons: "ten voting members include the heads of existing regulatory agencies, including the Federal Reserve, Federal Deposit Insurance Corporation, Securities Exchange Commission, alongside the Secretary of the Treasury and one independent member with insurance expertise."[129] Apart from these, there are also "five non-voting members, including the Director of the Office of Financial Research, who serve in an advisory capacity. It is chaired by the Secretary of the Treasury, and most decisions are taken by majority rule."[130]

Dodd–Frank Act states that the above-mentioned Council is entitled to monitor the potential risks endangering US financial security, but also to require from the Board of Governors of the FRB[131] to supervise the indicated non-credit financial institutions that might induce major risks to the US financial security under various circumstances, such as: material

[128] Beker, V. (2019, May 10–11). *Is the financial system prepared for a new financial crisis?* Paper presented at the 40th International Scientific Conference on Economic and Social Development—Buenos Aires.

[129] 12 U.S.C. §§ 5321(b)(1), 5331(b). The ten voting members include: the Secretary of the Treasury who chairs the council, the Chairman of the Federal Reserve, the Comptroller of the Currency, the Director of the CFPB, the Chairman of the U.S. Securities and Exchange Commission, the Chairman of the Federal Deposit Insurance Corporation, the Chairman of the Commodities Futures Trading Commission, the Director of the Federal Housing Finance Agency, the Chairman of the National Credit Union Administration Board, and an independent member with insurance expertise appointed by the president. See also Aikman, D., Bridges, J., Kashyap, A., & Siegert, C. (2019). Would macroprudential regulation have prevented the last crisis? *Journal of Economic Perspectives, 33*(1), 107–130.

[130] Idem.

[131] *Federal Reserve System.*

financial distress, crash or as a consequence of own businesses.[132] Similarly, the Dodd–Frank Act provides for the FSOC the recommendation toward FRB of highly prudent norms in respect to several selected nonbanking institutions,[133] being aware of the fact that FSOC is going to be helped by several regulatory authorities. In this respect, Dodd–Frank Act remedies several statutes, among which the Investment Advisers Act, for the authorization or orientation of some Federal authorities in supporting FSOC. Accordingly, FSOC needs to find the appropriate level of oversight in order to satisfy, on the one hand, the requests of the industry for lower levels of oversight as opposed to, on the other hand, the need for investor protection.

FSOC's overall mandate stands in the identification and response to risks endangering US financial stability, risks that might emerge either from banking or nonbanking institutions. Another duty of FSOC lies in the promotion of market discipline "by removing expectations that investors will be shielded from losses by the government."[134] Another task is that of facilitating the sharing of information between major regulatory bodies. One of its instruments resides in designating nonbank financial institutions presumed of being systemically important for increased control or supervision, this being a decision that needs to be backed by two-thirds of the members holding the right to vote. These being said, FSOC does not have other macroprudential powers. Therefore, in any other policy interference, the Council has the ability of issuing recommendations to other regulatory bodies.

There are voices who consider that FSOC "in its current form does not have sufficient powers to ensure financial stability."[135] Indeed, as scholars emphasize, "the FSOC may make recommendations to its member agencies to address threats to financial stability, but it cannot compel them to act even if there is a supermajority vote of the full membership. Similarly, although it provides a valuable forum for member agencies to meet and discuss issues, the council does not have the authority to force improved

[132] See the Dodd-Frank Act, Section 112.

[133] 15 U.S.C. § 77g.

[134] Aikman, D., Bridges, J., Kashyap, A., & Siegert, C. (2019). Would macroprudential regulation have prevented the last crisis? *Journal of Economic Perspectives, 33*(1), 107–130.

[135] Idem.

coordination on activities such as joint rule writing."[136] All these lead to the same conclusion: the FSOC needs additional authority to increase its capability of addressing these aspects concerning authority.[137] The same idea is supported also by Lothian (2017), who states that it remains to be seen if "the supervisory powers entrusted to the FSOC would be enough to prevent the next great financial panic."[138]

Problems associated with lack of power of the Financial Stability Oversight Council would be mitigated if other authorities had the tools and incentives to act. At the same time, with power comes also accountability. Due to this, there has been harsh criticism regarding FSOC's lack of openness although it has instituted a transparency policy in May 2014.[139] Trying to solve existing gaps, bills have been introduced in Congress having as main objective "to allow members of boards and commissions represented on the council, members of Congress who sit on FSOC oversight committees and FSOC member agency staff to be able to attend council meetings."[140]

However, there are also other regulations[141] which would subject the FSOC to the transparency provisions of the Government. Companies under review for being designated SIFI plead in favor of being better informed regarding every step of the respective process, at the same time being offered better and earlier chances to provide the FSOC with information and responses. They also underline the necessity of being presented the precise risks that the FSOC considers they pose to financial

[136] Baily, M.N., Klein, A., & Schardin, J. (2017). The Impact of the Dodd-Frank Act on financial stability and economic growth. *RSF: The Russell Sage Foundation Journal of the Social Sciences, 3*(1), 20–47. https://doi.org/10.7758/rsf.2017.3.1.02.

[137] Dugan, J. C., Fisher, P. R., & Muckenfuss, C. F. III. (2014). *Responding to systemic risk: Restoring the balance*. Washington, DC: Bipartisan Policy Center. https://bipartisanpolicy.org/wp-content/uploads/2019/03/BPC-Responding-to-Systemic-Risk.pdf. Accessed 26 July 2020.

[138] Lothian, T. (2017). *Law and the wealth of nations: Finance, prosperity, and democracy*. New York: Columbia University Press.

[139] Financial Stability Oversight Council. (2014). *Transparency policy for the Financial Stability Oversight Council*. www.treasury.gov/initiatives/Documents/FSOCtransparencypolicy.pdf. Accessed 15 July 2020.

[140] Baily, M. N., Klein, A., & Schardin, J. (2017). Op. cit.

[141] In this respect can be mentioned: The Sunshine Act, the Federal Advisory Committee Act and the Administrative Procedures Act.

stability, this being a basic condition in designating a SIFI. The designation of a SIFI was indeed subject to major debates. Scholars have however agreed that, in order that the FSOC remains effective, stakeholders must trust it. In this respect, several solutions have been offered to balance public need for information and the FSOC's ability to provide information on sensitive issues in their analyses concerning the designation process. The solutions involve that the "FSOC should augment its current transparency policy by releasing more detailed minutes of meetings, along the lines of the Federal Reserve's Federal Open Market Committee, which provides useful information and insights to the public through the release of its minutes subject to a three-week lag. The council would also be wise to improve its communication with companies under review for designation while continuing to protect confidential information. Notifying companies of their status in the designation process and allowing them to interact with council members at all stages would improve the process and lead to better outcomes."[142] Some of these suggestions were addressed by the FSOC in February 2015, in several amendments to the designation process.[143]

6.6.2.1 The Orderly Liquidation Authority

Another organization established by the Dodd–Frank Act is the Orderly Liquidation Authority ("the OLA").[144] The OLA stands as an organization empowered to deal with the liquidation of "too big to fail" financial institutions in periods of economic crisis.[145] The OLA is formed by regulators and experts with financial backgrounds, which is according to McMahon (2018) of major importance, since many of these financial regulators, "have spent their entire career working in the financial industry. Not only do these regulators possess an extensive knowledge

[142] Baily, M. N., Klein, A., & Schardin, J. (2017). Op. cit.

[143] Financial Stability Oversight Council. (2015). *Supplemental procedures relating to nonbank financial company determinations*. www.treasury.gov/initiatives/fsoc/designations/Documents/Supplemental%20Procedures%20Related%20to%20Nonbank%20Financial%20Company%20Determinations%20-%20February%202015.pdf. Accessed 16 June 2020.

[144] 12 U.S.C.A. § 5384 (2015).

[145] Lessambo, F. I. (2020). Bank bankruptcy. In *The U.S. banking system: Laws, regulations, and risk management* (pp. 297–315). London: Palgrave Macmillan. https://doi.org/10.1007/978-3-030-34792-5.

and understanding of the American and global financial markets, but they also possess the requisite contacts to coordinate large scale liquidation of financial institutions with offices across the world."[146] Additionally, the Orderly Liquidation Fund[147] was setup under Title II of the Dodd–Frank Act. The OLA is authorized by this fund to issue loans for financial organizations deemed as "systemically important." These loans were harshly criticized on the reason of serving as a façade for increasing taxpayer bailouts.[148] Still, these loans do not stand as taxpayer bailouts as the Dodd–Frank Act stipulates their being supported by the assets of the financial institutions.

Additionally, the regaining possession of the loans occurs during the resolution process, and in case this regaining is unattainable, loans can be retrieved from different big financial institutions.[149] At the same time, according to the current provisions of the OLA, regulators can start the liquidation proceedings, when appropriate, which stands as a critical subject because in this manner, regulators are able to prepare and accommodate foreign regulators to the process of bankruptcy. Contrarily, the last ones "are liable to seize the assets of the financial institution within their jurisdiction, which is often the 'death knell' for successful bankruptcies."[150] In addition, the Dodd–Frank Act urges for systemically big financial institutions to keep living wills providing a strategy for their resolution in the event that another major crisis would happen.[151] Seen as documents of major importance, the living wills make it easier for the OLA to plan and monitor both the industry and the individual financial firms with regards to signals of risks while acting against possible forthcoming financial stress, and planning suitable remedial measures. At

[146] McMahon, K. (2018). The Financial Banking Institute Act and the Financial CHOICE Act: The wrong choice for the American economy. *Journal of Business & Technology Law, 14*(1), 107–133.

[147] 12 U.S.C.A. § 5384 (2015).

[148] Gordon, J., & Roe, M. (2017). *Financial scholars oppose eliminating "Orderly Liquidation Authority" as crisis-avoidance restructuring backstop*. https://corpgov.law.harvard.edu/2017/05/26/financial-scholars-oppose-eliminating-orderly-liquidation-authority-as-crisis-avoidance-restructuring-backstop/. Accessed 28 June 2020.

[149] Idem.

[150] McMahon, K. (2018). Op. cit.

[151] Dodd-Frank Wall Street Reform and Consumer Protection Act § 165(d), 12 U.S.C. § 5325 (2012).

the same time, in the event of a financial crisis, OLA has the authorization of providing liquidity to financial corporations in absolutely necessary cases,[152] this being seen in the industry as vital for the stability of the financial corporations. Summing up, the OLA is an authority providing several important advantages for financial firms.

Another aspect that needs to be underlined at Title II is SPOE, which stands as a "progress toward a safer financial system."[153] Thus, even if the SPOE strategy was created to implement OLA under the Dodd–Frank Act, currently it is seen "as the most promising approach for the resolution of SIFIs from other jurisdictions as well."[154] Some of the reasons why the SPOE strategy was highly supported by financial industry groups, think tanks, rating agencies, foreign regulators, and other stakeholders[155] can be found in the list below:

- Greatly reducing the likelihood of systemically destabilizing disruptions to subsidiary operations;
- Imposing losses on the equity holders and creditors of the holding company, who are structurally subordinated to the creditors of operating subsidiaries;
- Mitigating potential cross-border coordination issues by keeping foreign subsidiaries open and operating; and
- Preserving the going-concern value of the SIFI, which should minimize losses for creditors and lessen the impact of the failure on the broader economy.[156]

Title IV revises "the Advisers Act" to impose the need for advisers of hedge funds and those of various private funds to register under the

[152] 12 U.S.C.A. § 5384 (2015).

[153] International Monetary Fund. (2020). *Law & financial stability.* Washington: International Monetary Fund. http://dx.doi.org/10.5089/9781513523002.071.

[154] Idem, p. 34.

[155] Guynn, R. (2014). Framing the TBTF problem: The path to a solution. In M. N. Baily & J. Taylor (Eds.), *Across the great divide: New perspectives on the financial crisis* (pp. 281–286). Stanford: Hoover Institution Press.

[156] International Monetary Fund. (2020). Op. cit., p. 36.

SEC.[157] That request was made by the Congress mainly since it considered data concerning dimension, strategies but also status of funds might prove essential for regulatory efforts with regard to possible, yet to come, crisis.[158] At the same time, this implies registered investment advisers to keep records and any other data that could be necessary and suitable for avoiding systemic risk, preventing fraud, and providing investors with useful data about the funds, thus trying to increase the protection of investors. Title IV builds up a new, innovative legislative regime for advisers to private funds. Accordingly, Dodd–Frank menaces to drive funds offshore, harm investors instead of protecting them, and make it more likely, not less, that these funds are going to be someday the recipients of government largesse. However, this represents an unfortunate evolution, as hedge funds and other private funds have usually appeared and disappeared as a consequence of market forces and not due to government intervention.

In particular, it is the Dodd–Frank Act that grants secondary obligations concerning "advisers to *private funds*." These types of funds might be considered entities acting as an "*investment company*" according to the "1940 Act," except the exemptions further specified in the 1940 Act.[159] These two exemptions are the most commonly used. Also, "the Dodd–Frank Act" points out the net value requirements that need to be met by the investors in a private fund.

Specifically, the Dodd–Frank Act eliminates the 14-or-fewer "private adviser exemption from SEC registration" that was previously offered by the Advisers Act.[160] However, it was only after the Madoff Ponzi scheme in 2008 (see Chapter 7), that regulators and commentators have turned to the question of whether and how the regulatory regime in force at the time was adequate to protect investors, forcing the Congress to remove the private adviser exemption. Dodd-Frank Act creates innovative exemptions from SEC registration, involving non-US based advisers meeting several conditions, advisers to family offices, and "advisers to venture

[157] Section 202(a)(29).

[158] Senate Committee Report, supra note 4, at 38.

[159] Section 3(c)(1) and (7).

[160] Through Section 203(b)(3).

capital funds."[161] The result of these changes was that many previously exempt advisers had to forcibly become registered to the SEC.

Thus, public authorities in the United States use two key instruments for facilitating the supervision of hedge fund managers: on the one hand mandatory disclosure and on the other hand, public enforcement.[162]

The implementation rules of Dodd–Frank stipulated that investment advisors would register under either Registered Investment Advisors ("RIAs"), a registered firm existing even prior to Dodd–Frank, or under Exempt Reporting Advisors ("ERAs"), which was created by the act.

The SEC is bound by the Dodd–Frank Act to exempt from registering requirements for investment advisers holding no more than USD 150 million in AUM.[163] Nevertheless, this is available only for investment advisers acting only as advisers for private funds while having also maximum USD 150 million AUM in the United States. Thus, in order to register with the SEC as an RIA, an investment advisor must have over USD 150 million in AUM. Also, an investment advisor must register if the state in which the advisor operates requires no registration or conducts no examinations of investment advisors.[164] After registering, RIAs fall under three types of obligations: "compliance requirements, government inspections, and disclosure obligations."[165]

Among the compliance requirements, there can be specified rules concerning recordkeeping, assigning a chief compliance officer, carefully observing several guidelines concerning performance fees, and solicitation of new clients. "Government inspections are onsite exams to assess a firm's fulfillment of compliance requirements, but they can also take the form of simple information requests. Disclosure obligations include filing Form ADV and, in some cases, Form PF. Form ADV focuses on general

[161] SEC. (2010). *Exemptions for advisers to venture capital funds, private fund advisers with less than $150 million in assets under management, and foreign private advisers*. Securities and Exchange Commission. http://www.sec.gov/rules/final/2011/ia-3222.pdf. Accessed 12 March 2020.

[162] DeMott, D. (2012). Regulatory techniques and liability regimes for asset managers. *Capital Markets Law Journal, 7*(4), 423–431. https://doi.org/10.1093/cmlj/kms034.

[163] Ibid.

[164] Section 408 of the Dodd-Frank Act.

[165] Restrepo, F. (2020). *Hedge fund regulation, performance, and risk-taking: Re-examining the effect of the Dodd-Frank Act*. http://dx.doi.org/10.2139/ssrn.3541916. Accessed 8 July 2020.

characteristics of the structure and operation of the investment advisor, including conflicts of interest, ownership structure, officers, clients, assets under management, accounting practices, and disciplinary history. Form PF is a new type of form created by the DFA, which focuses on portfolio information, including performance, risk, and financing data."[166] According to the Dodd–Frank, just RIAs holding over USD 150 million in AUM are required to file Form PF and the information disclosed in the form is therefore not disclosed.

Different from RIA, ERAs are restricted to several disclosure obligations[167] and as a consequence are exempt both from "inspections and compliance requirements."[168] This type of investment advisors "are eligible for this registration type if (1) they advise only venture capital funds or (2) they advise only private funds (hedge funds) and have less than USD 150 million in assets under management. Since only investment advisors with over USD 100 million in assets under management are eligible to register with the SEC, ERAs' assets must also be above that threshold."[169]

Another exemption stated by the Dodd–Frank Act consists of "venture capital fund advisers from registration under the Advisers Act."[170] In order to qualify for this, every adviser has to act like an investment adviser either for a single or for more venture capital funds.

One final exemption stipulated by Dodd–Frank Act is that of registering the *foreign private adviser*. This is defined as the investment adviser who places his financial company outside the American borders, who does not have more than 15 customers in America and American investing individuals investing money in private funds in compliance with the adviser's

[166] Idem.

[167] Namely, filing some portions of Form ADV.

[168] ERAs registered with the SEC file a portion of Form ADV but ERAs registered with the states file the entire form. ERAs do not have to file Form PF, are exempted by law from the majority of compliance requirements, and were exempted by the SEC from its examination program. See Dodd-Frank Act, § 407, § 408; Securities and Exchange Commission, Exemptions for Advisers to Venture Capital Funds, Private Fund Advisers With Less Than $150 Million in Assets Under Management, and Foreign Private Advisers, 76 Fed. Reg. 39,646, 39,666, Release No. IA-3222; File No. S7-37-10 (July 6, 2011); Mary Schapiro, Chairman, SEC, Opening Statement at SEC Open Meeting: Dodd-Frank Act Amendments to the Investment Advisers Act (June 22, 2011).

[169] Restrepo, F. (2020). Op. cit.

[170] Ibid.

advice, but who also has maximum USD 150 million in total AUM on behalf of this type of customers or investors.[171] They can also register with the SEC as ERAs.

The Dodd–Frank Act asks "FSOC to monitor the financial services marketplace"[172] in order to identify risks that might affect the US economic stability. Similarly, the Act enforces FSOC to gather facts from associated authorities in order to support its objectives.[173] According to Section 404, the SEC must compel advisers of private funds to maintain reports and fill in records,[174] due to the significance of their data for the SEC regarding the interests of the public. Other reasons are *the assessment of risk-exposure and the protection of the investors.* Therefore, if considered compulsory, FSOC could guide the "*Office of Financial Research*" (OFR) in gathering extra data from non-bank financial firms,[175] in order to increase investor protection.

A key aim of the Dodd–Frank Act[176] consists of minimizing future systemic risk-exposure. This can be achieved through empowerment of regulatory authorities to impose higher financial asset requirements, but also new limits in the control of corporations by creating regulatory, and market structures for financial derivatives, and by setting up systemic risk surveillance and provide particular officials to intervene.[177] The author of this book considers that a major problem emerges as the Dodd–Frank Act is generally focused on monitoring systemic risk, and consequently, the new legislation leaves many of the investor protection issues created by the hedge fund industry, unsolved.

There are two exemptions abolished by the Act.[178] The first is stipulated under Section 403, removing "the *de minimis* exemption from the

[171] Section 203(b)(3).

[172] Section 112(a)(2)(C) of the Dodd-Frank Act.

[173] Section 112(d)(1) of the Dodd-Frank Act.

[174] Section 404 of the Dodd-Frank Act.

[175] Sections 153 and 154 of the Dodd-Frank Act.

[176] Pub. L. 111-203 (2010).

[177] Gordon, J. N., & Muller, C. (2011). Confronting financial crisis: Dodd-Frank Act's dangers and the case for a systemic emergency insurance fund. *Yale Journal on Regulation, 28*(1), 151–211.

[178] http://www.gibsondunn.com/publications/pages/InvestmentAdviserstoPrivate Funds-InvestmentAdvisersActof1940.aspx. Accessed 12 May 2012.

Advisers Act."[179] This can be applied to that particular adviser: having maximum 15 customers along one year; not holding himself out under the title of investment adviser but also not advising registered investment firms. Usually, this exoneration is driven by individual fund administrators marketing maximum 15 funds due to the fact that each fund is usually considered one singular customer of the administrator regardless of the necessary number of investors.[180] Secondly, the same Section states the following: "advisers to private funds are not eligible to use the current exemption for investment advisers whose clients are all residents of the adviser's home state."[181]

Section 406 imposes authorized investment counselors of "private funds" to provide secondary data regarding every "private fund" administered by them to "the SEC and FSOC." According to the Act, the SEC has this obligation to lead examinations at regular intervals for the verification of every document "of private funds" administered by licensed investment counselors. Those documents are under the confidentiality clause without being disclosed to the wide public. These provisions become operational a year after the enactment of the Act.

Dodd–Frank Act additionally subjects every registered investment adviser who is adviser for private funds to new recordkeeping and reporting obligations. A registered investment adviser may be required to keep records, but also to file with the SEC some data regarding every advised private fund and to make such information available to the FSOC, and Federal department or agency, and to every self-regulatory organization.[182]

This information that should remain confidential will include:

- AUM and leverage use;
- Correspondent credit risk disclosure;
- Evaluation tactics and procedures;
- Categories of owned assets;

[179] Investment Management Group. (2010, July 21). *Financial Reform Act has broad impact on investment management industry. Investment Management Alert*. www.drinkerbiddle.com. Accessed 26 July 2020.

[180] According to "Rule 203(b)(3)-1 of the Advisers Act."

[181] Investment Management Alert. (2010). Op. cit., p. 1.

[182] Wilmarth, A. E. (2011). Op. cit., p. 954.

- Side agreements;
- Sale procedures.

In addition, the SEC and the FSOC are allowed to request additional data, as established at certain regular intervals.[183] However, it is questionable whether the Dodd–Frank Act provides hedge fund investors with sufficient information in order to adequately defend themselves from the unique informational challenges that are connected with hedge fund investments. These unique issues include a total lack of standardization in the hedge funds industry, especially as far as its disclosure practices, risk assessments, and valuation procedures are concerned. This lack of standardization, together with a narrow public disclosure regime, puts investors into difficulty to adequately study a certain hedge fund investment. Additionally, investors are not able to effectively choose an optimal hedge fund investment since the above-mentioned informational challenges make it hard to adequately compare a large range of hedge fund opportunities. It is our belief that this limits significantly investors' choice and competition within the industry, and as a consequence, investors' protection.

The standards controlling the qualification of natural persons as investors in private funds have also been changed. The net worth requirement to qualify "as an *accredited investor* under the Securities Act" shall not include the worth held by "the primary residence of such natural person."[184] In addition, for this four years period starting at the coming into force of the Act, the net worth threshold will be USD 1 million and thereafter, the threshold will be in excess of USD 1 million.[185]

A significant consequence of registration is that an investment adviser is restricted in his capability of charging effectiveness taxes on clients. Rule 205-3 provides an exemption for clients having minimum USD 750,000 AUM with the counselor. At the same time, the same exemption is available for those with a net value reaching at least USD 1.5 million. Customers who are "qualified purchasers" and certain employees of the adviser are also exempt.

[183] Fein, Melanie L. (2010). Op. cit., p. 24.

[184] Krainer, R. (2011). Regulating Wall Street: Dodd-Frank act and the new architecture of global finance. *Journal of Financial Stability, 8*(2), 121–133.

[185] Ibid.

6.6.2.2 *"International Collaboration"*

In order to evaluate risk, FSOC is compelled by the Dodd-Frank Act to coordinate its policies with those of the international authorities.[186] The collaboration can be individually essential for the systemic risk assessment connected to hedge funds and to different private funds since they usually operate internationally and make major investments in companies and financial markets at the international level.[187]

Several actors already admitted that it was absolutely necessary that an international regulation was enforced, particularly due to the globalized markets where both managers and funds alike operated.[188]

To this end, international regulatory coordination has been considered, mainly having in view the future financial crises. It becomes obvious that collecting constant and comparison-relevant data would definitely help with the international reporting of systemic risk and thus improve the usefulness of data dividing through US and foreign financial regulators. The first steps towards this accomplishment were Basel III and Dodd–Frank macro prudential measures which focused on facilitating financial stability.[189] In this regard, a more effective coordination and communication is required among standard setters and supervisors like the Basel Committee and national supervisors implied in the adoption of Basel III and the Dodd–Frank Act regulatory reforms, more transparent and more "authoritative" mandates are needed in making sure that the objectives of financial stability are achieved.

6.6.2.3 *Consumer Financial Protection Bureau*

The Dodd–Frank Act establishes under Title X the Consumer Financial Protection Bureau ("the CFPB").[190] This new authority had as main objective controlling most of the regulatory deficiencies, which led to the financial crisis of 2007/2008. The CFPB's perspective involved the

[186] Section 175 of the Dodd-Frank Act.

[187] Alexander, D., "Global Hedge Fund Assets Rebound to Just over $1.8 Trillion, Hedge Fund Intelligence" (2010).

[188] Group of Thirty. (2009). *Financial reform: A framework for financial stability*. https://group30.org/publications/detail/146. Accessed 20 July 2020.

[189] Ojo, M. (2012). *Harmonising Basel III and the Dodd Frank Act through greater collaboration between standard setters and national supervisors*. http://mpra.ub.uni-muenchen.de/36164/MPRA. Accessed 21 July 2020.

[190] 12 U.S.C. § 5491 (2012).

consolidation of an ample range of financial regulatory acts, the prevention of consumers from being "subordinated to regulatory concerns about bank profitability," and the guarantee that financial lawmakers possess the needed and essential financial expertise in order to ensure that effective regulations are being implemented on banks and non-banks institutions. With the empowerment from the Congress, the CFPB was able to create or promulgate regulations, supervise, being at the same time the enforcement body over various ranges of authorities which are subject to regulation of the consumer financial services industry. Other two major aspects regulated by the CFPB are transparency and stability, the CFPB having broad authority to impose stricter rules on major financial institutions in these regards, and especially for breaches of Federal consumer financial protection law. Granting vast authority on the financial markets enhanced many debates and particularly criticism, as we shall see below, from those who were afraid that holding this powerful authority, regulators would save failing financial institutions with taxpayer dollars. In this respect, the US Chamber of Commerce (2018) issued recently a report stating that the CFPB confides too much on "regulation by enforcement,"[191] at the same time criticizing several issues from the examinations of CFPB. The cost of regulation concerns was reflected in new proposals according to which, legislation must increase "the asset size threshold below which depository institutions are exempt from CFPB supervision and enforcement activities."[192]

Recently, in 2018, the Congress has passed, and the US President signed into law, regulation "(i) repealing CFPB's automobile lending regulations and (ii) exempting smaller banks that had been subject to its regulations."[193] In this case, the banks have won the battle, leaving the CFPB weak and muted.

[191] U.S. Chamber of Commerce. (2018). Consumer Financial Protection Bureau: Working Towards Fundamental Reform, Center for Capital Markets Effectiveness.

[192] See in this vein the Financial Regulatory Improvement Act of 2015, and the Consumer Financial Protection Bureau Examination and Reporting Threshold Act of 2017. Fuster, A., Plosser, M., & Vickery, J. (2018). *Does CFPB oversight crimp credit?* Staff Report No. 857. Federal Reserve Bank of New York Staff Reports.

[193] Coffee, J. C. Jr. (2019). The regulatory sine curve: What explains the retreat from systemic risk regulation (and why it was predictable). In S. O'Halloran & Th. Groll (Eds.), *After the crash: Financial crises and regulatory responses* (pp. 281–300). New York: Columbia University Press.

6.6.2.4 *Provisions Regarding Hedge Funds—The Volker Rule*

The Dodd–Frank Act introduced enhanced prudential standards for hedge funds and included particularly strict prohibitions regarding proprietary exchanging, but also hedge fund holding, innovative risk-based capital, leveraging, and liquidity stipulations. Indeed, the "Dodd-Frank Act"[194] represents a significant progress in tightening the regulation.

The 2010 "Dodd–Frank Act" plays an innovative role in prohibiting some assets exchanging processes by credit institutions associations, insured depository organizations and their partners. This condition or stipulation was called "the Volcker Rule." It is named after the previous "Federal Reserve Board Chairman," who supported and encouraged its adoption. The major objective of the Volcker Rule is to draw some boundaries or limits on bank activities as far as businesses with high degrees of risk are concerned, including asset exchanging, but also hedge fund and private equity[195] activities. The Volcker Rule stands as one of the most controversial parts of the Dodd–Frank Act due to the fact that it "prohibits banks from doing speculative activities such as proprietary trading. The purpose of the Rule is to prevent banks from overexposure to risk that might lead to inevitable bailouts."[196] The controversies are getting more relevant since the new administration under Donald Trump announced their wish of rolling back Dodd–Frank.

Standing as a key piece of regulation, the Dodd–Frank highly impacted the hedge fund industry. Generally speaking, "Dodd–Frank subjects most hedge funds to government inspections, requires them to register with the Securities and Exchange Commission ("SEC"), and imposes a number of disclosure and compliance obligations. Under the DFA, for example, hedge funds are required to maintain and report information on conflicts of interest, ownership structure, clients and officers, disciplinary history, assets under management, performance, risk exposure, and financing."[197] In a similar manner, newly registered funds are currently subject to the Presence Exam Initiative, compiled by the Office of Compliance Inspections and Examinations, which examines, among

[194] Omarova, S. T. (2011a). Wall Street as community of fate: Toward financial industry self-regulation. *University of Pennsylvania Law Review, 159*, 411–492.

[195] Fein, M. L. (2010). Op. cit., p. 24.

[196] Ho, V. T., & Ho, T. N. P. (2020). Regulations in the US and bond market liquidity. *Journal of Economic Development, 45*(1), 3–29.

[197] The Dodd-Frank Wall Street Reform and Consumer Protection Act.

others: the funds' valuation methodologies, allocation of expenses to investors, as well as other business practices.[198] Nevertheless, there has been plenty of criticism raising from these new regulations concerning the hedge fund industry, on grounds that, there was no need for new compliance requirements because hedge fund investors are sophisticated, at the same time signaling that all these obligations would finally lead to decreases in profitability and competitiveness of hedge funds, also impacting investors.[199]

The Volcker Rule sets up an official forbiddance for commercial banks which engage in proprietary trading.[200] This type of trading is perceived as high-risk trading, one of the most aggressive trading strategies in which bank employees engage generally, in highly speculative trading for making bank profit instead of profit for bank's clients.[201] Before the crisis, this was customary in spite of the fact that proprietary trading led to a major conflict of interest between big credit institutions and their clients. Getting involved into highly speculative and risky trading on the clients' side, can help banking institution in generating profits causing harm to their customers. Accordingly, the Volcker Rule comes to end these risky and uncertain practices accompanying proprietary trading.[202] There are researches which, however, find that the Volcker Rule "did not affect banks' overall risk-taking"[203] study outcomes indicating that the Volcker

[198] Bowden, A. (2014, May 6). Speech by the Director of the Office of Compliance, Inspections, and Examinations: Spreading sunshine in private equity. Private Equity International (PEI), Private Fund Compliance Forum, New York; Wyatt, M. (2015, May 13). *Speech by Acting Director, Office of Compliance, Inspections, and Examinations: Private equity: A look back and a glimpse ahead*. New York.

[199] Kaal, W. A. (2013). Hedge fund manager registration under the Dodd-Frank Act. *San Diego Law Review, 50*(2), 243–322.

[200] 12 U.S.C. § 1843 (2012) and 12 U.S.C. § 1851(a)(1) (2012) ("Unless otherwise provided under this section, a banking entity shall not—(A) engage in proprietary trading; (B) or acquire or retain any equity, partnership, or other ownership interest in or sponsor a hedge fund or a private equity fund.").

[201] Grant, G. S. (2014). International financial regulation through the G20: The proprietary trading case study. *Georgetown Journal of International Law, 45*, 1217–1221.

[202] McMahon, K. (2018). The Financial Banking Institute Act and the Financial CHOICE Act: The wrong choice for the American economy. *Journal of Business & Technology Law, 14*(1), 107–133.

[203] Elayana, F.A., Aktasb, R., Browna, K., & Pacharn, P. (2018). The impact of the Volcker rule on targeted banks, systemic risk, liquidity, and financial reporting quality. *Journal of Economics and Business, 96*, 69–89.

Rule is seen as a valid regulatory measure. Even if the Rule was scheduled to be statutory effective on July 21, 2012, its enactment was delayed as it was not ready by then. On December 10, 2013, the last version was released and it was only on January 31, 2014, that the final regulation was published in the Federal Register (2014), its implementation occurring on April 1, 2014. The Rule required banks having more than USD 50 billion worth of trading assets to start reporting from July 2014. At the same time, there was a conformance period for institutions to conform to the requirements. Therefore, banks did not need to entirely comply with the Volcker Rule until July 21, 2015.[204]

"The Volcker Rule" states that no *credit institution* can become involved in asset exchanges, sponsorship, or investment, be it in hedge funds or in private equity funds.[205] This Section, besides additional issues considers that a credit institution entity is considered "an insured depository institution, a company that controls an insured depository institution, a company treated as a bank holding company and any subsidiaries of such institutions or companies, including broker-dealer and fund manager subsidiaries."[206]

Nevertheless, despite the aforementioned interdiction, credit institutions can however promote either private equities or hedge funds, only if a certain number of requirements can be met. Thus, the first requirement is that the bank offers "*bona fide trust*," depositary or investment consultative assistances for the fund. Another condition stipulates that the fund is offered only in relation to consultative assistances and just for clients of the bank. Also, another condition is that the credit institution and its branches are not engaged in "covered transactions" with the fund and consider the fund to be some associate in order to attain the objectives contained in the Federal Reserve Act, to be more precisely, in Section 23B.[207] It is necessary that the credit institution lacks assurance of responsibilities or efficiency of the hedge fund or every umbrella fund. Another requirement is that neither the credit institution nor the fund

[204] Tandon, V. (2016). The Volcker rule: Clarifying the anti-evasion provision to facilitate compliance. *North Carolina Banking Institute, 20*(1), 385–411.

[205] Acharya, V. et al. (2011). *Regulating Wall Street: The Dodd-Frank Act and the New Architecture of Global Finance*. Hoboken, NJ: John Wiley & Sons, Inc.

[206] Investment Management Alert. (2010). Op. cit., p. 2.

[207] http://www.mofo.com/files/uploads/images/section23abchart.pdf. Accessed 22 March 2012.

is allowed to share one denomination or similar names. Another important condition is that only principals or credit institution staffs offering services in order to fulfill certain purposes of the fund are allowed to hold legal proprietorship interests in that particular fund.[208] At the same time, the bank must disclose to investors that the credit institution is not going to cause failures. One last condition is that the credit institutions make the so-called "seed investment," which means use of money to set up a new business or company, or different "*de minimis* investment"[209] within funds.

Another relevant rule of the Dodd–Frank Act is that it forbids credit institution holding firms, depository corporations, and their associates to promote or withhold "any equity, partnership, or other ownership interest in a hedge fund or a private equity fund,"[210] including several exemptions. Thus, "the prohibition comes with limited exceptions, allowing proprietary trading pertinent to the following activities: underwriting, market-making, risk-mitigating hedging, trading in domestic government debt, trading on behalf of customers, and trading by insurance companies."[211]

On the one hand, the so-called Volcker Rule imposes no interdictions on those companies controlled by the Board, which are not bank financial firms[212] although, on the other hand, it does require that they are subject to additional capital conditions and assets exchanging, hedge fund but also private equity fund activities. Even otherwise admitted processes, including promotion and investment both in a private equity and in a hedge fund, where the relevant requirements are met, the "Volcker Rule" forbids them to do this if the activity might lead to a conflict of interests with regard to materiality, which could occur between the credit institutions, on the one hand, and its clients, customers and third parties,

[208] Krainer, Robert E. Op. cit., p. 122.

[209] Ibid.

[210] Fein, M. L. (2010). Op. cit., p. 24.

[211] Tandon, V. (2016). The Volcker rule: Clarifying the anti-evasion provision to facilitate compliance. *North Carolina Banking Institute, 20*(1), 385–411.

[212] Jordan, N., Kawata, Y., Landa, L., & Rowland, G. S. (2011). *Advising private funds: A comprehensive guide to representing hedge funds, private equity funds and their advisers*. Minesota: Thomson West.

on the other hand.[213] Moreover, any transaction that would lead to risk-exposure or put forward any risk concerning the security and soundness of either credit institutions or the American financial security is forbidden.[214] Regulatory authorities are implementing regulations explicitly preventing processes in such a way.[215] While the conflicts of interest represent indeed the main harm that regulators are trying to address, the author considers that it may make sense to consider other solutions like additional disclosures and regulations to defend the public from that kind of conflicts. Therefore, it is the author's opinion that legislators focus on conflicts of interest that can be solved, as already mentioned above, through other methods, without any cost to diversification, economies of scope, and global competition.

In a recent Article, the conclusion confirms that banks take advantage by using adverse information about their client firms, just as it was anticipated by the Volcker Rule. At the same time, the article stipulates that "trading on adverse information about their client firms suggests that banks and investment advisers do not worry about potential conflicts of interests. By trading on adverse information, the banks and investment advisers publicize their clients' financial problems, prematurely depress their stock prices, and potentially make it more difficult for the client firms to solve their financial problems."[216] Considering the above conclusions, the problem of the existence of possible conflicts of interest between banks, non-banking institutions, and their clients is real.

As a consequence, the authors are in favor of the idea that "an added benefit of implementation of the Volcker Rule would be to eliminate the incentives to trade on material, non-public information about their clients that benefit the banks to the detriment of their clients, by eliminating proprietary trading by banks."[217] Thus, this is one more proof that, implementing the Volcker Rule helps enclosing part of the existing

[213] Ibid.

[214] Keppo, J., & Korte, J. (2016). Risk targeting and policy illusions—Evidence from the announcement of the Volcker rule. *Management Science, 64*(1), 215–234. https://doi.org/10.1287/mnsc.2016.2583.

[215] Jordan N. et al. (2011). Op. cit.

[216] Avci, S. B., Schipanr, C. A., & Seyhun, H. N. (2018). Eliminating conflicts of interests in banks: The significance of the Volcker rule. *Yale Journal on Regulation, 35*, 344–380.

[217] Avci, S. B., Schipanr C. A., & Seyhun, H. N. (2018). Op. cit., p. 380.

conflicts of interest which occur in the banking system as a consequence of the repealing of Glass–Steagall stipulations.

As a result of the Volcker Rule, leverage may become less readily available to or more expensive for bank-affiliated private equity funds because of increased risk weightings by financial institutions for loans to bank-sponsored funds. The Volcker Rule's ban on assets sale and significant limitations on promoting or "investing in private funds"[218] could result in financial institutions restructuring their private equity or hedge fund businesses or spinning out existing groups.

In this respect, there have already been several complaints on behalf of market participants according to whom "hedging has become more difficult since the financial crisis."[219] We mention in this vein, a letter from the Coalition of Derivatives End-Users to the Board of Governors, OCC, FDIC, CFTC, and SEC on October 17, 2018 where the impact of the Volcker Rule was highlighted, with main focus on effects associated with limited proprietary trading activity.[220]

The Volcker Rule was and still is subject to major debates. On one hand, there are scholars who are worried about the important side effect of the limitation of the market liquidity,[221] due to decreases in market making activities because of the possibility of being easily incorrectly considered proprietary trading. On the other hand, there are also voices in favor of this regulation, considering that since it impacts only particular dealers, "those that are unaffected would step in and make up for the

[218] "Indeed financial institutions have already begun to divest their interests in private fund businesses." e.g., Or, A. (2010, October 20). Front point managers take back majority stake from Morgan Stanley. *Wall Street Journal Online*. http://online.wsj.com/article/SB10001424052702304011604575564221698158651.html. Accessed 15 June 2020.

[219] Mixon, S., & Onur, E. (2020). *Risk appetite and intermediation by swap dealers*. https://www.cftc.gov/sites/default/files/2020-04/MIxon%20Onur%20Risk%20Appetite%20(2020)%20-%20ada.pdf. Accessed 18 July 2020.

[220] Mixon, S. (2018). Research issues in commodities and commodity derivatives. In H. K. Baker, G. Filbeck, & J. H. Harris (Eds.), *Commodities: Markets, performance, and strategies* (pp. 534–554). New York: Oxford University Press.

[221] Duffie, D. (2012). *Market-making under the Proposed Volcker Rule* (Working Paper). Stanford University. Financial Stability Oversight Council. (2011). Study and recommendations on prohibitions on proprietary trading and certain relationships with, hedge funds and private equity funds.

lack of market making activities from banks."[222] As a consequence, the liquidity will not be changed. Several researches also envisaged the market liquidity after the crisis, but their outcomes were not similar,[223] but the results are mixed.

As a concluding remark, all in all, the real challenges of the Dodd–Frank consist of:

1. Increased government reporting => increased investor protection.
2. Increased reporting to investors => increased investor protection.
3. Disclosure to both governing authority and investors => increased investor protection.

On the whole, one can say that the financial community has approved of the higher reporting requests concept under Dodd–Frank.

However, according to the above-mentioned issues, the Volker Rule has three different drawbacks. The first one is that it relies very much on regulatory interpretation and an equivocal separation of trading activities that are permitted and prohibited. Due to these ambiguities concerning the legal line, banks could avoid appropriately hedging risks. The second one is that restricting bank activities may increase bank fragility by restraining diversification, and thus, less diverse banks could be less secure. Last, the Volcker Rule, due to the fact that it restricts proprietary trading, can harm market liquidity, although it is clear that liquid markets are those supporting economic growth, the transparency of their prices, and the decrease of their costs of capital.

With regard to the Volcker Rule, it should also be mentioned that the Trump administration recently tried to repeal the Volcker Rule through Financial Choice Act, which passed the House of Representative on June 8, 2017. This aspect will be however thoroughly discussed in the next subchapter.

[222] Ho, V. T., & Ho, T. N. P. (2020). Op. cit., p. 4.

[223] Dick-Nielsen, J., & Rossi, M. (2016). *The cost of immediacy for corporate bonds* (Working Paper). Copenhagen Business School and Texas A&M University; Bao, J., Pan, J., & Wang, J. (2011). The illiquidity of corporate bonds. *The Journal of Finance, 66*(3), 911-9–6; Bessembinder, H., Jacobsen, S., Maxwell, W., & Venkataraman, K. (2018). Capital commitment and illiquidity in corporate bonds. *The Journal of Finance, 73*(4), 1615–1661.

6.6.3 *Repealing of the Dodd–Frank?*

Currently, Dodd–Frank is under attack. With the election of Donald Trump, a regulatory storm started to arise. Being a Republican, President Trump emitted several executive orders with the main aim of limiting government regulation of major economic segments. Also, in 2017, Congress took several measures to abrogate a lot of the Dodd–Frank Act. In this respect, on April 5, 2017, the Financial Institution Bankruptcy Act of 2017 (FIBA)[224] was passed by the House of Representatives. FIBA stipulates the invalidation of many of the provisions of Dodd–Frank, governing the liquidation of failing major financial institutions and at the same time introducing one new-subchapter in Chapter 11, where are mentioned financial institutions having minimum USD 50 billion in financial assets.[225]

In addition, two months later, on June 10, 2017 the House of Representatives passed the Financial CHOICE Act of 2017.[226]

Even if the Choice Act, by the time of this writing is unlikely to pass in the US Senate, still, it offers a comprehensive perspective of the Republican platform aiming at lessening what sees as the "regulatory stranglehold."[227] The Choice Act gathers 12 titles, substantially alters the Dodd-Frank Act as it abolishes the Volcker Rule,[228] eliminates most of the provision of the Orderly Liquidation Authority,[229] at the same time repealing the Fiduciary Duty rule and diminishing the protections of the CFPB.[230] Scholars were generally against these changes, arguing that "FIBA and the CHOICE Act place too much power and freedom back

[224] Financial Institution Bankruptcy Act of 2017, H.R. 1667, 115th Cong. (2017).

[225] Financial Institution Bankruptcy Act of 2017, H.R. 1667, 115th Cong. §§ 2(a)(9A)(B), 2(b)(1) (2017).

[226] H.R.10, 115th Cong. (as passed by House 2017–2018). The CHOICE Act passed in the House on June 8, 2017, by a 233-186 vote, largely along party lines.

[227] Magaldi, J., & Girasa, R. (2019). Reforming Dodd-Frank: Is the financial choice act or any subsequent act proposed—The right choice in this political environment? *North East Journal of Legal Studies, 38*, 70–102.

[228] The Financial CHOICE Act of 2016, H.R. 10, 115th Cong. § 901.

[229] The Financial CHOICE Act of 2016, H.R. 10, 115th Cong. § 111 (2017).

[230] Id. at § 711.

in the hands of those who bear substantial responsibility for the worst economic crisis since the Great Depression."[231]

Standing out an important period for the regulatory landscape in the United States, several analyses will be further made. The first important change proposed by the Choice Act can be found in Title I, Subtitle A, Ending "Too Big to Fail" and Bank Bailouts, Section 111, repealing the Orderly Liquidation Authority. We will first focus on Title I of the Financial Choice Act: Ending "Too Big to Fail" and Bank Bailouts, which repeals the Orderly Liquidation Authority.

In spite of the fact that this Title I focuses on the ending of taxpayer assistance to troubled banks, this is mainly done by the elimination of the Dodd–Frank Act instrument used to identify those financial institutions which are exposed to systemic risk.

Further on, instead of "identifying 'systemically important financial institutions' ('SIFIs') by FSOC under Title II of the Dodd-Frank Act and making them subject to enhanced prudential standards, the Choice Act substitutes a bankruptcy procedure for a 'covered financial corporation' defined as a bank holding company, which is corporation whose primary purpose is to own, control, or finance subsidiaries having a total consolidated assets of USD 50 billion or more, or such ownership or control of financial assets relating to depositary institutions represents 85 percent of the consolidated assets of the corporation."[232]

Consequently, many debates emerged on the proposed elimination of the orderly liquidation authority ("OLA") and the substitution of SIFI with an exclusive bankruptcy court. If adopted, FIBA would accordingly eliminate the OLA and offer more power to failing financial firms who can by this means restructure in bankruptcy process. Bearing in mind that OLA is made up of professionals having "knowledge and expertise of American and international financial markets; the ability to plan and monitor for the possibility of a financial meltdown; coordination; and liquidity,"[233] many scholars consider that "dissolving the OLA may actually hurt the efficacy of many of FIBA's key provisions. The stated purpose of the OLA is to quickly and efficiently liquidate failing financial firms in

[231] McMahon, K. (2018). The Financial Banking Institute Act and the Financial CHOICE Act: The wrong choice for the American economy. *Journal of Business & Technology Law, 14*(1), 107–133.

[232] Magaldi, J., & Girasa, R. (2019). Op. cit.

[233] McMahon, K. (2018). Op. Cit.

times of financial crisis. Simply put, bankruptcy courts are not as well situated to quickly and efficiently handle the liquidation of failing financial firms as the OLA is."[234]

This has led to much controversy. Scholars and commentators, as seen above, were against eliminating this mechanism. Thus, even if many acknowledged that the OLA is not perfect, at the same time they recognized it "as an essential tool for government regulators to ensure that the financial crisis attributable to a particular SIFI does not escalate to a broader financial crisis."[235] The same opinion is shared by a Harvard professor who states that, "although a bankruptcy mechanism usefully expands the channels for resolution of a failing financial firm, bankruptcy institutions alone cannot manage a full-blown financial crisis. Crisis management will need regulatory authorities. The difference in function, and the baseline uncertainty of success, could fan financial panic rather than stabilize the financial system, if there is no regulatory backup and support. While FIBA, particularly if made more robust than the current version, would be a valuable addition to the panoply of crisis tools, the economy and the financial system will still need OLA to make FIBA work. Hence, substituting FIBA for OLA risks exacerbating a financial crisis like that which the country faced in 2008–2009."[236]

Summing up, the OLA is an authority providing several important advantages for financial firms. As McMahon puts it, "the FIBA and the Financial CHOICE Act abolish the OLA and replace it with a court system that is ill-equipped to handle the dissolution of financial firms in times of economic crisis. The vigor of the system proposed by these acts would be severely diminished by the repeal of the OLA."[237] In his opinion, for this to be adopted OLA should be preserved not replaced.

By no means do scholars[238] agree to return to an era of deregulation when less than a decennium has passed since one of the greatest financial

[234] Idem.

[235] Idem.

[236] Gordon, J., & Roe, M. (2017). *Financial scholars oppose eliminating "Orderly Liquidation Authority" as crisis-avoidance restructuring backstop*. https://corpgov.law.harvard.edu/2017/05/26/financial-scholars-oppose-eliminating-orderly-liquidation-authority-as-crisis-avoidance-restructuring-backstop/. Accessed 28 June 2020.

[237] McMahon, K. (2018). Op. cit.

[238] Idem.

crises in the world. The Choice Act and the FIBA stand as a dangerous change in regulatory practices, due to the deregulations they imply.

6.6.3.1 Replacement of the CFPB with the "CLEA"

The new administration under Trump opposed the CFPB, launching attacks in court and lobbying for its replacement in Congress, the consequence being the significant limit of its influence.[239]

In the same document, the replacement of the CFPB with the Consumer Law Enforcement Agency (the "CLEA") is proposed.[240] Just as in the cases mentioned above, this new authority would inherit most of the same rulemaking powers of the CFPB, but will have no authority on conducting examinations or supervising the activities of major financial corporations. In addition, this new authority would focus mainly on cost–benefit, being forced to conduct such cost–benefit studies before each enforcement action, therefore, before the implementation of any regulation. Another difference between the CFPB and the CLEA is that it cannot "prohibit unfair, deceptive, and abusive acts or practices in consumer financial markets."[241] It can be therefore stated that, by these measures, the Financial CHOICE Act plans to replace the CFPB with the CLEA, a body having little power in putting an end to financially questionable banking practices.

In addition to the loosening of regulatory restrictions precipitated by the proposed changes to the CFPB, the Financial CHOICE Act also

[239] Financial CHOICE Act of 2017, H.R. 10, 115th Cong. (2017) (proposed that the CFPB must be replaced by an executive agency having a director who can be removed at-will); PHH Corp. v. Consumer Fin. Prot. Bureau, 881 F.3d 75, 110 (D.C. Cir. 2018) (en banc) (determined that the CFPB was constitutionally structured because its unitary director with for-cause removal protection does not impinge on the President's duties under Article II); Consumer Fin. Prot. Bureau v. RD Legal Funding, LLC, 332 F. Supp. 3d 729, 784 (S.D.N.Y. 2018) (in disagreement with the en banc holding of the D.C. Circuit in PHH Corp., which deemed instead the CFPB wholly invalid on the reason that its unitary director violated the principles involving the separation of powers); For more details see Hovie, L. (2019). A tragedy of novelty: Is for-cause removal protection for the consumer financial protection bureau's single director a fatal flaw? *Boston College Law Review, 60*(9), II.-100–II.-119., where several constitutional challenges to the CFPB are being presented.

[240] Labonte, M., Carpenter, D.H., & Davis, C.M. et al. (2017). *The Financial Choice Act in 115th Congress: Selected policy issues*. Congressional Research Service.

[241] Idem.

provides a "regulatory off-ramp" for major financial institutions.[242] These "off-ramp provisions" generally allow those financial corporations covered by the ongoing regulations to withdraw from enhanced regulatory standards for the sake of subjecting the institution to an increased leverage ratio summing up 10%. In this respect, researchers in banking finance raised doubts about the utility of the off-ramp provision since up to the present date no US bank was able to meet the 10% threshold. Also, questions concern whether relying only on one measure consisting of the leverage ratio is enough. At the same time, the off-ramp provisions, together "with the repeal of most of the other provisions in Title I, seem to imply that regulation of large banking institutions (whether on or off the ramp) is all that is necessary to address the sources of systemic risk. This approach runs counter to the widespread belief that much of the outsized risk in the US financial system in 2007–2008 originated in the unregulated or lightly regulated parts of the system. Addressing the diverse sources of systemic risk, especially those that may reside in the shadows of the regulated sector, is admittedly a difficult task."[243] In this respect, according to Meyerson et al. (2017), the CHOICE Act not only it does not try to find its own measures against this, but it does not even accept that such measures would be necessary.

All these changes stand as an abrupt shift in regulating finances in the United States, aiming at reducing dramatically the strength of the Dodd–Frank Act.[244]

One of the First CHOICE Act's key elements puts major limitations on the CFPB. Taking into account that the Financial CHOICE Act could pass, the state attorney generals consider manners to counteract deregulation. In this respect, "the Martin Act could be used to counteract financial deregulation. The Martin Act is a powerful piece of legislation that is interpreted broadly to protect investors from fraud. While the Martin Act

[242] Meyerson, L., Chorazak, M., Sloan, S., & Thacher, S. (2017). *Treasury Department Issues Recommendations on Reforming the U.S. Financial System*. https://corpgov.law.harvard.edu/2017/06/23/treasury-department-issues-recommendations-on-reforming-the-u-s-financial-system/. Accessed 18 July 2020.

[243] Idem.

[244] Lee, P. (2017). *The CHOICE Act is a bad choice for financial reform, the CLS blue sky blog: Columbia Law School's blog on corporations and the capital markets*. https://clsbluesky.law.columbia.edu/2017/04/12/the-choice-act-is-a-bad-choice-for-financial-reform/. Accessed 18 July 2020.

cannot be used to directly sue payday lenders and debt collectors for their abusive acts and practices, the Martin Act can be used to sue them for misleading their shareholders."[245]

6.6.3.2 Repeal of the Volcker Rule

Another measure of the Financial CHOICE ACT resides in the repealing of the Volcker Rule, found at Title IX,[246] this Rule restricting proprietary trading and whatever activity corresponding to highly speculative and risky trading, from which just credit institutions can make profit.[247]

Once more, repeal of the Volcker Rule would let credit institutions to engage in trade businesses which could harm national and global financial markets, leading to conflicts of interests between banks and clients. This is why most scholars are in favor of maintaining the Volcker Rule, so that financial institutions do not reiterate past behavior of unreliable trade practices and unchecked conflicts of interest. Currently, the system is healthy. In spite of this, "the Financial Choice Act seeks to repeal the very rule that prohibits a substantial amount of the activity that contributed to the financial crisis and once more allows large financial institutions the freedom to leverage the money of their own client for speculative gains of megabanks."[248]

A repeal of the Volcker Rule is not likely to happen, since in the Senate there are around 60 votes in minus for passing the regulation. However, changes will occur in order to make it better than it is nowadays. Scholars acknowledge that "policy makers have taken note of its difficulties. The OCC went so far as to open a comment period asking the public to provide their opinions on the Volcker Rule and ways to fix it. The five regulatory agencies which oversee the Volcker Rule are expected to explore ways to reform the rule by achieving congressional intent in the least burdensome means possible."[249] Even if not now, the Volcker Rule will be improved in the near future.

[245] DiNizo, A. (2018). The Martin Act: A tool for counteracting financial deregulation. *Stanford Journal of Law, Business & Finance 23*(2), 212–226.

[246] H.R. 10, 115th Cong. § 901 (2017).

[247] Grant, G., S. (2014). Op. cit.

[248] McMahon, K. (2018). Op. cit.

[249] Pasanisi, J. (2018). Revamping the Volcker rule. *International Financial Law Review*. https://www.iflr.com/article/b1lp1td3cg2hfb/revamping-the-volcker-rule. Accessed 3 May 2020.

As it could be seen, strong antipathy toward Dodd–Frank was proved by White House passage of the CHOICE Act. Still, the Act did not make it to the Senate. This lack of ability of the current Congress to win suggests that Dodd–Frank is seen as a good piece of regulation (lacks and drawbacks are normal) that will still stand for a while.[250]

6.6.4 Closing Remarks on Dodd–Frank Act

Starting from the analysis made in this chapter, it can be stated that there are clear gains but also costly trade-offs from the enactment of the Dodd–Frank Act. Also, there are obvious areas where progresses are still needed. Thus, Dodd–Frank's most valuable contributions have included higher prudential standards but also the creation of the CFPB. Additionally, the derivatives transactions were subject to greater transparency and oversight. At the same time, higher capital requirements made banking and non-banking institutions more flexible to financial pressure and crises. Another important shift resides in the FDIC[251] SPOE strategy that authorizes standard procedures for cautiously winding down a bankrupt institution, this leading to the improvement of the financial stability and also diminishing what means "too big to fail." From another perspective, the CFPB has two key roles; strengthens oversight duties, minimizing possible risky breaches in the US regulations, and improves protections for clients. In spite of all these, there is still room for improvement in all of these.

As seen, there are also other provisions that are difficult to assess, as they appear to bring about some advantages in spite of the important costs they imply. In this case the Volcker Rule can be mentioned. This prohibits proprietary trading on behalf of commercial banks and also the Lincoln Amendment, which bans entities engaged in swaps to receive federal assistance. There are critics complaining about the difficulties faced by regulators in implementing and overseeing the Volcker Rule. This regulation is complex, ambiguous, and expensive, and this also puts banks in difficulty when adhering to its stipulations. There are also scholars who consider that the Lincoln Amendment's provisions are more

[250] Taylor, C. (2018). The Dodd-Frank Death Knell. *Loyola University Chicago Law Journal, 49*, 655–668.

[251] Federal Deposit Insurance Corporation's.

or less the same as those of the Volker Rule, this leading to redundancy and rendering the Lincoln Amendment unnecessary.

There are also domains in which, the Dodd–Frank has made some progress, but there are still improvements to be made, and in this respect, we consider particularly the Financial Stability Oversight Council (FSOC).

In the author's opinion, the Dodd–Frank Act represents a step towards better regulation regarding hedge funds. According to the Dodd–Frank Act provisions, the hedge fund industry has been strongly affected. According to this Act, the large hedge funds might be seen as systemically major companies. The Act does not clearly state the size thresholds, the "*Federal Reserve System*" (FED) and FSOC being the ones who would have to decide on this matter. Hedge funds considered systemically crucial will fall under severe regulatory monitoring. At the same time, hedge funds could be under the impact of some extra conditions, as registering with the SEC in case their assets are larger than or equal to USD 150 million. The result of all these will be: stricter reporting and recordkeeping.

All the above-mentioned requirements will lead to consequences such as: limited gross margin, re-appraisal "of their balance sheets, amendments to their operational and legal entity structures and modifications to their tax procedures."[252] In this respect, it becomes obvious that the severe regulatory monitoring and the main clarifying requests on derivatives, might force funds to rearrange their own activities and diminish their own balance sheets to respect all provisions of the Act. The hedge funds margins of profit are likely to diminish in the future.

Campaigners for the Choice Act consider the Act "a major regulatory improvement that will restore market discipline while reducing the regulatory burden on the banking and financial industry."[253] Even if the Choice Act does not entirely dismiss the Dodd–Frank, "it calls for extensive changes to current financial regulation that include repealing certain portions of Dodd-Frank, amending other portions of Dodd-Frank

[252] Onorato, M., & Symeonidou, G. (2011). *Dodd-Frank Act Wall Street Reform and Consumer Protection Act: Business model implications*. Toronto: Algorithmics Trademarks LLC & Algorithmics Software LLC.

[253] Norbert, J. M. (2016, December 19). *Six recommendations for the CHOICE Act 2.0*. Heritage Found. https://www.heritage.org/report/six-recommendations-the-choice-act-20. Accessed 4 May 2020.

to provide regulatory relief, converting and restructuring the regulatory authority of certain government agencies, and implementing new government legislation to reduce the regulatory burden on the U.S. financial markets and the US economy."[254]

Currently, opinions are generally in favor of this Dodd–Frank Act. Thus, "the substantive success of Dodd-Frank is that it is helping produce a financial industry that is prosperous, less risky, and performing its various functions in a way that ensures the broader economy has been insulated from major assault."[255]

6.7 Concluding Remarks

This chapter analyzed the evolution of the hedge funds regulation in the United States. Thorough consideration has been given to the financial reform adopted via the ratification of "the Dodd–Frank Act," particularly regarding the regulation of investment advisers, and specifically of hedge fund managers and other alternative investment managers who were previously able to organize their operations in such a way as to avoid registration with the SEC.

The author of this book considered it necessary to first describe and examine all the laws concerning hedge funds regulation and the manner these contributed in the past to the shaping of this industry, in order to fully understand the revolutionary financial reform implied by "the Dodd–Frank Act." Thus, the ability of hedge funds to mitigate the risk of loss to investment portfolios has an important relationship to a fundamental policy objective of the US regulations. By disclosing material information and reducing the exposure of investment capital to losses, hedge funds complement the legislative and regulatory objective of investor protection.

This reform has to be read and analyzed also in the context of the twenty-first-century depression that has affected the world of global finances. In the aftermath of the crisis, governments were asked to implement strong financial reforms in order to avoid a Lehman Brothers scenario in the future. Since the crisis, major strides toward financial

[254] Idem.

[255] Barney, F. (2019). The economic and political implications of the Dodd-Frank Act. In S. O'Halloran & Th. Groll (Eds.), *After the crash: Financial crises and regulatory responses* (pp. 261–280). New York: Columbia University Press.

stability have been achieved. Meanwhile, regulations have forced the majority of hedge funds to insure investors' protection and greater transparency.

In addition, the author points out the strong impact that this reform has had on the hedge fund market. The so-called father of this post-modern hedge fund industry, George Soros, has decided to close all his hedge funds and establish a family office explaining his choice by the burdensome impact of "the Dodd-Frank Act" on this industry. The consequence of his decision could lead other hedge fund managers to end their businesses or to relocate to other more lightly regulated jurisdictions.

As seen so far, investor protection is a hallmark goal of federal securities law and the author accentuates the fact that this reform has had a major impact on the profits and risk-taking of the hedge fund industry. Dodd–Frank subjects most hedge funds to government inspections, requires them to register with the Securities and Exchange Commission ("SEC"), and imposes a number of disclosure and compliance obligations. The question which emerges is if the sector will cope with all these massive changes and in particular whether hedge funds will decide to stay and comply with all the reporting requirements, accepting the SEC's major principle oriented toward investor protection.

Since coming into power, President Trump and Republican supporter lawyers have pursued the deregulation of the Wall Street as a major priority. As Di Nizo puts it, "the Financial CHOICE Act is a piece of legislation that is viewed as a blueprint for how Republicans plan to scale back financial industry regulation."[256]

However, as it could be seen, strong antipathy toward Dodd–Frank was proved by White House passage of the CHOICE Act. Still, the Act did not make it to the Senate. This lack of ability of the current Congress to win suggests that Dodd–Frank is seen as a good piece of regulation (lacks and drawbacks are normal) that will still stand for a while.[257]

This chapter argues that the beneficial outcomes attained by hedge funds for their investors are widely attributable to the legal regime they operate under.

[256] DiNizo, A. (2018). The Martin Act: A tool for counteracting financial deregulation. *Stanford Journal of Law, Business & Finance 23*(2), 212–226.

[257] Taylor, C. (2018). The Dodd-Frank Death Knell. *Loyola University Chicago Law Journal, 49*, 655–668.

As it could be seen, in the United States, the imposition of new registration and reporting requirements, having as main scope the increase of transparency, seems to have diminished hedge funds' investment discretion. Among the most important changes during the last decade, both strong equity and bond markets can be enumerated, "making it harder for hedge funds to add value for investors the market."[258] All these challenges raise questions for investors concerning the performance of hedge funds in the near future.

References

Acharya, V. et al. (2011). *Regulating Wall Street: The Dodd-Frank Act and the New Architecture of Global Finance*. Hoboken, NJ: John Wiley & Sons, Inc.

Aikman, D., Bridges, J., Kashyap, A., & Siegert, C. (2019). Would macroprudential regulation have prevented the last crisis? *Journal of Economic Perspectives, 33*(1), 107–130.

Avci, S. B., Schipanr, C. A., & Seyhun, H. N. (2018). Eliminating conflicts of interests in banks: The significance of the Volcker rule. *Yale Journal on Regulation, 35*, 344–380.

Baily, M. N., Klein, A., & Schardin, J. (2017). The Impact of the Dodd-Frank Act on financial stability and economic growth. *RSF: The Russell Sage Foundation Journal of the Social Sciences, 3*(1), 20–47. https://doi.org/10.7758/rsf.2017.3.1.02.

Balotti, R. F., & Shaner, M. W. (2011). Safe Harbour for Officer Reliance: Comparing the Approaches of the Model Business Corporation Act and Delaware's General Corporation Law. *Law and Contemporary Problems, 74*(1), 161–174.

Bao, J., Pan, J., & Wang, J. (2011). The illiquidity of corporate bonds. *The Journal of Finance, 66*(3), 911–946.

Barbash, B., & Massari, J. (2008). The Investment Advisers Act of 1940: Regulation by Accretion. *Rutgers Law Journal, 39*, 627–656.

Barney, F. (2019). The economic and political implications of the Dodd-Frank Act. In S. O'Halloran & Th. Groll (Eds.), *After the crash: Financial crises and regulatory responses* (pp. 261–280). New York: Columbia University Press.

Baums, Th., & Cahn, A. (2004). *Hedge funds—Risks and regulation. Institute for Law and Finance Series*, 1. Berlin: De Gruyter.

[258] McCahery, J.F., & de Roode, A. (2019). The lost decade for hedge funds: Three threats, financing, hedge funds, investment decisions, management, performance. In D. Cumming, G. Wood, & S. Johan (Eds.), *Oxford handbook of hedge funds* (pp. 1–41). Series number: 486/2019. Oxford: Oxford University Press.

Beker, V. (2019, May 10–11). *Is the financial system prepared for a new financial crisis?* Paper presented at the 40th International Scientific Conference on Economic and Social Development—Buenos Aires.

Bessembinder, H., Jacobsen, S., Maxwell, W., & Venkataraman, K. (2018). Capital commitment and illiquidity in corporate bonds. *The Journal of Finance, 73*(4), 1615–1661.

Bowden, A. (2014, May 6). *Speech by the Director of the Office of Compliance, Inspections, and Examinations: Spreading sunshine in private equity*. Private Equity International (PEI), Private Fund Compliance Forum, New York.

Coffee, J. C. Jr. (2019). The regulatory sine curve: What explains the retreat from systemic risk regulation (and why it was predictable). In S. O'Halloran & Th. Groll (Eds.), *After the crash: Financial crises and regulatory responses* (pp. 281–300). New York: Columbia University Press.

Consumer Fin. Prot. Bureau v. RD Legal Funding, LLC, 332 F. Supp. 3d 729, 784 (S.D.N.Y. 2018).

Cumming, D., Dai, N., & Johan, S. (2019). Dodd-Franking the hedge Funds. *Journal of Banking and Finance*. https://doi.org/10.1016/j.jbankfin.2017.09.012.

Dancer, W. T., & Powell, D. (2018). Dodd-Frank repeal: Assessing the change in the day-to-day activities of financial institutions. *Journal of Accounting and Finance, 18*(7), 50–55.

DeMott, D. (2012). Regulatory techniques and liability regimes for asset managers. *Capital Markets Law Journal, 7*(4), 423–431. https://doi.org/10.1093/cmlj/kms034.

Dick-Nielsen, J., & Rossi, M. (2016). *The cost of immediacy for corporate bonds* (Working Paper). Copenhagen Business School and Texas A&M University. https://www.google.com/url?sa=t&rct=j&q=&esrc=s&source=web&cd=&ved=2ahUKEwjghK2franrAhVHPcAKHbSXCQQQFjAAegQIBxAB&url=http%3A%2F%2Fgcfp.mit.edu%2Fwp-content%2Fuploads%2F2016%2F09%2FDick-Nielsen-Rossi.pdf&usg=AOvVaw2M3h5eDLFmveo78XxW5VGp. Accessed 4 July 2020.

DiNizo, A. (2018). The Martin Act: A tool for counteracting financial deregulation. *Stanford Journal of Law, Business & Finance, 23*(2), 212–226.

Dodd-Frank Wall Street Reform and Consumer Protection Act § 165(d), 12 U.S.C. § 5325 (2012).

Duffie, D. (2012). *Market-making under the Proposed Volcker Rule* (Working Paper). Stanford University. https://www.google.com/url?sa=t&rct=j&q=&esrc=s&source=web&cd=&ved=2ahUKEwjpssr2r6nrAhWu_CoKHalCBbsQFjABegQIBRAB&url=https%3A%2F%2Fwww.darrellduffie.com%2Fuploads%2Fpolicy%2FDuffieVolckerRule.pdf&usg=AOvVaw2Aq-aGgvuyZ_7OYAqREIfR. Accessed 26 July 2020.

Duffie, D. (2019). Prone to fail: The pre-crisis financial system. *Journal of Economic Perspectives, 33*(1), 81–106. https://doi.org/10.1257/jep.33.1.81.

Dugan, J. C., Fisher, P. R., & Muckenfuss, C. F. III. (2014). *Responding to systemic risk: Restoring the balance*. Washington, DC: Bipartisan Policy Center. https://bipartisanpolicy.org/wp-content/uploads/2019/03/BPC-Responding-to-Systemic-Risk.pdf. Accessed 26 July 2020.

Easley, D., O'hara, M. O., & Yang, L. (2014). Opaque trading, disclosure, and asset prices: Implications for hedge fund regulation. *Review of Financial Studies*, *27*(4), 1190–1237. https://doi.org/10.1093/rfs/hht079.

Edwards, F. R. (2003, May 22). *The regulation of hedge funds: Financial stability and investor protection*. Paper presented at the Conference on Hedge Funds Institute for Law and Finance, Frankfurt.

Elayana, F.A., Aktasb, R., Browna, K., & Pacharn, P. (2018). The impact of the Volcker rule on targeted banks, systemic risk, liquidity, and financial reporting quality. *Journal of Economics and Business, 96*, 69–89.

Fein, M. L. (2010). *Dodd-Frank Act Wall Street Reform and Consumer Protection Act*. www.ssrn.com/abstract=1357452. Accessed 26 July 2020.

Financial Stability Oversight Council. (2011). *Study and recommendations on prohibitions on proprietary trading and certain relationships with, hedge funds and private equity funds*. https://www.google.com/url?sa=t&rct=j&q=&esrc=s&source=web&cd=&ved=2ahUKEwinlN-XsKnrAhUMxYsKHdrbCMAQFjAAegQIARAB&url=https%3A%2F%2Fwww.treasury.gov%2Finitiatives%2FDocuments%2FVolcker%2520sec%2520%2520619%2520study%2520final%25201%252018%252011%2520rg.pdf&usg=AOvVaw2MqmxEcAy_RRB4Pmn4oNBa. Accessed 26 July 2020.

Financial Stability Oversight Council. (2014). *Transparency policy for the Financial Stability Oversight Council*. www.treasury.gov/initiatives/Documents/FSOCtransparencypolicy.pdf. Accessed 15 July 2020.

Financial Stability Oversight Council. (2015). *Supplemental procedures relating to nonbank financial company determinations*. www.treasury.gov/initiatives/fsoc/designations/Documents/Supplemental%20Procedures%20Related%20to%20Nonbank%20Financial%20Company%20Determinations%20-%20February%202015.pdf. Accessed 16 June 2020.

Fuster, A., Plosser, M., & Vickery, J. (2018). *Does CFPB oversight crimp credit?* Staff Report No. 857. Federal Reserve Bank of New York Staff Reports. https://www.google.com/url?sa=t&rct=j&q=&esrc=s&source=web&cd=&ved=2ahUKEwijnaeDs6nrAhXbREEAHbkIDwEQFjAAegQIBBAB&url=https%3A%2F%2Fwww.newyorkfed.org%2Fmedialibrary%2Fmedia%2Fresearch%2Fstaff_reports%2Fsr857.pdf&usg=AOvVaw1jiUkMY4ggAbI3ff-SLQ8_. Accessed 16 June 2020.

Giancarlo, J.C., & Tuckman, B. (2018). *US commodity futures trading Comm'n, Swaps regulation version 2.0: An assessment of the current implementation of reform and proposals for next steps*. https://www.cftc.gov/sites/default/files/2018-04/oce-chairman-swapreg. Accessed 16 June 2020.

Gibbons, G., & Stone, H. M. (2011). PE managers as registered investment advisors. *The Journal of Private Equity, 15*(1), 8–15. https://doi.org/10.3905/jpe.2011.15.1.008.

Goldstein, D. A., & Kelly, B. (2004). SEC proposes rules requiring offshore advisers of offshore hedge funds to register under the Advisers Act. *Journal of Investment Compliance, 5*(2), 29–33. https://doi.org/10.1108/15285810410636127.

Gordon, J., & Roe, M. (2017). *Financial scholars oppose eliminating "Orderly Liquidation Authority" as crisis-avoidance restructuring backstop*. https://corpgov.law.harvard.edu/2017/05/26/financial-scholars-oppose-eliminating-orderly-liquidation-authority-as-crisis-avoidance-restructuring-backstop/. Accessed 28 June 2020.

Gordon, J. N., & Muller, C. (2011). Confronting financial crisis: Dodd-Frank Act's dangers and the case for a systemic emergency insurance fund. *Yale Journal on Regulation, 28*(1), 151–211.

Grant, G. S. (2014). International financial regulation through the G20: The proprietary trading case study. *Georgetown Journal of International Law, 45*, 1217–1221.

Group of Thirty. (2009). *Financial reform: A framework for financial stability*. https://group30.org/publications/detail/146. Accessed 20 July 2020.

Guynn, R. (2014). Framing the TBTF problem: The path to a solution. In M. N. Baily & J. Taylor (Eds.), *Across the great divide: New perspectives on the financial crisis* (pp. 281–286). Stanford: Hoover Institution Press.

Hammer, D. L. et al. (2005). *US Regulation of Hedge Funds*. Chicago: ABA Book Publishing.

Hanlon, A. P. (2002). *Proposal for Reform of Hedge Fund Regulation*. Harvard Law School.

Hayes, R., & Walker, R. S. (2006). Mandatory registration of hedge funds with the SEC and hedge fund activism in corporate decision. *Entrepreneurial Business Law Journal, 1*, 87–124.

Ho, V. T., & Ho, T. N. P. (2020). Regulations in the US and bond market liquidity. *Journal of Economic Development, 45*(1), 3–29.

Hong, X. (2014). The dynamics of hedge fund share restrictions. *Journal of Banking and Finance, 49*, 82–99.

Honigsberg, C. (2019). Hedge fund regulation and fund governance: Evidence on the effects of mandatory disclosure rules. *Journal of Accounting Research, 57*, 845–884.

Hovie, L. (2019). A tragedy of novelty: Is for cause removal protection for the consumer financial protection bureau's single director a fatal flaw? *Boston College Law Review, 60*(9), II.-100–II.-119.

H.R. 10, 115th Cong. § 111 (2017).

Hubbard, G. (2019). If IT happened again: A road map for regulatory reform chapter. In S. O'Halloran & Th. Groll (Eds.), *After the crash: Financial crises and regulatory responses* (pp. 47–56). New York: Columbia University Press.

International Monetary Fund. (2020). *Law & financial stability*. Washington: International Monetary Fund. http://dx.doi.org/10.5089/9781513523002.071.

International Trident Trust Group. (1999). *The chancellor offshore funds manual*. London: Chancellors Publications Limited.

Investment Management Group. (2010, July 21). Financial Reform Act has broad impact on investment management industry. *Investment Management Alert*. www.drinkerbiddle.com. Accessed 26 July 2020.

Jacoby, M. B. (2011). Dodd-Frank, regulatory innovation, and the safety of consumer financial products. *North Carolina Banking Institute, 15*. https://scholarship.law.unc.edu/ncbi/vol15/iss1/7. Accessed 26 July 2020.

Januzzi, F. V., Bressan, A. A., & Moreira, F. (2019). Opacity, risk, performance and inflows in hedge funds. *Revista de Administração Contemporânea, 24*(1), 77–99. https://doi.org/10.1590/1982-7849rac2020180233.

Jordan, N., Kawata, Y., Landa, L., & Rowland, G. S. (2011). *Advising private funds: A comprehensive guide to representing hedge funds, private equity funds and their advisers*. Minesota: Thomson West.

Kaal, W. A. (2013). Hedge fund manager registration under the Dodd-Frank Act. *San Diego Law Review, 50*(2), 243–322.

Kelleher, D. M., Hall, S. W., & Medina, F. (2016). The Dodd-Frank Act is working and will protect the American people if it is not killed before fully implemented. *North Carolina Banking Institute, 20*(1), 127–144.

Keppo, J., & Korte, J. (2016). Risk targeting and policy illusions—Evidence from the announcement of the Volcker rule. *Management Science, 64*(1), 215–234. https://doi.org/10.1287/mnsc.2016.2583.

Kling, L. R. et al. (1996–1997). Negotiated acquisitions of companies, subsidiaries and divisions. *Miami University Law Review, 1*(51), 5–34.

Krainer, R. (2011). Regulating Wall Street: Dodd-Frank act and the new architecture of global finance. *Journal of Financial Stability, 8*(2), 121–133.

Labonte, M., Carpenter, D. H., Davis, C. M. et al. (2017). *The Financial Choice Act In 115th Congress: Selected policy issues*. Congressional Research Service. https://www.google.com/url?sa=t&rct=j&q=&esrc=s&source=web&cd=&ved=2ahUKEwicpZWql6rrAhVvhosKHTahBg0QFjAAegQIARAB&url=https%3A%2F%2Ffas.org%2Fsgp%2Fcrs%2Fmisc%2FR44839.pdf&usg=AOvVaw0smiFr3f8sSYh88r_WnJAN. Accessed 26 July 2020.

Lee, P. (2017). *The CHOICE Act is a bad choice for financial reform, the CLS blue sky blog: Columbia Law School's blog on corporations and the capital markets*. https://clsbluesky.law.columbia.edu/2017/04/12/the-choice-act-is-a-bad-choice-for-financial-reform/. Accessed 18 July 2020.

Lessambo, F. I. (2020). Bank bankruptcy. In *The U.S. banking system: Laws, regulations, and risk management* (pp. 297–315). London: Palgrave Macmillan. https://doi.org/10.1007/978-3-030-34792-5.

Lothian, T. (2017). *Law and the wealth of nations. Finance, prosperity, and democracy*. New York: Columbia University Press.

Magaldi, J., & Girasa, R. (2019). Reforming Dodd-Frank: Is the financial choice act or any subsequent act proposed—The right choice in this political environment? *North East Journal of Legal Studies, 38*, 70–102.

McCahery, J. F., & de Roode, A. (2019). The lost decade for hedge funds: Three threats, financing, hedge funds, investment decisions, management, performance. In D. Cumming, G. Wood, & S. Johan (Eds.). *Oxford handbook of hedge funds* (pp. 1–41). Series number: 486/2019. Oxford: Oxford University Press.

McMahon, K. (2018). The Financial Banking Institute Act and the Financial CHOICE Act: The wrong choice for the American economy. *Journal of Business & Technology Law, 14*(1), 107–133.

Meyerson, L., Chorazak, M., Sloan, S., & Thacher, S. (2017). *Treasury Department Issues Recommendations on Reforming the U.S. Financial System*. https://corpgov.law.harvard.edu/2017/06/23/treasury-department-issues-recommendations-on-reforming-the-u-s-financial-system/. Accessed 18 July 2020.

Mixon, S. (2018). Research issues in commodities and commodity derivatives. In H. K. Baker, G. Filbeck, & J. H. Harris (Eds.), *Commodities: Markets, performance, and strategies* (pp. 534–554). New York: Oxford University Press.

Mixon, S., & Onur, E. (2020). *Risk appetite and intermediation by swap dealers*. https://www.cftc.gov/sites/default/files/2020-04/MIxon%20Onur%20Risk%20Appetite%20(2020)%20-%20ada.pdf. Accessed 18 July 2020.

Murray, I. (2015). *How Dodd–Frank Harms Main Street*. https://cei.org/content/how-dodd-frank-harms-main-street. Accessed 21 July 2020.

Murray, I. (2017). *Rethinking the Consumer Financial Protection Bureau*. Competitive Enterprise Institute. https://cei.org/shrinkinggov/cfpb. Accessed 16 June 2020.

Nat'l Regulatory Servs. & Inv. Advisers Ass'n (2007). *Evolution Revolution Report 4*. http://www.investmentadviser.org/public/evolution_revolution-2007.pdf. Accessed 21 July 2020.

Neiman, R. H., & Olson, M. (2014). *Dodd-Frank's missed opportunity: A road map for a more effective regulatory architecture*. Washington: Bipartisan Policy Center. http://bipartisanpolicy.org/wp-content/uploads/2014/12/BPC-FRRI-Dodd-Franks-Missed-Opportunity-April-2014.pdf#page=60. Accessed 27 June 2020.

Norbert, J. M. (2016, December 19). Six recommendations for the CHOICE Act 2.0. *Heritage Found*. https://www.heritage.org/report/six-recommendations-the-choice-act-20. Accessed 4 May 2020.

Ojo, M. (2012). *Harmonising Basel III and the Dodd Frank Act through greater collaboration between standard setters and national supervisors*. http://mpra.ub.uni-muenchen.de/36164/MPRA. Accessed 21 July 2020.

Omarova, S. T. (2011a). Wall Street as community of fate: Toward financial industry self-regulation. *University of Pennsylvania Law Review, 159*, 411–492.

Omarova, S. T. (2011b). The Dodd-Frank Act: A new deal for a new age? *North Carolina Banking Institute, 15*, 83–98.

Onorato, M., & Symeonidou, G. (2011). *Dodd-Frank Act Wall Street Reform and Consumer Protection Act: Business model implications*. Toronto: Algorithmics Trademarks LLC & Algorithmics Software LLC.

Or, A. (2010, October 20). Front point managers take back majority stake from Morgan Stanley. *Wall Street Journal Online*. http://online.wsj.com/article/SB10001424052702304011604575564221698158651.html. Accessed 15 June 2020.

Ordoñez, G. (2018). Sustainable shadow banking. *American Economic Journal: Macroeconomics, 10*(1), 33–56. https://doi.org/10.1257/mac.20150346.

Pacini, C., Paterson, J., & Ghahramani, S. (2011). The uncertain liability of accountants and other professionals in securities fraud cases: The shifting sands of Central Bank. *Journal of Forensic and Investigative Accounting, 3*(3), 46–67.

Pasanisi, J. (2018). Revamping the Volcker rule. *International Financial Law Review*. https://www.iflr.com/article/b1lp1td3cg2hfb/revamping-the-volcker-rule. Accessed 3 May 2020.

Peirce, H., & Broughel, J. (Eds.) (2012). *Dodd-Frank: What it does and why it's flawed*. Arlington: The Mercatus Center.

PHH Corp. v. Consumer Fin. Prot. Bureau, 881 F.3d 75, 110 (D.C. Cir. 2018).

Restrepo, F. (2020). *Hedge fund regulation, performance, and risk-taking: Re-examining the effect of the Dodd-Frank Act*. http://dx.doi.org/10.2139/ssrn.3541916. Accessed 8 July 2020.

Ricks, M. (2019). *Guarantor of last resort: Is there a better alternative?* Vanderbilt Law School Faculty Publications. https://scholarship.law.vanderbilt.edu/faculty-publications/1109. Accessed 12 June 2020.

Ritter, J. (1991). The long-run performance of initial public offerings. *Journal of Finance, 46*, 3–27.
Rosenblum, R. H. (2003). *Investment company determination under the 1940 Act: Exemptions and exceptions* (2nd ed.). Chicago: ABA Publishing.
Sandbu, M. (2015). *Europe's orphan. The future of the Euro and the politics of debt*. Princeton: Princeton University Press.
SEC. (2010). *Exemptions for advisers to venture capital funds, private fund advisers with less than $150 million in assets under management, and foreign private advisers*. Securities and Exchange Commission. http://www.sec.gov/rules/final/2011/ia-3222.pdf. Accessed 12 March 2020.
SEC v. Capital Gains Research Bureau, Inc., 375 U.S. 180, 191 (1963).
Sec. Act Release no 6389, Fed. Sec. L. Rep. (CCH) 83,106 (1982).
SEC v. Burton G. Friedlander, Civil Action No. 01 Civ. 4658 (S.D.N.Y.), Lit. Rel. No. 17021 (June 1, 2001).
Seligman, J. (2003). The New Uniform Securities Act. *Washington University Law Quarterly, 81*, 243–299.
Shelby, C. M. (2017). Closing the hedge fund loophole: The SEC as the primary regulator of systemic risk. *Boston College Law Review, 58*(2), 639–701.
Spangler, T., & Scholer, K. (2010). *A practitioner's guide to alternative investment funds* (2nd ed.). London: Sweet & Maxwell UK.
State Teachers Retirement Board v. Fluor Corp., 654 F.2d 843 (2d Cir. 1981).
Sterling, Th. F. (2004). *The Enron scandal*. New York: Nova Science Publishing.
Tandon, V. (2016). The Volcker rule: Clarifying the anti-evasion provision to facilitate compliance. *North Carolina Banking Institute, 20*(1), 385–411.
Taylor, C. (2018). The Dodd-Frank Death Knell. *Loyola University Chicago Law Journal, 49*, 655–668.
The White House. (2009). *Remarks of the President on Regulatory Reform*. http://www.whitehouse.gov/the_press_office/Remarks-of-the-President-on-Regulatory-Reform/. Accessed 4 June 2020.
Touche, Remnant & Company, SEC No-Action Letter (Aug. 27, 1984).
United States Congress. (2016, July 9). *The Dodd-Frank Act five years later: Are we more stable?* Hearing before the Committee on Financial Services. US House of Representatives. One Hundred Fourteenth Congress. First session.
Urska, V. (2017). Are the SEC's administrative law judges biased? An empirical investigation. *Washington Law Review, 92*(1), 315–370.
US Chamber of Commerce. (2018). *Consumer Financial Protection Bureau: Working towards Fundamental Reform, Center for Capital Markets Effectiveness*. https://www.google.com/url?sa=t&rct=j&q=&esrc=s&source=web&cd=&cad=rja&uact=8&ved=2ahUKEwivw8Xks6vrAhWRBGMBHQUIBwIQFjAAegQIBhAB&url=https%3A%2F%2Fwww.centerforcapitalmarkets.com%2Fresource%2Fworking-towards-fundamental-reform%2F&usg=AOvVaw3cuJWWqM8EZCLAsYfmGS1q. Accessed 17 June 2020.

Vasavada, N. (2010). *Taxation of US Investment partnerships and hedge funds: Accounting policies*. Hoboken, NJ: Wiley Publisher.

Vladimer, G. V., Manvelidze, R., & Manvelidze, L. (2019, April 29–30). Big financial crisis: Analysis, assessment. In A. L. da Silva, D. Tomic, & A. Grilec (Eds.), *Book of Abstracts of the 39th International Scientific Conference on Economic and Social Development—Sustainability from an Economic and Social Perspective*. Lisbon.

Wilmarth, A. E. (2011). The Dodd-Frank Act: A flawed and inadequate response to the too big to fail problem. *Oregon Law Review*, 87, 951–1058.

Wyatt, M. (2015, May 13). *Speech by Acting Director, Office of Compliance, Inspections, and Examinations: Private equity: A look back and a glimpse ahead*. New York.

CHAPTER 7

Litigation and Arbitration Regarding Hedge Funds

7.1 Introduction

Besides the prosecution of major fraud and insider trading schemes, including the Madoff, Stanford, and Petters cases, there has been a wave of litigation and arbitration cases filed against hedge fund managers in the aftermath of the financial crisis. Still, in the light of the new regulatory enforcements after the 2007–2008 crisis, such cases have turned currently rather rare than in the previous years, and definitely not as sound as they used to be. Indeed, nearly a decade ago, litigation and arbitration cases with regard to hedge funds regularly featured in the legal press,[1] astonishing the global community[2] and illustrating the lack of investor protection. These cases represented evidence that hedge funds investors needed more protection. They related to a diverse range of problems, as described below. For instance, in a process taken to court from the initiative of several funds versus a firm from Germany, it was concluded by the SDNY,[3] according to "the Exchange Act," respectively,

[1] Richards, T. (2008). The growth of third party funding. *CMS Dispute Resolution Newsletter*. www.cmslegal.com. Accessed 6 March 2012.

[2] Williams, G. (2012). *Trust but verify: Fraud in Victorian banking and its diminishment*. http://ssrn.com/abstract=1983633. Accessed 1 May 2012.

[3] Southern District of New York.

A. M. Fagetan, *The Regulation of Hedge Funds*,
https://doi.org/10.1007/978-3-030-63706-4_7

Section 10(b), that this has no intention of changing agreements referring to foreign accumulates. Another example is given by the "*Financial Industry Regulatory Authority*" (FINRA) legal procedure declaration versus Goldman Sachs concerning its failure to perform the analysis of its hedge fund client's cheat. Similarly, disputes arose between top broker Morgan Stanley and a hedge fund concerning a trading account limit condition that determined the failure of the hedge fund. Meanwhile, the New York Appellate Division concluded that a hedge fund compliance agent tending to use the funds with no liability,[4] working in retaliation due to analyzing duplicity, does not have a national regulatory countermeasure. In addition, tribunals from Cayman Islands and from British Virgin Islands, too, have concluded several cases referring to the equities of hedge fund stockholders who petitioned for bankruptcy.

Besides the well-known Madoff case, a similar case in dimension and scale can be seen with the scheme of Tom Petters, the architect of a USD 3.7 billion, ten-year deceit that was discovered in September 2008. A similar situation is that of Robert Allen Stanford, whose scheme emerged in February 2009 and is thought to have lasted ten years, involving the enormous amount of USD 8 billion, and S. Rothstein, who admitted to managing an approximate USD 1.2 billion Ponzi scheme at the end of 2009.[5]

The question arises as to why these unprecedented legal actions have occurred at this time. This chapter demonstrates exactly how the financial crisis effectively exhibited the vulnerabilities as expected for the traditional hedge funds pattern.[6] After almost a decade of prodigious, yet unbelievable development, major hedge funds seem now very passive and even damaged by litigation and arbitration. In fact, some hedge funds are entirely vanishing. Therefore, this chapter focuses on the *conflicts of interest* faced by hedge fund managers and the *regulatory measures* necessary to better protect hedge fund investors. This chapter provides

[4] At-will.

[5] In a Ponzi project, existing investors are rewarded with purported returns out of the funds that new investors add as a contribution. "Ponzi schemes tend to crash when it is hard to find new investors or when a great number of stockholders ask to cash out" (US SEC 2010).

[6] Cox, E. J. (2009). An economic crisis is a terrible thing to waste: Reforming the business of law for a sustainable and competitive future. *UCLA Law Review, 57,* 511–551, p. 512.

general background information about litigation and arbitration cases of hedge funds in the aftermath of the financial crisis up to the present date. Then it discusses the numerous conflicts of interest inherent in the hedge funds management, and makes the case that hedge fund investors were poorly protected from the injurious effects of these conflicts by both state and federal law. The conclusions of this chapter present, from the author's opinion, different proposals for mitigating and preventing conflicts of interest in hedge funds and therefore, recommend how hedge fund investors can be better protected from these cases and other risks they are exposed to.

In the aftermath of the financial crisis, many investments were lost due to hedge fund frauds. This has nourished important contradictory debates about whether authorities are able or not to control the hedge funds market. Negative associations and accusations used to be made concerning hedge funds, particularly concerning Bernie Madoff,[7] the "Ponzi scheme" accusation,[8] accusations of hedge fund "gambling,"[9] and other accusations of "manipulating markets."[10] Other accusations

[7] CONG. REC. S1654 (daily ed. Feb. 5, 2009) (statement of Sen. Schumer) ("I have a hedge fund I would like you to invest in called Madoff Securities, LLC").

[8] CONG. REC. H145 (daily ed. Jan. 9, 2009) (statement of Rep. Kucinich) ("We also have to address the issue of the fractional reserve system, which is how banks create money out of thin air. And then, as they do that, they've created the conditions where we've had this kind of Ponzi scheme collapsing, banks and the hedge funds working together").

[9] CONG. REC. S6054 (daily ed. July 21, 2010) (statement of Sen. Sanders) ("Do you remember those hedge fund managers on Wall Street who made $1 billion a year or several billion a year? They are going to benefit. Those are the guys—the people who drove us into the recession, who made huge amounts of money gambling on Wall Street").

[10] CONG. REC. S3359 (daily ed. Mar. 18, 2009) (statement of Sen. Harkin) (referring to Americans' view of "hedge fund hotshots" as manipulating markets and becoming further prosperous as a result).

concerned massive tax avoidance,[11] bankrupting Chrysler due to insisting on their rights as secured creditors[12] and the list can continue.

The hereby chapter presents several performance notices, which would be set on abnormal incomes generated by funds, as these are markers in terms of fraudulent risks-exposure from that period. Several cases of hedge funds being charged with violating the law are collected, but also studied over the course of this chapter, in view of the idea that regulation carries with it an implicit promise that laws are being enforced and at the same time, law breaches can be detected, because if this were not true, a misleading safety feeling could be indulged to investors.[13]

This chapter also addresses some of the main legal aspects involved in the extensive round of hedge fund litigation that is currently underway, namely, lawsuits—brought by one or more plaintiffs on behalf of a large group on a common legal claim. The author highlights in this chapter several probably major categories in the resolution of these cases:

- The differentiation of feasible *ex ante* presumptions, and active development concerning *ex post* profit losses;
- The differentiation of complete openness concerning the description of all underlying securities which are under securitization, but at the same time the openness to which industry members are being subjected regarding hedge funds profit losses;
- The differentiation between aspects apprehended by investors and industry members and things apprehended by particular corporations from inside the organized investment activity.

Similar to any debate on the future of hedge funds facing uncertainty as a result of the crisis and concerns about the effects of the Madoff fraud,

[11] CONG. REC. S8987 (daily ed. Dec. 14, 2010) (statement of Sen. Harkin) ("Another 33 for-profit education companies operating 65 more for-profit schools are at least partially owned by private equity investors or hedge funds. The result is that the vast majority of for-profit schools have prioritized growth over education in order to satisfy the demands of their investors").

[12] CONG. REC. H5047 (daily ed. Apr. 30, 2009) (statement of Rep. Miller) ("[B]ankruptcy will now be required only because of the greed of a few Wall Street hedge funds that held a portion of Chrysler's debt").

[13] Bollen, N. (2011). Suspicious patterns in hedge fund returns and the risk of fraud. *Review of Financial Studies, 25*(9), 1–43. https://doi.org/10.2139/ssrn.1569626.

this chapter discusses recent significant litigation cases brought to the courts of justice or to arbitration. Past stories such as Stanford, Petters, and Madoff can be labelled as not typical, due to the size of their collapse or due to the level of malfeasance connected with the fraud, but, however, the author considers that they help illustrating the reason why both regulators and supervisors are currently paying greater attention to hedge fund industry regulation and protection of investors.

7.2 Civil Litigation

7.2.1 Previously Reported Cases

This sub-section provides an update of the civil arbitration and litigation cases and highlights the cases of civil litigations, focusing also on enforcement processes related, particularly, to hedge funds industry. The main purpose is to present and analyze risks of investors induced by the absence of hedge funds regulation in the United States until the Dodd–Frank Act. Regarding the first case, it has been noted that tribunals largely used *Morrison*[14] *Company* as a "steamroller"[15] to include derivative securities referencing foreign assets.[16] The next presentation uses at first two cases of exploring the high disorientation following "the *Morrison* holding." Hence, the file regarding *Elliott Associates fund against Porsche Company* will be presented. This involves one agreement to swap concerning foreign assets. Furthermore, a similar case will be analyzed, consisting of the SEC against F. Tourre.[17] These two cases are important in revealing the limitations of the international regulatory frameworks at the global level,[18] and therefore the limitations regarding investors' protection before the enactment of the Dodd–Frank.

[14] U.S. 247 (2010).

[15] Bartlett, R., Cain, M. D., Fisch, J. E., & Davidoff, S. S. (2019). The myth of Morrison: Securities fraud litigation against foreign issuers. Faculty Scholarship at Penn Law. https://scholarship.law.upenn.edu/faculty_scholarship/2025. Accessed 29 July 2020.

[16] Idem.

[17] A former Goldman Sachs executive.

[18] Buxbaum, H. L. (2012a). Remedies for foreign investors under US federal securities law. *Law and Contemporary Problems, 75,* 161–186.

Section 10(b) does not apply for swap agreements regarding Foreign Securities, and here one can mention the case file of Elliott Associates against Porsche.[19] The complainants from Elliott involve several types of hedge funds—a part of them being structured according to American regulations, while others are organized according to non-US regulations. However, these have one thing in common: they are managed by administrators whose location is New York. These entered in agreements to swap concerning assets value of "Volkswagen" multinational from Germany. The litigant is represented by "Porsche," another multinational from Germany.

In the spring of 2010, an association of hedge funds brought legal charges in New York, more precisely in its Southern District against Porsche, alleging that it hid their real intention to buy VW, also arguing that its adoption in calculating exchanges aimed at hiding its correct stock standing was illegal. In compliance with hedge funds, most of them being retailers in VW stock, several misstatements were made, and also several laws were breached by Porsche, namely: Section 10(b),[20] as well as Rule 10b-5.[21] This determined the hedge funds to be deprived of more than USD 2 billion in protecting their own short sales.[22] Complainants lost more than USD 2 billion the very moment when suspects brought about the so-called massive short squeeze, according to Reuters, but also "a short squeeze" having outstanding dimensions, according to New York Times.[23] Subsequently to the amendment of this accusation of funds, according to the decision of the Supreme Court's agreement in the file conducted by *Morrison against NAB*,[24] Porsche attempted to dismiss the legal suit claiming mainly that the deceit dispositions in accordance

[19] Elliott Associates et al. (2010). Subcommittee Memorandum. Elliott Associates, L. P., et al. v. Porsche Automobil Holding SE, f/k/a Dr. Ing. h.c. F. Porsche A.G.

[20] Of the Exchange Act.

[21] Elliott Associates, L.P., et al. v. Porsche Automobil Holding SE, f/k/a Dr. Ing. h.c. F. Porsche A.G.; Black Diamond Offshore Ltd., et al., v. Porsche Automobil Holding SE, f/k/a Dr. Ing. h.c. F. Porsche AG; Wendelin Wiedeking; and Holger P. Haerter, Nos. 10 CV 0532 and 10 CV 4155 (S.D.N.Y. Dec. 30, 2010).

[22] Ibid.

[23] Rocker Mgmt., L.L.C. v. Lernout & Hauspie Speech Prods. N.V., No. 00-5965 (JCL), 2005 WL 1365465, at *2 n.5 (D.N.J. June 7, 2005).

[24] National Australia Bank -130 S. Ct. 2869 (2010).

with Section 10(b) was by no means available for securities undertakings that were not catalogued according to the American trades. Because most assets were held by the state or by different index funds, individuals who were short selling had "to close their positions at hugely inflated prices,"[25] which tripled VW's share prices. This turned VW into one of the biggest corporations at the global level, according to the estimation of the business shares. The severe liquidity impact emerged although the industry for "Volkswagen" shares proves usually highly productive.

Toward the end of December 2010, every hedge fund-related complaint registered in the Southern District of N.Y. was rejected.[26] The court of law declared that *Morrison* had put a limit to exchanges of securities according to Section 10(b)[27] catalogued on internal transactions and to internal exchanges in different securities. The funds were involved in domestic securities based on change settlements, which highly credited foreign VW capital.[28] Accordingly, VW denied their implication within internal exchanges in other securities, claiming to have done this only according to the aim of Section 10(b). Nevertheless, the tribunal discovered how change settlements have been the functional equal[29] to exchanging all implicit Volkswagen dividends within the Germanic stock and declared that it was revoltingly creating laws, which could cause the falling of external issuers not closely connected with America under their scope and thus their involvement in lawsuits for the simple fact that autonomous parties from that state signed a securities agreement regarding the foreign capital of the respective institution.[30] Pursuant to this, funds petitioned a Second Circuit at the very beginning of 2011.

[25] Korsmo, Ch. R. (2011). Mismatch: The misuse of market efficiency in market manipulation class actions. Faculty Publications, 61. https://scholarlycommons.law.case.edu/faculty_publications/61. Accessed 20 July 2020.

[26] Tatcher, S. (2011). Securities Law Alert, the Southern District of New York Dismisses Securities Fraud Actions against Porsche, Finding that Section 10(b) does not Protect Swap Agreements Referencing Foreign Securities. Securities Law Alert, p. 1. https://www.stblaw.com/docs/default-source/cold-fusion-existing-content/publications/pub1109.pdf?sfvrsn=2. Accessed 28 September 2020.

[27] Elliott Associates, L.P. Op, Cit., p. 8.

[28] Ibid.

[29] 130 S. Ct. 2869 (2010).

[30] Korsmo, Ch. R. (2011). Op. Cit.

It has been remarked that a major interrogation which emerges as a consequence of Porsche's reached resolution refers to the fact whether this predicts one tendency toward broadening the Morrison case above its initial objective. If this proves to be true, all funds having to do with the stock of a foreign issuing institution, or just signing financial agreements referencing the stock of a foreign issuing institution—are going to encounter no securities fraud remedies in the American tribunals. The real issues revealed by Elliott law case show that the so-called bright line test that Morrison fixed, might prove all-encompassing, allowing American regulation application within apparently absurd contexts.[31] Thus, courts might carefully take into consideration making attractive or acceptable "the bright-line test" through sustained efforts for a sensitive test use. Therefore, similar consequences are expected: rapid growth "of vaguely related variations on the test,"[32] which was harshly disapproved by the "Supreme Court" being considered one failure of the "old conduct and effects tests." In this case, political interests in diplomacy and accordingly, dispute avoidance, compete with political interests favoring the achievement of certainty and transparency of American regulations. All in all, it becomes clear that such failures are both unfair and inconsistent in terms of investor protection aim of the US securities laws. In this respect, the European Commission "strongly urge[d] ... against" a cross-border extension of Section 10(b), stated that an "extraterritorial application of the antifraud provisions of the United States' securities laws ... where the nexus is stronger with a foreign jurisdiction [] is liable to violate the EU's and its Member States' sovereignty, and to impede the proper development of [the] EU's securities regulation."[33] This point was supported by several comment letters which also noted that other jurisdictions offer investor protection that can be compared to the level of

[31] SEC versus Compania International Financiera S.A., no 11 Civ. 4904(DLC), 2011 WL 3251813 (S.D.N.Y. July 29, 2011).

[32] Morrison, 130 S. Ct. at 2880.

[33] SEC. (2012a). Study on the Cross-Border Scope of the Private Right of Action Under Section 10(b) of the Securities Exchange Act of 1934 As Required by Section 929Y of the Dodd-Frank Wall Street Reform and Consumer Protection Act. Securities and Exchange Commission (SEC). http://www.sec.gov/news/studies/2012/929y-study-cross-border-private-rights.pdf. Accessed 11 July 2013.

investor protection provided by the US securities laws.[34] A common argument advanced supporting the enactment of the conduct and effecting tests for Section 10(b) private actions is that this action could increase investor protection due to stronger enforcement of the federal securities laws.

Therefore, as seen above, the high pressures placed by liquidity and price will be probably more appreciated within markets that are less efficient than in those with increased performance indicators.[35] Bayou and Goldman Sachs have proved to be highly negative hedge fund misconduct examples, especially considering the great losses the investors were subjected to, and also the period and goal of the fraud.

7.2.2 Old Developments in Securities Litigation

Starting with the spring of 2010, many signs of litigations to come could be seen. First, the crisis filings were rejected, while around 1/2 of the decisions to date were motions to dismiss. Nevertheless, it is obvious that not only accusations but also products and defendants keep on changing, while lawsuits against particular accused litigants, among which one can mention especially those involving mainly CRAs,[36] successfully survived some motions for dismissal and will continue to do so. In addition, the current cases brought by the SEC increase insecurity regarding future directions, but also central points of the litigation.[37]

SEC v. Goldman Sachs & Co. They say about hedge funds that they used to be important buyers not only of Collateralised Debt Obligations, but also of CDO tranches[38] with subprime exposure. In this section, the author of this book identifies the major issues occurring due to the overestimation of investment tools like CDOs and "*Residential Mortgage-Backed Securities*" (RMBSs) which are considered to have

[34] See, for instance, letters from Government of France; Australian Government; Government of Switzerland; Canadian Bar Association.

[35] Aggarwal, K. A., & Wu, G. (2006). Stock market manipulations. *The Journal of Business, 79*(4), 1915–1954. https://doi.org/10.1086/503652.

[36] Credit Rating Agencies.

[37] Ibid., at 934.

[38] Bethel, J. E., Ferrell, A., & Hu, G. (2008). Law and economic issues in subprime litigation. Discussion Paper No. 612, 03/2008. Harvard Law School Cambridge. http://www.law.harvard.edu/programs/olin_center/. Accessed 29 July 2020, p. 28.

significantly contributed to the international economic crisis. According to data supplied by public area, the author of this book also explores the manners in which investment banks used to manage their assets, considered mainly the estimation of investment tools and whether there has been any conflict of interest in their study, this involving a conflict emerged from the banks' interests and those of their investors. The author analyses as paradigm case the context resulting from an unrelated US case regarding civil proceedings, respectively, Goldman Sachs.

In 2006, Goldman Sachs & Co. was the 4th most important Collateralised Debt Obligation contributor in America, pledging securities and investments equivalent to USD 16 billion. After Goldman Sachs became conscious of an important decrease in value of RMBS assets, it started to acquire short positions in order to gain advantage. Goldman Sachs was essentially hoping for the decline of RMBS industry. However, according to the American SEC, he kept on advertising, as well as selling CDOs.

During the same period, the SEC registered one civil implementation action within Unites States District Court for the SDNY[39] versus Goldman Sachs, but also versus one manager, F. Tourre, who confessed an undisclosed short interest. The SEC's complaint referred to the fact that at the end of 2004 and the commencement of 2005, Goldman Sachs delivered a correlation-trading portfolio, providing, among other things, the manufacture and marketing[40] of synthetic CDO generally known by the name of ABACUS.

It seems that the so-called Abacus 2007-AC1 was a financial tool made to fit precisely Paulson, an intimate organizational customer.[41] Starting with 2006, Paulson & Co, Inc. (hedge fund) changed its investment technique because they believed that some "mid-and-subprime RMBS rated Triple B",[42] namely debts at the supposed value BBB by Standard & Poor's or, according to the rating of Moody—Baa2, might be exposed to negative circumstances causing the significant fall of their value. In reality, Paulson considered that not just secondary place RMBSs, but also more senior AAA-rated tranches, could turn worthless. Paulson aimed

[39] Southern District of New York.

[40] Litigation, "SEC v Goldman Sachs & Co., US District Court for the SDNY", 10-cv-3229 (BSJ), 16 April 2010 ("SEC Complaint"), p 10.

[41] The manager of Paulson & Company. Schrieber, A. (2010b). The Investment Bank Job. The Kenan Institute for Ethics. Duke University, p. 2.

[42] Litigation, SEC v Goldman Sachs & Co., 2010, at 12.

at several RMBSs triple-B rated,[43] considering them as encountering significant difficulties. After that, Paulson discussed with Goldman Sachs and asked them to help it ensure safety by means of payment, through CDSs, by shorting an investment portfolio containing these RMBSs in an advantageous manner.[44]

The SEC stated that Paulson, assisted by Goldman Sachs, produced a synthetic CDO,[45] which included a portfolio of assets chosen by Paulson that Goldman Sachs could advertise to stockholders.

The SEC Complaint provided a number of examples of Goldman Sachs' data on the diminishing trend of the CDO market from 2007,[46] when they had a discussion with Paulson.[47] For instance, the SEC prepared for testimony an email from the litigant Tourre to a friend written on the January 23, 2007, in which Tourre confessed that due to the highly leveraged system, there was an imminent crash risk of the entire foundation at any moment.[48]

With that piece of information at hand, SEC affirmed that both Goldman Sachs and Tourre started to prepare the concealment of the fact that the short investor, Paulson, took part in this data hiding from other investors by saying that a professional, but also autonomous collateral manager from third-party selected those credit portfolios.[49] Goldman Sachs discussed ACA—a director they allegedly thought would consent to the choices of Paulson—to help as the "Portfolio Selection Agent."[50] ACA's part was of major relevance to the advertising and delivery of this CDO.

In the meantime, Paulson managed a verification of triple-B RMBSs. This verification was for the benefit of RMBS. It involved elevated scores

[43] Ibid., at 15.

[44] Ibid., at 15–16.

[45] Field, A. (2011). Deconstructing Goldman Sachs's Fraud Defense, apud Buell, S. W. (2011). What is securities fraud? *Duke Law Journal, 61*(3), 511–582.

[46] Gallu, J., & Harper, Ch. (2010, April 16). Goldman shares tumble on SEC fraud allegations. *Bloomberg News*.

[47] Calamari, A. M., et al. (2010). *United States. Securities and Exchange Commission v. Goldman Sachs & Co., and Fabrice Tourre Securities Fraud Complaint*. DC: US District Court, SDNY.

[48] Ibid.

[49] Litigation, SEC v Goldman Sachs & Co., 2010, at 19.

[50] Ibid., at 21–22.

of "rate mortgages, low borrower FICO scores, and a high concentration of mortgages"[51] in countries with high growth rates of houses value. On January 9, 2007, an amount of 123 RMBSs emerging from Paulson's verification were e-mailed to ACA, to be studied.[52] On February 26, 2007, Paulson and ACA consented to a citations portfolio of 90 RMBSs for ABACUS 2007-AC, which was made up mostly of Paulson's choices. The SEC has confirmed that ACA did not know of Paulson's intention to actually short that RMBS portfolio it was assisting.[53]

Thereafter, a few months after the managers at Goldman Sachs anticipated the decline of the RMBS market, a notice of almost 200 pages on ABACUS 2007-AC1[54] was finished. Paulson was not mentioned in this file. The SEC has affirmed that Goldman Sachs' advertising products used for ABACUS have been neither true, nor accurate.[55] The SEC further argued that during the organization of this business, Goldman Sachs made ACA falsely believe that Paulson planned to make investments in the fairness of ABACUS. This is very important because a fair play holder is the first to have a loss in case the portfolio fails. Thus, a fair play holder manifests the same permanent interest as other stockholders. In reality, on January 10, 2007 Tourre e-mailed ACA informing them that Paulson was an advocate of the *equity tranche*.[56]

During the organization phase of ABACUS 2007-AC1, both Goldman Sachs and Tourre started to search for investors. During the first four months of 2007, Goldman Sachs sent the bullet-point document, pictures book and offering reminder to IKB, a commercial bank having the headquarters in Dusseldorf. The SEC has declared that neither Goldman Sachs nor Tourre informed IKB of Paulson's role in the election activity of assets and its short position. Starting with the April 26, 2007, ABACUS 2007-AC1 was ended and bought "USD 50 million worth of Class A-1 notes

[51] Ibid., at 25.

[52] Fisher, J. Q. C., Cregan, C., Di Giulio, J., et al. (2011). Economic crime and the global financial crisis. *Law and Financial Markets Review*, *5*(4), 276–289. https://doi.org/10.5235/175214411796505642, p. 277.

[53] Ibid.

[54] Schrieber, A. (2010a). The US securities and exchange commission v. Goldman Sachs. Case Studies in Ethics at Duke University. http://ethics.iit.edu/eelibrary/node/7440. Accessed 29 August 2020.

[55] Litigation, SEC v Goldman Sachs & Co., 2010, at 36.

[56] Ibid., para. 47.

and USD 100 million worth of Class A-2 Notes,"[57] both rated in a similar way AAA by both S&P and Moody. In this regard, it has been stated that Goldman Sachs was expected to have the ability to acquire minimum USD 15 million and maximum USD 20 million[58] for organizing but also advertising ABACUS.

Both weak results "of ABACUS 2007-AC1" and consequent payout to Paulson are clear for all to see. IKB was effectively deprived of an investment comprising almost USD 150 million. Paulson received most of that invested amount, through successive transactions that Goldman Sachs and Paulson performed themselves. Around August 7, 2008, the RBS,[59] having bought the highest place in ABACUS 2007-AC1, offered Goldman Sachs an amount of USD 840 million to "separate its position." It is clear that a substantial money part went from Goldman Sachs to Paulson.[60]

The SEC litigation asserted in relevant part that [Goldman Sachs] as well as Tourre deliberately, riskily or maybe simply in a negligent manner mislead investors through material terms, presentation book and also through the memorandum offered regarding the ABACUS product, making them believe that it was ACA the one who selected that particular portfolio and omitting to mention that, in fact, Paulson held a major part in that selection. At the same time, the fund had strong financial interests in transactions, truly adverse not only to IKB, but also to ACA, as well as to ABN AMRO.[61] According to the same SEC litigation, [Goldman Sachs] as well as Tourre mislead ACA, persuading it about Paulson's investments "in the equity of ABACUS 2007-AC1,"[62] but also about the fact that the interest Paulson manifested in the collateral section activity was very similar to that of ACA. *De facto*, there was a *conflict of interests.*

[57] Schrieber, A. (2010). Op. Cit., p. 10.

[58] Schrieber, A. (2010). Op. Cit., p. 10.

[59] Royal Bank of Scotland.

[60] Ibid.

[61] Litigation, SEC v. Goldman Sachs & Co., 2010, para. 70.

[62] Ibid.

A week later, on April 27, 2010, after the registration of the SEC complaint, the Permanent Subcommittee on Investigations to the "Committee on Homeland Security and Governmental Affairs"[63] sustained several hearings examining several grounds, but also impacts of recent financial crisis.[64] The fourth section focused on the part of investment banks and moved around the attestation of a few head representatives from Goldman Sachs. The rumor came after the Subcommittee examined 18 months-worth of documents that Goldman Sachs and various organizations had acquired with particular reference to the RMBS market.[65]

In his declaration from the start, Senator Carl Levin depicted the results of the Subcommittee in connection with the operations of Goldman Sachs and various investment credit institutions. According to the proofs, most of the time, Goldman first took care of his own returns and incomes to the disadvantage of those of his customers. Similarly, his wrong use of glamorous but also complicated economic constructions contributed to the spreading of harmful mortgages all over the globe within the entire financial practices. What happened later was the rationale: global finances crashed due to the above-mentioned harmful mortgages. Obviously, Goldman took advantage of this. According to the company's data provided later to the SEC, it became clear that, although the Corporation used to sell risky derivates regarding mortgages, in the same manner it placed major confidence in this American industry.[66] The company continued to deny having taken significant bets despite all the proofs. The problem here is that Goldman misled their investors about the inexistence of any conflict of interest occurring between their company and the investors they had to counsel. The disputed aspect is

[63] Mitchell, M. (2010, April 20). Goldman Sachs, John Paulson, and the hedge funds that pumped and dumped our economy. *Deep Capture*. https://www.deepcapture.com/2010/04/goldman-sachs-john-paulson-and-the-hedge-funds-that-pumped-and-dumped-our-economy/. Accessed 29 July 2020.

[64] Subcommittee Memorandum, Elliott Associates, L.P., et al. v. Porsche Automobil Holding SE, f/k/a Dr. Ing. h.c. F. Porsche A.G.; Black Diamond Offshore Ltd., et al., v. Porsche Automobil Holding SE, f/k/a Dr. Ing. h.c. F. Porsche AG; Wendelin Wiedeking; and Holger P. Haerter, Nos. 10 CV 0532 and 10 CV 4155 (S.D.N.Y. Dec. 30, 2010).

[65] http://hsgac.senate.gov/public/index.cfm?FuseAction=Hearings.Hearing&Hearing_ID=f07ef2bf-914c-494c-aa66-27129f8e6282. Accessed 12 May 2012.

[66] Tuch, A. F. (2012). Conflicted gatekeepers: The Volcker rule and Goldman Sachs. *Virginia Law & Business Review*, 7(2), 365–420.

that whenever the investors were having financial problems, Goldman was doing well, while on the contrary, when their investors gained profit, Goldman was not. These realities reveal that Goldman's operations amounted to much more than being a simple market-marker, connecting buyers and sellers in a place. On this point, it has been noted that they acted as important speculations that the pledge securities industry, assisted at creating by Goldman, joined for an impressive comedown.[67]

On July 14, 2010, Goldman Sachs reached a concluding judgment.[68] Goldman Sachs offered USD 300 million in amends and USD 250 million as compensation to investors. IKB was declared to obtain USD 150 million while RBS was stated to obtain USD 100 million.[69] Moreover, while declaring that it neither recognized nor rejected the allegations of the complaint, Goldman affirmed that they were lacking data within those marketing products used for the ABACUS 2007-AC1 transaction. Most important, the biggest error consisted in the fact that those products stated that it was ACA who selected the portfolio, without mentioning Paulson's primordial function in its selection activity,[70] but also that Paulson's financial interest has been contrary to CDO investors. In the end, Goldman regretted the missing data from those staffs.

Goldman Sachs seems to have developed a market in CDOs, and then asked certain bonds for customers. Apparently, their customers could benefit from the trade failure, but also from the bankruptcy.[71] Thus,

[67] Litigation, SEC v Goldman Sachs & Co., 2010, para. 4.

[68] https://www.goldmansachs.com/investor-relations/financials/archived/8k/pdf-attachments/07-14-10-8k-doc.pdf. Accessed 22 May 2012.

[69] Gallu, J., & Scheer, D. (2010, July 21). SEC settlement with Goldman Sachs for USD 550 million approved by US judge. *Bloomberg*. www.bloomberg.com/news/2010-07-20/goldman-sachs-settlement-with-sec-for-550-million-approved-by-u-s-judge.html. Accessed 22 May 2012.

[70] Lehman Brothers Holdings Inc. (2010). Proceedings examiners report. Executive summary of the examiner's conclusions. https://www.worldcat.org/title/lehman-brothers-holdings-inc-chapter-11-proceedings-examiners-report/oclc/554260788. Accessed 22 May 2012.

[71] The Goldman PR made a statement saying that [Goldman] held no position within the organization, and that they were not "making markets in the company's bonds or credit-default swaps." This was however contradicted by Bloomberg news reports, according to which there existed emails that Goldman was transmitting to customers regarding these markets; in Paulden, P., & Harrington, S. D. (2009, December 17). Hoffa Says Goldman Sachs Driving YRC into Bankruptcy (Update1).

a major criticism is that CDO originators offered investors inadequate disclosure and warnings concerning different risks.

The SEC implementation operation against Goldman Sachs illustrates the problems faced by managers in resolving difficult securities transactions that involve a lot of groups and significant *conflicts of interest*. As a conclusion, in these cases, investors' interests are prejudiced by fund managers' conduct in the pursuit of their own interests at the fund investors' expense. In most cases, there was awareness among regulators regarding the risks beyond the regulatory perimeter and several steps should have been taken in order to address them by supporting self-regulatory approaches (for example, codes of conduct). Arguably, such behavior urges for the introduction of conduct of business regulation even in the context of unregulated funds. Any endeavor by the Department of Justice to register an identical complaint in a criminal operation would have encountered powerful resistance. That means it would have been claimed that Goldman Sachs lacked the intention to defraud IKB or other stockholders. On the other hand, the civil action caused indeed a settlement.

This represents an issue whose implicit meaning consists of the fact that the place where the location of transactions of investments is connected to the place of occurrence of the final agreement/settlement. This last act provides legal responsibility[72] for buying and selling. However, the parties are able to manipulate this.

One way to understanding the aspect presented above can be considered like a continuation of the principle according to which parts involved in the transactions of securities can employ forum clause and stipulations from the regulation for selecting the policy that will govern the transaction.[73] Nevertheless, the above-mentioned approach worked in a very restrictive manner.

Bloomberg News. http://www.bloomberg.com/apps/news?pid=20601087&sid=apCmuH.AP.VA. Accessed 12 July 2020.

[72] Paulden, P., et al. (2010). Op. Cit., for instance, Cascade, 2011 WL 1211511, 130 S. Ct. 2869 (2010).

[73] In, for instance, Richards v. Lloyd's of London, 135 F.3d 1289 (9th Cir. 1998); Roby v. Corp. of Lloyd's, 996 F.2d 1353 (2d Cir. 1993); Bonny v. Soc'y of Lloyd's, 3 F.3d 156 (7th Cir. 1993). They are largely discussed in Buxbaum, H. L. (2012b). Conflict of economic laws: From sovereignty to substance. *Vancouver Journal of International Law, 42*, 931–977.

Several issues were noticed in this regard. First, this was not broadened largely after the Lloyds case studies, which involved investing individuals who were truly experienced professionals. Then, the regulation selected for the above-mentioned cases seemed particularly similar to the US anti-fraud regulation.[74] Likewise, it has been stated that probably the courts would have been made no enforcement on those particular stipulations and that no removal of those claims would have been made from the attention and apprehension of the US regulation if the discussed foreign regulations were not so similar.[75] However, these provisions represent a consequence of a definite settlement,[76] the mediation of which needs to offer clearness, but also fairness. The ongoing perspective is that every individual selling stocks may easily locate himself/herself in other location than the United States while officially accepting, but also avoiding, being subjected to the US regulation.[77] In this regard, it has been noted that acting in such manner means not only being manipulative, but might as well signify being confusing for the other party. The allowance of determining the relevance of US regulation can thus withdraw some exchanges by protecting that particular regulation in the lack of protective stipulations usually attending "the contractual exercise of party autonomy."[78] Several measures were taken after this scandal. If implemented properly, they could restore investor confidence and prompt a new wave of primary issuances. For instance, Dodd–Frank Act recently resolved an issue concerning the necessity to inform investors and disclose information to them. Thus, Title IX, Subtitle D requires the SEC to pass disclosure requirements for asset-backed securities, including CDOs.

[74] Buxbaum, H. L. (2012). Op. Cit., p. 173.

[75] In, for instance "Bonny, 3 F.3d at 162" (focusing on the accessibility of remedies under British regulation that are not offending the policies regarding American securities regulations).

[76] In M/S Bremen v. Zapata Off-Shore Co., 407 US 1, 12 (1972).

[77] Buxbaum, H. L. (2012). Op. Cit., p. 173.

[78] Ibid.

7.2.3 *Recent Developments in Civil Litigations*

Among the new developments in securities litigations, two Citigroup affiliates can be mentioned,[79] who have agreed to pay USD 180 million to injured investors after reaching an agreement with the SEC. The SEC investigation and settlement established that Citigroup concealed problems at two of its hedge funds, the ASTA/MAT and Falcon Strategies funds, during the financial crisis. As a consequence, almost 4000 investors deposited about USD 3 billion in the funds, which Citigroup allegedly sold as a safe investment alternative to bonds. Plaintiffs had alleged the funds were actually highly leveraged, complex, and troubled. At first, Citigroup contested this stating that all the statements it made in its prospectuses were accurate. On August 17, 2015, the SEC accepted the settlement in which Citigroup did not admit wrongdoing.[80]

Citigroup also agreed to a settlement of USD 13.5 million in civil litigation involving its Corporate Special Opportunities fund. A group of investors brought a class action alleging that Citigroup:

1. induced investors to stay with the troubled fund through false assurances that the fund was "fundamentally sound,"
2. failed to disclose risky debt, and
3. failed to accurately represent risk controls just weeks before the fund's collapse during the financial crisis.

Citigroup responded that they were not in a direct contractual relationship with plaintiffs and that no specific false statements were identified. The fund, which primarily backed European private equity deals, was liquidated in 2008 due to the financial crisis and the fund's leverage. On August 10, 2015 documents reflecting the settlement were filed and the Southern District of New York has preliminarily approved the settlement.[81] The SEC announced on July 12, 2016 that Citigroup "has agreed to pay a USD 7 million penalty and admit wrongdoing to settle charges that a computer coding error caused the firm to provide

[79] Citigroup Global Markets Inc. and Citigroup Alternative Investments LLC.

[80] Citigroup Alternative Investments LLC and Citigroup Global Markets Inc., SEC Admin. Proc. No. 3-16757, 4 (Aug. 17, 2015).

[81] Beach et al. v. Citigroup Alternative Investments LLC et al., No. 1:12-cv-07717 (S.D.N.Y. Aug. 19, 2015).

the agency with incomplete "blue sheet" information about trades it executed."[82]

Further on, this chapter presents several Ponzi schemes. Some of these schemes imply the study of SEC's motivation policy failure to encourage thorough examinations of possible securities fraud. Also, the chapter analyses whether previous SEC employees currently working as independent professionals standing for customers investigated by the SEC induce excessive pressure on present SEC employees while solving litigations falling under the breach of securities regulation.[83]

7.3 Regulatory Enforcement

7.3.1 Developments in Ponzi Schemes Litigation

Investment fraud comprises every type of action taken with the purpose of getting some financial profit from investors by using deceit.[84] These types of frauds may be uncomplicated (for instance, the total stealing, when investors do not recover their money), or on the contrary, complicated schemes (for instance, Ponzi frauds). Similarly, these corporations may also act as governed either by the rule or principle or law, or not, capable also of taking various statutory shapes, starting from "joint stock companies to hedge funds or simple pools of assets."[85]

Prior to approaching the Thomas Petters, Robert Allen Stanford, and Bernie Madoff's schemes, it is important to understand first the Ponzi scheme concept. A Ponzi scheme represents mainly an illicit financial investment scheme where people who invest receive payment of their interests from the investments that new investors are making.[86] Regarding

[82] SEC. (2016). Press Release No. 2016-138. SEC: Citigroup Provided Incomplete Blue Sheet Data for 15 Years. Securities and Exchange Commission (SEC). https://www.sec.gov/news/pressrelease/2016-138.html. Accessed 22 July 2020. See also Winship, V., & Robbennolt, J. K. (2018). An empirical study of admissions in SEC settlements. *Arizona Law Review, 60,* 1–51.

[83] Perri, F. S., & Brody, R. G. (2011). The sleeping watch dog: AKA the securities and exchange commission. *Journal of Financial Regulation and Compliance, 19*(3), 208–221.

[84] Carvajal, A., Monroe, H., Pattillo, C., et al. (2009). *Ponzi schemes in the Caribbean* (International Monetary Fund Working Paper, p. 4).

[85] Carvajal, A., et al. (2009). Op. Cit., p. 5.

[86] Parsons, L. (2010). Gullible, greedy or just unlucky? How Bernie Madoff scammed about 15,000 investors. *National Legal Eagle, 16*(1), 5–10.

the operation of the scheme, the operator is said to guarantee in most cases huge profits regarding return rates. Also, this one makes sure that interest is going to be paid quickly,[87] as agreed, by generating significant spoken communication advertising sent on behalf of pleased investors.[88]

In this regard, the more new investments are performed, the more these schemes thrive. Still, the real problem emerges when not a single investor (or very few) is left and thus the operator finds himself incapable of paying the interest. It is then when the entire scheme crashes.[89] Similarly, it has been noticed that scammers have been using Ponzi schemes for some decades. The only difference is that, lately, they started to initiate bigger and by far more highly qualitative, quite exceptional schemes.[90]

The present economic crisis issued out of the real estate crisis revealed many Ponzi schemes starting with the Madoff scheme to the Palm Beach Capital scheme.[91] These used to be schemes no longer capable of masquerading and pretending to be an entity enjoying profitability, while in reality, the industry was melting down.[92] Fraudulent actions not only hurt investors, but also competitors. Also, investors are going to shy away from investing when there is the perception that neither the SEC nor other authorities are looking after their interests or protection.

Despite the fact that Madoff's story happened more than a decade ago, its consequences regarding hedge funds remained relevant. Even now, the SEC brings law implementation actions with regard to recently disclosed Ponzi schemes. Meanwhile, the SEC brings to trial different issues originating in ancient Ponzi schemes that have trapped new persons and new

[87] In re United Energy Corp., 944 F.2d at 590 n.1.

[88] Ibid.

[89] Carvajal, A., et al. (2009). Op. Cit., p. 5.

[90] Wilber, D. Q. (2009, June 12). Economic Downturn Accelerates Collapse of Ponzi Schemes. *Washington Post*. https://www.washingtonpost.com/wp-dyn/content/article/2009/06/11/AR2009061103993.html. Accessed 12 June 2020.

[91] See, e.g., SEC v. Bruce F. Prévost, David W. Harrold, Palm Beach Capital Mgmt. LP, and Palm Beach Capital Mgmt. LLC, Civil Action No. 10-cv-04235-PAM-SRN (October 14, 2010); SEC v. Med. Capital Holdings, Inc., No. SACV 09-818 DOC (RNBx), 2010 WL 809406 (C.D. Cal. Mar. 16, 2010); SEC v. Sunwest Management, Inc Et Al Case 6:09-Cv-06056-TC (D. Ct. Or. October 2, 2009); Kim, J. J. (2010, March 27). Cracking down on 'private placement' investments. *Wall Street Journal*; Stecklow, S. (2009, January 28). In echoes of Madoff, Ponzi cases proliferate. *Wall Street Journal*. http://www.pyramidschemealert.org/PSAMain/news/PonziCasesProliferate.pdf. Accessed 16 July 2020.

[92] Ibid.

funds. The most popular of them is by far the "*Bernard Madoff*'s Ponzi scheme," of course. This has been described as being of great amplitude, which apparently started two decades ago, involving far beyond USD 65 billion frauds money actually lost by investors. However, it was in December 2008 that everything became known.[93] Similar to the Madoff scandal in size and amplitude stands the fraud of *Tom Petters*, the planner of a USD 3.7 billion ten-year deceit discovered in the autumn of 2008. It is also the case of *Robert Allen Stanford*, whose fraudulent actions became known at the beginning of 2009, although they are considered to have lasted for ten years, and involved a total of USD 8 billion. Another similar case is that of *S. Rothstein*, who admitted toward the end of 2009 to have managed a Ponzi scheme estimated at around USD 1.2 billion.

The above Ponzi schemes have triggered major complaints in tribunals from the United States and other states. There are several ongoing cases against the authors of the Ponzi schemes themselves, while in other cases complainants have filed against feeder funds, banks, investment councilors, audit companies, and other groups who allegedly had a role in causing investors' losses.

While some cases still continue, many courts where this type of cases was pleaded conducted to essential resolutions regarding actual culpability of financial inspectors.[94] Several litigation and arbitration cases from the last decade are discussed below.

7.3.1.1 Thomas Petters

The above-mentioned fraud scandals widely covered by the media[95] have led to an increase in the hedge funds regulation. For this reason, these cases are important for the understanding of the nature of regulation and enforcement of hedge funds. The first case discussed in detail here is the Thomas Petters litigation case.

[93] Zweifach, L. J., & Khan, S. N. (2010). Recent developments in Ponzi scheme litigation. In M. P. Carroll, & R. J. Morvillo (Eds.), *Auditor liability in current environment: how to protect yourself* (pp. 99–132). New York: Practising Law Institute, p. 101.

[94] Lawrence, J., et al. (2010). Op. Cit., p. 101.

[95] Kelleher, L., Caplin & Drysdale. (2012). Liability & defense, hedge fund managers beware: Unless claims are assigned, managers do not have standing to sue for their funds. *Bloomberg Law Reports*. http://www.capdale.com/hedge-fund-managers-bewareunless-claims-are-assigned-managers-do-not-have-standing-to-sue-for-their-funds. Accessed 15 March 2020, p. 5.

Some hedge funds and their presidents were accused of complicity in fraud to an amount of USD 3.5 billion under the Ponzi scheme managed by Th. Petters.[96] Toward the end of 2009, he was found guilty.[97] Four months later, he received a 50 years[98] sentence.[99] Petters defrauded a large number of investors, including more than 100 clergy participants, several non-profit institutions, and some hedge fund managers. Many victims were deprived of their jobs while others were deprived of their entire life savings.[100] Two of the legal actions in Petters' case are discussed here, the case of SEC v. B. F. Prévost and D. W. Harrold, but also that of SEC v. Marlon Quan.

"*SEC v. B. F. Prévost but also D. W. Harrold*." After charging Petters with fraud, the SEC filed secondary accusations against Prévost, but also against Harrold on the account of facilitating Petters' Ponzi scheme.[101]

In October 2010, the SEC accused the two above-mentioned Florida fund directors of several laws infringements, including breaches of "Section 17(a) of the Securities Act, Section 10(b) of the Exchange Act and Rule 10b-5-communicated there under, Sections 206(1), 206(2) and Sections 206(4) of the Advisers Act and Rule 206-4(8)."[102] The two directors were said to have deceitfully inserted within Petters' scheme more than USD 1 billion.

These two directors supposedly, intentionally and deceptively guaranteed stockholders that their amounts of investments were going to be kept

[96] Pozza, C. L. Jr., Cox, Th. R., & Morad, R. J. (2009). A review of recent investor issues in the Madoff, Stanford and forte Ponzi scheme cases. *Journal of Business & Securities Law, 10*, 113–131.

[97] Hugues, A. (2009, December 2). Tom Petters found guilty of Ponzi scheme fraud. *Reuters*. http://www.reuters.com/article/idUSN024978920091202. Accessed 5 May 2020.

[98] Phelps, D., & Tevlin, J. (2008, November 2). The woman who brought down Tom Petters. *Star Tribune*. http://www.startribune.com. Accessed 5 May 2012.

[99] US v. Petters, No. 0:08-cr-00364 (D. Minn. Jan. 24, 2013).

[100] Phelps, D., & Tevlin, J. (2008, November 2). The woman who brought down Tom Petters. *Star Tribune*. http://www.startribune.com. Accessed 5 May 2012.

[101] Monitor Daily. (2011, March 30) *SEC blocks diversion of Petters Ponzi victim funds*. http://www.monitordaily.com/sec-blocks-diversion-petters-ponzi-victim-funds/. Accessed 9 May 2012.

[102] U.S. District Court District of Minnesota (Dmn) Civil Docket for Case #: 0:10-cv-04235-PAM -SRN (Filed: 10/14/2010).

safely in auxiliary accounts. They similarly depicted to investing individuals some false actions capable of ensuring the safety of investors' money. When Petters' scheme was discovered, Prevost and Harrold contrived some false paper exchange transactions with Petters having the intention to trap stockholders. Prevost and Harrold plainly traded old IOUs in exchange to new IOUs, falsely guaranteeing investors in monthly correspondence that the hedge funds had gained profits due to their money. Indeed, the SEC asserted that both Prevost and Harrold have injected capital into Petters' account over a period of four years, from 2004 to 2008, removing at the same time almost USD 58 million during the same period. At present, there are several pending actions including a liquidation process for Petters Group Worldwide,[103] a SEC operation against Petters and one of his hedge fund customers who avowedly took part in the fraud,[104] and a lot of civil legal processes, some of which contain claims against auditors.

Sec v. Marlon Quan. Another lawsuit related to the fraudulent scheme of Petters, dating back at the beginning of 2011, more precisely since March, testifies that the SEC authority received one imperative interdiction stopping M. Quan, who at that moment was a hedge fund director located in Connecticut, from moving in his own accounts settlement funds. These funds had been raised specifically for victims of these schemes.[105] M. Quan, as well as all the companies he managed, has been found to have previously transferred capital in the accounts held by Petters during the 2001–2008 period. Therefore, because of the above-mentioned issues not only Quan but also the funds he managed are considered to have breached Section 17(a) of the Securities Act, Section 10(b) of the Exchange Act and Rule 10b-5 there under, Section 206(4) of the Advisers Act, and Rule 206-4(8) there under.

At the same time, Quan was found to have made false guarantees to investors that his firms would ensure the security of investors' money. Rather than doing this, Quan is thought to have planned some complex exchanges together with Petters which were supposed to have reached the

[103] In re Petters Group Worldwide, LLC, Bky. Case no 08-45258 (D. Minn. June 27, 2019).

[104] SEC v. Petters, et al., No. 09-cv-1750 (D. Minn. Jul. 7, 2009).

[105] SEC v. Quan, No. 0:11-cv-00723 (D. Minn. Mar. 25, 2011).

large value of almost USD 187 million. This occurred with the particular desire of hiding the fraud made by Petters. These exchanges resulted directly in the fact that Quan's actions led to maintaining a fraud, counterfeit image of Petters, according to which, he was in fact delivering fees for all companies.

In order to prevent Quan from transferring more than USD 14 million into his own pockets, the SEC took into consideration the idea of creating a tribunal for critical situations. In this respect, Quan was forced to direct his capital to credit institutions from Germany or even from Bermuda, which was actually to his own benefit. Another accusation that the SEC brought to Quan dealt with him helping Petters to maintain his fraudulent activities, while receiving about USD 90 million during the period of the fraud. In this regard, Robert Khuzami stated that their actions proved once more that they were determined to steadily hunt illegal returns which were actually inappropriately taken out of the pockets of trustful investors by means of various Ponzi schemes.[106]

In a more recent litigation from 2014, SEC v. Marlon Quan et al., the Court imposed injunctions and monetary sanctions of over USD 80 million against Marlon Quan and his companies based on fraud verdict.[107] Accordingly, the Commission's complaint was filed in March 2011, alleging that Marlon Quan helped to facilitate the massive fraud of Tom Petters by funnelling several hundred million dollars of investor money into the Petters Ponzi scheme. In this respect, the two litigations are connected. Thus, according to the SEC's 2009 complaint against Tom Petters, promissory notes were sold to feeder funds like those controlled by Quan and his firms. Petters used some of the note proceeds to pay returns to earlier investors, meanwhile the rest of the money were being used for his own purposes. What Petters promised to investors was that "their money would be used to finance the purchase of vast amounts of consumer electronics by vendors who then re-sold the merchandise to such retailers as Wal-Mart and Costco."[108] However, what he promised

[106] Monitor Daily. (2011, March 30). *SEC blocks diversion of Petters Ponzi victim funds*. http://www.monitordaily.com/sec-blocks-diversion-petters-ponzi-victim-funds/. Accessed 9 May 2012.

[107] SEC v. Marlon Quan, et al., Civil Action No. 11-723. (ADM-JSM) (D. Minn., September 25, 2014).

[108] Idem.

never happened, since this was another Ponzi scheme as there were no inventory transactions.

According to the SEC, Quan and his firms invested hundreds of millions of hedge fund assets with Petters at the same time stealing tens of millions of dollars in fees. They falsely assured investors that their money would be protected by diverse safeguards such as "lock box accounts," but there was no real investor protection. When Petters was unable to make payments on investments held by the funds that Quan managed, the complaint also alleged and Quan and his firms concealed Petters' defaults from investors.

The Commission had previously charged Petters and Illinois-based fund manager Gregory M. Bell with fraud, and filed additional charges against Florida-based hedge fund managers Bruce F. Prévost and David W. Harrold for similarly defrauding their investors in connection with investments in the Petters Ponzi scheme. In a similar action, the SEC also charged James Fry, a Minnesota-based hedge fund manager, with the same misconduct.

On February 11, 2014, Marlon Quan and his three companies were found liable for securities fraud. In her September 19th Opinion and Order, Judge Montgomery permanently enjoined the Marlon Quan, Acorn, SIA and ACG II from violating, or aiding and abetting violations of Sections 17(a)(2) and (3) of the Securities Act, Section 10(b) of the Securities Exchange Act and Rule 10b-5 thereunder, and Section 206(4) of the Investment Advisers Act of 1940 and Rule 206(4)-8. Consequently, Marlon Quan and the other defendants were liable, jointly and severally, for disgorgement of USD 80,6213,589 together with prejudgment interest.[109]

Furthermore, the Robert Allen Stanford scheme represents the second Ponzi scheme of major relevance discussed herein. This particular lawsuit research enables the consideration of different ignored messages or major conditions characterizing the above-mentioned Ponzi scheme conducted by R. A. Stanford through his Financial Company.[110]

[109] Idem.

[110] Perri, F. S., et al. (2011). Op. Cit., p. 209.

7.3.1.2 Robert Allen Stanford

It becomes clear that, in recent years, there were many Ponzi schemes thriving apart from Madoff's, in spite of its being the most substantial. Thus, at the next level of financial frauds, one can find that of the Stanford Company, whose basis was set by A. Stanford, who also performed the managerial work while owning it. The Group crashed in 2009, after it was proved to be nothing but a Ponzi scheme.[111]

From 1997 onwards, the SEC suspected "R. Allen Stanford"[112] of managing a Ponzi scheme, which eventually cost stockholders almost USD 7 billion, but it took more than ten years before the SEC began to investigate him in a serious manner.[113] During 1997–2004, the SEC undertook four personnel searches, but it was unable to verify his businesses thoroughly until 2005. The first one was performed in 1997 and occurred two years after Stanford registered his company under the SEC. Thus, a SEC testing employee informed the local top-manager about carefully watching over that company and its managers, as for him everything looked similar to some Ponzi scheme that was about to burst sooner or later. However, SEC implementation officials did not pay attention to negative signals received from staff working at Stanford.

Robert Stanford was put under investigation for alleged deceit at the beginning of 2009. As mentioned in the allegations, Stanford sold deceitful deposit attestations in his bank, Stanford International Bank for at least ten years by deceiving the stockholders about the returning fees they could obtain on their investments while in fact planning a "USD 8 billion Ponzi scheme."[114] When confronted with the illicit allegations against him, Stanford pleaded not guilty. The case went to court in January 2011. The only one who actually recognized the charges was the former Chief Financial Officer.[115] The SEC case against Stanford and

[111] Warwick-Young Walsh, D., & Spalding, A. D. Jr. (2011). Recognizing and responding to red flags: The Stanford Ponzi scheme. *Journal of Legal Issues and Cases in Business,* p. 2.

[112] Texas financier.

[113] Perri, F. S., et al. (2011). Op. Cit., pp. 208–221.

[114] United States v. Stanford, 769 F. Supp. 2d 1083 (S.D. Tex. 2011); SEC v. Stanford Int'l Bank, No. 3:09-CV-0298-N (N.D. Tex. filed Feb. 17, 2009).

[115] Frean, A. (2010). Op. Cit. apud Perri, F. S., et al. (2011). Op. Cit., p. 108 (Accessed 3 April 2012).

his avowed co-partners still awaits a decision in connection with the illegal charges.

The pertinent question is why did the SEC fail to charge Stanford earlier? It seems that the SEC has been suspicious about Stanford's Ponzi scheme since 1997,[116] a scheme which eventually cost investors nearly USD 7 billion. Yet, the SEC started to really investigate ten years later. Four SEC examinations occurred since 1997 until 2004. "None of them managed to reveal his scamming before 2005."[117] In 1997, one SEC official examined the company and asked the branch supervisor to examine it as well, because the official suspected there was a Ponzi scheme involved,[118] which would eventually erupt. However, there were multiple warnings that the SEC authority received and ignored the warnings coming from internal employees working at Stanford. One particular example resides in the request made by Fort Worth authority, when it started to examine Stanford due to high returns, which could not have been real because the investment approach was a traditional one. Thus, when the SEC asked for particular data, Sanford declined.[119] Similarly, there was no reaction from the SEC, which, in the end, stopped pursuing this issue despite having obligatory empowerment.[120] Another example supporting these statements is that of Leyla Wydler[121] who has been asking demands regarding the company's doings regarding customers' investments.[122] Obviously, the bosses felt threatened, which led to her being fired.[123]

Leyla Wydler complained first to the NASD in 2003.[124] One year later she went to the SEC. She wrote a letter explaining that she was convinced that Stanford was seriously involved in fraudulent actions.

[116] Crittenden, M. R., & Scannell, K. (2010), apud Perri, F. S., et al. Op. Cit., p. 209.

[117] Issa, D. (2010). Perri, Frank S., et al. (2011). Op. Cit., p. 209.

[118] Crittenden, M. R., & Scannell, K. (2010). Perri, F. S., et al. (2011). Op. Cit., p. 209.

[119] Elliott, J. (2010). Perri, Frank S., et al. (2011). Op. Cit., p. 209.

[120] Elliott, J. (2010). Perri, Frank S., et al. (2011). Op. Cit., p. 209.

[121] Vice President of the company at the time.

[122] Goldfarb, Z. (2010). Perri, Frank S., et al. (2011). Op. Cit., p. 209.

[123] Crittenden, M. R., & Scannell, K. (2010). Perri, Frank S., et al. (2011). Op. Cit., p. 209.

[124] National Association of Securities Dealers, ibid.

SEC did not contact her before early 2009—when a case against Stanford was filed. At that moment, they contacted her to find out which were her accusations, finding out that officials from Fort Worth had hardly analyzed the document again, deciding that they should neither examine it, nor open investigation on that particular issue.[125]

This case raised two major problems. First, it was clear that the study of various Ponzi schemes was considered at that time to be a foolish waste of time, money, and other things involved. Second, the SEC refused to examine what was so easy to notice,[126] as the officials were concerned about the resources involved. These issues are backed up by the fact that former SEC employee, R. Sauer, stated that at the time that the local authorities were mainly concerned about the fact that examining this issue could take far too much time, and consequently decrease the number of reported lawsuits.[127]

Senior officials from the region where it all started considered vast lawsuits as being disapproved[128] since they were seen as too complex, so no rapid strike. This is why they were not encouraged to pursue them. Attorney Sauer also added that it is the state system the one creating shameful instigations. To impress legislative appropriators, the SEC's reported cases continued to increase yearly, which consequently led to new ways of favoring rapid lawsuits also against everything new or speculative.[129] Nevertheless, not all cases are similar, while the easiest cases are seldom the most important. Most of the time, the employees captive to the state treadmill implied increasing managerial problems which resulted in growing difficulties in either opening recent cases or in closing unsuccessful ancient cases. Most of the time, the official authorities tend to become slaves of the mass opinions, reacting very late to publicized frauds

[125] Goldfarb, Z. (2010), Perri, Frank S., et al. (2011). Op. Cit., p. 209.

[126] Perri, Frank S., et al. (2011). Op. Cit., p. 209.

[127] Sauer, R. C. (2010, July 17). Why the SEC missed Madoff. *The Wall Street Journal*. http://online.wsj.com/article/SB10001424052748704738404575347011129892600.html/. Accessed 12 July 2020.

[128] Westbrook, J., & Scheer, D. (2010). *Report finds SEC dropped the ball in Stanford case*. http://online.wsj.com/article/SB2000142405270230349130457518822 0570802084.html. Accessed 12 June 2020.

[129] Sauer, R. C. (2010, July 17). Why the SEC missed Madoff. *The Wall Street Journal*. http://online.wsj.com/article/SB10001424052748704738404575347011129892600.html/. Accessed 12 July 2020.

(and to allegations regarding the circumstances of its occurrence) through different examinations. Regrettably, the SEC often ignored all evidences of fraud presented by renowned financial academic scholars[130] until the press made an issue out of it.

Ten years after the second biggest investor fraud in US history, victims of the USD 8 billion Ponzi scheme run by disgraced financier R. Allen Stanford have recovered practically nothing.[131]

7.3.1.3 Bernard Madoff

As discussed above, the SEC has experienced a number of recent significant defeats, including a shameful one: SEC did not understand "Ponzi schemer Madoff." Several conservatives claimed that investor protection under the SEC was worse than without any investor protection at all, as the SEC was "just fostering the illusion of genuine regulatory effort-its own version of a con game."[132] However, moderate voices were more temperate, even if these admitted that the SEC was a hardly troubled institution in need of a massive reform. The so-called Madoff case is very instructive.

SEC's lack of success leads us to the idea of endless, highly connected problematic issues, beginning with the fact that frauds appearing too complicated tend to be ignored, and continuing with the regulatory officials who are not aware and do not know how hedge funds operate. Therefore, these officials are unable to prevent frauds. Finally, the list of debatable issues ends with the general opinion that the companies and the authorities attempt to regulate are seen as possible individuals to provide jobs if they abandon their career as public servants. So everything is inter-correlated.[133] Therefore, the request for legislative freedom, not only in fact but also in display, appears threatened and in this context, the regulatory enforcements become obligatory.

[130] Macey, J. (2010). The distorting incentives facing the US Securities and Exchange Commission. *Harvard Journal of Law and Public Policy, 33*(2), 639–670.

[131] SEC V. STANFORD INTERNATIONAL BANK, LTD., ET AL., No. 17-11073 (5th Cir. 2019). http://www.stanfordfinancialreceivership.com/documents/Receivers_16th_Interim_Report.pdf. Accessed 9 October 2019.

[132] Langevoort, D. C. (2009). The SEC and the Madoff Scandal: Three narratives in search of a story. Georgetown Law and Economics, Research Paper No. 1475433. https://doi.org/10.2139/ssrn.1475433, p. 3.

[133] Perri, F. S., et al. (2011). Op. Cit., pp. 209.

Bernard Madoff perpetrated the most complex economic crime from the entire American history.[134] In December 2008, federal researchers discovered what is thought to be the greatest Ponzi scheme ever, reportedly lasting for a period of twenty years and involving more than USD 6.4 thousand million. The scheme was devised by Bernard Madoff, who had been previously an investment advisor and the organizer of "Bernard L. Madoff Investment Securities, LLC (BLMIS)."

The information recently disclosed to the public regarding JP Morgan's handling of incensement securities provided by Bernard Madoff raises different, yet related thoughtful concerns. The custodian entrusted with the liquidation of Madoff's company[135] started a lawsuit at the Tribunal in Manhattan against JP Morgan Chase & Co seeking USD 6.4 billion, on December 2, 2010. In 2008, according to Davis and Wilson (2011), JP Morgan litigation got down payments on behalf of Madoff's investors totaling USD 5.5 billion.[136]

Madoff's fraudulent action caused many complaints, ranging from illicit accusations of Madoff and the individuals who supposedly participated in or alternatively helped at his fraudulent procedure, to parallel civil operations supported by the SEC and particular groups and cases brought to court by state attorney generals, and liquidation proceedings. Most remarkably, stockholders who were allegedly deprived of money for Madoff's benefit have started numerous civil lawsuits in the US and Europe area, in their attempt to recover funds from the credit institutions who provided them assistance or who made investments using their finances.

Madoff used to be president of this Corporation before his arrest at the end of 2008,[137] on a criminal charge. He confessed to securities deceit. The Department of Justice's information against Madoff, registered on March 10, 2010,[138] included more allegations: securities fraud,

[134] Shores, M. (2010). *Informal networks and white collar crime: An extended analysis of the Madoff scandal.* New York: Ithaca, p. 4.

[135] Fisher, J., et al. (2011). Op. Cit., p. 280.

[136] Davis, L. R., & Wilson, L. (2011b). Estimating JP Morgan Chase's profits from the Madoff Deposits. *Risk Management and Insurance Review, 14*(1), 107–119.

[137] Voreacos, D., & Glovin, D. (2008, December 12). Madoff confessed $50 billion fraud before FBI Arrest. *Bloomberg*. http://www.bloomberg.com/apps/news?pid=newsarchive&sid=atUk.QnXAvZY. Accessed 6 March 2012.

[138] In the U.S. District Court for the SDNY.

investment adviser trapping, mail fraudulent actions, false declarations, false testimony, filing false documents to the SEC, and stealing from an employer-sponsored retirement plan.[139] Bernard Madoff continued his fraudulent action by never processing any trades for his stockholders.[140] In the summer of 2010, federal accusers registered civil fine charges *contra* A. Bongiorno and J. Crupi, Modoff's back-office employees "seeking USD 5 million in assets."[141] The allegations state that each litigant consciously perpetrated the fraud, although no criminal charges have yet been made against Bongiorno and Crupi.[142]

His fraud illustrates two sides of this issue: on the one hand, major deficiencies in coordinating things and in supervising[143] with regard to market trade regulations. Thus, an obvious weakness of the internal controls meant to protect investors' assets from fraudulent activities could be observed. Also, at the feeder funds the Madoff or BMIS names were never mentioned. Final investors were thus not necessarily aware that they were investing with Madoff. When questioned on this point, the feeder distributors generally answered that their contract did not allow them to mention the Madoff or BMIS name. So this was another risk the investors were subjected to. However, while the Madoff scandal shows well how not only financial but also operational risks are related, it is primarily for investors a case of operational risk realization. The Madoff scandal clearly illustrates a bias that overtook many investors in whose minds performance overshadowed risks.

Madoff has been sentenced on June 29, 2009.[144] The Madoff case has brought light into these matters, raising public's and investors' attention, and that of financial market as a whole, with regard to this form of

[139] "US v. Madoff, N° 08 MAG 2735" (S.D.N.Y. filed Dec. 11, 2008).

[140] Ross, B. (2009). *The Madoff chronicles: Inside the secret world of Bernie and Ruth*. New York: Hyperion Publishing.

[141] US v. $304,041.01 on Deposit at Citibank, N.A., N° 10-cv-4858 (S.D.N.Y. filed June 22, 2010).

[142] Ross, B. (2009). Op. Cit., p. 185.

[143] Clauss, P., Roncalli, Th., & Weisang, G. (2009). Risk management lessons from Madoff fraud. *International Finance Review*. https://doi.org/10.2139/ssrn.1358086.

[144] Stolowy, H., Baker, R., Jeanjean, Th., & Messner, M. (2011). Information, trust and the limits of intelligent accountability in investment decision making: Insights from the Madoff case. *SSRN Electronic Journal*. https://doi.org/10.2139/ssrn.1930128.

financial investments, but also securities fraud.[145] However, the SEC was hardly criticized because they did neither recognize, nor reveal this fraud which lasted for more than two decades, particularly since it was provided precise and frequent warnings.[146]

Similar to the Stanford case, the SEC was informed about Madoff and his company several times before he confessed. Unknown parties filed at least three complaints to the SEC about Madoff, while another fund administrator examined alleged profits. In addition, several economic journals wrote about Madoff's unusual silence reputation and the unusual "consistency of his company's financial statements."[147] While SEC officials were in an unrelated thorough check of another company, they found Internet messages[148] showing that Madoff's records were false. Most importantly, in 2001, 2005, and 2007, H. Markopolos, the person who exposed this fraud, had filed clear but also meticulous complaints.[149] Nobody listened to him.

As seen in the Stanford case, although the supposed scheme was printed in the news, this was neglected as proof by the SEC, which therefore missed this chance of catching Madoff. Consequently, several reports published in Barron's and in MARHedge raised questions about SEC's examination procedures.[150] Following the above-mentioned warnings, SEC initiated about five inquiries, some of whom lasted 12 months, including thorough examinations of Madoff's reports.[151] Unfortunately, SEC officials did not go to the next phase required to expose the fraud. Why did the SEC's officials not reveal his lack of managing sales? Still, when criticized for failing to answer to all the complaints it had previously

[145] Jory, S., & Perry, M. J. (2011). Ponzi schemes: A critical analysis. *Journal of Financial Planning*. https://ssrn.com/abstract=1894206. Accessed 5 March 2020.

[146] Parsons, L. (2010). Op. Cit., p. 5.

[147] Issa, D. (2010), Perri, Frank S., et al. (2011). Op. Cit., p. 209.

[148] E-mails from that company's audit examination of Madoff.

[149] Markopolos, H. (2010). *No one would listen*. New York: Wiley.

[150] WebCPA Staff. (2009). *SEC admits missed opportunities in Madoff case*. www.webcpa.com/news/SEC-Admits-Missed-Opportunities-Madoff-Case-51607-1.html. Accessed 12 June 2020.

[151] Perri, F. S., et al. (2011). Op. Cit., p. 210.

received, SEC preferred to mention the number of new investigations opened.[152]

Again, as seen in the Stanford case, the SEC made the wrong decision that complex investigation was a waste of resources. Professor Macey supports this idea that investigating Ponzi schemes was regarded like a burning of resources.[153] He also concluded that the issue that seemed unusual consisted of the fact that, in reality, such a thorough check would have involved fewer resources than primarily considered.[154] Although the SEC received six major detailed complaints regarding Madoff, none of them was careful analyzed. Macey noticed:

According to the SEC authorities' testimony, a thorough check seemed very costly, but also monopolizing. At the same time, the SEC was unable to really see the proof, despite being conscious about it.[155]

The Madoff scam remains the largest documented Ponzi scheme in history, standing out as the first international Ponzi scheme which still haunts Wall Street and regulators. Scholars asses that "it claimed victims from Palm Beach to the Persian Gulf, from Canada to Brazil, from a teachers' pension plan in South Korea to a Catholic girls' school in St. Croix."[156] Even Madoff's declarations concerning the scale of his Ponzi scheme proved to be an underestimate. Thus, "his Ponzi scheme actually erased almost USD 65 billion in paper wealth supposedly held in investor accounts. He took almost USD 18 billion in cash from later investors and doled it out as fake profits to earlier investors."[157] Due to this immense fraud, Madoff stands in the record books being until his arrest, the biggest alleged Ponzi scheme in the United States' hedge funds fraud of around USD 4 billion.

December 11, 2019, marked the 11th anniversary of the Madoff Ponzi scheme being revealed to the world after Bernie Madoff was arrested. The trustee appointed to oversee the liquidation of Bernard L. Madoff

[152] Perri, F. S., et al. (2011). Op. Cit., p. 210.

[153] Perri, F. S., & Brody, Richard G. (2011). Op. Cit., p. 211.

[154] Macey, J. (2010). The distorting incentives facing the US Securities and Exchange Commission. *Harvard Journal of Law and Public Policy, 33*(2), 656.

[155] Markopolos, H. (2010). *No one would listen*. Hoboken, NJ: Wiley.

[156] Henriques, D. B. (2019). A case study of a Con Man: Bernie Madoff and the timeless lessons of history's biggest Ponzi scheme. In A. Mack (Ed.), *Cons and scams: Their place in American culture* (Vol. 85, pp. 745–766).

[157] Idem.

Investment Securities continues to pursue, on behalf of customers around the globe, the most far-reaching, historic and successful recovery initiative in American history.[158]

The US Securities and Exchange Commission Office of Inspector General put out a 477-page self-diagnosis, which investigated and documented "The Failure of the SEC to Uncover Bernard Madoff's Ponzi Scheme," along with making numerous, going-forward recommendations.[159] The Dodd–Frank Act was thereafter enacted in large part as the anti-fraud, legislative response to the Madoff scandal.[160] A decade later, that legislation sits at the heart of a fierce political debate over the proper levels of regulation and oversight needed for the securities and banking industries,[161] as well as whether and to what extent, the law should create monetary incentives for whistleblowers.

There are many lessons from the Madoff scandal that endure until today. Some include:

1. investors must perform their own rigorous due diligence;
2. investors must react and question warning signs or red flags;
3. investors must be skeptical of "exclusivity" investment pitches; and
4. investors must appreciate that there is no such thing as "guaranteed" returns (or its often stated corollary—if something seems too good to be true, it likely is).[162] Notwithstanding these and other lessons, the passage of Dodd–Frank, heightened SEC enforcement

[158] As of Sept. 30, 2018, over $13 billion, or more than 75 percent, of the lost principal (estimated to be just under USD 18 billion) has been recovered. Building the Customer Fund, Madoff Recovery Initiative.

[159] SEC. (2009, August 31). *Investigation of failure of the SEC to uncover Bernard Madoff's Ponzi scheme*. Report No. OIG-509. https://www.sec.gov/files/oig-509.pdf. Accessed 12 August 2020.

[160] Dodd-Frank Wall Street Reform and Consumer Protection Act, Pub. L. No. 11-203.

[161] On May 22, 2018, President Donald Trump signed into law the Economic Growth, Regulatory Relief, and Consumer Protection Act, partially repealing Dodd-Frank (exempting banks from certain core regulations). See Ramizez, K. (2018). *President Trump Signs Dodd-Frank Rollback into Law*. https://www.housingwire.com/articles/43464-president-trump-signs-dodd-frank-rollback-into-law/. Accessed 12 August 2020.

[162] Vonnegut, N. (2017, July 26). Three lessons from the Bernie Madoff scandal. *Enterprising Investor*. https://blogs.cfainstitute.org/investor/2017/07/26/three-lessons-from-the-bernie-madoff-scandal/. Accessed 19 July 2020.

in the aftermath of the crisis,[163] and deepened investor and industry awareness of what constitute "red flags," the Ponzi scheme and financial fraud generally continue to thrive, undeterred by frauds from the past. Negative history repeats itself on what seems like a daily basis.[164]

All in all, it is the author's opinion that, for many investors, being caught in a hedge fund fraud can also have major reputation and business connotations, which go far beyond the value of the actual investment loss. In this context, the role of the operational due diligence function is not only to stop monetary losses in the portfolio, but it can also be considered as a key function meant to protect the asset management business itself and, by this, investors as well.

Larson and Hinton found that, before the disclosure of Rothstein's fraudulent activity, the first two largest schemes filed by the SEC consisted of: first, Madoff's (USD 50 billion), second, Stanford's (USD 8 billion).[165] Since Larson and Hinton wrote their study, Tom Petters was convicted in a USD 3.7 billion Ponzi scheme.[166] That would mean that Rothstein's lawsuit currently represents "the fourth largest Ponzi scheme"[167] revealed until now.

[163] In the year after Madoff was arrested, more than 150 Ponzi schemes collapsed, totalling over USD 16.5 billion across all 50 states—nearly three and a half times that of 2008. See Busted Ponzi Schemes Quadrupled in 2009, CBS Money Watch (Dec. 28, 2009). By contrast, from 2014 to 2016, the number of uncovered schemes had dropped to an average of 63 schemes. See 2014–2016 Ponzi Scheme List, Ponzitracker. In 2017, SEC enforcement actions as a whole were at their lowest numbers since 2013, with 754 actions—down from its peak of 868 actions in 2016. Press Release, SEC, SEC Enforcement Division Issues Report on Priorities and FY 2017 Results (Nov. 15, 2017).

[164] See The Ponzi scheme authority (2020). Ponzitracker. http://www.ponzitracker.com. Accessed 12 June 2020.

[165] Larsen, J., & Hinton, P. (2009). *SEC settlements in Ponzi Scheme cases: Putting Madoff and Stanford in context* (NERA Economic Consulting White Paper).

[166] The New York Times. (2010, August 8). 50-year term for Minnesota Man in USD 3.7 Billion Ponzi Fraud. Associated Press. Reprinted in *The New York Times* B9. http://www.nytimes.com/2010/04/09/business/09ponzi.html. Accessed 12 June 2020.

[167] Davis, L., & Wilson, L. (2011a). Good timing? How one bank cut its link to a $1.2 billion Ponzi scheme. *Journal of Legal Economics, 18*(1), 1–26.

7.3.1.4 *Scott Rothstein*

One of the many important Ponzi schemes discovered so far is that of the American lawyer Scott Rothstein. The moment when his plan started to reveal itself, in the winter of 2009, Rothstein made a confession in front of the federal accusers, admitting fraud, money laundering, mail fraud, and wire fraud. Considering the allegations against him and his company, stockholders have attempted to procure shares in private settlement decisions. In fact, the settlements did not exist, and the investor hedge funds had already been used in order to continue Rothstein's Ponzi scheme.[168]

In January 2010, Rothstein admitted his guilt to all the criminal accusations against him and six months later he was convicted to 50 years in prison. Besides Rothstein, Debra Villegas, former Chief Operating Officer in his law company confessed her guilt.

At present, Rothstein's law company, Rothstein Rosenfeldt Adler, PA ("RRA") is in the process of liquidation operations in "the Southern District of Florida."[169] The Rothstein act of deceit has also caused civil lawsuits, most remarkably a 2200-plus page litigation in Florida State Court of Justice.[170]

Recently, in 2019, the US Court of Appeals for the Eleventh Circuit shot down an attempt by disbarred attorney and federal prisoner Scott Rothstein to reduce his 50-year sentence for running a USD 1.2 billion Ponzi scheme—among the largest in history. Rothstein was disbarred after pleading guilty to wire fraud, racketeering, conspiracy to commit money laundering and conspiracy to commit mail and wire fraud after it emerged, he used his then-Fort Lauderdale law firm Rothstein Rosenfeldt Adler to perpetuate the scheme. His arguments were that the US Attorney's Office breached its plea agreement by withdrawing a motion that under Federal Rule of Criminal Procedure 35 could have allowed his sentence to be reduced if he cooperated fully.

The government disagreed, arguing that Rothstein had provided false information. But Rothstein disputed that, requesting an evidentiary hearing and claiming he had been of "extraordinary assistance." The government filed the motion almost a year after Rothstein's sentencing,

168 US v. Rothstein, No. 09-6033 (S.D. Fl. filed Dec. 1, 2009).

169 In re Rothstein Rosenfeldt Adler, P.A., No. 09-34791-RBR (Bankr. S.D. Fla. Filed Nov. 19, 2009).

170 Razorback Funding LLC v. Rothstein, CACE09062943 (Fla. Cir. Ct. Broward Co. filed Nov. 20, 2009).

Table 7.1 History's biggest Ponzi Schemes

Schemer	*Year*	*Amount Scammed (in 2015 USD)*	*Year Prison Sentence*
Scott Rothstein	2010	USD 1 billion	50 years
Tom Petters	2009	USD 4 billion	50 years
Allen Stanford	2012	USD 8 billion	110 years
Bernie Madoff	2008	USD 73 billion	150 years

Source Williams (2017)

though it served as a placeholder at the time because his cooperation was not yet complete. If Rothstein did not comply, the motion said, it could be withdrawn.

Rothstein claimed he was not properly warned because his cooperation and plea agreements did not include the word "withdraw." The Eleventh Circuit was unconvinced, finding the cooperation agreement made no guarantees. It also pointed out that Rothstein's attorney signed the Rule 35 motion, which explained the government's ability to withdraw.[171]

The development of a cohesive regulation to respond to nefarious corporate behavior directed by managers who use their respective corporate entities is stringent. This necessity is further emphasized by the case describing how fraudsters can indirectly punish victims and creditors in relation to the current lack of coordination between the authorities and bankruptcy trustees. Protection of investors from undue losses can be performed with agreement among regulators to strongly consider prosecuting corporations used as vehicles for investment fraud aims. In these circumstances, doing so would be theoretically justified and also, from the practical point of view, adoptable, but also would further victim and creditor recovery so that would increase the equitable nature of both criminal forfeiture and bankruptcy proceedings connected to corporate fraud.

Summing up, Table 7.1 presents details concerning history's biggest Ponzi schemes and their major characteristics.[172]

The Petters, Rothstein, Madoff, and Stanford cases illustrate how the existence of pessimistic motivation structures for investigation can

[171] US v. Rothstein, No 18-11796 (S.D. Fl. Sept. 30, 2019).

[172] Williams, D. C. (2017). A timeline and fraud triangle analysis of the SEC's Madoff Ponzi scheme investigation. *International Journal of Business & Public Administration, 14,* 98–105.

effectively prevent the investigation of several types of cases. Moreover, the next sub-section exhibits market manipulation and misrepresentation cases.

7.3.1.5 Ponzi Schemes Over the Last Decade

Florida remains one of the "leading" states when it comes to economic fraud and Ponzi schemes.

In this respect the most recent Ponzi scheme will be presented, which was revealed by the SEC in 2019, that of Brenda A. Smith, of Philadelphia, Pennsylvania. She was the subject of a SEC suit that alleged she engaged in fraudulent, deceptive, and manipulative business practices and perpetrated a Ponzi-like scheme. According to the SEC, Ms. Smith took in more than USD 105 million from investors.[173]

Brenda A. Smith, who worked out of West Conshohocken, Pennsylvania, along with her co-Defendants, allegedly solicited approximately USD 105 million from investors in the Philadelphia area and elsewhere for purported investment in sophisticated securities trading strategies, according to the aforementioned Complaint.

Investor rights attorneys are investigating activity related to Brenda A. Smith's alleged Ponzi scheme. They were collecting evidence, interviewing individuals with direct knowledge of key aspects of Smith's alleged scheme, and identified a number of potential recovery options for investors. Their focus was on certain third parties that, they believed, played a role in assisting, enabling, or failing to prevent Smith's alleged fraud.

From February 2016 to present, it appears that Brenda Smith along with defendants Broad Reach Capital, LP, defendant Broad Reach Partners, LLC, and defendant Bristol Advisors, LLC[174] allegedly engaged in the aforementioned fraud. Smith, however, allegedly misused the vast majority of the funds she raised from investors for unrelated companies, to pay back other investors, and for personal use, and, in 2019, was confronted with at least one investor trying to redeem their investment. Smith then allegedly created a fictitious valuation of assets backed by false

[173] SEC v. BRENDA A. SMITH, BROAD REACH CAPITAL, LP, BROAD REACH PARTNERS, LLC, and BRISTOL ADVISORS, LLC, Case 2:19-cv-17213-MCA-LDW (New York Southern Court, August 27, 2019).

[174] All of which were entities she controlled.

claims that she held billions of dollars in assets through a company she owned.

Smith allegedly dominated and controlled the Entity Defendants such that they were essentially her so-called alter egos. From the Fund's inception, Smith purportedly raised approximately USD 105 million from at least 40 investors. The said investors are still owed more than USD 63 million in principal and the case has all the telltale signs of an alleged Ponzi scheme.

Brenda A. Smith has also been charged by the US Attorney's Office for the District of New Jersey with four counts of wire fraud and one count of securities fraud. Smith had previously been disciplined by FINRA in June, and her registration was revoked and she was barred from associating with any FINRA member. Finally, it is important to note that, as of the date of this writing, Smith was arrested on August 27, 2019. She is in an Essex County, N.J., prison awaiting trial. A grand jury has convened and she was charged with investment fraud, among other counts.

Currently, federal regulators have already obtained an emergency asset freeze against Brenda Smith and three of her investment companies. In addition, the agency is seeking all appropriate legal remedies. Specifically, this includes disgorgement of any ill-gotten gains, payment of full financial restitution, and further monetary penalties. It is worth mentioning that Brenda Smith has also been arrested. She is facing criminal fraud charges from the United States Department of Justice (DOJ).[175] In June 2020, she was indicted on six counts of wire fraud and one count of securities fraud.[176]

7.3.2 Securities Fraud Liability

Federal securities litigation was generous in 2019. Putting aside that plaintiffs continued filing securities lawsuits in crescent numbers, an important aspect resides in the fact that they constantly secured victories in cases on important aspects of law. The tone was set at the top with

[175] SEC. (2019). *SEC obtains emergency asset freeze, charges Pennsylvania Investment Adviser with USD 100 Million Fraud*. Securities and Exchange Commission (SEC). https://www.sec.gov/news/press-release/2019-162. Accessed 20 July 2020.

[176] Department of Justice. (2020). *Philadelphia woman indicted in $68 million securities fraud scheme*. https://www.justice.gov/usao-nj/pr/philadelphia-woman-indicted-68-million-securities-fraud-scheme. Accessed 20 July 2020.

the Supreme Court's notable opinion in Lorenzo v. SEC, as we shall see further on.

On March 27, 2019, the US Supreme Court issued a 6-2 decision in Lorenzo v. SEC[177] holding that an individual who is not a "maker" of a misstatement under Janus v. First Derivative Traders, 564 US 135 (2011) can nonetheless be held primarily liable under Section 10(b) of the Exchange Act and Rules 10b-5(a) and (c) thereunder for knowingly "disseminating" a misstatement made by another person. The Court's decision potentially expands the ability of private plaintiffs to bring Section 10(b) claims against those who knowingly or recklessly transmit false and misleading statements that were made by someone else, and could meaningfully erode the limits on primary liability under Section 10(b) established by the Court in Janus and Central Bank of Denver, N.A. v. First Interstate Bank of Denver, N.A., 511 US 164 (1994).

Francis Lorenzo, the defendant, was a director of an investment banking firm engaged in a USD 15 million bond offering. Lorenzo, under instructions of his supervisor, contacted via email potential investors stating that the issuer had intellectual property assets worth USD 10 million, while in reality the assets were almost worthless. Moreover, Lorenzo and his supervisor knew that the assets were almost worthless.

SEC Rule 10(b) implements Section 10(b) of the Securities Exchange Act of 1934 and contains three subsections prohibiting fraudulent conduct in connection with the purchase or sale of securities. Rule 10b-5(a) makes it unlawful to "employ any device, scheme or artifice to defraud"; Rule 10b-5(b) makes it unlawful to "make any untrue statement of a material fact;" and Rule 10b-5(c) prohibits engaging in "any act, practice, or course of business" that "operates … as a fraud or deceit." Claims asserted under Rule 10b-5(b) are often referred to as addressing "misstatement liability," while claims asserted under Rules 10b-5(a) and (c) are referenced as addressing "scheme liability."

In Janus, the Court considered the scope of Rule 10b-5(b), and ruled in a 5-4 decision that "misstatement liability" under Rule 10b-5(b) only extends to the "maker of a statement," which the Court held is "the person or entity with ultimate authority over the statement."[178]

[177] 139 S. Ct. 1094 (2019).

[178] 564 U.S.

In Lorenzo, the SEC charged Francis Lorenzo, the director of investment banking at a brokerage firm, with violating Rule 10b-5 by sending two false and misleading emails to potential investors.[179] However, Lorenzo argued (and the Court accepted as true for purposes of the appeal) that he had merely copied and pasted the false and misleading statements from an email that his supervisor sent him. Nevertheless, an ALJ concluded that Lorenzo acted with fraudulent intent and that his conduct violated Rules 10b-5(a), (b), and (c) of the Exchange Act.[180] In a split decision, the D.C. Circuit affirmed the ALJ's ruling on a "scheme liability" theory, finding that even though Lorenzo did not "make" the misstatements under Janus and thus could not be held liable under Rule 10b-5(b), he still violated Rules 10b-5(a) and (c) for his intentionally fraudulent "use" of the misstatements.[181]

On March 27, 2019, the Supreme Court affirmed in a 6-2 decision that "dissemination of false or misleading statements with intent to defraud" constitutes a violation of subsections (a) and (c) of Rule 10b-5, "even if the disseminator did not 'make' the statements."[182] The Court reasoned that subsections (a) and (c) "capture a wide range of conduct," and that it was "obvious" that the language is "sufficiently broad" to "prohibit the dissemination of false and misleading information," which would include Lorenzo's emails. As such, the Court concluded that both subsections can cover actors who disseminate misstatements that, under Janus, are "made" by someone else.[183]

In so ruling, the Court rejected Lorenzo's argument that each of the subsections of Rule 10b-5 "should be read as governing different, mutually exclusive spheres of conduct," and that one can only be liable for a misstatement under provisions that "refer specifically to false statements." Rather, the Court reasoned that there is "considerable overlap among the subsections," and that Rule 10b-5 is best read as "includ[ing] both

[179] Case No. 17-1077, 2019 WL 1369839 (U.S. Mar. 27, 2019).

[180] Francis v. Lorenzo, SEC Release No. 9762, 111 SEC Docket 1761, 2015 WL 1927763 (Apr. 29, 2015).

[181] Lorenzo v. SEC, 872 F.3d 578, 586 (D.C. Cir. 2017).

[182] Lorenzo, 2019 WL 1369839.

[183] Hurd, S., Gworek, M., & Glustrom, E. (2019). Lorenzo v. SEC: the supreme court rules on scheme liability under the federal securities laws. *Journal of Investment Compliance*. https://doi.org/10.1108/joic-04-2019-0021.

a general proscription against fraudulent practices and, out of an abundance of caution, a specific proscription against nondisclosure." Because Lorenzo, who did not challenge the appeals court's finding of intent, knew that his emails contained material misstatements and sent them with the "intent to deceive, manipulate, or defraud" investors, the Court concluded that there was "nothing borderline about this case."[184]

This case has provided the SEC and private parties with a major weapon. Starting from this case on, non-makers can be liable as primary violators under Rule 10b-5. In this vein, anybody, including investment bankers acting as underwriters or placement agents, could be held liable through their active and knowing participation in the distribution of a misstatement made by a different individual. Whether Lorenzo will actually translate in an increase in litigations by the SEC and private parties against investment bankers (or any other non-maker), however, is difficult to predict. This is because Lorenzo's outcome was facilitated by his admission of his knowingly disseminating a material misstatement. Similarly, this rule devised in Lorenzo could also apply overseas. In Robert Morrison v. National Australia Bank, 561 US 247 (2010),[185] the Supreme Court held that Rule 10b-5 applies any time a security is purchased or sold in the United States or if a security purchased or sold is listed on a US stock exchange. Lorenzo's holding, however, will not apply where the foreign securities transaction has no connection with the United States.

Remarkably, the majority opinion attests that "the case did not present a close call on the facts, and future courts will have to address "difficult problems of scope in borderline cases." More importantly, the claims in Lorenzo were brought by the SEC, not private shareholders, and the ruling will likely have limited impact on the scope of liability that companies and their executives face in private lawsuits brought by investors under Section 10(b)."[186]

According to the Court, in Lorenzo, private litigants must plead and give proofs of other aspects that the SEC does not, among which can be mentioned reliance on the alleged misstatements. There is major

[184] Idem.

[185] US 247 (2010). https://supreme.justia.com/cases/federal/us/561/247/. Accessed 21 July 2020.

[186] Hurd, S., Gworek, M., & Glustrom, G. (2019). Lorenzo v. SEC: The Supreme Court rules on scheme liability under the federal securities laws. *Journal of Investment Compliance*, Emerald Publishing Limited, p. 3.

difference between reliance and fraudulent intent (which Lorenzo conceded). Therefore, "reliance in private litigation is looked at not from the defendant's perspective, but from the perspective of the investor. Thus, in private actions, it does not matter for reliance purposes whether the defendant "intended" for shareholders to rely – the issue is whether they in fact did rely."[187]

Consequently, there will be still needed that private litigants would "plead and prove reliance, which will continue to serve as a barrier to expanded liability in private actions under the facts of Lorenzo. Indeed, the two potential investors who received Lorenzo's email would not have been able to sue him privately based on the record before the Court. There was no evidence that any individual even read his email, let alone relied on it in making the decision to pursue the investment opportunity at issue. Thus, the Lorenzo facts would preclude private liability in an individual action in the absence of pleading and proof of individual reliance."[188]

Besides, in spite of the fact that Lorenzo had distributed his email more widely, the classical presumption of reliance found in securities class actions could be applied since he made no statements to the market and, therefore, the "fraud on the market" presumption proved not available. In the absence of "the benefit of a presumption of reliance, a "class" of persons who received Lorenzo's email would still need to prove individual reliance on his statements, and the claims would be unable to proceed on a class basis for that reason."[189]

Accordingly, the Supreme Court clarified, in contrast to its 2011 decision in Janus Capital Group, Inc. v. First Derivative Traders,[190] that a person who does not "make" a fraudulent misstatement can nonetheless be held primarily liable for securities fraud under Section 10(b) of the Securities Exchange Act of 1934 (Exchange Act) and Rule 10b-5 thereunder for his or her role in disseminating the misstatement. In so ruling, the Supreme Court effectively eviscerated a popular defense in

[187] Idem.

[188] Idem.

[189] Idem.

[190] 564 U.S. 135 (2011).

fraud lawsuits since Janus and reaffirmed that the anti-fraud provisions of the securities laws covered a "wide range of conduct."[191]

Indeed, there were many other cases, in which federal courts ruled in favor of plaintiffs, establishing wide theories of liability for defendants.

7.3.2.1 Insider Trading

Meanwhile, the number of SEC insider trading cases diminished a lot, there were key aspects developing in criminal cases during the last years, and federal legislation that passed the House of Representatives might revamp insider trading law in the case it would be enacted.

Commentators repeatedly point out that the law of insider trading, in spite of being formally derived from Section 10(b) and Rule 10b-5 of the Securities Exchange Act of 1934, is best understood if read as a common law-like subject.[192] The reason for this is that "neither the statute nor the rule addresses insider trading explicitly, leaving to the judiciary to do all the work of fashioning legal doctrine about when and why insider trading operates as securities fraud. The SEC has acquiesced in this judicial law-making for the most part, preferring taking its chances in the courts (more often than anywhere else in the Southern District of New York) than putting the definition of insider trading up for political haggling. It has engaged in very specific rulemaking on a few contested issues, but been far from comprehensive"[193]; even when the Commission has adopted definitional rules (10b5-1 and -2), the courts do not always defer.[194] Up to now,[195] at least, the judiciary has "owned" insider

[191] 139 S. Ct. at 1101.

[192] Fisch, J. E. (2018). Constructive ambiguity and the judicial development of insider trading. *SMU Law Review, 71*(62), 749–757, citing Merrill, T. (1985). The common law powers of Federal Courts. *The University of Chicago Law Review, 52*, 21.

[193] Langevoort, D. C. (2019). *Watching insider trading law wobble: Obus, Newman, Salman, Two Martomas, and a Blaszczak*. Georgetown University Law Center. https://scholarship.law.georgetown.edu/cgi/viewcontent.cgi?article=3227&context=facpub. Accessed 12 July 2020.

[194] Coffee, J. C. Jr. (2013). Mapping the future of insider trading law: Of boundaries, gaps, and strategies. *Columbia Business Law Review, 2*, 281–317.

[195] In December 2019, the House of Representatives overwhelmingly passed a bill aiming at defining unlawful insider trading, maybe signalling a change in the locus of law-making. Insider Trading Prohibition Act, H.R. 2534,115th Cong., 1st Sess. (Dec. 5, 2019). What will happen to it is yet unknown.

trading law, for the most part choosing to give it broad reach. As the following cases will prove, the precise contours of insider trading law are not well-defined so far.

The regulations concerning insider trading represents a judge-made law constantly changing over the last half century, reaching a major deadlock in three recent decisions in the Second Circuit Court of Appeals: United States v. Newman, United States v. Martoma and United States v. Blaszczak. Opinions are not uniform between judges of the Second Circuit regarding the conduct that represents improper trading on material nonpublic information ("MNPI"), as regulation in this respect is confusing. The problems emerge from 10 years-old split within the judiciary about how to:

1. offer a fair securities marketplace, at the same time
2. being able to enable institutional analysts to probe for corporate information in pursuit of efficient market valuation of securities.

The insider trading current focus is on the misappropriation theory, which refers to the fact that a trader feigning loyalty to a company or an individual to get access to secrets eventually defrauds his source out of information the moment he misuses this data for trading.[196] A huge lack of clarity "stems largely from the fact that Congress has failed to enact a federal statute expressly defining and prohibiting insider trading."[197] Indeed, up to the present day, federal courts have essentially employed a

[196]This theory does not apply if the source granted valid permission for the trader to trade. Salman v. United States, 137 S. Ct. 420, 423 (2016) (recognizing that even without permission, traders may avoid liability if "they make appropriate disclosures ahead of time"). However, there is no protection where a trader has obtained permission to trade from someone who has no ultimate authority to grant it, in exchange for a personal benefit. Id. at 426–28; United States v. Martoma, 894 F.3d 64, 67–68 (2d Cir. 2017). For example, if a CEO shares secrets in exchange for reputational or pecuniary gains, or if a misappropriator shares her ill-gotten secret, the recipient is not permitted to trade on the newly acquired secret. Dirks, 463 US at 663–64. One who is tipped information in breach of a duty inherits that duty and violates the law as a tipper.

[197]Schipani, C., & Seyhun, H. J. (2016). Defining 'Material Nonpublic': What should constitute illegal insider information? *Fordham Journal of Corporate and Financial Law, XXI*(2), 327–378.

"make it up as you go" path,[198] which resulted in a "doctrinal mess,"[199] leading to intricate court decisions[200] and a plethora of questions like "what's so wrong with insider trading anyway?"[201] or "should the recipient of a gift of information be allowed to trade on it?"[202] With corporate data breaches and rising insider "expert net-works,"[203] the necessity for clarity and consensus-building in the United States having to do with insider trading rules stands as imminent.

In United States v. Newman, judges of the Second Circuit established there were several defendants who, in spite of being convicted, were not guilty.[204] In the end, the Court's ruling and interpretation of the regulation conducted to cancellations of other convictions; at the same time several allegations were discharged, even for defendants who stated they were culpable of insider trading.[205]

This was reversed only three years later, when a different panel of the Second Circuit in: United States v. Martoma ended up issuing a ruling that categorically opposed to that in Newman.[206] A dissenting judge disagreed, stating that the majority's mistaken rule should be ignored as *dictum*.[207] The Congress became particularly interested in this regulation,

[198] Henning, P. J. (2018). Making up insider trading law as you go. *Washington University Journal of Law & Policy, 56,* 101–120, p. 101.

[199] Kim, S. (2014). Insider trading as private corruption. *UCLA Law Review, 61,* 928–1008.

[200] Knight, T. B. (2017). Salman v. US: Another insider trading case. *Cato Supreme Court Review, 2016–2017,* 181–203.

[201] Thomson-DeVeaux, A. (2016). What's so wrong with insider trading anyway? *Five Thirty-Eight*. https://fivethirtyeight.com/features/whats-so-wrong-with-insider-trading-anyway/. Accessed 12 June 2020.

[202] United States v. Martoma, 894 F.3d 64, 78 (2d Cir. 2017).

[203] Edde, J., Kumar, N., & Waite, S. (2018). Investors are paying $1300 per hour for 'Expert' chats. *Bloomberg*.

[204] United States v. Newman, 773 F.3d 438, 443 (2d Cir. 2014).

[205] United States. v. Conradt, 2015 U.S. Dist. LEXIS 16263 (S.D.N.Y. Jan. 22, 2015).

[206] United States v. Martoma, 869 F.3d 55, 61 (2d Cir. 2017), opinion amended and superseded, 894 F.3d 64 (2d Cir. 2017).

[207] United States v. Martoma, 869 F.3d at 74 (Pooler, J., dissenting).

and is currently taking into account redefining the insider trading prohibition.[208] Meanwhile Congress is currently taking into account a bill that should provide much needed clarity, there are scholars who consider that there may be some problems with the current draft as it "embraces a 'parity of information' vision for the securities market by prohibiting any trades while in possession of material nonpublic information ("MNPI") obtained through a breach of a confidentiality obligation. In so doing, the bill gives too little regard for the competing interest of market efficiency. It is the conflict between these two important interests that mired the courts in debate for decades. If passed, the bill's blanket prohibition could materially impact institutional investors' ability to investigate corporate information, a task that is vital to accurate securities valuations."[209] Indeed, in the wake of Newman/Martoma/Blaszczak, maybe the Senate needs to take a more careful look at the insider trade regulation in order to gain better insights and by consequence find better solutions. As Park states, in spite of the fact that "the bill has the benefit of clarity, it may discourage institutional analysts from seeking out nonpublic information that illuminate the true condition of companies they analyze. If that happens, the market's ability to value securities may become less reliable—instead, a company's public representations about itself may become the predominant basis of its stock price."[210] Consequences are not clear so far with regard to the efficiency of the marketplace. However, there are scholars who consider "that the core of the matter concerns the marginal contribution of insider trading law to the existing body of contract law: the creation of an extra limit on informed trading and an extra layer of enforcement. These differences are justified where traders react too much in protecting themselves *ex ante* and too little in protecting themselves *ex post*. That is to say we should have insider trading law in domains where traders and intermediaries are likely to withdraw from markets due to widespread informed trading—especially in high-volume intermediated markets—and where experts are able to develop expertise in a wide variety

[208] Insider Trading Prohibition Act, H.R. 2534,115th Cong., 1st Sess. (Dec. 5, 2019) (as approved by H.R. Fin. Serv. Comm., May 8, 2019, and committed to the H. Comm. of the Whole, Sept. 27, 2019).

[209] Park, T. H. (2019). Newman/Martoma: The insider trading law's impasse and the promise of congressional action. *Fordham Journal of Corporate & Financial Law, XXV*, 3–95, p. 4.

[210] Idem, p. 5.

of somewhat fungible but complex assets, the value of which to single litigants may be too low relative to the overall social value."[211]

The major problematic cases concerning insider trading focus currently either on "personal benefit test" or on the "remote tippees," individuals who get their information from a chain of tippers or from friends, not from the corporate insider himself.

In the case United States v. Newman (2014), for instance, two hedge fund portfolio managers collected around USD 72 million in profits by trading on documents giving details about sheets to become public in the near future concerning corporate earnings. This data was received from analysts with social connections to corporate insiders, which were their friends. In spite of being convicted, their decisions were overturned by the Second Circuit Court of Appeals since, even if the traders seemingly knew the data was material and nonpublic, there were no evidences that the original tip came from an insider, or there were no proofs concerning the existence of personal benefits in exchange for the tip. Starting from the Newman decision, many different federal convictions and pending cases were dismissed.[212]

Todd Newman and co-defendant Anthony Chiasson challenged the Government at trial.[213] In spite of the fact that the Government prevailed before a jury, the case was reversed and dismissed in the Second Circuit, due to the fact that Judge Winter[214] reiterated the key aspect of personal benefit.[215] In so doing, the Court took the unusual step of broadly criticizing the Government's "recent insider trading prosecutions, which are increasingly targeted at remote tippees many levels removed from corporate insiders."[216]

Both Newman and Chiasson were portfolio managers, the first at Diamondback Capital Management, LLC ("Diamondback"), and the last

[211] Verstein, A. (2019). Crypto assets and insider trading law's domain. *Iowa Law Review, 105*, 1–59.

[212] Goldstein, M. (2015). US Prosecutor to drop insider trading cases against seven. *The New York Times*.

[213] United States v. Newman, 773 F.3d 438, 442 (2d Cir. 2014).

[214] the author of the comprehensive dissent and concurring opinion in Chestman.

[215] United States v. Newman, 451.

[216] Idem at 448.

at Level Global Investors, L.P. ("Level Global").[217] This case implied two different insider tippers working for two firms: Rob Ray at Dell, and Chris Choi of Nvidia.[218]

With regard to Dell securities, Ray tipped Dell's earnings results, pre-public announcement, to Sandy Goyal, an analyst at an investment firm Neuberger Berman.[219] At the same time, Goyal tipped Diamondback analyst Jesse Tortora who further on tipped his manager, defendant Newman.[220] Summing up, as to Dell, Newman was three steps removed from the insider. It could not be proved that he was aware that Ray was the source of the insider information.[221] Tortora also tipped the Dell information to Level Global analyst, Spyridon Adondakis.[222] "Adondakis then passed along the Dell information to [defendant] Chiasson," who was his manager.[223] Therefore, Chiasson was four steps removed from the insider and, like Newman, it could not be proved that Chiasson knew that Ray was the source.[224]

As far as Nvidia securities are concerned, insider Choi tipped somebody he knew from church, Hyun Lim, regarding Nvidia's quarterly earnings information pre-public announcement.[225] Hyun Lim tipped Danny Kuo—analyst working at investment company Whittier Trust, and "Kuo circulated the information to the group of analyst friends, including Tortora and Adondakis, who in turn gave the information to Newman and Chiasson. This made Newman and Chiasson four levels removed from the [Nvidia] inside tippers."[226]

The Second Circuit focused on the ultimate defendant tippee's requested level of knowledge. Trying to connect the personal benefit and the violation of duty subject, the Court decided that the Government would have to prove that the ultimate tippee was aware of the insider

[217] Idem at 442.

[218] Id.

[219] Id.

[220] Id.

[221] Id.

[222] Id.

[223] Id.

[224] Id.

[225] Id.

[226] Id.

tipper's personal benefit, since the exchange of confidential information for personal benefit is tied to the insider's fiduciary breach. Consequently, the fiduciary breach triggers liability for securities fraud under Rule 10b-5. For insider trading liability, confidential information disclosed by the insider, standing alone, does not represent a breach.[227]

The Government was not satisfied, but the Court discharged the objections as "overreliance on our prior dicta,"[228] characterizing the prior cases as involving "tippees who directly participated in the tipper's breach (and therefore had knowledge of the tipper's disclosure for personal benefit) or tippees who were explicitly apprised of the tipper's gain by an intermediary tippee."[229] In response, the Court answered it was not aware of "a single case in which tippees as remote as Newman and Chiasson have been held criminally liable for insider trading."[230]

The Supreme Court soundly confirmed that "insider trading liability is based on breaches of fiduciary duty, not on informational asymmetries. This is a critical limitation on insider trading liability that protects a corporation's interests in confidentiality while promoting efficiency in the nation's securities markets."[231]

The Newman Court stated that a "corporate insider breach[es] his fiduciary duty by (a) disclosing confidential information to a tippee (b) in exchange for a personal benefit; [and] the tippee knew of the tipper's breach, that is, he knew the information was confidential and divulged for personal benefit."[232] By referring to the above-mentioned ideas, the decision was "that a defendant could be criminally liable for insider trading merely if such defendant knew that an insider had divulged information that was required to be kept confidential. But a breach of the duty of confidentiality is not fraudulent unless the tipper acts for personal benefit, that is to say, there is no breach unless the tipper 'is in effect selling the information to its recipient for cash, reciprocal information, or other things of value for himself'."[233]

[227] Id. at 448.

[228] Id.

[229] Id.

[230] Id.

[231] Id. at 449.

[232] Id. at 450.

[233] Id. (citing Dirks, 463 U.S. at 664).

Therefore, in this part of the opinion, Newman could be seen as having put the brakes on the Government. But, further on, when the Court stipulates what "personal benefit" stands for, it added a new requirement, which had not been expressly contained in Dirks: "To the extent Dirks suggests that a personal benefit may be inferred from a personal relationship between the tipper and tippee, where the tippee's trades 'resemble trading by the insider himself followed by a gift of the profits to the recipient,' we hold that such an inference is impermissible in the absence of proof of a meaningfully close personal relationship that generates an exchange that is objective, consequential, and represents at least a potential gain of a pecuniary or similarly valuable nature."[234]

Since "the evidence of the insiders' personal benefit in tipping involved nothing more than 'career advice' or membership in the same church, without any expectation of a *quid pro quo*, the Government had adduced insufficient evidence of a violation of fiduciary duty and the convictions had to be reversed." At the same time, the Court stated that "the Government presented absolutely no testimony or any other evidence that Newman and Chiasson knew that they were trading on information obtained from insiders, or that those insiders received any benefit in exchange for such disclosures, or even that Newman and Chiasson consciously avoided learning of these facts."[235]

Although friends were implied, the Newman Court held the information needed to be in exchange for something meaningful instead of simply good personal feelings.

Undeniably, some types of trading on material nonpublic information stand currently as legal. Keefe stated in this vein that, "[t]he truth is that if you operate a hedge fund and care to structure your business around the gaping loopholes that the Supreme Court has implicitly endorsed, insider trading is now effectively legal in the United States."[236] Currently, insider trading law in the United States has plenty of gaps, which could to some extent satisfy scholars in favor of making insider trading legal. Post-Newman, several reasons were offered concerning the limitations on insider trading prosecutions: the involvement of the government in "the

[234] Id. at 452.

[235] Id.

[236] Keefe, P. R. (2015, October 27). Making insider trading legal. *The New Yorker*. https://www.newyorker.com/business/currency/making-insider-trading-legal. Accessed 5 March 2020.

free market" is not good; innocent activities tend to be over-criminalized; defendants simply act as human when holding valuable information; regulation is unclear as to non-insiders.[237]

The Martoma Saga. The Martoma court held that "an insider or tipper personally benefits from a disclosure of inside information whenever the information was disclosed 'with the expectation that [the recipient] would trade on it' ... and the disclosure 'resemble[s] trading by the insider followed by a gift of the profits to the recipient'," no matter if there was a close personal friendship between tipper and tippee or not.[238]

The Court's opinion in Martoma case proved the strong fracture within the Second Circuit. The different decisions in United States v. Martoma[239] proved that the policy fight between information parity and market efficiency, keeps on being waged among fair-minded judges.[240]

Working with the SAC Capital hedge funds, Martoma, the portfolio manager in this fund, traded the stock of Elan Corporation and Wyeth Pharmaceuticals after having several meetings with Dr. Stanley Gilman, the alleged tipper.[241] Both Elan and Wyeth were at that moment collaborating for an experimental drug known under the name of bapineuzumab in their desire to treat Alzheimer's disease.[242] With the aim of learning more about this drug, Martoma asked the help of expert networking companies and settled in this vein paid consultations with doctors with a rich experience in Alzheimer's disease.[243] With the help of this network, Martoma came along with two doctors working on the clinical trial, Joel Ross and Dr. Gilman,[244] the last one being chairman of the safety monitoring committee for the bapineuzumab clinical trial.[245]

[237] Dorfman, J. (2015, March 22). Make insider trading legal to stop hurting ordinary investors. *Forbes*.

[238] Klotz, M., Schachter, M. S., Gray, E. P., et al. (2017). Second circuit eliminates 'meaningfully close personal relationship' test. *The Investment Lawyer, 24*(11), 34.

[239] United States v. Martoma, 869 F.3d 58 (2d Cir. 2017), opinion amended and superseded, 894 F.3d 64 (2d Cir. 2017).

[240] Martoma, 869 F.3d at 58.

[241] Id. at 61.

[242] Id.

[243] Id.

[244] Id.

[245] Id.

Despite their implications concerning confidentiality, both doctors Gilman and Ross disclosed confidential information concerning the progress of the trial to Martoma.[246] However, the main "insider"—like in Newman, Dr. Gilman, was not charged although he testified against Martoma. His not being charged was due to signing a non-prosecution agreement with the Government.[247] After a jury trial, the decision was that Mathew Martoma was convicted of insider trading.[248] On appeal, he mentioned the Newman case, stipulating that legal standards were not complied also adding that there were not enough proofs to support the conviction.[249]

According to his declaration, Martoma stated that the relation he had with Dr. Gilman was not a "meaningfully close personal relationship," at the same time stating that Dr. Gilman did not receive any "objective, consequential ... gain of a pecuniary or similarly valuable nature" in exchange for his sharing of information with Mathew Martoma.[250] On these grounds, Martoma requested a retrial.[251]

His claims were rejected with majority (two of the three-judge panel). Thus, two separate opinions were issued by Chief Judge Robert Katzmann and Judge Denny Chin, over the dissent of Judge Rosemary Pooler.[252] The two opinions departed sharply from Newman case opinion.[253]

United States v. Lee. Even if, at some point the Martoma saga seemed closed, another long-running insider trading matter was temporarily brought back to life. Thus, in June 2019, a federal judge established

[246] Id. at 62.

[247] Jacobs, B. (2016, February 9). Non-prosecution agreements: Reserved for VIPs? *Forbes*. https://www.forbes.com/sites/insider/2016/02/09/non-prosecution-agreements-reserved-for-vips/#684b1e572bdd. Accessed 25 July 2020.

[248] Stevenson, A., & Goldstein, M. (2014, February 6). Ex-SAC trade convicted of securities fraud. *The New York Times*. https://dealbook.nytimes.com/2014/02/06/former-sac-trader-found-guilty-of-insider-trading/. Accessed 20 July 2020.

[249] Martoma, 869 F.3d at 61.

[250] Id. at 64–65.

[251] Id.

[252] United States v. Martoma, 869 F.3d 58 (2d Cir. 2017), opinion amended and superseded, 894 F.3d 64 (2d Cir. 2017).

[253] Martoma, 869 F.3d at 67; Martoma, 894 F.3d at 77–78.

the necessity for a retrial for Richard Lee, a former hedge fund portfolio manager who had pled guilty for securities fraud and conspiracy to do securities fraud.[254]

In July 2013, Lee had pled guilty to insider trading by exchanging information from tippers at public companies and investment firms. According to his declaration, he had knowledge about other individuals who had breached a fiduciary duty or duty of confidentiality, while they were offering him various pieces of information.

Several years later, in 2017, due to evolutions in litigation (see the Newman trial), Lee decided in favor of withdrawing his guilty plea, considering it not enough regarding the personal benefit requirement. Lee's action had as a basis an issue in Newman's case not eroded by Salman and Martoma: the necessity for a tippee to know that the tipper disclosed MNPI in exchange for a personal benefit.

According to the court, Lee's plea proceeding did not explore "(1) who the corporate insiders were; (2) whether Lee knew who they were; (3) to whom the corporate insiders disclosed material non-public information, or (4) the nature of the relationship between the tippers and those to whom they disclosed material non-public information."[255] By consequence, the court held Lee's guilty plea to be factually insufficient due to the lack of any information speaking "directly or indirectly to Lee's knowledge of any personal benefit the corporate insiders received as a result of divulging confidential information."[256]

In the end, the Government dismissed the case on November 7, 2019, before the scheduled December retrial.

As we have seen, in the Newman case, in the center of the decision was not the "personal benefit," but the fact that the tippee must know that the tipper received a personal benefit. Starting from this, the Lee court noticed that, "[p]rior to Newman, it was not clear that a breach of fiduciary duty [by the tipper] by definition includes a personal benefit to the tipper. Newman clarifies this point, which the Supreme Court later confirmed in Salman."[257] Because of this clarification of the law, the court

[254] United States v. Lee, No. 13 CR 539 (PGG), S.D.N.Y. June 21, 2019.

[255] Id.

[256] Id.

[257] Id.

saw "no reason to believe that Lee – in using the phrase 'breach of fiduciary duty' during his 2013 allocution – understood that phrase to include the liability components later explicated in Newman and Salman."[258]

The question that arises is when does information become sufficiently "public" for trading?

The Lee case needs further attention and solutions concerning the above-mentioned question, so that insiders can avoid new information that is not "public" and safely trade it. If in the beginning Lee pleaded guilty to trading on tips of MNPI, he changed his mind later on, stating that the traded information was at the time public. His argument was however rejected by the Court, stating that "[i]nformation is not 'fully impounded' into the price of a stock if the price is rising as one is trading … At best, the information is in the process of being 'impounded' into the share price by virtue of the trades that are contemporaneously occurring."[259]

Taking into account that (i) Lee offered no proof "as to how many or which [research-firm] clients received this information, or when they received it," (ii) the research firm had disclosed the information only to "a special group – [its] clients," and (iii) the issuer's "share price continued to rise while Lee was trading, demonstrating that the information he had obtained was not fully impounded into the share price," there was no proof that the information at issue was public when Lee received it and began to trade.

Second Circuits Holds that No Personal Benefit Required for Criminal Insider Trading Cases Brought under Title 18. In late December 2019, the Second Circuit issued a decision in United States v. Blaszczak[260] stating that the personal benefit test cannot be applied in every insider trading cases. The government has traditionally brought insider trading cases as violations of the general anti-fraud provisions found in Section 10(b) of the Exchange Act.[261] A long line of insider trading cases (Dirks, Newman, Salman, and Martoma) urged for proof of a direct or indirect personal benefit to the tipper to settle liability. In recent times, several criminal prosecutors have brought insider trading cases as violations of the criminal

[258] Id.

[259] Id.

[260] United States v. Blaszczak, 947 F.3d 19 (2d Cir. 2019).

[261] Title 15 of the US Code.

wire fraud and/or securities fraud statutes under Title 18 of the US Code additionally to charging violations of Section 10(b) of the Exchange Act, arguing that the personal benefit requirement does not apply to charges brought under Title 18.[262] The Blaszczak case has to do with allegations that two hedge funds illegally traded on MNPI dealing with medical treatment reimbursement rates they received from a consultant (Blaszcak), who was informed by a friend who worked at a medical center. Additionally to violations of Section 10(b), the prosecutors charged defendants with violations of Sections 641 (conversion), 1343 (wire fraud), and 1348 (securities fraud) under Title 18. At trial, the defendants were acquitted on the Section 10(b) charges, but convicted of violations of Title 18. On appeal, the defendants argued that their wire fraud and securities fraud convictions under Title 18 should be overturned because the district court did not apply Dirks and require the government to prove that the CMS employee received a personal benefit for tipping the information. In a split decision, the Second Circuit stated the convictions and held that the personal benefit requirement did not apply to the Title 18 wire fraud and securities fraud statutes.[263]

The Second Circuit's decision broadens criminal prosecutors' power in insider trading cases. In spite of the fact that decades of case law have established that the government must prove a personal benefit in Section 10(b) cases, prosecutors may now convict a defendant under other criminal statutes without proving that the tipper of MNPI received a personal benefit in exchange for that information. As the mixed verdicts in Blaszczak prove, this lower burden can be crucial to the outcome in some cases. It remains to be seen whether prosecutors will now charge defendants with securities fraud and wire fraud in insider trading cases with less than overwhelming evidence of a personal benefit, but company employees and others with access to MNPI should be on notice about the potentially increased risk of prosecution.

According to Langevoort, "information use and dissemination from inside public companies is immensely weighty as a matter of policy,

[262] The SEC may only bring civil enforcement actions and does not have the authority to charge violations of criminal statutes. See Securities and Exchange Commission Division of Enforcement (2017). Enforcement Manual Office of Chief Counsel, November 28, 2017. https://www.sec.gov/divisions/enforce/enforcementmanual.pdf. Accessed 20 July 2020.

[263] Blaszczak, 947 F.3d at 36-37.

much more than the simplistic invocation of embezzlement can bear. "Akin to" is not the same as "is." Reference to breach of fiduciary duty is required in ordinary classical and misappropriation enforcement proceedings in order to address the "fine distinctions" between good and bad ways of obtaining or using material nonpublic information. Existing doctrine could surely do better, but it would require something more than reference to stolen goods."[264] Consequently, the outcome encourages bringing challenging tipper-tippee cases (especially chain-link ones) as criminal rather than civil cases, in spite of the fact that insider trading enforcement is meant to work in a different manner.

The regulation concerning insider trading and more precisely tipping has attracted attention during the last several years, "and will likely continue to be in flux as the Second Circuit and other courts grapple with complex issues relating to the Supreme Court's decision in Salman and the Second Circuit's decisions in Newman and Martoma. For now, Martoma II has embraced a broad theory that tippers are liable when they give material, nonpublic information to a tippee with an intent to benefit the tippee, which can be proven based on circumstantial evidence. Judge Pooler's strong dissent insisting that this theory is not consistent with precedent suggests that the issue is not settled."[265] It is true also that Martoma has filed a petition for certiorari,[266] but this was denied.

Half a century after the "evolving" judge-made law of insider trading, the Newman/Martoma impasse has finally driven Congress to undertake the difficult task of defining the law of insider trading.

[264] Langevoort, D. C. (2019). *Watching insider trading law wobble: Obus, Newman, Salman, Two Martomas, and a Blaszczak*. Georgetown University Law Center. https://scholarship.law.georgetown.edu/cgi/viewcontent.cgi?article=3227&context=facpub. Accessed 12 July 2020.

[265] Cahn, M. D., Mitchell, E. L., & WilmerHale, B. A. (2019). *Better the devil you know? Tipping liability, Martoma and the rise of 18 U.S.C. § 1348*. Harvard Law School Forum on Corporate Governance. https://corpgov.law.harvard.edu/2019/06/02/better-the-devil-you-know-tipping-liability-martoma-and-the-rise-of-18-u-s-c-%C2%A7-1348/. Accessed 20 July 2020.

[266] Sherry, A. (2019). Martoma seeks SCOTUS review of 'Dirks-defying' insider trading decision. https://lrus.wolterskluwer.com/news/securities-regulation-daily/martoma-seeks-scotus-review-of-dirks-defying-insider-trading-decision/71839/. Accessed 28 July 2020.

7.4 New Regulatory Developments

The new regulatory changes have been prompted by the necessity "for coherence in the law, especially when it can result in a prison sentence or substantial monetary penalties for a violation. Statutes give us some comfort that a legislative body has thought about the reason certain conduct is designated as wrongful, and why the moral opprobrium of the community should be visited on offenders. At least, that is what we hope would happen. But, when the law develops in a different way, through ad hoc judicial decisions, administrative regulations, and legislative inaction to correct or redirect its application, then there is a fear that traditional notions of due process and fair notice have not been adequately addressed. Those concerns have not had an impact, however, in the world of securities fraud for one of its prime areas: insider trading."[267]

Insider trading captured attention from regulators, authorities, and financial professionals. Accordingly, "in light of the implications of insider trading law to the country's securities market, few laws demand congressional attention more than this one."[268] Scholars agree on this subject[269] stating even that "Congress should act"[270] and faced with several uncertainties, many commentators have called for a legislative solution.[271] This necessity was also favored by the fact that, "allowing this errant doctrine to become firmly lodged in the law would needlessly leave many socially undesirable trades unpunished and hence undeterred."[272]

[267] Henning, P. J. (2018). Making up insider trading law as you go. *Washington University Journal of Law & Policy, 56,* 101. https://openscholarship.wustl.edu/law_journal_law_policy/vol56/iss1/12. Accessed July 28, 2020.

[268] Spacone, A. C. (2019). The second circuit's curious journey through the law of tippee liability for insider trading: Newman to Martoma. *Roger Williams University Law Review, 24*(1), Article 2. https://docs.rwu.edu/rwu_LR/vol24/iss1/2. Accessed July 27, 2020.

[269] Hostert, J. (2019). Great expectations, good intentions, and the appearance of the personal benefit in insider trading: why the stage needs reset after Martoma. *Southern Illinois University Law Journal, 43,* 703–748. See also Spacone, A. C. (2019). Op. Cit.

[270] Murdock, C. W. (2019). The future of insider trading after Salman: Perpetuation of a Flawed analysis or a return to basics. *Hastings Law Journal, 70*(6), 1547–1612.

[271] Fisch, J. E. (2018). Constructive ambiguity and judicial development of insider trading. Faculty Scholarship at Penn Law. 2028. https://scholarship.law.upenn.edu/faculty_scholarship/2028. Accessed July 27, 2020.

[272] Fox, M. B., & Tepe, G. N. (2018). Personal benefit has no place in misappropriation tipping cases. *SMU Law Review, 71,* 767–782.

As a consequence, after several drafts, in 2019, the House passed the ITPA.[273] Still, in the final voice vote on December 5, 2019, there was an amendment of the bill inserting a personal benefit aspect, requested by the Republican Representative Patrick McHenry. This new version stipulates that trading is unlawful in the case in which information was achieved in one of the following cases: breach of a fiduciary duty, confidentiality agreement, or breach of a contract "for a direct or indirect personal benefit (including pecuniary gain, reputational benefit, or a gift of confidential information to a trading relative or friend)."[274]

The amendment previously mentioned was added in the lack of fact-finding hearing or analysis. In spite of the fact that the final bill that passed provides bigger weight to market efficiency interests than all the other drafts issued, there is still room for improvement as the bill incorporated a similar language regarding personal benefit that has raised judges one against the other, without providing any illumination concerning the meaning of the term. According to "by using the word 'including,' does the bill mean to suggest that 'personal benefits' is not necessarily limited to pecuniary gain, reputational benefit, or gift to a relative or friend, and might include merely a charitable desire to gift information to a perfect stranger as Martoma II's majority concluded? That reading likely is not one Congressman McHenry would agree with since it tends to dilute the force of a personal benefit element. But it is a fair reading of the language."[275]

At the same time another question that rises is what represents a "friend" who can receive as gift confidential information that constitutes a crime? Is this the case of Newman, namely a person who is very close, or a casual friend can be seen as enough? Professor John Coffee of Columbia Law School was one of the proponents of the first draft for this bill. In this case, he expressed his disappointment with this late proposed and voted amendment, affirming that the switch removed the "key element"

[273] Insider Trading Prohibition Act, H.R. 2534,115th Cong., 1st Sess. (Dec. 5, 2019) § 16A (as approved by H.R. Fin. Serv. Comm., May 8, 2019, and committed to the H. Comm. of the Whole, Sept. 27, 2019)/ITPA.

[274] Insider Trading Prohibition Act, H.R. 2534,115th Cong., 1st Sess. (Dec. 5, 2019). § 2 at 16A(c)(1)(D) (2019).

[275] Park, T. H. (2019). Newman/Martoma: The insider trading law's impasse and the promise of congressional action. *Fordham Journal of Corporate & Financial Law, XXV*, 3–95, p. 95.

that would have offered deep clarification.[276] The regulation of insider trading is a challenge that "cannot be addressed by simply adopting the language with which courts have struggled. An empirical study of what kind of marketplace the country needs may lead to clearer language about the scope of prohibition on trading."[277] ITPA can however, if carefully considered, "unmoor the offense from its current fraud-based rubric."[278]

7.5 Arbitration Cases

SEC v. Quantek Asset Management LLC. The SEC considers it suitable and important to citizens that public administrative and C&D[279] processes be implemented according "to Section 8A of the Securities Act of 1933 - Securities Act, Sections 203(e), 203(f), and 203(k) of the Investment Advisers Act of 1940 - Advisers Act, and Section 9(b) of the Investment Company Act of 1940 Investment Company Act"[280] against Quantek Asset Management, LLC (Quantek), Bulltick Capital Markets Holdings (LP Bulltick), Javier Guerra (Guerra), but also Ralph Patino (Patino) all in all considered Respondents.

On May 29, 2012, the SEC accused a fund adviser located in Miami of having deceived investing individuals regarding the managers' investments made in a fund located in Latin America.[281]

According to the examination performed by the SEC, it was discovered that different misleading representations have been made by Quantek regarding "skin in the game along with investors in the USD 1 billion

[276] Kragie, A., & Godoy, J. (2019). House Passes 1st Explicit Ban on Insider Trading, LAW360 (Dec. 5, 2019). https://www.law360.com/articles/1225615/house-passes-1st-explicit-ban-on-insider-trading. Accessed 28 July 2020.

[277] Park, T. (2019). Op. Cit., p. 95.

[278] Nagy, D. M. (2020). Chiarella v. United States and its Indelible Impact on Insider Trading Law (July 1, 2020). *Tennessee Journal of Law and Policy, 15*. https://papers.ssrn.com/sol3/papers.cfm?abstract_id=3650626. Accessed 12 July 2020.

[279] Cease-and-desist.

[280] http://www.lexissecuritiesmosaic.com/gateway/sec/press-release/2012_33-9326.pdf. Accessed June 16, 2020.

[281] SEC. (2012b). Miami Hedge Fund Adviser Charged for Misleading Investors About 'Skin in the Game' and Related-Party Deals. US Securities and Exchange Commission. https://www.sec.gov/news/press-release/2012-2012-104htm. Accessed 27 July 2020.

Quantek Opportunity Fund."[282] Similarly, it has been noted that "skin in the game," under this fund management given circumstance, represents that particular situation in which the adviser/executive decides to invest his/her own capital in that company. This is considered, in the opinion of each fund investor a major means of aligning all advisers' interests to his/her own, leading to a better control and to a better risk management.[283]

In fact, Quantek's managers never invested their capital in the Funds. Similarly, the SEC's research revealed how Quantek manipulated investors regarding investments of those funds it managed,[284] but also some connected-party exchanges involving manager Guerra, as well as his previous owning corporation Bulltick LP.

In the enactment process conducted by the SEC, Quantek, and several persons including Bulltick, Guerra, and Ralph Patino have been accused together.[285] They paid the total amount of USD 3.1 million, while Guerra, just like Patino was forced to assent to securities industry bars.[286]

Besides, the SEC has discovered a crucial element, namely, that information was not accurately revealed to investors by neither Quantek nor Guerra or Bulltick. This proved to be another key element in this file. Thus, around four or even five years ago, due to the fact that Opportunity Funds allowed related-party exchanges between the parent entity belonging to Quantek, Bulltick but also various associates, investors had been alerted with regard to exchanges improperly disclosed. Both Quantek's and Bulltick's staff took care but also backdated omitted capital lent data.

[282] Ibid.

[283] Ibid.

[284] Forkey, R. (2012, June 9). Investment Advisor and Broker/Dealer Investment Fraud and Mismanagement Litigation and FINRA. Investment Advisor Magazine.

[285] SEC. (2012). http://www.sec.gov/litigation/admin/2012/33-9326.pdf. Accessed 16 June 2020.

[286] Ibid.

Javier Guerra resigned on September 28, 2011.[287] According to press reports,[288] the portfolio manager of QAM[289] and Quantek Opportunity Fund, LP (Partnership or Feeder Fund), submitted his relinquishment of responsibility (he resigned) leaving the job due to losses in arbitration to Aris.[290]

According to the arbitration bureau, it was reported that Quantek Asset Management introduced Aris by fraud for investing in the Feeder Fund (USD 15 million were invested[291]) while, at the same time, it commanded Guerra to pay losses worth USD 1 million.

Quantek procured incorrect notifications to investors regarding some connected-party exchanges by the funds. Through its processes, Quantek broke several anti-fraud, compliance and records management agreements from "the Advisers Act and Securities Act." Guerra, Quantek's manager and its former operations manager, Ralph Patino, had made misstatements concerning Quantek's account. Bulltick had helped and encouraged this, causing several of Quantek's violations.[292]

Quantek,[293] Guerra,[294] Bulltick,[295] and Patino[296] established charges in the absence of any guilt confession.

[287] Vardi, N. (2012). Hedge Fund Manager of Former USD 1 Billion Fund Quits after Arbitration Loss. http://www.forbes.com/sites/nathanvardi/2011/10/03/hedge-fund-manager-of-former-1-billion-fund-quits-after-arbitration-loss/. Accessed 12 June 2012.

[288] Pitaro, V. (2010). New York state supreme court dismisses hedge funds of funds' complaint against accipiter hedge funds based on exculpatory language in accipiter fund documents and absence of fiduciary duty among constituent limited partners. *The Hedge Fund Law Report, 3*(7).

[289] Quantek Asset Management.

[290] Aris Multi-Strategy Fund.

[291] Greenstein, A. (2011). Fund of hedge funds Aris multi-strategy fund wins arbitration award against underlying manager based on allegations of self-dealing. *The Hedge Fund Law Report, 4*(39).

[292] Forkey, R. (2012). Investment advisor and broker/dealer investment fraud and mismanagement litigation and FINRA. Investment Advisor on Saturday, June 9, 2012.

[293] Quantek Asset Management, LLC.

[294] Javier Guerra, from Miami, Florida, "the lead principal of Quantek and the portfolio manager for the Opportunity Funds."

[295] Bulltick Capital Markets Holdings, LP founded by Javier Guerra and his associates, parent company of Quantek and two Commission registered broker-dealers.

[296] Ralph Patino from Miramar, Florida, Quantek's director of operations.

In this regard, Quantek and Guerra decided in favor of paying around "USD 2.2 million in disgorgement and prejudgment interest, and financial penalties of USD 375,000 and USD 150,000. Bulltick agreed to pay a penalty of USD 300,000, while Patino accepted to pay a penalty of USD 50,000. Guerra consented to a five-year securities industry bar, and Patino consented to a securities industry bar of one year."[297] Censorship was granted by Quantek and Bulltick.

As seen above, this claim of malpractice was resolved by monetary penalties, censorship and securities industry bars. Nevertheless, it should be clear that every broker's obligation is stated to investors as accurate as possible, always providing them the best solutions and recommendations which best suit each investor. Accordingly, the stage of life, soundness, but also financial complexity, or its lack, must represent major indexes for each broker. The law and the SEC are there to help protect investors, and here they helped in that particular case to correct a dangerous path the company was taking.

As of November 2017, FINRA "operates the largest securities dispute resolution forum in the United States,"[298] through its wholly owned subsidiary, FINRA Dispute Resolution. At this time, 99% of the securities-related disputes in the United States are managed through FINRA's arbitration process. This process includes a review for conflicts of interest,[299] a background investigation, and a general obligation of a continuing duty to disclose special interests of the arbitrator as they arise.[300] Further, for each dispute, the arbitrators are selected randomly, through the Neutral List Selection System, which creates a random computer-generated roster of arbitrator candidates that parties may select for a given dispute.[301] The number of arbitrators for each dispute, which ranges from one to three, is determined by the amounts at issue in the dispute, with claims up to USD 100,000 heard by a single arbitrator, and claims involving amounts

[297] Forkey, Russell, Investment Advisor and Broker/Dealer.

[298] Gross, J. (2016). The historical basis of securities arbitration as an investor protection mechanism. *Journal of Dispute Resolution*, 171–186 at 184 (noting that FINRA "administers more than 99% of securities arbitrations in the country").

[299] FINRA. (2016). Your duty to disclose. Financial Industry Regulatory Authority. https://www.finra.org/sites/default/files/FINRA-duty-disclose-training.pdf. Accessed 1 October 2019.

[300] Id.

[301] Id.

greater than USD 100,000 heard by three arbitrators.[302] Recovery of punitive damages in securities disputes is a pro-investor characteristic of FINRA securities arbitration, as ability to obtain punitive damages in securities disputes in federal courts is limited. In 2018, FINRA reported average turnaround time for an arbitration claim, from the beginning of the dispute through its resolution, was 14.5 months.[303] In cases involving simplified decisions, or in cases expedited due to the advanced age of the customer bringing the claim, the turnaround time can be cut by nearly half, to an average of 7.3 months.[304] In contrast, a federal lawsuit involving a securities transaction on average takes 689 days or nearly 23 months to resolve. In 2018, FINRA:

- "Levied USD 39.5 million in fines.
- Ordered USD 27.9 million in restitution to harmed investors.
- Referred more than 827 fraud and insider trading cases to the SEC and other agencies for litigation and/or prosecution."[305]

James Lee v. Kylin Management LLC, et al. James Lee, a managing director set a dispute against Kylin Management LLC, a hedge fund, before the United States District Court for the Southern District stating that the hedge fund illegally withheld "over USD 3 million in compensation to which Lee was entitled."[306] In motion for summary judgment, the hedge fund sought to dismiss each of the managing director's claims on various grounds, but primarily argued that the NYLL claim should be dismissed on the ground that carried interest and performance bonuses are not "wages" under the statute. On July 31, 2019, the United

[302] FINRA. (2017). Arbitrator selection. Financial Industry Regulatory Authority. https://www.finra.org/arbitration-and-mediation/arbitrator-selection. Accessed 27 July 2020. See also FINRA (2017). Rules r. 12403 (Fin. Indus. Regulatory Auth. 2017).

[303] See FINRA. (2019) Dispute Resolution Statistics 2018. Financial Industry Regulatory Authority. http://www.finra.org/arbitrationand-mediation/dispute-resolution-statistics. Accessed 12 July 2020.

[304] Idem.

[305] FINRA (2020). Annual Financial Report 2019. Financial Industry Regulatory Authority. https://www.finra.org/sites/default/files/2020-06/2019-annual-financial-report.pdf. Accessed 12 July 2020.

[306] Lee v. Kylin Mgmt. LLC, No. 17-CV-7249 (JMF), 2019 WL 917097 (S.D.N.Y. Feb. 25, 2019).

States District Court for the Southern District denied the hedge fund's motion for summary judgment. Relying upon clear precedent in the New York Court of Appeals and Second Circuit, the Court held that "although 'incentive pay' like the disputed bonus amounts in this case 'does not constitute a wage until it is actually earned and vested,' when it is 'guaranteed under [a] formula to be a percentage of the revenues ... generated' and 'not left to [the employer's] discretion,' it constitutes protected 'wages' under the Labor Law."[307] The District Court allowed the managing director's claims, including for liquidated damages, prejudgment interest, and attorneys' fees under the NYLL, to proceed and ordered the parties to prepare for trial.

7.6 Concluding Remarks

The cases presented above are some of the most recent and most famous. According to Poser, unlike Madoff's scheme that seems to have been an impressive, immense fraud, most of litigations and arbitrations involved fraudulent actions widely spread in the entire funds market,[308] seriously affecting investors. Poser noted that due to SEC's inability or unwillingness to fulfil its enforcement responsibilities investors have lost billions of USD.[309] Since 2000, regulators were unsuccessful in taking appropriate and efficient action to restrict abuses in relation to hedge funds, which leads to the conclusion that both *regulatory enforcement and investors' protection are highly necessary.*

With regard to why the regulators failed in the above cases it has been remarked that: the explanations include conflicts of interest among employees, poor employees' training, constraints related to finances, and a devised nature of the regulatory system.[310] The various players in these litigation and arbitration cases acted in ways that in the end turned out to be against their own interest. A high number of sophisticated but also ordinary hedge fund investors favored these funds for a long period and lost money. The administrators and the auditors were willing to accept

[307] Quoting Reilly v. Natwest Mkts. Group. Inc., 181 F.3d 253, 271 (2d Cir. 1999).

[308] Ibid.

[309] Poser, N. S., & Fanto, J. A. (2007). *Broker-dealer law & regulation* (4th ed.). New York: Aspen Publishers.

[310] Poser, N. S. (2009). Why the SEC failed: Regulators against regulation. *Brooklyn Journal of Corporate, Financial & Commercial Law, 3*(2), 289–324.

the manager's explanations, if any. Still, this acceptance led to disastrous consequences for their funds or business. Above all, the SEC did not assure too much protection for investors.

Nevertheless, the basic motivation explaining failures is the anti-regulatory atmosphere, supported by academically generated anti-regulatory approach that has pervaded government during the last twenty or thirty years. Apparently, the SEC's major aim shifted: it no longer protects investing persons, but rather it protects those firms and investment companies that it regulates. As one commentator concluded, in spite of having been made particularly for protecting investors, the SEC changed into some authority protective with financial scammers.[311] This is an exaggeration, of course, but it needs to be taken into consideration.

Now, it is likely that conflicts concerning both redemptions and distressed hedge funds will end up in court during the years to come. The conflicts of interest in these cases concern not only instances of confessed fraud that emerge as bankruptcy declines and losses rise, but also valuation conflicts and controversies between stockholders and hedge repositories over the timing of salvations. Many of these demands have been litigated in other countries, but US complaints are also on the rise.

A shift in the modern view of hedge fund investments but also organizational audit is underway. These consequences rising from the Madoff crisis, together with the current recession, is going to affect hedge funds' due diligence, mainly with respect to operational risk. On this point, it has been remarked that not only investors, but also funds are going to obligatory reconsider prior rigorous due diligence assumptions. In order to survive in the post-Madoff world, they ought to make themselves ready to paying prices related to the growing resources necessary to be invested in order to efficiently solve "operational due diligence."[312]

During recent years, new regulatory modifications have been suggested. The political requirement to enact new measures quickly, however, has led to proposed alterations that are adapted to the specific features of the hedge reserves fraud. Unfortunately, there does not seem to have been a complete assessment of the present regulatory system for hedge funds.

[311] Lewis, M., et al. (2009, January 3). The End of the Financial World as We Know It. *The New York Times*, p. 9.

[312] Scharfman, J. (2009). *The Madoff identity: A new operational due diligence paradigm in a post-Madoff world*. http://ssrn.com/abstract=1435024. Accessed 29 August 2020.

This chapter described several case studies concerning various claims that financial organizations and investors might encounter if a regulatory enforcement crashes. It is certain that, due to the worldwide financial circumstances, claims against financial institutions are going to grow. The following quote from Johnson et al. (2010) sums up much of the recent debate following these cases:

"In the aftermath of a Ponzi scheme's collapse, financial institutions, whether direct or indirect participants, will almost certainly face litigation risks for even the most remote involvement in financial frauds."[313] Recently, it was seen that litigations and arbitrations are changing, respectively, persecuted investors tend to become more and more innovative, prosecuting every financial sound company, generally financial companies that could have played significant roles. The economic situation is standing still while indignation is going stronger in people's lives due to light regulation of the financial market, which can become a model.

While stories such as Stanford's, Petters', and Madoff's can be labelled as atypical due to the size of their collapse or due to the level of malfeasance connected with the fraud, they help to illustrate the reason why both regulators and the public in general must pay greater attention to hedge fund industry regulation and the protection of investors.

As highlighted above, substantive regulation directed toward the elimination and governance of conflicts of interest has its limits. It is the author's opinion that where these limits emerge, only mandatory and voluntary disclosure is able to offer the necessary protection by shifting part of the responsibility for the protection of investors to the investors themselves. This is especially because, as it is well-known, disclosure offers the foundation for the regulations and especially of investor protection laws.

In addition to explaining many of these risks and conflicts of interests associated to hedge fund management, this chapter demonstrated the risks that they induced to hedge fund investors, particularly sophisticated, but also to indirect investors who were often not aware of their hedge fund investment.

Lately, due to the increase of arbitration and litigation cases, hedge fund investors, specifically institutional investors, have been intensifying their requests for better safeguard. Therefore, investors within the hedge

[313] Johnston, K., et al. (2010). Op. Cit., p. 55.

fund industry lost their confidence and have come to understand that improved investor protection was imperative.

The increased attention on the issue has led to the creation of hedge fund "*best practices*" documents, making a multitude of suggestions that, if made, could greatly improve the level of investors' interests protection. Still, *best practices* are generally voluntary suggestions that, so far, hedge fund managers have proven little desire of adopting and implementing.

Recently, in the United States, the most important factor driving hedge funds litigations and arbitrations is regulatory risk, primarily involving the Securities and Exchange Commission (SEC). As seen so far, the SEC stays very focused on the securities investments, including the SEC's enforcement program. Lately, a high number of litigations as well as enforcement actions were with regard to investment advisers, valuations, Foreign Corrupt Practices Act (FCPA) violations and insider trading. In this respect, Financial Industry Regulatory Authority (FINRA) and other state-level regulatory authorities also have been very active over the last several years on regards of hedge funds. Arbitration is often used to solve claim disputes, particularly if they are cross-border. But even if arbitration is generally quicker than litigation, and usually cheaper, litigations are still leading in cases. Lately, many hedge funds litigation decisions seem overwritten opinions that attempt to legislate a better regulation. However, until new regulatory enforcements are made, risks must be carefully considered. Currently, all these problems that appear in hedge funds litigations indicate that in the next future, hopefully, the Congress will take up the difficult and dangerous task of turning a common law crime into a real statute.

As a concluding remark, it is necessary that regulators take action to ensure that hedge fund investors receive adequate protection from the funds' many risks and conflicts of interest. Through the introduction of increased transparency to hedge fund investment and standardization of the valuation process, regulators are able to defend investors' rights without eliminating the specific flexibility that enables hedge funds to confer major benefits on the markets.

References

Aggarwal, K. A., & Wu, G. (2006). Stock market manipulations. *The Journal of Business, 79*(4), 1915–1954. https://doi.org/10.1086/503652.

Bartlett, R., Cain, M. D., Fisch, J. E., & Davidoff, S. S. (2019). The myth of Morrison: Securities fraud litigation against foreign issuers. *Faculty Scholarship at Penn Law*. https://scholarship.law.upenn.edu/faculty_scholarship/2025. Accessed 29 July 2020.

Beach et al. v. Citigroup Alternative Investments LLC et al., No. 1:12-cv-07717 (S.D.N.Y. Aug. 19, 2015).

Bethel, J. E., Ferrell, A., & Hu, G. (2008). *Law and economic issues in subprime litigation* (Discussion Paper No. 612, 03/2008). Harvard Law School Cambridge. http://www.law.harvard.edu/programs/olin_center/. Accessed 29 July 2020.

Black Diamond Offshore Ltd., et al., v. Porsche Automobil Holding SE, f/k/a Dr. Ing. h.c. F. Porsche AG; Wendelin Wiedeking; and Holger P. Haerter, Nos. 10 CV 0532 and 10 CV 4155 (S.D.N.Y. Dec. 30, 2010).

Bollen, N. (2011). Suspicious patterns in hedge fund returns and the risk of fraud. *Review of Financial Studies, 25*(9), 1–43 (2011). https://doi.org/10.2139/ssrn.1569626.

Bonny v. Soc'y of Lloyd's, 3 F.3d 156 (7th Cir. 1993).

Buell, S. W. (2011). What is securities fraud? *Duke Law Journal, 61*(3), 511–582.

Buxbaum, H. L. (2012a). Remedies for foreign investors under US federal securities law. *Law and Contemporary Problems, 75*, 161–186.

Buxbaum, H. L. (2012b). Conflict of economic laws: From sovereignty to substance. *Vancouver Journal of International Law, 42*, 931–977.

Cahn, M. D., Mitchell, E. L., & WilmerHale, B. A. (2019). *Better the devil you know? Tipping liability, Martoma and the rise of 18 U.S.C. § 1348*. Harvard Law School Forum on Corporate Governance. https://corpgov.law.harvard.edu/2019/06/02/better-the-devil-you-know-tipping-liability-martoma-and-the-rise-of-18-u-s-c-%C2%A7-1348/. Accessed 20 July 2020.

Carvajal, A., Monroe, H., Pattillo, C., et al. (2009). *Ponzi schemes in the Caribbean* (International Monetary Fund Working Paper). https://www.google.com/url?sa=t&rct=j&q=&esrc=s&source=web&cd=&ved=2ahUKEwjxlIf0uavrAhWD2aQKHcPeD7IQFjABegQIBRAB&url=https%3A%2F%2Fwww.imf.org%2Fexternal%2Fpubs%2Fft%2Fwp%2F2009%2Fwp0995.pdf&usg=AOvVaw3FpriLdVMURHTRcY1imyDf. Accessed 20 July 2020.

Citigroup Alternative Investments LLC and Citigroup Global Markets Inc., SEC Admin. Proc. No. 3-16757, 4 (Aug. 17, 2015).

Clauss, P., Roncalli, Th, & Weisang, G. (2009). Risk management lessons from Madoff fraud. *International Finance Review*. https://doi.org/10.2139/ssrn.1358086.

Coffee, J. C., Jr. (2013). Mapping the future of insider trading law: Of boundaries, gaps, and strategies. *Columbia Business Law Review, 2,* 281–317.
CONGRESSIONAL RECORD—HOUSE. 145 (daily ed. Jan. 9, 2009).
CONGRESSIONAL RECORD—HOUSE. 5047 (daily ed. Apr. 30, 2009).
CONGRESSIONAL RECORD—SENATE 1654 (daily ed. Feb. 5, 2009).
CONGRESSIONAL RECORD—SENATE 3359 (daily ed. Mar. 18, 2009).
CONGRESSIONAL RECORD—SENATE 6054 (daily ed. July 21, 2010).
CONGRESSIONAL RECORD—SENATE 8987 (daily ed. Dec. 14, 2010).
Cox, E. J. (2009). An economic crisis is a terrible thing to waste: Reforming the business of law for a sustainable and competitive future. *UCLA Law Review, 57,* 511–551.
Davis, L. R., & Wilson, L. (2011a). Good timing? How one bank cut its link to a $1.2 billion Ponzi scheme. *Journal of Legal Economics, 18*(1), 1–26.
Davis, L. R., & Wilson, L. (2011b). Estimating JP Morgan Chase's profits from the Madoff deposits. *Risk Management and Insurance Review, 14*(1), 107–119.
Department of Justice. (2020). *Philadelphia woman indicted in $68 million securities fraud scheme.* https://www.justice.gov/usao-nj/pr/philadelphia-woman-indicted-68-million-securities-fraud-scheme. Accessed 20 July 2020.
Dorfman, J. (2015, March 22). Make insider trading legal to stop hurting ordinary investors. *Forbes.* https://www.forbes.com/sites/jeffreydorfman/2015/03/22/a-modern-insider-trading-law-would-recognize-the-victims-of-current-law/. Accessed 20 July 2020.
Edde, J., Kumar, N., & Waite, S. (2018). Investors are paying $1,300 per hour for 'Expert' chats. *Bloomberg.* https://www.bloomberg.com/news/articles/2018-02-28/investors-are-paying-1-300-per-hour-for-expert-chats. Accessed 20 July 2020.
Elliott Associates et al. (2010). Subcommittee memorandum. Elliott Associates, L.P., et al. v. Porsche Automobil Holding SE, f/k/a Dr. Ing. h.c. F. Porsche A.G.
Field, A. (2011). Deconstructing Goldman Sachs's fraud defense. https://www.aol.com/2010/04/19/deconstructing-goldman-sachss-fraud-defense/?guccounter=1&guce_referrer=aHR0cHM6Ly93d3cuZ29vZ2xlLmNvbS91cmw_c2E9dCZyY3Q9aiZxPSZlc3JjPXMmc291cmNlPXdlYiZjZD0mdmVkPTJhaFVLRXdqTl9fR3B2cXZyQWhVQ0MyTUJIU3k0RHIwUUZqQUFlZ1FJQmhBQiZ1cmw9aHR0cHMlM0ElMkYlMkZ3d3cuYW9sLmNvbSUyRjIwMTAlMkYwNCUyRjE5JTJGZGVjb25zdHJ1Y3RpbmctZ29sZG1hbi1zYWNoc3MtZnJhdWQtZGVmZW5zZSUyRiZ1c2c9QU92VmF3MlFPN1JVbUdzb3ZpbUd2cWZ5dVBrYw&guce_referrer_sig=AQAAAI_yzTV8wqDB76EWHpKEWqBzjS65dNSqBEXZ0PxfbJou2edWhsTNiAsZainDtJABu_4TCbDiPj9QCU3Z5IJLSQWT3V5VxcCe0mS_QWZWo68Vay-RaysIT3p-

AgvMXQbWmZi8GXvjyZgvd4yff36lUBDhXoEPRIg0yW0WQQvN0GIT. Accessed 20 July 2020.

FINRA. (2016). *Your duty to disclose*. Financial Industry Regulatory Authority. https://www.finra.org/sites/default/files/FINRA-duty-disclose-training.pdf. Accessed 1 October 2019.

FINRA. (2017). *Arbitrator selection*. Financial Industry Regulatory Authority. https://www.finra.org/arbitration-and-mediation/arbitrator-selection. Accessed 27 July 2020.

FINRA. (2019). *Dispute resolution statistics 2018*. Financial Industry Regulatory Authority. http://www.finra.org/arbitrationand-mediation/dispute-resolution-statistics. Accessed 12 July 2020.

FINRA. (2020). *Annual financial report 2019*. Financial Industry Regulatory Authority.https://www.finra.org/sites/default/files/2020-06/2019-annual-financial-report.pdf. Accessed 12 July 2020.

Fisch, J. E. (2018). Constructive ambiguity and the judicial development of insider trading. *SMU Law Review, 71*, 749–757.

Fisher, J. Q. C., Cregan, C., Di Giulio, J., et al. (2011). Economic crime and the global financial crisis. *Law and Financial Markets Review, 5*(4), 276–289. https://doi.org/10.5235/175214411796505642.

Forkey, R. (2012, June 9). Investment advisor and broker/dealer investment fraud and mismanagement litigation and FINRA. *Investment Advisor Magazine*.

Fox, M. B., & Tepe, G. N. (2018). Personal benefit has no place in misappropriation tipping cases. *SMU Law Review, 71*, 767–782.

Francis v. Lorenzo, SEC Release No. 9762, 111 SEC Docket 1761, 2015 WL 1927763 (Apr. 29, 2015).

Gallu, J., & Harper, Ch. (2010, April 16). Goldman shares tumble on SEC fraud allegations. *Bloomberg News*.

Gallu, J., & Scheer, D. (2010, July 21). SEC settlement with Goldman Sachs for USD 550 million approved by US judge. *Bloomberg*. www.bloomberg.com/news/2010-07-20/goldman-sachs-settlement-with-sec-for-550-million-approved-by-u-s-judge.html. Accessed 22 May 2012.

Goldstein, M. (2015, October 23). US prosecutor to drop insider trading cases against seven. *The New York Times*. https://www.nytimes.com/2015/10/23/business/dealbook/us-prosecutor-to-drop-insider-trading-cases-against-seven.html. Accessed 12 July 2020.

Greenstein, A. (2011). Fund of hedge funds Aris multi-strategy fund wins arbitration award against underlying manager based on allegations of self-dealing. *The Hedge Fund Law Report 4*(39). https://www.hflawreport.com/2542656/fund-of-hedge-funds-aris-multi-strategy-fund-wins-arbitration-award-against-underlying-manager-based-on-allegations-of-self-dealing.thtml. Accessed 12 July 2020.

Gross, J. (2016). The historical basis of securities arbitration as an investor protection mechanism. *Journal of Dispute Resolution, 2016,* 171–186.

Henning, P. J. (2018). Making up insider trading law as you go. *Washington University Journal of Law & Policy, 56,* 101–120.

Henriques, D. B. (2019). A case study of a Con Man: Bernie Madoff and the timeless lessons of history's biggest Ponzi scheme. In A. Mack (Ed.), *Cons and Scams: Their Place in American Culture* (Vol. 85, pp. 745–766).

Hostert, J. (2019). Great expectations, good intentions, and the appearance of the personal benefit in insider trading: Why the stage needs reset after Martoma. *Southern Illinois University Law Journal, 43,* 703–748.

Hugues, A. (2009, December 2). Tom Petters found guilty of Ponzi scheme fraud. *Reuters.* http://www.reuters.com/article/idUSN02497892009l202. Accessed 5 May 2020.

Hurd, S., Gworek, M., & Glustrom, E. (2019). Lorenzo v. SEC: The supreme court rules on scheme liability under the federal securities laws. *Journal of Investment Compliance.* https://doi.org/10.1108/joic-04-2019-0021.

Insider Trading Prohibition Act, H.R. 2534,115th Cong., 1st Sess. (Dec. 5, 2019).

Jacobs, B. (2016, February 9). Non-prosecution agreements: Reserved for VIPs? *Forbes.* https://www.forbes.com/sites/insider/2016/02/09/non-prosecution-agreements-reserved-for-vips/#684b1e572bdd. Accessed 25 July 2020.

Jory, S., & Perry, M. J. (2011). Ponzi schemes: A critical analysis. *Journal of Financial Planning.* https://ssrn.com/abstract=1894206. Accessed 5 March 2020.

Keefe, P. R. (2015, October 27). Making insider trading legal. *The New Yorker.* https://www.newyorker.com/business/currency/making-insider-trading-legal. Accessed 5 March 2020.

Kelleher, L., Caplin & Drysdale (2012). Liability & defense, hedge fund managers beware: Unless claims are assigned, managers do not have standing to sue for their funds. *Bloomberg Law Reports.* http://www.capdale.com/hedge-fund-managers-bewareunless-claims-are-assigned-managers-do-not-have-standing-to-sue-for-their-funds. Accessed 15 March 2020.

Kim, J. J. (2010, March 27). Cracking down on 'private placement' Investments. *Wall Street Journal.* https://www.wsj.com/articles/SB10001424052748704211704575139831790780958. Accessed 15 July 2020.

Kim, S. (2014). Insider trading as private corruption. *UCLA Law Review, 61,* 928–1008.

Klotz, M., Schachter, M. S., Gray, E. P., et al. (2017). Second circuit eliminates 'meaningfully close personal relationship' test. *The Investment Lawyer.* https://www.google.com/url?sa=t&rct=j&q=&esrc=s&source=web&cd=&ved=2ahUKEwjq25O16bDrAhUGxYsKHcbVB9kQFjAAegQIBBAB&url=

https%3A%2F%2Fwww.willkie.com%2F-%2Fmedia%2Ffiles%2Fpublications%2F2017%2F08%2Fsecond_circuit_eliminates_meaningfully_close_personal_relationship_test.pdf&usg=AOvVaw1yBJTatZtnVJlDLA3n1GT-. Accessed 19 July 2020.

Knight, T. B. (2017). Salman v. US: Another insider trading case. *Cato Supreme Court Review, 2016–2017,* 181–203.

Korsmo, Ch. R. (2011). Mismatch: The misuse of market efficiency in market manipulation class actions. *Faculty Publications*, 61. https://scholarlycommons.law.case.edu/faculty_publications/61. Accessed 20 July 2020.

Kragie, A., & Godoy, J. (2019). House passes 1st explicit ban on insider trading, LAW360 (Dec. 5, 2019). https://www.law360.com/articles/1225615/house-passes-1st-explicit-ban-on-insider-trading. Accessed 28 July 2020.

Langevoort, D. C. (2009). The SEC and the Madoff scandal: Three narratives in search of a story. *Georgetown Law and Economics*, Research Paper No. 1475433. https://doi.org/10.2139/ssrn.1475433.

Langevoort, D. C. (2019). *Watching insider trading law wobble: Obus, Newman, Salman, Two Martomas, and a Blaszczak.* Georgetown University Law Center. https://scholarship.law.georgetown.edu/cgi/viewcontent.cgi?article=3227&context=facpub. Accessed 12 July 2020.

Larsen, J., & Hinton, P. (2009). *SEC settlements in Ponzi scheme cases: Putting Madoff and stanford in context.* NERA Economic Consulting White Paper. https://www.google.com/url?sa=t&rct=j&q=&esrc=s&source=web&cd=&ved=2ahUKEwiJhKTR17DrAhXGjqQKHVtSDmYQFjAAegQIAhAB&url=http%3A%2F%2Fwww.knowledgemosaic.com%2Fgateway%2Fsec%2Ftestimony%2Fwww.securitieslitigationtrends.com_PUB_Ponzi_Schemes_0309.pdf&usg=AOvVaw0L57pZimYio67pzB4nT435. Accessed 17 July 2020.

Lee v. Kylin Mgmt. LLC, No. 17-CV-7249 (JMF), 2019 WL 917097 (S.D.N.Y. Feb. 25, 2019).

Lehman Brothers Holdings Inc. (2010). Proceedings examiners report. Executive summary of the examiner's conclusions. https://www.worldcat.org/title/lehman-brothers-holdings-inc-chapter-11-proceedings-examiners-report/oclc/554260788. Accessed 22 May 2012.

Lewis, M., et al. (2009, January 3). The end of the financial world as we know it. *The New York Times*, p. 9. https://www.google.com/url?sa=t&rct=j&q=&esrc=s&source=web&cd=&cad=rja&uact=8&ved=2ahUKEwjY2uLw2LDrAhWCyaQKHenfArgQFjAAegQIBxAB&url=https%3A%2F%2Fwww.nytimes.com%2F2009%2F01%2F04%2Fopinion%2F04lewiseinhorn.html&usg=AOvVaw2CMAboJH95KLlrYEflxT1U. Accessed 27 July 2020.

Lorenzo v. SEC, 872 F.3d 578, 586 (D.C. Cir. 2017).

M/S Bremen v. Zapata Off-Shore Co., 407 US 1, 12 (1972).

Macey, J. (2010). The distorting incentives facing the US Securities and Exchange Commission. *Harvard Journal of Law and Public Policy, 33*(2), 639–670.

Markopolos, H. (2010). *No one would listen*. New York: Wiley.

Mitchell, M. (2010, April 20). Goldman Sachs, John Paulson, and the hedge funds that pumped and dumped our economy. *Deep Capture*. https://www.deepcapture.com/2010/04/goldman-sachs-john-paulson-and-the-hedge-funds-that-pumped-and-dumped-our-economy/. Accessed 29 July 2020.

Monitor Daily. (2011, March 30). *SEC blocks diversion of Petters Ponzi victim funds*. http://www.monitordaily.com/sec-blocks-diversion-petters-ponzi-victim-funds/. Accessed 9 May 2012.

Murdock, C. W. (2019). The future of insider trading after Salman: Perpetuation of a flawed analysis or a return to basics. *Hastings Law Journal, 70*(6), 1547–1612.

Nagy, D. M. (2020, July 1). Chiarella v. United States and its indelible impact on insider trading law. *Tennessee Journal of Law and Policy, 15*. https://papers.ssrn.com/sol3/papers.cfm?abstract_id=3650626. Accessed 12 July 2020.

Park, T. H. (2019). Newman/Martoma: The insider trading law's impasse and the promise of congressional action. *Fordham Journal of Corporate & Financial Law, XXV*, 3–95.

Parsons, L. (2010). Gullible, greedy or just unlucky? How bernie Madoff scammed about 15,000 investors. *National Legal Eagle, 16*(1), 5–10.

Paulden, P., & Harrington, S. D. (2009, December 17). Hoffa says Goldman Sachs driving YRC into bankruptcy (Update1). *Bloomberg News*. http://www.bloomberg.com/apps/news?pid=20601087&sid=apCmuH.AP.VA. Accessed 12 July 2020.

Paulden, P., et al. (2010). Op. Cit., for instance, Cascade, 2011 WL 1211511, 130 S. Ct. 2869 (2010).

Perri, F. S., & Brody, R. G. (2011). The sleeping watch dog: AKA the securities and exchange commission. *Journal of Financial Regulation and Compliance, 19*(3), 208–221.

Petters Group Worldwide, LLC, Bky. Case no 08-45258 (D. Minn. June 27, 2019).

Phelps, D., & Tevlin, J. (2008, November 2). The woman who brought down Tom Petters. *Star Tribune*. http://www.startribune.com. Accessed 5 May 2012.

Pitaro, V. (2010). New York state supreme court dismisses hedge funds of funds' complaint against accipiter hedge funds based on exculpatory language in accipiter fund documents and absence of fiduciary duty among constituent limited partners. *The Hedge Fund Law Report, 3*(7). https://www.hflawreport.com/2539816/new-york-state-supreme-court-dismisses-hedge-funds-of-funds-complaint-against-accipiter-hedge-funds-based-on-exculpatory-lan guage-in-accipiter-fund-documents-and-absence-of-fiduciary-duty-among-constituent-limited-partners-.thtml. Accessed 13 August 2020.

Poser, N. S. (2009). Why the SEC failed: Regulators against regulation. *Brooklyn Journal of Corporate, Financial & Commercial Law, 3*(2), 289–324.

Poser, N. S., & Fanto, J. A. (2007). *Broker-dealer law & regulation* (4th ed.). New York: Aspen Publishers.

Pozza, C. L., Jr., Cox, Th R, & Morad, R. J. (2009). A review of recent investor issues in the Madoff, stanford and forte Ponzi scheme cases. *Journal of Business & Securities Law, 10*, 113–131.

Ramizez, K. (2018). *President trump signs Dodd-Frank rollback into law*. https://www.housingwire.com/articles/43464-president-trump-signs-dodd-frank-rollback-into-law/. Accessed 12 August 2020.

Razorback Funding LLC v. Rothstein, CACE09062943 (Fla. Cir. Ct. Broward Co. filed Nov. 20, 2009).

Reilly v. Natwest Mkts. Group. Inc., 181 F.3d 253, 271 (2d Cir. 1999).

Richards, T. (2008). The growth of third party funding. *CMS Dispute Resolution Newsletter*. www.cmslegal.com. Accessed 6 March 2012.

Richards v. Lloyd's of London, 135 F.3d 1289 (9th Cir. 1998).

Roby v. Corp. of Lloyd's, 996 F.2d 1353 (2d Cir. 1993).

Rocker Mgmt., L.L.C. v. Lernout & Hauspie Speech Prods. N.V., No. 00-5965 (JCL), 2005 WL 1365465, at *2 n.5 (D.N.J. June 7, 2005).

Ross, B. (2009). *The Madoff chronicles—Inside the secret world of Bernie and Ruth*. New York: Hyperion Publishing.

Rothstein Rosenfeldt Adler, P.A., No. 09-34791-RBR (Bankr. S.D. Fla. Filed Nov. 19, 2009).

Salman v. United States, 137 S. Ct. 420, 423 (2016).

Sauer, R.C. (2010, July 17). Why the SEC missed Madoff. *The Wall Street Journal*. http://online.wsj.com/article/SB10001424052748704738404575347011129892600.html/. Accessed 12 July 2020.

Scharfman, J. (2009). The Madoff identity: A new operational due diligence paradigm in a post-Madoff world. http://ssrn.com/abstract=1435024. Accessed 29 August 2020.

Schipani, C., & Seyhun, H. J. (2016). Defining 'Material Nonpublic': What should constitute illegal insider information? *Fordham Journal of Corporate and Financial Law, XXI*(2), 327–378.

Schrieber, A. (2010a). The US Securities and Exchange Commission v. Goldman Sachs. Case Studies in Ethics at Duke University. http://ethics.iit.edu/eelibrary/node/7440. Accessed 29 August 2020.

Schrieber, A. (2010b). *The investment bank job*. The Kenan Institute for Ethics. Duke University. https://www.google.com/url?sa=t&rct=j&q=&esrc=s&source=web&cd=&ved=2ahUKEwiInpmH7cXrAhVp6uAKHYRND0YQFjAAegQIAhAB&url=https%3A%2F%2Fkenan.ethics.duke.edu%2Fwp-content%2Fu

ploads%2F2018%2F01%2FGoldmanSachs_TN2015.pdf&usg=AOvVaw1TeHPfdLmbn4dgSTnQ2-B5. Accessed 29 August 2020.

SEC v. Stanford Int'l Bank, No. 3:09-CV-0298-N (N.D. Tex. filed Feb. 17, 2009).

SEC v. Goldman Sachs & Co., US District Court for the SDNY, 10-cv-3229 (BSJ), 16 April 2010 ("SEC Complaint").

SEC v. Bruce F. Prévost, David W. Harrold, Palm Beach Capital Mgmt. LP, and Palm Beach Capital Mgmt. LLC, Civil Action No. 10-cv-04235-PAM-SRN (October 14, 2010).

SEC v. Med. Capital Holdings, Inc., No. SACV 09-818 DOC (RNBx), 2010 WL 809406 (C.D. Cal. Mar. 16, 2010).

SEC v. Sunwest Management, Inc Et Al Case 6:09-Cv-06056-TC (D. Ct. Or. October 2, 2009).

SEC v. Petters, et al., No 09-cv-1750 (D. Minn. Jul. 7, 2009).

SEC v. Quan, No 0:11-cv-00723 (D. Minn. Mar. 25, 2011).

SEC V. STANFORD INTERNATIONAL BANK, LTD., ET AL., No. 17-11073 (5th Cir. 2019). http://www.stanfordfinancialreceivership.com/documents/Receivers_16th_Interim_Report.pdf. Accessed 9 October 2019.

SEC versus Compania Internacional Financiera S.A., no. 11 Civ. 4904(DLC), 2011 WL 3251813 (S.D.N.Y. July 29, 2011).

SEC v. Marlon Quan, et al., Civil Action No. 11-723. (ADM-JSM)(D. Minn., September 25, 2014).

SEC v. BRENDA A. SMITH, BROAD REACH CAPITAL, LP, BROAD REACH PARTNERS, LLC, and BRISTOL ADVISORS, LLC, Case 2:19-cv-17213-MCA-LDW (New York Southern Court, August 27, 2019).

SEC. (2009, August 31). *Investigation of failure of the SEC to uncover Bernard Madoff's Ponzi scheme*. Report No. OIG-509. https://www.sec.gov/files/oig-509.pdf. Accessed 12 August 2020.

SEC. (2012a). Study on the cross-border scope of the private right of action under Section 10(b) of the securities exchange act of 1934 as required by Section 929Y of the Dodd-Frank Wall Street reform and consumer protection act. Securities and Exchange Commission (SEC). http://www.sec.gov/news/studies/2012/929y-study-cross-border-private-rights.pdf. Accessed 11 July 2013.

SEC. (2012b). Miami hedge fund adviser charged for misleading investors about 'skin in the game' and related-party deals. US Securities and Exchange Commission. https://www.sec.gov/news/press-release/2012-2012-104htm. Accessed 27 July 2020.

SEC. (2016). Press Release No. 2016-138. SEC: Citigroup provided incomplete blue sheet data for 15 years. Securities and Exchange Commission (SEC). https://www.sec.gov/news/pressrelease/2016-138.html. Accessed 22 July 2020.

SEC. (2019). *SEC obtains emergency asset freeze, charges Pennsylvania Investment Adviser with USD 100 Million Fraud*. Securities and Exchange Commission (SEC). https://www.sec.gov/news/press-release/2019-162. Accessed 20 July 2020.

Securities and Exchange Commission Division of Enforcement. (2017, November 28). Enforcement Manual Office of Chief Counsel. https://www.sec.gov/divisions/enforce/enforcementmanual.pdf. Accessed 20 July 2020.

Sherry, A. (2019). Martoma seeks SCOTUS review of 'Dirks-defying' insider trading decision. https://lrus.wolterskluwer.com/news/securities-regulation-daily/martoma-seeks-scotus-review-of-dirks-defying-insider-trading-decision/71839/. Accessed 28 July 2020.

Shores, M. (2010). *Informal networks and white collar crime: An extended analysis of the Madoff scandal*. New York: Ithaca. https://www.google.com/url?sa=t&rct=j&q=&esrc=s&source=web&cd=&ved=2ahUKEwj2z_bn7bDrAhUGcBQKHZqXD3wQFjABegQIARAB&url=https%3A%2F%2Fcore.ac.uk%2Fdownload%2Fpdf%2F4913109.pdf&usg=AOvVaw2054hzIHKuaKossEdjftju. Accessed 28 July 2020.

Spacone, A. C. (2019). The second circuit's curious journey through the law of tippee liability for insider trading: Newman to Martoma. *Roger Williams University Law Review, 24*(1), 1–45.

Stecklow, S. (2009, January 28). In echoes of Madoff, Ponzi cases proliferate. *Wall Street Journal*. http://www.pyramidschemealert.org/PSAMain/news/PonziCasesProliferate.pdf. Accessed 16 July 2020.

Stevenson, A., & Goldstein, M. (2014, February 6). Ex-SAC Trade Convicted of Securities Fraud. *The New York Times*. https://dealbook.nytimes.com/2014/02/06/former-sac-trader-found-guilty-of-insider-trading/. Accessed 20 July 2020.

Stolowy, H., Baker, R., Jeanjean, Th, & Messner, M. (2011). Information, trust and the limits of intelligent accountability in investment decision making: insights from the Madoff case. *SSRN Electronic Journal*. https://doi.org/10.2139/ssrn.1930128.

Tatcher, S. (2011). Securities Law Alert, the Southern District of New York Dismisses Securities Fraud Actions against Porsche, Finding that Section 10(b) does not Protect Swap Agreements Referencing Foreign Securities. *Securities Law Alert,* p. 1. https://www.stblaw.com/docs/default-source/cold-fusion-existing-content/publications/pub1109.pdf?sfvrsn=2. Accessed 28 September 2020.

The New York Times. (2010, August 8). 50-Year Term for Minnesota Man in USD 3.7 Billion Ponzi Fraud. Associated Press. Reprinted in *The New York Times* B9. http://www.nytimes.com/2010/04/09/business/09ponzi.html. Accessed 12 June 2020.

The Ponzi Scheme Authority. (2020). *Ponzitracker*. http://www.ponzitracker.com. Accessed 12 June 2020.

Thomson-DeVeaux, A. (2016). What's so wrong with insider trading anyway? *Five Thirty-Eight*. https://fivethirtyeight.com/features/whats-so-wrong-with-insider-trading-anyway/. Accessed 12 June 2020.

Tuch, A. F. (2012). Conflicted gatekeepers: The Volcker rule and Goldman Sachs. *Virginia Law & Business Review, 7*(2), 365–420.

United States v. Blaszczak, 947 F.3d 19 (2d Cir. 2019).

United States v. Lee, No. 13 CR 539 (PGG), S.D.N.Y. June 21, 2019.

United States v. Martoma, 869 F.3d 55, 61 (2d Cir. 2017), opinion amended and superseded, 894 F.3d 64 (2d Cir. 2017).

United States v. Martoma, 869 F.3d 58 (2d Cir. 2017), opinion amended and superseded, 894 F.3d 64 (2d Cir. 2017).

United States v. Martoma, 894 F.3d 64, 67–68 (2d Cir. 2017).

United States v. Martoma, 894 F.3d 64, 78 (2d Cir. 2017).

United States v. Newman, 773 F.3d 438, 442 (2d Cir. 2014).

United States. v. Conradt, 2015 U.S. Dist. LEXIS 16263 (S.D.N.Y. Jan. 22, 2015).

United States v. Stanford, 769 F. Supp. 2d 1083 (S.D. Tex. 2011).

US v. $304,041.01 on Deposit at Citibank, N.A., No 10-cv-4858 (S.D.N.Y. filed June 22, 2010).

US v. Madoff, No 08 MAG 2735 (S.D.N.Y. filed Dec. 11, 2008).

US v. Petters, No. 0:08-cr-00364 (D. Minn. Jan. 24, 2013).

US v. Rothstein, No 09-6033 (S.D. Fl. filed Dec. 1, 2009).

US v. Rothstein, No 18-11796 (S.D. Fl. Sept. 30, 2019).

Vardi, N. (2012). Hedge Fund Manager of Former USD 1 Billion Fund Quits after Arbitration Loss. http://www.forbes.com/sites/nathanvardi/2011/10/03/hedge-fund-manager-of-former-1-billion-fund-quits-after-arbitration-loss/. Accessed 12 June 2012.

Verstein, A. (2019). Crypto assets and insider trading law's domain. *Iowa Law Review, 105*, 1–59.

Vonnegut, N. (2017, July 26). Three lessons from the Bernie Madoff Scandal. *Enterprising Investor*. https://blogs.cfainstitute.org/investor/2017/07/26/three-lessons-from-the-bernie-madoff-scandal/. Accessed 19 July 2020.

Voreacos, D., & Glovin, D. (2008, December 12). Madoff confessed $50 billion fraud before FBI arrest. *Bloomberg*. http://www.bloomberg.com/apps/news?pid=newsarchive&sid=atUk.QnXAvZY. Accessed 6 March 2012.

Warwick-Young Walsh, D., & Spalding, A. D. Jr. (2011). Recognizing and responding to red flags: The Stanford Ponzi scheme. *Journal of Legal Issues and Cases in Business*. https://www.google.com/url?sa=t&rct=j&q=&esrc=s&source=web&cd=&ved=2ahUKEwjJnP6v_LDrAhUVmVwKHSKIDhkQFjAAegQIAhAB&url=https%3A%2F%2Fwww.aabri.com%2Fmanuscripts%2F1

1829.pdf&usg=AOvVaw2Z6dD3c505Q2oss8Mn-1H8. Accessed 12 June 2020.

WebCPA Staff. (2009). *SEC admits missed opportunities in Madoff case*. www.webcpa.com/news/SEC-Admits-Missed-Opportunities-Madoff-Case-51607-1.html. Accessed 12 June 2020.

Westbrook, J., & Scheer, D. (2010). *Report finds SEC dropped the ball in Stanford case*. http://online.wsj.com/article/SB20001424052702303491304575188220570802084.html. Accessed 12 June 2020.

Wilber, D. Q. (2009, June 12). Economic downturn accelerates collapse of Ponzi schemes. *Washington Post*. https://www.washingtonpost.com/wp-dyn/content/article/2009/06/11/AR2009061103993.html. Accessed 12 June 2020.

Williams, G. (2012). Trust but verify: Fraud in Victorian banking and its diminishment. http://ssrn.com/abstract=1983633. Accessed 1 May 2012.

Williams, D. C. (2017). A timeline and fraud triangle analysis of the SEC's Madoff Ponzi scheme investigation. *International Journal of Business & Public Administration, 14*, 98–105.

Winship, V., & Robbennolt, J. K. (2018). An empirical study of admissions in SEC settlements. *Arizona Law Review, 60*, 1–51.

Zweifach, L. J., & Khan, S. N. (2010). Recent developments in Ponzi scheme litigation. In M. P. Carroll & R. J. Morvillo (Eds.), *Auditor liability in current environment: How to protect yourself* (pp. 99–132). New York: Practising Law Institute.

Final Conclusions

The main goal of this book is to establish the framework for global regulation of hedge funds, focusing on investor protection, in a continuously changing and challenging regulatory field: on the one hand, due to Trump's deregulatory approach and, on the other hand, due to United Kingdom's decision to leave the EU.

As noted, during the last decade, hedge funds have always been on the top of regulators' agenda. This book concludes that there is indeed a strong case for increased investor protection in hedge funds, on an international approach. Hence, as financial products become more complex and innovative, financial regulation, and investor protection need to be equally innovative, creative, and proactive. A comprehensive research on the possible costs and benefits of such regulation concludes that the benefits are likely to be greater than the costs, stipulating that regulators need to be aware of regulation excesses and overregulation dangers. Therefore, an international hedge funds regulation focused on investor protection, transparency, and risk mitigation is the best answer for the global financial area.

It is a proven fact that the shifts in the legal field have seriously affected hedge funds operations. These shifts were caused among others by the financial crisis, the urgency to mitigate risks, the necessity to better control hedge funds, the need to increase investors' protection, and the transparency of hedge funds. As observed, all regulators acknowledged the potential benefits but also the shortcomings of tighter regulation such

A. M. Fagetan, *The Regulation of Hedge Funds*,
https://doi.org/10.1007/978-3-030-63706-4

as, for example, a strategic method to face risks in the hedge funds area and increase funds competitiveness, controlling their impact on the hedge funds market and the international financial system, on the one hand. On the other hand, tighter regulation implies diversification and competition.

Nevertheless, there are still regulators who hesitate to tighten the controls on hedge funds. In this vein, the general opinion among investors is that, a more regulated industry could turn into an obstacle to future development of the hedge funds market. Additionally, the more regulated the hedge funds industry will be, the less appealing hedge funds managers will find to settle their funds in certain jurisdictions, particularly in the offshore ones. In addition, even in the United States, the imposition of new registration and reporting requirements, having as main scope the increase of transparency, seems to have diminished hedge funds' investment discretion. All these challenges raise questions for investors concerning the performance of hedge funds in the near future.

The European and American authorities have much considered lately hedge funds, and in this direction, the author acknowledged the cross-border nature of the hedge funds sector and, therefore, the need to create an internationally harmonized regulation regime for hedge funds. As they have fallen beyond the boundaries of global public regulation, hedge funds have often been considered the proof that international financial markets have exceeded the states' ability to competently regulate and control them, this industry seemingly reinforcing arguments about the transnational ascension of both authorities and regulations. The consequence of the international financial crisis proclaimed the necessity for the emergence of regulatory authority in a globally coordinated manner over this industry. Since the crisis, major strides towards financial stability have been achieved.

As acknowledged, there is a close connection between the regulatory course of the European authorities and the corresponding regulatory actions in the United States. While European hedge funds regulators were capable, to a certain extent, of generating innovative issues but also legislative answers, in some cases they ran behind Washington's policies, at least up to 2017, when President Trump came along. Unfortunately, since coming into power, President Trump and Republican supporter lawyers have pursued the deregulation of the Wall Street as a major priority, which raises many questions regarding the future of hedge funds' regulatory framework in the United States. Currently, a decade after the crisis, recent views on regulations are challenging against the financial system: Trump's populist approach to financial regulations and United Kingdom's Brexit, threatening with disintegration of the international and EU system of regulation.

Requisite discussion highlights the polarization in the regulation of hedge funds under the law of different EU member states. This book has examined and compared the hedge funds regulation in several onshore and offshore jurisdictions such as the United States, the United Kingdom, Italy, France, Ireland, Luxembourg, Malta, Switzerland (onshore), and offshore jurisdictions: Cayman Islands, British Virgin Islands, Mauritius, and Delaware, after the twenty-first-century depression. The book pursued to depict the progress achieved at regulatory level after the financial crisis, with major focus on investor protection. Along our journey, the reforms introduced in the regulatory field were described and analyzed, such as UCITS Directives (IV, V, and VI), AIFM Directive and MiFID (Level I and II) and other major sources of Community Legal Rules in the EU and the Dodd–Frank Act in the United States.

The hedge funds industry undergoes pressures from private financial groups as well as from the opinions of major elite policy makers concerning market discipline and self-regulatory mechanisms. It is true that the shockwaves produced by the financial crisis generated a shift in the domestic politics of the largest financial powers, the essence of international rules changing accordingly. What is clear is that, despite the fact that hedge funds contributed to the development of the 2007/2008 crisis, they cannot be held responsible for it. All in all, the author considers that regulators must develop their rules and requirements, by constantly gathering substantial collection of data from advisers/managers. This collection is intended to help investors and assist the regulatory and examination efforts of both the United States Securities and Exchange Commission ("SEC") and the European Parliament, in prompting investor-centric regulation and in enhancing protection for investors' interests, by mitigating some of the higher risk behavior of hedge funds.

Major regulators also changed their opinion on the merits of market discipline and self-regulation according to the lessons learned during the financial crisis. At the same time, it was assessed that many private actors also came to approve the regulation not only for defensive reasons at a time of weakened political legitimacy, but also for more positive reasons of improving the operation of their hedge funds industry, bringing back confidence, and/or increasing market shares. As the most powerful states agreed, to a greater or smaller extent, to move toward tighter official regulation for domestic purposes, they had major reasons—as noted in the book—to become sure that the content of international rules changed in the same direction of investor protection.

Analyses emphasizing inter-state power relations could be tempted to consider the end of self-regulation to be a result of the decrease of the United States and United Kingdom power and the favorable outcome of states with more interventionist predilections among which one mentions France and Italy in overcoming their rivalry. In the author's opinion, however, this interpretation would neglect the importance of the domestic changes in the United States and the United Kingdom in explaining the shift to direct regulation. Accordingly, this book states that analysts focusing on inter-state power relations would be right to consider the growing capacity of the EU to act as a whole both unilaterally and at global level as an important development in this story. As shown above, this shift increasingly constrained United Kingdom's autonomy in global regulatory politics, maybe to a certain extent even prompting Brexit, simultaneously with causing global outcomes to be influenced by regulatory bodies such as the ECB, the EC, and the European Parliament.

Both the US and the EU have imposed major regulation and reporting requests on hedge funds, which were completely analyzed and approached both in the United States (Chapter 6) and in the EU (Chapter 2).

The AIFM Directive, thoroughly examined and discussed in this book (Chapter 2), comprises authorization, risk management, operational risk, depositories, valuation tools, liquidity, capital, leverage, conduct of business, and marketing for these funds. Therefore, the author considers that further negotiations and debates could be needed when transposing it into national law, in order to achieve the correct equilibrium between the two main parties involved: the international or global nature of this market, on the one hand and the local nature of the investors, on the other hand. The AIFM Directive, will definitely: (a) diminish systemic risks and the leverage use; (b) improve investor protection while increasing the transparency, too; (c) enhance the integrity and the efficiency of the sector; (d) promote the sector for the supervision of corporations. The impact of the AIFM Directive on local jurisdictions in Europe is also described (Chapter 3).

Regarding the hedge funds in the United States, *ab initio* it can be stated that there are clear gains but also costly trade-offs from the enactment of the Dodd–Frank Act. Also, there are obvious areas where progresses are still needed. Thus, Dodd–Frank's most valuable contributions have included higher prudential standards but also the creation of the CFPB. Additionally, the derivatives transactions were subject to greater transparency and oversight. At the same time, higher capital requirements made banking and non-banking institutions more flexible to financial pressure and crises. Another important shift resides in the FDIC[1] SPOE strategy that authorizes standard procedures for cautiously winding down a bankrupt institution, this leading to the improvement of the financial stability and also diminishing what means "too big to fail." From another perspective, the CFPB has two key roles; strengthens oversight duties, minimizing possible risky breaches in the US regulations, and improves protections for clients. In spite of all these, there is still room for improvement in all of these.

As seen, there are also other provisions that are difficult to assess, as they appear to bring about some advantages in spite of the important costs they imply. In this case the Volcker Rule can be mentioned. This prohibits proprietary trading on behalf of commercial banks and also the Lincoln Amendment, which bans entities engaged in swaps to receive federal assistance. There are critics complaining about the difficulties faced by regulators in implementing and overseeing the Volcker Rule. This regulation is complex, ambiguous, and expensive, and this also puts banks in difficulty when adhering to its stipulations. There are also scholars who consider that the Lincoln Amendment's provisions are more or less the same as those of the Volker Rule, this leading to redundancy and rendering the Lincoln Amendment unnecessary.

There are also domains in which, the Dodd–Frank has made some progress, but there are still improvements to be made, and in this respect, we consider particularly the Financial Stability Oversight Council (FSOC).

After examining this multitude of attempts to mitigate risks by means of legislation, another major conclusion of the study refers to the involvement of jurisdiction. There are two major concerns regarding hedge funds, consisting of very small charges and little or no divulgement, particularly in offshore jurisdictions. Generally, hedge funds have the opportunity to choose the most sympathetic location. Also, when a state changes major stipulations, be it taxes, laws, or divulgement requests,

[1] Federal Deposit Insurance Corporation's.

principals, and fund managers can change location easily. This effortlessness in changing the location does not prove providential at all for any state because funds are synonymous with high revenues, as this is the essential reason for jurisdictions not agreeing to funds changing their residence. Every residence change reduces not only incomes, but also risk mitigation efforts. Therefore, state cooperation has a double purpose: first, to solve problems that involve residence authority, and second, to diminish global risk that can otherwise cause depressions. These risks, also called "systemic risks," have been widely analyzed by global authorities and officials. Another signaled problem is that, although there are important differences between both regulations and investor taxes, there is little academic research differentiating between onshore and offshore hedge funds. To anyone's surprise, most offshore hedge funds are successful in tax heavens. As already seen in Chapter 5, there are plenty of benefits for hedge funds in moving offshore, the most important being for sure the tax neutrality, these locations being known also under the name of "tax havens." Indeed, these locations offer strongly favorable tax terms as a stimulus to start up new business, taxes that lead, on the one hand to big profits and on the other hand to major benefits for the host country as well, no matter if it is a small or a big country.

From the offshore jurisdictions analyzed in Chapter 5, the Cayman Islands represent the largest HF offshore jurisdiction, both United States and United Kingdom based managers preferring it mainly due to (1) its good reputation among institutional investors, this helping HFs with their fund-raising effort, and also due to (2) its strong supporting infrastructure. There are many factors which explain the Cayman Islands' popularity such as: the stability of its government, the public policies oriented toward business, the advanced legal system—as well as its major various tax-free incentives with low financial regulation and oversight. However, Cayman can be compared rather to Luxembourg, as this acts as an important hub for European investment funds, than to Switzerland.

In a similar manner, Delaware's HF infrastructure is strong, being generally used by United States-based HFs. Additionally, Delaware has a business-friendly legal system and its location offers a high level of confidence for institutional investors. Also, it should be stipulated that Delaware ranks first place as a domicile location among the US (offshore) hedge funds.

Both the UK and US hedge funds are attracted by the British Virgin Islands, mainly because this country is historically tied to the United

Kingdom and geographically close to the United States. The British Virgin Islands stands as one of the best, highly respected hedge funds' domiciles, globally speaking. In addition to its modern, efficient banking system stands the government's public policies focused mainly on developing strict money laundering and tax evasion standards, this earning for the British Virgin Islands a leading reputation in the financial world.

Mauritius is the favorite offshore center for the Far East investing. The overall advantages offered by these jurisdictions are crystal clear: light legislation, easy registration, high confidentiality, low reporting standards, and last but not least, low taxes. Cayman Islands stand as one node in the triangle with the United States and the United Kingdom. As hedge fund managers are extremely concentrated in these two last jurisdictions, hedge fund support services are usually provided either by Cayman, Ireland, or the United States. By consequence, the legal domiciles of these funds are concentrated primarily in the Cayman Islands, meanwhile British Virgin Islands and Delaware act rather as secondary centers. It has therefore been concluded that the Cayman Islands act as a central element of the global Anglo-American hedge fund industry.

Every risk assumed by each particular person investing in funds, every component of the economic and financial structure, as well as Europe's objective of making "a single market" place nowadays funds on the first place in terms of interest not only at the European, but also at international level. Starting with 2007, when Germany became President of the "Group of 8," funds turned into a major issue discussed within multiple meetings, with transparency as the main focus. Nowadays, it seems that hedge funds market understood that there are many advantages for everyone involved within this business, if scammers are annihilated. Accordingly, regulatory bodies and fund managers cooperate in the attempt to build a healthy funds market regardless of the fact they are based onshore or offshore.

Another concluding remark is that EU and US legislators are deeply concerned both about the hedge funds' strategies and about the associated risks, in terms of the fund's properties estimations and investor protection. Vast legislation resulted from these concerns regarding systemic and particular risks affecting especially the investors. Still, legislators and regulatory bodies must understand hedge funds and the impact of such tighten regulation on the achievement of a reasonable legal framework that will not jeopardize their activities and their very existence. This is the reason for stimulating and developing initiatives such as the researches on the AIFM Directive and the Dodd–Frank Act developed in this book.

Another quite intuitive observation is necessary: in the present world, globalization leads to the interconnection of markets, as financial aspects ignore state borders when the law is enclosed within a defined location, creating a disjunction between territorial regulation and international activities. This remark is general, but it can easily apply to hedge funds and could prove to be one of the biggest challenges faced by the financial law. Indeed, operations and investors in various jurisdictions come together with likely conflicting regulations problems, and with high compliance costs. At the same time, another risk should be emphasized—that of forum shopping, since the lack of globally coordinated approach enables hedge funds to move away to less rigid jurisdictions out of the regulatory authority's reach, which is certainly not good news for the systemic risk mitigation efforts. The author considers that global economic challenges require a global answer. International multilateralism within intergovernmental and supranational *fora* is the *sine qua non* of an effective resolution to the analyzed industry challenges and a sound reform of the international hedge funds industry especially from offshore jurisdictions.

Overall, despite all regulations and regulators, offshore funds regulation is still one major issue to be solved. All regulatory reforms seem passive as compared to it. It is clear that a coordinated onshore–offshore approach to regulation could prove much more effective and it could lead to costs cuts.

If at the beginning of the twenty-first century the achievement of an international harmonized legal framework for hedge funds seemed utopian, now it is not the case anymore, in spite of United Kingdom's withdraw from the EU. On the contrary, the international financial architecture developed as a solution to the necessity of a common system of global financial risk oversight. The author considers that policies must be structured around global institutions to achieve collective objectives such as prudential/financial stability regulations, market conduct regulations and trading practices, general market integrity regulations and investor protection regulation. The international financial architecture is intended to deal with international financial regulation. Supervision and regulation are two sides of the same coin.

As demonstrated in this book, there are common objectives of the United States and the EU financial regulatory frameworks, but the current reform proposals did not size yet the opportunity of contingency for promoting a coordinated international approach. One thing needs to be pointed out clearly: this book supports the idea of global financial regulation and encourages an international framework.

Indeed, several deep philosophical and cultural differences have shaped various perceptions regarding regulation in general and hedge funds regulation in particular. On the one side, there seems to be the United Kingdom and the United States, offshore jurisdictions but also, to a smaller extent Italy, which is in favor of a flexible approach to hedge fund regulation. On the other side, there is France, which keeps pushing for more regulation, mainly because it has nothing to lose. Acknowledging these divergences is the first step to overcome them and to develop a global legal framework. It is true that these differences may first of all originate in the very perception of the state role. While France has a tight state intervention tradition, the United States, offshore jurisdictions, and the United Kingdom have a quite liberal one. This may also come from the role of the law itself in each of the abovementioned countries. Hence, France has always been a highly regulated state with a massive legislative activity, while the US offshore jurisdictions and the United Kingdom regulate more lightly and only if necessary.

The hedge funds approach of each of the states discussed in this book is at the same time influenced by the significance of the funds industry in these states. Accordingly, France is not really concerned about the impact of hedge fund regulation on its economy due to the fact that this impact could not be so significant (since funds based in France are few, although diverse). On the contrary, the United Kingdom and the United States have a strong motivation to maintain their competitiveness, as they are the two major financial centers for hedge funds. Finally, there seems to be a competition between the jurisdictions analyzed in this book to impose their own regulation perceptions in a very chauvinistic manner, which may prove prejudicial in the author's opinion.

An important question deals with United Kingdom's decision to leave the EU. The government's persistence to leave the single EU market raises major concerns regarding the way in which financial services will be impacted both in the United Kingdom and in the rest of the world. If the United Kingdom remains in the EEA, the impact will be lower since both British managers and funds will continue to be seen as similar to EU entities, meanwhile, if the United Kingdom leaves the EEA, they will be considered third-country entities, which will make it more difficult to access the EU market. The path to go is yet unknown, but both regulators and investors prepare for both scenarios.

Brexit prompts hard choices for both the UK and the EU. In the middle of all these changes, a major question concerning hedge funds emerges: will/should the United Kingdom keep on co-existing under the EU regulations or it can consider applying a certain divergence from them?

The author makes several remarks concerning the United Kingdom. First, it becomes obvious that Brexit is going to introduce additional, complex, layers of regulations but also costs for the UK hedge funds market. At the same time, there is little, if any guarantee concerning the future Single market access rights. In a more positive note, markets and financial regulation are constantly changing and co-evolving. Consequently, Brexit can have also a positive aspect for the United Kingdom, and new benefits can be found in terms of hedge funds regulation.

Second, the United Kingdom's future choices regarding the hedge funds regulations are important in the context of United Kingdom's maintaining the key, top position on international financial markets, as a global financial center. As already seen, "over the short to medium term, the UK should ensure it is likely to be deemed equivalent under EU law."[2] In this case, the current access to the European Single market can continue as much as possible, and consequently, the United Kingdom's hedge funds industry can market and manage funds at least to some point within the Common market.

Nevertheless, there can be sections within UK hedge funds regulation, which can emerge some limited divergence. This can occur "provided that the UK remains in line with international standards, and (ideally) continues to be recognizably similar to remain equivalent. This certainly holds true in the event that equivalence is interpreted as more of a holistic assessment that could extend to embrace an element of regulatory competition."[3]

In the long term, Brexit should, on behalf of both EU and the UK, stimulate broader negotiations concerning longer term challenges that

[2] Howell, E., (2020), Post-Brexit UK fund regulation: Equivalence, divergence or convergence? *European Business Organization Law Review*. https://doi.org/10.1007/s40804-020-00177-w.

[3] Idem.

the hedge funds market is going to face in the post-Brexit era. From this perspective, Brexit should also imply innovative and proportionate solutions for the reinforcement and strengthening of this important industry.

The author's firm belief is that, unless action is taken to harmonize the regulation of hedge funds at global level, the confidence of investors in the safety of invested assets through a collective investment vehicle would continue to be poor. The other way round, it seems it is a favorable moment for an international legal framework in the hedge fund industry but, unfortunately, governments and regulators still struggle to overcome their national particularities, which leads to a deadlock. Harmonization of legal frameworks seems to be illusory since regulators continue to contemplate national-based reforms when an effective prevention of systemic risk requires international cooperation. The proposal presented in this book considers this structural situation requiring significant effort. It acknowledges the obvious tendency of jurisdictions to handle regulation on a national-basis. The national prerogatives to regulate as each state sees appropriate are not denied by the creation of a global database of systemic risk. Instead, this promotes an international cooperation framework via an information-sharing system superimposed on national regulations. This would be for sure one of the most far-reaching innovations of post-crisis financial regulation, as it will oversee the market as a whole, particularly monitoring investor protection.

The author concludes that the 2007 global financial crisis marked the passing of post-modern finance, while revealing the excesses of finance and the failures of a lightly regulated and self-regulated system. This is why investor protection should be placed at the top of all rules and principles, be they national or European. And above all, global hedge funds regulation represents a stringent necessity.

Therefore, the author opts for a global hedge funds regulation because she considers that the rationale for international financial regulation establishes prudential rules for hedge funds operating in various states on the global financial services market. A comprehensive global financial regulation is able to meet the challenges in coordinating highly divergent national regulations that frequently overlap other higher level regulations.

There are still many open questions about the need for consumer protection. What constitutes harm and when should a regulator act? When is consumer protection needed? What is the impact of existing regulations on the hedge funds industry, on investors and fund managers?

Going forward, there is a major need for scholars to further engage in research dealing with hedge funds on consumer protection, as it is my true belief that they have the ability to influence policies and regulators in their decision-making. Altogether, it is the author's intent and hope that this research stimulates the careful debate of this issue by scholars and regulators. At the same time, it is the author's credo that regulation should not be made *ad infinitum*.

Index

A. M. Fagetan, *The Regulation of Hedge Funds*,
https://doi.org/10.1007/978-3-030-63706-4

U

V

The manufacturer's authorised representative in the EU is Springer Nature Customer Service Centre GmbH, Europaplatz 3, 69115 Heidelberg, Germany. If you have any concerns regarding our products, please contact ProductSafety@springernature.com

Printed and bound by CPI Group (UK) Ltd, Croydon, CR0 4YY
30/09/2026
02225702-0020